The Practice
of Social Research

The Practice
of Social Research

Earl R. Babbie

University of Hawaii

Wadsworth Publishing Company, Inc.
Belmont, California

Designer: Nancy Benedict
Sociology Editor: Stephen Rutter
Copy Editor: Elizabeth Bagwell
Production Editor: Susan Yessne

ISBN 0-534-00381-8
L. C. Cat. Card No. 74-15633
Printed in the United States of America

  2 3 4 5 6 7 8 9 10—79 78 77 76 75

Also available:
Practicing Social Research by Earl R.
Babbie and Robert Huitt, a practical guide to
accompany *The Practice of Social
Research*

Dedication

Georg von Bekesy
(1899–1972)

Werner Erhard

Table of Contents

Preface

The purpose of this book is to introduce readers to the *logic* and the *skills* of social scientific research. The book will have been successful if a reader comes away from it able to *do* social research and understanding *why* it is done the way it is done. The acid test of the book will come when a reader attempts an empirical research project, finds that the particular field conditions do not exactly match anything dealt with in the book, and is able to figure ·out those *compromises* that represent the best bridge between the particular field conditions and the fundamental logic of scientific inquiry. I want to dwell on this point, since it is central to the purpose and history of this book.

In my own experience as a student and as an instructor, I have found it much easier to understand the logic of science than to bring that understanding across the bridge into the real world of actually doing research. On one side of the bridge, things are perfectly neat, logical, and "scientific." On the other side, chaos reigns: there are only incomplete lists to sample from, subjects don't show up for experiments, interviewers make mistakes and lose questionnaires, people lie and misunderstand, and nothing correlates "well enough" with anything else.

I found the discrepancies between these two worlds especially troublesome when I first began to teach research methods. It seemed as though I had to choose between (1) presenting the *logic* of science, hoping my students would eventually learn how to apply it in practice, or (2) giving detailed and specific "cookbook" instructions on *doing* research, hoping my students would eventually figure out why research was done the way I told them to do it. I was unable to find a book that resolved the dilemma.

A book that would solve this dilemma would have to do three things. First, it should present the fundamental logic of scientific research, addressing social science and social research by extension. Second, it should describe in detail many of the most conventional techniques used in research, showing how they flowed from the fundamental logic of science: *why* they were "conventional." Finally, based on the understanding of both logic and techniques, such a book should prepare readers to handle the variety of compromises they would have to make in the design and execution of actual research. In my teaching, I had found the progression of logic-to-techniques-to-compromises the most effective in training well-rounded and flexible researchers, and, in part, I decided to write *The Practice of Social Research* in order to accomplish that goal.

I have also grown convinced through my writing and my teaching that the fundamental logic of scientific inquiry was the same for survey research, experiments, content analysis, field research, and the other methods employed by social scientists. In the case of *quantitative analysis,* in fact, many of the techniques as well as the logic were the same, regardless of the initial method of data collection. This book also has its origins, then, in this sense of the commonality of method in social research.

Some of the materials concerning survey research are taken from my earlier book, *Survey Research Methods.* Readers familiar with that book will recognize those portions. All of the sections in this book dealing with methods other than survey research, however, are completely new, and many of the topics covered in the earlier book have been substantially reconceptualized and rewritten. For example, the discussion of conceptualization and operationalization is greatly expanded here, reflecting the more general concern of this book. The chapter on *causation* is an example of the many topics that were not covered in the earlier book.

The Practice of Social Research is organized as follows. Part One addresses some of the basic, logical considerations that lie at the foundation of scientific inquiry. The chapters in this part of the book give readers a "feel" for those very general considerations that make *scientific* inquiry different from nonscientific inquiry. At the same time, readers should develop an awareness of the many similarities that cross-cut *all* kinds of inquiry.

Part Two is addressed to matters of study design. It presents a picture of the ways in which social scientists begin to organize and specify their research interests and plans. While the specific topics covered in Part Two are more directly related to some methods than to others, my purpose has been to deal with those fundamental issues of research design that apply to most kinds of projects.

Part Three discusses the different methods of data collection available to social researchers. There are a number of issues and procedures that cut across several such methods, but I have kept them separate here in the belief that a student wishing to learn about content analysis, for example, should be able to find out about it in one coherent section of the book, rather than having to skip around. While it would be impossible to exhaust fully all the different data-collection methods available to social researchers, I have attempted to cover all those that students are likely to engage in.

In Part Four, the distinction between different data-collection methods is once again set aside. The basic logic and skills of *quantitative* analysis apply no more or less to one data-collection method than to another. They apply to *data,* not to methods of collecting data. The chapters comprising Part Four mix discussions of the fundamental logic of descriptive and explanatory analysis with guides and concrete illustrations for *doing* data analysis.

In Part Four and throughout the book, I have stressed *fundamental,* even rudimentary, logic and techniques rather than more advanced and sophisticated materials. This is done intentionally in the belief that unless people understand the fundamentals of research *fully,* they will have difficulty

understanding and utilizing wisely the more advanced and powerful techniques available to social scientists.

Robert Huitt of Texas A&I University and I have prepared a compan-
ion guide, *Practicing Social Research*, for this book. It includes questions
designed to reinforce a reader's understanding of the text material, as well as
offering at least three extended activities for each chapter of the book. These
activities are designed to get readers *doing* research, thereby extending their
knowledge of research concepts.

Ultimately, I hope to convey the basic perspective and manner of the
social researcher. I would like the reader to learn how a social researcher
thinks about things. In this sense, I have been more interested in training
detectives than technicians. I guess I've always had the romantic notion that
Sherlock Holmes and Inspector Gideon could have given Sam Stouffer and
Paul Lazarsfeld a run for the money as social scientists.

Acknowledgements

It would be impossible to acknowledge adequately all the people who have been influential, directly or indirectly, in forming what this book contains. My previous book, *Survey Research Methods*, was dedicated to Samuel Stouffer, Paul Lazarsfeld, and Charles Glock; I would like to repeat the acknowledgement of my debt to them.

Turning to the present book, I am particularly grateful to Steve Rutter at Wadsworth for a variety of editorial and psychic supports that are too numerous to list. In an important way, this is Steve's book as well as mine. I would also like to offer a special acknowledgement to John Lofland, a friend and colleague. It was clear to me from the start that I had the least expertise in the general area of field research. John's truly excellent little book, *Analyzing Social Settings*, was invaluable in my own education in this area, and his willingness to have portions of that book reproduced here have added much to this book.

I am grateful for the intellectual comradeship I have enjoyed with Joe Seldin, a colleague here at Hawaii. Joe has been a fountain of insight, a demanding critic, and an inexhaustible source of information.

Special thanks go to my coauthor Robert Huitt for his invaluable work on *Practicing Social Research*.

Pat Horton, Jesse Ohta, and Janet Tanahara were invaluable in handling the thousands of clerical matters that are the bridge between a good idea and a book. In addition, I am grateful to the Haas Community Fund for a generous grant that paid for additional clerical assistance.

Thanks also go to the editorial assistants at Wadsworth, Dee Baer Farneth, Annette "Sam" Kauffman, and Carrie Bagala, for their assistance throughout the publishing process; to Elizabeth Bagwell for her excellent editing; and to Susan Yessne for producing the book from the manuscript.

I would also like to thank Professors Andy B. Anderson, Purdue University; David J. Bordua, University of Illinois at Urbana-Champaign; Thomas J. Dimieri, Wellesley College; Dean Dorn, California State University, Sacramento; Billy J. Franklin, Wright State University; David B. Graeven, California State University, Hayward; Bernard C. Hennessy, California State University, Hayward; Robert E. Huitt, Texas A & I University; Judson R. Landis, California State University, Sacramento; Ronald Miller, CUNY, Brooklyn College; David Nasatir, University of California, Berkeley; and, Charles

Wellford, Florida State University, Tallahassee, for their constructive criticism of the manuscript.

I will avoid the customary tip-of-the-hat to my wife, Sheila, since such a gesture would be wholly inadequate and inappropriate. I have acknowledged my many debts to her directly and will continue to do so.

Finally, I would like to dedicate this book on social research to two people neither of whom would be regarded as a social scientist. Georg von Bekesy was a distinguished physiologist whom I had the pleasure of knowing for about four years prior to his death in 1972. Professor von Bekesy was perhaps the last of the Renaissance Men: interested in and unaccountably insightful in everything, winner of the 1961 Nobel Prize in Medicine-Physiology, possessor of a dozen or so doctorates and as many fluent languages, an expert in fine art, the gentlest of men, and the compleat scientist. Despite our short acquaintance, I gained a feel for doing science from Professor von Bekesy that I would be hard-pressed to describe or acknowledge in words.

The second dedication is to Werner Erhard, founder of the Erhard Seminars Training (*est*). Werner is not even a scientist within the customary meaning of that term, and yet his influence pervades the whole book. In June 1973, in the midst of writing the book, I took the *est* training. I suppose I took the training out of curiosity as much as anything else, because my personal life and career were both unquestionably successful at the time.

At the time I took the week-long training, the textbook was progressing satisfactorily, having reached the point of a craftsmanly chore whose initial novelty and excitement had worn off. Following the training, I found myself becoming more enthusiastic and more effective in everything I was doing. The book became a genuine pleasure again, truly a work of love that was more exciting in any given moment than it had been before. My enjoyment of writing, moreover, seemed to clarify and deepen my understanding of what I wanted to write; and the deeper, clearer understanding further fueled my enjoyment in a continuing spiral. Soon, in addition to understanding the logic of scientific inquiry, I began "getting it" the way you may get a joke as distinguished from having it explained to you until you understand it. That spiral of enjoying, understanding, and getting my discipline continues for me, and I want to acknowledge Werner for his assistance in getting it started and for the book that happened along the way.

Part One:
Introduction to Inquiry

This book has two chief purposes: to familiarize students with the underlying logic of scientific—especially *social* scientific—research and to describe some of the specific research techniques that have grown out of the use of scientific thinking in relation to social phenomena. The purpose of Part I of the book is to present the underlying logic of science.

Dr. Benjamin Spock, the renowned author-pediatrician, begins his books on child care by assuring new mothers that they already know more about child care than they think. A similar beginning would be wholly appropriate in this book as well. You do know more about scientific research than you may think. More important, you have been conducting scientific research, or a reasonable facsimile, all your life. All this book will do is assist you in improving your knowledge and abilities.

Chapter 1 begins with an examination of native human inquiry—how we go about learning things about the world we live in. Following that introduction, the chapter turns to science as a refined approach to human inquiry. Special attention is paid to ways scientific inquiry often differs from nonscientific inquiry. Much of the chapter is addressed to some of the foibles of nonscientific human inquiry and some of the ways in which science offers safeguards against those foibles. You should come away from Chapter 1 with a well-rounded understanding of what science is all about.

Chapter 2 deals specifically with social scientific inquiry. The lessons of Chapter 1 are applied to the study of human social behavior. You will discover that, while special considerations are involved in studying people, the basic logic of all science is the same.

1
Human Inquiry and Science

1.1
Introduction

"Science" is a familiar word used by everyone. Yet images of science differ greatly. For some, science is mathematics; for others it is white coats and laboratories. It is often confused with technology or equated with difficult high school or college courses.

Science is, of course, none of these things per se. It is difficult, however, to specify exactly what science is. The purpose of this chapter is to clarify the term sufficiently at the outset for the remainder of this book to make sense. Science, as we shall see, is a special form of human inquiry. It provides us with ways for learning about the world we live in. To appreciate what makes science special, we will find it useful to consider briefly some daily examples of human inquiry.

1.2
Native Human Inquiry

Practically all people, and many lower animals as well, exhibit a desire to predict their future circumstances. They seem willing, moreover, to undertake this task using causal and probabalistic reasoning. First, it is generally recognized that future circumstances are somehow caused or conditioned by present ones. People learn that walking against a traffic light may result in their being hit by a car, that swimming beyond the reef may bring an unhappy encounter with sharks. Sharks, on the other hand, may learn that hanging around the reef may bring a happy encounter with unhappy swimmers. Students may learn that studying hard will result in better examination grades than will not studying hard.

People, and seemingly other animals, learn also that such patterns of cause and effect are probabalistic in nature: the effects occur more often when the causes occur than when the causes are absent. Thus, students learn that studying hard in most instances produces good examination grades; but this may not happen every time. We recognize the danger of swimming beyond the reef—with reference to the probability or likelihood of being eaten by sharks—without necessarily believing that every such swim will be fatal.

We will return to these two concepts throughout the book. As we shall see, science makes such concepts more explicit and provides techniques for dealing with them more rigorously than is the case in casual human inquiry.

It is important to distinguish prediction from understanding. Often we are able to predict without understanding—as in the case of the ability to predict rain on the basis of an aching trick knee. And often, even in the absence of understanding, we are willing to act on the basis of a demonstrated predictive ability. The race track buff who finds that the third-ranked horse in the third race of the day always wins will probably keep betting without knowing (or caring) why it works out that way.

Frequently, the ability to predict comes from simple observation. The family dog can predict that punishment will result from his nestling into an expensive chair in the living room. A young child may learn to expect reprimands for wandering into the street. Neither is likely to understand why the given action produces the given result; but each observes that this is the case, and the power to predict is born.

We can learn to predict through the observation of patterns of regularities. We discover, and other animals discover, that life is not a series of random occurrences. Some events exhibit a pattern of regularity over time: commuter traffic is always heaviest during the morning rush hour. Other events exhibit a pattern of regularity with regard to conditions: commuter traffic will be relatively light during, say, a truckers' strike. Life is full of regularities, and we observe and recognize them.

Whatever drives or instincts provide the most primitive motivation for human beings and other animals, their satisfactions depend heavily on the ability to predict future circumstances. It comes as no surprise, then, that people, and perhaps other animals, seek to discover regularities. People, perhaps alone among the animals, do not just passively note regularities; they actively observe, compare, try to remember, and even experiment in the hope of uncovering new patterns.

People also seek to expand their recognition of regularities through understanding. Understanding why observed regularities occur has two important functions for the power to predict. First, understanding why a pattern occurs helps us evaluate its reliability; we can anticipate the conditions under which it would fail. Second, fully understanding the nature of one regular pattern may point to the probability of other previously unrecognized patterns. Thus, the hunter who concludes that a particular game animal is found in a specific wooded area because of the cool shade may then seek out game in other cool places.

Ultimately, people seek generalized understanding, for this provides a maximum predictive power from a minimum of direct observation. It would be simply impossible for us to discover very many of the regularities around us through direct observation alone. We must rely on our ability to reason logically.

The search for generalized understanding typically takes two distinct approaches: induction and deduction. **Induction** is the process of establishing general principles from specific observations; **deduction** is the process of deriving specific expectations from general principles. The development and the use of generalized understanding involve both of these processes in concert. For example, a student may observe that his instructor reacts favorably to students who speak out in class. The student may conclude (induction) that, as a general principle, the instructor enjoys interaction with his students. The student might further conclude on the basis of that general principle (deduction) that the instructor would react favorably to students who spoke to him after class and visited him during office hours.

The student in our example might observe later, however, that only the first of his expectations (deductions) proved correct. His subsequent observations might help him refine his understanding of the general principle at work, and the refinement might suggest other specific expectations that could be tested through further observation.

This cyclical process of inductive and deductive inquiry with its goal of generalized understanding is deeply imbedded in our daily lives. As we shall see, it is also fundamental to scientific inquiry. In science the specific expectations that we derive from general principles are called **hypotheses.** Checking these expectations against subsequent experiences is called **hypothesis-testing,** and the whole process of developing generalized understanding is called **theory construction.**

1.3
Sources of Understanding

If the preceding discussion has made human inquiry seem a totally individual and logical process, the record should be set straight. While every person discovers patterns of regluarities on his own, his social life plays a significant role—both assisting and hindering inquiry. At least two social sources of understanding—tradition and authority—deserve brief consideration here.

Tradition

Every person inherits a culture made up, in part, of accepted knowledge about the workings of the world. He may learn from others that planting corn in the spring will gain the greatest assistance from the gods, that sugar from too much candy will decay his teeth, that building airstrips will bring cargo planes, that the circumference of a circle is approximately twenty-two-sevenths the length of the radius, and that masturbation will make him blind. He may or may not test these "regularities" independently, and persons from a different culture may or may not agree as to their validity.

Tradition, in this sense of the term, has some clear advantages for human inquiry. No individual is forced to start from scratch in his search for regularities and understanding. Knowledge is cumulative, and an inherited body of generalized understanding is the jumping-off point for the development of more.

At the same time, tradition is often detrimental to human inquiry. The person who seeks a different understanding of something that "everyone already understands and has always understood" may be marked the fool for his efforts. More to the point, it may never occur to him to seek a different understanding at all.

Authority

During his own lifetime, a person may fall beneficiary to newly recognized regularities and understandings. Often acceptance of these new acquisitions will be related to the status of their discoverer. The successful hunter who declares that game animals seek out cool places will, perhaps, be more readily believed than the unsuccessful hunter. The biologist who declares that the common cold can be transmitted through kissing will probably be believed more than one's maiden aunt.

Like tradition, authority can both assist and hinder human inquiry. Especially in the face of contradictory explanations for a given phenomenon, we do well to trust in the judgment of the person possessing the authority of special training and expertise in the realm of the phenomenon. At the same time, inquiry can be greatly hindered by the legitimate authority who errs within his own special province. Inquiry is also hindered by dependence on the "authority" of one speaking outside his special realm of expertise, such as the government official who, lacking any biochemical expertise, declares marijuana to be a dangerous drug.

I shall turn now to science as another source of understanding. I will compare and contrast it with the type of inquiry we all practice in our daily lives.

1.4
The Traditional View of Science

I have already acknowledged the difficulty of specifying precisely what science is. At the same time, you should come away from this chapter with a fuller understanding of what science is than you had before. In this section, I will describe the scientific process in a fashion that I suspect is rather typical of introductory science courses and textbooks. The traditional view of science, unfortunately, can make the subject seem relatively straightforward, precise, and even routine. When it does this, it does not give the student a very realistic impression of what a scientist does; nor does it prepare him to undertake scientific research of his own.

For all its shortcomings, however, the traditional view of science provides a useful starting point for our discussions. Subsequent sections of this chapter will present less traditional views. If you are able to balance these several perspectives, you will have a healthy understanding of what science is, and you will be in a position to learn how to do scientific research.

Scientific Research

Scientists, we are told, begin with an interest in some aspect of the world around them. They may be interested in knowing how blood pressure is regulated in the body, why one strain of rice is hardier than another, what determines the paths of comets, or what causes cancer. Their interest in such things frequently may be spurred by observed inconsistencies or contradictions. The scientist then engages in a logical, theoretical exercise aimed at identifying the relevant aspects of the phenomenon under study and at suggesting logical relationships among those aspects. The result of this exercise may be a set of statements describing conditions and relationships in general, abstract terms.

On the basis of his theory, the scientist then derives hypotheses: predictions about events or conditions. Often, hypotheses are of an if-then form. If event A were to occur, then event B would follow. Since this relationship is warranted by the general theory, the failure of event B to follow event A in real life would call into question the validity of the theory itself.

A well-known illustration from the physical sciences should clarify this process further. One of Aristotle's legacies left to Western science was the assertion that heavy objects fell to earth faster than light ones, with their speeds being proportional to their weights. Centuries after Aristotle, however, Galileo, a father of the experimental method, found that this was simply not the case. Dropping objects of different weights simultaneously from atop a high tower, he discovered that they reached the earth about the same time—the heavier one preceding the lighter one by only the width of a few fingers. Galileo's experiments, then, contradicted Aristotle's assertion that speed was a direct function of weight.

Galileo further challenged the Aristotelian position through purely logical deductions. Let us suppose we have a heavy object, H, and a light object, L, Galileo reasoned. According to Aristotle, H should fall faster than L. If they were tied together and dropped, then, the relatively slower speed of L should somewhat hold back the progress of H, while the relatively faster speed of H should pull L along somewhat faster than it would normally fall. The speed of the two objects tied together should be somewhere between the independent speeds of H and L. On the other hand, Galileo pointed out, the combined weight of L and H tied together would be greater than that of H alone; hence, the combined package should fall even faster than H. Since these two conclusions contradict each other, the only reasonable alternative would be that all objects fall at the same speed regardless of their weights.

Galileo's ingenious deductions, while apparently demolishing the Aristotelian position, still left Galileo with a problem. His own experiments seemed to contradict the assertion that all objects fall at the same speed. The heavy ones always arrived a bit earlier than the light ones. Galileo then turned to other observations. He noted that heavy objects fell much faster than light ones when they descended through water as opposed to air, and the difference was greater still when water was replaced by mercury. Aha! The three media differed greatly in the amount of resistance they offered to objects passing through them. And while air offered the least resistance, it offered some. Galileo concluded that the resistance of the air accounted for the greater speed of cannon balls, as opposed to musket balls, dropped from the top of the tower.

This line of reasoning led Galileo to a hypothesis: objects of grossly different weights would fall at the same speed *through a vacuum*. Unfortunately, Aristotle had also declared vacuums impossible. Hence there were none available in which Galileo could test his hypothesis.

Operationalization

Theoretical hypotheses are often very general and abstract predictions about the nature of things. While Galileo's hypothesis regarding travel through a vacuum is not difficult for us to understand, it was far more difficult for many of his contemporaries. Similarly, many of the hypotheses of modern science would be impossible for most of us to understand.

The next step in the scientific process being described here is called **operationalization**. Most simply put, this means that the scientist must describe in detail the operations that might be performed in order to test the truth of his hypothesis in the real world. Typically, he describes a set of operations that produce some kind of observed result. Certain observed results, he tells us, would confirm his hypothesis while other observed results would deny it.

To test Galileo's hypothesis, it would be necessary for us to specify the operations that would result in the creation of a vacuum, the manner in which objects would be allowed to fall through it, and the manner in which we would measure their speeds. We would further specify that observing the two objects to fall at the same speed would constitute confirmation of the hypothesis and that observing them to fall at different speeds would deny it.

Experimentation

The final stage in the process would involve the execution of an experiment based on the operationalized hypothesis. If the hypothesis is confirmed by the experiment, then the general theory from which the hypothesis was derived is also partially confirmed. If the hypothesis is not confirmed, the general theory is called into question; and the scientist goes back to the drawing board. Whatever the outcome of the experiment, the scientist presumably publishes his findings, he gets academic tenure, and the world presumably becomes a little better place to live.

Summary

Because the scientist operates in accord with rational and objective procedures, his conclusions are presumably of a higher quality than the subjective impressions and prejudices of the layman. The scientist deals with facts and figures; and, we are told, figures do not lie.

As we shall see later in the chapter, scientific inquiry is typically a refinement of native human inquiry, but science is not as neat and clean as the above description might suggest.

1.5

The Debunking of Science

In recent years, some students have been given an image of science and of scientists that is quite different from the traditional perspective. This more iconoclastic view of science has a number of dimensions.

First, scientists are motivated by the same human emotions and hindered by the same human frailties as are other human beings. Scientists, we are told, frequently select their subjects of study on the basis of personal biases; and some may devote all their energies to "proving" some pet hunch. Rather than framing and executing experiments objectively, they design research as a continuing search for data to substantiate their prejudices.

Similarly, the cults and cliques of the scientific world have been held up to public view. A scientific paper submitted for publication may be judged more on the basis of the researcher's credentials (degrees, schools, etc.) than on the intrinsic merits of the paper itself. A journal editor trained under Professor X may tend to reject all papers submitted by students of Professor Y. Moreover, accepted ideas in scientific disciplines are very difficult to challenge. A research paper presenting a radically new perspective on an old and presumably settled issue may never see publication.

We are told that grantsmanship has replaced scholarship in science, that many researchers evaluate a prospective research project in terms of the likelihood of foundation funding more than in terms of its possible contribution to understanding. In these terms, a researcher may be judged by the number of research assistants he employs rather than by the quality of his research findings.

Since so much scientific research is conducted within universities, the growing criticism of the publish-or-perish norm attributed to most contemporary academic departments is worth noting. Faculty members are often expected to publish research reports in academic journals or as books in order to gain promotion, tenure, or even renewal of contract. Under the pressure of this nonscientific norm of the scientific community, researchers sometimes look more toward the quantity than the quality of research projects and reports. A forthright rejection of the norm may deny them the basic resources for research altogether.

Finally, scientific researchers—social and other—have been on the receiving end of growing criticism regarding their participation in research that carries negative social implications. Researchers have been criticized for directly or indirectly supporting national war efforts or colonialism or for providing the tools of social control that may then be used to subjugate people at home or abroad. Scientific researchers are receiving demands that they exercise a social conscience even in the exercise of their scientific research.

These criticisms of modern science have been fueled by a number of candid research biographies published in recent years by noted scientists.[1] Increasingly, practicing scientists have attempted to present honest accounts of their research projects, to place their findings in proper perspective, and to provide guidance to aspiring researchers. Since these accounts have pointed to errors, oversights, and other practical problems, many of the contemporary critics of science have taken these as inside admissions that all of science is bunk.

The recent criticism of science is probably a healthy turn of events. For too long, science has been regarded as a mystical enterprise and scientists as infallible superhumans. If science is a rational and objective activity, then it should withstand objective and rational evaluation. Those aspects that do not survive such a critique should probably not remain a part of science.

There is a danger inherent in the current widespread criticisms of science: they may serve as an excuse for dismissing science altogether. Especially for those who may have difficulty understanding science, it is easier to dismiss the whole thing as meaningless, ritualistic, or even evil than to master it and make it better.

I am, of course, biased on this topic. (See how candid scientists are.) I believe that science is a distinctive form of human inquiry. While many activities that may be called scientific are not so in my opinion, there are many scientific activities that are importantly different from other human activities; and understanding those differences is extremely important.

The primary problem here lies with the inaccuracy of the traditional perspective of the scientific method as it is conventionally presented to beginning science students. Science in practice does not correspond fully to the traditional image of science, but at the same time it is not as bad as its severest critics contend. The following section aims at describing science in practice as distinguished from the traditional image. Then we shall turn to those features that make science distinct from other human activities.

1.6

Science in Practice

Although the traditional perspective suggests that the scientist moves directly from an interest in some subject to the logical derivation of a theory, this is seldom the case. His initial interest in the subject often stems from some previous empirical research, perhaps some curious findings

---

1. See, for example, James D. Watson, *The Double Helix* (New York: The New American Library, Inc., 1968) for a candid account of the research which resulted in the discovery of the DNA molecule. For other candid research biographies, see Phillip E. Hammond, ed., *Sociologists at Work* (New York: Basic Books, 1964).

generated by his own research or that of some other researcher. Thus, he may begin with a very specific discovery—that event A is usually followed by event B or that two variables are empirically related to each other—and then set out to derive a more general understanding of why that is the case.

Theories are almost never the result of a totally deductive process. They are more typically the end result of a long chain of inductive and deductive activities: observation and interpretation, looking and thinking. At one point, the scientist may have a tentative explanation for an empirical relationship; he may test it partially through the collection of more data, use the results to modify his explanation, collect more data, and so forth.

Theories are seldom confirmed at a given time because there are relatively few critical experiments in science—experiments upon which a whole theory stands or falls. Instead, evidence is built up over time to lend support to a continually modified theory. Some form of the theory may eventually become generally accepted, but we can seldom point to a given time at which it was "proven." Moreover, all theories continue to undergo modifications even after they have been generally accepted.

The empirical definition of concepts is never as clear-cut as the traditional image of science may suggest. Most scientific concepts lend themselves to a variety of interpretations. Thus, the researcher typically specifies tentative empirical definitions of those concepts, and the results of his studies are used for evaluating the measurement procedures as much as for testing hypotheses.

Where concepts can be operationalized in a reasonably unambiguous manner, experimental results are seldom conclusive in an absolute sense, even with regard to specific hypotheses. A hypothesis is seldom confirmed or rejected fully on the basis of a single test. Theories are normally accepted on the basis of a weight of evidence amassed over the course of several experiments. If a large number of empirical observations are better explained by a given theory than by any other theory available, that theory will probably be accepted for the time being.

Finally, the impression that empirical testing of ideas is a routine activity is totally incorrect. The traditional image of science suggests that brilliance is required in the derivation of theories and in the design of experiments, but that the execution of the experiments themselves is pretty dull and unimaginative stuff. In practice, the execution of an experiment requires countless critical decisions. Unexpected situations arise. Bizarre observations are recorded suggesting measurement errors. Data may be lost or falsified or both. The operationalization of concepts is rarely completely unambiguous and must be further specified during the experiment. Each of these situations requires decisions that will influence the outcome of the experiment and, by extension, the hypothesis and the theory from which it may have been derived.

This is an important point in the context of the present volume. Many of today's students have served or know others who have served as research workers on scientific projects. Most can attest to the disparity between the project design and the day-to-day work on the project. Especially in the case of a poorly supervised project, the research worker may take a rather jaundiced view of the scientific-sounding description of the project as reported in an academic journal. Such a student may conclude that all science is unscientific.

I emphasize this point for two purposes. First, I would stress (and will do so throughout the book) that the very quality of a research project can depend greatly on the seemingly mundane decisions and activities that go into the collection and processing of data. The project director who does not involve himself in such activities runs a serious risk that the project will be meaningless. However, the implications of routine decisions are not always easily apparent. Not every decision will have important consequences. It takes skill to know when what might seem a sloppy procedure to a student research worker might not in fact affect the study significantly. The capacity to make good decisions and to evaluate the implications of bad ones depends on a well-founded understanding of the logic of science as a distinctive activity. It is this latter topic to which we will now turn.

1.7
Science and the Foibles of Human Inquiry

Science, I have suggested, is in no way magically distinct from the sort of inquiry all of us engage in day to day; but I do not mean to imply that science is no different from, or no better than, casual human inquiry. The point to be made here is that casual human inquiry often goes astray and falls into error. While scientific inquiry often does the same thing, certain characteristics of science make errors less likely. We shall turn now to a consideration of some of the more common foibles of casual human inquiry and see the ways in which scientific inquiry provides safeguards against them.

Inaccurate Observation

Observation is perhaps the keystone of inquiry; thus, inaccurate observations can mislead inquiry. An American tourist in France may be rudely treated by several strangers and conclude that Frenchmen are rude, while the offenders may actually have been German tourists. A primitive tribesman may observe someone emerging from a dark cave and believe the person to be a certain fellow tribesman. When the fellow tribesman later suffers a severe fever and dies, the cave may be viewed as the cause of the fever, when in fact someone else altogether was seen there. A meteor streaking across the sky may be mistaken for a flying saucer and held responsible for the earthquake that occurs the following day.

Science is based on careful observation and measurement, and the care with which scientific observations are made is an important norm of science—one that students of science are taught early in their training. Whereas the layman often observes casually and, perhaps, semiconsciously, the scientist is trained to make observation a conscious, calculated endeavor.

Simply making observation more deliberate has the effect of reducing errors.

In many sciences, both simple and complex measurement devices help to guard against inaccurate observation. At the same time, these add a degree of precision well beyond the capacity of the unassisted human senses. These are two of the ways in which science guards against inaccurate observations. However, such safeguards are not 100 percent effective, and errors are sometimes made.

Overgeneralization

Man discerns patterns and develops understanding on the basis of particular observations, and the desire for generalized understanding may often lead him to imagine broad patterns on the basis of relatively few specific observations. Let's imagine an escaped prisoner of war moving across a strange countryside. Will the local inhabitants protect him or betray him? If his first contact results in protection, he may conclude that all the local inhabitants will react similarly. The journalist under pressure to understand and report overall student reactions to a militant demonstration may be tempted to generalize from the consistent responses of the first three students interviewed, and may spend his remaining time trying to explain why the student body as a whole feels that way.

Probably the tendency to overgeneralize is greatest when the pressure to arrive at a generalized understanding is greatest. Yet it also occurs casually in the absence of pressure. Whenever it does occur, it can misdirect or even block further inquiry.

Although generalization is one of the primary characteristics of science, a number of safeguards against overgeneralization exist as well. The replication of research under slightly varying conditions is perhaps the chief safeguard. For example, the layman observing that an iron bar oxidizes when exposed to air for a period of time might assume that this is a general characteristic of all metal. The scientist, however, would test this possibility by actually exposing samples of several different metals to air under controlled conditions. He would discover that some metals oxidize while others do not. He would then turn to the task of developing a generalized understanding of why some do and others do not. What are the common characteristics of metals in the two groups?

A later discussion in Chapter 17 concerning the elaboration model and the concept of specification in particular will illustrate this safeguard further. Ironically, it is the scientist's desire for generalizability that leads him to attempt ever more general applications of an observed pattern, and this in turn points to the limits of the generalization.

Selective Observation

A danger of overgeneralization is that it may lead to selective observation. Once we have concluded that a particular pattern exists and have developed a generalized understanding of why, we are tempted to heed future observations that correspond with the pattern and to ignore contradictory ones. Racial and ethnic prejudices, for example, depend heavily on selective observation for their persistence. Having been cheated by a shopkeeper and having observed him to be Jewish—perhaps mistakenly—a man may overgeneralize that all Jewish shopkeepers are dishonest. Subsequently, he may take special note of dishonest actions by other Jewish shopkeepers while ignoring honest Jews and dishonest non-Jews. Others may take special note of all lazy blacks observed, while ignoring energetic blacks and lazy whites.

Whereas the layman may unconsciously limit his observations to those cases that generally confirm an already formed theory, the scientist has a degree of protection from this foible. Frequently the scientist does not begin his analysis and interpretation of data until a predetermined set of observations has been completed. In the oxidization example, a scientist may have designed a lengthy experiment in which different metals were to be exposed to air for a specified period of time. Once the predetermined period of exposure had passed, he would systematically examine the oxidation that had occurred with each sample. While a layman could unconsciously overlook an exposed and unoxidized piece of metal, the scientist conducting a careful experiment would be unlikely to do so as easily.

The scientist's commitment to a predetermined set of observations, which is worth underscoring, should be distinguished from the traditional image of science discussed at the outset of this chapter. In the illustration just given, there is no reason to suppose that the scientist in question designed his experiment on the basis of a carefully derived theory or even that he suspected that some metals would not oxidize. Indeed, he may have firmly believed that all metals shared this characteristic. As a scientist, however, he would be obliged to "document the obvious" (more about this later) by designing a reasonable test and deferring his conclusions until all the facts were in.

In a somewhat different sense, however, selective observation is inherent in all human inquiry. Indeed, in the scientific effort to discover what causes a given event or situation, the scientist spends much of his time ruling out those things that do not constitute the cause. In the best circumstances, possible causes are ruled out on the basis of empirical tests, but the possible causes are always so numerous as to make this impossible in every case. Thus some variables are ruled out on the basis of established theories, logic, common sense, or simple oversight. Probably no one has ever carefully tested the effect of a falling object's color on its acceleration.

There is no simple or single guard against the dangers of selective observation in this sense. Only the cumulative and progressive nature of science, the search for ever better answers, work against it in the long term.

Deduced Information

Observations contradicting one's understanding sometimes cannot be ignored. The Jewish shopkeeper who walks four miles to return the anti-Semite's lost wallet, the black who is energetic and hard-working, and the native tribesman who picnics in the tabu cave without injury—all present problems to prejudiced people. A solution to the problem, of course, is to conclude that one's earlier understanding of the situation was incorrect.

Deducing unobserved information on the basis of one's understanding is another solution. The anti-Semite has two immediate deductive possibilities: (1) the shopkeeper in question is not really Jewish, or (2) he has a hidden, diabolical purpose in returning the wallet. The hard-working black may be seen as seeking an executive post in which he can be lazy. And the tabu-violating tribesman may be regarded as suffering from a not yet apparent malady.

Scientists, too, sometimes must resolve the problem of observations that contradict hypotheses. And if the hypothesis is a dearly held one, the data may be questioned. The scientist, however, is unlikely to dismiss them out of hand. He may suggest replicated or additional observations that would resolve the ambiguity without threatening the hypothesis, but he then tests his explanation through new observations. If further observations do not fulfill his expectations, he continues looking and perhaps revises his hypothesis.

I do not wish to suggest that all scientists are perfect in this regard, or even that any scientist always behaves this way. Adherence to this norm, however, is one of the things that distinguishes scientific from nonscientific inquiry.

Illogical Reasoning

Without attempting a rigorous, epistemological definition of logic, we may nonetheless conclude that man often employs what must be regarded as illogical reasoning, often as a solution to the dilemma presented by observations that contradict his understanding. Surely, one of the most amazing creations of the human mind is "the exception that proves the rule." Whereas deducing a new conclusion requires a complex framework of understanding and may be mentally taxing, this alternative brushes away contradictions in a simple stroke of illogic.

What statisticians have labeled the gambler's fallacy provides another illustration. A consistent run of either good or bad luck is presumed to foreshadow its opposite. An evening of bad luck at poker may kindle the belief that a winning hand is due. Or conversely, an extended period of pleasant weather may lead to the conclusion that it is certain to rain on the weekend.

The scientific method has a number of general and specific safeguards against illogical reasoning. As a specific example, probability theory works against both the exception that proves the rule and the gambler's fallacy. Flipping a coin is an activity governed by probability theory. Each time a normal coin is flipped, the probability of its landing heads is .5 or 50 percent. This probability is unaffected by the results of previous flips. Thus, if we have flipped ten heads in a row—an unlikely event—the probability of getting heads the eleventh time is still .5. Thus, the scientist does not fall into the trap of the gambler's fallacy.

Because the likelihood of getting heads each time is 50 percent, flipping a coin ten times in a row is most likely to result in five heads and five tails. Thus, getting ten heads in a row is unlikely. Should this happen, however, the scientist is spared from proclaiming the exception that proves the rule, since probability theory permits—even demands—that rare events happen occasionally. Indeed, probability theory tells us approximately how often they should happen.

More generally, scientists avoid illogical reasoning by using systems of logic consciously and explicitly. Probability theory, mentioned above, is not merely common sense; it is a rigorously explicated system based on logical deductions and empirical observations. While logical systems in science change from time to time—and specific systems may be proven faulty—scientists use such systems carefully and deliberately rather than casually. Recall the illustration earlier in this chapter concerning Galileo's logical reasoning that the situation of two objects tied together proved Aristotle's theory of falling objects logically impossible. The two objects tied together could not logically fall faster than the heavier one alone and also fall slower than the heavier one alone.

In Chapter 2, as well as in several chapters in Part Four of the present work, more concrete illustrations are provided of logical reasoning in science. Scientists are far from perfect in their reasoning, however. Every scientist sometimes reasons illogically. When he does this, though, his colleagues will usually set him straight, thereby providing still another safeguard.

The Premature Closure of Inquiry

Overgeneralization, selective observation, deduced information, and the defensive use of illogical reasoning all characterize the premature closure of inquiry. We have seen that man seeks the ability to predict the future through generalized understanding. He wants success in that endeavor. As a result, he wants assurance that he has been successful, and one important form of assurance is the positive declaration of success. This may be an individual or a social act.

The anti-Semite who says, "I understand Jews; don't try to confuse me," has effected a personal closure on inquiry. The private foundation or government agency that refuses to support further research on a topic that is "already understood" effects closure as a social act, and so does the denominational college that prohibits scholarship that might challenge the existence of God. And more generally, tradition and authority may have this effect.

I have already pointed out that science is an open-ended enterprise in which conclusions are constantly being modified. This is an explicit norm of science. *Experienced* scientists, therefore, accept this as a fact of life and expect established theories to be overturned eventually. And if one scientist considers a line of inquiry to be completed forever, his colleagues may not. If a whole generation of scientists closes inquiry on a given topic, a later generation of scientists is likely to set about testing the old ideas and changing many of them.

Ego-Involvement in Understanding

The search for regularities and generalized understanding is not a trivial intellectual exercise. It critically affects our personal lives. Our understanding of events and conditions is often of special psychological significance to us. The man who has lost his job or has failed to be promoted may "understand" his plight as a consequence of an insidious, foreign conspiracy. This understanding of the situation avoids any explanation involving his personal inabilities. Any challenge to the idea that a Wall-Street-communist-Jewish-Jesuit conspiracy exists is a challenge, indirectly, to his self-image. As another example, his more successful co-worker may be ego-involved in the general understanding that hard work and ability result in success.

Similarly, our willingness, or even the necessity, to act on our understandings creates ego-involvement in them. Thus, the religious ascetic who "understands" that earthly sacrifice will be rewarded after death is not likely to challenge the existence of an after-life, nor is he likely to respond positively to others who do so. The man who invests his precious savings in a Rolls Royce on the "understanding" that it will bring him increased status may subsequently rule out the possibility that a Bentley may have conferred even higher standing.

In the same way, social institutions, associations, and societies, too, often develop something like ego-involvement in understandings. Thus physicians as a group have an ego-involvement in the understanding that all chiropractors are quacks. A nation may become chauvinistically committed to the understanding that it was the object of aggression just before it launched its massive military attack. Such commitments impede further inquiry.

Because scientists are human beings, it is not surprising that they may suffer from an egotistical defensiveness regarding their own ideas and conclusions. An astronomer who has a comet named after him is not likely to brook lightly a challenge to its existence. The biochemist who has a life-saving vaccine named after him may react emotionally to a later suggestion that it is ineffective. A scientist who has devoted his life to a particular line of inquiry will not easily agree that it represents a meaningless dead end. Even so, a full commitment to the norms of science may bring a scientist to recognize his own errors. If not, there are always his colleagues; and in the end, science will overcome the problem even if the individual scientist does not.

The Mystification of Residuals

None of us can hope to understand everything. No matter how intelligent or how diligent we may be in our inquiry, there will always be countless events and situations that we do not understand. Man may never fully understand the origin of the universe; a given individual may never in his lifetime understand why he failed calculus in his freshman year of college.

One common response to this problem is to attribute the phenomenon to mystical or supernatural causes that man cannot understand. I am not referring to religious or magical systems that offer reasonable, though supernatural, explanations of events. I mean the simple assertion that there are causes ultimately beyond human comprehension. Quite possibly this may be true of some events and situations in life. Perhaps this is the result of some supernatural design, or perhaps some phenomena are not part of a regular pattern, but are truly random. Unfortunately we cannot know in advance which, if any, manifestations fall into this category. In any event, human inquiry is impeded by the assumption that some things are beyond human comprehension. Inquiry is enhanced by the perhaps incorrect belief that everything may be understood ultimately.

Scientific inquiry is predicated on the belief that rational explanations exist for just about everything. Thus the scientist is loath to admit that anything lies beyond the ultimate grasp of scientific inquiry. Scientists will readily acknowledge that a given problem is currently unsolved, even that it may be insoluble in the immediate future; but they would not say that man cannot solve it.

Science versus the Foibles
of Inquiry in Perspective

I have attempted to indicate some of the ways in which scientists may escape the foibles of less systematic human inquiry. As I have pointed out repeatedly, scientists are not immune to any of the pitfalls previously discussed. Each pit contains the forgotten bones of scientists long since passed, and more will join them in the future. Two factors guide scientists away from these pits, however.

First, scientific inquiry is particularly self-conscious. While laymen observe and reason casually, the scientist is taught to pay close attention to his observing and reasoning activities. Moreover, he is taught to accept the validity of the several norms of scientific inquiry discussed earlier and is given the skills appropriate to them.

Second, interrelations among scientists improve the quality of inquiry and help to weed out errors. The most cordial collegiality can have this effect, and so can the most ruthless competition among scientists. While much human inquiry is done in private and goes unnoticed, scientific inquiry is more likely to be examined publicly. Whereas the criticized layman can keep the nature of his private inquiries to himself, the scientist simply cannot do this and still practice his profession.

1.8
Summary

The purpose of this chapter has been to start you thinking about scientific research. It began with a discussion of native human inquiry, and then it looked quickly at the traditional view of what science is like. Next we saw that the traditional view of science is being challenged and questioned increasingly these days. Some people have appeared more or less hostile in challenging the "sacred cow" status of science. Among scientists themselves, many have become more honest in describing how science is really done.

Against this backdrop, I have attempted to describe what science is like in practice. I have pointed out that science bears many similarities to nonscientific, human inquiry. In a sense, science is merely a refinement of native, human inquiry, with safeguards against common foibles.

1.9
Main Points

1. Inquiry is a natural human activity.

2. Man seeks generalized understanding about the world around him.

3. To understand, man observes and seeks to discover patterns of regularities in what he observes.

4. Science represents a special form of human inquiry.

5. The traditional image of science includes: theory, operationalization, and experimentation.

6. The traditional image of science is not a very accurate picture of how scientific research is actually conducted.

7. The special character of science can best be seen in relation to the common foibles of human inquiry: inaccurate observation, overgeneralization, selective observation, deduced information, illogical reasoning, premature closure of inquiry, ego-involvement in understanding, mystification of residuals.

8. Though science provides no guarantee against these foibles of inquiry, it does seem to provide some protection.

1.10
Annotated Bibliography

Butterfield, Herbert, *The Origins of Modern Science* (New York: Macmillan, 1960). An excellent, readable history of the development of science which illustrates many of the central issues involved in scientific inquiry. Understanding some of the stages through which science has passed can clarify what it is that now distinguishes scientific inquiry from nonscientific inquiry.

Irvine, William, *Apes, Angels, and Victorians* (New York: Meridian Books, 1959). An account of the social and religious furor which surrounded Darwin's publications on evolution and natural selection and Thomas Huxley's propounding of Darwin's ideas. In addition to casting science within a social context, this engaging little book offers excellent insights into the personal doubts and vacillations of a great scientist at work.

Kaplan, Abraham, *The Conduct of Inquiry* (San Francisco: Chandler, 1964). A standard reference volume on the logic and philosophy of science and social science. Though rigorous and scholarly, it is eminently readable and continually related to the real world of inquiry.

Kuhn, Thomas, *The Structure of Scientific Revolution* (Chicago: University of Chicago Press, 1962). An exciting and innovative recasting of the nature of scientific development. Kuhn disputes the notion of gradual change and modification in science, arguing instead that established "paradigms" tend to persist until the weight of contradictory evidence brings their rejection and replacement by new paradigms. This short book is at once stimulating and informative.

Watson, James, *The Double-Helix* (New York: New American Library, 1968). An informal and candid research biography describing the discovery of the DNA molecule, written by a principal in the drama. This account should serve as a healthy antidote to the "traditional" view of science as totally cool, rational, value-free, and objectively impersonal.

2
Social Scientific Inquiry

2.1
Introduction

One of the livelier academic debates of recent years has concerned the "scientific" status of those disciplines gathered under the rubric of the social sciences—typically including sociology, political science, social psychology, economics, anthropology, and sometimes fields such as geography, history, communications, and other composite and specialty fields. Basically at issue is whether human behavior can be subjected to scientific study. Whereas the previous chapter has pointed to the confusion that surrounds the term "science" in general, it should come as no surprise that academicians have disagreed about the social sciences.

Opposition to the idea of social sciences has risen both within the fields and outside them. Within the fields, the movement toward social science has represented a redirection and, in some cases, a renaming of established academic traditions. Increasingly, departments of government have been replaced by departments of political science. There are today few university departments of social studies, while sociology departments abound.

In many cases, the movement toward social science has represented a greater emphasis on systematic explanation where the previous emphasis was on description. In political science, it has meant a greater emphasis on explaining political behavior rather than describing political institutions. In anthropology, it has represented a lessening of the emphasis on ethnography. The growth of such subfields as econometrics has had this effect in economics, as has historiography in history. Some geographers have moved from the enumeration of imports and exports to mathematical models of migration. Quite understandably, professionals trained and experienced in the more traditional methods of these fields have objected to the new orientations.

Outside the social science departments, similar opposition has come from the physical sciences: from physicists, biologists, chemists, and so forth. Sometimes informed by the traditional image of science discussed in the previous chapter, the physical scientists have often objected that the scientific method could not be applied to human social behavior.

All too often, the advocates of social science have fueled the debate through the blind emulation of the trappings and rituals of the established sciences. This has taken many forms: a fascination with laboratory equipment, often inappropriate uses of statistics and mathematics, the development of obscure terminology, and the wholesale adoption of theories and terminology from the physical sciences.

For the most part, these errors would seem to have grown out of an acceptance of the traditional image of science and a lack of understanding of the logic of science in practice. Would-be social scientists have too often attempted to reach understanding through methods that do not work even for the physical scientists. The result frequently has been ridicule from physical scientists, professional colleagues, and laymen.

It is the firm assumption of this book that human social behavior can be subjected to scientific study as legitimately as can atoms, cells, and so forth. This assumption must be understood within the context of the earlier discussion of science in practice, however. From this perspective, there would seem to be no significant difference between the physical and social sciences.

Like physical scientists, social scientists seek to discover regularity and order. The social scientist looks for regularity in social behavior. He does this through careful observation and measurement, the discovery of relationships, and the framing of models and theories.

2.2
The Search for Social Regularities

Measuring Social Phenomena

The first building block of science is measurement, or systematic observation. There is no fundamental reason why social scientists cannot measure phenomena relevant to their inquiry. The age and sex of people can be measured. Place of birth and marital status can be measured in a number of different ways, varying in accuracy and economy.

Aggregate social behavior can be measured systematically as well. The political scientist can determine the election-day voting behavior of the entire electorate or of individual precincts. The amount of traffic over a given section of highway can be measured at different points in time.

Attitudes may also be measured, although this is a point of broad disagreement. For example, anti-Semitic prejudice can be measured by determining individual acceptance or rejection of beliefs and perspectives representing such prejudice. Religiosity, political liberalism and conservatism, authoritarianism, and similar variables can be measured in similar fashion.

Attitude measurement is frequently challenged as unscientific; and, while later sections of this chapter and of subsequent chapters in this book are addressed to this issue, a word or two of comment is in order here. It must be recognized that all such measurements (all measurements, in fact) are arbitrary at base. The social scientist cannot unequivocally describe one person as "religious" and another as "irreligious." Rather, he will describe people as *more or less* religious. This is by no means unique to social science, however, as evidenced by the hardness scale used by physical scientists, the Richter scale for earthquakes, and so forth.

Ultimately, all scientific measurements must be judged on the basis of their utility for inquiry, rather than on the basis of absolute Truth. The social scientist can never hope to describe a person as "religious" in an absolute sense any more than the chemist can ever describe a given element as "hard." The religiosity/hardness of a given person/element has meaning only in relation to other persons/elements.

It may be charged that social scientists continually revise their measurements of variables and that two social scientists at a given time differ in their methods, but this is not unique to social science, either. The openness of all science demands continual change.

Discovering Social Regularities

There is a tendency to regard the subjects of the physical sciences as more regular than those of the social sciences. A heavy object falls to earth every time it is released, while a man may vote for a candidate in one election and against him in the next. Similarly, ice always melts when heated, while seemingly religious people do not always attend church. While these particular examples are generally true, there is a danger in going on to discount the existence of social regularities altogether. The existence of observable social norms denies this conclusion.

Some social norms are prescribed by the formal institutions of a society. For example, only persons of a certain age or older are permitted to vote in elections. In American society, men were drafted into the armed forces, but women were not. Such formal prescriptions, then, regulate, or regularize, social behavior.

Aside from formal prescriptions, other social norms can be observed. Registered Republicans are more likely to vote for Republican candidates than are registered Democrats. University professors tend to earn more money than unskilled laborers. Women tend to be more religious than men.

Reports by social scientists of such regularities are often subject to three types of criticism. First, it may be charged that the report is trivial, that everyone was aware of the regularity. Second, contradictory cases may be cited, indicating that the observation is not wholly true. And third, it may be argued that the people involved could upset the observed regularity if they wished.

The charge that many of the social scientist's discoveries are trivial or already well known has led many would-be social scientists to seek esoteric or obscure findings that would prove that social science is more than pretentious common sense. This is inappropriate from a number of standpoints. To begin, there are so many contradictions in the broad body of common sense, that it is essential to systematically weed out the existing misconceptions. Even where a proposition is unchallenged by laymen, it is necessary to test it empirically.

Many social science methodology instructors begin their classes by revealing a set of "important discoveries" that have come from social science, derived from studies conducted by Samuel A. Stouffer during World War II.[1] These "discoveries" include findings that (1) Negro soldiers were happier in Northern training camps than in Southern ones, (2) soldiers in the Army Air Corps, where promotions were rapid, were more likely to feel that the promotion system was fair than were those in the Military Police, where promotions were very slow, and (3) more educated soldiers were more likely to resent being drafted than those with less education. Once students have begun to dismiss the "important discoveries" as obvious, the instructor then reveals that each of them was disproven by the studies and explains why the observed relationships are susceptible to logical understanding, though requiring greater sophistication. (These findings will be examined in detail in Chapter 17.)

In short, "documenting the obvious" is a valuable function of any science, physical or social. This is not a legitimate criticism of any scientific endeavor. (Darwin coined the term "fool's experiment" in ironic reference to much of his own research.)

The criticism that given generalizations from social science are subject to disconfirmation in specific cases is not a sufficient challenge to the scientific character of the inquiry either. Thus it is not sufficient to note that a given man is more religious than a given woman. Social regularities represent probabilistic patterns, and a general relationship between two variables need not be true in 100 percent of the observable cases.

Physical science is not exempt from this challenge. In genetics, for example, the mating of a blue-eyed person with a brown-eyed person will *probably* result in a brown-eyed offspring. The birth of a blue-eyed offspring does not challenge the observed regularity, however, since the geneticist states only that the brown-eyed offspring is more likely and, further, that brown-eyed offspring will be born in a certain percentage of the cases. The social scientist makes a similar, probabilistic prediction—that women overall will be more likely to appear religious than men. And with an adequately tested measurement device, he may be able to predict the percentage of women who will appear more religious than men.

Finally, the charge that observed social regularities could be upset through the conscious will of the actors is not a sufficient challenge to social science, even though there does not seem to be a parallel situation in the physical sciences. (Presumably an object cannot resist falling to earth "because it wants to.") There is no denying that the religious, right-wing bigot could go to the polls and vote for an agnostic, left-wing radical black if he wanted to upset the political scientist studying the election. All voters in an election could suddenly switch to the underdog so as to frustrate the pollster. By the same token, workers could go to work early or stay home from work and thereby prevent the expected rush-hour commuter traffic. But these things do not happen sufficiently often to seriously threaten the observation of social regularities.

---

1. Samuel A. Stouffer, *et al., The American Soldier* (Princeton, N.J.: Princeton University Press, 1949).

The fact remains that social norms do exist, and the social scientist can observe those norms. When norms change over time, the social scientist can observe and explain those changes. Ultimately, social regularities persist because they tend to make sense for the people involved in them. Whereas the social scientist may suggest that it is logical to expect a given type of person to behave in a certain manner, those people may very well agree with the logical basis for the expectation. Thus, while the religious, right-wing bigot *could* vote for the agnostic, left-wing radical black candidate, he would consider it stupid to do so.

Creation of Social Theories

Social scientists have not yet developed theories of social behavior comparable with the theories developed by physical scientists. Of course, there have been countless theories of social behavior dating back centuries, but none of these is seriously defended as adequate. This observation must be made in the context of the history of many, now inadequate, theories pertaining to the physical world, however. The ultimate demise of the Ptolemaic theory of epicycles does not deny the scientific standing of present-day astronomy. Nor even does the knowledge that contemporary theories in physics will eventually be supplanted deny the scientific status of that field.

Nevertheless, at present, the social sciences do not have formal theories comparable with those existing in other fields. In part, this is due to the fact that systematic scientific methods have not been applied to social behavior for as long as they have been applied to physical phenomena. And at the same time, the reluctance to admit the susceptibility of social behavior to scientific study has limited the resources made available for the development of social sciences.

In addition, however, this textbook grows out of the conviction that the scientific development of the social sciences has been seriously handicapped by a misunderstanding of the logical nature of science in general. A commitment to the traditional image of science, as opposed to an understanding of science in practice, has had this effect. In view of this, we shall turn now to a discussion of the characteristics of social science.

2.3
The Characteristics of Social Science

In Chapter 1, in discussing the ways in which science guards against the foibles of casual human inquiry, I hinted at some of the general characteristics of science. The present section is directly about those characteristics. While our ultimate concern here is with understanding the characteristics of *social* science, we shall see that they are the same as for science in general.

Logical Reasoning

Science is fundamentally a rational activity, and scientific explanations must make sense. Religions may rest on revelations, customs, or traditions, gambling on faith; but science must rest on logical reason.

Logic is a difficult and complex branch of philosophy, and a full delineation of systems of logic is well beyond the scope of this textbook. Perhaps a few examples will illustrate what is meant by science being logical. For example, a given event cannot, logically, cause another event that occurred earlier in time. The movement of a bullet cannot cause the explosion of the gunpowder propelling it. Thus science takes a different approach from the *teleological* views assumed by some religions. For example, some Christians believe that Jesus was destined to be crucified, and that this destiny thereby caused him to be betrayed and tried. Such a view could not be accepted within the logic of science.

In the logic of science, it is impossible for an object to have two mutually exclusive qualities. The flip of a coin cannot result in both a head and a tail. By contrast, we might note that many deeply prejudiced people argue that Jews are both "clannish" (refusing to mix with non-Jews) and "pushy" (forcing themselves in with non-Jews). Faced with such an assertion, the scientist would suggest that either one or both of the characterizations of Jews are untrue or that the two characteristics are being defined in such a way that they are not mutually exclusive.

Similarly, a given event cannot have mutually exclusive results. Thus, getting a college education cannot make a man both wealthier and poorer at the same time. It is possible for a college education to result in wealth for one man and poverty for another, just as some Jews might be described as clannish and others pushy, but contradictory results or descriptions fly in the face of logic and are intolerable to science.

All this is not to say that science in practice is wholly devoid of illogical assertions. Many readers will already realize that physicists currently regard light as both particles and waves, even though these are contradictory descriptions of the nature of light. This particular contradiction exists in science since light behaves as particles under some conditions and as waves under others. As a result of this situation, physicists continue to use the two contradictory conceptualizations as they may be appropriate in given conditions. Nevertheless, such a situation represents a strain for the logic of science.

Beyond this common-sense notion of logic, there are two distinct logical systems important to the scientific quest, referred to as *deductive logic* and *inductive logic*. Beveridge describes them as follows:

> Logicians distinguish between inductive reasoning (from particular instances to general principles, from facts to theories) and deductive reasoning (from the general to the particular, applying a theory to a particular case). In induction one starts from observed data and develops a generalization which explains the relationships between

the objects observed. On the other hand, in deductive reasoning one starts from some general law and applies it to a particular instance.[2]

The classical illustration of deductive logic is the familiar syllogism: "All men are mortal; Socrates is a man; therefore Socrates is mortal." A researcher might then follow up this deductive exercise with an empirical test of Socrates' mortality. This is essentially the approach discussed as the "traditional perspective of science" early in this chapter.

Using inductive logic, the researcher might begin by noting that Socrates is mortal and observing a number of other men as well. He might then note that all the *observed* men were mortals, thereby arriving at the tentative conclusion that *all* men are mortal.

Deductive logic is very old as a system, dating at least to Aristotle. Moreover, this system was predominant in Western philosophy until the sixteenth or seventeenth century. The birth of modern science was marked by the rise of inductive logic in a variety of scientific contexts. Increasingly, the general conclusions derived from careful observations contradicted the general postulates that represented the anchoring points of many deductive systems.

In astronomy, for example, Ptolemy accounted for observed variations from this model by developing an *epicyclical* model in which stars and planets rotated—in circles—around points in space which, in turn, rotated around the stationary earth in circles. As further variations were noted, the system was made more and more complicated in order to retain the key beliefs of circular motion and a stationary earth.

Copernicus attacked the Ptolemaic system by suggesting that the sun, rather than the earth, was the center of the universe. This radically new perspective was derived on the basis of observed celestial motion rather than from an initial commitment to the earth as the center of the universe. Copernicus, however, did not challenge the assumption of circular motion. "The later astronomer, Kepler, said that Copernicus failed to see the riches that were within his grasp, and was *content to interpret Ptolemy rather than nature*." [3] Kepler, on the other hand, was determined to interpret nature—in the form of the voluminous empirical data that he inherited from the Danish astronomer, Tycho Brahe. As Butterfield goes on to tell us:

> We know how with colossal expenditure of energy he tried one hypothesis after another, and threw them away, until he reached a point where he had a vague knowledge of the shape required, decided that for purposes of calculation an ellipse might give him at any rate approximate results, and then found that an ellipse was right.[4]

2. W. I. B. Beveridge, *The Art of Scientific Investigation* (New York: Vintage Books, 1950), p. 113.
3. Herbert Butterfield, *The Origins of Modern Science* (New York: Macmillan, 1960), p. 24, emphasis added.
4. *Ibid.*, p. 64.

This example should illustrate the rise of inductive logic in science. Similar dramas occurred in other fields of inquiry during the fertile sixteenth and seventeenth centuries. A century or so later, the inductive, scientific research of Charles Darwin clashed with yet another tradition.

It should not be concluded from the foregoing historical account that deductive logic is inherently incorrect or that it is now outmoded. An exercise in deductive logic is as good as its internal consistency and the truth of its beginning assumptions. And inductive logic, on the other hand, is only as good as its internal consistency and the accuracy of its observations.

Let's examine these two logical models somewhat differently for a moment. The following two graphic illustrations may clarify the manner in which the deductive and inductive models are employed in the conduct of scientific research.

The first illustration (see Figure 2-1) contrasts the deductive and inductive methods through a descriptive rather than an explanatory example. Let's assume that an archeologist is studying the building methods of an ancient civilization. Let's assume further that his research on the culture and technology of that civilization leads him to hypothesize that nearly square, rectangular bricks would have been used in the construction of buildings in that civilization. His hypothesis is indicated graphically in the first half of Figure 2-1.

Now let's suppose that the archeologist has uncovered a fragment of a brick during his digging at the site of the ancient civilization under study. The irregular shape marked "reality" in Figure 2-1 represents the shape of that fragment. Using the deductive method, the archeologist must now decide whether the brick fragment which he possesses confirms or contradicts his hypothesis regarding the shape of bricks used by the civilization he is studying. In Figure 2-1 note that the rectangular shape representing his hypothesis has been superimposed over the irregular shape representing the brick fragment. Clearly, the expected and observed shapes do not correspond perfectly. Thus, the archeologist must decide whether the correspondence is close enough to support his theoretical hypothesis.

The second half of Figure 2-1 illustrates the inductive method, using this same archeological example. Note that the researcher begins with the brick fragment, the observed "reality". Next he attempts to find a general or regular pattern which closely corresponds to the observed reality. In this case, he notes that a nonrectangular parallelogram corresponds quite closely to the actual brick fragment. The correspondence is not perfect, but it is very close.

Using the inductive method, the researcher reaches a tentative conclusion regarding the shape of bricks used for construction in the ancient civilization.

Neither the inductive nor the deductive method, as illustrated above, is free from the danger of error. The deductive researcher—depending on the degree of correspondence which he requires for the confirmation of his hypothesis—may conclude that rectangular bricks were used in the civilization, assuming that the actual brick fragment he possesses originally had that shape.

THE DEDUCTIVE METHOD

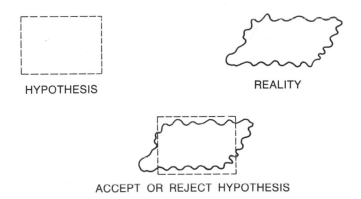

HYPOTHESIS   REALITY

ACCEPT OR REJECT HYPOTHESIS

THE INDUCTIVE METHOD

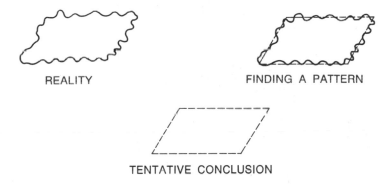

REALITY   FINDING A PATTERN

TENTATIVE CONCLUSION

Figure 2-1

At first glance, the inductive method may seem superior. The researcher has no preconceived ideas to distort his perception of reality. Indeed, the pattern arrived at by the inductive researcher corresponds much more closely to the observed reality than does the hypothesized pattern of the deductive researcher. Unfortunately, the inductive researcher has no assurance that the brick fragment now under examination is typical of bricks used in the ancient civilization. Quite possibly, the civilization did in fact use rectangular bricks, and the one in hand has been chipped away to a different shape over the centuries.

On balance, the deductive researcher has the advantage of a logical, theoretical support for his hypothesis even though it does not match perfectly a specific instance of reality. The inductive researcher, on the other hand, reaches a conclusion that closely reflects the specific instance, but he may lack theoretical support for generalizing from it.

      Let's turn now to an illustration, Figure 2-2, involving the relationship between two variables, X and Y. Let's assume that we have some reason to believe that variable X will cause, to some degree at least, variable Y. For example, variable X might represent people's education, and variable Y might represent their income.

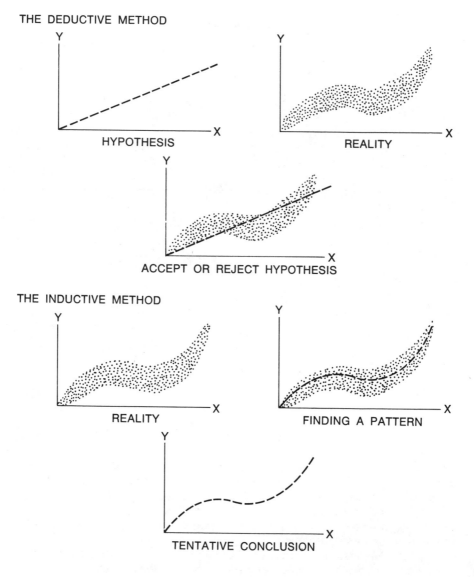

Figure 2-2

Using the deductive method, a researcher might derive a theoretical hypothesis regarding the nature of the relationship between these two variables. This is represented in Figure 2-2 by the straight dashed line, which suggests that the greater a person's education (X), the greater his income (Y). If we knew the amount of education a person had received, the hypothesis (represented by the dashed line) would permit us to estimate that person's income.

"Reality" is shown in Figure 2-2 as a *scattergram*. Each dot in the scattergram represents an individual person, in terms of variables X and Y. The first half of Figure 2-2 shows the hypothesis superimposed upon the observed reality. We note once more that the two clearly do not correspond exactly. The researcher, thus, must decide whether the correspondence is close enough to warrant accepting his hypothesis or whether it should be rejected.

Using the inductive method, the researcher begins with the observed reality. Next he attempts to find a general, regular pattern that closely corresponds to that reality. The pattern that he decides upon, as in the illustration of the brick fragment, then becomes his tentative conclusion regarding the relationship between variables X and Y.

Once again the tentative conclusion reached by the inductive method corresponds more closely to the observed reality than does the hypothesis used in the deductive method. (This need not be the case, but it frequently is.) Scientific conclusions should have both *theoretical* and *empirical* support. Generally speaking, the deductive method is stronger in the former, while the inductive method is stronger in the latter.

Quite clearly, the best scientific research would involve both the inductive and deductive methods, used in a cyclical fashion. The researcher might begin with a derived hypothesis, modify it inductively, rethink his theoretical system, reformulate his hypothesis, and seek new observations. Replication is the key to this process and resolves the previously mentioned problems of both the deductive and inductive methods. Only repeated observation, yielding the same result or conclusion (replication), can assure the scientist that he has discovered—deductively, inductively, or both—a general principle.

Determinism

Science is based on the assumption that all events have antecedent causes that can be identified and logically understood. For the scientist, nothing "just happens"; it happens for a reason. If a man catches a cold, if it rains today, if a ball seems to roll uphill, the scientist assumes that each of these events is susceptible to rational explanation.

Several caveats should be entered in this regard, however. First, scientists do not know, nor do they pretend to know, the specific causes of all events. They simply assume that such causes exist and can be discovered.

Second, science accepts multiple causation. A given event may have several causes; the voting decision may have resulted from a number of different factors. And one event may have one cause, while a similar event may have a different cause. Two men may vote for the same candidate for different reasons, but it is assumed that reasons exist in each case.

Finally, much science is based on a probabalistic form of determinism.[5] Thus, Event A may result in Event B 90 percent of the time, or 70 percent of all Republicans may vote for a given political candidate, while only 23 percent of the Democrats do so. In this sense, then, political party affiliation would be said to determine voting behavior, even though the determination was not complete. (Other factors might be introduced to explain the discrepancies.)

This characteristic of social science seems often at odds with common sense, as some earlier discussions in this chapter have indicated. The social scientist may conclude that a group of people behave in a certain fashion because of a number of prior events and conditions: for example, recall the voting behavior of the religious, right-wing bigot in an earlier discussion. In this sense, the conditions of religiosity, prejudice, the right-wing political orientations *determine* the man's voting behavior. This is not to deny that the man in question *could* vote for the agnostic, left-wing radical black candidate; he is simply unlikely to do so.

The deterministic posture of the social sciences represents its most significant departure from more traditional, humanistic examinations of social behavior. Whereas a biographer, for example, might consider the soul-searching and agonies by which a given man will weigh the relative merits and demerits of a given action, arriving at a considered decision, the social scientists would more typically look for the general determinants of such a decision among different aggregates of persons. Where the biographer would argue that the decision reached by each individual person represented the outcome of an idiosyncratic process, the social scientist would say it could be fit into a much simpler, general pattern.

In Chapter 16, which deals with the logic of causation, we shall see how determinism provides the logical basis for the examination of cause and effect in social scientific analyses. We shall also consider determinism with regard to the charge of "dehumanization" in social science.

Generalization

Science aims at general understanding rather than at the explanation of individual events. The scientist is typically less interested in understanding why a given ball falls to the earth when released from a height than in understanding why all such balls tend to do so. Similarly, the scientist is less

---

5. The reader should be warned that this issue is far more complicated than suggested here, and there remains a good deal of disagreement in the scientific community on it. Some scientists argue that there is a probabilistic element in all real-world phenomena. Others argue that the universe is totally determinate but that our sciences are not yet sufficient to understand that determinate system. Still others use the terms "deterministic" and "probabilistic" as antithetical.

interested in explaining why a given man voted as he did than in understanding why large groups of people voted as they did.

This characteristic of science is related to its probabilistic determinism. It is conceivable that we could completely explain the reasons lying behind a given event—why a given man voted for Candidate X. The scientist might conceivably discover every single factor that went into the voting decision. If he were successful in this, then presumably he could predict the voting behavior of identical persons with perfect accuracy. In the long run, however, such a capability would not provide much useful information about voting behavior in general. First, it is doubtful that the scientist would ever find another person with exactly the same characteristics. More important, his discoveries might help him very little in understanding the voting behavior of people with other characteristics. The scientist, then, would be happier with less than 100 percent understanding if he were able to understand voting behavior in general.

This is the sense in which the scientist and the historian differ in their approaches to the same subject matter. The historian aims at understanding everything about a specific event, while the scientist would be more interested in generally understanding a class of similar, though not identical, events. By the same token, the psychologist and the therapist would differ in their approaches to human behavior. The psychologist would examine schizophrenic behavior among several individuals in an effort to arrive at a general understanding of schizophrenia, while the therapist would take advantage of existing general knowledge in an effort to help a specific individual.

Generalizability, thus, is an important characteristic of scientific discoveries. The discovery that red balls fall to earth at a given acceleration is less useful than the discovery that balls of all colors do so. Similarly, it is less useful to know that balls fall with a given acceleration at sea level, than to know that the acceleration of all falling balls can be determined from their altitude.

To the social scientist, a theory of voting behavior that applies only to whites is less useful than one that applies to voters of all races. A theory of religiosity that applies only to Christians is less useful than one that applies to people of all religions—or people with no religion at all.

While the social scientist often begins with an attempt to explain a rather more limited range of social behavior or the behavior of a limited subset of the population, his goal is normally to expand his findings to explain other forms of behavior and other subsets of the population.

Parsimony

As the previous sections indicate, the scientist spends much of his effort in the attempt to discover the factors that determine types of events. At the same time, he attempts to discover those factors that do not determine the events. Thus, in determining the acceleration of a falling object, we discount its color as being irrelevant.

Like the physical scientist, the social scientist attempts to gain the most explanatory power out of the smallest number of variables. In many cases, the additional consideration of new variables adds explanatory and predictive power, but it also results in a more complicated model. And, in practice, the addition of more variables often reduces the generalizability of the explanation, since certain variables may have one effect among members of one subset of the population and a different effect among those of other subsets.

It should be noted that the parsimonious character of social science, like its deterministic posture, opens it to criticism from those holding a more individualistic view of human behavior. Whereas they would tend to explore the depths of idiosyncratic factors resulting in a decision or action on the part of a given person, the social scientist consciously attempts to limit such inquiry.

The social scientist, then, might attempt to explain overall voting behavior through the observation of, say, three or four variables. The critic might object that each of the voters had many other, individual, reasons for voting as he did, that the limited number of variables did not adequately explain the depth of decision making for any of the subjects under study. The problem here is that the social scientist has a special goal in all this. He is consciously attempting to gain the greatest amount of understanding from the smallest number of variables. Neither the scientist nor his critic in such a case is more correct than the other; they simply have different goals. We must fully understand the scientist's goal, however, in order to recognize that this criticism is not a valid one.

Ultimately, the scientist attempts to understand the reasons for the events, using as few explanatory factors as possible. In practice, of course, the number of explanatory factors taken into account typically increases the degree of determination achieved. One political scientist may achieve a certain degree of explanation of voting behavior through the use of only two factors, say party affiliation and social class. Another might achieve a more complete understanding by also taking into account such other factors as race, region of upbringing, sex, education, and so forth. Frequently, the scientist is forced to choose between simplicity, on the one hand, and degree of explanation on the other. Ideally, he tries to maximize both. In part, this accounts for the elegance of Einstein's famous equation: $E = mc^2$.

Specificity

The social scientist, like the physical scientist, must specify his methods of measurement. Perhaps this is especially important in the social sciences, since they deal with concepts more vaguely defined in common discourse. While the physicist defines "acceleration" more rigorously than the layman, the scientific definition is not greatly at variance with the common understanding of the term. Concepts such as "religiosity" and "prejudice," however have such varied meanings in common language that their rigorous definitions are not readily apparent.

In conducting a research project on the topic of prejudice, then, the scientist must generate a *specific* operationalization of the concept prejudice: for example, agreement with several questionnaire statements that seem to indicate prejudice. In reporting his research, he will be careful to describe his operationalizations in detail so that the reader will know precisely how the concept has been measured. While a given reader may disagree with the operationalization, he will at least know what it is.

Often the generalizability of a given discovery is substantiated through the use of different operationalizations of the concepts involved. If a given set of factors results in prejudice as measured in a number of different ways, the researcher (or the scientific community) may conclude that those factors result in prejudice *in general,* even though prejudice itself is not susceptible to a single measurement that would be accepted by everyone.

Empirical Verification

Science at its best results in the formulation of general laws or equations describing the world around us. Such formulations, however, are not useful unless they can be verified through the collection and manipulation of empirical data. A general theory of prejudice would be useless unless it suggested ways in which data might be collected and unless it predicted the results that would be obtained from the analysis of those data.

There is another way of viewing this characteristic, however. In a sense, no scientific theory can ever be *proved.* Let's consider the case of gravity. Physicists tell us that a body falls to earth because of the general attraction that exists between physical bodies and that this relationship is affected by the mass of the bodies involved. Since Earth has a vast mass, a ball thrown out a window will move toward Earth.

Such an explanation of gravity is empirically verifiable. A researcher can throw a ball out a window and observe that it falls to the earth. This does not prove the truth of the theory of gravity, however. Rather, the researcher specifies that if the ball does *not* fall to the earth, then the theory of gravity is incorrect. Since the ball is, in fact, observed to behave as expected, the theory of gravity *has not been disconfirmed.*

Thus, when we say that a scientific explanation must be subject to empirical testing, we mean, more precisely, that the researcher must be able to specify conditions under which the theory would be disproved. As he consistently fails to disprove the theory, then, he may become confident that the theory is correct. But it is important to realize that he will never have proved it.

In the example of falling bodies, another theorist might note that the experimental ball was of the same color as the ground to which it fell. He might suggest, therefore, that bodies of the same color are attracted to each other—for whatever reason he might devise. The initial experiment, then, would lend confirmation to both of the competing theories. The second theory, however, suggests a method of disconfirmation. If a ball differing in color from the earth were thrown out the window, it should not fall to the earth. To do so would disconfirm the second theory. An appropriate second experiment would, hopefully, result in an empirical disconfirmation of the color-attraction theory.

To be useful, social scientific propositions and theories must also be testable in the real world. Thus it is useless to assert that religiosity is positively associated with prejudice without suggesting ways in which the two variables might be measured and the proposition tested. As in the physical sciences, the social scientist must be able to describe empirical conditions under which a given proposition would be judged incorrect, ways in which it might be disproved.

Religious beliefs, such as the existence of God, for example, are not susceptible to empirical verification. Similarly, the assertion that members of a religious or racial group are disloyal "in their hearts" even when they appear to act in a loyal manner is not subject to empirical verification. The same would be true of propositions predicting human social behavior in the event that the sun did not rise on a given morning.

At the same time, a great many hypotheses regarding human social affairs *can* be tested empirically. For example, it has been commonly believed in America that women were incapable of reasoning as logically as men. Instead, women have been characterized as "flighty" and "emotional" in their thinking processes. This notion—so comfortable for American men—could be tested empirically. Moreover, the recent success of women in the "thinking professions" suggests that a controlled empirical test would wipe out the common, comfortable belief.

As indicated elsewhere in this book, much social research is addressed to testing, with empirical data, those items of "common-sense" that "everybody knows are true." Where "common-sense" notions are imprecise, the social scientist doggedly specifies them in a testable form and tests them. Then, he respecifies them in another testable form and retests them. Frequently, he discovers that "common-sense" doesn't make much sense in terms of the empirical reality.

Intersubjectivity

It is frequently asserted that science is "objective," but such an assertion typically results in a good deal of confusion as to what "objectivity" is. Moreover, it has been noted increasingly in recent years that no scientist is completely objective in his work. All scientists are "subjective" to some extent—influenced by their personal motivations.

In saying that science is "intersubjective," I mean that two scientists with different subjective orientations would arrive at the same conclusion if each conducted the same experiment. An example from political science should clarify this.

The tendency for intellectuals in America to align themselves more with the Democratic Party than with the Republican Party has led many people to assume that Democrats as a group are better educated than Republicans. It is reasonable to assume that a Democratic scientist would be happy with this view while a Republican scientist would not. Yet, it would be possible for the two scientists to agree on the design of a research project that would collect data from the American electorate relating to party affiliation and educational levels. The two scientists could then conduct independent studies of the subject, and both would discover that Republicans as a whole have a higher educational level than do Democrats. (This is due to the fact that the Democratic Party also attracts a larger proportion of working-class voters than does the Republican Party in America, while businessmen are more attracted to the Republican Party.) Both scientists—with opposite subjective orientations—would arrive at the same empirical conclusion.

Clearly, scientists often disagree among themselves. They may offer grossly different explanations for a given event. Such disagreements, however, typically involve questions of conceptualization and definition. Thus, one social scientist may report that religiosity is positively related to prejudice, while another disagrees. The disagreeing scientist will, in all likelihood, suggest that either or both of the variables have been incorrectly measured. He may conduct his own study, measuring the two variables differently, and report a negative relationship between them. If the first researcher had reported the design and execution of his study in precise and specific details, however, and the second were to replicate that study exactly, he should arrive at the same finding. This is what is meant by the *intersubjectivity* of science.

Openness to Modification

It should be clear from the previous section that "science" does not provide a set of easy steps to the attainment of Truth. Two scientists, both adhering to the previously discussed characteristics of science, may arrive at quite different explanations of a given phenomenon. At a given time, moreover, there may be no way of evaluating their relative merits. If the two explanations contradict one another, presumably both cannot be correct. Either one or both will later be proven incorrect, or else it will be discovered that the two explanations are not mutually exclusive after all.

Countless "scientific" theories of the past have subsequently been disproved and replaced by better ones. Current theories will eventually be replaced. More basically, we shall probably never discover Truth in any area of inquiry.

In an important sense, science does not even seek Truth, but rather utility. Scientific theories should not be judged on their relative truth value, but on the extent to which they are useful in understanding the world around us.

In the final analysis, the characteristics of science that have been discussed above provide a set of guidelines that enhance the utility of discoveries and theories. Inquiries that seek to adhere to these characteristics will, in the long run, produce more useful discoveries than inquiries of another sort. Thus, one man may be able to predict the weather more accurately on the basis of his "trick" knee than all the scientific meteorologists in the world. But, in the long run, the scientists will contribute more to our general understanding of the nature of the weather.

No social theory is likely to survive indefinitely. Either a growing weight of disconfirming evidence will bring it down, or a newer, more parsimonious, replacement will be found. In any event, no social science finding can be expected to withstand the long-term test of time.

In practice, of course, the social scientist deals with phenomena that also come under the purview of ideology: religious, political, and philosophical. And ideologies are less open to modification than science. When the social scientist explains religiosity in terms of background variables, he challenges basic religious beliefs about moral behavior, religious reward and punishment systems, and so forth. When the political scientist concludes that the working class in America is more authoritarian than the middle class, he challenges left-wing political ideology. And the deterministic posture of the social sciences in general flies in the face of a philosophical free-will image of man that has a long history in Western civilization.

The danger is that individual social scientists may be so personally committed to particular ideological stances that their commitment will prevent them from maintaining the openness of their science. Thus, the committed left-wing political scientist may be unwilling to consider, undertake, or accept research activities which might lead to the conclusion that the working class is more authoritarian than the middle class.

As found in earlier discussions, this situation is not unique to the *social* sciences. Physical science inquiry has challenged and continues to challenge accepted ideological belief systems. And individual physical scientists have been handicapped by ideological commitments that reduced the openness of their scientific activities.

2.4
Scientists and Detectives

The primary purpose of these first two chapters has been to give you a relatively balanced view of what science is like. It might be useful to conclude these discussions by likening scientific inquiry to the work of a detective. Like detectives, scientists work at finding the answers to questions: who killed Cock Robin, what causes cancer? It is essential that you understand that *finding the answer* is what makes a good scientist just as it makes a good detective. Merely going through a set of steps generally associated with scientific research or criminal investigation does not make you a scientist or a detective.

In one sense, how you get the answer is irrelvant as long as you can substantiate the soundness of your answer. Intuition, for example, is perfectly acceptable in science as in detective work. An answer to a problem is no less valid because it came to the investigator originally through intuition. A detective may "get a feeling" that "the butler did it"; a scientist may "get a feeling" that harsh toilet training explains subsequent fear of flying.

Luck is perfectly all right in science and in detective work, too. The detective who just happens to be at the scene of the murder when the murderer sneaks back to erase a clue is simply lucky. Kepler was lucky when he decided to use an ellipse as the approximate model for the movement of planets and then discovered that the ellipse was exactly right. Such lucky events do not diminish the validity of the answers which they provide.

If intuition and luck are acceptable in the solution of scientific and detective problems, then why worry about specialized methods of scientific and detective investigation? The specialized methods and the logic underlying them serve two important functions in careful inquiry. First, the methods typically followed by professional scientists and detectives increase the likelihood that intuition, insight, or good luck will occur. The detective's standard methods of criminal investigation place him at the scene of the crime; Kepler's training in mathematics and geometry made it possible for him to employ a more sophisticated approximation than others would have done. Thus, the standard methods of science and detecting tend to put you where the luck happens.

Second, while intuition is legitimate in obtaining the answer to a problem, it is not sufficient to demonstrate that you really have the answer. Thus, the detective may have a feeling that the butler is guilty, but such a feeling is not enough—nor should it be—to convict the butler. A gut feeling that harsh toilet training results in a fear of flying does not prove the case. The standard methods of inquiry, and especially the logic that underlies them, provide rules of proof. Thus, the detective might be led by intuition to seek hard evidence showing the butler's guilt, and the scientist might be led by intuition to conduct a rigorous scientific experiment on the effects of harsh toilet training on the fear of flying.

2.5
Summary

Chapter 2 began by asking whether social *science* is possible. Can social phenomena be subjected to scientific inquiry like nonhuman phenomena? Happily, the discussion concluded that social science *is* possible, that the most frequently raised objections to the scientific study of human social behavior do not hold up under careful scrutiny. It is possible to *measure* social phenomena; we have observed many *regularities* in society; and there are no fundamental reasons why *general social theories* cannot be developed. If social science is in some ways more challenging than the physical sciences, it is by no means impossible.

The chapter concluded with an examination of several general characteristics of social scientific inquiry. These characteristics apply equally to science in general, and they represent the reasons why scientific inquiry is different from other modes of human inquiry.

It should be clear to you by now that there is no such thing as *the* scientific method. Science operates in many different ways and often involves seemingly nonscientific elements. The general characteristics of science that have been discussed in these first two chapters are a good general guide to what science is.

Having discussed the general characteristics of science, and having conceded that social science is possible, we shall turn now to *how* social scientific research is conducted.

2.6
Main Points

1. Social science is the application of scientific logic and methods to social phenomena.

2. Social science seeks to understand social behavior through:
    a. the measurement of social phenomena
    b. the discovery of social regularities
    c. the creation of social theories.

3. Induction is the process of reasoning from specific observations to general principles.

4. Deduction is the process of reasoning from general principles to specific instances.

5. Social science employs both inductive and deductive methods.

6. Social science requires the use of logical reasoning, as compared with natural human inquiry which is often illogical.

7. Social science is based, implicitly, on a deterministic image of man: everything the social scientist studies is caused by something else.

8. Social science attempts to generate ever more general explanations for social behavior.

9. Social science is parsimonious, attempting to generate the greatest amount of understanding from the least amount of information.

10. "Specificity" in social science refers to the clear, precise description of how the social scientist has made measurements and how he reached his conclusions.

11. Empirical verification is a key element in the logic and methods of social science. Explanations for social behavior must make sense and they must correspond to what is actually observed.

12. "Intersubjectivity" refers to research conditions in which different social scientists, with different perspectives, would arrive at the same conclusions.

13. A final, important characteristic of social science is its openness to modification: social scientific understandings of the world are constantly changing.

2.7
Annotated Bibliography

Babbie, Earl, *Survey Research Methods* (Belmont, California: Wadsworth, 1973), Chapter 3. An application of the basic ideas developed in this chapter to the method of survey research. This short discussion should further clarify your understanding of the characteristics of science and social science as these appear in practice.

Campbell, Donald, and Stanley, Julian, *Experimental and Quasi-Experimental Designs for Research* (Chicago: Rand McNally, 1963). A somewhat different approach to the logic of social science than has been presented in this chapter. The authors begin with the logic of the controlled experiment and show how it is approximated in other social research designs.

Franklin, Billy, and Osborne, Harold (eds.), *Research Methods: Issues and Insights* (Belmont, California: Wadsworth, 1971), Parts One and Two. An excellent collection of papers dealing with various aspects of social research. The selections in Parts One and Two provide a variety of stimulating perspectives on the general logic of social research, asking whether social science is "scientific," where it fits into our comprehensive understanding of people, and the links between theory and research in the social sciences.

Wallace, Walter, *The Logic of Science in Sociology* (Chicago: Aldine-Atherton, 1971). An eminently readable overview of the logic connecting the several stages of social research. This remarkable little book leads you around the unending circle of observation to generalization to theory to hypothesis to observation and on and on.

Part Two:
The Structuring of Inquiry

Posing problems properly is often far more difficult than answering them. Indeed, a properly phrased question often seems to answer itself. You may have discovered the answer to a question just through the process of making the question clear to someone else.

At base, scientific research is a process for achieving generalized understanding through observation. Part Three of this book describes some of the specific methods of social scientific observation; Part Two deals with what should be observed. Put differently, Part Two considers the posing of proper scientific questions, the structuring of inquiry.

Chapter 3 considers the beginnings of research efforts. It examines some of the purposes of research, the units of analysis and topics of social scientific research, and the reasons scientists get involved in research projects.

The topics of research are considered in further detail in Chapter 4 on *conceptualization* and *operationalization*. Once you have made a general decision to study, say, why some sectors of the community are hostile to college students, you must decide more precisely what you mean by "hostility." This is called *conceptualization*. Next you must determine what kinds of observed events in the real world would represent hostility toward students or the lack thereof. This is called *operationalization*.

Chapter 5 provides a practical application for the lessons of Chapter 4. Many modes of observation in the social sciences, most notably survey research, involve the use of a questionnaire or other standardized form as a guide to observation. Such instruments represent the ultimate operationalization of the topics of study in relation to observations. Learning how to construct good questionnaires will be of practical value to you, as well as improving your understanding of the basic logic of conceptualization and operationalization.

Chapters 6 and 7 are devoted to the targets—the units of analysis—of research. Who or what is to be observed? Very often, a scientist is unable to make all the observations that might be relevant to his research interest. Scientific sampling is a reflection of the parsimony discussed as a characteristic of science in Chapter 1. It is often possible to reach generalized understandings about a large population of people or other subjects of study on the basis of observations of a much smaller fraction of the population's members. Chapter 6 examines the logic of this and the techniques for doing it. Chapter 7 presents several real examples of sample designs to clarify further the various sampling procedures.

What you learn in Part Two will bring you to the verge of making controlled social scientific observations. Part Three shows you how to take the next step.

3
Research Design

3.1
Introduction

The preceding chapter asked whether social science is possible and answered "yes." In the present chapter, we shall see that the possibilities for social scientific research are almost limitless. Indeed, the wide range often makes it difficult for a beginning researcher to know where to begin.

We shall begin with a discussion of three general purposes which social scientific research may serve. Following that, we shall turn to some of the different possible *units of analysis* for research: whom or what are you going to study? Next, we shall examine some potential topics of research—what characteristics of those units of analysis will you study?

These first three sections will sketch out some of the very broad parameters of social scientific research. If anything, this could increase your paralysis regarding the initial design of a study. Thus, the final section of the chapter addresses the question of how you begin, how you pin down a manageable research project. The section describes some typical motivations for research. At least the last of these, on *involuntary research,* may offer some assistance to students who are required to undertake research for course or thesis purposes.

3.2
Purposes of Research

There are probably as many different reasons for conducting social scientific research as there are research projects. While there are too many such purposes to enumerate here, three general objectives crosscut these many concerns: *exploration, description,* and *explanation.* Although a given study may (and usually does) aim at satisfying more than one of these objectives, it will be useful to examine them as distinct for present purposes.

Exploration

A great deal of research is done for the purpose of exploring a topic to familiarize the researcher and his subsequent audiences with it. This would be the case especially when the researcher is just beginning his studies of a given topic or when the topic itself is new.

As an example, let's suppose that widespread taxpayer unhappiness with the government erupts into a taxpayers' revolt: people begin to refuse to pay their taxes and to organize around that issue. A social scientist might wish to learn more about the movement: how widespread it is, what levels and degrees of support there are within the community, how the movement is organized, what kinds of people are active in it, and so forth. He might undertake an exploratory study to obtain at least approximate answers to some of these questions. He might check figures with tax-collecting officials, he could collect and study the literature of the movement, he could attend meetings and interview leaders.

Exploratory studies are also appropriate in the case of more persistent phenomena. Perhaps a college student is unhappy with the college's dormitory regulations and wants to work toward changing them. He might study the history of dormitory regulations at his college, meet with college officials to learn the reasons for the regulations, and talk to a number of students to get a rough idea of student sentiments on the subject. This latter activity would not necessarily yield a precise and accurate picture of student opinion, but it would provide some guide to what probably would be discovered in a more careful study.

Exploratory studies are most typically done for three purposes: (1) simply to satisfy the researcher's curiosity and desire for better understanding, (2) to test the feasibility of undertaking a more careful study, and (3) to develop the methods to be employed in a more careful study. As an example of the last of these, a number of researchers at a major university, during the mid-to-late 1960s, were interested in studying the extent, sources, and consequences of the changes in student attitudes occurring at about that time. It was evident to a casual observer that many students were becoming active in radical politics, others were becoming "flower children," and still others seemed to have maintained a commitment to the more traditional collegiate orientations. The researchers were interested in learning the relative proportions of the student body in each category, the reasons for commitment to the various positions, and what the consequences might be in terms of school performance, occupational plans, and so forth.

A large-scale survey of students was planned ultimately, but a difficulty was foreseen in devising a questionnaire to measure the several student orientations. In view of this, a small-scale exploratory study was made in which open-ended interviews were conducted with approximately fifty students, selected so as to have some who seemed to fit into each of the categories initially considered. In the interviews, respondents were asked very general questions about their orientations to college and to the society and were encouraged to give their answers in depth and in their own words. The answers given in the exploratory study provided many insights as to the complexities of the different major orientations and suggested ways in which those complexities could be tapped in a more structured questionnaire to be administered to a much larger sample.

Exploratory studies are very valuable in social scientific research.

They are essential whenever a researcher is breaking new ground, and they can almost always yield new insights into a topic for research. The chief shortcoming of exploratory studies is that they seldom provide satisfactory answers to research questions. They can hint at the answers and can provide insights into the research methods that could provide definitive answers. The reason exploratory studies are seldom definitive in themselves is the issue of representativeness, discussed at length in Chapter 6 in connection with sampling. Once you understand sampling and representativeness, you will be able to know whether a given exploratory study actually answered a given research problem or only pointed the way toward an answer.

Description

A major purpose of many social scientific studies is to describe situations and events. The researcher observes, and then he describes what he has observed. Since scientific observation is careful and deliberate, however, scientific descriptions are typically more accurate and precise than casual descriptions.

The United States Census is an excellent example of a descriptive social scientific research project. The goal of the census is to describe, accurately and precisely, a wide variety of characteristics of the United States' population, as well as the populations of smaller areas such as states and counties. Other examples of descriptive studies are the computation of age-sex profiles of populations done by demographers and the computation of crime rates for different cities.

A Gallup Poll conducted during a political election campaign has the purpose of describing the voting intentions of the electorate. A product marketing survey has the purpose normally of describing the people who use, or would use, a particular product. A researcher who carefully chronicles the events which take place during a student political demonstration has, or at least serves, a descriptive purpose. A researcher who computes and reports the number of times individual legislators voted for or against organized labor also has or serves a descriptive purpose.

Two aspects of social scientific description discussed in more detail in later chapters are worth mentioning at this point. They are the *quality* of descriptions and the *generalizability* of them. The first of these considerations will be examined in Chapter 4 which deals, among other things, with the quality criteria for measurement. The second consideration will be dealt with in Chapter 6 on sampling.

Explanation

The third general purpose of social scientific research is to explain things. Whereas reporting the voting intentions of an electorate is a descriptive activity, reporting *why* some people plan to vote for Candidate A and others for Candidate B is an explanatory activity. Reporting *why* some cities have higher crime rates than others is a case of explanation, whereas simply reporting the different crime rates is a case of description. A researcher has an explanatory purpose if he wishes to know why a student demonstration ended in a violent confrontation with police, as opposed to simply describing that it happened.

The logic of explanation is the subject of several chapters in Part Four of this book, and it is much too complicated to be summarized here. It is sufficient now for us to realize that explanation normally involves the examination of many different aspects of a situation or event simultaneously. In the design of a research project, then, it is essential that all those aspects be incorporated in the plan for observation and analysis.

3.3
Units of Analysis

In social scientific research, there is a wide range of variation in what or whom is studied. By this, I do not mean the *topics* of research but what are technically called the **units of analysis.** To clarify this further, I may note that social scientists most typically perhaps have individual people as their units of analysis. The researcher may make observations describing the characteristics of a large number of individual people, such as their sexes, ages, regions of birth, attitudes, and so forth. He then aggregates the descriptions of the many individuals so as to provide a descriptive picture of the population that those several individuals comprise. For example, he may note the age and sex of each individual student enrolled in Political Science 110 and then characterize the students as a group as being 53 percent men, 47 percent women, and as having a mean age of 18.6 years.

What I have just described would be a descriptive analysis of the students taking Political Science 110. While the final description would be of the class as a whole, the individual students in it would be the units of analysis, the units whose individual characteristics are aggregated for purposes of describing some larger group.

The same situation would exist in an explanatory study. Suppose that the researcher wished to discover whether students with a high grade point average received better grades in Political Science 110 than did students with a low grade point average. A relevant study would measure the grade point averages and the P.S. 110 grades of individual students. The researcher might then aggregate all those students with a high grade point average and aggregate all those with a low grade point average and see which group received the best grades in the course. The purpose of the study would be to explain why some students do better in the course than others (looking at overall grade point averages as a possible explanation), but individual students would still be the units of analysis.

Units of analysis, then, are those units that we initially describe for the ultimate purpose of aggregating their characteristics in order to describe some larger group or explain some abstract phenomenon. This concept should be clarified further as we now consider some possible social science units of analysis.

Individuals

As mentioned above, individual human beings are perhaps the most typical units of analysis for social scientific research. We tend to describe and explain social groups and interactions by aggregating and manipulating the descriptions of individual persons.

Any kinds of individuals may be the units of analysis for social scientific research. This point is more important than it may seem at first reading. The norm of *generalized understanding* in social science would suggest that scientific findings are most valuable when they apply to *all* kinds of people. In practice, however, social scientists seldom study all kinds of people. At the very least, their studies are typically limited to the people living in a single country, though some comparative studies stretch across national boundaries. Often, our studies are even more circumscribed.

Examples of circumscribed groups whose members may be units of analysis—at the individual level—would be students, residents, workers, voters, parents, and faculty members. Note that each of these terms implies some population of individual persons. The term "students" implies some population of *all* students (at a given school, in a given class, etc.); "residents" implies a population of all residents (of a certain place). The term "population" will be considered in some detail in Chapter 6 on sampling. At this point, it is sufficient to realize that descriptive studies that have individuals as their units of analysis typically aim at describing the population that those individuals comprise, whereas explanatory studies aim at discovering the social dynamics operating within that population.

Groups

Social groups may also be the units of analysis for social scientific research. Realize that this case is not the same as studying the individuals within a group. Families, for example, might be the units of analysis in a study. The researcher might describe each family in terms of its total annual income and according to whether or not it had a color television set. He could aggregate families and describe the mean income of families and the percentage with color television sets. He would then be in a position to determine whether families with higher incomes were more likely to have color television sets than those with lower incomes. The individual *family* in such a case would be the unit of analysis.

Other units of analysis—at the group level—could be friendship cliques, street gangs, married couples, or census blocks. Realize that each of these terms also implies some population. "Street gangs" implies some population that includes all street gangs. The population of street gangs could be described, say, in terms of its geographical distribution throughout a city, and an explanatory study of street gangs might discover, say, whether large gangs were more likely to engage in intergang warfare than were small ones.

When social groups are the unit of analysis, their characteristics may be derived from the characteristics of their individual members. Thus, a family might be described in terms of the age, race, or education of its head. In a descriptive study, then, we might examine and report the percentage of all families that have a college-educated head-of-family. In an explanatory study, we might determine whether families with a college-educated head have, on the average, more or fewer children than families with heads who have not graduated from college. In each of these examples, however, the family would be the unit of analysis. (Had we asked whether college graduates—college-educated *individuals*—have more or fewer children than their less educated counterparts, then the individual *person* would have been the unit of analysis.)

Social groups, and also individuals, may be characterized in other ways: for instance, in terms of their environments or their membership in larger groupings. Families, for example, might be described in terms of the type of dwelling unit they reside in, and we might want to determine whether rich families are more likely to reside in single-family houses (as opposed, say, to apartments) than are poor families. The unit of analysis would still be the family.

Individuals, as the units of analysis, may be characterized in terms of their membership in social groupings. Thus, an individual may be described as belonging to a rich family or to a poor one, or he may be described as having a college-educated father or not having one. We might examine in a research project whether people with college-educated fathers are more likely to attend college than are those with non-college-educated fathers, or whether high school graduates in rich families are more likely to attend college than those in poor families. In each case, the individual would be the unit of analysis—not his father nor his family.

Organizations

Formal social organizations may also be the units of analysis in social scientific research. An example would be corporations, implying, of course, a population of all corporations. Individual corporations might be characterized in terms of their number of employees, their net annual profits, gross assets, number of defense contracts, percentage of employees who are from racial or ethnic minority groups, and so forth. In a descriptive study, we might examine the average net profit of all corporations. In an explanatory study we might determine whether large corporations employ a larger percentage of minority-group employees or a smaller percentage than is true of small corporations.

Other examples of formal social organizations suitable as units of analysis would be churches, colleges, army divisions, academic departments, and supermarkets. Each of these units of analysis could be characterized in terms of its organizational characteristics, descriptions of its elements, or descriptions of larger groupings to which it belonged.

A further set of related examples should point out the possible complexity of the issue of units of analysis. If a researcher asks whether companies whose employees have many preschool-age children are more likely to establish day care programs than companies whose employees have few preschool-age children, this question suggests that his unit of analysis is the company. If he asks whether workers with many preschool-age children are more likely to work at companies with day care programs than are workers with fewer preschool-age children, this question suggests his unit of analysis is the individual worker. If, finally, he asks whether children whose parents work for companies with day care programs are more likely to attend *some* day care program than is true of children whose parents do not work at such companies, this question suggests that the unit of analysis is the individual child.

If all this seems unduly complicated, you may take some assurance that in most research projects you are likely to undertake, the unit of analysis will be relatively clear to you. When the unit of analysis is not so clear, however, it is absolutely essential to determine what it is; otherwise, it will be impossible to determine what observations are to be made about whom or what.

Some studies have the purpose of making descriptions or explanations pertaining to more than one unit of analysis. In these cases, it is imperative that the researcher anticipate what conclusions he wishes to draw with regard to what units of analysis.

Social Artifacts

There is another large group of possible units of analysis that may be the focus of social scientific research to which we might refer generally as *social artifacts,* or the products of social beings or their behavior. One class of artifacts would include social objects such as books, poems, paintings, automobiles, buildings, songs, pottery, jokes, and scientific discoveries.

Each of these objects implies a population of all such objects: all books, all novels, all biographies, all introductory sociology textbooks, all cookbooks. A description of an individual book might characterize it in terms of its size, weight, length, price, content, number of pictures, volume of sales, or descriptions of its author. The population of all books or of a particular kind of book could be analyzed for the purpose of description or explanation.

A social scientist could analyze whether paintings by Russian, Chinese, or American artists showed the greatest degree of working-class consciousness, taking paintings as the units of analysis and describing each, in part, by the nationality of its creator. He might examine a local newspaper's editorials regarding a local university for purposes of describing, or perhaps explaining, changes in the newspaper's editorial position on the university over time; individual editorials would be the units of analysis.

Social interactions form another class of social artifacts suitable for social scientific research. Weddings would be an example of this. Weddings might be characterized as racially or religiously mixed or not, religious or secular in ceremony, resulting in divorce or not, or in terms of descriptions of one or both of the marriage partners. Realize that when a researcher reports that weddings between partners of different religions are more likely to be performed by secular authorities than is the case for those between partners of the same religion, the weddings are the units of analysis and not the individual partners to them.

Other examples of social interactions that might be the units of analysis in social scientific research are friendship choices, court cases, traffic accidents, divorces, fistfights, ship launchings, airline hijackings, race riots, and Congressional hearings.

Summary

The purpose of this section has been to stretch your imagination somewhat regarding possible units of analysis for social scientific research. While individual human beings are typically the units of analysis, this need not be the case. Indeed, many research questions could more appropriately be answered through the examination of other units of analysis.

The concept of the unit of analysis may seem more complicated than it needs to be. It is irrelevant whether you classify a given unit of analysis as a group, a formal organization, or a social artifact. It is essential, however, that you be able to identify what your unit of analysis *is*. You must decide whether you are studying marriages or marriage partners, crimes or criminals, families or heads of families, hijackings or hijackers, corporations or corporate executives. Unless you keep this point in mind constantly, you run the risk of making assertions about one unit of analysis based on the examination of another.

This is an appropriate point at which to introduce, briefly, two important concepts related to units of analysis: the *ecological fallacy* and *reductionism*. The first of these concepts, the *ecological fallacy,* means the danger, just mentioned, of making assertions about one unit of analysis based on the examination of another. Let's consider a hypothetical illustration of this.

Suppose we are interested in learning something about the nature of electoral support received by a female political candidate in a recent city-wide election. Let's assume that we have the vote tally for each precinct so that we can tell which precincts gave her the greatest support and which gave her the least. Assume also that we have census data describing some of the characteristics of those precincts.

Our analyses of such data might show that those precincts whose voters were relatively young gave the female candidate a greater proportion of their votes than those precincts whose voters had an older average age. We would be tempted to conclude from these findings that young voters were more likely to vote for the female candidate than were older voters, that age affected support for the woman. In reaching such a conclusion, we run the risk of committing the *ecological fallacy* in that it may have been the older voters in those "young" precincts who voted for the woman. Our problem in this is that we have examined *precincts* as our units of analysis and wish to draw conclusions about *voters.*

The same problem would arise if we discovered that crime rates were higher in cities having large black populations than in those with few blacks. We would not know if the crimes were actually committed by blacks. Or if we found suicide rates higher in Protestant countries than in Catholic ones, we still could not know for sure that more actual suicides were committed by Protestants than Catholics.

In another example, let's assume that the students attending High School A come from families having a higher average income than those students attending High School B. Assume further that High School A sends a higher proportion of its students on to college than does High School B. This, in and of itself, does not necessarily mean that students from wealthy families are more likely to attend college than those from poor families. It is possible—in both schools—that rich and poor students have the same likelihood of attending college, and that those in High School A are more likely overall to attend college than those in High School B.

It should be noted that very often the social scientist must address a particular research question through an ecological analysis such as those mentioned above. Perhaps the most appropriate data are simply not available to him. For example, the precinct vote tallies and the precinct characteristics mentioned in our initial example might be easily obtained, but he does not possess the resources necessary to conduct a postelection survey of individual voters. In such cases, the social scientist may reach a tentative conclusion, recognizing and noting the risk he runs in terms of the ecological fallacy.

The second concept that I wish to mention at this point is *reductionism.* Basically, **reductionism** refers to an overly strict reduction or limiting of the kinds of concepts and variables to be considered relevant to understanding a broad range of human behavior. Sociologists may tend to consider only sociological variables (values, norms, roles); economists may consider only economic variables (supply and demand, marginal value); psychologists may consider only psychological variables (personality types, traumas). For example, what caused the American Revolution? A shared commitment to the value of individual liberty, the economic plight of the colonies in relation to Britain, the megalomania of the Founding Fathers, or what? Scientists from different disciplines would tend to look at different types of answers and would ignore others. Explaining all or most human behavior in terms of economic factors is referred to as *economic reductionism;* explaining all or most human behavior in terms of psychological factors is referred to as *psychological reductionism;* and so forth.

This concept is related to our present discussion, since reductionism of any type tends to suggest particular units of analysis as being more relevant than others. If we were to regard shared values as the cause of the American Revolution, our unit of analysis would be the individual colonist. An economist, on the other hand, might choose the thirteen different colonies as his units of analysis and examine the economic organizations and conditions of each colony. The psychologist might choose individual leaders as the units of analysis for purposes of examining their personalities.

This fault, like the ecological fallacy, occurs with the use of "inappropriate" units of analysis. The "appropriate" unit of analysis for a given research question, however, is not always clear, and it is often debated by social scientists, especially across disciplinary boundaries.

3.4
Topics for Research

The preceding discussion of different possible units of analysis has frequently made references to their *characteristics.* Now we turn to the range of possible characteristics, seen as *topics* for research. In order to present a general overview of this range, I shall consider three classes: *conditions, orientations,* and *actions.*

Conditions

To begin, the various units of analysis may be characterized in terms of their conditions or their states of being. Individual persons might be characterized by such states as sex, age, height, marital status, deformities, region of origin, or hearing ability. Social groups and formal organizations might be characterized, for example, by their size, structure, location, and aggregated descriptions of their members. Physical objects as social artifacts might be described in terms of their physical characteristics such as size, weight, and color, or by the characteristics of the humans associated with them. Social interactions as units of analysis might be characterized in terms of where they occur, when they occur, or by the characteristics of the people involved.

These examples are not intended to represent an exhaustive list of possibilities. Nevertheless, they should suggest the kinds of conditions that may be used to characterize the units of analysis.

Orientations

In the study of individual people as the units of analysis, we frequently investigate what are called *orientations:* attitudes, beliefs, personality traits, prejudices, predispositions, and the like. Individuals might be characterized as religious, politically liberal, anti-Semitic, intellectually sophisticated, superstitious, scientific.

Social groups and formal organizations, similarly, might be characterized in terms of their purposes, policies, regulations, procedures, or in terms of the aggregated orientations of their members.

Social interactions might be similarly characterized. Airline hijackings might be characterized as politically or nonpolitically motivated. So could court cases and Congressional hearings.

Actions

Sometimes social *action* is the focus of research. We may observe directly, or accept secondhand accounts of, individual human actions such as voting, bond buying, investing, striking, dropping out of school, going to church, buying Brand X toothpaste. Secondhand accounts of actions may be obtained from the participants themselves or from other sources. Thus, to find out whether a given person has registered to vote, we might ask him, or we might check the list of registered voters.

Social groups and formal organizations act as well. Families may go on picnics, pray together, fight over money, or move to another city. Fraternities may sponsor concerts, sororities may collect money to send girls to camp. Corporations may contribute to political campaigns, merge with other corporations, fix prices, or go bankrupt.

Since social interactions are actions themselves, it is a little more difficult to imagine them engaging in actions. Nevertheless, marriages succeed or fail, court cases result in conviction or acquittal, fistfights cool off or get out of hand.

Summary

Like the earlier discussion of units of analysis, the present section on topics for research is intended as a mind-expanding exercise, not as a definitive statement of all the possible or legitimate topics. It matters little at this point whether you regard a person's score on an I.Q. test as a condition, an orientation, or an action, only that you recognize it as a possible focus of study.

Chapter 4 will return to all this with a more rigorously analytical perspective.

3.5
The Time Dimension

Time plays a number of roles in the design and execution of research, quite aside from the time one takes to do research. When we examine causation in detail in Part Four, we shall find that the time sequence of events and situations is a critical element in determining causation. Time is also involved in the issue of the generalizability of research findings. Do the descriptions and explanations which result from a particular study accurately represent the situation of ten years ago, ten years from now, or do they represent only the present state of affairs?

Thus far in this chapter, we have regarded research design as a process for deciding *what aspects* we shall observe, *of whom,* and *for what purpose.* Now we must consider another set of options that is time-related and that crosscuts each of these earlier considerations. Our observations may be made at more or less one point in time, or they may be deliberately stretched over a longer period.

Cross-Sectional Studies

Many research projects are designed to study some phenomenon by taking a cross section of it at one point in time and analyzing that cross section carefully. Exploratory and descriptive studies are often **cross-sectional.** A single United States Census, for instance, is a study aimed at a description of the United States population at a given point in time.

Many explanatory studies are also cross-sectional. A researcher who conducted a large-scale national survey to examine the sources of racial and religious prejudice would, in all likelihood, be dealing with a single time frame in the ongoing process of prejudice.

Explanatory, cross-sectional studies have an inherent problem. Typically, they are directed at the understanding of causal processes which occur over time, yet the conclusions are based on observations made at only one point in time. This problem is somewhat akin to that of determining the speed of a moving object on the basis of a high-speed, still photograph which "freezes" the movement of the object. A subsequent subsection of this chapter as well as Chapter 16 will present some of the ways in which researchers deal with this difficult problem.

Longitudinal Studies

Other research projects are designed to permit observations over an extended time period. An example of this is a researcher who participates in and observes the activities of a radical political group from the time of its inception to its demise. The analysis of newspaper editorials or Supreme Court decisions over time provides other examples. In the latter instances, it would be irrelevant whether the researcher's observations and analyses were made at one point in time or over the course of the actual events under study.

Three special types of **longitudinal studies** should be noted here. **Trend studies** are those which study changes within some general population over time. Examples would be a comparison of United States Censuses over time, showing growth in the national population, or a series of Gallup Polls during the course of an election campaign, showing trends in the relative strengths and standing of different candidates.

Cohort studies examine more specific subpopulations (cohorts) as they change over time. An example would be a series of national surveys, conducted perhaps every ten years, to study the economic attitudes of the cohort comprised of those persons born during the Depression years of the early 1930s. A sample of persons 20–25 years of age might be surveyed in 1950, another sample of those 30–35 years of age in 1960, and another sample of those 40–45 years of age in 1970. Although the specific set of people studied in each of those surveys would be different, each sample would represent the survivors of the cohort born between 1930 and 1935.

Panel studies are similar to trend and cohort studies except that the same set of people is studied each time. One example would be a voting study in which the same sample of voters were interviewed every month during an election campaign and asked for whom they intended to vote. Such a study would make it possible to analyze overall trends in voter preferences for different candidates, but it would have the added advantage of showing the precise patterns of persistence and change in intentions. For example, a trend study which showed that Candidates A and B each had exactly half of the voters on September first and on October first as well could indicate that none of the electorate had changed voting plans, that everybody had changed his intention, or something in between. A panel study would eliminate this confusion by showing what kinds of voters switched from A to B, what kinds switched from B to A, and other facts.

Longitudinal studies have an obvious advantage over cross-sectional ones in providing information describing processes over time. But very often, this advantage comes at a heavy cost of both time and money, especially in a large-scale survey: observations may have to be made at the time events are occurring, and the method of observation may require the employment of many research workers.

Approximating Longitudinal Studies

Often it is possible to draw approximate conclusions about processes that take place over time even when only cross-sectional data are available. It is worth noting some of the ways to do this.

Sometimes, cross-sectional data imply processes over time on the basis of simple logic. For example, a study of student drug use was conducted at the University of Hawaii in 1969–71. Students were asked to report whether they had ever tried each of a number of illegal drugs. With regard to marijuana and LSD, it was found that some students had tried both drugs, some had tried only one, and others had not tried either. Since these data were collected at one point in time, and since some students presumably would experiment with drugs later on, it would appear that such a study could not tell the *order* in which students were likely to experiment with marijuana and LSD: were students more likely to try marijuana or LSD first?

A closer examination of the data showed, however, that while some students reported having tried marijuana but not LSD, there were no students in the study who had tried only LSD. From this finding it was inferred—as common wisdom suggested—that marijuana use preceded LSD use. If the process of drug experimentation occurred in the opposite time-order, then a study at one point in time should have found some students who had tried LSD but had not gone on to try marijuana, and it should have found no students who had tried only marijuana.

Logical inferences may also be made whenever the time-order of variables is clear. If we discovered in a cross-sectional study of college students that those educated in private high schools received better college grades than those educated in public high schools, we would conclude that we had discovered an effect of the type of high school on college grades, rather than one of college grades on the type of high school attended. Thus, although the study collected data at only one point in time, we would feel justified in this case in drawing conclusions about processes taking place over time.

As in the previous example, cross-sectional studies often attempt to deal with longitudinal situations by asking people to report information from previous times. Suppose, for example, that we wish to find out if those people who supported Senator Eugene McCarthy for President in 1968 tended to support Senator George McGovern in 1972. We might examine this question by asking people which candidates they supported for President in each of those years, even though our study might take place subsequent to both of those election campaigns. The inherent danger in asking people for information about prior times, however, is that their reports may not be altogether accurate. We shall consider this issue more fully in Chapter 5.

Sometimes the examination of cohorts in a cross-sectional study can shed light on processes that occur over time. The inherent danger is that some set of peculiar historical circumstances may explain the differences among cohorts rather than their different locations in a process.

Let's suppose that a cross-sectional study shows college seniors to be more intellectually sophisticated than freshmen. We might conclude from that finding that students become more intellectually sophisticated as they progress through their college education. But perhaps the particular freshman class under study was intellectually unsophisticated for special historical reasons. It might be the case that college education has no effect on intellectual sophistication: the freshmen class under study might emerge as unsophisticated as they entered; the senior class under study might have been just as sophisticated when they were freshmen as when they were studied during their senior year.

This danger is guarded against through the replication of studies and their findings. The persistence of the cross-sectional pattern, then, supports the view that it accurately represents a process that occurs over time.

3.6

Motivations for Research

Thus far, the present chapter has sketched out some of the various options available to social scientific research—purposes, units of analysis, topics, and the time dimension. It is important that you develop and maintain a very broad perspective of what is possible for social scientific research, since a narrower perspective limits imagination and flexibility. A broad perspective can be dysfunctional, however, in that too many options make it difficult to develop a specific, limited research design.

Very often, people who have been schooled in the skills and even the logic of research have great difficulty getting started *doing* research. And a conventional understanding of the traditional model of science as discussed in Chapter 1 doesn't seem to help very much when a social science student is instructed simply to "do a research project" or when a junior faculty member is advised that a few research publications are expected if he is to be promoted, have his contract renewed, or be given tenure.

In the remainder of this chapter, I shall describe several of the ways in which social scientific research gets started, whether the researcher is a professional with the traditional perspective of science or a student writing a term paper. I hope these several models will provide some guidance to prospective (and even involuntary) researchers.

Testing Formal Theories

Sometimes, rather ambitious social scientists attempt to frame an understanding of all or a sizeable portion of social reality. (This is not advisable as a class project.) For a hypothetical illustration of this process, discussed previously in Chapter 1, let's try our hands at deriving a comprehensive theory of social behavior.

A formal, deductive theory begins with one or more postulates, or basic premises. (Realize, of course, that these will have grown out of prior observations, including, perhaps, rigorous empirical research.) Let's begin with the postulate: *All social behavior is based on self-interest.* We might further specify this postulate as follows: *Given a choice among alternative action possibilities, a person will choose that action which best corresponds to his own self-interest.*

No sooner have we printed this neatly at the top of a clean page in our "Big 5" tablet than we immediately think of hundreds of examples of people acting in ways that go directly contrary to their self-interest. Further specification is clearly in order. We might begin by introducing the notion of *perceived* self-interest, thereby allowing a person to choose the "wrong" action thinking it was the "right" one. Correspondingly, we would want to introduce the notion of a *perceived* choice to take account of those who did not know they had a choice. We would want to be sure to build in *no action* as one of the choices for the situation in which a person does not perceive any one of the action possibilities as being more in his self-interest than the others.

Before long, we would be forced to delineate various types of perceived self-interest: biological, economic, psychological, and others. Having done this, we might address the issue of priority ranking of the different types, either as might apply universally among all people or as might apply among different kinds of people or under different conditions. This consideration would permit us to handle those situations in which one action most closely corresponds to the actor's economic self-interest while another corresponds most closely to his psychological self-interest. (Will he accept a promotion at work, acquiring a raise in pay but also the insecurity of added responsibilities?)

As we pursue this sort of activity, we shall develop two types of statements: those that we postulate as the basic premises upon which our theory is grounded, and those that are derived logically from the beginning premises. In all this, we would have two goals: (1) to develop a comprehensive theory of social behavior, covering all its aspects, and (2) to arrive at more specific statements about the types of behavior to be expected in different types of situations. Statements of this latter kind are called *hypotheses.* In stating a hypothesis, the social scientist says that (a) if his basic premises are correct and (b) if his derivations are logically correct, then the behavior specified in the hypothesis should be observed in reality.

For purposes of illustration, let's suppose that our derivation of a "self-interest" theory of social behavior has progressed to the point at which we are prepared to state the following hypothesis: *Persons who experience economic deprivation during socialization will place a higher priority on economic self-interest later in life than will be true for those persons not experiencing economic deprivation during socialization.* Now we would have a hypothesis, but one that could not be tested immediately. Prior to testing the hypothesis, we would have to (a) specify the several concepts contained in it, (b) select a research method and research setting appropriate to testing, and (c) determine and obtain the resources needed. In practice, these several decisions are interwoven, and their relative importance will vary from one situation to another.

The specification of our concepts, for example, might be already pretty clear in our minds. Indeed, the hypothesis may have been suggested in part by some real-life situation that could imply the most appropriate method and setting, and having settled these factors, we could determine the amount and kind of resources needed.

On the other hand, it might be that we were qualified in the use of only a particular research method, say, survey research, participant observation, or small-group experimentation. If so, we would be limited in the ways in which we might specify our concepts and test the hypothesis. Or we might find ourselves effectively limited to a particular research setting, say, students enrolled in a social science methods class. This latter example is a typical limit to the resources available for research.

Although a large, national grant-giving agency would be unlikely to be interested in funding a test of the particular hypothesis in our illustration, very frequently it would be appropriate to seek support for research. Possibly we could obtain support for basic research on a theory of social behavior, but we would be more likely to do so if we envisioned a more or less practical concern to which the hypothesis might be related. Typically, this would require testing the hypothesis within a broader setting, but since the hypothesis itself is already part of a broader theoretical context, a large-scale research project might test a substantial portion of the theory.

For purposes of our illustration, though, let's assume that there is no support for the research; we are, for some reason, interested in testing only our particular hypothesis; and we do not have much time to devote to it. (Please note: this exercise in realism is not intended as a lesson on how research ought to be done.) Thus, we test the hypothesis among that class of methodology students we mentioned before.

Although these conditions do not inexorably fix the research method to be used, it seems likely that we would choose survey research because of

economy and efficiency. We decide, therefore, to administer a questionnaire
to the class. To do this, we must construct a questionnaire that will solicit data
relevant to testing our hypothesis. There are, of course, many ways in which
we might do this, but let's consider only one or two examples here.

Our hypothesis contains two key variables: *economic deprivation
during socialization* and *current priority of economic self-interest.* (Chapter 4
discusses the nature of *variables* in detail.) Our questionnaire, then, should
measure both variables among the students being studied. We might measure
economic deprivation during socialization in a number of ways: ask for
subjective assessments from the students, ask them for estimates of family
income during the period in question, or ask for reports on various
possessions of their families during the period. In the first of these, for
example, we might ask: "During most of the time you were growing up, would
you say your family was better off financially than other families, worse off, or
about the same as other families?" As to specific possessions, we might ask:
"How many cars, if any, did your family have when you started school?" In
practice, we would design several questions similar to these examples,
attempting to tap several different aspects of economic deprivation and
asking for both objective and subjective reports.

Current priority of economic self-interest might also be measured in
a number of ways. Since the units of analysis are all students, we might ask:
"In thinking of your future career, how important would you say it is for you to
earn a high salary? Extremely important, very important, fairly important, not
very important." Or, we might ask them to rank "a high salary" with other
possible characteristics of their careers such as responsibility, helping
people, or creativity.

These two sets of questions, and others, would permit us to classify
students in terms of the two key variables in the hypothesis. They could be
ranked in terms of their relative economic deprivation during socialization and
in terms of their current concern over economic self-interest. We would,
therefore, administer the questionnaire, process the data, and analyze the
relationship between the two variables.

Although survey research seems to be the likely method in this
situation, we might have tested the hypothesis in other ways. For example, we
might note that certain college majors are generally assumed to lead to
higher-paying jobs than others: engineering is assumed to be better than
English, for example. Moreover, we might surmise that students economically
deprived during socialization would be more likely to need financial assistance during college than others. These premises would suggest, therefore,
that engineering majors should be overrepresented among those seeking
financial aid (loans, student jobs) and English majors should be underrepresented. Perhaps the Student Aid office at our university would provide us with
a tally of the majors of loan and job applicants. Let's assume that engineering
majors make up 10 percent of the total student body, but they make up 20
percent of the loan and job applicants; and let's assume that English majors
make up 15 percent of the total student body but only 2 percent of the loan
and job applicants. These findings would support our hypothesis.

Many readers may feel rather uneasy about this second "test" of our
hypothesis; it is so indirect and involves additional assumptions. It should be

noted that it is hardly the ideal test, involving, as it does, a great many tenuous assumptions, but the example is described in order to make three additional points. First, a scientist seldom can undertake the best test of his hypothesis for lack of time and other resources. An effective scientist, therefore, must develop an ingenuity which permits him to test his hypotheses in the best *feasible* ways. Second, a strong, general theory should explain a wide variety of events and situations. Thus, it is important to determine the breadth of a theory's applicability.

Finally, it must be recalled from an earlier discussion in the present book that we never *prove* a theory correct; we can merely fail to *disprove* it. Moreover, we seldom if ever base the testing of a theory or a hypothesis on a single investigation. A thorough test of our present hypothesis might involve the two examples presented above plus several other, different tests. If each such test fails to disprove the hypothesis, we might gain confidence that it is essentially correct. If one or more of the tests does seem to disprove the hypothesis, we would attempt to decide whether: (1) the general hypothesis is incorrect, (2) it applies to a more limited range of phenomena, or (3) the particular test does not really test the hypothesis after all.

Although the research situation described above, testing a general theory, is perhaps the most well known, it is nonetheless the least typical. One good example, however, would be Samuel Stouffer's attempt to test a portion of Talcott Parsons' general theory of action: that portion dealing with *pattern variables*.[1]

In part, Parsons' theory dealt with standards that determine social action. He considered situations in which *universalistic* standards would be applied—standards that are the same regardless of which *social actors*[2] are involved in a situation. For example, a judge should apply the same standards to all defendants appearing before him in court. Parsons also considered situations in which *particularistic* standards would be applied—different standards for different people. In a family, for example, parents might have different standards for older children than for younger ones. (Realize that these concepts have far more general applicability than these specific examples suggest.)

Parsons was also concerned, at a general theoretical level, with situations in which universalistic and particularistic standards might conflict. Consider, for example, the policeman who discovers his own son burglarizing a store or speeding. His role as policeman would in all likelihood conflict with his role as father.

Stouffer directed his attention specifically at the question of role conflict with regard to particularistic and universalistic standards. His research, in this instance, consisted of a survey of Harvard students; in it they were presented with hypothetical situations in which they witnessed friends of theirs breaking laws and rules. Would they act in accord with the universalistic standards pertaining to law-breaking, or in accord with the particularistic standards more appropriate to friendship relations?

---

1. See Talcott Parsons and Edward A. Shils, *Toward a General Theory of Action* (Cambridge, Mass.: Harvard University Press, 1954), pp. 479–496.
2. See glossary.

Stouffer's research, while testing Parsons' theoretical derivations, contributed to the theory itself by pointing to additional specifications required for a full understanding of social behavior. In addition, it provides an excellent example of the procedures involved in making concrete measurements appropriate to abstract theoretical concepts (a topic to be addressed in detail in Chapter 4).

The Parsons/Stouffer example also illustrates the frequent "division of labor" in the social sciences. A separation of theory and research has characterized the social sciences in recent decades: some social scientists are primarily noted for the derivation of social theories, while others are primarily noted for their empirical research efforts. Thus, we frequently find some social scientists conducting research in order to test or refine the theories developed by others. To the extent that specialization promotes better theories and better research, this situation is advantageous to the progress of social science. At the same time, it can be dysfunctional. Researchers may not fully understand the theories they attempt to test; theorists might develop better theories if they more fully understood the logic of scientific research methods.

Testing Limited Hypotheses

In practice, few research projects in the social sciences seek to test substantial portions of general theories. While some empirical research is aimed at testing portions of comprehensive theories, more research is concerned with developing and testing limited theoretical hypotheses. Often these hypotheses have no direct reference to general theories. Sometimes the social scientist will begin with a particular interest in some area of social life, attempt to derive a theoretical understanding of it, and then conduct research aimed at testing his limited hypothesis.

Let's suppose he has an interest in "super-patriotic" political movements in the United States. Whereas the desire to frame a general and comprehensive theory of social behavior would lead him to a consideration of first principles, a more limited interest such as this one would probably begin with a review of his own observations and previous research, perhaps by others, on the specific topic. He might then attempt to place the specific topic within a more general theoretical context. How do super-patriotic political movements fit into the context of political attitudes and movements of all types, and perhaps even nonpolitical attitudes and movements?

He may discard the notion that members of super-patriotic movements are simply more patriotic than other people, based on his own interpretation of the idea of patriotism as loyalty to one's country. Thus, he looks for another explanation.

Being a good social scientist, he may note that group membership has as one of its functions an effect on the member's social identification. Thus, membership in a super-patriotic political movement would lead to a member's being identified as super-patriotic, or perhaps clearly and unquestionably patriotic to the United States. Such an identity might, of course, be desired by most if not all Americans, but why do only a small minority seek such identification through involvement in such a movement? Our social scientist might conclude that some people feel a greater need for patriotic certification than others. "Aha!" he says. "Those people whose loyalty to the United States might be questioned by others will be more in need of certification of their loyalty than others. Therefore, they will be more likely to join a 'super-patriotic' political movement."

This line of reasoning would lead our social scientist to think about the ways in which a person's loyalty to the United States might be subject to question. First, he notes that members of the New Left—often criticized as disloyal and subversive—are, by definition, absent from the movements under consideration. Then, especially if he is a sociologist, our scientist asks whether there might be some other social statuses that might raise questions of loyalty.

"Aha!" he says again, knowingly. "Persons who feel they might be identified with some other nation might feel their loyalty to the U.S.A. could be doubted." Thus, he concludes that persons identified, by themselves or by others, as foreigners might feel their American loyalty was subject to doubt, and they might attempt to prove loyalty through participation in super-patriotic organizations.

Having framed his hypothesis, he would then set about specifying it in terms of some research methodology and study design. He might, for example, analyze the membership lists of super-patriotic organizations, identifying "hyphenated" Americans—Italian-Americans, German-Americans, Polish-Americans—and compare the proportion of such members with their proportion in the total population. In this manner, he might determine whether such people are disproportionately represented in super-patriotic organizations.

As an alternative approach, our scientist might design and conduct a survey of the general population, asking questions about national origins and about participation in super-patriotic organizations. In this instance, he might wish to collect additional information about political attitudes in general and also information about respondents' perceptions of how others might view their loyalty.

The manner in which a limited hypothesis might be tested is the same as that described earlier in the case of a comprehensive theory. The only differences lie in the manner in which the hypothesis is derived and in the implications of the results of testing it. In the case of a comprehensive theory, the results will reflect on the theory from which the hypothesis is derived, while in a test of a limited hypothesis, the implications are for the hypothesis only. (If the hypothesis in our example were disconfirmed, the scientist would begin again to look for reasons for participation in super-patriotic organizations.)

Exploring Unstructured Interests

Quite often, a scientist will take an interest in a topic without having any clear ideas about what to expect in the way of relationships among variables. Let's suppose that a social science graduate student is particularly interested in the issue of student representation on the standing committees of the department in which he is enrolled. Perhaps he believes that students deserve representation and that they would be able to make meaningful contributions to the operation of the department. Each time the matter is raised, however, he may get the feeling that faculty members are generally opposed to the idea. He wants to learn more about the situation and to understand the reasons for opposition if such really exists.

Initially, our graduate student has no general theory of behavior from which to derive formal hypotheses regarding faculty attitudes toward student participation. Probably he has no hypotheses relating to this particular issue. Let's assume that all he has are concern and curiosity. Since the situation is so unstructured, he can choose from a number of methods for beginning his inquiry. Let's consider a few of them briefly.

He could find out whether other researchers have examined this issue. The student might begin with a review of appropriate literature, utilizing the various indexing sources of the campus library, academic journals, and so forth. If he finds relevant prior research, he should assess its applicability to the situation in his own department. Do the conditions studied by the prior researchers seem similar to or different from the conditions in his own department? Do the findings of the earlier studies make sense intuitively as he attempts to apply them to his department? Perhaps this exercise will adequately satisfy the student's curiosity regarding faculty attitudes toward student participation. Perhaps he will decide to replicate one or more of the prior studies within his own department, or perhaps the prior studies will suggest elements of a rather different study design.

As a different approach, the student might examine the several departments comprising his college. Contact with the various departmental offices, for example, might provide him with information about student representation on the committees of assorted departments. If he discovers that students have representation in some departments but not in others, he would then begin investigating the characteristics of those departments granting representation and those not granting it. He might consider such variables as number of faculty members, their average age, academic field, and ethnic and sex composition of faculty. If this examination produces fairly clear patterns of differences between those departments with and those without student representation, such patterns may help to explain the situation in his own department.

If he has discovered that some departments have student representation on committees, he might undertake an historical study of how such representation came about in those cases. He might be given access to the minutes of departmental meetings on the issue of representation. If he is barred from that, he might be able to construct a history of events through informal interviews with the students and faculty members who were involved.

Coming closer to home, the student might conduct unstructured interviews with *informants* (in the less sinister, anthropological, sense) in his own department. He may discover that some faculty members can give him a good picture of the situation, based on their own knowledge of the faculty and discussions of the issue. Such interviews might be coupled with some careful observations at faculty meetings—if he is permitted to attend. (Bugging faculty meetings or faculty restrooms is not an acceptable research technique.)

Finally, our graduate student might feel the necessity of a formal study of faculty attitudes within his department. Having been properly socialized in social research techniques, he decides to conduct a survey to assess the nature and sources of faculty attitudes on the issue of student representation on departmental committees. The design and content of his survey questionnaire will reflect the various insights gained from the research methods and activities previously discussed. He may replicate portions of earlier surveys, if any, and he will attempt to collect data relevant to the possible explanations suggested by his examination of other departments and his informal examination of his own.

The analysis of data collected in such a survey would be necessarily open-ended, since the student would have no formal hypotheses to test. For this situation, it is rather difficult to provide a set of guidelines for undertaking the analysis, but a few general comments may be made.

Typically, studies of this sort aim at determining the sources and consequences of something: what causes it, and what does it cause? If there is no other specific design, the most useful analytical format would appear to be the following. The researcher begins by constructing a workable measure of the *something* that constitutes the primary focus of the study—in this case, faculty attitudes toward student representation on committees. For example, our student may have asked several questions in the questionnaire that reflect such attitudes. He might then construct an index or scale to measure such attitudes in general. (See Chapter 15 for methods of index and scale construction.)

Next he should examine the relationship between the *something,* on the one hand, and those variables which precede it in time. In our present example, the student might look for a possible correlation between such variables as age, sex, academic rank, and tenure status and attitudes toward student representation. If he discovers several variables related to the attitudes in question, he should ask what else those variables may have in common and attempt to develop a general understanding of the sources of the attitudes.[3]

In our present example, the analysis might conclude with the formulation of specific hypotheses about the sources of faculty attitudes toward student representation, but frequently the researcher goes on to explore how his key variable affects other things.[4] In this example, the

---

3. An example of this may be found in Charles Y. Glock, Benjamin B. Ringer, and Earl R. Babbie, *To Comfort and to Challenge* (Berkeley, Calif.: University of California Press, 1967). Having discovered church involvement to be affected by sex, age, family status, and socio-economic status, the researchers were forced to consider what those disparate variables had in common; the result was the concept of social deprivation.
4. Having determined the sources of church involvement (*ibid.*), the researchers then set about to determine what difference it made. What effect might it have on other orientations and behaviors? As another example of this general approach to analysis, see Earl R. Babbie, *Science and Morality in Medicine* (Berkeley, California: University of California Press, 1970), a study that attempted to (a) measure the scientific orientations of medical school faculty members, (b) discover why some of

researcher might examine how faculty attitudes toward student representation are related to other attitudes and actions.

Since there is a tendency among social scientists to regard the exploration of unstructured ideas as Inferior to more structured inquiries, I should note that that is not my position. Often research efforts that are largely unstructured at the outset may be more fruitful ultimately than those that are prestructured. In a structured inquiry, analysis all too often concludes with the testing of a prespecified hypothesis. In an unstructured inquiry, however, it concludes with the researcher satisfying himself that he has discovered the best available answer to his general research question or that he is presently unable to discover an answer. There is a constant danger that structured inquiries may overlook relationships not anticipated by formal hypotheses. All this is not said to encourage chaos and anarchy among social researchers. Rather, it is to suggest that there are many legitimate paths to scientific discovery, perhaps thereby helping those who fear to take the first step in the belief that all empirical inquiries must be preceded by the framing of formal hypotheses.

Contracted Research

With increased frequency, social scientists are being commissioned to engage in specific research projects, usually of an applied nature. A city government may commission a survey of unemployment rates; a business firm may commission an evaluation of its new apprenticeship program; a political aspirant may commission a poll of voters. Although researchers may occasionally be asked to undertake research that will add to basic, scientific knowledge, contracted research typically is predicated on a need for specific facts and findings with policy implications. In other words, persons or agencies requesting such research usually plan to determine future courses of action on the basis of the research results. (Whether they ultimately do so is quite another matter.)

This research situation differs importantly from the earlier ones in the present chapter. Whenever the social scientist seeks to test a formal theory or an isolated hypothesis or when he seeks to explore an unstructured interest, it is the scientist himself who decides what will be the focus of inquiry. In contracted research, this decision is made by someone else. The scientist's response to a request for such research involves a number of considerations and decisions. The priority of considerations and the order of decisions will vary in different situations.

Presumably, the scientist considers the social value of the proposed research, as well as any ethical issues that it may involve. He will probably be concerned about the ultimate use of the project findings, including whether they will be made a part of the public domain of scientific research. (He will probably think to ask about this in the case of privately funded projects, but

them were more scientifically oriented than others, and (c) determine the consequences of scientific orientations on such things as humanitarian patient care.

he would be advised to raise the issue in the case of publicly funded ones as well.)

In the context of the ideas discussed in this chapter, our scientist will probably consider whether the specific applied concern of the proposed project can be placed within the scope of some more general scientific and theoretical issues. In a great many cases, the proposed project will have a descriptive purpose, and the scientist will be able to add an explanatory component. For example, he may be asked to undertake a sample survey to determine the unemployment rate in a given city, and he will be able to broaden the study design so as to address the question of why some groups of people have higher unemployment rates than others. Even when the proposed study has an explanatory purpose to begin with, he may be able to place it in a more general context. For example, he may be asked to determine the sources of support and opposition regarding a potential political candidate; a broader study design might permit him to explore the more general sphere of political decision-making.

Whenever the scientist attempts to broaden the scope and purpose of a proposed study, he is under an ethical obligation to make his intent known to the person or agency requesting that he undertake the study in the first place. The scientist may reasonably make this broadening a condition of his accepting the study request, but he should make sure that the sponsor understands the situation. The revised study design may even serve the interests of the sponsor better than the original, more limited one. Indeed, the ability to see this potential is part of the professional expertise that the scientist brings to the enterprise.

The involvement of nonresearchers in the decision-making process has both advantages and disadvantages. An advantage is communication. The sponsor's involvement can help to assure that the study will indeed meet the needs for which it was envisioned, and help to prevent the scientist from designing a study that has scientific interest but no direct relevance to the agency's needs.

The disadvantage is that people who ask a scientist to undertake a study usually do not fully understand research methods themselves. Not only must the scientist design a study relevant to a purpose he may not fully understand, but he must also conduct a course of instruction in research methods. Anyone who has engaged in this type of research undertaking, either as a scientist or as a sponsor, will probably agree that I have underrepresented the difficulties involved.

Be of good cheer, however. There is a relatively foolproof solution to the communication difficulties of contracted research. While the solution requires some resocialization on the part of both parties to the contract, it is undoubtedly worth the effort.

I have written elsewhere that "The first step in *organized* research is the drafting of the final report." This is an especially valuable guideline for contract research. The person requesting the research should be asked to prepare a rough draft of the report that he wishes to have once the project is completed. This draft should contain all relevant narrative sections and tables, with blank spaces provided for the data to be collected and reported. The first draft of a narrative portion might read, "The most economically depressed areas of the city are . . ." The scientist would then be able to specify different ways to operationalize such a statement, perhaps producing a revised statement such as "Those census blocks with the lowest median household incomes are . . ." The result of this drafting effort would be (a) a clear understanding by the sponsor of precisely what he is going to get from the study and (b) a clear guide to the scientist concerning what is to be said about whom in what form, so that he can design the most appropriate study for the sponsor's purpose.

The final report from a study may not look like the predesign draft. Too many fruitful discoveries occur later during the analysis stage for that to happen very often. Nevertheless, a predesign draft constitutes a minimal assurance that the basic purposes of the study will be met.

Involuntary Research

The theme of this final subsection is of a somewhat different order than the earlier ones. We have seen that researchers may be motivated to test general theories, to test limited hypotheses, to explore unstructured interests, and to undertake research contracts. Now we shall consider a motivation that often crosscuts those previously discussed.

A fair amount of the social research undertaken these days might reasonably be called *involuntary*, in that the researcher undertakes it as a result of external pressures to do so. The two most typical examples are of (1) the faculty member whose professional security or advancement depends, in part, on scientific publications and (2) the student who must do a research project to fulfill course requirements. I shall not comment on either the positive functions or the fallacies of such pressures. Rather, this subsection is addressed to the question: What do you do if you find yourself in the position of an involuntary researcher? The answer to the question involves what is called *research design*—the topic of this entire chapter.

Basically, research design involves a set of decisions regarding *what topic* is to be studied among *what population* using *what research methods* for *what purpose*. Whereas the earlier sections of this chapter—dealing with research purposes, units of analysis, topics—aimed at broadening your perspective in all these regards, research design is the process of narrowing, or focusing, your perspective for purposes of a particular study.

In the case of involuntary research, many aspects of research design may have been specified for you in advance. If you must do a project for a course in experimental methods, the method of research will have been specified for you. If the project is for a course in voting behavior, the research topic will have been somewhat specified. Since it would not be feasible for me to anticipate all such constraints, the following discussion will assume there are none.

In designing a research project, you will find it useful to begin by assessing three things: your own interests, your abilities, and the resources available to you. Each of these considerations will suggest a large number of possible studies.

Simulate the beginning of a more conventional research project: ask yourself what you are interested in understanding. Surely there are several questions you have about social behavior and attitudes. Why are some people politically liberal and others politically conservative? Why are some people more religious than others? Are college students becoming more vocationally oriented or less so? Do colleges and universities still discriminate against women faculty members? Are interracial marriages more or less successful than others? Do students learn more in large classes or small ones? Is the United States' economy more or less dependent on war and defense than in the past? Sit for awhile and think about the kinds of questions that interest and concern you.

Once you have a few questions you would be interested in answering for yourself, think about the kind of information that would be needed to answer them. What research units of analysis would provide the most relevant information: college students, corporations, voters, cities, or what? This question will probably be inseparable in your thoughts from the question of research topics. Then ask: what *aspects* of the units of analysis would provide the information you need to answer your research question?

Once you have some ideas about the kind of information relevant to your purpose, ask yourself how you might go about getting that information. Are the relevant data likely to be already available somewhere (say, in a government publication), or would you have to collect them yourself? If you think you would have to collect them, how would you go about doing that? Would it be necessary to interview a large number of people? Could you learn what you need to know by attending meetings of certain groups? Could you glean the data you need from books in the library?

As you answer these questions, you are well into the process of research design. Keep in mind your own research abilities and the resources available to you, however. Do not design the perfect study when you will be unable to carry it out. You may want to attempt to use research methods that you have not used before, since research should be a learning experience in many ways, but you should not put yourself at too great a disadvantage.

Once you have a general idea of what you want to study and how, you should carefully review previous research in journals and books to see how other researchers have addressed the topic and what they have learned about it. Your review of the literature may lead you to revise your research design: perhaps you will decide to use a previous researcher's method or even attempt to replicate his study; or perhaps you will decide to study some aspect that you feel has been previously overlooked.

Having refined your ideas about what you will study and how, you should turn to the subsequent chapters of this book to learn exactly how to proceed. If you have found a topic that really interests you, you will have a good start on a successful project.

3.7
Summary

Chapter 3 has dealt with the process of research design. It has posed the question: What aspects of whom (or what) will be studied in what fashion and for what purpose? As we have seen, in social science, the answers can be numerous.

The chapter began by examining the three major purposes of research: exploration, description, and explanation. Then, it considered the variety of units of analysis appropriate to social scientific research: we saw that social scientists can study individual people, groups, social organizations, and social artifacts. Next, we examined the different aspects of those units of analysis that might serve as topics of study: the conditions in which people and groups exist, people's orientations, and their actions.

Social science methods can be used to study social phenomena at a single point in time or across time. Different research designs serve these different approaches.

The chapter closed with a description of several motivations for undertaking social research, from traditional images of research—testing theories and hypotheses and exploring unstructured interests—to the kind with which students are likely to be more familiar, involuntary research.

3.8
Main Points

1. Exploration is the attempt to develop an initial, rough understanding of some phenomenon.

2. Description is the precise measurement and reporting of the characteristics of some population or phenomenon under study.

3. Explanation is the discovery and reporting of relationships among different aspects of the phenomenon under study. Whereas descriptive studies answer the question "what's so?" explanatory ones tend to answer the question "why?"

4. Units of analysis are the people or things whose characteristics social researchers observe, describe, and explain. Typically, the unit of analysis in social research is the individual person, but it may also be a group, a formal organization, or a social artifact.

5. Cross-sectional studies are those based on observations made at one point in time. While such studies are limited by this characteristic, inferences can be made about processes that occur over time.

6. Longitudinal studies are those in which observations are made at many points in time. Such observations may be made of samples drawn from

general populations (trend studies), samples drawn from more specific subpopulations (cohort studies), or the same sample of people each time (panel studies.)

7. A theory is a general and more or less comprehensive set of statements relating different aspects of some phenomenon.

8. A hypothesis is a statement of specific expectations about the nature of things, derived from a theory. Much research is devoted to hypothesis-testing, determining whether theoretical expectations are confirmed by what goes on in the real world.

3.9
Annotated Bibliography

Hammond, Phillip (ed.), *Sociologists at Work* (New York: Basic Books, 1964). A collection of candid research biographies written by several eminent social science researchers, discussing the studies which made them eminent. A variety of research motivations and designs are illustrated in these honest reports of how the research actually came about and unfolded. Take two chapters every four hours to relieve the discomfort of believing that social science research is routine and dull.

Miller, Delbert, *Handbook of Research Design and Social Measurement* (New York: David McKay, 1970). A useful reference book for introducing or reviewing numerous issues involved in design and measurement. In addition, the book contains a wealth of practical information relating to foundations, journals, and professional associations.

Stouffer, Samuel, *Social Research to Test Ideas* (New York: Free Press of Glencoe, 1962). A stimulating and downright inspirational posthumous collection of research articles by one of the giants of social research. In these reports, you will see how an ingenious man formulates an idea, designs the perfect study for testing it, is prevented from conducting the study, and then devises another feasible method for testing the same idea. Especially enlightening are Paul Lazarsfeld's introduction and Chapter 6 in which Stouffer reports on the effects of the Great Depression on the family.

4

Conceptualization and Operationalization

4.1
Introduction

Chapter 4 is a detailed discussion about topics of research. Examples and illustrations in the preceding chapter showed that social scientists study varied topics such as prejudice, religiosity, marital success, and corporate price-fixing. Each of these examples is a *concept* that may mean something to the reader, but is too general for precise communication

The several sections of the present chapter are about decisions and procedures by means of which the researcher moves from general concepts that interest him to specific methods of identifying and measuring those concepts in the real world. Let's suppose that during your reading of Chapter 3, you developed a deep and abiding interest in learning whether college students are becoming increasingly vocationally oriented. By the time you finish Chapter 4, you should be able to develop ways to recognize a "vocationally oriented" student when you see one. More important, you should complete the chapter with a realization of the difficulty of that accomplishment.

4.2
Conceptualization

Conceptualization is the process of refining general, theoretical ideas—essentially, concept definition. Although laymen may use a term such as "prejudice" rather casually, without defining precisely what they mean, scientists are not afforded this luxury. It is essential that scientists tell exactly what they mean by research concepts.

Definitions of the term *concept* are many and often complicated, partly because the term represents a concept itself. In the present context, however, it will be most useful to think of concepts as abstract summaries of related observations in the world. We spend much of our lives observing concrete objects, conditions, and events. Rather than regarding each of them as unique, we constantly attempt to fit them into groups of similar objects, conditions, and events. When we perceive similarities, we form a concept. For example, the term "chair" is a verbal representation of a concept that would refer to a large variety of observed objects. Other examples of concepts are "shelter," "happiness," "high rise," "poverty," "marriage," and "success."

To make matters more complicated, every object, condition, and event can be included in many concepts. Consider the humble packing crate. It might be regarded as a container, a chair, a table, a wood product, an artifact of modern society, a possession, a mass of molecules, a clue that someone is moving, or a source of anxiety. (An important element of science is discovering new ways of looking at old things.)

Concepts, then, are abstractions or mental images summarizing a diversity of specific objects, conditions, and events. You have never seen, touched, or sat on a concept, although you have surely thought about ("conceived") many. In communicating about concepts, we give them verbal labels or *terms*. If I describe someone to you as being "upper-class," this term represents a concept that I have in my mind and evokes a concept you have in your mind. Unfortunately, the concepts that the term "upper-class" represents for you and me may not be the same. If you were to meet the person I had called "upper-class," you might very well disagree with my description.

Conceptualization, then, is a mental process through which the scientist refines and specifies what his research concepts mean to him. In communicating his conceptualization to others, he defines the terms that he uses to represent his concepts verbally. How does the scientist define his terms?

Real Definitions

Beginning social science students often ask questions such as: "How do you define 'social class?' What does it *really* mean? Is it income, education, occupation, social position, or what?" Unfortunately, there are no "real" definitions of broad terms such as these. As Carl G. Hempel has cautioned:

> A "real" definition, according to traditional logic, is not a stipulation determining the meaning of some expression but a statement of the "essential nature" or the "essential attributes" of some entity. The notion of essential nature, however, is so vague as to render this characterization useless for the purposes of rigorous inquiry.[1]

The plain fact is that many terms, such as "social class," have been used over the years to represent a variety of concepts. This is true among social scientists as well as among laymen. Karl Marx used the term "social

---

1. Carl G. Hempel, "Fundamentals of Concept Formation in Empirical Science," *International Encyclopedia of Unified Science II*, No. 7 (1952), p. 6.

class" to mean a person's position in relation to economic production. W. Lloyd Warner used it more or less in reference to social prestige within a community.

Many subsequent social scientists have preferred the term "socio-economic status" (SES), which refers to the ranking of people in a society on a continuum running from "low" to "high." Yet, "socioeconomic status" is still only a term used to represent a concept, and just as with "social class," different social scientists have slightly different concepts in mind when they use the term. Although it is possible to list some of the commonly measured aspects of SES—income, education, wealth, power, prestige—there is no "real" definition of SES.

Nominal Definitions

We face a dilemma. Scientists must define their terms in order to promote the communication of scientific research findings, but none of the terms used have real definitions. The scientist solves this dilemma simply by being specific in stating *his* definition. He may state that for purposes of his research project, he will define socioeconomic status as a combination of formal education and income, further specifying how those two components are to be defined and combined.

What is the function of such a personal definition? One reader of the research report may conclude that the definition given coincides exactly with his own concept of socioeconomic status. Another reader may decide that the definition is very different from his own concept. Both readers will know exactly what the scientist means when he uses the term, however, and they may gauge their evaluation of his research findings accordingly.

A definition that is simply assigned to a term, without regard to the question of its real or ultimate meaning, is called a *nominal definition.* It stands to reason, therefore, that a given term might be assigned different nominal definitions by different researchers. Each would assign a definition appropriate to his concept, his mental image.

Conceptualization in science is not quite as chaotic or anarchistic as the above comments might suggest. In framing even nominal definitions, the researcher is not wholly without guidance. One constraint is common language usage: it is unlikely that a social scientist would define socioeconomic class as a person's height times his weight. For example, we might define "Democrat" as someone who votes for Democratic party candidates more often than for candidates of other political parties.

Within the traditional realm of science, the researcher's nominal definition of his terms would be guided by his general theory. A deductive theory relating to socioeconomic status would, in all likelihood, indicate which aspects commonly associated with that term were appropriate.

Further guidance is to be found in the previous work of other researchers. Unless the researcher is exploring a totally uncharted topic, he will want to consider the conceptualizations and definitions of other scholars. Adopting previously used definitions will have the added advantage of facilitating the comparison of his research with prior research, thereby contributing to the cumulative development of science.

Finally, a number of commonly used terms have been more or less standardized, and the researcher will probably use those standardized definitions. The United States Census, for instance, has defined such terms as "housing unit," "labor force," and "family." Common intelligence and personality tests provide other examples. Realize, however, that none of these are "real" definitions, only commonly accepted ones.

Even when general consensus exists with regard to a term or a concept, a researcher may choose to use a different definition. His deductive theory may suggest to him that a new definition would be more fruitful, or perhaps he simply has a feeling that the conventional definition conceals more than it reveals. Whatever his reasons are and whatever definition is used, he must state explicitly in the reporting of his research. We shall turn now to how definitions are made clear.

Operational Definitions

The preceding comments may have suggested to you that good research reports always contain such a sentence as, "In this study, prejudice was defined as . . ." If you review a number of published research reports, however, you may be surprised to find such a sentence missing in many of them. In its place you may find, "In this study, prejudice was *measured* as follows: . . ." Very frequently, *measurement* is substituted for *definition,* a subtle and important difference.

An example of this substitution may be found in the research by Charles Y. Glock and his colleagues attempting to measure church involvement among American Episcopalians.[2] Glock felt that one test of involvement would be church members' participation in church organizations, such as Altar Guilds, Women's Auxiliaries, or couples' clubs. Thus, the more church organizations a person participated in, the more involved he was in the life of the church. Glock noted, however, that people differ generally in the extent to which they participate in *any* kind of organizations. "Thus, it might be more significant that an 'organization-phobe' belongs to one church organization than that an 'organization-phile' belongs to three."[3]

As a result of this consideration, Glock chose to define (measure) organizational involvement as follows:

> A superior measure of organizational involvement in the church, therefore, is one which specifies the degree to which a given parishioner's total organizational connections are church related. In this way, varying dispositions toward "joining" in general could be

2. Charles Y. Glock, Benjamin B. Ringer, and Earl R. Babbie, *To Comfort and to Challenge* (Berkeley: University of California Press, 1967).
3. *Ibid.,* p. 23.

accounted for and parishioners would be distinguished in terms of the proportion of their organizational energy to the church.

Since parishioners in the study were asked to list all the organizations to which they belonged, it was possible to score each on the proportion of his organizational memberships which were religious. This measure will be called the Index of Organizational Involvement.[4]

Without using the term "definition," these paragraphs specify the **operational definition** of organizational involvement in the church: a specification of the *operations* that result in the measurement of the concept, in this case, organizational involvement. The number of religious organizations to which a parishioner belongs is to be divided by the total number of organizations to which he belongs. Thus a person belonging to six organizations of which three were religious (Index = .50) would be less organizationally involved than one belonging to four organizations of which three were religious (Index = .75).

It is instructive to consider some possible criticisms of this procedure. First, this operational definition means that a person belonging to nine religious organizations and one secular one would be judged less organizationally involved than a person belonging to one religious organization and no secular ones. Second, the operational definition takes no account of the time and energy devoted to organizations; it considers only simple membership. Third, the operational definition depends on information obtained by a questionnaire given to parishioners who might make errors—most likely errors of omission. Fourth, a person may belong to a religious organization for strictly nonreligious reasons: a young man may join the young people's club for the sole purpose of meeting young women.

The list of possible objections could go on and on. Three general points are important here. In reality, no operational definition is likely to correspond with everyone's conceptualization of what it is intended to represent. Also, operational definitions draw attention to possible, or even probable, errors of measurement. Furthermore, an operational definition has the virtue of communicating *exactly* what the corresponding term represents; thus, although a reader might disagree with Glock's definition of organizational involvement, there can be no misunderstanding of his meaning in the statement, "Women are more organizationally involved in church than men."

Ultimately, all conceptualization and definition in empirical research come down to operational definitions, whether or not they are presented explicitly in a research report. When a researcher observing a campus political movement reports, "The more radical members were totally opposed to the proposed meeting with the campus administrators," this statement implies an operational definition of "radical," even though the researcher may not state that operational definition explicitly.

A mark of good scientific reporting is the explicitness with which

---

4. *Ibid.*, p. 23.

operational definitions are presented. Clearly, we cannot gauge the full meaning of research findings unless we know exactly what they represent. Research cannot be replicated unless it is possible to use the same operational definitions in each study.

Nevertheless, many operational definitions are not stated explicitly. You should be aware of one of the reasons for this tendency, since you are likely to experience it yourself in conducting research and in reading about the research of others. Explicit operational definitions often seem to rob concepts of their richness of meaning.

Take the earlier example of "radical" political orientations of students, for example. The term "radical" is likely to evoke a rich imagery for every reader; it is irrelevant whether the imagery is essentially positive or negative. Perhaps the term stirs in you memories of previous events you have witnessed or pictures of people you would regard as radical. It will kindle different feelings whether you imagine acts of altruistic heroism and dedication or acts of subversion and disloyalty.

No operational definition is likely to capture satisfactorily all of these personal reactions to the term "radical." Partly, this is because each of us has a slightly different personal reaction to the term. But another cause is that many of our reactions to the term exist within us and cannot be observed directly in the stimulus to which we react. An operational definition must be limited to those things that can be observed, either directly or indirectly.

A precise operational definition of "radical" within the research context described above might be one who was observed in such acts as: publicly proposing some action that would be against the law, voting at a meeting in favor of an illegal action, using the term "liberal" in a derisive fashion, publicly identifying himself as a radical, or identifying himself as a radical in response to a direct question by the researcher. Each of these acts could be observed by the researcher. I would imagine that each bears some resemblance to your own personal image of acts typical of a "radical," and I am sure that no combination of them fully matches your image.

A precise operational definition of "radical" would describe exactly what operations or observations would identify someone as a radical, or as being more or less radical than someone else. No such definition will be fully satisfying to you, nor to others. Yet if you refuse to be explicit, you will make it impossible for anyone to know what dfinition is being used.

We shall return to this issue later in the present chapter when we consider the criteria for measurement quality, especially *validity* and *reliability.*

Since the preceding discussion may possibly make social science seem "unscientific," some words of perspective are in order. All that has been said about definitions applies to the physical sciences as well. There are no "real" definitions in the physical sciences, only nominal and operational ones. Acceleration is not "really" the rate of change in an object's velocity: the operational definition of feet per second per second has no ultimate truth value; it is merely a convention accepted by physicists.

The reason the issue seems less problematic in the physical sciences is that most people do not have a very rich, personal imagery attached to such concepts as "acceleration." Consider, however, the concept of "life." Hempel quotes a biologist's definition of a living organism:

> . . . a discrete mass of matter, with a definite boundary, undergoing continual interchange of material with its surroundings without manifest alteration of properties over short periods of time, and, as ascertained either by direct observation or by analogy with other objects of the same class, originating by some process of division or fractionation from one or two pre-existing objects of the same kind.[5]

Try to write a definition of human life using similar terminology to make more specific the definition just presented. Now relate that definition to the contemporary social controversies regarding abortion, mercy killing, capital punishment, wartime atrocities, and mass murders. The definition suddenly seems rather sterile. "Surely," you are saying, "there is more to life than that."

Explicit, operational definitions are essential to science, whether physical or social. As a general rule, the more explicit the definitions are, the more superficial they may seem.

The ultimate criterion for any definition should be its utility, its usefulness. As we look next at how definitions and measurements are actually used by researchers, perhaps the problem we have been discussing will not seem quite so difficult.

4.3
Definitions and Research Purposes

Recall from Chapter 3 that two of the general purposes of research are *description* and *explanation*. The distinction between them has important implications for the process of definition and measurement. If you have formed the opinion that description is a simpler task than explanation, you will be surprised to learn that definitions are more problematic for descriptive research than for explanatory research. This point will be discussed more fully in Part Four, but it is important that you have a basic understanding of why it is so before we turn to a detailed discussion of research measurement techniques.

The importance of definitions for descriptive research should be clear. If our task is to describe and report the unemployment rate in a city, our definition of "being unemployed" is critical. That definition will depend on our definition of another term: the "labor force." If it seems patently absurd to regard a three-year-old child as being unemployed, it is because such a child is not considered a member of the labor force. Thus, we might follow the

---

5. G. Evelyn Hutchinson, quoted in Hempel, *op. cit.*, p. 7.

United States Census Bureau's convention and exclude all persons under 14 years of age from the labor force.

This convention alone, however, would not give us a satisfactory definition, since it would count as unemployed such people as high school students, the retired, the disabled, and housewives. We might follow the census convention further by defining the labor force as "all persons 14 years of age and over who are employed, looking for work, or waiting to be called back to a job from which they have been laid off or furloughed." Unemployed persons, then, would be those members of the labor force who are not employed. If a student, housewife, or retired person is not looking for work, such a person would not even be included in the labor force.

But what does "looking for work" mean? Would it be necessary for a person to register with the State Employment Service or go from door to door asking for employment? Would it be sufficient to "want a job" or "be open to an offer of employment?" Conventionally, "looking for work" is defined operationally as saying "yes" in response to an interviewer's asking "Have you been looking for a job during the past seven days?" (Seven days is the conventional time period specified, but for some research purposes it might make more sense to shorten or lengthen it.)

I have spelled out these considerations in some detail so that you will realize that the conclusion of a descriptive study about the unemployment rate, for example, depends directly on each of them. Increasing the period of time during which people are counted as "looking for work" would have the effect of adding more unemployed persons to the labor force as defined, thereby increasing the reported unemployment rate. If we follow another convention and speak of the *civilian* labor force and the *civilian* unemployment rate, we are excluding military personnel; this, too, increases the reported unemployment rate, since military personnel would be employed— *by definition.*

Thus the descriptive statement that the unemployment rate in a city is 3 percent, or 5 percent, or whatever it might be, depends directly on the specific operational definitions employed. If that seems clear in this example, it is because there are a number of accepted conventions relating to the labor force and unemployment. Consider how difficult it would be to get agreement about the definitions you would need in order to make a descriptive statement such as this: "Forty-five percent of the students are politically conservative." This percentage, like the unemployment rate above, would depend directly on one's definition of what is being measured. A different definition might result in the statement, "Five percent of the student body are politically conservative."

Ironically, definitions are less problematical in the case of explanatory research. Let's suppose that we are interested in explaining political conservatism: why are some people conservative while others are not? More specifically, let's suppose we are interested in whether old people are generally more conservative than young people. What if you and I have twenty-five different operational definitions of "conservative," and we can't agree on which definition is the best one? We would seem to have an insurmountable obstacle to our research *unless we discovered that the definition didn't really matter.* Suppose that we found old people generally more conservative than young people in terms of each of the twenty-five definitions! To make matters clearer, let's suppose that we found old people generally more conservative than young people in terms of *every* reasonable definition of conservatism we could think of. In this case, it wouldn't matter what our definition was. We would conclude that old people are generally more conservative than young people even though we couldn't agree on what a conservative "really" is.

In practice, explanatory research seldom results in findings quite as unambiguous as the above example suggests; nonetheless, the general pattern is quite common in actual research. The important point is that this situation is extremely unlikely in descriptive research. Changing definitions almost inevitably results in arriving at different descriptive conclusions.

Now that we have examined the process of conceptualization from a general, logical perspective, let's move on to more concrete matters. We shall begin by giving deliberate attention to certain terms that have been used rather casually in previous discussions.

4.4
Attributes and Variables

Thus far, we have covered numerous examples of *concepts.* From the standpoint of scientific research, it is useful to distinguish two kinds of concepts.

Many of the concepts mentioned above refer to **attributes** or characteristics of persons or things. Examples of these might include such terms as tall, heavy, blue, upper-class, four years old, male, and so forth. Any given object or event could be conceptualized in terms of its attributes.

Variables, on the other hand, are logical groupings of attributes. Thus, for example, "male" and "female" would be attributes, while "sex" or "gender" would be variables comprised of those two attributes. "Color" would be a variable comprised of such attributes as red, blue, and green. "Social class" would be a variable comprised of a set of attributes such as upper-class, middle-class, and lower-class, or some similar divisions.

The relationship between attributes and variables lies at the heart of both description and explanation in science. For example, we might describe a college class in terms of the variable "sex" by reporting the observed frequencies of the attributes "male" and "female": "Sixty percent of the class are men; forty percent are women." An unemployment rate can be thought of as a description of the variable "employment status" of a labor force in terms of the attributes "employed" and "unemployed." Even the report of "average family income" for a city is a summary of the attributes comprising that variable: $3,124, $10,980, $35,000, etc.

The relationship between attributes and variables is more complicated in the case of explanation, and much of Part Four of the book is addressed to this. By way of a simple illustration, however, let's return to the earlier example of age and conservatism. For simplicity, let's define the variable "conservatism" as comprised of the attributes "conservative" and "nonconservative," without worrying too much about the definitions of those attributes. In the same spirit, let's define the variable "age," in terms of two attributes, "young" and "old." We would conclude that age partially "explains" conservatism if we found a pattern connecting the attributes of those two variables: if, for example, we found that 80 percent of those people with the attribute "old" also had the attribute "conservative," while only 30 percent of those with the attribute "young" had the attribute "conservative."

The next section of the present chapter will deal with the various ways in which attributes are grouped—the structures that are formed by the attributes making up a given variable. Before turning to that topic, however, we should consider two structural features common to all variables.

First, the group of attributes comprising a variable must be *exhaustive.* Thus, for example, he would not say that the attributes "red" and "blue" comprise the variable "color." They are *some of* the attributes comprising that variable. Similarly, the attributes "5 years old" and "6 years old" do not comprise the variable "age." The importance of this requirement will become more evident when we discuss actual techniques for measurement in research.

Second, the group of attributes comprising a variable must be *mutually exclusive.* No more than one attribute of a variable can be applicable in describing whatever is being described in terms of that variable. Thus, the attributes "male" and "female" can appear in the same variable, but the attributes "male" and "college graduate" cannot, since a given person could be both.

Realize that these two requirements, like all such requirements, are somewhat flexible in practice, especially the requirement for exhaustiveness. There are conditions under which the variable "color" might include only the attributes "red" and "blue" or maybe "red," "blue," and "other." And although we typically limit the variable "sex" to the attributes "male" and "female," there are research situations in which "neuter" should be added. And if the variable were "human sexual identity," an extended continuum from "totally male" to "totally female" might be needed to include an exhaustive grouping of attributes.

4.5
Levels of Measurement

Now we shall see how the structure of a variable—the way in which its attributes are grouped—has important implications for the tasks of measurement and association. The requirements of mutual exclusiveness and exhaustiveness apply to all sets of attributes comprising variables. However, attributes form other structures as well. Because of these additional structural features, different variables may represent different *levels of measurement.*[6] We shall examine four levels of measurement in this section: *nominal, ordinal, interval,* and *ratio.*

---

6. An excellent treatment of this topic is to be found in James A. Davis, *Elementary Survey Analysis* (Englewood Cliffs, N.J.: Prentice-Hall, 1971), pp. 9ff. Most treatments of these levels of measurement

Nominal Measures

Variables whose attributes have *only* the characteristics of exhaustiveness and mutual exclusiveness represent **nominal measures.** Examples of these would be sex, religious affiliation, political party affiliation, college major, hair color, and birthplace. While the attributes comprising each of these variables—"male" and "female" comprising the variable "sex"—are distinct from one another (and exhaust the possibilities of gender among people), they have none of the additional structures mentioned below.

It might be useful to imagine a group of people being characterized in terms of one such variable and physically grouped by the applicable attributes. Imagine asking a large gathering of people to stand together in groups according to the states in which they were born: all those born in Vermont together in one group, those born in California in another, and so forth. (The variable would be "place of birth"; the attribute would be "born in California," or "born in Vermont.") All the people standing in a given group would share at least one thing in common; the people in any group would differ from the people in all the other groups in that same regard. Where the individual groups formed, how close they were to one another, or how the groups were arranged in the room, would all be irrelevant. All that would matter would be that all the members of a given group share the same state of birth, and that each group have a different shared state of birth.

Ordinal Measures

Variables whose attributes may be logically *rank-ordered* represent **ordinal measures.** The different attributes represent relatively more or less of the variable. Variables of this type are social class, religiosity, conservatism, alienation, prejudice, intellectual sophistication, and the like.

Note that each of the examples provided above would be subject to serious differences of opinion as to its definition. Many of the ordinal variables used in social scientific research have this quality, but that need not be the case. In the physical sciences, hardness is the most frequently cited example of an ordinal measure. We may say that one material (e.g., diamond) is harder than another (e.g., glass) if the former can scratch the latter and not vice versa (e.g., diamond scratches glass, but glass does not scratch diamond). By attempting to scratch various materials with others, we might eventually be able to arrange the several materials in a row, ranging from the softest to the hardest. It would not ever be possible to say how hard a given material was in absolute terms, but only in relative terms—which materials it was harder than, and which it was softer than.

Let's pursue the earlier example of grouping the people at a social gathering, and imagine that we asked all the people with a college education to stand in one group, all those with a high school education (but who were

use the term "scale" (e.g., *nominal scale*), following the example of S. S. Stevens, "On the Theory of Scales of Measurement," *Science,* Vol. 103 (1946), pp. 677–680. Since this book uses the term "scale" in a different sense, I have avoided its use in this context.

not also college graduates) to stand in another group, and all those who had not graduated from high school to stand in a third group. This manner of grouping people would satisfy the requirements for exhaustiveness and mutual exclusiveness discussed earlier. In addition, however, we might logically arrange the three groups in terms of the relative amount of formal education (the shared attribute) each had. We might arrange the three groups in a row, ranging from most to least formal education. This arrangement would provide a physical representation of an ordinal measure. If we knew which groups two individual people were in, we could determine that one had more, less, or the same formal education as the other; in a similar way, one individual object could be ranked as harder, softer, or of the same hardness as another object.

It is important to note that in the previous example it would be irrelevant how close or far apart the educational groups were from one another. They might stand five feet apart or five hundred feet apart; the college and high school groups could be five feet apart, while the less-than-high-school group might be five hundred feet farther down the line. These actual distances would not have any meaning. The college group, however, should be closer to the high school group than to the less-than-high-school group or else the rank order would be incorrect.

Interval Measures

For the attributes comprising some variables, the actual distance separating those attributes has meaning. Such variables are **interval measures.** For these, the logical distance between attributes can be expressed in meaningful standard intervals. A physical science example would be the Fahrenheit (or the Celsius, but not the Kelvin) temperature scale. The difference, or distance, between 80 degrees and 90 degrees is the same as that which separates 40 degrees and 50 degrees. Eighty degrees Fahrenheit is not twice as hot as 40 degrees, however, since the zero point in the Fahrenheit scale (and the Celsius, but not the Kelvin), is an arbitrary one; zero degrees does not really mean a lack of heat, nor does -30 degrees represent 30 degrees less than no heat. (The Kelvin scale is based on an *absolute zero* which does mean—for a physicist at least—a complete lack of heat.)

About the only interval measures commonly used in social scientific research are those constructed measures such as standardized intelligence tests that have been more or less accepted. The interval separating IQ scores of 100 and 110 may be regarded as the same as the interval separating scores of 110 and 120 by virtue of the distribution of observed scores obtained by many thousands of people who have taken the tests over the years. (A person who received a score of 0 on a standard IQ test could not be regarded, strictly speaking, as having *no* intelligence, although we might feel he was unsuited to be a college professor or even a college student.)

Most of the social scientific variables meeting the minimum require-ments for interval measures also meet the requirements for **ratio measures** (see below).

Ratio Measures

The attributes comprising some variables, besides having all the structural characteristics mentioned above, are based on a true zero point. I have already mentioned the Kelvin temperature scale in contrast to the Fahrenheit and Celsius scales. Examples from social scientific research would include age, length of residence in a given place, the number of organizations belonged to, the number of times attending church during a particular period of time, the number of times married, and the number of Arab friends.

Returning to the illustration of methodological party games at a social gathering, we might ask people to group themselves according to age. All the one-year-olds would stand (or sit or lie) together, the two-year-olds together, the three-year-olds, and so forth. The fact that members of a single group shared the same age and that different groups had different shared ages would satisfy the minimum requirements for a nominal measure. The several groups could be arranged in a line running from the youngest to the oldest, thereby meeting the additional requirements of an ordinal measure and permitting us to determine if one given person was older, younger, or the same age as another. It would also be reasonable to arrange the groups in such a way as to have the same distance between each pair of adjacent groups, thereby satisfying the additional requirements of an interval measure and permitting us to say *how much* older one person was than another. Finally, since one of the attributes included in age represents a true zero (babies carried by women about to give birth), the phalanx of hapless party-goers would also meet the requirements for a ratio measure, permitting us to say that one person was twice as old as another.

Implications of Levels of Measurement

Since it is unlikely that you will undertake the physical grouping of people described above (try it once, and you won't be invited to many parties), I should draw your attention to some of the practical implications of the differences that have been distinguished. Primarily, these implications appear in the analysis of data (discussed in Part Four), but those analytical implications should be anticipated in the structuring of your research project.

Certain analytical techniques require variables of certain minimum levels of measurement. For example, if a technique involves addition, subtraction, multiplication, or division, then interval or ratio measures are needed. If only addition and subtraction are involved, interval measures would suffice. To the extent that the variables to be examined in your research project are limited to a particular level of measurement—say, ordinal—you should plan your analytical techniques accordingly. More precisely, you should anticipate drawing research conclusions appropriate to the levels of measurement used in your variables. For example, you might reasonably plan to undermine and report the mean age of a population under study (add up all the individual ages and divide by the number of people), but you should not plan on reporting the mean religious affiliation, since that is a nominal variable. (You could report the *modal*—the most common—religious affiliation.)

At the same time, it is important to realize that some variables may be treated as representing different levels of measurement. A variable representing a given level of measurement—say, ratio—may also be treated as representing a "lower" level of measurement—say, ordinal. Recall, for example, that age is a ratio measure. Thus, the researcher would be justified in computing a *regression equation* (requiring at least interval-level variables) linking age and height. If the researcher wished to examine only the relationship between age and some ordinal-level variable—say, self-perceived religiosity: high, medium, and low—he might choose to treat age as an ordinal-level variable as well. He might characterize the subjects of his study as being "young," "middle-aged," and "old," specifying what age range comprised each of those groupings. Finally, age might be used as a nominal-level variable for certain research purposes. People might be grouped as being members of the post-World-War-II "baby boom" or not; they might be grouped as being born during the Depression of the 1930s or not. Another nominal measurement, based on birthdate rather than just age, would be the grouping of people by astrological signs.

The analytical uses planned for a given variable, then, should determine the level of measurement to be sought, with the realization that some variables are inherently limited to a certain level. If a variable is to be used in a variety of ways, requiring different levels of measurement, the study should be designed in such a fashion as to achieve the highest level required. (For example, if the subjects in a study are asked their exact ages, they can subsequently be organized into ordinal or nominal groupings.)

You need not necessarily treat variables at their highest level of measurement, however. If you are sure to have no need for ages of people at higher than the ordinal level of measurement, you may simply ask people which among several age ranges they belong in: their twenties, thirties, and so forth. In a study of the wealth of corporations, you may use Dun and Bradstreet reports, which list many United States corporations and classify them according to net worth. If your research purposes require only ordinal measurement of corporate wealth, you might choose to use Dun and Bradstreet data to rank corporations rather than seeking more precise information. Whenever your research purposes are not altogether clear, however, it is advisable to seek the highest level of measurement possible. While ratio measures can subsequently be reduced to ordinal ones, it is not possible to convert an ordinal measure to a ratio one. That is a one-way street worth remembering.

4.6
An Operationalization Framework

The preceding section discussions and topics of this chapter have described various aspects of the conceptualization process. At the same time, they have moved on occasion into what is called operationalization. We might logically distinguish these two processes as follows. **Conceptualization** is the refinement of abstract ideas—variables and attributes—while **operationalization** is the development of specific research procedures (operations) that will result in empirical observations representing those concepts in the real world.

For example, we might conceptualize age as the number of years that have passed since a person's birth. Even more specifically, we might limit our conceptualization to the number of *full* years, treating alike the person who is eighteen years and two months old and the person who is eighteen years and six months old. Or we might follow the practice of insurance companies and conceptualize age as based on a person's nearest birthday, rounding off ages to the nearest number of full years.

Operationalization involves the act of measurement. Thus we might operationalize the measurement of age by conducting personal interviews in which the people in the study are to be asked, "How old are you?" The operational definition (see section 4.2) of age, then, would be "the age indicated by a subject's response to the question 'How old are you?' "

In practice, the distinction between conceptualization and operationalization is not always clear, and you should not worry about this. The remainder of the present section will be devoted to some guidelines for the operationalization of concepts in the design of a research project, and we shall frequently touch on matters of conceptualization as well. The combined conceptualization-operationalization process is somewhat cyclical in practice. Typical end-products of the process include the following:

1. A specification, if appropriate, of the various aspects or dimensions of the abstract theoretical concept. When an abstract concept means different things to different people, those things are the dimensions of the concept.

2. A specification of each dimension as a variable comprised of a set of attributes.

3. The identification of operations by the researcher that would result in empirical observations about each of the attributes of each variable. These observations are also referred to as *empirical indicators* of the variable in the sense that they indicate which attribute of a given variable is applicable to a given research subject.

Suppose a researcher wishes to study student participation in the college class he is teaching. Perhaps he is interested in learning why some students participate more than others and what effects participation has on their comprehension of the subject matter. One dimension of participation might be classroom discussion. This dimension would be a variable comprised of the attributes "joins in" and "does not join in." The act of asking a question in class or making a comment might then be regarded as an empirical indicator of classroom participation. Or more precisely, the teacher-researcher might establish as his operational measurement that *observing* a student asking a question or making a comment in class would be sufficient for applying the attribute "joins in" to that student. No less important, observing that a given student did not ask questions or make comments in class would be sufficient for applying the attribute "does not join in" to that student.

Alternatively, the teacher-researcher might specify the variable "classroom discussion" as being comprised of the attributes: "never joined in," "joined in once," "joined in twice," and so forth. Operationally, the number of times he *observed* a given student asking a question or making a comment would be the indicator determining which of the possible attributes should be applied to that student.

Consider a different operationalization of the variable "classroom discussion." The teacher-researcher might prepare and circulate a questionnaire among the students in his class asking: "Who do you think joins in most in classroom discussions?" Each student would be asked to write in the name of the student he felt joined in the most. The teacher-researcher might then tally the number of times each student was named. The attributes comprising the variable in this instance would be: "not named," "named once," "named twice," and so forth.

It is important to recognize that the two measurement operations described above provide different operational definitions of "classroom discussion." The measurement operations involved are different, the attributes comprising the variable are different, and, perhaps more significantly, one measures *frequency of joining in* while the other measures what we might call *appearance of joining in the most often.*

Every empirical indicator or set of indicators considered should be related back to the general concept that you wish to study. In the present example, you should ask whether the act of asking a question or making a comment in class reflects what you have in mind by "participation." A useful technique for doing this is to imagine circumstances in which the indicator might be observed without representing what you have in mind: in all likelihood, asking "May I go to the bathroom?" would not qualify as "participation." The same might be said for comments that a student makes when called on by the teacher. This exercise will usually result in a further specification of empirical indicators and, in turn, of variables.

The process of specifying the dimensions of a general concept and identifying empirical indicators can take one of two directions in practice, similar to the *deductive* and *inductive* methods mentioned in Chapter 2. On the one hand, the researcher may delineate abstractly the several dimensions of the general concept and then set about identifying empirical indicators appropriate to each. Or, on the other hand, he may begin by listing a variety of empirical indicators that he might associate with the general concept and then attempt to determine what different dimensions those various indicators represent.

Perhaps an illustration will clarify these two approaches further. Let's take the example of *religiosity,* or religiousness. I suspect that most readers will have some personal image of what constitutes religiosity—what distinguishes religious people from nonreligious people. Probably no single reader will have a perfectly clear image of this, however, and surely different readers would have diverse images. Plainly, the term "religiosity" is used casually in reference to a number of dissimilar things: religiosity has many dimensions. Charles Y. Glock, who is one of several social scientists who have attempted to distinguish and refine the assorted dimensions of religiosity, suggests there are at least five important dimensions.[7]

Ritual involvement refers to participation in such activities as—for Christians, say—weekly church services, communion, and prayers before meals. (Note that each of these examples suggests an operationalization.) *Ideological involvement* concerns the acceptance of traditional religious beliefs. *Intellectual involvement* refers to the extent of one's knowledge about religion. *Experiential involvement* means personal, religious experiences such as, say, hearing God speak, seeing religious visions, or having religious seizures. Finally, Glock suggests *consequential involvement* as the extent to which social behavior is motivated by religious concerns and in accord with religious teachings. Being honest as a result of one's religious beliefs would be an example of this.

This specification of dimensions of religiosity is only one among many that have been developed within the social sciences. Some scholars would distinguish church attendance from private prayers, calling the latter a *devotional* dimension. Others conceive of having close friends within the same religion as constituting a *communal* dimension. Many other dimensions and subdivisions of those already mentioned have been suggested by still other scholars.

Were you to attempt a study of religiosity, then, you might begin by making a list of all the conceivable dimensions that relate somewhat to the general concept you have in mind. You would probably be guided by the work of other scholars in this. At the same time, you might be working within a theoretical framework that would impose special constraints on the dimensions specified. If you were developing a purely social-psychological model of religiosity, you might possibly ignore behavioral aspects of religiosity, accepting ideological involvement while ignoring ritual involvement, for example.

As an alternative approach, you might begin by listing all the empirical indicators that come to mind when you think about the general concept of religiosity: attending church, praying, reading the Bible, giving to charity, believing in God, referring to religious teachings in conversation. Having listed all those specific empirical indicators you can think of, you should then attempt to organize them into somewhat more general dimen-

---

7. Charles Y. Glock and Rodney Stark, *Religion and Society in Tension* (Chicago: Rand McNally, 1965), pp. 18–38.

sions of religiosity. The identification of dimensions in this fashion will probably suggest to you more dimensions and indicators that you did not think of initially.

Either of the two approaches described above is legitimate in conceptualization and operationalization. In practice, you will probably use both. This, too, is legitimate, even desirable.

Your goal should be the fullest possible view of what you are studying. Do not try to reach a decision as to a single indicator to represent a given attribute; to the extent that your research plans and resources will permit, you should select many indicators. You should plan to make observations permitting a variety of measurements of your variables, representing a variety of operational definitions. It is both safer and more fruitful to decide which is the best definition on the basis of your analyses of the data you will collect. (There will be more about how to do this in Part Four.)

A Note on Opposites

Before we move on, our attention should be given to a frequently troublesome technicality in conceptualization and operationalization. When we speak of "religiosity" as a research variable, we tend to think of attributes comprising that variable as ranging from, say, "very religious" to "not religious." Thus, for example, the empirical indicator "attends church every day" might represent the attribute "very religious," while the indicator "never attends church" might represent the attribute "not religious." But we might conceive of the range of variation in religiosity as extending even further in the negative direction. Some people, for example, might be considered "antireligious." Burning down churches, shooting religious leaders, or publicly denouncing all religions would be possible empirical indicators of antireligiosity.

In the conceptualization-operationalization process, then, you must decide on the range of variation relevant to your research purposes. If you were to pursue the example given just above, would it be sufficient for your purposes to group together those people who are simply nonreligious with those who are rabidly antireligious, or would it be important to separate those types of people? Would it be sufficient to distinguish people who are prejudiced from those who are not, or would it be important to further distinguish those who might be called "antiprejudiced?" (The refusal to admit that blacks and whites are different in *any* way or the belief that bigots should be shot down in the streets might be indicators of this.)

In research practice, this kind of question is resolved in varying ways. In most studies of religiosity and of prejudice, for example, the lesser ranges of variation described above have typically been used, though the "antireligious" and the "antiprejudiced" have been studied on occasion. In the case of political orientations, on the other hand, it is more conventional to consider an extreme range of variations, from, say, "very conservative" to "very liberal."

Ultimately, empirical indicators such as the examples we have considered above are clues to the applicability or inapplicability to a given unit of analysis of particular attributes comprising a given variable or dimension of a variable. If church attendance is considered an empirical indicator of the attribute "religious," the observation that someone attends church is taken to mean that the attribute applies to that person; the observation that someone does not attend church is taken to mean that the attribute does not apply to that person. A difficulty arises, however, in the determination of what attribute to apply whenever the specified indicator is not observed. What do we call a person who does not attend church: "nonreligious" or "antireligious?" Or, to turn the example around, we might reasonably call a church-burner "antireligious," but would we be justified in attaching the attribute "religious" to a person who has never burned down a church?

The complexity of this problem should not be underestimated. The foregoing discussion should highlight, moreover, the ambiguities involved in the terms we use to label conditions, acts, and orientations. The terms we associate with concepts, variables, and attributes are, after all, only terms. They have no intrinsically *real* meanings, only greater or lesser consensus as to their agreed-upon meanings. If there is greater consensus as to the meaning of "acceleration" than of "religiosity," that does not make the accepted meaning of the former any *truer* than that of the latter, only less troublesome in the practice of research.

4.7
Criteria for Measurement Quality

There is no doubt a danger that the extreme nominalism of the preceding sections of this chapter may lead some readers to imagine that there are no standards whatever governing definition and measurement. If a term such as "religious" has no ultimate meaning, can't you define and measure religiosity any way you jolly well please? You can do precisely that, of course, but people may not be interested in reading about your research if you take that position in the extreme. You will not get good grades on your term papers; you will not get tenure.

The tone of the preceding sections has been taken in order to expand your research consciousness, not to turn you to research anarchy. There *are* standards governing definition and measurement, and those standards are not merely the accepted dictates of some scientific establishment. They are intrinsically meaningful and functional for good scientific research.

To begin, measurements can be made with varying degrees of *precision.* The description of a man as "43 years old" is more precise than "In his forties." "Eleven-and-a-half inches long" is a more precise description than "about a foot long."

As a general rule, precise measurements are superior to imprecise ones, as common sense would dictate. There are no conditions under which imprecise measurements would be intrinsically superior to precise ones. Precision is not always necessary or desirable, however. If your research purpose is such that knowing a man to be in his forties is sufficient, then any additional effort invested in learning his precise age is wasted. The operationalization of concepts, then, must be guided partly by an understanding of the degree of precision required. If your needs are not clear, strive for greater precision rather than lesser.

Precision must not be confused with *accuracy*. The description of something as being "eleven and a half inches long" may be relatively precise, but if the object is actually twelve and a half inches long, the less precise description, "about a foot long," would have been more accurate.

The term "reliability" is used to refer to the extent to which a given measurement operation is likely to yield consistent observations of the same empirical reality. An *operational definition* of reliability would be the extent to which a given measurement method yields the same observation in several independent measurements of the same empirical phenomenon. Suppose, for example, that we ask several people to estimate independently the thickness of this textbook—using no instruments other than their eyes and brains. It is unlikely that they would all report exactly the same thickness. Now suppose we ask them to repeat the task, using an expensive set of scientific calipers. In all likelihood, the second exercise would yield less variation in measurements—more reliability—as well as greater precision.[8]

For a social science example, let's return to the earlier example of ritual involvement as a dimension of religiosity. Suppose we ask people to tell us how many times they attended church during the past year. To the extent that they were willing to give us an exact number in response to this question, we might regard our measurement of ritual involvement as precise, but is it likely to be reliable? As a practical matter, it seems unlikely that many people would remember how many times they attended church over such a long period of time, except for those who never attended and those who attended regularly.

Recalling the operational definition of reliability, a researcher might ask people how many times they had attended church during the past year, wait awhile, and then ask the same people the same question again. To the extent that people gave different answers on the two occasions, the measurement method would be regarded as unreliable. (Realize that if we were actually to do this, people might remember what they had told us the first time, thereby concealing the unreliability of the measure.)

The final criterion to be considered here is *validity*. In conventional usage, this term refers to the extent to which an empirical indicator adequately reflects the *real meaning* of the general concept under consideration. For example, the validity of "church attendance" as an indicator of religiosity is the extent to which measuring church attendance really taps what is meant by the more general concept of religiosity. To the extent that church attendance actually represents something other than religiosity, it lacks validity as an indicator of religiosity.

---

8. Strictly speaking, a "reliable" measure need not be an "accurate" one; the measure might contain a "bias" (see Chapter 5). In the above example, the calipers might be built so as to always underestimate the thickness of the book by, say, 2 millimeters.

All this is likely to seem a little ironical in a textbook that has already taught that concepts such as "religiosity" have no ultimate meanings. Recall, however, that we have spoken previously of greater or lesser consensus or agreement as to the meaning of a concept. Specific indicators, then, may vary in the degree to which they approach the agreed-upon meaning which exists for a given concept. It is unlikely, for instance, that we would take a person's shoe size as an indicator of his religiosity.[9]

Recall the previously prescribed practice of trying to imagine circumstances in which an empirical indicator might be observed without really reflecting the general concept. This is an excellent method for determining the *face validity* of an indicator, the extent to which it logically appears to be appropriate. Thus, we might imagine someone attending church only because a parent or spouse insisted on it. Given this possible circumstance, we might arrive at one of several decisions regarding the validity of church attendance as a measure.

First, we might assume that this circumstance was sufficiently rare as to represent only a small number of cases. Or we might feel it to be sufficiently frequent and so far removed from our general understanding of "religiosity" as to make church attendance an invalid and unworthy indicator. Finally, we might decide that church attendance—whatever the motivation for it—was a valid indicator of ritual involvement, but emphasize that that in turn was only one dimension of religiosity.

Face validity is only one kind of validity, however. Chapter 15, dealing with the construction of scales and indexes, will consider validity of indicators as an empirical question.

4.8
Summary

Chapter 4 has addressed a related set of topics that are critical to the understanding and execution of research—social or other. In large part, the chapter has dealt with the question of definition: how the researcher defines what it is he wishes to study. This process involves the transition from a vague imagery about what is to be studied to a specific statement of how it would be observed in the real world.

The chapter began with the process of conceptualization: the theoretical refinement of general ideas. We began by discussing "real" definitions, attempts to define the "true" and "essential" nature of concepts, and we found such notions useless. It became apparent that general concepts such as "religiosity," "liberalism," "social class," and so forth are

---

9. There is every reason to believe that we would find a negative association between foot size and such measures of religiosity as church attendance, prayer, and belief, however. People with small feet would, on the average, appear to be more religious than those with large feet. The reason for this is to be found in the variable *sex*. Women consistently appear more religious than men in studies of religiosity, and women have smaller feet than men on the average. Regardless of this empirical association, however, foot size is foot size and not religiosity.

really nothing more than terms: terms that have been commonly associated with some general images people have had about the world around them. Such terms, however, do not have any ultimately "true" meanings. We noted, though, that people can more or less agree on the meanings to be associated with such terms, and these agreements are called *nominal definitions.*

The ultimate refinement and specification of concepts results in *operational definitions,* precise descriptions of the procedures, or operations, to be undertaken in making observations in the real world that will be related to concepts. Thus, we may operationally define "academic excellence" as the earning of a grade point average of 3.8 or better. Such an operational definition does not represent ultimate truth; it is merely a precise description of the meaning to be assigned to a given term in a given research study.

Next, the chapter turned to the relationship between definitions and purposes of research. We saw that an operational definition might be appropriate for one purpose, but quite a different operational definition of the same concept might be more appropriate to another research purpose. This further illustrated the point that there are no ultimately "true" definitions of concepts, only more or less useful ones.

More specific attention was given to the details of definitions and measurement in the discussion of *attributes* and *variables.* Recall that attributes are the characteristics of units of analysis. Examples of attributes would be "male," "tall," "religious." Certain logically related sets of attributes comprise variables. For example, the variables that would include the attributes listed above would be "sex," "height," and "religiosity." The researcher, then, observes which attributes of given variables characterize each of his units of analysis. The purpose of description is served by the determination and reporting of the distribution of attributes of a given variable among some population. An example would be the reporting of the number of men and women in some population. The purpose of explanation is served by the determination of associations (to be discussed later) between certain attributes of different variables.

The remainder of the chapter was concerned with the nature and characteristics of different kinds of measurements. We discussed different levels of measurement, an operationalization framework, and different criteria quality in measurements.

4.9
Main Points

1. Conceptualization is the process of refining and specifying the vague imagery of theoretical ideas.

2. There are no ultimately "true" definitions for concepts; they are merely terms agreed upon to describe certain aspects of the world around us.

3. Operationalization is the process of specifying the concrete procedures to be followed in observing and identifying concepts in the real world. It is the development of operational definitions.

4. Attributes are the characteristics of units of analysis.

5. Variables are logically related sets of attributes. "Political orientation" would be a variable comprised of the attributes "liberal," "conservative," and "middle-of-the-road," or some similar set of attributes.

6. Nominal measures refer to those variables whose attributes are simply different from one another. An example would be "sex."

7. Ordinal measures refer to those variables whose attributes may be rank-ordered along some progression from "more" to "less." An example would be the variable "prejudice" as comprised of the attributes "very prejudiced," "somewhat prejudiced," "slightly prejudiced," and "not at all prejudiced."

8. Interval measures refer to those variables whose attributes are not only rank-ordered but also are separated by a uniform distance between them. An example would be I.Q.

9. Ratio measures are the same as interval measures except that ratio measures also are based on a true zero point. Age would be an example of a ratio measure, since that variable contains the attribute "zero years old."

10. A given variable can sometimes be measured at different levels of measurement. Thus, age, potentially a ratio measure, may also be treated as interval, ordinal, or even nominal. The most appropriate level of measurement employed depends on the purpose of the measurement.

11. The refinement of concepts often involves the specification of *dimensions,* different aspects of a variable. Thus, "political orientations" might be further specified into "domestic political orientations" and "international political orientations."

12. There are three criteria for the quality of measurements: precision, reliability, and validity.

13. Precision refers to the exactness of the measure used in an observation or description of an attribute. For example, the description of a person as being "six feet, one and three-quarters inches tall" is more precise than the description "about six feet tall."

14. Reliability refers to the likelihood that a given measurement procedure would yield the same description of a given phenomenon if that measurement were repeated. For example, estimating a person's age by asking his friends would be less reliable than asking the person himself or checking his birth certificate.

15. Validity refers to the extent to which a specific measurement provides data that relate to commonly accepted meanings of a particular concept. For example, the frequency of church attendance would be a more valid measure of religiosity than would the frequency of a person's use of the word "God," since this latter measure would result in attributing a high degree of religiosity to people who swear a lot.

4.10
Annotated Bibliography

Franklin, Billy, and Osborne, Harold (eds.), *Research Methods: Issues and Insights* (Belmont, California: Wadsworth, 1971), Part 5A. Three articles providing different overviews of measurement in social research. The Lazarsfeld-Barton article on qualitative measurements offers a useful balance to the generally quantitative orientation of this chapter.

Lazarsfeld, Paul, and Rosenberg, Morris (eds.), *The Language of Social Research* (New York: Free Press of Glencoe, 1955), Section I. An excellent and diverse collection of descriptions of specific measurements in past social research. These fourteen articles present extremely useful accounts of actual measurement operations performed by social researchers as well as more conceptual discussions of measurement in general.

Wallace, Walter, *The Logic of Science in Sociology* (Chicago: Aldine-Atherton, 1971), Chapter 3. A brief and lucid presentation of concept formation within the context of other research steps. This discussion relates conceptualization to observation on the one hand and to generalization on the other.

5
Questionnaire Construction

5.1
Introduction

This chapter continues the earlier discussion of *operationalization.* It is one possible conclusion to that discussion, although the chapters in Part Three will provide other conclusions as well.

Operationalization is the process through which the researcher devises procedures—operations—that will result in observations relevant to the general concepts he is interested in studying. If he is interested in studying religiosity among a group of people, for example, he must devise operations that will result in observations from which he can draw conclusions about which people are religious and which are not.

One very popular mode of operationalization in the social sciences is the **questionnaire.** Concepts are operationalized in the form of questions which are then asked of the people under study. Their answers, observed and analyzed by the researcher, indicate whether they are religious or not, whether they are liberal or conservative, whether they are men or women, and so forth.

Questionnaires are the backbone of survey research. They are also frequently used in experiments and in field research. Sometimes, questionnaires are designed so as to be self-administered by the people under study; sometimes they are designed for interviewers to use in questioning the people under study.

Questionnaires provide a perfect example of operationalization. Since the questions must be written down in a specific form, we can easily see all the considerations involved in specifying concepts to the point of empirical observation. Whether a given item in a questionnaire is a good or bad operationalization of a given concept, we know exactly *what* the item is; we know exactly how the concept has been operationalized. Ultimately, questionnaire items are the operational definitions of concepts.

The specificity of the operational definitions that questionnaire items represent is sometimes a source of dissatisfaction for people, including some researchers. To take an oversimplified example, our operational definition of religiosity may be persons' answers to the question: "How religious are you? Very religious, somewhat religious, slightly religious, or not at all religious?" Surely, there is more to religiosity than this.

It is important to recognize that all scientific observation is based on the asking of questions—whether they are asked of a subject under study, an informant, or of the researcher himself; whether they are asked explicitly or implicitly. Observations don't just happen. They are, to some extent, structured. Therefore, the manner in which observations are structured—the questions that are asked—has important implications for the meaning of the observations—the answers. This is true for all forms of scientific observation, but it is simply more evident in the case of standardized questionnaires.

As operational structures for scientific observation, questionnaires have three advantages over less explicit operationalizations. First, questionnaire construction provides an opportunity for a deliberate and careful operationalization of concepts. A questionnaire item is written down, examined, criticized, revised, and reexamined. Probably the knowledge that one's colleagues will subsequently examine and criticize one's questionnaire items provides additional incentive to do a good job. Second, as indicated above and earlier, questionnaires make perfectly clear *what* the operationalization is. We may disagree on its quality but not on what it is. Third, questionnaires insure that the *same* structure is used in observing all the subjects under study. Imagine for the moment that we seek to learn how religious several people are, and we ask each of them a different question. Realizing that the question asked will affect the answer given to some extent, we would have no way of comparing the answers of different subjects. Whatever the possible defects of a given questionnaire item, we at least would know that all subjects responded to the same stimulus.

The "best" questionnaire item for operationalizing a given concept will depend on what the concept is, who the subjects of study are, and the purpose for which the concept is to be used. No textbook could possibly point to the "best" questionnaire items for a particular study. Nevertheless, there are a number of general guidelines that apply to most questionnaire construction efforts. The remainder of this chapter will discuss some of those guidelines.

5.2
Guides to Question Construction

Questions and Statements

The term "questionnaire" suggests a collection of questions, but an examination of a typical questionnaire will probably reveal as many statements as questions. This is not without reason. Often, the researcher is interested in determining the extent to which respondents hold a particular attitude or perspective. If he is able to summarize the attitude in a fairly brief statement, he will often present that statement and ask respondents whether they agree or disagree with it. Rensis Likert has greatly formalized this procedure through the creation of the "Likert scale," a format in which respondents are asked to "strongly agree," "agree," "disagree," or "strongly disagree," or perhaps "strongly approve," "approve," and so forth.

Both questions and statements may be used profitably. Using both in a given questionnaire gives the researcher more flexibility in the design of items and can make the questionnaire more interesting as well.

Open-Ended and Closed-Ended Questions

In asking questions, the researcher has two options. He may ask *open-ended* questions in which case the respondent is asked to provide his own answer to the question. For example, the respondent might be asked, "What do you feel is the most important issue facing the United States today?" and be provided with a space to write in his answer (or be asked to report it verbally to an interviewer).

In the other case, *closed-ended* questions, the respondent is asked to select his answer from among a list provided by the researcher. Closed-ended questions are very popular since they provide a greater uniformity of responses and because they are more easily processed. Open-ended responses must be coded prior to keypunching and there is a danger that some respondents will give answers that are essentially irrelevant to the researcher's intent. Closed-ended responses, on the other hand, can often be keypunched directly from the questionnaire and in some cases can be marked directly on optical-sensing sheets by respondents for automatic punching.

The chief shortcoming of closed-ended questions lies in the researcher's structuring of responses. Where the relevant answers to a given question are relatively clear, this may present no problem. In other cases, however, the researcher's structuring of responses may overlook some important responses. In asking about "the most important issues facing the United States," for example, the researcher might provide a checklist of issues, but in doing so he might overlook certain issues that respondents would have said were important.

In the construction of closed-ended questions, you should be guided by the two structural requirements discussed earlier in connection with variables and attributes. The response categories provided should be *exhaustive:* they should include all the possible responses that might be expected. Often, researchers insure this by adding a category labeled something like: "Other (Please specify.)_____"

Second, the answer categories must be *mutually exclusive:* the respondent should not feel compelled to select more than one. (In some cases, you may wish to solicit multiple answers, but these may create difficulties in data processing and analysis later on.) To insure that your categories are mutually exclusive, you should carefully consider each combination of categories, asking whether a person could reasonably choose more than one answer. In addition, it is useful to add an instruction to the question asking the respondent to "select the *one best* answer," but this technique is not a satisfactory substitute for a carefully constructed set of responses.

Make Items Clear

It should go without saying that questionnaire items should be clear and unambiguous, but the broad proliferation of unclear and ambiguous questions in surveys makes the point worth stressing here. Often the researcher becomes so deeply involved in the topic under examination that opinions and perspectives are clear to him but will not be clear to his respondents—many of whom have given little or no attention to the topic. Or, on the other hand, the researcher may have only a superficial understanding of the topic and fail to specify the intent of his question sufficiently. The question "What do you think about the proposed antiballistic missile system?" may evoke in the respondent a counterquestion: "*Which* proposed antiballistic missile system?" Questionnaire items should be precise so that the respondent knows exactly what the researcher wants an answer to.

Avoid Double-Barreled Questions

Very frequently, researchers ask respondents for a single answer to a combination of questions. This seems to happen most often when the researcher has personally identified with a complex position. For example, he might ask respondents to agree or disagree with the statement "The United States should abandon its space program and spend the money on domestic programs." While many people would unequivocally agree with the statement and others would unequivocally disagree, still others would be unable to answer. Some would want to abandon the space program and give the money back to taxpayers. Others would want to continue the space program, but also put more money into domestic programs. These latter respondents could neither agree nor disagree without misleading the researcher.

As a general rule, whenever the word "and" appears in a question or questionnaire statement, the researcher should check whether he is asking a double-barreled question.

Respondents Must Be Competent to Answer

In asking respondents to provide information, the researcher should continually ask himself whether they are able to do so reliably. In a study of child rearing, he may ask respondents to report the age at which they first "talked back" to their parents. Quite aside from the problem of defining "talking back to parents," it is doubtful if most respondents would remember with any degree of accuracy.

As another example, student government leaders occasionally ask their constituents to indicate the manner in which students' fees ought to be spent. Typically, respondents are asked to indicate the percentage of available funds that should be devoted to a long list of activities. Without a fairly good knowledge of the nature of those activities and the costs involved in them, the respondents cannot provide meaningful answers. ("Administrative costs" will receive little support although they may be essential to the program as a whole.)

One group of researchers examining the driving experience of teen-agers insisted on asking an open-ended question concerning the number of miles driven since receiving a license. Although consultants argued that few drivers would be able to estimate such information with any accuracy, the question was asked nonetheless. In response, some teen-agers reported driving hundreds of thousands of miles.

Questions Should Be Relevant

Similarly, questions asked in a questionnaire should be relevant to most respondents. When attitudes are requested on a topic that few respondents have thought about or really care about, the results are not likely to be very useful. Of course, the respondents may express attitudes even though they have never given any thought to the issue, and the researcher runs the risk of being misled.

This point is illustrated occasionally when researchers ask for responses relating to fictitious persons and issues. In one study of political images, respondents were asked whether they were familiar with each of 15 political figures in the community. In regard to one purely fictitious figure, 9 percent of the respondents said they were familiar with him. Of those respondents, about half reported seeing him on television and reading about him in the newspapers.

When responses are obtained with regard to fictitious issues, the researcher can disregard those responses. But when the issue is real, he may have no way of telling which responses genuinely reflect attitudes while others reflect meaningless answers to an irrelevant question.

Short Items Are Best

In the interest of being unambiguous and precise and pointing to the relevance of an issue, the researcher is often led into long and complicated items. This should be avoided. That the intent of an item is clear when studied carefully is irrelevant for respondents who do not give it the necessary study. The respondent should be able to read an item quickly, understand its intent, and select or provide an answer without difficulty. In general, the researcher should assume that respondents *will* read items quickly and provide quick answers; therefore, he should provide clear, short items that will not be misinterpreted under those conditions.

Avoid Negative Items

The appearance of a negation in a questionnaire item paves the way for easy misinterpretation. Asked to agree or disagree with the statement "The United States should not recognize mainland China," a sizable portion of the respondents will read over the word "not" and answer on that basis. Thus, some will agree with the statement when they are in favor of recognition, while others will agree when they oppose it. And the researcher may never know which is which.

In a study of civil liberties support, respondents were asked whether they felt "the following kinds of people should be prohibited from teaching in public schools," and were presented with a list including such items as a Communist, a Ku Klux Klansman, and so forth. The response categories "yes" and "no" were given beside each entry. A comparison of the responses to this item with other items reflecting support for civil liberties strongly suggested that many respondents gave the answer "yes" to indicate willingness for such a person to teach, rather than to indicate that such a person should be "prohibited." (A subsequent study in the series gave as answer categories "permit" and "prohibit" and produced much clearer results.)

Avoid Biased Items and Terms

Recall from the earlier discussion of conceptualization and operationalization that there are no ultimately true meanings for any of the concepts that we typically study in social science. "Prejudice" has no ultimately correct definition, and whether a given person is "prejudiced" depends on our definition of that term. This same general principle applies to the responses that we obtain from persons completing a questionnaire.

The meaning of someone's response to a question in a questionnaire depends in large part on the actual question that was asked. This is true of every question and answer. At the same time, some questions would seem to encourage particular responses more than other questions. Questions that encourage respondents to answer in a particular way are called **biased.**

Most researchers would recognize the likely effect of a question that began "Don't you agree with the President of the United States in the belief that . . ." and no reputable researcher would use such an item. Unhappily, the biasing effect of items and terms is far subtler than this example suggests.

The mere identification of an attitude or position with a prestigious person or agency can bias responses. The item "Do you agree or disagree with the President's proposal to . . ." would have this effect. "Do you agree or disagree with the recent Supreme Court decision that . . ." would have a similar effect. I should make it clear that I am not suggesting that such wording will necessarily produce consensus or even a majority in support of the position identified with the prestigious person or agency, only that support would likely be increased over what would have been obtained without such identification.

Questionnaire items can be biased negatively as well as positively. "Do you agree or disagree with the position of Adolf Hitler when he stated that . . ." would be an example. In recent years in the United States, it has been very difficult to ask questions relating to China. Identifying the country only as "China" would result in confusion between mainland China and Taiwan. Referring to "Red China" or "Communist China" would evoke a more negative response from many respondents. At the same time, of course, the researcher's purpose must be taken into account. Referring to "mainland China" might produce less hostile responses when anticommunist feelings were an important aspect of the research.

As in all other examples, the researcher must carefully examine the purpose of his inquiry and construct items that will be most useful to it. He should never be misled into thinking there are ultimately "right" and "wrong" ways of asking the questions.

5.3
General Questionnaire Format

The format of a questionnaire can be just as important as the nature and wording of the questions asked. An improperly laid out questionnaire can lead respondents to miss questions, can confuse them as to the nature of the data desired, and, in the extreme, can lead to respondents throwing the questionnaire away. Both general and specific guidelines can be suggested.

As a general rule, the questionnaire should be spread out and uncluttered. The researcher should maximize the "white space" in his instrument. Inexperienced researchers tend to fear their questionnaires will look too long, and as a result, they squeeze several questions on a single line, abbreviate questions, and try to use as few pages as possible. All these efforts are ill-advised and even dangerous. Putting more than one question on a line will result in some respondents skipping the second question. Abbreviating questions will result in misinterpretations. And more generally, the respondent who finds he has spent considerable time on the first page of what seemed a short questionnaire will be more demoralized than the respondent who quickly completed the first several pages of what initially seemed rather long. Moreover, the second respondent will have made fewer errors and will not have been forced to reread confusing, abbreviated questions. Nor will he have been forced to write a long answer in a tiny space.

The desirability of spreading questions out in the questionnaire cannot be overemphasized. Squeezed-together questionnaires are disastrous whether they are to be completed by the respondents themselves or to be used by trained interviewers.

Formats for Responses

A variety of methods are available for presenting a series of response categories for the respondent to check in answering a given question. It has been my experience that *boxes* adequately spaced apart are the best. If the questionnaire is to be set in type, this can be accomplished easily and neatly. It is also possible to do this with a typewriter, however.

If the questionnaire is typed on a typewriter with brackets, excellent boxes can be produced by a left-bracket, a space, and a right-bracket: [ ]. If brackets are not available, parentheses work reasonably well in the same fashion: ( ). The researcher should be discouraged from utilizing slashes and underscores, however. First, this technique will require considerably more typing effort; and second, the result is not very neat, especially if the response categories must be single-spaced. Figure 5-1 provides a comparison of the different methods.

```
[ ] Yes          ( ) Yes          / / Yes
[ ] No           ( ) No           / / No
[ ] Don't know   ( ) Don't know   / / Don't know
```

Figure 5-1

Of the three methods shown, the brackets and the parentheses are clearly the neatest; the slash-and-underscore method simply looks sloppy. Since every typewriter at least has parentheses, there is no excuse for using the slashes and underscores. (It is also much easier to type the brackets or parentheses.)

The worst method of all is to provide open blanks for check marks, since respondents will often enter rather large check marks and it will not be possible to determine which response was intended. As a general rule, moreover, it is always best to double-space between response categories to avoid ambiguous check marks.

A very different method might also be considered. Rather than providing boxes to be checked, the researcher might consider entering code numbers beside each response and ask the respondent to *circle* the appropriate number. This has the added advantage of specifying the number to be punched later in the processing stage. I have had little experience with this method, but my initial experimentation has been favorable. If this method is used, however, the researcher should provide clear and prominent instructions to the respondent, as many will be tempted to cross out the appropriate number, thereby making punching even more difficult. (*Note:* The technique can be used more safely in those studies in which interviewers will administer the questionnaires, since they can be specially instructed and supervised.) Figure 5-2 illustrates this last method.

1. Yes
(2.) No
3. Don't know

Figure 5-2

Contingency Questions

Quite often in questionnaires, certain questions will clearly be relevant only to some of the respondents and irrelevant to others. In a study of birth control methods, for instance, you would probably not want to ask men if they take birth control pills.

Frequently, this situation will arise when you wish to ask a series of questions about a certain topic—realizing that the topic is relevant only to some respondents. You may want to ask whether your respondents belong to a particular organization and, if so, how often they attend meetings, whether they have held office in the organization, and so forth. Or, you might want to ask whether respondents have heard anything about a certain political issue and then learn the attitudes of those who have heard of it.

The subsequent questions in series such as these are called **contingency questions**—whether they are to be asked and answered is contingent on responses to the first question in the series. The proper use of contingency questions can facilitate the respondent's task in completing the questionnaire in that he is not faced with the problem of answering questions that are irrelevant to him.

There are several formats for contingency questions. The one shown in Figure 5-3 is probably the clearest and most effective. Note two key elements in this format. First, the contingency question is isolated from the other questions by being set off to the side and by being enclosed in a box. Second, an arrow connects the contingency question to the answer upon which it is contingent. In the illustration, only those respondents answering "yes" are expected to answer the contingency question. The rest of the respondents should simply skip it.

It should be noted that the questions shown in Figure 5-3 could have been dealt with in a single question. The question might have read: "How many times, if any, have you smoked marijuana?" The response categories, then, might read: "Never," "Once," "2 to 5 times," and so forth. Such a single question, then, would apply to all respondents, and each would find an appropriate answer category. Such a question, however, would appear to put some pressure on respondents to report having smoked marijuana, since the main question asks how many times they have smoked it, even though it allows for those *exceptional cases* who have *never smoked marijuana even once*. (The emphases used in the previous sentence give a fair indication of how respondents might read the question.) The contingency question format illustrated in Figure 5-3 should reduce the subtle pressure on respondents to report having smoked marijuana. All the foregoing discussion should point out the way in which seemingly theoretical issues of *validity* and *reliability* are involved in so mundane a matter as how to put questions on a piece of paper.

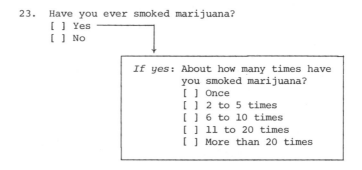

Figure 5-3

Used properly, even rather complex sets of contingency questions can be constructed without confusing the respondent. Figure 5-4 illustrates a more complicated example.

Sometimes it may be the case that a set of contingency questions is so long as to extend over several pages. Suppose you were studying political activities of college students, and you wished to ask a large number of questions of those students who had ever voted in a national, state, or local election. You could separate out the relevant respondents with an initial question such as "Have you ever voted in a national, state, or local election?" but it would not make sense to place all the contingency questions in a box stretching over several pages. Instead, it would make more sense to enter instructions in parentheses after each answer telling respondents whether to answer or skip the contingency questions. Figure 5-5 provides an illustration of this.

14.   Have you ever heard anything about
      the Model Cities Program?
      [ ] Yes ─────────────────────┐
      [ ] No   │
                                    ↓
      ┌──┐
      │ *If yes:*   │
      │   │
      │ a. Do you generally approve or   │
      │   disapprove of that program?   │
      │   [ ] Approve   │
      │   [ ] Disapprove   │
      │   [ ] No opinion   │
      │   │
      │ b. Have you ever attended a Model   │
      │   Cities resident meeting?   │
      │   [ ] Yes ──────────────┐   │
      │   [ ] No   │   │
      │   ↓   │
      │   ┌─────────────────────────────────────┐   │
      │   │ *If yes:* When did you last   │   │
      │   │   attend a meeting?   │   │
      │   │   │   │
      │   │   ─────────────────────   │   │
      │   └─────────────────────────────────────┘   │
      └──┘

Figure 5-4

In addition to these instructions, it would be of additional value to place an instruction at the top of each of the subsequent pages containing only the contingency questions. For example, you might say, "This page is only for respondents who have ever voted in a national, state, or local

13.   Have you ever voted in a national, state, or local
      election?
      [ ] Yes   (Please answer questions 14-25)
      [ ] No   (Please skip questions 14-25. Go directly
                to question 26 on page 8.)

Figure 5-5

election." Clear instructions such as these spare respondents the frustration of reading and puzzling over questions that are irrelevant to them as well as increasing the likelihood of responses from those for whom the questions are relevant.

Matrix Questions

Quite often, you will want to ask several questions that have the same set of answer categories. This is typically the case whenever the Likert response categories are used. In such cases, it is often possible to construct a matrix of items and answers as illustrated in Figure 5-6.

17. Beside *each* of the statements presented below, please indicate whether you Strongly Agree (SA), Agree (A), Disagree (D), Strongly Disagree (SD), or are Undecided (U).

	SA	A	D	SD	U
a. What this country needs is more law and order.	[ ]	[ ]	[ ]	[ ]	[ ]
b. The police should be disarmed in America. .	[ ]	[ ]	[ ]	[ ]	[ ]
c. During riots, looters should be shot on sight.	[ ]	[ ]	[ ]	[ ]	[ ]

etc.

Figure 5-6

This format has a number of advantages. First, it is efficient in its use of space. Second, respondents will probably find it faster to complete a set of questions presented in this fashion. In addition, this format may increase the comparability of responses given to different questions for the respondent as well as the researcher. Since the respondent can quickly review the answers given to earlier items in the set, he might choose between, say, "strongly agree" and "agree" on a given statement by comparing his strength of agreement with that which he indicated in responding to earlier items in the set.

There are some dangers inherent in using this format as well. Its advantages may encourage you to include items in a matrix that might be more appropriately presented in a different format. For example, you might try to structure the item so as to use the responses being called for in the matrix when a different, more idiosyncratic, set of responses might be more appropriate.

Also, the matrix-question format can foster a *response-set* among some respondents—they may develop the pattern of, say, agreeing with all the statements. This would be especially likely if the set of statements began with several that indicated a particular orientation (e.g., a liberal political perspective) with only a few, later ones that represented the opposite orientation. Respondents might assume that all the statements represented the same orientation and, reading quickly, misread some of them, thereby giving the wrong answers. This problem can be reduced somewhat by alternating statements representing different orientations and by making all statements short and clear.

5.4
Ordering Questions in a Questionnaire

The *order* in which questions are asked can also affect the answers given. First, the appearance of one question can affect the answers given to subsequent ones. For example, if a number of questions have been asked about the dangers of communism to the United States and a subsequent question asks respondents to volunteer (open-ended) what they believe to represent dangers to the United States, "communism" will receive more citations than would otherwise be the case.

If respondents are asked to assess their overall religiosity ("How important is your religion to you in general?"), their responses to later questions concerning specific aspects of religiosity will be aimed at consistency with the prior assessment. The converse would be true as well. If respondents are first asked specific questions about different aspects of their religiosity, their subsequent overall assessment will reflect the earlier answers.

Some researchers attempt to overcome this effect by "randomizing" the order of questions. This is usually a futile effort. To begin, a "randomized" set of questions will probably strike the respondent as chaotic and worthless. It will be difficult for him to answer, moreover, since he must continually switch his attention from one topic to another. And, finally, even a randomized ordering of questions will have the effect discussed above—except that the researcher will have no control over the effect.

The safest solution is sensitivity to the problem. Although the researcher cannot avoid the effect of question order, he should attempt to estimate what that effect will be. Thus, he will be able to interpret results in a meaningful fashion. If the order of questions seems an especially important issue in a given study, the researcher might construct more than one version of the questionnaire containing the different possible orderings of questions. He would then be able to determine the effects. At the very least, he should pretest his questionnaire in the different forms.

The desired ordering of questions differs somewhat between self-administered questionnaires and interviews. In the former, it is usually best to begin the questionnaire with the most interesting set of questions. The potential respondent who glances casually over the first few questions should *want* to answer them. Perhaps they will ask for attitudes that he is aching to express. At the same time, however, the initial questions should not be threatening. (It might be a bad idea to begin with questions about sexual behavior or drug use.) Requests for duller demographic data (age, sex, and the like) should generally be placed at the end of the self-administered questionnaire. Placing these questions at the beginning, as many inexperienced researchers are tempted to do, gives the questionnaire the initial appearance of a routine form, and the person receiving it may not be motivated to complete it.

Just the opposite is generally true for interview surveys. When the potential respondent's door first opens, the interviewer must begin quickly gaining rapport. After a short introduction to the study, the interviewer can best begin by enumerating the members of the household, getting demographic data about each. Such questions are easily answered and generally nonthreatening. Once the initial rapport has been established, the interviewer can then move into the area of attitudes and more sensitive matters. An interview that began with the question "Do you believe in God?" would probably end rather quickly.

5.5
Instructions

Every questionnaire, whether it is to be completed by respondents or administered by interviewers, should contain clear instructions and introductory comments where appropriate.

General Instructions

It is useful to begin every self-administered questionnaire with basic instructions to be followed in completing it. Although many people these days are pretty familiar with forms and questionnaires, it is useful to begin by telling them exactly what you want: that they are to indicate their answers to certain questions by placing a check mark or an X in the box beside the appropriate answer, or by writing in their answer when asked to do so. If many open-ended questions are used, respondents should be given some guide as to whether brief or lengthy answers are expected. If you wish to encourage written-in answers to elaborate on responses given to closed-ended questions, that should be noted.

Introductions

If a questionnaire is arranged into content subsections—political attitudes, religious attitudes, background data—it is useful to introduce each section with a short statement concerning its content and purpose. For example, "In this section, we would like to know what people around here consider the most important community problems." Demographic items at the end of a self-administered questionnaire might be introduced thus: "Finally, we would like to know just a little about you so we can see how different types of people feel about the issues we have been examining."

Short introductions such as these help make sense out of the questionnaire for the respondent. They make the questionnaire seem less chaotic, especially when it taps a variety of data. And they help put the respondent in the proper frame of mind for answering the questions.

Specific Instructions

Some questions may require special instructions to facilitate proper answering. This is especially true if a given question varies from the general instructions pertaining to the whole questionnaire. Some specific situations will illustrate this.

Despite the desirability for mutually exclusive answer categories in closed-ended questions, it is often the case that more than one answer will apply for respondents. If the researcher wants a single answer, he should make this perfectly clear in the question. An example would be "From the list below, please check the *primary* reason for your decision to attend college." Often the main question can be followed by a parenthetical note: "Please check the *one* best answer." If, on the other hand, the researcher wishes the respondent to check as many answers as apply, that should be made clear as well.

When a set of answer categories are to be rank-ordered by the respondent, the instructions should indicate as much, and a different type of answer format should be used (for example, blanks instead of boxes). These instructions should indicate how many answers are to be ranked (for example, all, first and second, first and last, most important and least important) and the order of ranking (for example, "place a 1 beside the most important, a 2 beside the next most important, and so forth"). (*Note:* Rank-ordering of responses is often difficult for respondents, since they may have to read and reread the list several times.)

In multiple-part matrix questions, it is useful to give special instructions unless the same format is used throughout the questionnaire. Sometimes the respondent will be expected to check one answer in each *column* of the matrix, while in others he will be expected to check one answer in each *row*. Whenever the questionnaire contains both types, it will be useful to add an instruction clarifying which is expected in each case.

Interviewer Instructions

Whereas a confusing self-administered questionnaire can lower the morale of the respondent, a confusing interview questionnaire can lower the morale of both the respondent and the interviewer and will endanger the efficiency of the latter. It is particularly important, then, to provide clear supplementary instructions where appropriate to interviewers.

It is essential in an interview questionnaire that different formats be used for those instructions that the interviewer is to read to the respondents and those that are not to be read. For example, the latter might always be typed in parentheses or in capital letters. An interview could be destroyed by an interviewer reading aloud something on the order of "If the respondent is nearly illiterate, then . . ."

It is equally important that an interview questionnaire contain a *verbatim script* for the interviewer to read in interviewing. In ideal circumstances, an interviewer should be able to conduct an entire interview from initial introduction ("Hello, my name is . . .") to final remarks ("That completes the interview. We would like to thank you for . . .") without ad-libbing a single word. All transitional statements throughout the questionnaire should be included ("Now we would like to turn from community problems to national problems . . .") so that the verbatim script sounds natural and conversational. The same is true for the demographic enumeration of household members. Rather than instructing the interviewer to obtain the age of each family member, the researcher should provide a standardized question for each ("How old was [he/she] on January 1, 1971?"). Chapter 11 will stress the importance of the interviewer following the questionnaire wording exactly, but it should be recognized in advance that this will not be possible unless the questionnaire is properly constructed.

5.6
Precoding the Questionnaire

In laying out the format for a questionnaire, the researcher should give special attention to the method of data processing that will be used. This is essential, especially if the questionnaire is to be keypunched directly. The following suggestions will facilitate punching directly from the questionnaire.

The questionnaire should be precoded to facilitate punching (or coding for that matter). Items of data should be assigned to cards and columns in advance, and notations in the questionnaire should indicate those assignments. There are two types of precoding. First, card and column assignments should be indicated, although it is normally not necessary to enter separate notations for each column. Since experienced keypunchers will not check each column number as it is punched, it is normally sufficient to enter the range of column numbers assigned to a questionnaire page or section of a page. Then, the keypuncher can check once or twice per page to insure he is punching the correct column.

The second type of precoding concerns punch assignments with a given column. Wherever a given column contains three or fewer response categories, precoding can normally be omitted, as the keypuncher can easily determine the appropriate punch if logic assignments are made. Whenever

there are more than three response categories, it is normally safest to enter
the punch assignments. Figure 5-7 presents examples of precoding appropriate for punching directly.

14.   Beside each of the political figures listed below,
      please indicate whether you strongly approve (SA),
      approve (A), disapprove (D), or strongly disapprove
      (SD) of that person's political philosophy as you
      understand it.

                                          SA   A   D   SD
                     (23-29)   ___ ___ ___ ___
                                          1   2   3   4

      a. Richard Nixon.............. [ ] [ ] [ ] [ ]
      b. Eugene McCarthy............ [ ] [ ] [ ] [ ]
      c. Edmund Muskie.............. [ ] [ ] [ ] [ ]
      d. George Wallace............. [ ] [ ] [ ] [ ]
      e. Spiro Agnew................ [ ] [ ] [ ] [ ]
      f. George McGovern............ [ ] [ ] [ ] [ ]
      g. Eldridge Cleaver........... [ ] [ ] [ ] [ ]

15.   What is your political party affiliation, if any?

                     (30)

      Democratic Party......................... 1 [ ]
      Republican Party......................... 2 [ ]
      American Independent Party............... 3 [ ]
      Peace and Freedom Party.................. 4 [ ]
      Other, please specify:_____ 5 [ ]
      None, no party identification............ 6 [ ]

                    Figure 5-7

        Several things should be noted in Figure 5-7. First, note that the
column assignments are presented in parentheses; columns 23 to 29 are
assigned to approval/disapproval of the political figures, while column 30 is
assigned to political party identification. The punch assignments for question
14 are presented above the response category columns. In question 15, with
only one set of responses, the punch assignments are presented beside the
spaces for checking answers.
        Finally, note that all responses in the two questions are located on
the same side of the page. This is important as it facilitates punching. The
keypuncher is able to punch both questions without moving his eyes back
and forth across the page. If the location of responses moves around on the
page, the keypuncher will work more slowly and will be more likely to miss
items.
        Whenever precoding is used on a self-administered questionnaire, it
is normally a good idea to mention the precoding in an introductory note to
the questionnaire. ("The numbers shown in parentheses and beside answer

categories should be ignored; they are included only to assist the processing of your answers.") In any event, precoding should be kept as inconspicuous as possible, since it may confuse the respondent. If the questionnaire is set in type, the precoding should be entered in a smaller type face.

Even if the questionnaire is not to be punched directly, the format should take intended processing methods into account. Most of the suggestions made above will facilitate hand coding. If the questionnaire is to be read by an optical-sensing machine, then the researcher must check his format against the requirements of that machine.

One further technique facilitates both coding and keypunching whenever more than one card is required for recording the questionnaire responses. Experience has shown that both coders and keypunchers work more efficiently if they are able to code or punch a given set of responses (a single card) for several questionnaires in a series rather than coding or punching all cards for a given questionnaire before moving on to the next questionnaire. This is especially true for keypunching, since the keypunch machine can be set to make automatic skips. Thus it is more efficient for the keypuncher, for example, to punch all of the "card 1's" before moving on to the "card 2's" and so forth.

To facilitate this, card and column assignments should be made so as to begin each new card at the top of a questionnaire page. If necessary, the last few columns of the previous card can be left blank. Doing this will make it easier for keypunchers or coders to work on one card at a time. Going one step further, moreover, all the questionnaire pages assigned to a particular card can be pulled out of the questionnaire and stapled into a "packet." If this is done for each card, then different keypunchers or coders can be working on different cards simultaneously, thus speeding the processing. (*Note:* It is essential in such a case that the same identification number be placed on the first page of each packet prepared for a given questionnaire.)

5.7
Reproducing the Questionnaire

Having constructed a questionnaire that will collect data relevant to the researcher's aims and one that will be efficiently processed, it is necessary to produce enough copies for the actual data collection. The method of reproducing the questionnaires is important to the overall success of the study, as a neatly reproduced instrument will encourage a higher response rate, thereby providing better data.

There are several alternative methods for reproducing questionnaires, and the researcher's decision will depend on funds available, local facilities, and timing. Ditto or mimeograph reproductions are generally cheaper and more readily available, but they are the least professional looking in quality. Photo-offsetting a typed copy of the questionnaire provides better quality and, beyond a certain number of copies, it may even be cheaper. (A single photo-offset master will make countless copies, while a ditto or mimeograph master must be recut after a few hundred copies have been run off.)

The best method of reproduction from the standpoint of professional quality is printing from set type. This is also the most expensive, however, and it may not be feasible for some projects. Also, printing from set type generally takes longer than other methods. In any event, the researcher should explore the local possibilities, balancing the relative values of time, money, and quality.

The questionnaire can be produced in several different forms, also. In some cases, it may be appropriate to print the questionnaire on an oversized single sheet of paper to be folded into a quasi-booklet of unfolding panels. If several pages are required for the questionnaire, it may be appropriate to connect them with a corner staple. The most professional looking long questionnaire is the printed booklet held together with a saddle stitch. Again, this is the most expensive as well.

One final concern in the reproduction of the questionnaire is how many to order. In arriving at this decision, the researcher must consider his sample size, the number of follow-up mailings, if any, in a mail survey, and the possible need for discussion copies, samples for other researchers, copies for inclusion as appendixes in research reports, code books, and so forth. As a rough rule of thumb, the researcher should estimate the number required for data collection and multiply that figure by a factor of 1.5 to 2.0 in determining the number to be ordered. Bear in mind that additional copies produced in the initial run of the questionnaires will be far cheaper than a second run.

5.8
A Composite Illustration

It might be useful to conclude this chapter with an illustration of a real questionnaire similar to one you might construct. Figure 5-8 is a portion of a 30-page questionnaire developed by University of Hawaii students for the purpose of a student survey in 1969. The purpose of the survey was to create a comprehensive file of information about student attitudes and orientations in a variety of areas: politics, religion, education, and others.

I have chosen this questionnaire since it employed no expensive production techniques—it was typed and then photo-offset—and because it covers subject matter that you might want to study sometime yourself. On the whole, it is a pretty good questionnaire. Still, it is not perfect. As you read through the questionnaire, you will find marginal notations (e.g., NOTE 1). Whenever such a notation appears, you might try to figure out how the questionnaire could have been improved at that point. At the end of the illustration questionnaire, I have told how I feel it could have been improved.

To improve your critical skills in questionnaire construction, you should also look for mistakes that I have *not* marked.

GENERAL INSTRUCTIONS: Either a pen or pencil may be used
to complete this questionnaire. Most of the questions may be
answered by simply placing an X in the appropriate box; other
questions ask for written-in answers. However, you may write
in additional comments whenever you wish to do so. Please ignore
the numbers beside the questions and answers; they are for machine
tabulation only.

A. POLITICAL ORIENTATIONS   NOTE 1

(1-4, 5/1)

1. Beside each of the statements listed below, please indicate
whether you strongly agree (SA), agree (A), disagree (D),
strongly disagree (SD), or don't know (DK).

(6-15)	SA 1	A 2	D 3	SD 4	DK 5
a. It would be a good thing if the United Nations were someday converted into a world government. .	[ ]	[ ]	[ ]	[ ]	[ ]
b. People who defile the American flag should be put in prison. . .	[ ]	[ ]	[ ]	[ ]	[ ]
c. The United States is too ready to interpret the actions of communist nations as threatening . . .	[ ]	[ ]	[ ]	[ ]	[ ]
d. The United States is spending too much money on defense	[ ]	[ ]	[ ]	[ ]	[ ]
e. Communism is probably the best form of government for some countries	[ ]	[ ]	[ ]	[ ]	[ ]
f. The Central Intelligence Agency has too much power.	[ ]	[ ]	[ ]	[ ]	[ ]
g. The NLF (Viet Cong) are mostly invaders from North Vietnam . . .	[ ]	[ ]	[ ]	[ ]	[ ]
h. The United States was justified in using nuclear weapons against Japan in 1945	[ ]	[ ]	[ ]	[ ]	[ ]
i. If it were not for the power of the United States, most nations of the world would be taken over by the communists	[ ]	[ ]	[ ]	[ ]	[ ]
j. We should support our country's policies even when they are wrong	[ ]	[ ]	[ ]	[ ]	[ ]

Figure 5-8

2. In general, how do you feel about each of the following possible U.S. policies regarding the war in Vietnam? Please indicate beside each whether you approve (A), disapprove (D), or don't know (DK).

	A 1	D 2	DK 3
(16-25)			
a. Maintenance of present level of U.S. military activities	[ ]	[ ]	[ ]
b. Immediate beginning of unilateral withdrawal of U.S. forces	[ ]	[ ]	[ ]
c. Withdrawal of U.S. forces into strategic hamlets in South Vietnam.	[ ]	[ ]	[ ]
d. Bombing of strategic targets in North Vietnam	[ ]	[ ]	[ ]
e. Invasion of North Vietnam by U.S. ground forces.	[ ]	[ ]	[ ]
f. Invasion of North Vietnam by South Vietnamese ground forces.	[ ]	[ ]	[ ]
g. Use of nuclear weapons against North Vietnam if recommended by U.S. military leaders	[ ]	[ ]	[ ]
h. Cessation of all U.S. bombing in South Vietnam	[ ]	[ ]	[ ]
i. Granting U.S. military leaders complete freedom to handle the war as they see fit .	[ ]	[ ]	[ ]
j. Continuation of the Paris peace talks . . .	[ ]	[ ]	[ ]

3. As a general rule, do you personally tend to believe or doubt the validity of *official* U.S. government reports regarding the following aspects of the war in Vietnam?

	Believe 1	Doubt 2	Don't know 3
(26-28)			
a. Reports of enemy casualties	[ ]	[ ]	[ ]
b. Reports of Viet Cong atrocities . .	[ ]	[ ]	[ ]
c. Proclamations of U.S. goals in Vietnam	[ ]	[ ]	[ ]

4. Is there anything else you would like to say about the war in Vietnam? (Additional space is provided at the end of the questionnaire.)
(29-30)

Figure 5-8 (Continued)

5. Listed below are some statements people have made regarding
    the student peace movement in America. Beside each, please
    indicate whether you strongly agree (SA), agree (A), disagree
    (D), strongly disagree (SD), or don't know how you feel (DK).

	SA	A	D	SD	DK
(31-36)	1	2	3	4	5
a. Peace demonstrators threaten the peace more than they enhance it .	[ ]	[ ]	[ ]	[ ]	[ ]
b. A person's moral convictions should take precedence over national policies of war.	[ ]	[ ]	[ ]	[ ]	[ ]
c. Peace demonstrators are primarily interested in personal publicity.	[ ]	[ ]	[ ]	[ ]	[ ]
d. Pacifism is simply not a practical philosophy in the world today.	[ ]	[ ]	[ ]	[ ]	[ ]
e. Burning one's draft card should *not* be considered a crime	[ ]	[ ]	[ ]	[ ]	[ ]
f. Peace demonstrators should be drafted and sent to Vietnam . . .	[ ]	[ ]	[ ]	[ ]	[ ]

6. In November, 1968, two U.S. Marines sought sanctuary on the
    UH campus as a protest against the war in Vietnam. Which of
    the following do you believe *should* have been the policy of
    the university administration?

(37)   NOTE 2
    1 [ ] The university should have granted official sanctuary.
    2 [ ] The university should have permitted them to stay on
           campus without granting official sanctuary.
    3 [ ] The university should have forced them to leave the
           campus.

                                                                        NOTE 3
7. There has been disagreement recently as to whether the uni-
    versity should permit military recruiters and antidraft
    counselors to come on the UH campus to talk with students.
    Do you personally feel the university should permit both,
    only one, or neither to come on campus to talk with students?

(38)
    1 [ ] Should permit *both* military recruiters and antidraft
           counselors
    2 [ ] Should permit only *military* recruiters
    3 [ ] Should permit only *antidraft* counselors
    4 [ ] Should permit *neither*
    5 [ ] I don't know

Figure 5-8 (Continued)

8.   Which of the following, if any, do you believe should be suf-
     ficient grounds for exemption from military service? (Please
     check 'yes' if you believe it should be sufficient and 'no'
     if you believe it should not be sufficient.)

	Yes	No	Don't know
(39-43)	1	2	3
a. Membership in a religious group with strong pacifist principles.	[ ]	[ ]	[ ]
b. Strong personal religious pacifist principles.	[ ]	[ ]	[ ]
c. Strong personal moral or philosophical (nonreligious) pacifist principles. . . .	[ ]	[ ]	[ ]
d. Strong objections to a particular war . .	[ ]	[ ]	[ ]
e. Other (Please specify: _____ _____) . .	[ ]	[ ]	[ ]

9.   Have you personally supported the current peace movement in
     any of the following ways?

	Yes	No
(44-50)	1	2
a. Attended a peace rally.	[ ]	[ ]
b. Participated in a peace march	[ ]	[ ]
c. Written a letter intended for publication . . .	[ ]	[ ]
d. Spoken at a peace rally	[ ]	[ ]
e. Written a letter to a public official	[ ]	[ ]
f. Campaigned for a peace candidate.	[ ]	[ ]
g. Distributed peace literature.	[ ]	[ ]
h. Participated in *mild* direct action subject to arrest (trespassing, disturbing the peace, etc.)	[ ]	[ ]
i. Participated in *strong* direct action subject to arrest (destruction of property, inter- fering with military operations, etc.).	[ ]	[ ]
j. Was arrested for peace movement activities. . .	[ ]	[ ]
k. Other (Please specify: _____ _____)	[ ]	[ ]

10. Which government would you prefer to have represented in the
     United Nations: the Nationalist government on Taiwan or the
     Communist government on the mainland of China?
   (55)   NOTE 4
        1   [ ] Only the Nationalist government on Taiwan
        2   [ ] Only the Communist government on the mainland
        3   [ ] Both governments should be represented

Figure 5-8 (Continued)

11. Please indicate whether you agree (A), disagree (D), or are
    undecided (U) about each of the following possible United
    States' policies toward mainland China.

	A 1	D 2	U 3
(56-61)			
a. Granting diplomatic recognition to China. .	[ ]	[ ]	[ ]
b. Seeking economic trade with China	[ ]	[ ]	[ ]
c. Offering economic aid to China.	[ ]	[ ]	[ ]
d. Seeking cultural exchange programs with China	[ ]	[ ]	[ ]
e. Seeking to contain China militarily	[ ]	[ ]	[ ]
f. Seeking to destroy China's military power .	[ ]	[ ]	[ ]

12. The question of military intervention has come up many times
    in the past. The following is a list of instances in which
    the U.S. had to decide whether or not to intervene militar-
    ily. In each case, please indicate whether or not you feel
    the U.S. should have intervened with military force.

	Should have intervened 1	Should not have intervened 2	Not sure 3
(62-72)			
a. Chinese Communist Revolu- tion, 1948-49	[ ]	[ ]	[ ]
b. Korean conflict, 1950 . . . . ·	[ ]	[ ]	[ ]
c. Hungarian revolt, 1956. . . .	[ ]	[ ]	[ ]
d. Bay of Pigs invasion, 1961. .	[ ]	[ ]	[ ]
e. Vietnam buildup, 1964-65. . .	[ ]	[ ]	[ ]
f. Dominican Republic revolt, 1965.	[ ]	[ ]	[ ]
g. Rhodesian independence, 1965.	[ ]	[ ]	[ ]
h. Greek military coup d'etat, 1965.	[ ]	[ ]	[ ]
i. Israeli-Arab conflict, 1967 .	[ ]	[ ]	[ ]
j. Capture of U.S.S. Pueblo, 1968.	[ ]	[ ]	[ ]
k. Russian occupation of Czecho- slovakia, 1968.	[ ]	[ ]	[ ]

Figure 5-8 (Continued)

13. In general, how would you characterize your own political orientation? How would you characterize the political orientations of your parents? (Please answer for each.)

	Yourself	Your Father	Your Mother	NOTE 5
Right radical.	1 [ ]	1 [ ]	1 [ ]	
Very conservative.	2 [ ]	2 [ ]	2 [ ]	
Moderately conservative.	3 [ ]	3 [ ]	3 [ ]	
Moderately liberal	4 [ ]	4 [ ]	4 [ ]	
Left radical	5 [ ]	5 [ ]	5 [ ]	
Other (Please specify: _____				
_____) . .	6 [ ]	6 [ ]	6 [ ]	
Don't know	7 [ ]	7 [ ]	7 [ ]	

14. Do you normally identify yourself with any particular political party? (Please indicate *which party*, if any, you identify with.)

    (76)   NOTE 6
        1 [ ] Democratic party
        2 [ ] Republican party
        3 [ ] American Independent party
        4 [ ] Peace and Freedom party
        5 [ ] Other (Please specify: _____)
        6 [ ] No party identification, independent

15. Were you eligible to vote in the November, 1968, general election?

    (77-78)   NOTE 7
        1 [ ] Yes**   15a. ** If *yes*, did you vote? 1 [ ] Yes
        2 [ ] No   2 [ ] No

16. Whether or not you were eligible to vote in November, 1968, which of these Presidential candidates, if any, did you prefer?

    (79)
        1 [ ] Hubert Humphrey
        2 [ ] Richard Nixon
        3 [ ] George Wallace
        4 [ ] Eldridge Cleaver
        5 [ ] None of these

    (80/R)

Figure 5-8 (Continued)

NOTE 1 This is not a serious problem, but since the full questionnaire dealt with a variety of topics, it would have been useful to insert a short introductory comment at this point to inform respondents of what was contained in the section. This would have been even more useful in later sections, where respondents were asked implicitly to switch their thinking to different topics. An appropriate introduction might have been "In this first section, we are interested in learning how you feel about a variety of foreign and domestic political issues."

NOTE 2 Since Question 5 has its answer spaces to the right of the answers, it would have been better to follow the same pattern with Questions 6 and 7. Switching the placement of answer spaces on the same page will make processing somewhat difficult for keypunchers and will increase the likelihood of errors.

NOTE 3 The list of response categories for Question 6 is probably not exhaustive. In fact, some respondents wrote in answers of their own. It would have been better to provide an "Other (Please specify:)_____" category for this purpose. (Incidentally, the university administration chose the second alternative, and everything worked out just fine.)

NOTE 4 Rather whimsically, the answer spaces for Question 10 have been placed to the left, while those for Questions 11 and 12 are on the right. See Note 2 above if you've forgotten why this is a bad idea.

NOTE 5 "Very liberal" is missing from the list of response categoeies. As a result, the spectrum of political orientations is unbalanced. This omission is the result of a simple typing error and the failure to proofread the questionnaire carefully enough. It is worth noting that this error occurred after hours of considered debate over the proper terms to be used in labeling different political orientations—especially at the extremes. The most careful conceptualization can go for naught unless every step in the research process is taken with sufficient caution.

NOTE 6 There go the answer spaces across the page again. Since Question 15 contains a contingency question, making it awkward to place the answer spaces to the right, it would have been better to place those for Question 13 on the left.

NOTE 7 This is not a very good format for the contingency question. See Figure 5-3 earlier in this chapter for a better format. Also, note how crowded the questionnaire is at this point. There is a danger that many respondents would get confused and miss the contingency question altogether. Can you determine why the researchers crowded questions together so much here? (The answer is to be found in the precoding instructions and in the final paragraph of section 5-6 earlier in this chapter.)

5.9
Summary

Chapter 5, on questionnaire construction, should be regarded as a continuation of the preceding chapter on conceptualization and operationalization. The construction of a questionnaire is a concrete example of these processes. Moreover, the specific questions contained in a questionnaire and the answers to them may be regarded as the operational definition of concepts.

The chapter began with some general guidelines for the construction of questions to be included in a questionnaire. For the most part, these guidelines seem perfectly straightforward and even obvious. You should be warned, however, that it is very easy to lose sight of them when you actually set about the task of preparing a questionnaire.

Next, we looked at some of the considerations involved in the format of a questionnaire. The physical layout of questions is sometimes as important as the wording of the questions themselves in assuring that the information elicited will be that which is needed for the research purposes. Several different types of question formats were discussed.

Also important is the order in which questions are asked in a questionnaire. The act of thinking about and answering one question may affect the answers given to subsequent questions. For example, if a person is asked to rank the importance of, say, ten problems facing the nation, and is then asked to indicate, in his own words, what he believes to be the one most important national problem, he will very likely pick one from the earlier list.

Next, the chapter dealt with the use of instructions in questionnaires. There are basically two kinds of instructions: those addressed to the person answering the questionnaire, and those special instructions addressed to the interviewer if the questionnaire is administered by an interviewer.

Finally, the chapter examined methods of precoding questionnaires for easier data processing later on and some of the nitty-gritty issues surrounding the physical reproduction and manufacture of questionnaires. The chapter concluded with an illustration of a real questionnaire.

5.10
Main Points

1. Questionnaires are used frequently in social research as a method for collecting information about people.

2. Questionnaire construction is a concrete example of the conceptualization and operationalization processes.

3. Information about people may be collected through the use of questions to be answered or statements to which the people are asked to react.

4. Open-ended questions are those which are to be answered in the respondent's own words; closed-ended questions have a set of answers from which the respondent is to select.

5. Questionnaire items must be clear in their meaning if they are to provide relevant information.

6. Double-barreled questions are those that actually contain more than one question. They should be avoided.

7. It is essential that respondents be asked to answer only questions that they are competent to answer.

8. If attitudinal items are used in a questionnaire, they should be limited to those attitudes that are likely to interest the respondents. Questions about attitudes and issues that are generally irrelevant to the respondents are unlikely to provide useful information.

9. Where possible, short items are preferred over long ones.

10. Negative terms should be avoided in questionnaire items, since they are subject to misinterpretation.

11. Bias is the phrasing of questionnaire items in such terms as to tend to encourage a certain kind of response over another. This should be avoided.

12. Contingency questions are those that should be answered only by those persons giving a particular response to some preceding question. The contingency question format is very useful in that it saves asking people to answer questions that have no meaning for them. For example, a question about the number of times a person has been pregnant should be asked only of women.

13. Matrix questions are those in which a standardized set of closed-ended response categories are to be used in answering several questionnaire items. This format can facilitate the presentation and completion of items.

14. Precoding a questionnaire refers to the assignment of data processing codes to different questions and responses on the questionnaire itself. This practice facilitates keypunching later on.

5.11
Annotated Bibliography

Miller, Delbert, *Handbook of Research Design and Social Measurement* (New York: David McKay, 1970). A useful reference work. This book, especially Part IV, cites and describes a wide variety of operational measures used in prior social research. In a number of cases, the questionnaire formats used are presented. Though the quality of these illustrations is uneven, they provide excellent examples of the variations possible.

Oppenheim, A. N., *Questionnaire Design and Attitude Measurement* (New York: Basic Books, 1966). An excellent and comprehensive treatment of the construction of questionnaires and their relation to measurement in general. Although the illustrations of questionnaire formats are not always the best, this comes the closest of any book available to being the definitive work on questionnaires. Its coverage ranges from the theoretical to the nitty-gritty.

Payne, Stanley, *The Art of Asking Questions* (Princeton, N.J.: Princeton University Press, 1951). A dated but still instructive treatment of questionnaires. This book is decidedly practical, anecdotal, and folksy. Special attention is paid to the field of the meanings of words and the implications of that on questionnaire construction. In that regard, it should be inspirational as well as specifically instructive.

6
The Logic of Sampling

6.1
Introduction

The preceding two chapters have been addressed to the *topics* of research—the concepts, variables, and attributes studied. Chapters 6 and 7 are addressed to the units of analysis of research—the people, events, or things, which may be characterized in terms of variables.

In an earlier discussion of units of analysis, I said that individual people are the typical subjects of social scientific research. We describe people in terms of variables, and we do this by observing them. Very often, however, we cannot observe all the people who might be relevant to our research concerns. If we wished to know the average age of the American population, we would probably be unable to determine the age of every man, woman, and child in order to compute the average. The same problem frequently occurs when the subjects of study are not people. If we wished to examine shifts in the editorial leanings of a given newspaper over the course of a hundred-year publication history, it would be unlikely that we could read and evaluate all 36,500 issues.

Fortunately, a variety of *sampling* methods make it possible for us to observe only a portion of our subjects of study and still draw conclusions about the larger population from which the sample was selected. Thus, we might interview only a sample of Americans and still estimate the average age of all Americans.

Chapter 6 discusses the logic and methods of sampling. Since social sampling techniques have been developed and used in connection with survey research, the bulk of the chapter will consider sampling within that context. While examining survey sampling in detail, we shall also consider, more briefly, the implications of sampling for other modes of observation. While rigorous sampling methods in social science have been associated predominantly with survey research, the logic of probability sampling and many of the techniques can be applied profitably to other research methods.

Why Sample?

Most readers can no doubt give two reasons for sampling: time and cost. The interviewing alone for a comprehensive interview survey may require one to three hours and $20 to $30 per interview. The savings in studying 2,000 people rather than, say, 500,000 are apparent. A survey project requiring a two-month interviewing period at a cost of $40,000 might very well be judged feasible, while a 10-year interviewing project costing $10 million very probably would not. Thus sampling often makes a project possible, whereas a refusal to sample would rule out the study altogether.

Sampling should not be regarded as a necessary evil, however. It is not generally recognized, perhaps, but sample surveys are often *more accurate* than would be the case for a total census—interviewing every member of a given population. There are several reasons for this seemingly bizarre fact, growing out of the logistics of survey interviewing.

First, an enormous interviewing project would require a very large staff of interviewers. Although researchers typically attempt to limit their staffs to the best available interviewers, such a project would probably require them to employ everyone in sight, with the result that the overall quality of interviewers would be lower than usually achieved. The quality of data collected would be reduced by the decreased quality of interviewers. Also, a smaller scale study would permit more diligent follow-up procedures, thereby increasing the rates of interview completion.

Second, interviewing all members of a given large population would require a lengthy interviewing period. As a result, it would be difficult if not impossible to specify the *time* to which the data refer. If the study were aimed at measuring the level of unemployment in a given large city, the unemployment rate produced by the survey data would not refer to the city as of the beginning of interviewing or as of the end. Rather, the researcher would be forced to attribute the unemployment rate to some hypothetical date—representing perhaps the midpoint of the interviewing period. (Asking respondents to answer in terms of a uniform date introduces the problem of inaccurate recall.) While this problem is inherent in any interviewing project that is not executed all in one moment, the seriousness of the problem grows with the duration of interviewing. If the interviewing were to take 10 years to complete—with the unemployment rate presumably changing during that period—the resultant rate would be meaningless.

Finally, the managerial requirements of a very large survey would be far greater than normally faced by survey researchers. Supervision, record keeping, training, and so forth would all be more difficult in a very large survey. Once again, the quality of data collected in a very large survey might be lower than that obtained in a smaller, more manageable one. (It is worth noting that the Bureau of the Census follows its decennial census with a sample survey for purposes of evaluating the data collected in the total enumeration.)

Are Sample Data Really Accurate?

Despite the foregoing, many readers no doubt still feel somewhat uneasy about sampling. Since it is clearly possible for a sample to misrepresent the population from which it is drawn, there is an inevitable danger to the researcher who utilizes sampling methods. Nevertheless, as will be shown in this chapter, established sampling procedures can reduce this danger to an acceptable minimum. Ultimately, sample surveys can provide very accurate estimates about the populations that they portray. However, the sample survey researcher must be prepared to tolerate a certain ambiguity: we are seldom able to determine exactly how accurate our sample findings are.

Political pollsters are one group of survey researchers who are given an opportunity to check the accuracy of their sample findings. Election day is the final judgment for political pollsters, and their mixed experiences are instructive in the more general question of sample survey accuracy.

Most critics of sample survey methods are familiar with the 1936 *Literary Digest* poll that predicted Alfred M. Landon to win over Franklin D. Roosevelt by a landslide. Polling a sample of more than 2 million voters by mail, the *Digest* predicted that Landon would beat Roosevelt by nearly 15 percentage points. The primary reason for this failure lay in the *sampling frame* (see below) used by the pollsters. The *Digest* sample was drawn from telephone directories and automobile registration lists. This sampling procedure had seemed sufficient in the 1920, 1924, 1928, and 1932 elections, but by 1936 it did not provide a representative cross section of American voters. In the wake of the Depression, and in the midst of the New Deal, unprecedented numbers of poor Americans came to the polls. These people, however, were not adequately represented by telephone directories and automobile registration lists since they could not afford telephones and automobiles.

In 1936, George Gallup correctly predicted that Roosevelt would win a second term. Gallup's sampling procedures differed from those of the *Literary Digest*, however. Gallup's American Institute of Public Opinion had pioneered in the use of *quota sampling* (see below), which better insured that all types of American voters—rich and poor—would be adequately represented in the survey sample. Where the *Digest* poll failed to reach and question the poor—and predominantly Democratic—voters, Gallup's quota sampling did.

Twelve years later Gallup, and most political pollsters, suffered the embarrassment of predicting victory for Thomas Dewey over Harry Truman. As Goodman Ace acidly noted, "Everyone believes in public opinion polls. Everyone from the man in the street . . . up to President Thomas E. Dewey." [1] A number of factors conspired to bring about the 1948 polling debacle. For one thing, most pollsters finished their polling too soon despite a steady trend toward Truman over the course of the campaign. The large numbers of voters who said they did not know whom they would vote for went predominantly to Truman. Most important, however, the failure in 1948 pointed to serious shortcomings inherent in quota sampling—the method that was such an improvement over the *Literary Digest* sampling methods. In 1948 a number of academic survey researchers had been experimenting with *probability sampling* methods. By and large, they were far more successful than the quota samplers, and probability sampling remains the most respected method used by survey researchers today.

---

1. Requoted in *Newsweek*, July 8, 1968, p. 24.

The brief discussion above has presented a partial history of early survey sampling in America but has perhaps done so at the expense of the reader's modicum of faith in sample survey methods. To counterbalance this possible effect, it will be useful to consider the more recent score sheet of political polling accuracy. In November 1968, Richard Nixon received 42.9 percent of the popular vote for President. In their latest preelection polls, George Gallup and Louis Harris respectively predicted Nixon would receive 43 and 41 percent. This accuracy was accomplished, moreover, in the face of the uncertain effect of George Wallace's third-party candidacy. And, in place of the 2 million voters polled by the *Literary Digest* in 1936, approximately 2,000 voters were sufficient to predict the voting of some 73 million who went to the polls in 1968.

Sample surveys can be extremely accurate. At the same time, we should concede that they often are not, even today. The remainder of this chapter is devoted to presenting the reasons and rules for accuracy in sampling.

Two Types of Sampling Methods

It is useful to distinguish two major types of sampling methods: *probability* sampling and *nonprobability* sampling. The bulk of this chapter will be devoted to probability sampling, as it is currently the most respected and useful method. A smaller portion of this chapter will consider the various methods of nonprobability sampling.

We shall begin with a discussion of the logic of probability sampling, followed by a brief glossary of sampling concepts and terminology. Then we shall turn to the concept of sampling distribution: the basis of estimating the accuracy of sample survey findings. Following these theoretical discussions, we shall turn to a consideration of populations and sampling frames—focusing on practical problems of determining the target group of the study and how to begin selecting a sample. Next, we shall examine the basic types of survey designs: simple random samples, systematic samples, stratified samples, and cluster samples. Then, a short discussion and description of nonprobability sampling is presented.

Subsequent chapters in Part Three will consider nonsurvey uses of sampling methods in such fields as content analysis, participant observation, and historical analyses. Hopefully, the reader will have become so familiar with the *logic* of survey sampling that he will be able to profit from that knowledge in a broader variety of situations.

6.2
The Logic of Probability Sampling

It should be apparent from the history of political polling that sample surveys can be very accurate. At the same time it should be equally apparent that samples must be selected in a careful fashion. We might consider briefly why this is the case.

The Implications of Homogeneity and Heterogeneity

If all members of a population were identical to one another in all respects, there would be no need for careful sampling procedures. In such a case, any sample would indeed be sufficient. In this extreme case of homogeneity, in fact, *one* case would be sufficient as a sample to study characteristics of the whole population.

Before you dismiss this idea as impossible, recall that much scientific sampling is carried out on this basis. In the physical sciences, it is sometimes safe to make this assumption and proceed on the basis of it in research. The chemist who wishes to test certain properties of carbon, for example, need not undertake a painstaking enumeration of all the carbon molecules in the world and then carefully select a probability sample of carbon molecules for study.

By the same token, the medical scientist—or the practicing physician—who wishes to examine a person's blood need not draw out all of the person's blood and select a probability sample of blood cells. Again, for most purposes, any sample of blood from the person may suffice.

Faced with variation or heterogeneity in the population under study, however, more controlled sampling procedures are required. The broader applicability of this principle—beyond social research—is worth noting. The origins of modern sampling theory are to be found in agricultural research, especially in the work of R. A. Fisher whose name is still attached to some commonly used survey statistics.

For our purposes, it is more important to note the heterogeneity of social groups. People differ in many ways. A given human population, then, is comprised of varied individuals. A sample of individuals from that population, if it is to provide useful descriptions of the total population, must contain essentially the same variation as exists in the population. Probability sampling provides an efficient method for selecting a sample that should adequately reflect the variation that exists in the population.

Conscious and Unconscious Sampling Bias

Of course anyone could select a survey sample, even without any special training or care. To select a sample of 100 university students, a person might go to the university campus and begin interviewing students found walking around campus. This kind of sampling method is often used by untrained researchers, but it has very serious problems.

To begin, there is a danger that the researcher's own personal biases may affect the sample selected in this manner—hence the sample would not truly represent the student population. Let's assume that the researcher is personally somewhat intimidated by "hippy-looking" students, feeling that they would ridicule his research effort. As a result, he might consciously or semiconsciously avoid interviewing such people. Or, he might feel that the attitudes of "straight-looking" students would not be relevant to his research purposes and would avoid interviewing such students. Even if he sought to interview a "balanced" group of students, he probably would not know the proper proportions of different types of students making up such a balance, or he might be unable to identify the different types just by watching them walk by.

Even if the researcher made a conscientious effort to interview every tenth student entering the university library, this would not insure him of a *representative* sample, since different types of students visit the library with different frequencies. Thus, the sample would overrepresent students frequenting the library more often.

Representativeness and Probability of Selection

Survey samples must represent the populations from which they are drawn if they are to provide useful estimates about the characteristics of that population. Realize that they need not be representative in all respects; **representativeness,** as it has any meaning in regard to sampling, is limited to those characteristics that are relevant to the substantive interests of the study. (This will become more evident in the discussion of stratification below.)

A basic principle of probability sampling is the following: *A sample will be representative of the population from which it is selected if all members of the population have an equal chance of being selected in the sample.*[2] Samples that have this quality are often labeled **EPSEM** samples (equal probability of selection method). While we shall discuss variations of this principle later, it is the primary one providing the basis of probability sampling.

Moving beyond this basic principle, we must realize that samples— even carefully selected EPSEM samples—are seldom if ever *perfectly* representative of the populations from which they are drawn. Nevertheless, probability sampling offers two special advantages for researchers.

First, probability samples, while never perfectly representative, are typically *more representative* than other types of samples because the biases discussed in the preceding section are avoided. In practice, there is a greater likelihood that a probability sample will be representative of the population from which it is drawn than that a nonprobability sample would be.

Second, and more important, probability theory permits the researcher to estimate the accuracy or representativeness of his sample.

---

2. We shall see shortly that the size of the sample selected as well as the actual characteristics of the larger population affect the *degree* of representativeness.

Conceivably, an uninformed researcher might, through wholly haphazard means, select a sample that nearly perfectly represents the larger population. The odds are against his doing so, however, and he would be unable to estimate the likelihood that he has achieved representativeness. The probability sampler, on the other hand, can provide an accurate estimate of his success or failure.

Following a brief glossary of sampling terminology, we shall examine the means whereby the probability sampler estimates the representativeness of his sample.

6.3
Sampling Concepts and Terminology

The following discussions of sampling theory and practice utilize a number of technical terms. To facilitate the reader's understanding of those discussions, it is important to quickly define those terms. For the most part, I will employ terms commonly used in other sampling and statistical textbooks so that readers may better understand those other sources.

In presenting this glossary of sampling concepts and terminology, I would like to acknowledge a debt to Leslie Kish and his excellent textbook on survey sampling.[3] While I have modified some of the conventions used by Kish, his presentation is easily the most important source of our discussion.

Element

An *element* is that unit about which information is collected and which provides the basis of analysis. Typically, in survey research, elements are people or certain types of people. It should be recognized, however, that other kinds of units might constitute the elements for a survey; families, social clubs, or corporations might be the elements of a survey. (*Note:* Elements and units of analysis are often the same in a given study.)

Universe

A *universe* is the theoretical and hypothetical aggregation of all elements, as defined for a given survey. If the individual American is the element for a survey, then "Americans" would be the universe. A survey universe is wholly unspecified as to time and place, however, and is essentially a useless term.

---

3. Leslie Kish, *Survey Sampling* (New York: John Wiley, 1965).

Population

A *population* is the theoretically specified aggregation of survey elements. While the vague term "Americans" might be the universe for a survey, the delineation of the population would include a definition of the element Americans (for example, citizenship, residence) and the time referent for the study (Americans as of when?). Translating the universe "adult New Yorkers" into a workable population would require a specification of the age defining "adult" and the boundaries of New York. Specifying the term "college student" would include a consideration of full-time and part-time students, degree candidates and nondegree candidates, undergraduate and graduate students, and similar issues.

While the researcher must begin with a careful specification of his population, poetic license usually permits him to phrase his report in terms of the hypothetical universe. For ease of presentation, even the most conscientious researcher normally speaks of "Americans" rather than "resident citizens of the United States of America as of November 12, 1971." The primary guide in this matter, as in most others, is that the researcher should not mislead or deceive his readers.

Survey Population

A *survey population* is that aggregation of elements from which the survey sample is actually selected. Recall that a population is a theoretical specification of the universe. As a practical matter, the researcher is seldom in a position to guarantee that every element that meets the theoretical definitions laid down actually has a chance of being selected in the sample. Even where lists of elements exist for sampling purposes, the lists are usually somewhat incomplete. Some students are always omitted, inadvertently, from student rosters. Some telephone subscribers request that their names and numbers be unlisted. The survey population, then, is the aggregation of elements from which the sample is selected.

Often researchers may decide to limit their survey populations more severely than indicated in the above examples. National polling firms may limit their "national samples" to the 48 adjacent states, omitting Alaska and Hawaii for practical reasons. A researcher wishing to sample psychology professors may limit the survey population to psychology professors who are serving in psychology departments, omitting those serving in other departments. (In a sense, we might say that these researchers have redefined their universes and populations, in which case they must make the revisions clear to their readers.)

Sampling Unit

A *sampling unit* is that element or set of elements considered for selection in some stage of sampling. In a simple, single-stage sample, the sampling units are the same as the elements. In more complex samples, however, different levels of sampling units may be employed. For example, a researcher may select a sample of census blocks in a city, then select a sample of households on the selected blocks, and finally select a sample of adults from the selected households. The sampling units for these three stages of sampling are, respectively, census blocks, households, and adults, of which only the last of these are the elements. More specifically, the terms "primary sampling units," "secondary sampling units," and "final sampling units" would be used to designate the successive stages.

Sampling Frame

A **sampling frame** is the actual list of sampling units from which the sample, or some stage of the sample, is selected. If a simple sample of students is selected from a student roster, the roster is the sampling frame. If the primary sampling unit for a complex population sample is the census block, the list of census blocks comprises the sampling frame—either in the form of a printed booklet, a card file, or a magnetic tape file.

In a single-stage sample design, the sampling frame is a list of the elements comprising the survey population. In practice, the existing sampling frames often define the survey population rather than the other way around. The researcher often begins with a universe or perhaps a population in mind for his study; then he searches for possible sampling frames. The frames available for his use are examined and evaluated, and the researcher decides which frame represents a survey population most appropriate to his needs.

The relationship between populations and sampling frames is critical and one that has not been given sufficient attention. A later section of the present chapter will pursue this issue in greater detail.

Observation Unit

An *observation unit,* or unit of data collection, is an element or aggregation of elements from which information is collected. Again, often the unit of analysis and unit of observation are the same—the individual person—but this need not be the case. Thus the researcher may interview heads of households (the observation units) to collect information about all members of the households (the units of analysis).

The researcher's task is simplified when the unit of analysis and observation unit are the same. Often this is not possible or feasible, however, and in such situations the researcher should be capable of exercising some ingenuity in collecting data relevant to his units of analysis without actually observing those units.

Variable

As discussed in Chapter 4, a *variable* is a set of mutually exclusive attributes such as sex, age, employment status, and so forth. The elements of a given population may be described in terms of their individual attributes on a given variable. Typically, surveys aim at describing the distribution of attributes comprising a variable in a population. Thus a researcher may describe the age distribution of a population by examining the relative frequency of different ages among members of the population.

It should be noted that a variable, by definition, must possess *variation;* if all elements in the population have the same attribute, that attribute is a *constant* in the population, rather than part of a variable.

Parameter

A *parameter* is the summary description of a given variable in a *population.* The mean income of all families in a city and the age distribution of the city's population are parameters. An important portion of survey research involves the estimation of population parameters on the basis of sample observations.

Statistic

A *statistic* is the summary description of a given variable in survey sample. Thus the mean income computed from a survey sample and the age distribution of that sample are statistics. Sample statistics are used to make estimates of population parameters.

Sampling Error

Sampling error will be discussed in more detail below. Probability sampling methods seldom, if ever, provide statistics exactly equal to the parameters that they are used to estimate. Probability theory, however, permits us to estimate the degree of error to be expected for a given sample design.

Confidence Levels and Confidence Intervals

Confidence levels and *confidence intervals* will also be discussed more fully below. The computation of sampling error permits the researcher to express the accuracy of his sample statistics in terms of his level of confidence that the statistics fall within a specified interval from the parameter. For example, he may say he is "95 percent confident" that his sample statistics (for example, 50 percent favor Candidate X) are within plus or minus (±) 5 percentage points of the population parameter. As the confidence interval is expanded for a given statistic, his "confidence" increases and he may say that he is 99.9 percent confident that his statistic falls within ±7.5 percentage points of the parameter.

6.4
Probability Sampling Theory and Sampling Distribution

This section will examine the basic theory of probability sampling as it applies to survey sampling, and we shall consider the logic of sampling distribution and sampling error with regard to a **binomial variable**—a variable comprised of two characteristics.

Probability Sampling Theory

The ultimate purpose of survey sampling is to select a set of elements from a population in such a way that descriptions of those elements (statistics) accurately describe the total population from which they are selected. Probability sampling provides a method for enhancing the likelihood of accomplishing this aim, and it also provides methods for estimating the degree of probable success.

Random selection is the key to this process. A random selection process is one in which each element has an equal chance of selection that is independent of any other events in the selection process. Flipping a perfect coin is the most frequently cited example, whereby the "selection" of a head or a tail is independent of previous selections of heads or tails. Rolling a perfect set of dice is another example.

Such images of random selection seldom apply directly to survey sampling methods, however. The survey sampler more typically utilizes tables of random numbers or computer programs that provide a random selection of sampling units. The wide availability of such research aids makes this an adequate beginning point for our discussion of random sampling.

The reasons for using random selection methods—using random-number tables or computer programs—are twofold. First, this procedure serves as a check on conscious or unconscious bias on the part of the researcher. The researcher who undertakes the selection of cases on an intuitive basis might very well select cases that would support his research expectations or hypotheses. Random selection, then, erases this danger.

More important, random selection offers the researcher access to the body of probability theory, which provides the basis for his estimates of population parameters and estimates of error. We shall turn now to an examination of this latter aspect.

Binomial Sampling Distribution

To discuss the concept of sampling distribution, it will be clearest to utilize a simple survey example. Let us assume for the moment that we wish to study the student population of State University to determine approval or disapproval of a student conduct code proposed by the administration. The survey population will be that aggregation of students contained in a student roster: the sampling frame. The elements will be the individual students at SU. The variable under consideration will be attitudes toward the code, a binomial variable: approve and disapprove. We shall select a random sample of students for purposes of estimating the entire student body.

Figure 6-1 presents an *x* axis that represents all possible values of this parameter in the population—from 0 percent approval to 100 percent approval. The midpoint of the axis—50 percent—represents the situation in which half the students approve of the code while the other half disapprove.

0   50   100

Percent of students approving of the student code

Figure 6-1

Let us assume for the moment that we have given each student on the student roster a number and have selected 100 random numbers from a table of random numbers. The 100 students having their numbers selected are then interviewed and asked for their attitudes toward the student code: whether they approve or disapprove. Let us further assume that this operation provides us with 48 students who approve of the code and 52 who disapprove. We may represent this statistic by placing a dot on the *x* axis at the point representing 48 percent.

Now let us suppose that we select another sample of 100 students in exactly the same fashion and measure their approval or disapproval of the student code. Perhaps 51 students in the second sample approve of the code, and this might be represented by another dot in the appropriate place on the *x* axis. Repeating this process once more, we may discover that 52 students in the third sample approve of the code.

Figure 6-2 presents the three different sample statistics, representing the percentages of students in each of the three random samples who approved of the student code. The basic rule of random sampling is that such samples drawn from a population provide estimates of the parameter that pertains in the total population. Each of the random samples, then, gives us an estimate of the percentage of students in the total student body who approve of the student code. Unhappily, however, we have selected three samples and now have three separate estimates.

To retrieve ourselves from this dilemma, let's go on to draw more and more samples of 100 students each, question each of the samples as to their approval or disapproval of the code, and plot the new sample statistics on our summary graph. In drawing many such samples, we will begin to discover that

Percent of students approving of the student code

Figure 6-2

some of the new samples provide the same estimates given by earlier samples. To take account of this situation, we shall add a y axis to the figure, representing the number of samples providing a given estimate. Figure 6-3 is the product of our new sampling efforts.

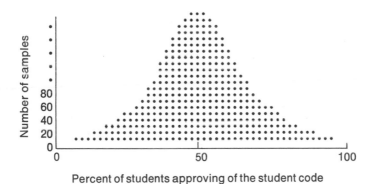

Percent of students approving of the student code

Figure 6-3

The distribution of sample statistics provided in Figure 6-3 is called the *sampling distribution*. We note that by increasing the number of samples selected and interviewed, we have also increased the range of estimates provided by the sampling operation. In one sense we have increased our dilemma in attempting to guess the parameter in the population. Probability theory, however, provides certain important rules regarding the sampling distribution presented in Figure 6-3.

First, if many independent random samples are selected from a population, the sample statistics provided by those samples will be *distributed around the population parameter* in a known way. While we see that there is a wide range of estimates, more of them are in the vicinity of 50 percent than elsewhere in the graph. Probability theory tells us, then, that the true value is in the vicinity of 50 percent.

Second, probability theory provides us with a formula for estimating *how closely* the sample statistics are clustered around the true value. This formula contains three factors: the parameter, the sample size, and the *standard error* (a measure of sampling error).

Formula: $S = \sqrt{\dfrac{PQ}{n}}$

Symbols: *P, Q:* the population parameters for the binomial; if 60 percent of the student body approves of the code and 40 percent disapproves, *P* and *Q* are 60 percent and 40 percent, or .6 and .4. Note that $Q = 1 - P$ and $P = 1 - Q$.

   n: the number of cases in each sample.

   s: the standard error.

Let us assume that the population parameter in the study survey example is 50 percent approving of the code and 50 percent disapproving. Recall that we have been selecting samples of 100 cases each. When these numbers are put into the formula, we find that the standard error equals .05 or 5 percent.

In terms of probability theory, the standard error is a valuable datum, for it indicates the extent to which the sample estimates will be distributed around the population parameter. Specifically, probability theory indicates that certain proportions of the sample estimates will fall within specified increments of standard errors from the population parameter. Approximately 34 percent (.3413) of the sample estimates will fall within one standard error above the population parameter, and another 34 percent will fall within one standard error below the parameter. In our example, the standard error is 5 percent, so we know that 34 percent of our samples will give estimates of student approval between 50 percent (parameter) and 55 percent (one standard error above); another 34 percent of the samples will give estimates between 50 percent and 45 percent (one standard error below the parameter). Taken together, then, we know that roughly two-thirds (68 percent) of the samples will give estimates within (plus or minus) 5 percent of the parameter.

Moreover, probability theory dictates that roughly 95 percent of the samples will fall within plus or minus two standard errors of the true value, and 99.9 percent of the samples will fall within plus or minus three standard errors. In our present example, then, we know that only one sample out of a thousand would give an estimate lower than 35 percent approval or higher than 65 percent.

The proportion of samples falling within one, two, or three standard errors of the parameter are constants for any random sampling procedure such as the one just described, providing that a large number of samples are selected. The size of the standard error in any given case, however, is a function of the population parameter and the sample size. If we return to the formula for a moment, we note that the standard error will increase as a function of an increase in the quantity: P times Q. Note further that this quantity reaches its maximum in the situation of an even split in the population. If $P = .5$, $PQ = .25$; if $P = .6$, $PQ = .24$; if $P = .8$, $PQ = .16$; if $P = .99$, $PQ = .0099$. By extension, if P is either 0.0 or 1.0 (either 0 percent or 100 percent approve of the student code), the standard error will be 0. If everyone in the population has the same attitude (no variation), then every sample will give exactly that estimate.

The standard error is also a function of the sample size—an *inverse* function. As the sample size increases, the standard error decreases. As the sample size increases, the several samples will be clustered nearer to the true value. Another rule of thumb is evident in the formula: because of the square root in the formula, the standard error is reduced by half if the sample size is *quadrupled.* In our present example, samples of 100 produce a standard error of 5 percent; to reduce the standard error to 2.5 percent, it would be necessary to increase the sample size to 400.

All the foregoing is provided by established probability theory in reference to the selection of large numbers of random samples. If the population parameter is known, and very many random samples are selected, we are able to predict how many of the samples will fall within specified intervals from the parameter. These conditions do not typically pertain in survey sampling, however.

Typically, the survey researcher does not know the parameter, but he conducts a sample survey in order to estimate that value. Moreover, he does not typically select large numbers of samples, but he selects only one sample. Nevertheless, the preceding discussion of probability theory provides the basis for inferences about the typical survey situation.

Whereas probability theory specifies that 68 percent of the samples will fall within one standard error of the parameter, the survey sampler infers that a given random sample has a likelihood of 68 percent of falling within that range. In this regard we speak of **confidence levels:** the researcher is "68 percent confident" that his sample estimate is within one standard error of the parameter. Or he may say he is "95 percent confident" that the sample statistic is within two standard errors of the parameter, and so forth. Quite reasonably, his confidence increases as the margin for error is extended. He is virtually positive (99.9 percent confident) that he is within three standard errors of the true value.

While he may be confident (at some level) of being within a certain range of the parameter, we have already noted that he seldom knows what the parameter is. To resolve this dilemma, the survey sampler substitutes his sample estimate for the parameter in the formula; lacking the true value, he substitutes the best available guess.

The result of these inferences and estimations is that the survey researcher is able to estimate a population parameter and also the expected degree of error on the basis of one sample drawn from a population. Beginning with the question "What percentage of the student body approves of the student code?" the researcher could select a random sample of 100 students and interview them. He might then report his best estimate is that 50 percent of the student body approves of the code, and that he is 95 percent confident that between 40 and 60 percent (plus or minus two standard errors) approve. The range from 40 to 60 percent is called the **confidence interval.**

This then is the basic logic of probability sampling. Random selection permits the researcher to link his sample survey findings to the body of probability theory for purposes of estimating the accuracy of those findings. All statements of accuracy in sampling must specify both a confidence level and a confidence interval. The researcher may report that he is x percent confident that the population parameter is between two specified values. It does not make sense, however, for a researcher to report that his findings are "x percent accurate."

The foregoing discussion has considered only one type of statistic: the percentages produced by a *binomial* or dichotomous variable. The same logic, however, would apply to the examination of other statistics, such as mean income for example. Since the computations are somewhat more complicated in such a case, I have chosen to consider only binomials in this introduction.

The reader should be cautioned that the survey uses of probability theory as discussed above are not wholly justified technically. The theory of sampling distribution, for example, makes assumptions that almost never apply in survey conditions. The number of samples contained within specified increments of standard errors, for example, assumes an infinitely large population, an infinite number of samples, and sampling with replacement. Moreover, the inferential jump from the distribution of several samples to the probable characteristics of one sample has been grossly oversimplified in the above discussion.

The above cautions are offered for reasons of perspective. Researchers often appear to overestimate the precision of estimates produced by the use of probability theory in connection with survey research. As will be mentioned elsewhere in this chapter and throughout the book, variations in sampling techniques and nonsampling factors may further reduce the legitimacy of such estimates. Nevertheless, the calculations discussed in this section can be extremely valuable to the researcher in understanding and evaluating his data. Although the calculations do not provide as precise estimates as some researchers might assume, they can be quite valid for practical purposes; they are unquestionably more valid than less rigorously derived estimates based on less rigorous sampling methods.

Most important, the reader should be familiar with the basic *logic* underlying the calculations. If he is so informed, he will be able to react sensibly to his own data and to those reported by others.

6.5

Populations and Sampling Frames

The immediately preceding section has dealt with a theoretical model for survey sampling. While it is necessary for the survey consumer, student, or researcher to understand that theory, it is no less important that he appreciate the less-than-perfect conditions that exist in the field. The present section is devoted to a discussion of one aspect of field conditions that requires a compromise with regard to theoretical conditions and assumptions. We shall consider the congruence of, or disparity between, populations and sampling frames.

Simply put, a sampling frame is the list, or reasonable facsimile, of elements from which a probability sample is selected. The following section will deal with the methods for selected samples, but we must first consider the sampling frame itself. Properly drawn samples will provide information appropriate for describing the population of elements comprising the sampling frame—nothing more. It is necessary to make this point in view of the all-too-common tendency for researchers to select samples from a given sampling frame and then make assertions about a population similar to, but not identical to, the survey population defined by the sampling frame. The problem involved here is the broader social scientific one of generalization and is akin to studying a small Lutheran church in North Dakota for purposes of describing religion in America.

In the remainder of this section, we shall examine different survey purposes and discuss the good and bad sampling frames that might be used to satisfy those purposes.

Surveys of organizations are often the simplest from a sampling standpoint because organizations typically have membership lists. In such cases, the list of members constitutes an excellent sampling frame. If a random sample is selected from a membership list, the data collected from that sample may be taken as representative of all members—*if all members are included in the list*. If some members are omitted from the membership list, an effort must be made to sample those nonlisted members, or else the sample survey findings can be taken as representative only of those members on the list.

Populations that often can be sampled from good organizational lists include elementary school, high school, and university students and faculty; church members; factory workers; fraternity or sorority members; members of social, service, or political clubs; and members of professional associations.

The above comments apply primarily to local organizations. Often statewide or national organizations do not have a single membership list easily available. There is, for example, no single list of Episcopalian church members. However, a slightly more complex sample design could take advantage of local church membership lists: by first sampling churches, and then subsampling the membership lists of those churches selected. (More about this below.)

Other lists of individuals may be especially relevant to the research needs of a particular survey. Government agencies maintain lists of registered voters, for example, that might be used if the researcher wishes to conduct a preelection poll or a more detailed examination of voting behavior —but the researcher must insure that the list is up-to-date. Similar lists contain the names of automobile owners, welfare recipients, taxpayers, business permit holders, licensed professionals, and so forth. Although it may be difficult to gain access to some of these lists, they may provide excellent sampling frames for specialized research purposes.

Realizing that the sampling elements in a survey need not be individual persons, we may note that lists of other types of elements also exist: universities, businesses of various types, cities, academic journals, newspapers, unions, political clubs, professional associations, and so forth.

Telephone directories are frequently used for "quick and dirty" public opinion polls. Undeniably they are easy and inexpensive to use, and this is no doubt the reason for their popularity. And, if one wishes to make assertions about telephone subscribers, the directory is a *fairly good* sampling frame.[4] Unfortunately, telephone directories are all too often taken to be a listing of a city's population or of its voters. There are many defects in this reasoning, but the chief one involves a social-class bias. Poor people are less likely to have telephones; a telephone directory sample, therefore, is likely to have a middle- or upper-class bias.

The class bias inherent in telephone directory samples is often hidden. Preelection polls conducted in this fashion are sometimes quite accurate. The reason for this would seem to be in the class bias evident in voting itself: poor people are less likely to vote. Frequently, then, these two biases nearly coincide and the results of a telephone poll may come very close to the final election outcome. Unhappily, the pollster never knows for sure until after the election. And sometimes, as in the case of the 1936 *Literary Digest* poll, he may discover that the voters have not acted according to the expected class biases. The ultimate disadvantage of this method, then, is the researcher's inability to estimate the degree of error to be expected in his sample findings.

Street directories and tax maps are often used for easy samples of households, but they may suffer from some of the same disadvantages as the telephone directory: incompleteness and possible bias. For example, in strictly zoned urban regions, "illegal" housing units are unlikely to appear on official records. As a result, such units would have no chance of selection, and sample findings could not be representative of those units, which are often poorer and more overcrowded than the average.

Review of Populations and Sampling Frames

Surprisingly little attention has been given to the issues of populations and sampling frames in survey research literature. With this in mind, I

---

4. Realize, of course, that a given directory will not include new subscribers or those who have requested unlisted numbers. Sampling is further complicated by the inclusion in directories of nonresidential listings.

have devoted special attention to them here. To further emphasize the point, it seems appropriate to list, in review, the main guidelines to be borne in mind.

1. Sample survey findings can be taken only as representative of the aggregation of elements that comprise the sampling frame.

2. Often, sampling frames do not truly include all the elements that their names might imply. (Student directories do not include all students; telephone directories do not include all telephone subscribers.) Omissions are almost inevitable. Thus a first concern of the researcher must be to assess the extent of omissions and to correct them if possible. (Realize, of course, that he may feel he can safely ignore a small number of omissions that cannot easily be corrected.)

3. Even to generalize to the population comprising the sampling frame, it is necessary for all elements to have equal representation to the frame: typically, each element should appear only once. Otherwise, elements that appear more than once will have a greater probability of selection, and the sample will, overall, overrepresent these elements.

Other, more practical, matters relating to populations and sampling frames will be treated elsewhere in this book. For example, the form of the sampling frame is very important: a list in a publication, a 3x5 card file, mailing address plates, machine-readable cards, or magnetic tapes. It should be noted here that such considerations may often take priority over scientific considerations: an "easier" list may be chosen over a "harder" one, even though the latter is more appropriate to the target population. We should not take a dogmatic position in this regard, but every researcher should carefully weigh the relative advantages and disadvantages of such alternatives. Most important of all, he must be aware—and must so inform his reader—of the shortcomings of whatever sampling frame is chosen.

6.6
Types of Sampling Designs

Introduction

Perhaps the reader will have reached this point in his reading somewhat aghast at the importance and difficulties of organizing his sampling frame; such a feeling would be altogether appropriate and healthy. Once it has been established, the researcher must then actually select a sample of elements for study.

Up to this point, we have focused on *simple random sampling.* And, indeed, the body of statistics typically used by survey researchers assumes such a sample. As we shall see shortly, however, the researcher has a number of options in choosing his sampling method, and he seldom if ever chooses simple random sampling. There are two reasons for this. First, with all but the simplest sampling frame, simple random sampling is not possible. Second, and probably surprisingly, simple random sampling may not be the best (not the most accurate) method available. We shall turn now to a discussion of simple random sampling and the other options available.

Simple Random Sampling

As noted above, **simple random sampling** (SRS) is the basic sampling method assumed in survey statistical computations. The mathematics of random sampling are especially complex, and we shall detour around them in favor of describing the field methods of employing this method.

Once a sampling frame has been established in accord with the discussion above, the researcher may then assign numbers to each of the elements in the list—assigning one and only one number to each and not skipping any number in the process. A table of random numbers could then be used in the selection of elements for the sample. (See Appendix C.)

If the researcher's sampling frame is in a machine-readable form— cards or magnetic tape—a simple random sample could be selected automatically through the use of a computer. (In effect, the computer program would number the elements in the sampling frame, generate its own series of random numbers, and print out the list of elements selected.)

Systematic Sampling

Simple random sampling is seldom used in practice. As we shall see in later sections, it is not usually the most efficient sampling method and, as we have already seen, it can be rather laborious if done manually. SRS typically requires a list of elements; when such a list is available, researchers usually employ a *systematic* sampling method rather than simple random sampling.

In systematic sampling, every *k*th element in the total list is chosen (systematically) for inclusion in the sample. If the list contains 10,000 elements and the researcher desires a sample of 1,000, he will select every tenth element for his sample. To insure against any possible human bias in using this method, the researcher selects the first element at random. Thus, in the above example he would begin by selecting a random number between 1 and 10; the element having that number would be included in the sample, plus every tenth element following it. This is technically referred to as a "systematic sample with a random start."

Two terms are frequently used in connection with systematic sampling. The **sampling interval** is the standard distance between elements selected in the sample: 10 in the example above. The **sampling ratio** is the proportion of elements in the population that are selected: one-tenth in the example above.

In practice, systematic sampling is virtually identical to simple random sampling. If, indeed, the list of elements is "randomized" in advance of sampling, one might argue that a systematic sample drawn from that list is in fact a simple random sample. By now, debates over the relative merits of simple random sampling and systematic sampling have been resolved largely in favor of the simpler method: systematic sampling. Empirically, the results are virtually identical. And, as we shall see in a later section, systematic sampling, in some instances, is slightly more accurate than simple random sampling.

There is one danger involved in systematic sampling. The arrangement of elements in the list can make systematic sampling unwise. This danger is usually referred to by the term *periodicity*. If the list of elements is arranged in a cyclical pattern that coincides with the sampling interval, it is possible that a grossly biased sample may be drawn. Two examples should suffice.

In one study of soldiers during World War II, the researchers selected a systematic sample from unit rosters. Every tenth soldier on the rosters was selected for the study. The rosters, however, were arranged in a table of organization: sergeants first, then corporals and privates, squad by squad—and each squad had 10 members. As a result, every tenth person on the roster was a squad sergeant. The systematic sample selected contained only sergeants. It could, of course, have been the case that no sergeants were selected for the same reason.

As another example suppose we wish to select a sample of apartments in an apartment building. If the sample were drawn from a list of apartments arranged in numerical order (for example, 101, 102, 103, 104, 201, 202, and so on), there would be a danger of the sampling interval coinciding with the number of apartments on a floor or some multiple thereof. In such a case, the samples might include only northwest-corner apartments or only apartments near the elevator. If these types of apartments had some other particular characteristic in common (for example, higher rent), the sample would be biased. The same danger would appear in a systematic sample of houses in a subdivision arranged with the same number of houses on a block.

In considering a systematic sample from a list, then, the researcher should carefully examine the nature of that list. If the elements are arranged in any particular order, he should ascertain whether that order will bias the sample to be selected and should take steps to counteract any possible bias (for example, take a simple random sample from cyclical portions).

In summary, however, systematic sampling is usually superior to simple random sampling, in convenience if nothing else. Where problems exist in the ordering of elements in the sampling frame, these can usually be remedied quite easily.

Stratified Sampling

In the two preceding sections we have discussed two alternative methods of sample selection from a list. **Stratified sampling** is not an alternative to these methods, but it represents a possible modification in their use.

Simple random and systematic sampling are important in that they insure a degree of representativeness and permit an estimate of the error present. Stratified sampling is a method for obtaining a greater degree of representativeness—decreasing the probable sampling error. To understand why this is the case, we must return briefly to the basic theory of sampling distribution.

We recall that sampling error is reduced by two factors in the sample design. First, a large sample produces a smaller sampling error than does a small sample. Second, a homogeneous population produces samples with smaller sampling errors than does a heterogeneous population. If 99 percent of the population agree with a certain statement, it is extremely unlikely that any probability sample will greatly misrepresent the extent of agreement. If, on the other hand, the population is split fifty-fifty on the statement, then the sampling error will be much greater.

Stratified sampling is based on this second factor in sampling theory. Rather than selecting his sample from the total population at large, the researcher insures that appropriate numbers of elements are drawn from homogeneous subsets of that population. In a study of university students, for example, the researcher may first organize his population by college class and draw appropriate numbers of freshmen, sophomores, juniors, and seniors. In a nonstratified sample, representation by class would be subjected to the same sampling error as other variables. In a sample stratified by class, the sampling error on this variable is reduced to zero.

The researcher might wish to utilize an even more complex stratification method. In addition to stratifying by class, he might also stratify by sex, by grade point average, and so forth. In this fashion he might be able to insure that his sample would contain the proper numbers of freshman men with a 4.0 average, of freshman women with a 4.0 average, and so forth.

The ultimate function of stratification, then, is to organize the population into homogeneous subsets (with heterogeneity, between subsets) and to select the appropriate number of elements from each. To the extent that the subsets are homogeneous on the stratification variables, they may also be homogeneous on other variables as well. Since age is related to college class, a sample stratified by class will be more representative in terms of age as well. Since occupational aspirations still seem to be related to sex, a sample stratified by sex will be more representative in terms of occupational aspirations.

The choice of stratification variables typically depends on what variables are available. Sex can often be determined in a list of names. University lists are typically arranged by class. Lists of faculty members may indicate their departmental affiliation. Governmental agency files may be arranged by geographical region. Voter registration lists are arranged according to precinct.

In selecting stratification variables from among those available, however, the researcher should be concerned primarily with those that are presumably related to variables that he wishes to represent accurately. Since sex is related to many variables and is often available for stratification, it is often used. Education is related to many variables, but it is often not available for stratification. Geographical location within a city, state, or nation is related to many things. Within a city, stratification by geographical location usually increases representativeness in social class, ethnic group, and so forth. Within a nation, it increases representativeness in a broad range of attitudes as well as in social class and ethnicity.

Methods of stratification in sampling vary. When a researcher is working with a simple list of all elements in the population, two are predominant. First, the researcher may group the population elements into discrete groups based on whatever stratification variables are being used. On the basis of the relative proportion of the population represented by a given group, he selects—randomly or systematically—a number of elements from that group constituting the same proportion of his desired sample size. For example, if freshman men with a 4.0 average comprise 1 percent of the student population and the researcher desires a sample of 1,000 students, he would select 10 students from the group of freshman men with a 4.0 average.

As an alternative method, he may group students as described above and then put those several groups together in a continuous list: beginning with all the freshman men with 4.0 average and ending with all the senior women with a 1.0 or below. He would then select a systematic sample, with a random start, from the entire list. Given the arrangement of the list, a systematic sample would select proper numbers (within an error range of 1 or 2) from each of the subgroups. (*Note:* A simple random sample drawn from such a composite list would cancel out the stratification.)

The effect of stratification is to insure the proper representation of the stratification variables to enhance representation of other variables related to them. Taken as a whole, then, a stratified sample is likely to be more representative on a number of variables than would be the case for a simple random sample. Although the simple random sample is still regarded as somewhat sacred, it should now be clear that a researcher can often do better.

Implicit Stratification in Systematic Sampling

It was mentioned above that systematic sampling can, under certain conditions, be more accurate than simple random sampling. This is the case whenever the arrangement of the list is such as to create an implicit stratification. As already noted, if a list of university students is already arranged by class, then a systematic sample will provide a stratification by class where a simple random sample would not. Other typical arrangements of elements in lists can provide the same feature.

If a list of names comprising the sampling frame for a study is arranged alphabetically, then the list is somewhat stratified by ethnic origins.

All the McTavishes are collected together, for example, as are the Lees, Wongs, Yamamuras, Schmidts, Whitehalls, Weinsteins, Gonzaleses, and so forth. To the extent that any of these groups comprise a substantial subset of the total population, that group will be properly represented in a systematic sample drawn from an alphabetical list.

In a study of students at the University of Hawaii, after stratification by school class, the students were arranged by their student identification numbers. These numbers, however, were their social security numbers. The first three digits of the social security number indicate the state in which the number was issued. As a result, within a class, students were arranged by the state in which they were issued a social security number, providing a rough stratification by geographical origins.

The researcher should be aware, therefore, that an ordered list of elements may be more useful to him than an unordered, randomized list. This point has been stressed here in view of an unfortunate belief that lists should be randomized before systematic sampling. Only if the arrangement presents the problems discussed earlier should the list be rearranged.

Multistage Cluster Sampling, General

The four preceding sections have dealt with reasonably simple procedures for sampling from lists of elements. Such a situation is ideal. Unfortunately, however, much interesting social research requires the selection of samples from populations that cannot be easily listed for sampling purposes. Examples would be the population of a city, of a state, or of a nation, all university students in the United States, and so forth. In such cases, it is necessary to create and execute a more complex sample design. Such a design typically involves the initial sampling of *groups* of elements—clusters —followed by the selection of elements within each of the selected clusters.

The varieties and procedures of multistage cluster sampling will be spelled out in some detail in the sampling examples of Chapter 7. Nevertheless, it is appropriate here to outline the method.

Cluster sampling may be used when it is either impossible or impractical to compile an exhaustive list of the elements comprising the target population. All church members in the United States would be an example of such a population. It is often the case, however, that the population elements are already grouped into subpopulations, and a list of those subpopulations either exists or can be created practically. Thus, church members in the United States belong to discrete churches, and it would be possible to discover or create a list of those churches. Following a cluster sample format, then, the list of churches would be sampled in some manner as discussed above (for example, a stratified, systematic sample). Next, the researcher would obtain lists of members from each of the selected churches. Each of the lists obtained would then be sampled, to provide samples of church members for study.[5]

---

5. For an example, see Charles Y. Glock, Benjamin B. Ringer, and Earl R. Babbie, *To Comfort and to Challenge* (Berkeley: University of California Press, 1967), app. A.

Another typical situation concerns sampling among population areas such as a city. While there is no single list of a city's population, citizens reside on discrete city blocks or census blocks. It is possible, therefore, to select a sample of blocks initially, create a list of persons living on each of the selected blocks, and subsample persons on each block.

In a more complex design, the researcher might sample blocks, list the households on each selected block, sample the households, list the persons residing in each household, and, finally, sample persons within each selected household. This multistage sample design would lead to the ultimate selection of a sample of individuals but would not require the initial listing of all individuals comprising the city's population.

Multistage cluster sampling, then, involves the repetition of two basic steps: listing and sampling. The list of primary sampling units (churches, blocks) is compiled and, perhaps, stratified for sampling. Then a sample of those units is selected. The selected primary sampling units are then listed and perhaps stratified. The list of secondary sampling units is then sampled, and so forth. The actual methods of listing and sampling will be spelled out in considerable detail in the examples in Chapter 7.

Cluster sampling is highly recommended by its efficiency, but that efficiency comes at a price in terms of accuracy. Whereas a simple random sample drawn from a population list is subject to a single sampling error, a two-stage cluster sample is subject to two sampling errors. First, the initial sample of clusters will represent the population of clusters only within a range of sampling error. Second, the sample of elements selected within a given cluster will represent all the elements in that cluster only within a range of sampling error. Thus, for example, the researcher runs a certain risk of selecting a sample of disproportionately wealthy city blocks, plus a sample of disproportionately wealthy households within those blocks. The best solution to this problem lies in the number of clusters selected initially and the number of elements selected within each.

Typically, the researcher is restricted to a total sample size; for example, he may be limited to conducting 2,000 interviews in a city. Given this broad limitation, however, the researcher has several options in designing his cluster sample. At the extremes he might choose one cluster and select 2,000 elements within that cluster; or he might select 2,000 clusters with one element selected within each. Of course, neither of these extremes is advisable, but the researcher is faced with a broad range of choices between them. Fortunately, the logic of sampling distributions provides a general guideline to be followed.

Recall that sampling error is reduced by two factors: an increase in the sample size and an increased homogeneity of the elements being sampled. These factors operate at each level of a multistage sample design. A sample of clusters will best represent all clusters if a large number are selected and if all clusters are very much alike. A sample of elements will best represent all elements in a given cluster if a large number are selected from the cluster and if all the elements in the cluster are very much alike.

With a given total sample size, however, if the number of clusters is increased, the number of elements within a cluster must be decreased. In this respect, the representativeness of the clusters is increased at the expense of more poorly representing the elements comprising each of those clusters, or vice versa. Fortunately, the factor of homogeneity can be used to ease this dilemma.

Typically, the elements comprising a given natural cluster within a population are more homogeneous than are all elements comprising the total population. The members of a given church are more alike than are all church members; the residents of a given city block are more alike than are all the residents of a whole city. As a result, relatively fewer elements may be needed to adequately represent a given natural cluster, while a larger number of clusters may be needed to adequately represent the diversity found among the clusters. This fact is most clearly seen in the extreme case of very different clusters that are comprised of exactly identical elements within each. In such a situation, a large number of clusters would adequately represent the variety among clusters, while only one element within each cluster would adequately represent all its members. Although this extreme situation never exists in reality, it is closer to the truth in most cases than its opposite: identical clusters comprised of grossly divergent elements.

The general guideline for cluster design, then, is to maximize the number of clusters selected while decreasing the number of elements within each cluster. It must be noted, however, that this scientific guideline must be balanced against an administrative constraint. The efficiency of cluster sampling is based on the ability to minimize the listing of population elements. By initially selecting clusters, the researcher must list only the elements comprising the selected clusters, not all elements in the entire population. Increasing the number of clusters, however, goes directly against this efficiency factor in cluster sampling. A small number of clusters may be listed more quickly and more cheaply than a large number. (Remember that all the elements in a selected cluster must be listed even if only a few are to be chosen in the sample.)

The final sample design will reflect these two constraints. In effect, the researcher probably will select as many clusters as he can afford. Lest this issue be left too open-ended at this point, one rule of thumb may be presented. Population researchers conventionally aim for the selection of five households per census block. If a total of 2,000 households are to be interviewed, the researcher would aim at 400 blocks with five household interviews on each. We shall return to this rule of thumb in the later examples of sample designs, but it is mentioned at this point to buoy up the spirits of the reader.

Before turning to more detailed procedures available to cluster sampling, it bears repeating that this method almost inevitably involves a loss of accuracy. The manner in which this appears, however, is somewhat complex. First, as noted earlier, a multistage sample design is subject to a sampling error at each of its stages. Since the sample size is necessarily smaller at each stage than the total sample size, the sampling error at each stage will be greater than would be the case for a single-stage random sample of elements. Second, sampling error is estimated on the basis of observed variance among the sample elements. When those elements are drawn from among relatively homogeneous clusters, the estimates of sampling error will be too optimistic and must be corrected in the light of the cluster sample design. (This will be discussed in detail in the later consideration of univariate analysis.)

Multistage Cluster Sampling, Stratification

Thus far, we have discussed cluster sampling as though a simple random sample were selected at each stage of the design. In fact, it is possible to employ stratification techniques as discussed earlier to refine and improve the sample being selected.

Later examples will detail possible methods of stratification, but for the present we should note that the basic options available are essentially the same as those possible in single-stage sampling from a list. In selecting a national sample of churches, for example, the researcher might initially stratify his list of churches by denomination, geographical region, size, rural or urban location, and perhaps by some measure of social class. United States Census information may be used by population researchers to stratify census blocks in terms of ethnic composition, social class, property values, quality of structures, nature of property ownership, and size.

Once the primary sampling units (churches, blocks) have been grouped according to the relevant, available stratification variables, either simple random or systematic sampling techniques could be used to select the sample. The researcher might select a specified number of units from each group or *stratum*, or he might arrange the stratified clusters in a continuous list and systematically sample that list.

To the extent that clusters are combined into homogeneous strata, the sampling error at this stage will be reduced. The primary goal of stratification, as before, is homogeneity.

There is no reason why stratification could not take place at each level of sampling. The elements listed within a selected cluster might be stratified prior to the next stage of sampling. Typically, however, this is not done. (Recall the assumption of relative homogeneity within clusters.)

Probability Proportionate to Size (PPS) Sampling

Thus far, we have spoken in a general way about the assignment of sample elements to selected clusters: how many clusters should be selected, how many elements within each cluster? This section discusses in greater detail two options available to the researcher.

To insure the overall selection of a representative sample of elements, the researcher should give each element in the total population an equal chance of selection. The simplest way to accomplish this in a cluster sample would be to give each cluster the same chance of selection and to select a given *proportion* of elements from each selected cluster. Thus with a population of 100,000 elements grouped in 1,000 clusters (of varying sizes) and a total sample target of 1,000 elements, the researcher might select one-tenth of the clusters (100) with equal probability and subselect one-tenth of the elements in each of the clusters initially chosen. In this fashion approximately 1,000 elements would be selected and each element in the population would have had the same $(1/10 \times 1/10 = 1/100)$ probability of selection. While this type of sample selection technique is the clearest and simplest, it is not the most efficient.

Most cluster sampling involves clusters of grossly different sizes (in numbers of elements). The religion researcher finds very large churches and very small ones. The population researcher finds city blocks containing many people and blocks containing very few. Moreover, it is often the case that the small clusters outnumber the large ones, although the large ones may account for a large proportion of the total population. Thus a few, very large, city blocks may contain a large proportion of a city's population, while a large number of small blocks actually contain only a small proportion of the population.

The selection of clusters with equal probability, with a fixed proportion of elements being taken from the selected clusters, will result in the following situation. (1) A relatively small number of large clusters would be selected in the first stage of sampling. (2) The elements selected to represent all elements in large clusters would be drawn from very few such clusters. In the extreme, then, all of a city's population residing on 10 large city blocks · might be represented by a people living in only one of those blocks.

An earlier section on cluster sampling discussed the greater efficiency inherent in the selection of many clusters with few elements being drawn from each of those clusters. This principle is put into practice through the method of **probability proportionate to size** (PPS) sampling. This method provides for the selection of more clusters, insures the representation of elements contained in large clusters, and also gives each element in the population an equal chance of selection.

Clearly, PPS cluster sampling is not possible unless the researcher knows the number of elements in each of his clusters. As will be illustrated in the final example of Chapter 7, however, it is not necessary for him to know exactly how many elements are in each cluster. A set of fairly good estimates is sufficient. Corrections can be made during later stages of the sampling process to account for erroneous estimates.

In the first stage of sampling, each cluster is given a chance of selection proportionate to its size (in number of elements). Large clusters have a better chance of selection than small ones. In the second stage of sampling, however, the same *number* of elements are chosen from each selected cluster. The effect of these two procedures is to equalize the ultimate probabilities of selection of all elements, since elements in large clusters stand a poorer chance of selection *within* their cluster than those in small clusters. For example, a city block containing 100 households will have 10 times the chance of selection as a block containing only 10 households. However, if both blocks are selected, and the same number of households is selected from each, households on the large block will have only $\frac{1}{10}$ the chance of selection of those on the small one. The following formula indicates a given element's probability of selection in a PPS sample design.

If 100 clusters are selected and 10 elements are selected from each of those out of a total population of 100,000, the overall probability of

$$
\begin{bmatrix} \text{Element} \\ \text{Probability} \end{bmatrix} = \begin{bmatrix} \text{Number of} \\ \text{Clusters} \\ \text{Selected} \end{bmatrix} \times \begin{bmatrix} \dfrac{\text{Cluster Size}}{\text{Population Size}} \end{bmatrix} \times \begin{bmatrix} \dfrac{\text{Elements} \\ \text{Selected} \\ \text{per Cluster}}{\text{Cluster Size}} \end{bmatrix}
$$

selection for each element will be 1,000/100,000 or 1/100. In a cluster containing 100 elements, that cluster has a probability of selection equal to 100 (clusters to be selected) times 100/100,000 (cluster size/population size) or 1/10; each element has a chance of 10/100 (elements per cluster/cluster size) or 1/10 of being selected *within* that cluster; the element's overall chance of selection in this case is 1/10 times 1/10 or 1/100. For a cluster containing only 10 elements, that cluster's probability of selection is 100 times 10/100,000 or 1/100, but each element's chance of selection within the cluster is 10/10 or 1, making the overall chance of selection equal to 1/100.

Regardless of the number of elements in a cluster, then, each element has the same probability of selection ultimately. This may be seen more clearly in the formula when we note that cluster size appears in both the numerator and the denominator and may be cancelled out: the probability of selection then becomes the number of clusters to be chosen times the number of elements to be chosen from each selected cluster, divided by the population size. This is, of course, the sample size divided by the population size.

Two modifications are typically made in this PPS sample design. First, the researcher may feel it is imperative that *very large* clusters be represented in the sample; he may wish to insure that all city blocks (or churches) with more than, say, 1,000 elements be included in the sample. In such a case, he may select all those clusters in the beginning (with a probability of 1.0) and the elements in those clusters should be given a probability equal to the overall sampling ratio. In the previous example, 1/100 of the elements on each of the large blocks might be selected.

The second modification concerns small clusters. If a standard number of elements is to be selected from each of the clusters chosen, clusters containing fewer elements than that standard number present a problem. If the target is 10 households from each selected city block, what will he do with blocks containing five households? The usual solution to this problem is to combine small clusters so that each combination contains at least the standard number to be selected. (If the clusters are stratified, combinations should be accomplished within strata. Similarly, small clusters may be attached to larger ones if this procedure will insure a greater homogeneity within the combined cluster.) The example of an area cluster sample in Chapter 7 indicates the necessity of taking this step to insure the consideration of blocks believed to have no households on them.

By way of summary, cluster sampling is a difficult though important sampling method—it may be required whenever it is impossible to compile a list of all the elements comprising the population under study. The preceding discussion of cluster sampling has been regrettably abstract, but the example given in Chapter 7 will provide a clearer picture of the actual steps involved in a complex sample selection.

Disproportionate Sampling and Weighting

Ultimately, a probability sample is representative of a population if all elements in the population have an equal chance of selection in that sample. Thus, in each of the preceding discussions we have noted that the various sampling procedures result in an equal chance of selection—even though the ultimate selection probability is the product of several partial probabilities.

More generally, however, a probability sample is one in which each population element has a *known nonzero* probability of selection—even though different elements may have different probabilities. If controlled probability sampling procedures have been used, any such sample may be representative of the population from which it is drawn if each sample element is assigned a weight equal to the inverse of its probability of selection. Thus, where all sample elements have had the same chance of selection, each is given the same weight: 1. (This is called a "self-weighting" sample.)

Disproportionate sampling and weighting come into play in two basic ways. First, the researcher may sample subpopulations disproportionately to insure sufficient numbers of cases from each for analysis. For example, a given city may have a suburban area containing one-fourth of its total population. Yet the researcher may be especially interested in a detailed analysis of households in that area and may feel that one-fourth of this total sample size would be too few. As a result, he may decide to select the same number of households from the suburban area as from the remainder of the city. Households in the suburban area, then, are given a disproportionately better chance of selection than those located elsewhere in the city.

As long as the researcher analyzes the two area samples separately or comparatively, he need not worry about the differential sampling. If he wishes to combine the two samples to create a composite picture of the entire city, however, he must take the disproportionate sampling into account. If n is the number of households selected from each area, then the households in the suburban area had a chance of selection equal to n divided by one-fourth of the total city population. Since the total city population and the sample size are the same for both areas, the suburban-area households should be given a weight of $\frac{1}{4}n$ while the remaining households should be given a weight of $\frac{3}{4}n$. This weighting procedure could be simplified by merely giving a weight of 3 to each of the households selected outside the suburban area. (This procedure would give a *proportionate* representation to each sample element. The population figure would have to be included in the weighting if population estimates were desired.)

Disproportionate sampling and weighting procedures are sometimes used in situations involving the errors and approximation that are often inherent in complex, multistage sampling. This will be discussed in some detail in the example of an area cluster sample in Chapter 7, but it is appropriate to list here the basic conditions under which weighting is often required.

1. In stratified cluster sampling, a given number of clusters may be selected from each stratum, although the sizes of the different strata will vary. Differential weighting may be used to adjust for these variations.

2. A given cluster may be selected in a PPS sample design on the basis of its expected or estimated size, but a field investigation may later indicate the initial estimate was in error. Thus the cluster was given a disproportionately high or low chance of selection, and weighting may be used to adjust for that error.

3. A sample design may call for the selection of one-tenth of the elements in a cluster, but the cluster might contain 52 elements, only five of which are selected for study. Weighting can be used to adjust for the .2 element which logically could not be selected.

4. Ten elements might have been selected for study within a cluster, but two of these could not be studied (for example, refused to be interviewed). Assuming homogeneity within the cluster, the researcher might assign a weight of 1.25 to each of the studied elements to make up for the two that were not studied.

All of these uses of weighting will be illustrated in the final sampling example of Chapter 7. With the exception of case 4 above, however, the researcher can derive his own weighting procedure by carefully determining the probability of selection—step-by-step—for each sample element and assigning a weight equal to the inverse of that probability. Three further points should be discussed before moving on from the topic of weighting.

Degrees of Precision in Weighting

In any complex sample design, the researcher faces a number of options with regard to weighting in connection with purposively or inadvertently disproportionate sampling. He may compute weights for each element to several decimal places, or he may assign rough weights to account for only the grossest instances of disproportionate sampling. In the previous case of the city in which the suburban area was oversampled, it is unlikely that the population of that area comprised exactly one-fourth of the city's population: suppose it actually comprised .25001, .2600, or .2816 of the total population. In the first instance, it seems quite likely that the researcher would choose to apply the rough overall weighting of cases described if no other disproportionate sampling were involved at other stages in the sample design. Perhaps he would do the same in the second and third instances as well. The precision he will seek in weighting should be commensurate with the precision he desires in his findings. If his research purposes can tolerate errors of a few percentage points, he will probably not waste his time and effort in weighting exactly. In deciding the degree of precision required, moreover, he should take into account the degree of error to be expected from normal sampling distribution, plus all the various types of nonsampling error.

Ultimately, there is no firm guideline for the researcher to follow in determining the precision to be sought in weighting. As in so many other aspects of survey design, he is afforded considerable latitude. At the same time, however, he should bear his decision in mind when reporting his findings. He should not employ only a rough weighting procedure and then suggest that his findings are accurate within a minuscule range of error.

Methods for Weighting

Having outlined the scientific concerns for determining the degree of precision desired in weighting, I should note that the choice will often be made on the basis of available methods for weighting. There are three basic methods for weighting.

1. For the rough weighting of samples drawn from subpopulations, weighted tables can be constructed from the unweighted tables for each of the subsamples. In the earlier example, the researcher could create a raw table of distributions for the suburban sample and for the nonsuburban sample separately, triple the number of cases in each cell of the nonsuburban table, add the cases across the two tables, and compute percentages for the composite table.

2. For more extensive and faster, though still rough, weighting, machine-readable cards can be mechanically reproduced for those cases requiring weights. In the previous example two additional copies of each card relating to a nonsuburban household could be made (for a total of three each), the enlarged nonsuburban file could then be combined with the suburban file, and the entire card file could be analyzed as though three times as many nonsuburban households had been studied.

3. If the data are to be analyzed by computer, a special program may be designed to assign a precise weight to each case in the original data file. Only this latter method is appropriate to refined weighting, since it is impossible to reproduce fractions of cards with any meaning.

As mentioned at the outset of this section, scientific concerns in weighting are usually subjugated to practical concerns in this instance as in others. If the analysis is to be conducted through cards only, weighting must of necessity be approximate rather than precise.

Weighting and Statistical Inference

The reader should be advised that the weighting procedures described in this section have serious effects on most computations related to statistical inference. Researchers whose research purposes require precise statistical inferences (for example, population estimates) on the basis of carefully weighted data should consult a special source[6] on this matter or, better yet, should consult a sampling statistician *before the sample is designed*.

Probability Sampling in Overview

The preceding lengthy and detailed discussion has been devoted to the key sampling method utilized in controlled survey research: probability sampling. In each of the variations examined, we have seen that elements are chosen for study from a population on a basis of random selection with known nonzero probabilities.

Depending on the field situation, probability sampling can be very simple, or it can be extremely difficult, time-consuming, and expensive. Whatever the situation, however, it remains the most effective method for the selection of study elements. There are two reasons for this.

First, probability sampling avoids conscious or unconscious biases in element selection on the part of the researcher. If all elements in the population have an equal (or unequal and subsequently weighted) chance of selection, there is an excellent chance that the sample so selected will closely represent the population of all elements.

Second, probability sampling permits estimates of sampling error. While no probability sample will be perfectly representative in all respects, controlled selection methods permit the researcher to estimate the degree of expected error in that regard.

Having discussed probability sampling at some length, we shall turn now to a briefer examination of some popular methods of nonprobability sampling.

6.7
Nonprobability Sampling

Despite the accepted superiority of probability sampling methods in survey research, nonprobability methods are sometimes used instead—usually for situations in which probability sampling would be prohibitively expensive or when precise representativeness is not necessary. The primary methods of nonprobability sampling are described briefly below.

Purposive or Judgmental Sampling

Occasionally it may be appropriate for the researcher to select his sample on the basis of his own knowledge of the population, its elements, and

---

6. For example, Kish, *op. cit.*

the nature of his research aims. Especially in the initial design of his questionnaire, he might wish to select the widest variety of respondents to test the broad applicability of questions. While the survey findings would not represent any meaningful population, the test run might effectively uncover any peculiar defects in his research instrument. This situation would be referred to as a pretest, however, rather than a survey proper.

In some instances, the researcher may wish to study a small subset of a larger population in which many members of the subset are easily identified but the enumeration of all would be nearly impossible. For example, he might want to study the leadership of a student protest movement; many of the leaders are easily visible, but it would not be feasible to define and sample all leaders. In studying all or a sample of the most visible leaders, he may collect data sufficient for his purposes.

In a multistage sample design, the researcher may want to compare left-wing and right-wing students. As he may not be able to enumerate and sample from all such students, he might decide to sample the memberships of Students for a Democratic Society and Young Americans for Freedom. Although such a sample design would not provide a good description of either left-wing or right-wing students as a whole, it might suffice for general comparative purposes.

Sampling of selected precincts for political polls is a somewhat refined judgmental process. On the basis of previous voting results in a given area (city, state, nation), the researcher purposively selects a group of voting precincts that, in combination, produces results similar to those of the entire area. Then, in subsequent polls, he selects his samples solely from those precincts. The theory is, of course, that the selected precincts provide a cross section of the entire electorate.

Each time there is an election that permits the researcher to evaluate the adequacy of his group of precincts, he considers revisions, additions, or deletions. His goal is to update his group of precincts to insure that it will provide a good representation of all precincts.

To be done effectively, selected precinct sampling requires considerable political expertise. The researcher should be well versed in the political and social history of the area under consideration so that the selection of precincts is based on an *educated* guess as to its persistent representativeness. In addition, this system of sampling requires continuing feedback to be effective. The researcher must be in a position to conduct frequent polls and must have periodic electoral validations.

Quota Sampling

Quota sampling begins with a matrix describing the characteristics of the target population. The researcher must know what proportion of the population is male and what proportion female, for example; and for each sex, what proportion falls into various age categories, and so forth. In establishing a national quota sample, he must know what proportion of the national population is say, urban, Eastern, male, under 25, white, working class, and the like, and all the other permutations of such a matrix.

Once such a matrix has been created and a relative proportion assigned to each cell in the matrix, the researcher collects data from persons having all the characteristics of a given cell. All the persons in the given cell are then assigned a weight appropriate to their portion of the total population. When all the sample elements are so weighted, the overall data should provide a reasonable representation of the total population.

There are a number of inherent problems in quota sampling. First, the quota frame (the proportions that different cells represent) must be accurate, and it is often difficult to get up-to-date information for this purpose. The Gallup failure to predict Truman as the presidential victor in 1948 was due partly to this problem.

Second, biases may exist in the selection of sample elements within a given cell—even though its proportion of the population is accurately estimated. An interviewer, instructed to interview five persons meeting a given, complex set of characteristics, may still avoid persons living at the top of seven-story walk-ups, having particularly run-down homes, or owning vicious dogs.

In recent years, attempts have been made to combine probability and quota sampling methods, but the effectiveness of this effort remains to be seen. At present, the researcher would be advised to treat quota sampling warily.

Reliance on Available Subjects

Stopping people at a street corner or some other location is almost never an adequate sampling method, although it is employed all too frequently. It would be justified only if the researcher wanted to study the characteristics of people passing the sampling point at specified times.

University researchers frequently conduct surveys among the students enrolled in large lecture classes. The ease and inexpense of such a method explains its popularity, but it seldom produces data of any general value. It may serve the purpose of a pretest of a questionnaire, but such a sampling method should not be used for a study purportedly describing students as a whole.

6.8
Summary

Chapter 6, a rather lengthy one, has presented the basic logic and some of the techniques of probability sampling. In addition, it has discussed, more briefly, some methods for nonprobability sampling. Since rigorous sampling methods have been developed and used primarily within the context of survey research, most of the discussions have focused on that method. It is important for you to realize, however, that the basic logic and many of the specific techniques of sampling discussed in this chapter are equally applicable to other research methods, such as content analysis, experimentation, and even field research.

The chapter began with an introductory discussion of what sampling is and why sampling methods are used. We noted that social researchers are often interested in describing and explaining certain characteristics of very large populations. Since it is often impossible—in terms of time and money—to observe all the members of such populations, the researcher may select a smaller subset—a sample—of members from that population. He then observes his sample and infers that what he learns about the sample will also be true of the population from which it was drawn.

We noted that the history of sampling in social research has been a rather spotty one, containing the well-known snafus of the *Literary Digest* poll of 1936 and the Gallup poll of 1948. More recently, however, sampling techniques have yielded results that are extremely accurate reflections of the characteristics of large populations.

Most of the chapter dealt with the logic of probability sampling, based on probability theory. We noted that these controlled sampling methods have three basic advantages: (1) they rule out the human biases that might be involved in the more casual selection of people to be observed, (2) they enhance the likelihood that a sample drawn from a population will be representative, that is, it will have essentially the same distribution of characteristics as the population from which it is drawn, and (3) probability theory provides a set of computational methods for estimating the degree of error to be expected in a given sample. The basic principle involved in probability sampling is that every member of the total population shall have a known, nonzero probability of being selected into the sample. In the simplest case, each member will have the same probability of being selected.

The chapter then illustrated the logic of probability sampling by introducing the notion of a sampling distribution, the expected variety of samples that would be drawn from a given population. Although none of the samples would be likely to reflect *perfectly* all the characteristics of the total population, we saw the distribution of different degrees of error (sampling error) in such samples. This model was then turned inside out to permit the estimation of the accuracy of a single sample in describing the larger population.

Next, the chapter turned to an examination of sampling frames, the lists or quasi-lists of population members that constitute the fundamental resource in the selection of a sample. We discussed the relative quality of several commonly used sampling frames.

The remainder of the chapter was devoted to some of the many concrete sampling techniques that are used in sample selection. Most of this discussion focused on different types of probability sampling techniques, with less attention given to some of the available nonprobability sampling techniques.

6.9
Main Points

1. A sample is a special subset of a population that is observed for purposes of making inferences about the nature of the total population itself.

2. Although the sampling methods used earlier in this century often produced misleading inferences, current techniques are far more accurate and reliable.

3. The chief criterion of the quality of a sample is the degree to which it is representative—the extent to which the characteristics of the sample are the same as those of the population from which it was selected.

4. Probability sampling methods provide one excellent way of selecting samples that will be quite representative.

5. The most carefully selected sample will almost never provide a perfect representation of the population from which it was selected. There will always be some degree of sampling error.

6. Probability sampling methods make it possible for the researcher to estimate the amount of sampling error that should be expected in a given sample.

7. The chief principle of probability sampling is that every member of the total population have some known nonzero probability of being selected into the sample.

8. An EPSEM sample is one in which every member of a population has the same probability of being selected.

9. A sampling frame is a list or quasi-list of the members of a population. It is the resource used in the selection of a sample. A sample's representativeness depends directly on the extent to which a sampling frame contains all the members of the total population that the sample is intended to represent.

10. Simple random sampling is logically the most fundamental technique in probability sampling, though it is seldom used in practice.

11. Systematic sampling involves the selection of every *k*th member from a sampling frame. This method is functionally equivalent to simple random sampling, with a few exceptions, and it is a more practical method.

12. Stratification is the process of grouping the members of a population into relatively homogeneous strata prior to sampling. This practice has the effect of improving the representativeness of a sample by reducing the degree of sampling error.

13. Multistage cluster sampling is a more complex sampling technique that is frequently used in those cases in which a list of all the members of a population does not exist. An initial sample of groups of members

(clusters) is selected first. Then, all the members of the selected clusters are listed, often through direct observation in the field. Finally, the members listed in each of the selected clusters are subsampled, thereby providing the final sample of members.

14. Probability proportionate to size (PPS) is a special efficient method for multistage cluster sampling.

15. If the members of a population have unequal probabilities of selection into the sample, it is necessary to assign weights to the different observations made in order to provide a representative picture of the total population. Basically, the weight assigned to a particular sample member should be the inverse of its probability of selection.

16. Purposive sampling is a type of nonprobability sampling method in which the researcher uses his own judgment in the selection of sample members. It is sometimes called a judgmental sample.

17. Quota sampling is another nonprobability sampling method. The researcher begins with a detailed description of the characteristics of the total population (quota matrix) and then selects his sample members in such a fashion as to include different composite profiles that exist in the population. The representativeness of a quota sample depends in large part on the accuracy of the quota matrix as a reflection of the characteristics of the population.

18. In general, nonprobability sampling methods are regarded as less reliable than probability sampling methods. On the other hand, they are often easier and cheaper to use.

6.10
Annotated Bibliography

Kish, Leslie, *Survey Sampling* (New York: John Wiley, 1965). Unquestionably the definitive work on sampling in social research. Let's not beat around the bush: if you need to know something more about sampling than was contained in this chapter, there is only one place to go. Kish's coverage ranges from the simplest matters to the most complex and mathematical. He is both highly theoretical and downright practical. Easily readable and difficult passages intermingle as Kish exhausts everything you could want or need to know about each aspect of sampling. It seems to me altogether possible that nobody will ever write another book on this subject.

7
Examples of Sample Designs

7.1
Introduction

Chapter 6 presented the basic logic of survey sampling and outlined some of the procedural options available to the researcher. This chapter will present four case studies of sample designs, representing different sampling situations and designs.

The first example is a stratified systematic sample of students attending the University of Hawaii during the fall 1968 semester. The second example is a cluster sample of medical school faculty members, with the primary sampling units selected with equal probability. The third concerns a cluster sample of Episcopal women in northern California, using a PPS (probability proportionate to size) design for primary sampling unit selection. The final example is a complex area sample designed for a household survey In Oakland, California, in 1966.

7.2
Sampling University Students

The purpose of this study was to survey, with a self-administered instrument, a representative cross section of students attending the main campus of the University of Hawaii in 1968. The following sections will describe the steps and decisions involved in selecting that sample.

Survey Population and Sampling Frame

The obvious sampling frame available for use in this sample selection was the magnetic registration tape maintained by the university administration. The tape contained students' names, local and permanent addresses, social security numbers, and a variety of other information such as field of study, class, age, sex, and so forth.

The registration tape, however, contains files on all persons who could, by any conceivable definition, be called students, many of whom seemed inappropriate to the purposes of the study. As a result, it was necessary to define the *survey population* in a somewhat more restricted fashion. The final definition included those 15,225 day program degree candidates registered for the fall 1968 semester on the Manoa campus of the university, including all colleges and departments, both undergraduate and graduate students, and both American and foreign students. The computer program used for sampling, therefore, limited consideration to students fitting this definition.

Stratification

The sampling program also permitted the stratification of students prior to sample selection. In this instance, it was decided that stratification by college class would be sufficient, although the students might have been further stratified within class if desired, by sex, college, major, and so forth.

Sample Selection

Once the students had been arranged by class (by the sampling program), a systematic sample was selected across the entire rearranged list. The sample size for the study was initially set at 1,100. To achieve this sample, the sampling program was set to employ a 1/14 sampling fraction. The program, therefore, generated a random number between 1 and 14; the student having that number and every fourteenth student thereafter were selected in the sample.

Once the sample had been selected in this fashion, the computer was instructed to print each student's name and mailing address on six self-adhesive mailing labels. These labels were then simply transferred to envelopes for mailing the questionnaires.

Sample Modification

The preceding describes the initial design of the sample for the study of university students. Prior to the mailing of questionnaires, it was discovered that unexpected expenses in the production of the questionnaires made it impossible to cover the costs of mailing to some 1,100 students. As a result, one-third of the mailing labels were systematically selected (with a random start) for exclusion from the sample. The final sample for the study was thereby reduced to about 770.

This modification to the sample is mentioned here to illustrate the frequent necessity to change aspects of the study plan in midstream. Since a systematic sample of students was omitted from the initial systematic sample, the resulting 770 students could still be taken as reasonably representing the survey population. The reduction in sample size did, of course, increase the range of sampling error.

7.3

Sampling Medical School Faculty

This section reports the sample design employed to select a sample of medical school faculty members for a national survey on the effects of scientific orientations on humane patient care. The study design called for a national sample of medical school faculty members in the departments of medicine and pediatrics.

Under ideal conditions, the researcher would have obtained or constructed a single list of all faculty members in the two departments and would have selected his sample from that list. Unfortunately, no such list appeared to exist, so the decision was made to select a two-stage cluster sample. In the first stage, a sample of medical schools would be selected; then faculty members would be selected from each of those schools.

The sample design was hampered by unavailable data from the very beginning. The study design called for an examination of both full-time and part-time faculty members. While there were approximately 3,700 full-time faculty in the two departments nationally at the time of the study, there were no good data concerning the numbers of part-time faculty. An analysis of existing data, however, suggested that the total number of both full-time and part-time faculty was around 12,000. For the purposes of the study, it was decided that a sample of 2,000 would be sufficient (an overall sampling fraction of 1/6).

The Selection of Medical Schools

At the time of the study, there were 84 four-year medical schools belonging to the Association of American Medical Colleges. These schools comprised the survey population of schools. The schools were arranged into geographical strata, and they were then arranged by size (number of students) within strata.

The stratified list of schools was numbered from 1 to 84, and a random number was selected between 1 and 6 (the sampling interval). The school having the number so selected and every sixth school thereafter were selected at the first stage of sampling. Letters were then sent to the deans of the selected schools, explaining the purpose of the survey and asking their assistance in getting a list of the faculty members in their departments of medicine and pediatrics.

Fourteen medical schools were initially selected. Not all deans were willing to cooperate with the study, however. As refusals were received, an alternative school for each was selected from the list: a school adjacent on the list to the refusing school was chosen through the toss of a coin.

Faculty Member Selection

As soon as a medical school dean agreed to cooperate with the survey, a list was compiled of all the faculty members in the departments of medicine and pediatrics at his school. All such faculty were included in the final sample and were mailed survey questionnaires.

It should be noted that this sample design was not the best one that might have been employed. The entire sample of faculty members was selected from relatively few schools. A better design would have selected more schools, with fewer faculty selected from each. For example, one-third of the schools might have been selected, with half the faculty at each studied.

The actual sample design was prompted by administrative rather than scientific concerns. A pilot study in the project had shown the difficulty of gaining approval and cooperation from deans. Even when a dean agreed to cooperate with the study, he might be rather slow in providing a list of faculty members. The main bottleneck in sampling came at this point. Increasing the number of schools would directly increase the time and problems involved in the overall sample selection. For this reason alone, the decision was made to take one-sixth of the schools and all the appropriate faculty at each.

7.4
Sampling Episcopal Churchwomen

The purpose of this study was to examine the attitudes of women members of churches in a diocese of the Episcopal Church. A representative sample of all churchwomen in the diocese was desired. As the reader will by now expect, there was no single list of such women, so a multistage sample design was created. In the initial stage of sampling, churches were selected, and then women were selected from each. Unlike the medical school sample, the church sample was selected with *probability proportionate to size* (PPS).

Selecting the Churches

The diocese in question publishes an annual report that contains a listing of the 100 or so churches comprising it with their respective sizes in terms of membership. This listing constituted the sampling frame for the first stage of sampling.

A total of approximately 500 respondents were desired for the study, so the decision was made to select 25 churches with probability proportionate to size and take 20 women from each of those selected. To accomplish this, the list of churches was arranged geographically, and then a table was created similar to the partial listing shown in Table 7-1.

Beside each church in the table, its membership was entered, and that figure was used to compute a cumulative total running through the list.

Table 7-1. Form Used in Listing of Churches

Church	Membership	Cumulative Membership
Church A	3,000	3,000
Church B	5,000	8,000
Church C	1,000	9,000

The final total came to approximately 200,000. The object at this point was to select a sample of 25 churches in such a way that each would have a chance of selection proportionate to the number of members in it. To accomplish this, the cumulative totals were used to create ranges of numbers for each church equaling the number of members in that church. Church A in the table above was assigned the numbers 1 through 3,000; Church B was assigned 3,001 through 8,000; Church C was assigned 8,001 through 9,000; and so forth.

By selecting 25 numbers ranging between 1 and 200,000, it would be possible to select 25 churches for the study. The 25 numbers were selected in a systematic sample as follows. The sampling interval was set at 8,000 (200,000/25) and a random start was selected between 1 and 8,000. Let us say the random number was 4,538. Since that number fell within the range of numbers assigned to Church B (3,001–8,000), Church B was selected.

Increments of 8,000 (the sampling interval) were then added to the random start, and every church within whose range one of the resultant numbers appeared was selected into the sample of churches. It should be apparent that in this fashion, each church in the diocese had a chance of selection directly proportionate to its membership size. A church with 4,000 members had twice the chance of selection as a church of 2,000 and 10 times the chance of selection as one with only 400 members.

Selecting the Churchwomen

Once the sample of churches was selected, arrangements were made to get lists of the women members of each. It is worth noting here that in practice the lists varied greatly in their form and content. In a number of cases, lists of all members (men and women) were provided, and it was necessary to sort out the women before sampling the lists. The form of the lists varied from typed lists to 3 x 5 cards printed from mailing address plates.

As the list arrived from a selected church, a sampling interval for that church was computed on the basis of the number of women members and the number desired (20). If a church contained 2,000 women, the sample interval, therefore, was set at 100. A random number was selected and incremented by the sampling interval to select the sample of women from that church. This procedure was repeated for each church.

Note that this sample design ultimately gives every woman in the diocese an equal chance of selection *only* if the assumption is made that half the members of each church are women (or if a constant proportion of them are). This is due to the fact that churches were given a chance of selection based on their *total* membership (numbers of women were not available). Given the aims of this particular study, the slight inequities of selection were considered insignificant.

A more sophisticated sample design for the second stage would have resolved this possible problem. Since each church was given a chance of selection based on an assumed number of women (assuming 1,000 women in a church of 2,000), the sampling interval could have been computed on the basis of that assumption rather than on the actual number of women listed. If it were assumed in the first stage of sampling that a church had 1,000 women (out of a membership of 2,000), the sampling interval could have been set at 50 (1,000/20). Then this interval could have been used in the selection of respondents regardless of the actual number of women listed for that church. If 1,000 women were in fact listed, then their church had the proper chance of selection and 20 women would be selected from it. If 1,200 women were listed, that would mean that the church had too small a chance of selection, but this would have been remedied through the selection of 24 women using the preestablished sampling interval. If only 800 women were listed, on the other hand, only 16 would have been selected.

7.5
Sampling Oakland Households

This final example represents one of the most complex sample designs typical of survey research: an *area cluster sample.* The purpose of this study, conducted in 1966, was to collect data relevant to the study of poverty in the poorer areas of Oakland, California, using the remainder of the city for purposes of comparison. Since the findings of the survey were to be used, in part, to support requests for federal funding for Oakland, it was essential that the data collected provide an accurate description of the city.

For purposes of the study, the city was divided into seven areas; four were officially designated poverty areas, while the remaining three were traditionally viewed as distinct sections of the city. (See Figure 7-1.) The total sample size for the city was set at 3,500 households on the basis of computations whose complexity exceeds the scope of this book. It is worth noting, however, that the determination of the sample size began with policy discussion concerning the "chance" city officials were willing to take that the survey would—through normal sampling error—underestimate poverty and unemployment levels sufficiently to disqualify the city in its request for funding. If these levels were, in fact, high enough to warrant the award of funds, then a perfectly accurate sample would demonstrate this fact. With a small sample, however, the range of sampling error opened the possibility of underestimation. As the sample size was increased, of course, the chance of this underestimation was reduced. It was in this manner, then, that the ultimate sample size of 3,500 was established. (*Note:* This is the way sample sizes *should* be established.)

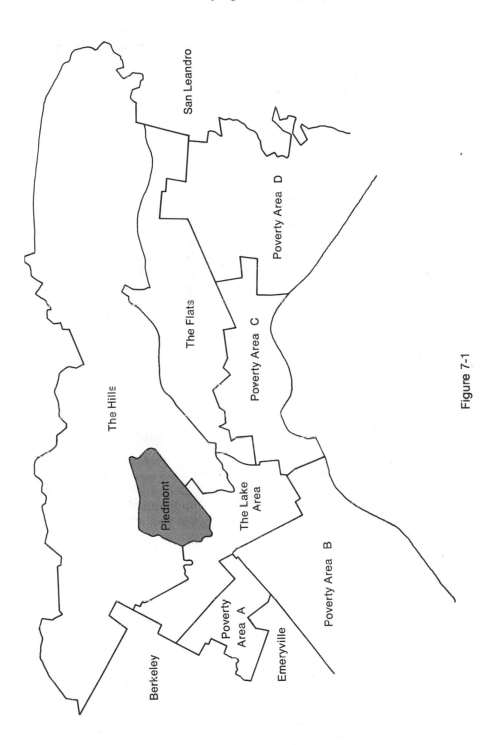

San Leandro

Poverty Area D

The Flats

Poverty Area C

The Hills

Piedmont

The Lake Area

Poverty Area B

Berkeley

Poverty Area A

Emeryville

Figure 7-1

Since the study called for the comparison of all seven areas of the city with one another, it was important that all areas be described with equal degrees of accuracy. Therefore the sample was designed so as to select 500 households from each area even though they differed greatly in their total numbers of households. The remainder of this discussion will be devoted to the sample selection procedures used in only one of the seven areas, since the procedures were essentially replicated for each.

General Considerations

As noted above, an area cluster sample was designed for the study. At the first stage of sampling, a stratified sample of census blocks was to be selected with probability proportionate to size. Blocks selected in this manner were to be listed; enumerators would visit each selected block physically and prepare lists of all the households found there. Then a systematic sample of five households was to be selected from each of those blocks.

As noted in the preceding chapter, five households per block is a common convention in area cluster sampling. Both sampling theory and survey experience suggest that five households represents the point of diminishing returns in the description of blocks. Five households will provide a reasonably accurate description of a given block, due to the homogeneity typically found among households on a single block. While six households, of course, provide a more accurate description of that block, this advantage would be more than offset by the corresponding decrease in the accuracy of the sample of blocks selected in describing the population of all blocks. (This assumes that the total survey sample size is fixed.) To illustrate this point in the extreme, the researcher could limit his sample to all those households found on a single block; this would provide a perfectly accurate description of that block, but the block in itself would not provide a very accurate description of all blocks and, by extension, of all households in the city.

Since 500 households were to be selected from each area of the city, this meant that 100 blocks would be selected, with five households taken from each. Moreover, to permit rigorous analyses of the variance in descriptions of households, it was decided to organize the blocks into relatively homogeneous strata and to select two blocks from each stratum. Thus, the initial task in each area was to create 50 strata, then two blocks would be selected from each and, finally, five households would be selected from each block—making a total of 500 households in the area.

The First-Stage Sampling Frame

Two kinds of data were required for describing census blocks. Most importantly, it was necessary to know approximately how many households there were on each of the blocks so that a PPS block sample could be selected. For purposes of stratification, however, it was also necessary to know certain relevant characteristics about the blocks, such as their racial composition and socioeconomic levels.

Both kinds of data were available to the research team in the form of the 1960 United States Census block statistics. This file indicated the 1960 size of all blocks (in numbers of housing units) and also provided such variable descriptions as (1) percent nonwhite, (2) percent renter-occupied, (3) percent deteriorating, and (4) value of the structures (either rent or valuation). Unfortunately, however, the study was being conducted six years after the census data had been collected, so it was anticipated that many of the housing counts would be out of date.

Before the sampling began, two months were spent examining city planning maps of each area. Housing units constructed or demolished since the 1960 census were noted, and these data were used to correct the estimated number of households per block. At the conclusion of this process, a machine-readable card was prepared for each census block in the city—showing its current expected size (in households) and the several characteristics compiled in the 1960 census (there was no way of updating these).

The following comments describe the sample selection procedures used in Poverty Area D, which had an estimated 9,938 households at the time of sampling. Since the sample target for the area was 500 households, the overall sampling fraction was 1/20.

Large Block Selection

Each of the areas of the city had some census blocks that contained very large numbers of households. Some of these were large blocks in geographical size; others contained several large apartment houses. Since the presence of these blocks might hinder the stratification techniques planned for the study, and since they were considered very important blocks for purposes of the study, an initial decision was made that every block containing 200 or more households would be included automatically in the sample. Each such block would be listed, and 1/20th (overall sampling ratio for the area) of the households listed would be selected for interviewing.

In Poverty Area D, the large blocks contained a total of 702 households. Therefore 35 households were to be selected from those blocks, leaving 465 to be selected from the remainder of the area.

Handling Small Blocks and Zero Blocks

Several blocks in Poverty Area D (and elsewhere) contained very few households, and some were estimated to contain none. These blocks presented a special problem. First, a block having an expected size of zero would have no chance of selection. If the estimates were incorrect and the block did in fact have households on it, then those households would have no chance of selection.

Second, since the basic sample design called for the selection of five households from each selected block, those having fewer than five would present a problem. Moreover, if the size estimates were incorrect, some blocks believed to contain more than five households might in fact have fewer.

To resolve these problems, each zero block and each block with an expected size of fewer than 10 was "attached" to an adjacent block. The number of households expected on the small block—if any—was added to the number for the adjacent block and the pair of blocks were treated as a single block for purposes of sampling. The pair had a chance of selection proportionate to their combined size, and if the pair were selected in the sample of blocks, both were listed and sampled as though they were a single block.

Stratification

Since 35 households were to be taken from the very large blocks, 465 were to be selected from the remainder of the area with its total of 9,236 estimated households. With five households to be taken from each sample block, 93 blocks would be required. And, since two blocks would be taken from each stratum, the task at this point was to create 47 (rounded from 46.5) strata.

Each of these strata—or groups of blocks—had to have two characteristics. First, the blocks in the stratum should be as similar to one another as possible, in terms of racial composition, SES (socioeconomic status), and so forth. This would insure that all types of blocks would be selected in their proper proportion for the total sample. Second, each of the strata should contain a total of approximately 200 households. Since 10 households were to be selected from each stratum (two blocks, five households from each), a stratum size of 200 would produce an ultimate sampling fraction of 1/20: the fraction established for the whole area. Of course, all the blocks contained specified numbers of households, so it was not possible to create strata containing *exactly* 200 households. (A later discussion will deal with the statistical correction for such variations.)

In creating homogeneity among the blocks grouped in a given stratum, it was possible to employ the block characteristics provided by the 1960 census. To avoid confusion in the following empirical descriptions, it should be noted that the creation of homogeneity was undertaken on a largely ad hoc and arbitrary basis. While one might be tempted to create a stratification format on theoretical grounds at the outset (for example, all blocks with more than 75 percent nonwhite residents, more than 50 percent renter-occupied, and with average monthly rent less than $150 would be combined into a stratum), such an approach would not necessarily be appropriate to the nature of the blocks being stratified. Instead, each group of blocks (comprising an area of the city or a subset thereof) was examined to determine the variations of its characteristics, and a stratification system was developed to suit those particular characteristics. This meant that different areas of the city were stratified differently; moreover, it should be recognized that the particular stratification format for a given area was only one of several, perhaps equally appropriate, possibilities.

As a general rule, however, the available stratification variables were considered in a set order for each area of the city: racial composition, percent renter- or owner-occupied, property value, and deterioration. To begin, then, an attempt was made to create relatively homogeneous groups of blocks in terms of racial composition. Each of those groups would then be subdivided into relatively homogeneous subgroups in terms of percentages occupied by renters or by owners, and so forth. Whenever this ordering of stratification variables was inappropriate to a given area, the inappropriate variables were simply ignored or considered at a different point in the stratification. For example, one area of the city of Oakland was, at the time of study, virtually all white. As a result, it made little sense to try stratifying the blocks in that area in terms of racial composition, even though it would have been possible to group together those blocks with *any* nonwhite residents. If, on the other hand, one small group of blocks in the area had, say, 20 percent or more nonwhite residents, these might have been put in a separate stratum.

As a general rule, however, the stratification variables were considered, and typically employed, in the order described above. Prior to the consideration of those variables, however, a somewhat different variable was used to divide each of the seven areas of the city for the first step of stratification.

When the updated machine-readable cards were created for each census block, a notation was made as to the number of housing units constructed subsequent to the 1960 census. Since it was felt that blocks containing new construction would differ from others, this datum was used as the first stratification variable. All those blocks in Poverty Area D containing any new units, then, were pulled out for separate stratification. Altogether these blocks contained an estimated 1,254 households. At 200 households per stratum, the "growth" blocks were to be grouped into six strata.

The second stratification variable used was racial composition. All the growth blocks were arranged in terms of the percentage nonwhite living in each. Some of the blocks were found to have 80 percent or more nonwhite residents. Taken together, these blocks contained 247 households. As this was relatively close to the target of 200 households per stratum, these blocks were designated as the first stratum.

The blocks containing between 30 and 79 percent nonwhite residents had a total of 385 households, so it was decided to create two strata from these. The second stratification variable was the percentage of households occupied by renters (as opposed to owners). In the present case, those blocks with 36 percent or more of the households occupied by renters had a total of 214 households; the remaining 171 households were on blocks with less than 36 percent renters. These two groups of blocks were designated as the second and third strata. (*Note:* There is nothing intrinsically meaningful about the cutting point of 36 percent renters. The goal here was to create strata of equal size, so the cutting point that accomplished the goal was used.)

Blocks having less than 30 percent nonwhite residents contained 622 households, calling for three strata. In examining these blocks in terms of all the stratification variables, it was discovered that one group of blocks had more than 10 percent of its households designated as "deteriorating" by the census. These blocks contained a total of 214 households. Since 10 percent deterioration is quite high in the context of all blocks, this group was designated as the fourth stratum.

The remaining blocks contained 408 households, calling for two strata. When renter-occupation was examined, it was discovered that those blocks with 86 percent or more renters contained 201 households, and these were designated as the fifth stratum. The blocks containing the remaining 207 households were designated the sixth stratum.

In view of the complexity of this procedure, Table 7-2 presents a schematic summary of the stratification of the growth blocks in Poverty Area D. The groups of blocks designated as strata are indicated by the notation S1, S2, and so forth.

Recall that the goal of stratification was to create relatively homogeneous groups of blocks. We might pause for a moment to note the characteristics that all the blocks in Stratum 5 have in common: (1) all are located in Poverty Area D of Oakland; (2) all have fewer than 200 households; (3) all have experienced a growth in households since 1960; (4) all have less than 36 percent nonwhite residents; (5) all have less than 10 percent of their structures deteriorating; and (6) all have more than 85 percent renters. The extreme homogeneity of this group of blocks should be apparent.

Table 7-2. Stratification of Growth Blocks in Poverty, Area D

All Growth Blocks (1254hh*)	
80% or more nonwhite (247 hh)	S1
30–79% nonwhite (385hh)	
36% or more renters (214 hh)	S2
35% or fewer renters (171 hh)	S3
29% or fewer nonwhite (622 hh)	
10% or more deteriorating (214 hh)	S4
9% or fewer deteriorating (408 hh)	
86% or more renters (201 hh)	S5
85% or fewer renters (207 hh)	S6

* hh = household. This term has been used rather than the technically more correct term—dwelling unit—to assist the reader who is having his first contact with survey sampling. A dwelling unit is a room or set of rooms intended for the residential use of a person or a family; a household is the person or group of people residing in a dwelling unit.

The reader will do well to recognize that the above discussion is limited to the creation of six strata in Poverty Area D. Forty-one more strata were created in this fashion in the same area, and the whole process was replicated six more times for the other areas of the city. With the use of a desk calculator and a counter-sorter-puncher, the actual stratification required about 30 man-hours of intensive work.

Block Selection within Strata

Two blocks were to be selected from each stratum with probabilities proportionate to their sizes. Stratum 1 in the previous example, containing 247 households, will be used to illustrate the procedure used in block selection.

Table 7-3. Block Selection Procedure

Census Tract	Census Block	Number of Households	Cumulative Total	Cumulative Range
27	18	12	12	1–12
27	5	30	42	13–42 (selected)
27	23	26	68	43–68
28	4	80	148	69–148
27	14	48	196	149–196 (Selected)
28	2	51	247	197–247

Total hh/2 = 123.5; random number between 1 and 123.5 = 35; random number + total hh/2 = 158.5.

To begin, all the blocks (cards) in Stratum 1 were shuffled to approximately "randomize" their order. Then, Table 7-3 was created from the household estimates for each block.

The first two columns in the table simply identify the blocks by census tract number and census block number (within the tract). The third column presents the estimated block sizes, followed by the cumulative total across the six blocks. The final column in the table presents the range of numbers assigned to each block on the basis of its size.

Since two blocks were to be selected, the cumulative total for the stratum (247) was divided by 2 (123.5). A random number (35) was then selected between 1 and 123.5. Block 27/5, with a range of 13–42, contained this random number, so it was selected into the sample of blocks. The random number was then added to 123.5. Block 27/14, with a range of 149–196, contained this new number (158.5), so it was the second block selected into the sample.

For this particular study, a computer program was prepared to carry out most of the steps described above. The cards representing the blocks were grouped by strata. The computer read the cards in a given stratum, computed and printed the cumulative totals for that stratum, divided the total by 2 and printed that number, and finally generated and printed a random number between 1 and the half-total. The researcher then determined which blocks were to be included in the sample.

Household Selection within Blocks

The procedure described above resulted in the selection of approximately 700 census blocks throughout the city of Oakland. Five households (usually) were to be interviewed on each block. To accomplish this, maps were prepared to identify clearly each of the selected blocks, and enumerators were sent to prepare a list of all the households on each block. The lists were prepared through the use of standard forms and looked something like the example presented as Table 7-4.

To prepare the listing, the enumerator went to a designated corner of the block and proceeded to walk around it in a circle until returning to the starting point, entering on the form each household as it appeared. Each household, whether it was a single-family house, half a duplex, or an apartment, was entered separately. As it was entered on the list, each household was assigned a number in continuous serial order.

The listing process provided a new estimate of the number of households on each block. (Since enumerators could make mistakes in listing, this should still be regarded as an *estimate*.) However, we should recall that each block was selected on the basis of an earlier estimate of its size. To take account of discrepancies between these two estimates, the researchers employed a technique mentioned in the earlier discussion of sampling Episcopal churchwomen.

Table 7-4. Sample List Sheet

Hh Number	Street Name	Street Number	Apartment Number or Other Identification
01	Walnut St.	2301	
02	Walnut St.	2303A	Duplex
03	Walnut St.	2303B	
04	Tenth Ave.	(102?)	No number; brown house with hedge
05	Tenth Ave.	104	Apt. 101
06	Tenth Ave.	104	Apt. 102
07	Tenth Ave.	104	Apt. 201
. . .	. . .	. . .	. . .
47	Ninth Ave.	103	
48	Ninth Ave.	101	

The sampling interval to be used in selecting households from a given block was computed on the basis of the earlier estimate of its size and the five households intended to be selected. If the block size had been estimated at 50 households, then the sampling interval was set at 10. This interval was used in household selection, even if the listed size of the block was larger or smaller. If the block contained 60 households instead of the estimated 50, 6 households were selected in the sample; if it contained only 40, then 4 were selected. (A more precise correction was also employed, and this will be discussed shortly.)

The selection of households was accomplished by selecting a random number between 1 and the sampling interval. That random number was then incremented by the sampling interval. The households listed in the list sheet as having that random number and the numbers resulting from the incrementation process were designated for interviewing.

When the initial estimates of block size were greatly inaccurate and when the procedures just outlined would produce only 1 or 2 sample households (or would produce more than 10), a different procedure was used. In such cases, an arbitrary number of households (no more than 10) was selected, and a note was made to weight those interviews separately during the analysis. (See below.)

This completes the set of procedures used in the selection of some 3,500 households throughout the city of Oakland, California, in 1966. Including the updating of census block sizes and the listing of sample blocks, the whole process took about five months and a staff of approximately 20 people at its peak.

Weighting the Sample Households

In the simple sample design, each element in the population has the same probability of selection. As a result, the aggregated sample can be taken as representative of the population from which it was selected. If 2,000 respondents were selected from a population of 2,000,000, then each respondent would be taken to "represent" an additional 999 people who were not selected. To estimate the *number* of people in the population who have a given characteristic, we would multiply the number having that characteristic in our sample times 1,000. This *weight* is the inverse of respondents' probabilities of being selected into the sample. When all respondents have the same probability of selection, weighting is irrelevant except for estimating *numbers* in the population.

When respondents have different probabilities of selection, weighting becomes more important—relevant even in the computation of percentages. The Oakland study provides an example of the need for, and methods of, weighting sample elements in a complex sample design. No matter how complex the sample design, however, the basic principle still holds: a respondent's weight is the inverse of his probability of selection into the sample.

In computing a given respondent's overall probability of selection, we must recall that if several stages of sampling are employed with separate probabilities of selection at each stage, these probabilities must be multiplied by each other to determine the overall probability. If the respondent belongs to a group (church, block) that has a 1/10 chance of selection and he has a 1/10 chance of selection *within* that group, his overall probability of selection is 1/100.

In the computation of household weights for the Oakland sample, we must take into account two separate probabilities of selection: the probability of a block being selected and the probability of a household being selected within that block. These two probabilities would be computed as follows.

Block Probability   Each block had a probability of selection equal to its estimated size (EBS) divided by the size of the stratum (SS) times 2 (two blocks selected per stratum). We will write this as 2EBS/SS. Note that this formula takes account of the PPS sampling plus the variation in strata sizes. Block 27/5 in our earlier example had an estimated size of 30 households in a stratum containing 247; its probability of selection therefore was .2429.

Household Probability   Within a given block, each selected household had a probability of selection equal to the number selected on the block (n) divided by the actual number (ABS) listed for the whole block: n/ABS. If Block 27/5 was found in listing to have 34 households (instead of 30) and 5 of those were selected, each would have a probability of selection equal to .1471.

Overall Probability   Putting together the separate formulas, we have the following: $(2EBS)(n)/(SS)(ABS)$. For the example used above, the overall probability of selection is .0357 or about 1/28. Note that this probability is less than the target sampling fraction of 1/20 for Poverty Area D. This is due to the fact that Stratum 1 had 247 households instead of the target of 200, and Block 27/5 had 34 households instead of the 30 estimated. As a result, each of the five households selected on Block 27/5 had a lesser probability of selection than had been intended initially.

Note, however, that if the estimated and actual block size were identical, the probability formula would be reduced from $(2EBS)(n)/(SS)(ABS)$ to $2n/SS$, or twice the number of households selected divided by the number of households in the stratum. And if the SS = 200, the target sampling fraction of 1/20 would be achieved, since five households would have been selected on the block.

Weighting the Households   All the differences in probabilities of selection were taken care of in the assignment of weights equal to the inverse of a household's overall probability of selection. In the first example above, each of the households interviewed on Block 27/5 would have been assigned a weight of 28. Each of those households would be assumed to represent itself plus another 27 households in the city of Oakland.

Additional Weighting for Nonresponse   One final comment should be made. Surveys of this sort never succeed in interviewing *all* the households initially selected in the sample. Some persons in the sample will refuse to be interviewed, others will be unavailable.

In this particular study, an additional weight was assigned to households to take account of such nonresponse. It was assumed that households that could not be interviewed were more like those that had been interviewed on the same block than any other possible estimate. As a result, each completed interview was assigned a weight equal to the number of households selected on that block divided by the number actually completed. If four out of five were completed, each of the completed interviews received an additional weight of 1.25. If all selected households were successfully interviewed, of course, the assigned weight was 1.

7.6
Summary
The preceding four examples of sample designs have been presented to give the reader a more realistic picture of the sampling situations that he is likely to face in practice. While these examples do not exhaust the range of variation in field conditions, study objectives, and sampling techniques, they illustrate the most typical ones. Hopefully, these examples will have illustrated the basic logic behind survey sampling and will better equip the reader to improvise wisely when faced with a novel problem.

7.7
Annotated Bibliography

The following research reports provide reasonably detailed discussions of the sampling methods employed.

Almond, Gabriel, and Verba, Sidney, *The Civic Culture* (Princeton, N.J.: Princeton University Press, 1963).

Babbie, Earl R., *Science and Morality in Medicine* (Berkeley: University of California Press, 1970).

Glock, Charles Y., and Stark, Rodney, *Christian Beliefs and Anti-Semitism* (New York: Harper & Row, 1966).

————, Ringer, Benjamin B., and Babbie, Earl R., *To Comfort and to Challenge* (Berkeley: University of California Press, 1967).

Stouffer, Samuel A., *Communism, Conformity, and Civil Liberties* (New York: John Wiley, 1966).

Part Three:
Modes of Observation

For many beginning researchers, doing research means making observations, collecting data, or, if you will, creating data. Any readers of that persuasion will probably have grown impatient by now. It bears repeating, however, that the structuring of inquiry is an integral part of research. The time has come to move to some of the techniques employed by social scientists in the collection of data.

Chapter 8, on field research, examines what is perhaps the most natural form of data collection employed by the social sciences: the direct observation of social phenomena in natural settings. As we shall see, some researchers go beyond mere observation to participate in what they are studying—to obtain a more intimate view and a fuller understanding.

Chapter 9 discusses content analysis, a method of collecting social data through carefully specifying and counting social artifacts such as books, songs, speeches, and paintings. Without making any personal contact with people, social researchers can use this method to examine a wide variety of social phenomena.

It is often possible to bring aspects of social life into the laboratory for close and controlled examination. Experiments have played a central role in the progress of the natural sciences; in Chapter 10 we shall see some of the ways they can be employed in the social sciences.

One of the most popular data collection methods in the social sciences is survey research: getting information directly from the responses of (usually large) samples of individuals or groups. Questionnaire construction and sampling were dealt with in Part Two; Chapter 11 will focus on methods of administering survey instruments.

Finally, Chapter 12 will describe briefly some additional modes of observation employed by social scientists. The materials in this chapter should round out your appreciation of the variety of approaches that may be taken to the study of people.

Before we turn to the actual descriptions of the several methods, two points should be made. First, you will probably discover that you have been using most of these scientific methods quite casually in your daily life. You use some form of field research every day. You are employing a crude form of content analysis every time you judge an author's motivation or orientation from his writings. You engage in at least casual experiments frequently. The chapters of Part Three will show you how to improve your use of these methods to avoid the foibles and pitfalls of casual, uncontrolled observation.

Second, none of the data-collection methods described in the following chapters is appropriate to all research topics and situations. I have tried to give you some ideas, early in each chapter, of when a given method might be appropriate. Still, it would not be possible to anticipate all the possible research topics that may one day interest you. As a general guideline, it is always best to employ a variety of techniques in the study of any topic. Since each of the methods has its weaknesses, the use of several methods can help to fill the gaps left by each; and, if the different, independent approaches to the topic all yield the same conclusion, this can constitute a form of replication.

8
Field Research

8.1
Introduction

Chapter 8 deals with a mode of observation that is, in a sense, very closely related to the opening discussion in this book concerning human inquiry. It involves the collection of data about social phenomena through the direct observation of, and perhaps participation in, that which is being studied. I have used the term *field research* to include methods of research sometimes referred to as *participant observation, direct observation,* or *case studies.*

Field research is at once very old and very new in social science. It is very old in that many of the techniques to be discussed in this chapter have been used by social researchers for centuries. It is very new in that it has received increasing methodological attention and has been refined in recent years. It should be noted, moreover, that this method is employed by many people who might not, strictly speaking, be regarded as social science researchers. Newspaper reporters are one example; welfare department case workers are another.

It bears repeating that field research is constantly used in everyday life, by all of us. In a sense, we do field research whenever we observe or participate in social behavior, whether at a corner tavern, in a doctor's waiting room, on an airplane, or anywhere. Whenever we look around us and observe what is happening and try to understand it, we are engaging in field research. Whenever we report our observations to others, we are reporting our field research efforts. The purpose of this chapter is to discuss this method in some detail, providing a logical overview of the method, and suggesting some of the specific skills and techniques that make scientific field research more useful than the casual observation we all engage in.

Field observation differs from some other models of observation in that it is not only a data-collecting activity. Frequently, perhaps typically, it is a theory-generating activity as well. The field researcher seldom approaches his task with precisely defined hypotheses to be tested. More typically, he attempts to make sense out of an ongoing process that cannot be predicted in advance—making initial observations, developing tentative general conclusions that suggest particular types of further observations, making those observations and thereby revising his conclusions, and so forth. The alternation of induction and deduction, discussed in Chapter 2 of this book, is perhaps nowhere more evident and essential than in good field research.

8.2
Topics Appropriate to Field Research

One of the key strengths of field research, as will be discussed at the close of this chapter, is the comprehensiveness of perspective that it provides to the researcher. By going directly to the social phenomenon under study and observing it as completely as possible, the researcher may develop a deeper and fuller understanding of it. This mode of observation, then, is especially, though not exclusively, appropriate to those research topics and social studies that appear to defy simple quantification. The field researcher may recognize several nuances of attitude and behavior that might escape researchers using other methods.

Somewhat differently, field research is especially appropriate to the study of those topics for which attitudes and behaviors can best be understood within their natural setting. Experiments and surveys, for example, may be able to measure behaviors and attitudes in somewhat artificial settings, but not all behavior is best measured this way. For example, field research provides a superior method for studying the dynamics of religious conversion at a revival meeting.

Finally, field research is especially appropriate to the study of social processes over time. Thus, for example, the field researcher might be in a position to examine the rumblings and final explosion of a riot as events actually occur rather than trying to reconstruct them afterwards.

Other good studies for field research methods would be campus demonstrations, courtroom proceedings, labor negotiations, public hearings, or any similar events taking place within a relatively limited area and time. Several such observation efforts must be combined in a more comprehensive examination across time and space.

John Lofland, in his *Analyzing Social Settings*, has suggested six different types of social phenomena that might be addressed by the field researcher.[1]

In thinking about presenting the examples in an orderly fashion, it seemed best to arrange them along a continuum from the most *microscopic* social phenomenon to the most *macroscopic.* While the materials in fact shade one into another, in order to be more precise, I have chopped the continuum into six categories. Ranging from microscopic to macroscopic, these are as follows:

1. *Acts.* Action in a situation that is temporally brief, consuming only a few seconds, minutes, or hours.

---

1. John Lofland, *Analyzing Social Settings* (Belmont, California: Wadsworth, 1971), 14–15.

2. *Activities*. Action in a setting of more major duration—days, weeks, months—constituting significant elements of persons' involvements.

3. *Meanings*. The verbal productions of participants that define and direct action.

4. *Participation*. Persons' holistic involvement in, or adaptation to, a situation or setting under study.

5. *Relationships*. Interrelationships among several persons considered simultaneously.

6. *Settings*. The entire setting under study conceived as the unit of analysis.

The vague term "social phenomenon" used above can now be seen to translate into at least six more specific categories. Instead of asking "What are the characteristics of a social phenomenon, the forms it assumes, the variations it displays?", we can now ask: What are the characteristics of acts, activities, meanings, participation, relationships, and settings, the forms they assume, the variations they display?

Let me emphasize, however, that there is nothing magic or immutable in this set of six terms. It is merely a device, useful, I hope, in making an orderly and therefore more understandable presentation of many years of accomplished qualitative analysis in sociology.

8.3

The Various Roles of the Researcher

I have used the term "field research" rather than the frequently used term "participant observation" since field researchers need not always participate in what they are studying, though they usually will study it directly at the scene of the action. Raymond Gold[2] has discussed four different roles

---

2 Raymond L. Gold, "Roles in Sociological Field Observation," in George J. McCall and J. L. Simmons, Eds., *Issues in Participant Observation* (Reading, Mass: Addison-Wesley, 1969), pp. 30–39.

that field researchers may play in this regard: *complete participant, participant-as-observer, observer-as-participant,* and *complete observer.*

Gold described the complete participant as follows:

> "The true identity and purpose of the complete participant in field research are not known to those whom he observes. He interacts with them as naturally as possible in whatever areas of their living interest him and are acceptable to him in situations in which he can play or learn to play requisite day-to-day roles successfully." [3]

The complete participant, in this sense, may be a genuine participant in what he is studying (e.g., a participant in a campus demonstration), or he may pretend to be a genuine participant. In any event, the complete participant lets people see him *only* as a participant, not a researcher.

Clearly, if the field researcher is not a genuine participant in that which he is studying, he must learn to behave as though he were. If he is studying a group made up of uneducated and inarticulate people, it would not be appropriate for him to talk and act like a university professor or student.

Here let me draw attention to an ethical issue involved in the research situation under discussion. Social researchers themselves are divided on this issue. Is it ethical for a researcher to deceive the people he is studying in the hope that they will confide in him as they will not confide in an identified researcher? Do the interests of science—the scientific values of the research—offset such ethical considerations? Although many professional associations have addressed this issue, the norms to be followed remain somewhat ambiguous when applied to specific situations.

Related to this ethical consideration is a scientific one. No researcher deceives his subjects solely for the purpose of deception. Rather, he does it in the belief that his data will be more valid and reliable, that his subjects will be more natural and honest with him if they do not know that he is doing a research project. If the people being studied know they are being studied by a researcher, they might modify their behavior in a variety of ways. First, they might expel the researcher. Second, they might modify their speech and behavior so as to appear more "respectable" than would otherwise be the case. Third, the social process itself might be radically changed. Students making plans to burn down the university administration building, for example, might give up the plan altogether once they learn that one of their group is a social scientist conducting a research project.

On the other side of the coin, the researcher as a complete participant may affect what he is studying. To play the role of participant, the researcher must *participate.* Yet, his participation may importantly affect the social process he is studying. Suppose, for example, the participant researcher is asked for his ideas as to what the group should do next. No matter

---

3. *Ibid.;* p. 33.

what he says, he will affect the process in some fashion. If he makes a suggestion that is followed by the group, his influence on the process is obvious. If he makes a suggestion that is not followed, the process whereby the suggestion is rejected may importantly affect what happens next. Finally, if he indicates that he just doesn't know what is to be done next, this may add to a general feeling of uncertainty and indecisiveness in the group.

Ultimately, *anything* that the participant observer does or does not do will have some effect on that which he is observing; this is simply inevitable. More seriously, what he does or does not do may have an *important* effect on what happens. There is simply no complete protection against this, though sensitivity to the issue may provide a partial protection. (This influence, called the Hawthorne effect, is discussed more fully in Chapter 10.)

Because of these several considerations, ethical and scientific, the field researcher frequently chooses a different role from that of complete participant. In Gold's terminology, he might choose the role of participant-as-observer. In this role, he would participate fully with the group under study, but he would make it clear that he was also undertaking research. There are dangers in this role also, however. First, the people being studied may shift much of their attention to the research project rather than focusing on the natural social process, and the process being observed may no longer be typical. Or, conversely, the researcher himself may come to identify too much with the interests and viewpoints of the participants. He may begin to "go native" and lose much of his scientific objectivity.

The observer-as-participant is one who identifies himself as a researcher and interacts with participants in the social process but makes no pretense of being a participant himself. A good example of this would be a newspaper reporter who is learning about a social movement; for instance, the unionization of migrant farm workers. He might interview leaders and also visit workers where they live, watch strawberry picking, go with an injured worker to the hospital, and so on.

The complete observer, at the other extreme, is one who only observes a social process without becoming a part of it in any way. Quite possibly, the subjects of study might not realize they are being studied by virtue of the researcher's unobtrusiveness. Sitting at a bus stop for the purpose of observing jaywalking behavior at a nearby intersection would be an example of this. While the complete observer is less likely to affect that which he studies and less likely to "go native" than the complete participant, he is also less likely to develop a full appreciation of what he is studying. His observations may be more sketchy and transitory.

It bears repeating that different situations require different roles to be played by the researcher. Unfortunately, there are no clear guidelines to be employed in making this choice, and the researcher must rely on his understanding of the situation and his own good judgment. In making his decision, however, the researcher must be guided by both methodological and ethical considerations. Since these often conflict with one another, his decision will frequently be a difficult one, and he may find sometimes that his role limits his study.

8.4
Preparing for the Field

Let's assume for the moment that you have decided to undertake field research regarding a campus political organization. Let's assume further that you are not a member of that group, that you do not know a great deal about it, and that you will identify yourself to the participants as a researcher. This section will discuss some of the ways in which you might prepare yourself before undertaking direct observation of the group.

As is true of all research methods, you would be advised to begin with a search of the relevant literature. Depending on the popularity and the age of the group, there may be published material about it. Perhaps the group itself has published something. You would be advised, as a beginning, to read everything you can find relating to the group. Whether or not there are writings available on this specific group, you surely will find some that are at least indirectly relevant. There has been a large volume of research on student politics in general; there is an even larger volume of research literature on social movements. Reviewing such literature will assist you in refining whatever theoretical framework you may bring to your particular study, thereby attuning you to the most relevant things to observe.

The above remarks regarding the importance of library research prior to study design and data collection are part of the common sense of scientific research in general, and they would apply to all types of research methods. There is a sense in which it might be argued that they should be *ignored* in the case of field research, however. Since this method is less "structured" than others, field researchers have a greater danger of unconsciously observing only what they *expect* to find: *selective perception* is the term normally used in this regard. There is a danger, in other words, that a field researcher might familiarize himself with previous research on a topic, accept the conceptual frameworks and the conclusions of past studies as reasonable, and proceed to observe only those things that confirm the earlier studies. This would not happen, of course, if he were unfamiliar with the prior research.

Again, I can provide no handy guideline. "To read or not to read" is not a question I can answer for you. As with all the other "gray areas" in social research, I can only suggest that sensitivity to the problem should help to alleviate it. Certainly, no one should avoid a review of the literature on a topic out of laziness, but you should know that there may be legitimate scientific grounds for doing so.

In the next phase of your research, you may wish to make use of *informants*. You might wish to discuss the student political group with others who have already studied it, or with anyone else who is likely to be familiar with it. In particular, you might find it useful to discuss the group with a member of it. Perhaps you have a friend who is a member, or you can meet someone who is. This aspect of your preparation is likely to be more effective if your relationship with the informant extends beyond your research role. In dealing with members of the group as informants, you should take care that your initial discussions do not compromise or limit later aspects of your research. Realize that the impression you make on the member-informant, the role you establish for yourself, may carry over into your later effort. For example, creating the initial impression that you may be an undercover FBI agent is unlikely to facilitate later observations of the group.

Prior to making your first contact with the student group, then, you should be already quite familiar with it as well as understanding the general, theoretical context within which it exists.

There are a variety of ways in which to establish your initial contact with the people you plan to study. How you do it will depend, in part, on the role you intend to play. Especially if you are to take on the role of complete participant, you must find a way of developing an identity with the people to be studied. If you wish to study dishwashers in a restaurant, the most direct method would be to get a job as a dishwasher. In the case of the student political group, you might simply answer their call for new members.

Many of the social processes appropriate to field research are sufficiently open as to make your contact with the people to be studied rather simple and straightforward. If you wish to observe a mass demonstration, simply be there. If you wish to observe patterns in jaywalking, simply hang around busy streets.

Whenever you wish to make a more formal contact with the people and wish to identify yourself as a researcher, you must be able to establish a certain rapport with them. You might contact a participant with whom you feel comfortable and gain that person's assistance. If you are studying a formal group, you might approach the group leaders. Or you may find that one of your informants who has studied the group is able to introduce you to it.

In making a direct, formal contact with the people you want to study, you will be required to give them some explanation of the purpose of your study. Here again, you face an ethical dilemma. Telling them the complete purpose of your research might lose you their cooperation altogether or importantly affect their subsequent behavior. On the other hand, giving only what you believe would be an acceptable explanation may involve outright deception. Realize in all this that your decisions—in practice—may be largely determined by the purpose of your study, the nature of what you are studying, observations you wish to use, and other such factors.

Previous field research offers no fixed rule—methodological or ethical—to be followed in this regard. Your appearance as a researcher, regardless of stated purpose, may result in a warm welcome from people, flattered that a scientist finds them important enough to study. Or, it might result in your being totally ostracized or worse. (Do not, for example, burst into a meeting of an organized crime syndicate and announce that you are writing a term paper on organized crime.)

8.5
Sampling in Field Research

Earlier chapters of this book discussed the logic and the more conventional techniques involved in probability sampling in social research.

Although the general principles of representativeness in that context should be remembered in field research, controlled sampling techniques are normally inappropriate. This section will discuss the matter of sampling as it typically applies in field research.

To begin, the population and the units of analysis in a field research project may be somewhat ambiguous. In studying the campus political group mentioned above, are you interested in studying that group only, the members of the group, student political behavior in general, political behavior more generally, or what? If you are studying three juvenile gangs in a particular city, are the gangs your units of analysis, the individual juveniles, or the city? Are you interested only in describing the gangs under study, or does your interest extend to juvenile peer-relations in general? It is important that you ask yourself what population you wish to make general assertions about when you are finished with your research. The answer to this will not always be obvious to you, and it may change over the course of your research. A limited initial concern may be expanded later, as you conclude that certain of the phenomena that you are observing apply well beyond your specific subjects of study. Although this general issue may not be easily resolved in practice, sensitivity to it should help to clarify your goals and methods.

The field researcher attempts to observe everything within his field of study; thus, in a sense, he does not sample at all. In reality, of course, it is impossible to observe everything. To the extent that the field researcher observes only a portion of what transpires, then, that which he does observe is a *de facto* sample of all the possible observations that might have been made.

The concept of sampling, in connection with field research, is more complicated than in the situation dealt with in the earlier chapters. Of the communications and behaviors under study, those observed represent a sample of all those that occur. If several people are shouting support for the speaker in a religious revival meeting, those shouts that the researcher hears and understands represent a sample of all such shouts. Or if a researcher observes acts of violence during a riot, the observed acts are a sample of all such acts of violence. The field researcher will seldom be able to select a controlled sample of such observations, but he should bear in mind the general principles of representativeness and interpret his observations accordingly.

Sometimes, however, the field researcher will be in a position to sample among possible observations. If he is studying the development of a student political organization over time, for example, he may choose to interview different members of that organization by making a list of all the members and then selecting a probability sample. This might not be the best method of sampling for his purposes, however. McCall and Simmons[4] suggest three types of sampling methods that are specifically appropriate to field research: the *quota* sample, the *snowball* sample, and *deviant cases*.

To begin, if the group or social process under study has fairly clearly defined categories of participants, some kind of **quota sample** might be

---

4. McCall and Simmons, *op. cit.*, pp. 64–67.

employed: persons representing all the different participation categories should be studied. (See Chapter 6 for a more detailed discussion of quota sampling as a general procedure.) In the study of a formal group, for example, you might wish to interview both leaders and nonleaders. In studying a student political organization, it might be useful to interview both radical and more moderate members of that group. In general, whenever representativeness is desired, you should use quota sampling and interview both men and women, young people and old people, and the like.

Second, McCall and Simmons mention the **snowball sample.** If you wish to learn, for example, the pattern of recruitment to a religious organization over time, you might begin by interviewing a fairly recent convert, asking him who introduced him to the group. You might then interview the person named, asking, in part, who introduced *him*. In studying a loosely structured political group, you might ask one of the participants who he believes to be the most influential members of the group. You might interview those people and, in the course of the interviews, ask who *they* believe to be the most influential. In each of these examples, your sample would "snowball" as each of your interviews suggested others.

Finally, McCall and Simmons draw attention to the importance of *deviant cases*. Often, our understanding of fairly regular patterns of attitudes and behaviors is further improved through the examination of those cases that do not fit into the regular pattern. Thus, for example, you might gain important insights into the nature of school spirit as exhibited at a pep rally by interviewing those people who did not appear to be caught up in the emotions of the crowd, or by interviewing students who did not attend the rally at all.

Aside from sampling individuals for interviewing, there are other field research situations in which it may be possible to undertake a conscious sampling procedure. In a study of jaywalking, you might wish to make observations on a number of different city streets. You might pick the sample of locations through standard probability methods; or, more likely, you might employ a rough quota system, observing wide streets and narrow ones, busy streets and quiet ones, or including samples from different times of day, or of common types of pedestrians. In a study of the ways in which people interact or fail to interact at a bus stop, you would make observations at a number of different kinds of bus stops and of other variations in that situation.

In practice, controlled probability sampling is seldom employed in field research. To the extent that he may consciously sample at all, the field researcher is more likely to employ what has been called a **purposive sample.** He selects a sample of observations that he believes will yield the most comprehensive understanding of his subject of study, based on the intuitive "feel" for the subject that comes from extended observation and reflection. Nonetheless, understanding the principles and logic of more formal sampling methods is likely to result in more effective "intuitive" sampling in field research.

In all this, bear in mind two stages of sampling. First, to what extent are the total situations *available* for observation representative of the more *general class* of phenomena you wish to describe and explain? Are the three juvenile gangs you are observing representative of all gangs? Second, are your *actual* observations within those total situations representative of all the *possible* observations? Have you observed a representative sample of the members of the three gangs, have you observed a representative sample of the interactions that have taken place? Even when controlled probability sampling methods are impossible or inappropriate, the logical link between representativeness and generalizability still holds.

8.6
Recording Observations

Finally, the basic tools of field research are the notebook—or *field journal*—and a pencil. Even tape recorders and cameras cannot capture all the relevant aspects of social processes. The greatest advantage of the field research method is the presence of an observing thinking researcher on the scene of the action. If possible, you should take notes on your observations *as you observe.* When this is not possible, you should write down your notes as soon as possible afterwards.

Your notes should include both your empirical observations and your interpretations of them. You should record what you "know" has happened and what you "think" has happened. It is important, however, that these different kinds of notes be identified for what they are. For example, you might note that person X spoke out in opposition to a proposal made by a group leader, that you *think* this represents an attempt by Person X to take over leadership of the group, and that you *think* you heard the leader comment to that effect in response to the opposition.

Just as you cannot hope to observe everything, neither can you record everything that you do observe. Whereas your observations represent a *de facto* sample of all possible observations, so do your notes represent a sample of your observations. Rather than recording a random sample of your observations, however, you should, of course, record your "most important" observations.

Some of the "most important" observations can be anticipated in advance of beginning the study; others will become apparent as your observations progress. Sometimes your note-taking can be facilitated by the advance preparation of standardized forms for recording. In a study of jaywalking, for example, you might anticipate the characteristics of pedestrians that are the most likely to be useful for analysis—age, sex, social class, ethnicity, and so forth—and prepare a form in which actual observations can be recorded easily. Or, you might develop a symbolic shorthand in advance to speed up recording. For studying audience participation at a mass meeting, you might want to construct a numbered grid representing the different sections of the meeting room; then, you would be able to record the location of participants easily, quickly, and accurately.

None of this advanced preparation should limit your recording of unanticipated events and aspects of the situation. Quite the contrary, speeding up the handling of anticipated observations can give you more freedom to observe the unanticipated.

Every student is somewhat familiar with note taking, just as every human being is somewhat familiar with field research in general. Like *good* field research, however, *good* note taking requires more careful and deliberate attention, and there are some specific skills that can be learned in that regard.

Excerpted below is John Lofland's excellent discussion of this skill in his field research textbook, *Analyzing Social Settings.*[5]

For better or worse, the human mind forgets massively and quickly. The people under study forget massively and quickly, too. In order, then, to have any kind of an edge on the participants in articulating and understanding their world, it is necessary to have some means to overcome forgetting. Writing is such a device. Without the sustained writing down of what has gone on, the observer is in hardly a better position to analyze and comprehend the workings of a world than are the members themselves. Writing, in the form of continued notes with which the forgotten past can be summoned into the present, is an absolutely necessary if not sufficient condition for comprehending the objects of observation. Aside from getting along in the setting, the fundamental concrete task of the observer is the taking of field notes. Whether or not he performs this task is perhaps the most important determinant of later bringing off a qualitative analysis. Field notes provide the observer's *raison d'etre.* If he is not doing them, he might as well not be in the setting.

1. Mental Notes

Let us assume the observer is somewhere—meeting with persons, attending an event, etc. The first step in taking field notes is to evoke one's culturally common sense and shared notion of what constitutes a descriptive report of something happening. From reading newspapers, magazines, and the like, one is already familiar with the character of sheer reportage. It concerns such matters as who and how many were there, the physical character of the place, who said what to whom, who moved about in what way, and a general characterization of an order of events.

The first step in the process of writing field notes is to orient one's consciousness to the task of remembering items of these (and, as the research develops) other kinds. This act of directing one's consciousness in order to remember at a later point may be called *mental notes.* One is preparing oneself to be able to put down on paper what he is now seeing.

5. Lofland, *op. cit.*, pp. 101–108.

2. Jotted Notes

If one is writing field notes *per se* only at the end of a period of observation or at the end of a day—which is a relatively typical practice—it will be helpful to preserve these mental notes as more than electrical traces in the brain. Such traces have a very high rate of decay. One way in which provisionally to preserve them is with *jotted notes.* Jotted notes are constituted of all the little phrases, quotes, key words, and the like that one puts down during the observation and at inconspicuous moments in order to have something physically to refer to when one actually sits down to write his field notes. Jotted notes have the function of jogging one's memory at the time of writing field notes.

Many field workers carry small, pocket-sized tablets or notebooks precisely for the purpose of jotting down notes. Any surface will do, however—the cover of a book, a napkin, the back of a pamphlet, etc.

Previously Forgotten. In the field, a present observation will often bring back a memory of something that happened on a previous occasion that one has forgotten to put in his field notes. Include these memories in one's jotted notes also.

Don't Jot Conspicuously. Whether one is a known or an unknown observer, the general rule of thumb is "don't jot conspicuously." Of course, one may also be doing interviewing in the field while observing. In that case, in order to seem competent, one should take notes of the kind described [elsewhere in Lofland's book]. In an interaction defined as an interview, the interviewee will expect one to take some kind of notes in order to indicate that you are indeed seriously interviewing him! And there may be other occasions when someone expects one to write something down on the spot.

But in ordinary day-to-day observation it seems wisest not to flaunt the fact that one is recording. If one is a known observer, the observed are already well aware of being observed. One need not increase any existing anxieties by continuously and openly writing down what is being viewed. Rather, jot notes at moments of withdrawal and when shielded: for example, in rest rooms, and sometimes in cars, hallways, and offices, etc. In some settings that have "meetings," members will sometimes themselves make notes. Under such conditions one can feel free to go along with the crowd.

Fuller Jottings. In addition, and before getting to the full field notes, an observer may—on the way home, waiting for a bus, before going to bed, etc.—make more elaborate jottings.

3. The Full Field Notes

At the end of a day (or of a shorter observation period), the observer must cloister himself for the purpose of doing *full field notes.* All those mental notes and jottings are *not* field notes until one has converted them to a running log of observations.

Mechanics *Write Promptly.* As a general rule, full field notes should be written no later than the morning after observation on the previous day. If one observed only in a morning, then write them up that afternoon. If one observed only in an afternoon, do the notes that evening. The underlying rule is to minimize the temporal span between observation and writing field notes.

Among the useful findings of psychologists is that forgetting is very slight in the first time units after a learning experience but then accelerates in a rather geometric fashion as more time passes. To wait a day or more is to forget a massive amount of material. Happily, it has also been found that memory decays very little during sleep. That is, forgetting has more to do with the acquisition of new experience than with the sheer passage of time. Therefore, it is reasonably safe to sleep on a day's or evening's observations and to write them up the first thing the next morning, thus avoiding the necessity of staying up half the night. But if one waits for days, he is likely to remember only the barest outlines of the observation period.

Personal Discipline and Time. Let me not deceive the reader. The writing of field notes takes *personal discipline* and *time.* It is all too easy to put off actually writing notes for a given day and to skip one or more days. For the actual writing of the notes may take as long or longer than did the observation! Indeed, a reasonable rule of thumb here is to expect and plan to spend as much time writing notes as one spent in observing. This is, of course, not invariant. Some observers spend considerably less time and are still able to perform good analysis. Many others have been known to spend considerably more than equal time in writing up their notes. How much time one actually spends depends, too, on the demands of the setting one is observing and the proportion of one's total time being devoted to the study.

But one point is inescapable. All the fun of actually being out and about mucking around in some setting must also be matched by cloistered rigor in committing to paper—and therefore to future usefulness—what has taken place.

Dictating versus Writing. Some observers have access to the luxury of dictating machines and transcribing secretaries. And, it seems, talking one's field notes takes much less time than writing them. Such affluents need the same advice here as was given for intensive interviewing: Get the transcriptions as soon as possible and review and pore over them, making further notes in the process. While talking rather than writing saves time, it also removes one from really having to think about what has happened and from searching out analytic themes. Writing rather than talking stimulates thought, or, at least, so it seems for a great number of people.

Since I prefer writing and believe most observers to be poor, I assume, in what follows, writing rather than dictating observers.

Handwriting versus Typewriting. I am afraid that an observer should know how to type. Typing is faster than writing, and it is easier to read. As discussed below, copies of the notes are going to be needed. If humanly possible, learn how to type before undertaking any significant piece of field research. I am mindful, nonetheless, that the great works of anthropological field work and works even today are performed well without such an aid. But, then, because many tasks *can* be performed by brute force is not to say that mechanical aids would not help enormously. Thus, one cannot be certain that dictating and computerized transcription will not soon replace typewriting.

Number of Copies. Even the least affluent of observers should make at least an original and two carbons of his field notes. The typical practice is to retain one set of notes undisturbed as the running, raw material of observation. Thus, context, sequence, and the like can more easily be summoned up at points of quandary and inquiry at later dates. The other two copies will be literally cut up, filed, and otherwise manipulated. . . .

To the slightly more affluent or resourceful, I should like to recommend a practice described by George McCall. Each day's notes can be typed directly onto ditto, spirit, mimeograph, or other inexpensive duplicating masters. Whatever number of copies one wants are then made, and the masters retained in case one wants even more copies (McCall and Simmons, 1969:76). In such a way, one attains maximum flexibility in manipulating one's observational material.

What Goes In?   What do field notes consist of? At the most general level they are a more or less chronological log of what is happening, to and in the setting and to and in the observer. Beyond this general statement, the following materials typically and properly appear in field notes.

Running Description. For the most part, they consist of a running description of events, people, things heard and overheard, conversations among people, conversations with people. Each new physical setting and person encountered merits a description. Changes in the physical setting or persons should also be recorded. Since one is likely to encounter the same physical settings and persons again and again, such descriptions need not be repeated, only augmented as changes occur. Observers often draw maps into their field notes, indicating the approximate layouts of locations and the physical placement of persons in scenes, indicating also gross movements of persons through a period of observation.

Since the notes will be heavily chronological, records can be kept of approximate times at which various events occurred.

The writing of running descriptions can be guided by at least two rules of thumb.

Be concrete. Rather than summarizing or employing abstract adjectives and adverbs, attempt to be behavioristic and concrete. Attempt to stay at the lowest possible level of inference. Avoid, as much as possible, employing the participants' descriptive and interpretative terms as one's own descriptive and interpretative terms. If person A thought person B was happy, joyous, depressed, or whatever, today, report this as the imputation of person A. Try to capture person B's raw behavioral emissions, leaving aside for that moment any final judgment as to B's "true state" or the "true meaning" of his behavior. The participant's belief as to the "true meaning" of objects, events and people are thus recorded as being just that.

Recall distinctions. Truman Capote has alleged his ability to recall verbatim several hours of conversation. Such an ability is strikingly unusual. More typically, people recall some things verbatim and many other things only in general. Whether or not one is giving a verbatim account should be indicated in one's field notes. One might consider adopting notations such as those employed by Anselm Strauss *et al.* in their study of a mental hospital: "Verbal material recorded within quotations signified exact recall; verbal material within apostrophes indicated a lesser degree of certainty or paraphrasing; and verbal material with no markings meant reasonable recall but not quotation" (Strauss, Schatzman, Bucher, Ehrlich, and Sabshin, 1964:29).

Previously Forgotten, Now Recalled. As observation periods mount up, one finds himself recalling—often at odd moments—items of information he now remembers that he has not previously entered into the field notes. An occurrence previously seen as insignificant, or simply forgotten, presents itself in consciousness as meriting of record. Summoning it up as best one can, enter the item's date, content, context, and the like into the current day's notes.

Analytic Ideas and Inferences. If one is working at it at all, ideas will begin to occur about how things are patterned in this setting; how present occurrences are examples of some sociological or other concept; how things "really seem to work around here"; and the like. Some of these ideas may seem obvious and trivial; some may seem far fetched and wild; and many may seem in between. *Put all of them into the field notes.*

The only proviso about putting them in is to be sure to mark them off as being analytic ideas and inferences. This can be done with various characters that appear on a typewriter keyboard—especially brackets [ ].

When one eventually withdraws from the setting and concentrates upon performing analysis he should thus have more than only raw field material. The period of concerted analysis is greatly facilitated if during the field work itself one is also assembling a background, a foundation of possible lines of analysis and interpretation.

Analytic ideas are likely to be of three varieties. (1) Ideas about the master theme or themes of the study. "What will be the main notions around which all this minutiae is going to be organized?" (2) "Middle-level" chunks of analysis. "Although the topic could not carry the entire analysis, here seems to be developing a set of materials in the field notes that hang together in the following way . . . taking up perhaps ten to twenty pages in the final report." "Relative to this topic, I want to consider . . ." (3) Minute pieces of analysis. "Here is a neat little thing that will perhaps work out in this way . . . taking a few pages to write up in the final report."

One is very likely to have many more of these memos on analytic directions included in his field notes than he will ever include in the final report. But, by building a foundation of memos and tentative pieces of and directions for analysis, the analytic period will be much less traumatic. Analysis becomes a matter of selecting from and working out analytic themes that already exist. (This is in decided contrast to the pure field note grubber who has no ideas and faces the trauma of inventing analysis during the subsequent period of writing the report. Such people tend not to write the reports or to write highly undisciplined description.)

Personal Impressions and Feelings. The field notes are not only for recording the setting; they are for "recording" the observer as well. The observer has his personal opinions of people; he has emotional responses to being an observer and to the setting itself. He can feel discouraged, joyous, rejected, loved, etc. In order to give himself some distance on himself, the observer should also be recording whatever aspect of his emotional life is involved in the setting. If he feels embarrassed, put down, looked upon with particular favor, if he falls in love, hates someone, has an affair, or whatever, this private diary should be keeping track of such facts. Such keeping track can serve at least two important functions. (1) In being at least privately honest with oneself about one's feelings toward objects, events, and people, one may find that some of the participants *also* feel quite similar things and that one's private emotional response was more widespread, thus providing a clue for analysis. In feeling, for instance, that some person in the setting is getting screwed by a turn of events, and getting privately angry over it, one may also discover later that many other people privately felt the same way. And a fact of this kind may lead into important analytic trails. (2) Periodically, one will review his notes, and during analysis one will work with them intensively. A concurrent record of one's emotional state at various past times, might, months later and away from the setting in a cooler frame of mind, allow one to scrutinize one's notes for obvious biases he might have had. One becomes more able to give the benefit of the doubt in cases where one was perhaps too involved or uninvolved in some incident. This running record of one's opinions, impressions, emotions, and the like should, of course, also be labeled as such in the notes.

Notes for Further Information. Any given day's observations are likely to be incomplete. An account of an incident may lack adequate description of given persons' behavior or their conscious intentions. The event, or whatever, may only be sketchily known. A well-described incident may lead one to want to look for further occurrences of events of that kind. In other words, a given day's notes raise a series of observational questions. It is reasonable to make note of these as one is writing up the notes. One can then review the notes and assemble all these queries as reminders of questions unobtrusively to ask of particular people or of things to look for.

Other Aspects   *How Long and Full?* There is the inevitable question of how many pages notes should run for a given observation period. It happens that observers differ enormously in the detail and length of their field notes. Some seem to be frustrated novelists and have been known to write 40 or more single-spaced pages on a three-hour period of observation. Other observers might write only a few pages. Here there are no set rules. Settings differ enormously. Observers' verbal compulsions differ enormously. The kinds of phenomena to which observers are sensitive vary quite widely. One possible rule of thumb is that the notes ought to be full enough adequately to summon up for one again, months later, a reasonably vivid picture of any described event. This probably means that one ought to be writing up, at the very minimum, at least a couple of single-spaced typed pages for every hour of observation. It is quite likely that one will want to write much more.

Let It Flow. Field notes are typically quite private documents, or at least accessible only to one's trusted friends, as in most team observer situations. One need not attempt, then, always to employ correct grammar, punctuate with propriety, hit the right typewriter keys, say only publicly polite things, be guarded about one's feelings—and all those other niceties we affect for strangers. The object in field notes, rather, is to get information down as correctly as one can and to be as honest with one's self as possible. Since they will *never* be public documents—such as a letter or a paper—one can—to modify a current metaphor—*write on.* Let all those mental and jotted notes flow out, typing like a madman with a compulsion.

Field notes are, after all, behind the scenes. It is at the next stage—concerted analysis—that all of this is processed for propriety.

Their Warhol Flavor. I have perhaps made field notes sound intimate and revealing and therefore fascinating reading. To a degree they are. But the overwhelming portion of field notes is constituted of the first category described, "running descriptions."

Thus, they are much like the early movies of Andy Warhol. They are largely mundane, uneventful, and dull. Indeed, if they were otherwise, people would simply publish their field notes. It is precisely because they are little in and of themselves that it is necessary to do analysis. Therefore, do not begin by believing that the field work venture and field notes in particular are always zap-zing affairs. Patience, persistence, drudgery, and dullness occur here, as everywhere else in social life. However, take heart. Field work can also be punctuated by periods of elation and joy over events and the occurrence of insights, ideas, and understandings.

Field Notes as Compulsion. Take heart, too, in the following likely occurrence. Once a regime of jotting regularly and then making disciplined, full notes is established, it can come to have a demand and a logic of its own. The observer can get to feel that unless something he remembers appears in his full notes he is in peril of losing it. He experiences a compulsion to write it up lest it be lost to him, and he does. Upon reaching that level of felt responsibility for logging information in his field notes, the observer is fully *engaged* in field work.

The Sense of Betrayal. Somewhat independently of how much or how little the observer "grooves" with the people observed, some special problems of the observer's orientation arise out of this process of note taking and analysis.

These jottings and cloisterings for drawing up field notes place the observer in a peculiar relation to the people under observation. While they are forgetting and going on to live their lives, he is cloistered somewhere remembering and contemplating their world. Even when an unknown observer, he is playing a different role than they, despite the documentation part of his life not being visible to them. But *he* knows what he is doing. And what he is doing is playing to a different audience. To engage in a regime of documentation and analysis is necessarily to compromise one's local loyalties and intimacies. While the participants forget, the observer remembers.

It happens that participants everywhere do and say many things they would prefer to forget or prefer not to have known, or at least not widely known. In the process of writing up his notes, the observer necessarily violates these participant preferences.

Unless the observer is bent upon presenting the setting in the most self-serving and idealistic fashion, a disparity must necessarily arise. The comprehensive portrait he is likely to present is unlikely to be the one that the participants would want promoted as the best possible public image. The observer is likely to recognize this.

This skewing of understanding becomes all the more poignant because the observer typically forms personal attachments to some, if not all, of the observed. They are likely to confide in him as friends and persons, rather than simply as observed and observer. And, alas, the products of such attachments and diffuseness must go into his field notes and eventually into his reports.

8.7
Data Processing

Chapter 13 of this textbook describes the process whereby social scientific researchers transform their original observations into something that can be manipulated by card sorters and computers. Those remarks are appropriate to *quantitative* social scientific analyses, and they may sometimes apply to portions of field research projects. At the same time, field research is more typically an example of *qualitative* social scientific research, and the comments in Chapter 13 regarding mechanized data processing are inappropriate to much of what the field researcher does. We shall therefore consider field research data processing separately.

The preceding section of this chapter dealt with the ways in which the field researcher observes and records his observations. The section following this one deals with the analysis of field research data. Lying between those two activities is a data processing stage as important to field research as to other methods. It is typically different from the comparable activity in other methods, however, by virtue of the qualitative nature of the data. In the case of field research, data processing is typically a *filing* activity.

Again, I could do no better than to present John Lofland's excellent discussion of this activity.[6]

Establish Files

Perhaps foremost among concrete procedures is the establishment of some kind of *files*. Good filing devices include file folders—often having third-cut tabs—combined with "hanging files," which have overhanging metal "ears" that sit on metal rails in a file drawer. Using folders and hanging files, one can avoid the plague of "falling files" and can place several file folders into a single hanging file. Thus, one has maximum flexibility in grouping and regrouping data into categories of observations and ordering and reordering topics. Another possibility is to employ boxes, such as those in which more expensive bond paper is sold, and to establish shelves of these boxes containing material on various topics. Such boxes may be bought empty and in bulk from wholesale paper dealers. (See also C. W. Mills' discussion of filing in his "On Intellectual Craftsmanship," 1959: 195–226.)

Whatever the concrete details of the physical filing, the aim is to get the material out of the sheer chronological narrative of one's field or interview notes and into a *flexible storage, ordering,* and *retrieval* format. It is here that the advice to have *multiple copies* of one's notes assumes supreme importance. The more copies of a

---

6. *Ibid.*, pp. 118–121.

particular observation/interview response or analytic idea one has, the more categories it can be filed under. Thus, the previously mentioned practice of putting notes on spirit masters seems a particularly good suggestion (see above and also McCall and Simmons, 1969:76). Multiple carbons perform the same function, even though they produce fewer copies. And even if one lacks sufficient copies, cross-referencing notes can be made.

Types of Files

Mundane Files Although I began by speaking of files as crucial stimulants to the analytic process, I want to emphasize that this is not their only function. Nor are analytic files the only kind one wants to keep, at least initially. Files must also be used simply to keep track of *people, places, organizations, documents, and the like.* Such mundane files are organized very much like those in any business enterprise, with information grouped under the most obvious catego-ries, the better to locate it again. Thus, one will almost certainly want to have a folder on each person—or each leading person—under observation. The material that one accumulates through time on the most obvious of units can help—through review—to point up crucial things not considered about the unit. The bulk of such material may reveal patterns not previously contemplated.

Even a study of a highly limited setting and number of people can produce a very complex set of facts, activities, etc., for which one needs aids in simply keeping the most mundane matters straight. Mundane files facilitate laying hands on a record of something that happened, let us say, several months in the past. One can easily spend hours trying to locate it in chronological notes or analytic files, but a mundane file locates the material immediately.

Analytic Files Mundane files are likely to provide a stark contrast to the physically separate, analytic files. Any given piece of information is easily imbued with multiple and diverse analytic significance. While a given piece of information has—by intent—only one or a very few locations in one's mundane files, that same piece of information can—and should—have a variety of locations in one's analytic files. While one is tame in his mundane files, one can and should be wild in his analytic files. When a given episode, or whatever, suggests several kinds of notions or significances, write them up in a brief (or extended) fashion (along with the empirical materials), label file folders, and enter those folders into one's fuller set of analytic files. Additional pieces of information may then be added to each of these file folders if they suggest the same kind of significance.

Early-on in this process of building analytic files one need not be terribly concerned over whether a given category is indeed viable in the long run, ultimately makes any kind of sense, or whatever. The aim, rather, is to set up as many separate items (literally, file folders) as one is prompted to and feels reasonably excited about. The hard day of finally reckoning with one's analytic impulses comes later, during the period of concerted analysis.

The content categories (literally, file folder headings) of one's analytic files are categories such as those described [earlier]. The six categories described there, however, are only *example paradigms* of categories for analytic files. One should feel free not only to adopt into his analytic files any, some, or all of those six example paradigms, but also to strike off into other directions. Often a simple idea that at the moment fits together with nothing else will seem worthy of having its own folder in one's analytic files.

The most general point is that analytic files are an *emergent coding scheme* by means of which to extract from an order the unordered flux of raw reality. Most important, the coding scheme embodied in the analytic files is an emergent, *sociological-analytic coding scheme.*

Field Work File   In addition to mundane and analytic files, one ought also to have a folder in which he accumulates material on the process of doing the research itself. It is a relatively standard practice for the researcher to include in his report an account of how the research was done. A file already built on this topic will facilitate later writing of such an account.

Periodicity in Filing

The exigencies of interviewing and observation and other facets of one's life will presumably govern the frequency with which one engages in filing sessions. One might prefer to do it every day, once a week, or even once a month, depending upon the rate of one's interviewing and observation and the accumulation of material that needs to be managed. One might vary, too, in how frequently he performs mundane filing as opposed to analytic filing. Simply to keep track of material at a gross level, one might want to do mundane filing more frequently. One is "saved" from the necessity of doing analytic filing daily by virtue of assiduously placing analytic ideas in the running notes. The idea about the category is thus preserved for later physically storing it in a distinctive place, along with subsequent accumulations on the same category.

Scissors, Circling, and Filing

At a very concrete level, all of this means that one needs to disassemble copies of his notes for the purpose of splitting them up into various kinds of categories. If one has a limited number of copies, one will be literally scissoring the notes into small bits of paper and putting them into file folders, boxes, or whatever. If one has many copies of his notes, he can simply circle or otherwise mark the relevant information on a page or pages before placing them into the files. If one has only a few copies of his notes or other material, cross-referencing notes can be entered in various files.

File Everything?

There is the inevitable consternating question of how much material should be filed, especially analytically. Some pieces of information will seem to have no interesting analytic significance whatsoever. Or, a given piece of information may be the fiftieth instance of a category and by then terribly redundant.

For this problem I can offer no firm answer, save perhaps to counsel a middle way. If one finds analytic significance in only a very small part of his materials and therefore files little, that fact itself ought to be made a central problem of the study. If one spends an enormous amount of time filing and files practically everything in sight, then one might ask himself whether a means has been transformed into an end, with consequent deleterious effects upon the *real* end, which is to write an excellent qualitative analysis.

Like anything done in excess, too soon, or compulsively, filing can be a vice. It seems likely that one will want to do only the most gross of mundane filing right in the beginning of his study. One will want, however, to be writing down analytic ideas as they occur. But since there is a record of them, and since such ideas shift constantly, it may be of little use to enshrine each and every one in a file folder of its own. Instead, wait until some minimum of stability is attained in analytic formulations. One will be able to discern this by the constant recurrence of ideas in connection with recurrent material in one's field notes.

One Set of Materials Intact

All of this splitting of the materials into mundane, analytic, and field work files facilitates being on top of what is happening and evolving an analysis. But it tends to obscure that nebulous quality called "context." In scrutinizing a particular piece of filed material, the question can arise: What else was happening then that seemed irrelevant at the time but now seems important? One wants then to look back at the more general context. In order to do so most easily, one needs an intact chronological record of the past. A full set of one's materials should therefore be kept in the order in which they were originally collected.

A chronologically intact set of materials is useful, also, simply for locating information itself that is not obviously available in one or another of the mundane or analytic files. And, it is useful simply for reading and reviewing from beginning to end, as a stimulus for thinking about larger patterns that develop only over longer periods of time and for "larger" units of comprehension.

8.8
Data Analysis

Through the previous discussions, I have omitted a direct discussion of what are the most critical aspects of field research: how the researcher determines what is important to observe, and how he formulates his analytical conclusions on the basis of those observations. I have indicated that observation and analysis are interwoven processes in field research. Now it is time to say something about that interweaving.

As perhaps the most general guide, the field researcher looks especially for *similarities* and *dissimilarities*. (That just about covers everything he is likely to see.) On the one hand, he looks for those patterns of interaction and events that are generally common to what he is studying. In sociological terms, he looks for *norms* of behavior. What do all the participants in a situation share in terms of behavior patterns? Do all jaywalkers check for policemen before darting across the street? Do all the participants in a campus political rally join in the same forms of supportive behavior during speeches? Do all the participants in a religious revival meeting shout "Amen" at the appropriate times? Do all hookers dress seductively? In this sense, then, the field researcher is especially attuned to the discovery of *universals*. As he first notices these, he becomes more deliberate in observing whether they are truly universal in the situation he is observing. If they are essentially universal, he asks why that should be the case. What function do they serve, for example? This explanation may suggest conditions under which the "universals" would not appear, and he may look around for those conditions in order to test his expectations.

On the other hand, the field researcher is constantly alert to *differences*. He is on the watch for deviation from the general norms he may have noted. Although most of the participants in a religious revival meeting murmur "Amen" throughout the leader's sermon, he may note a few who do not. Why do they deviate from the norm? In what other ways are they different from the other participants?

Sometimes the researcher will find aspects of behavior that are more characterized by dissimilarity and similarity in general; there is no easily identifiable norm. How do different people handle the "problem" of standing in line for tickets at a movie theater? Some stare into space, some strike up conversations with strangers, some talk to themselves, some keep standing on tiptoes to see if the line is really moving, some keep counting their money, some read, and so forth. An important part of the field researcher's initial task in such situations is to create a *taxonomy* of behaviors: an organized listing of the variety of types. Having done this, he then seeks to discover other characteristics associated with those different types of behavior. Are the "rich-looking" or "poor-looking" moviegoers more likely to recount their money? Do men strike up more conversations with strangers than women? Do old people talk to themselves more than young people? His purpose in all this is the discovery of general patterns.

To the field researcher, the formulation of theoretical propositions, the observation of empirical events, and the evaluation of theory are typically all part of the same on-going process. While his actual field observations may be preceded by deductive theoretical formulations, the field researcher seldom if ever merely tests a theory and lets it go at that. Rather, he develops theories, or generalized understandings, over the course of his observations. About each new set of empirical observations, he asks what it all represents in terms of general social scientific principles. His tentative conclusions, so arrived at, then provide the conceptual framework for further observations. In the course of his observations of jaywalking, for example, it may strike him that whenever a well-dressed and important-looking person jaywalks, others are encouraged to follow him. Having noticed this apparent pattern, the field researcher might pay more attention to this aspect of the phenomenon, thereby testing more carefully his initial impression. He might subsequently observe that his initial impression held true only when the jaywalking "leader" was also middle-aged, for example, or perhaps only if he were caucasian. These more specific impressions would simultaneously lead the field researcher to pay special attention to the new variables and require that he consider what general principle might be underlying the new observations.

There is an inherent advantage in field research in that the interaction between data collection and data analysis affords a greater flexibility than is typically found in connection with other research methods. The survey researcher, for example, must at some point commit himself to a questionnaire, thus limiting the kind of data that will be collected. If his subsequent analyses indicate that he has overlooked the most important variable of all, he is out of luck. The field researcher, on the other hand, is in a position to modify continually his research design as indicated by his observations, his developing theoretical perspective, or changes in what he is studying.

This advantage in field research comes at the price of an accompanying danger. As the researcher develops theoretical understanding of what he is observing, there is a constant risk that he will observe only those things that support his theoretical conclusions. Having concluded, for example, that a religious group under study will, under certain conditions, intensify its attempts to gain new members, he is likely to pay more attention to such attempts whenever the conditions exist. He may even misinterpret what is happening in such a way as to support his developing theoretical perspective. This is not to suggest that such *selective perceptions* and misinterpretations will be conscious on the part of the researcher. Rather, he will not even be aware of them.

This danger may be at least partially avoided in a number of ways.

First, the field researcher may augment his qualitative observations with quantitative ones. If he expects religious proselytization to be greater under some conditions than under others, he might formulate a concrete operational definition of proselytization and begin counting under the different conditions. For example, he might note the number of group members who raised this topic, the number of members assigned to the task, or perhaps the number of new converts added to the group. Even rough quantifications such as these might provide a safeguard against selective perception and misinterpretation.

Second, we should recall that one of the norms of science is its *intersubjectivity*. The field researcher, then, might enlist the assistance of others as he begins to refine his theoretical conclusions. In the case of religious conversion, for example, he might ask colleagues to attend several meetings of the group over time and to indicate their observations as to the relative stress placed on proselytization in each of the meetings.

Finally, as with all such problems, sensitivity and awareness may provide sufficient safeguards. Merely by being aware of the problem, the researcher may be able to avoid it.

In connection with the combined process of data collection and data analysis, the following general procedure usually would be advisable. As already mentioned, the researcher should record his observations in detail either during or immediately after making them. Following each period of observation and notation, he should review his notes, adding recollections and interpretations. After spending the day with jaywalkers, for example, he might spend the evening reviewing, revising, and interpreting his notes. It is important that this review process be carried on continually. Reviewing his notes while an event is still fresh in his mind will be of far greater value than doing so once the event has dimmed in his memory.

In all social science research methods, there is a large gap between understanding the skills of data analysis and actually using those skills effectively. Typically, experience is the only effective bridge across the gap. This situation applies more to field research than to any other method. It is worth recalling the parallel between the activities of the scientist and those of the investigative detective. While fledgling detectives can be taught technical skills and can be given general guidelines, insight and experience separate good detectives from mediocre ones. The same is true of field researchers.

8.9
Strengths and Weaknesses of Field Research

I have already touched on some of the particular strengths and weaknesses of field research as compared with other methods available to the social scientist. It will be useful at this point to review those earlier comments and to consider additional strengths and weaknesses.

As indicated earlier, field research is especially effective for studying the subtle nuances of attitudes and behavior, and for examining social processes over time. For these reasons, the chief strength of this method lies in the depth of understanding that it may permit. Although other research methods may be challenged as "superficial," that charge is seldom lodged against field research.

Flexibility is another advantage of field research. In this method, you may modify your research design at any time, as discussed earlier. Moreover, you are always prepared to engage in field research, whenever the occasion should arise, whereas you could not as easily initiate a survey or an experiment.

Field research can be relatively inexpensive. Whereas other social scientific research methods may require expensive equipment or an expensive research staff, field research typically can be undertaken by one researcher with a notebook and a pencil. This is not to say that field research is never expensive. The nature of the research project, for example, may require a large number of trained observers. Expensive recording equipment may be required. Or the researcher may wish to undertake participant observation of customer-waitress interactions in expensive Paris nightclubs.

Field research has a number of weaknesses as well. First, being qualitative rather than quantitative, it seldom yields precise descriptive statements about a large population. Observing casual political discussions in laundromats, for example, would not yield trustworthy estimates of the future voting behavior of the total electorate. Nevertheless, the study could provide important insights into the process of political attitude formation.

More generally, the conclusions drawn from qualitative field research are often regarded as suggestive rather than definitive. In part this is a function of the informal sampling and uncertain representativeness of the observations made and recorded. Also involved is the nature of operational definition and measurement in field research. Since field research depends so heavily on the judgments and total comprehension of the researcher, operating within the context of the phenomenon under study, field research seldom involves the uniform application of precise operational definitions. Thus, for example, the field researcher may draw general conclusions regarding the "radical" and the "moderate" members of a student political organization, based on his overall assessment of the attitudes and actions of individuals. He might be unable, ultimately, to specify his definitions and to tell exactly why he labeled a given student as "radical" and another as "moderate"; another observer might draw different conclusions.

The chief weaknesses of field research, then, are in relation to the scientific norms of *generalizability* and *intersubjectivity.* This is not to say that a particular set of field research conclusions are not generally applicable, nor that two field researchers would not arrive at the same research conclusion. We simply have less assurance in these regards than would be the case for more structured research methods.

Overall, field research is an excellent vehicle for "exploratory" research, and it is is quite weak in terms of "descriptive" research as discussed in Chapter 3. As to "explanatory" research, it has the great advantage of dealing with processes occurring over time, though it is advisable to replicate the explanatory conclusions of field research using more rigorously controlled research designs.

8.10
Summary

Chapter 8 has described some of the characteristics and techniques involved in one particular method of observation, or data collection, in social research: field research. Basically, this technique is the direct observation of events by the researcher at the scene of the action. As noted at the outset, this is a research method that you have been using all your life and one that is used by other professionals such as newspaper reporters.

The chapter began with a discussion of the topics most appropriate to field research. First, it is effective in the study of those phenomena that can be understood adequately only in their full, natural settings. Moreover, we noted that it is especially useful for the study of some processes taking place over time, such as the development and course of a riot.

One of the procedural options open to the field researcher is the choice of several different *roles* that he may assume. Essentially, these choices revolve around (1) whether he identifies himself as a researcher to those people he is observing and (2) whether he participates in the events under study. The several different possibilities in these regards were discussed in terms of their ethical and scientific aspects.

Next, the chapter took up the details of getting ready for field research and beginning to make observations. We saw some of the preparatory steps, such as library research and the interviewing of informants, that can make for more fruitful subsequent observations in the field.

Sampling in field research is usually handled differently than in other methods of observation. Although the field researcher is guided by the same basic concern as other researchers for representativeness, he may achieve this differently. In particular, he is likely to pay more attention to unusual or deviant cases than other researchers. The different types of sampling methods employed in field research were described.

The specific techniques for making and recording observations were the next focus of the chapter. Note taking, we saw, is an essential skill in field research, yet it is a difficult skill to master. Note-taking suggestions were made.

In field research, observation, data processing, and analysis are interrelated activities far more than is the case for other social research methods. The field researcher makes and records a set of observations, reviews and organizes them, and looks for meaningful patterns in what he has observed; the recognition of patterns and the development of generalized understanding then suggest a modified strategy for subsequent observations. The new observations may then reveal new patterns, modifying the researcher's understanding further, and revising his observational strategy.

The chapter concluded with a discussion of the special strengths and weaknesses of field research. We found it especially useful as a way of developing a fuller comprehension of social processes in their natural settings but discovered that it is weakest in terms of the scientific norms of *generalizability* and *intersubjectivity*.

8.11
Main Points

1. Field research is a social research method that involves the direct observation of social phenomena in their natural settings.

2. The researcher may or may not identify himself as a researcher to the people he is observing. Identifying himself as a researcher may have some effect on the nature of what he is observing, but concealing his identity may involve deceit.

3. The researcher may or may not participate in that which he is observing. Participating in the events may make it easier for him to conceal his identity as a researcher, but participation is likely to affect what is being observed.

4. Since controlled probability sampling techniques are usually impossible in field research, a rough form of quota sampling may be used in the attempt to achieve better representativeness in observations.

5. Snowball sampling is a method through which the researcher develops an ever increasing set of sample observations. He asks one participant in the event under study to recommend others for interviewing, and each of the subsequently interviewed participants is asked for further recommendations.

6. Often, the careful examination of deviant cases in field research can yield important insights into the "normal" patterns of social behavior.

7. The field journal is the backbone of field research, for this is where the researcher records his observations. Journal entries should be detailed, yet concise. If possible, observations should be recorded as they are made; otherwise, they should be recorded as soon afterward as possible.

8. Field research is a form of qualitative research, although it is sometimes possible to quantify some of the observations that are being recorded.

9. In field research, observation, data processing, and analysis are interwoven and cyclical processes.

8.12
Annotated Bibliography

Becker, Howard, Geer, Blanche, Hughes, Everett, and Strauss, Anselm, *Boys in White: Student Culture in Medical School* (Chicago: University of Chicago Press, 1961). An excellent and important illustration of field research methods. This study, involving continued interaction with medical school students over the course of their professional training, examines the impact of their experiences on their values and orientations. An informal biography of this project, by Blanche Geer, may be found in Phillip Hammond (ed.), *Sociologists at Work* (New York: Basic Books, 1964) and is also reprinted in McCall-Simmons (see below).

Lofland, John, *Analyzing Social Settings* (Belmont, California: Wadsworth, 1971). An unexcelled presentation of field research methods from beginning to end. This eminently readable little book manages successfully to draw the links between the logic of scientific inquiry and the nitty-gritty practicalities of observing, communicating, recording, filing, reporting, and everything else involved in field research. In addition, the book contains a wealth of references to field research illustrations.

Lofland, John, *Doomsday Cult: A Study of Conversion, Proselytization, and Maintenance of Faith* (Englewood Cliffs, N.J.: Prentice-Hall, 1966). Another excellent illustration of field research methods in practice. This study examines the dynamic development of a deviant religious movement still active today. A shorter report of this study may be found in John Lofland and Rodney Stark, "Becoming a World-Saver: Conversion to a Deviant Perspective," *American Sociological Review*, 30:862–875 (December, 1965).

McCall, George, and Simmons, J. L., (eds.), *Issues in Participant Observation: A Text and Reader* (Reading, Mass.: Addison-Wesley, 1969). An excellent collection of important articles dealing with field research. The thirty-two selections cover most aspects of field research, both theoretical and practical. Moreover, many of the selections provide illustrations of actual research projects.

9

Content Analysis

9.1
Introduction

Content analysis, the subject of this chapter, differs from the other modes of observation considered in the book in that individual people are *not* typically the units of analysis. Nor are people observed directly as, for example, in field research. Rather, human communications are the topics of study, and communication units such as books, paragraphs, broadcasts, or songs are the units of analysis. Content analysis studies a type of social artifact as mentioned in Chapter 3.

Such communications may be studied through content analysis either for the purpose of understanding communication processes or for understanding the originators of the communication. It is primarily in the latter sense that we consider content analysis in this chapter.

I shall treat content analysis as another mode of observation through which to obtain information suitable for describing and explaining social phenomena. To determine whether a given newspaper might more appropriately be characterized as "liberal" or "conservative," we might ask the newspaper's editor for a self-assessment in a survey, or we might undertake a content analysis of the paper's editorial positions on various issues.

9.2
Topics Appropriate to Content Analysis

Content analysis methods may be applied to virtually any form of communication. Among the possible artifacts for study are books, poems, newspapers, songs, paintings, speeches, letters, laws, and constitutions, as well as any component or collections thereof. Are popular French novels more concerned with love than American ones? Was the popular American music of the 1960's more politically cynical than the popular German music during that period? Do political candidates who primarily address "bread and butter" issues get elected more often than those who address issues of principle? Each of these questions addresses a social scientific research topic: the first might address "national character," the second political orientations, and the third political process. While such topics might be addressed through the observation of individual people, content analysis provides another approach.

The paradigmatic question in communication research is: "Who says what, to whom, how, and with what effect?" [1] Holsti[2] suggests adding "why?" to this formulation. Content analysis, as a mode of observation, involves the standardized coding of the *what* in this formulation, and the analysis of data collected in this mode may be addressed to the *why* and the *with what effect*.

9.3
Sampling in Content Analysis

In the study of communications, as in the study of people, it is often impossible to observe directly all the possible subjects of study. If we were to study, for example, the relative use of metaphors by French and American politicians, we surely would be unable to examine every utterance of every French and American politician. For practical purposes, therefore, it would be essential that we select a sample for observation.

As we shall see, the logic and technique of sampling in content analysis very closely parallel those described in Chapter 6. In this section, we shall begin with an examination of the *units of analysis* that may be examined in content analysis; then we shall review some appropriate sampling techniques.

Units of Analysis

You will recall from Chapter 6 that the units of analysis are the individual units about which or whom descriptive and explanatory statements are to be made. If we wished to examine the orientation of American voters, for example, the individual American voter would be the unit of analysis in that study. If we wished to compute the average family income, the individual family would be the unit of analysis. If we wished to compare divorce rates between religiously mixed and unmixed marriages, the individual marriage would be the unit of analysis.

It was pointed out in Chapter 6 that determining the appropriate unit of analysis is not always a simple task. For example, in computing the average family income, we might ask individual members of families how much money they make. Individual people, then, would be the units of observation, but the individual family would still be the unit of analysis. Similarly, we may wish to compare crime rates of different cities in terms of their sizes, geographical regions, racial compositions, and other differences. Even though the characteristics of these cities are partly a function of the behaviors and characteristics of their individual residents, cities would ultimately be the units of analysis.

---

1. See Harold B. Lasswell, Daniel Lerne, and I. de S. Pool, *The Comparative Study of Symbols* (Stanford: Stanford University Press, 1952).
2. Ole R. Holsti, *Content Analysis for the Social Sciences and Humanities* (Reading, Mass.: Addison-Wesley, 1969).

The complexity of this issue is often more apparent in content analysis than in other research methods. This is especially the case when the units of observation differ from the units of analysis. A few examples should clarify this distinction.

Let's suppose we are interested in learning about sex discrimination and the legal system in America. Suppose, as a start, that we want to find out whether criminal law or civil law makes the most distinctions between men and women. In this instance, individual laws would be both the units of observation and the units of analysis. We might select a sample of, say, a state's criminal and its civil laws, and we might then categorize each law in the sample in terms of whether it makes a distinction between men and women. In this fashion, we would be able to determine whether criminal or civil law distinguishes most by sex.

Somewhat differently, we might wish to determine whether states that enacted laws distinguishing between different racial groups were more likely to enact laws distinguishing between men and women than was true of states that did not distinguish races. While the examination of this question would involve, like the previous one, the examination and coding of individual acts of legislation, the unit of analysis in this latter case would be the individual state.

Let's suppose we are interested in representationalism in painting. If our interest is in comparing the relative popularity of representational and nonrepresentational paintings, the individual paintings would be our units of analysis. If, on the other hand, we wish to discover whether representationalism in painting is more characteristic of wealthy or impoverished painters, of educated or uneducated painters, of capitalist or socialist painters, individual painters would be our units of analysis.

It is essential that this issue be clear, since sample selection depends largely on what the unit of analysis is. If individual writers are the units of analysis, the sample design should select all or a sample of the writers appropriate to the research question. If books, on the other hand, are the units of analysis, we would select a sample of books, regardless of their authors.

All this is not to suggest that sampling is to be based solely on the units of analysis. Indeed, we may often subsample—select samples of subcategories—for each individual unit of analysis. Thus, if writers are the units of analysis, we might (1) select a sample of writers from the total population of writers, (2) select a sample of the books written by each writer selected, and (3) select portions of each selected book for observation and coding.

Sampling Techniques

In content analysis of written prose, sampling may occur at any or all of the following levels: words, phrases, sentences, paragraphs, sections, chapters, books, writers, or the contexts relevant to the works. Other forms of communication may also be samples at any of the conceptual levels appropriate to them.

Any of the conventional sampling techniques discussed in Chapter 6 may be employed in content analysis. We might select a *random* or *systematic* sample of French and American novelists, of laws passed in the state of Mississippi, or of Shakespearean soliloquies. We might select (with a random start) every twenty-third paragraph in Tolstoy's *War and Peace.* Or, we might number all of the songs recorded by The Beatles and select a random sample (using a random number table) of 25.

Stratified sampling is also appropriate to content analysis. To analyze the editorial policies of American newspapers, for example, we might first group all newspapers by region of the country, size of the community in which they are published, frequency of publication, or average circulation. We might then select a stratified random or systematic sample of newspapers for analysis. Having done this, we might then select a sample of editorials from each selected newspaper, perhaps stratified chronologically.

Cluster sampling is equally appropriate to content analysis. Indeed, if individual editorials were to be the unit of analysis in the previous example, then the selection of newspapers at the first stage of sampling would be a cluster sample. In an analysis of political speeches, we might begin by selecting a sample of politicians; each politician would represent a "cluster" of political speeches.

It should be repeated that sampling need not end when we reach the unit of analysis. If novels are the unit of analysis in a study, we might select a sample of novelists, subsamples of novels written by each selected author, and a sample of paragraphs within each novel. We would then analyze the content of the paragraphs for the purpose of describing the novels themselves.

Let us turn now to a more direct examination of "analysis," which has been mentioned so frequently in the previous discussions. At this point, "content analysis" will refer to the coding or classification of material being observed. Part IV of this book will deal with "analysis" in terms of manipulating those classifications to draw descriptive and explanatory conclusions.

9.4
Coding in Content Analysis

As a mode of observation, content analysis is essentially an operation of coding. Communications—oral, written, or other—are coded or classified in terms of some conceptual framework. Thus, for example, newspaper editorials may be coded as "liberal" or "conservative". Radio broadcasts might be coded as "propagandistic" or not. Novels might be coded as "romantic" or not. Paintings might be coded as "representational" or not. Political speeches might be coded as "containing character assassinations" or not. Recall that terms such as these are subject to many interpretations, and the researcher must specify his definitions clearly.

Coding in content analysis involves the logic of conceptualization and operationalization as these have been discussed in Chapter 4. In content analysis, as in other research methods, you must refine your conceptual framework and develop specific methods for observing in relation to that framework. This section discusses those processes in the context of content analysis.

Manifest and Latent Content

As discussed earlier in the context of questionnaires and of field research, social researchers often face a decision between *specificity* and *depth* of understanding. By their very nature, standardized questionnaires represent the epitome of specificity. The operational definitions of concepts are totally clear since they are comprised of specific questions and specific sets of answers contained in a questionnaire administered to all subjects in the research project. Because of this very trait, the survey method may often seem to be superficial. Field research, on the other hand, tends to involve less specificity in the definition and measurement of concepts, characterizing people, for example, more on the basis of total impressions: actions, words, and gestures within their natural context. In this sense, field research provides a greater depth of understanding while having less specificity.

The content analyst faces this same issue in organizing his coding activities. Coding the **manifest content** of communication would more closely approximate the use of standardized questionnaires. To determine, for example, how "erotic" certain novels are, he might simply count the number of times the word "love" appears in each novel, or the average number of appearances per page. Or, he might use a list of words, such as "love," each of which might serve as an indicator of the "erotic" nature of the novel. This method would have the advantages of ease and *reliability* in coding and of letting the reader of the research report know precisely how eroticism was measured. It would have a disadvantage, on the other hand, in terms of *validity.* Surely the term "erotic novel" conveys a richer and deeper meaning than the number of times the word "love" is used.

Alternatively, you may code the **latent content** of the communication. In the present example, you might read an entire novel or a sample of paragraphs or pages and make an overall assessment of how "erotic" the novel was. Although your total assessment might very well be influenced by the appearance of words such as "love" and "kiss", it would not depend fully on the frequency with which such words appeared.

Clearly, this second method would appear better designed for tapping the underlying meaning of communications, but this advantage comes at a cost of reliability and specificity. Especially if more than one person were coding the novel, somewhat different definitions or standards might be employed. A passage that might be regarded as "erotic" by one coder might seem "nonerotic" to another. Even if you do all of the coding yourself, there is no guarantee that your definitions and standards will remain constant throughout the enterprise. Moreover, the reader of your research report would be generally uncertain as to the definitions you have employed.

Wherever possible, the best solution to this dilemma is to employ *both* methods. A given unit of observation should receive the same character-ization from both methods if coding *manifest* content has validity and coding *latent* content has reliability. If the agreement produced by the two methods is fairly close though imperfect, the final score might reflect the scores assigned in the two independent methods. If, on the other hand, coding manifest and latent contents produces gross disagreement, you would be well advised to reconsider your theoretical conceptualization.

Conceptualization and the Creation of Code Categories

In all research methods, conceptualization and operationalization typically involve the interaction of theoretical concerns and empirical obser-vations. If, for example, you believe some newspaper editorials to be "liberal" and others to be "conservative", ask yourself *why* you believe that to be the case. Read some editorials, asking yourself which ones are liberal and which ones are conservative. Why did you feel that way? Was the political orientation of a particular editorial most clearly indicated by its manifest content, or by its tone? Was your decision based on the use of certain terms (e.g., "pinko," "right-winger," etc.), or on the support or opposition given to a particular issue or political personality?

Both inductive and deductive methods should be employed in this activity. If you are testing theoretical propositions, your theories should suggest empirical indicators of concepts. If you have begun with specific empirical observations, you should attempt to derive general principles relating to them and then apply those principles to other empirical observa-tions.

Throughout this activity, you should remember that the operational definition of any variable is comprised of the *attributes* included in it. Such attributes, moreover, should be mutually exclusive and exhaustive. A newspa-per editorial, for example, should not be described as both "liberal" and "conservative," though you should probably allow for some to be "middle-of-the-road." It may be sufficient for your purposes to code novels as being "erotic" or "nonerotic," but you may also want to consider a range of variation in this extending to novels that are "antierotic." Paintings might be classified as "represensational" or not, if that satisfied your research purpose, or you might wish to further classify them as "impressionistic," "abstract," "allegorical," and so forth.

Realize, further, that different levels of measurement may be em-ployed in content analysis. You may, for example, use the *nominal* categories of "liberal" and "conservative," for characterizing newspaper editorials, or you might wish to use a more refined *ordinal* ranking ranging from "extremely liberal" to "extremely conservative." It is important that you bear in mind, however, that the level of measurement implicit in your coding methods does not necessarily represent that level of measurement in terms of your variables. If you were to count the number of times the word "love" appeared in a novel, the raw score assigned to that novel would be a *ratio* measurement. If the word "love" appeared 100 times in novel A and 50 times in novel B, you would be justified in saying that the word "love" appeared twice as often in novel A but not that novel A was twice as "erotic" as novel B. This is true for the same reason that agreeing with twice as many anti-Semitic statements in a questionnaire does not make one twice as anti-Semitic.

No coding scheme should be used in content analysis until it has been carefully *pretested*. You should decide what manifest or latent contents of communications will be regarded as indicators of the different attributes comprising your research variable, write down these operational definitions, and then use them in the actual coding of several units of observation. If more than one person is to be engaged in the coding phase of the final project, each of them should independently code the same set of observations. With several coders, you should then determine the extent of agreement produced. In any event, you should take special note of any difficult cases: those observations that were not easily classified in terms of the operational definition. Finally, you should review the overall results of the pretest effort to insure that such results will be appropriate to your analytical concerns. If, for example, all of the pretest newspaper editorials have been coded "liberal," you may want to reconsider your definition of that attribute.

As with other types of quantitative research, it is not essential that you commit yourself in advance to a specific definition of each concept. Often, you will do better to devise the most appropriate definition of a concept on the basis of your subsequent quantitative analyses. In the case of "erotic" novels, for example, you might do well to count separately the frequency with which different "erotic" words appear. This procedure would provide you with the resources for determining, during your later analysis, which of the words, if any, or which combination thereof provided the most useful indication of your variable. (Part Four—especially Chapter 15—of this book will tell you how to do that.)

Counting and Record-Keeping

If a quantitative analysis of your content analytic data is to be undertaken, it is essential that your coding operation be amenable to data processing. Chapter 13 of this book will explain the requirements of data processing, but some specific comments are in order at this point.

First, the end product of your coding must be *numerical*. If you are counting the frequency of appearance of certain words, phrases, or other manifest content, this will necessarily be the case. Even if you are coding latent content on the basis of overall judgments, it will be necessary to represent your coding decision numerically: 1 = "very liberal," 2 = "moderately liberal," 3 = "moderately conservative," and so on.

Second, it is essential that your record keeping clearly distinguishes between your units of analysis and your units of observation, especially if these two are different. Your initial coding, of course, must relate to your units of observation. If novelists are your units of analysis, for example, and you wish to characterize them through a content analysis of their novels, your primary records will represent novels. You may then combine your scoring of individual novels for purposes of characterizing each of the individual novelists.

Third, when counting, it will normally be important to record the *base* from which the counting is done. It would probably be useless to know the number of "realistic" paintings produced by a given painter without knowing the number that he had painted altogether; he would be regarded as a "realistic" painter if a high percentage of his paintings were of that genre. Similarly, it would tell us little that the word "love" appeared 87 times in a novel if we did not know about how many words there were in the novel altogether.

The issue of observation base is most easily resolved if *every* observation is coded in terms of one of the attributes making up the variables in question. Rather than simply counting the number of "liberal" editorials in a given collection, for example, code each editorial examined in terms of its political orientation, even if it must be coded "no apparent orientation."

In all cases, the end product of coding should be essentially the same. A set of numerical scores must be assigned to each of the units of analysis, as will be discussed in greater detail in Chapter 13. Figure 9-1 is a hypothetical illustration of a portion of a tally sheet that might result from the coding of newspaper editorials.

Note in the illustration that newspapers are the units of analysis. Our purpose in this hypothetical project is to describe and explain the editorial policies of different newspapers. Each newspaper has been assigned an identification number to facilitate mechanized processing. In the second column in the illustration, we have a space for indicating the number of editorials coded for each newspaper. This will be an important piece of information, since we want to be able to say "22 percent of all the editorials were pro-United Nations," not just "there were 8 pro-United Nations editorials."

There is a column in the illustration for assigning a "subjective" overall assessment of the newspapers' editorial policies. (Such assignments might subsequently be compared with the several "objective" measures.) Other columns provide space for recording the numbers of editorials reflecting specific editorial positions. In a real content analysis, there would be additional spaces for recording other editorial positions as well as other noneditorial information about each newspaper, such as region in which published, circulation, and so forth.

9.5
Strengths and Weaknesses of Content Analysis

Probably the greatest advantage of content analysis is its economy in terms of both time and money. It might be feasible for a single college student to undertake a content analysis, whereas undertaking a survey, for example, might not be feasible. There is no requirement for a large research staff; no special equipment is required. As long as you had access to the material to be coded, you could undertake content analysis.

Newspaper ID	Number of editorials evaluated	SUBJECTIVE EVALUATION 1. Very liberal 2. Moderately liberal 3. Middle-of-road 4. Moderately conservative 5. Very conservative	Number of "anticommunist" editorials	Number of "pro-UN" editorials	Number of "anti-UN" editorials
001	37	2	0	8	0
002	26	5	10	0	6
003	44	4	2	1	2
004	22	3	1	2	3
005	30	1	0	6	0

Figure 9-1. Sample Tally Sheet (Partial)

Safety is another advantage of content analysis. If you discover that you have botched up a survey or an experiment, you may be forced to repeat the whole research project with all the attendant costs in time and money. If you botch up your field research, it may be simply impossible to redo the project; the event under study might no longer exist. In content analysis, although you might be forced to repeat a portion of the study, that more likely would be feasible than in the case of other research methods. You might be required, moreover, only to recode a portion of your data rather than to repeat the entire enterprise.

Another important, and nearly unique, strength of content analysis has to do with *historical research.* As long as historical records exist, content analysts easily may study past periods of history or make comparisons over time. You might focus on the imagery of blacks conveyed in American novels of 1850–1860, for example, or you might examine changing imagery from 1850 to the present.

Finally, content analysis has the advantage of being *unobtrusive* (see Chapter 12). That is, the content analyst seldom has any effect on that which he is studying. Since the novels have already been written, the paintings already painted, the speeches already presented, subsequent content analyses can have no effect on them. This advantage is not present in all research methods.

Content analysis has disadvantages as well. For one thing, content analysis is limited to the examination of *recorded* communications. While such communications may be oral, written, or graphic, they must be recorded in some fashion to permit analysis.

Another problem in content analysis, that of validity, has already been discussed. You may have difficulty developing counting and coding methods that adequately represent your theoretical concepts. At base, this is no different from the problem that you face in constructing a standardized questionnaire. In the case of content analysis, however, you have less freedom and flexibility in the matter. You cannot, for example, dictate the population of words that may be used in writing novels. Rather, you must work with the communications that have been produced and are available for analysis. These difficulties notwithstanding, content analysis may be fruitfully employed in the analysis of a variety of social research topics.

9.6
Summary

Chapter 9 has addressed content analysis as a mode of observation in social research. We saw that this method is different from most other research methods in that it does not focus on people per se but on social artifacts, very often on social communications such as books, songs, paintings, and so forth. While content analysis is often used in the study of communication processes, it is also appropriate to the study of other social phenomena. The chapter began with a discussion of some of the topics appropriate to content analysis.

The sampling methods employed in content analysis are essentially those discussed in Chapter 6. Only the units of analysis and sampling units are importantly different. The content analyst may sample words, sentences, paragraphs, books, or similar units of communication, whereas the survey researcher would sample people. The logic and techniques for sampling are the same, however.

Conceptualization and operationalization are essential in content analysis, and these processes must be carried out more explicitly than in field research. The content analyst can develop operational definitions based on either the *manifest* or the *latent* content of communications.

Coding is the primary observation and recording process in content analysis. It was pointed out that coding is an important element in data processing, no matter by what mode of observation the data have been produced.

The chapter concluded with a discussion of the special strengths and weaknesses of content analysis. It has been found to be an economical and unobtrusive research method, but one that is limited to the analysis of recorded communications.

9.7
Main Points

1. Content analysis is a social research method appropriate for studying human communications. Besides being used to study communication processes, it may be used to study other aspects of social behavior.

2. Units of communication, such as words, paragraphs, and books, are the usual units of analysis in content analysis.

3. Standard probability sampling techniques are appropriate in content analysis.

4. *Manifest content* refers to the directly visible, objectively identifiable characteristics of a communication, such as the specific words in a book, the specific colors used in a painting, and so forth. This is one focus for content analysis.

5. *Latent content* refers to the meanings contained within communications. The determination of latent content requires judgments on the part of the researcher.

6. *Coding* is the process of transforming raw data—either manifest or latent content—into standardized, quantitative form.

9.8

Annotated Bibliography

Berelson, Bernard, "Content Analysis," in Lindzey, Gardner (ed.), *Handbook of Social Psychology* (Reading, Mass.: Addison-Wesley, 1954), Vol. 1, 488–522. A somewhat dated but classic overview of content analysis. The author discusses the various aspects of content analysis, describing the options available to the analyst, and provides many illustrations and citations of the use of this method.

Funkhouser, G. Ray, "The Issues of the Sixties: An Exploratory Study of the Dynamics of Public Opinion," *Public Opinion Quarterly*, 37:62–75 (Spring, 1973). A recent illustration of content analysis. This article reports a content analysis of the most prominent issues of the 1960s. News articles appearing in *Time, Newsweek,* and *U.S. News* provide the basis for the analysis. In addition, Gallup Polls of the period are analyzed to determine the issues considered most important by the general public. The relationships between these two rankings are compared. (Vietnam was number one in both.)

Holsti, Ole, *Content Analysis for the Social Sciences and Humanities* (Reading, Mass.: Addison-Wesley, 1969). A more recent, comprehensive overview of content analysis as a method. This excellent book examines the place of content analysis within the context of studying communication processes, discusses and illustrates specific techniques, and cites numerous reports utilizing this method. The book concludes with a substantial discussion of the use of computers in both the coding and analysis of content.

Zuckerman, Harriet, "Nobel Laureates in Science: Patterns of Productivity, Collaboration, and Authorship," *American Sociological Review*, 32:391–403 (June, 1967). Another illustration of the use of content analysis. The author examines aspects of professional behavior among the nation's most eminent scientists through a content analysis of, among other things, whether Nobel laureate co-authors list themselves as "first" authors on articles or whether they give this status to their collaborators.

10
Experiments

10.1
Introduction

Chapter 8 discussed a research method most closely associated with natural human inquiry; Chapter 10 addresses a research method that is probably most frequently associated with structured science in general. We shall discuss the *experiment* as a mode of social scientific observation.

It is worth noting at the outset that experiments also are used often in nonscientific human inquiry. We experiment copiously in our attempt to develop generalized understanding about the world we live in. All adult skills are learned through experimentation: eating, walking, talking, riding a bicycle, swimming, and so forth. Students discover how much studying is required for academic success through experimentation. Professors learn how much preparation is required for successful lectures through experimentation.

At base, experiments involve (A) taking action and (B) observing the consequences of that action. In preparing a stew, for example, we add salt, taste, add more salt, and taste again. In defusing a bomb, we clip a wire, observe whether the bomb explodes, and clip another.

This chapter will discuss some of the ways in which social scientists may employ experiments in the development of generalized understandings. We shall see that, like other methods available to the social scientist, experimenting has special strengths and weaknesses.

10.2
Topics Appropriate to Experiments

Experiments are especially well suited to research projects involving relatively limited and well-defined concepts and propositions. The traditional image of science, discussed earlier in this book, and the *experimental model* are closely related to one another. Experimentation, then, is especially appropriate for hypothesis testing. It is better suited to explanatory than to descriptive purposes.

Let's assume, for example, that we are interested in studying antiblack prejudice and in discovering ways of reducing it. We might hypothesize that acquiring an understanding of the contribution of blacks to

American history might have the effect of reducing prejudice. We might test this hypothesis experimentally. To begin, we might test the level of antiblack prejudice among a group of experimental subjects. Next, we might show them a documentary film depicting the many ways in which blacks have contributed importantly to the scientific, literary, political, and social development of the nation. Finally, we might remeasure the levels of antiblack prejudice among our subjects to determine whether the film has actually reduced prejudice.

Experimentation would also be appropriate and has been successful in the study of small group interaction. Thus, we might bring together a small group of experimental subjects and assign them a task, such as making recommendations for popularizing carpools. We might observe, then, the manner in which the group organizes itself and deals with the problem. Over the course of several such experiments, we might vary the nature of the task or the rewards for handling the task successfully. By observing differences in the way groups organize themselves and operate under these varying conditions, we would learn a great deal about the nature of small group interaction.

We typically think of experiments as being conducted in laboratories. Indeed, most of the examples to be used in this chapter will involve such a setting. This need not be the case, however. As we shall see, social scientists often study what are called *natural experiments:* "experiments" that occur in the regular course of social events. Increasingly, moreover, social scientists have begun addressing themselves to real-life experiments in the form of *evaluation research.* The latter portion of this chapter will deal with such research.

10.3

The "Classical" Experiment

The most conventional type of experiment, in the natural as well as social sciences, involves three major components: (1) independent and dependent variables, (2) experimental and control groups, and (3) pretesting and posttesting. This section of the chapter will deal with each of those components and how they are put together in the execution of the experiment.

Independent and Dependent Variables

Essentially, an experiment examines the effect of an **independent variable** on a **dependent variable.** (Typically, the independent variable takes the form of an experimental stimulus, which is either present or absent; i.e., it is typically a **dichotomous variable**—having two attributes. This need not be the case, however, as later sections of this chapter will indicate.) In the example concerning antiblack prejudice mentioned above, prejudice would be the dependent variable, and exposure to black history would be the independent variable. The researcher's hypothesis would suggest that prejudice depends, in part, on a lack of knowledge of black history. The purpose of the experiment would be to test the validity of this hypothesis. The independent and dependent variables appropriate to experimentation are nearly limitless. It should be noted, moreover, that a given variable might serve as an independent variable in one experiment and as a dependent variable in another.

It is essential that both independent and dependent variables be operationally defined for purposes of experimentation. Such operational definitions might involve a variety of observation methods. Responses to a questionnaire, for example, might be the basis for defining antiblack prejudice. Speaking to black subjects, agreeing with the black subjects, disagreeing with black subjects, or ignoring the comments of black subjects, might be elements in the operational definition of interaction with blacks in a small group setting.

Conventionally, the experimental model has required the operational definition of such variables in advance of the experiment. This need not be the case, however. As was seen with content analysis and will be seen in connection with survey research, it is sometimes appropriate to make a wide variety of observations during data collection and determine the most useful operational definitions of variables during the subsequent analyses. Ultimately, however, experimentation, like other quantitative methods, requires specific and standardized measurements and observations.

Pretesting and Posttesting

In the classical experimental model, subjects are measured in terms of a dependent variable, are exposed to a stimulus representing an independent variable, and then are remeasured in terms of the dependent variable. Differences noted between the first and last measurements on the dependent variable are then attributed to the influence of the independent variable.

In the example of antiblack prejudice and exposure to black history, we might begin by measuring the extent of prejudice among our experimental subjects. Using a questionnaire asking about attitudes toward blacks, for example, we would be able to measure the extent of prejudice exhibited by each individual subject and the average prejudice level of the whole group. After exposing the subjects to the black history film, we might then administer the same questionnaire again. Responses given in the second administration of the questionnaire would permit us to measure the later extent of prejudice for each subject and the average prejudice-level of the group as a whole. If we discovered a lower level of prejudice during the second administration of the questionnaire, we might conclude that the film had indeed reduced prejudice.

In the experimental examination of attitudes such as prejudice, we face a special practical problem relating to validity. As you may have already imagined, it is possible that the subjects would respond differently to the questionnaires the second time, even if their attitudes remained unchanged.

During the first administration of the questionnaire, the subjects may have been unaware of its purpose. By the time of the second measurement, they might have figured out that the researchers were interested in measuring their prejudice. Since no one wishes to seem prejudiced, the subjects might "clean up" their answers the second time around. Thus, the film would seem to have reduced prejudice while this was not, in fact, the case.

This is an example of a more general problem that plagues many forms of social scientific research. The very act of studying something may change it. As we shall see in the following subsection, and elsewhere in this chapter, there are a variety of techniques for dealing with this problem in the context of experimentation.

Experimental and Control Groups

The foremost method of offsetting the effects of the experiment itself is the use of a *control* group. Laboratory experiments seldom if ever involve only the observation of an experimental group to which a stimulus has been administered. In addition, observations are made of a control group to which the experimental stimulus has *not* been administered.

In the example of prejudice and black history, two groups of subjects might be examined. To begin, each group would be administered a question-naire designed to measure their antiblack prejudice. Then, one of the groups—the experimental group—would be shown the film. Subsequently, the researcher would administer a posttest of the prejudice of *both* groups. Figure 10-1 presents a diagrammatic illustration of this basic experimental design.

The use of a control group serves the purpose of ruling out, or "controlling," the effects of the experiment itself. If participation in the experiment were to lead the subjects to exhibit, or even to have, less prejudice against blacks, this should occur in both the experimental and control groups. If the overall level of prejudice exhibited by the control group were reduced between the pretest and posttest as much as for the experimental group, then the apparent reduction in prejudice would be a function of the experiment per se or some external factor rather than a function of the film specifically. If, on the other hand, prejudice were reduced *only* in the experimental group, such reduction would seem to be a consequence of exposure to the film. Or, alternatively, if prejudice were reduced *more* in the experimental group than in the control group, that, too, would be grounds for assuming that the film reduced prejudice.

The need for control groups in social research became clear in connection with a series of studies of employee satisfaction conducted by F. J. Roethlisberger and W. J. Dickson in the late 1920s and early 1930s.[1] These two researchers undertook a series of experiments concerning working conditions in the telephone "bank wiring room" of the Western Electric

---

1. F. J. Roethlisberger and W. J. Dickson, *Management and the Worker* (Cambridge: Harvard University Press, 1939).

Hawthorne Works in Chicago, attempting to discover what changes in working conditions would improve employee satisfaction and productivity.

To the researchers' great satisfaction, they discovered that making working conditions "better" consistently increased satisfaction and productivity. As the workroom was brightened up through better lighting, for example, productivity went up. Lighting was further improved, and productivity went up again. To further substantiate their scientific conclusion, the researchers then dimmed the lights: *productivity again improved!*

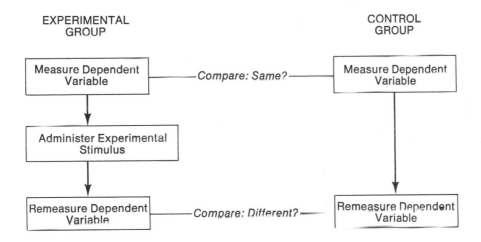

Figure 10-1. Diagram of Basic Experimental Design

It became evident that the wiring room workers were responding more to the *attention* given them by the researchers than to the "Improvement" of working conditions. As a result of this phenomenon, often referred to as the *Hawthorne Effect,* social researchers have become more sensitive to and cautious about the possible effects of experiments themselves. The utilization of a proper control group—studied intensively without any of the working conditions changed otherwise—would have pointed to the existence of this effect in the wiring room study.

The need for control groups in experimentation has been nowhere more evident than in medical research. Time and again, patients have appeared to improve by participation in medical experiments, and it has been unclear how much of the improvement has been due to the experimental treatment and how much to the experiment. In testing the effects of new drugs, then, medical researchers frequently administer a *placebo* (e.g., "sugar pills") to a control group. Thus, the control group of patients believe they, like the experimental group, are receiving an experimental drug. Often, they improve. If the new drug is effective, however, those receiving that drug will improve more than those receiving the placebo.

In social scientific experiments, control groups are important as a guard not only against the effects of the experiments themselves but also against the effects of events that may occur outside the laboratory during the course of experiments. In the example of the study of antiblack prejudice, suppose that a relatively popular black leader were assassinated in the middle of, say, a week-long experiment. Such an event might very well horrify the experimental subjects, requiring them to examine their own attitudes toward blacks, with the result of reduced prejudice. Since such an effect should happen about equally for members of the control and experimental groups, a *greater* reduction of prejudice among the experimental group would, again, point to the impact of the experimental stimulus: the documentary film.

10.4
Selecting Subjects

It seems very likely that most social scientific laboratory experiments are conducted with college undergraduates as subjects. Typically, the experimenter asks students enrolled in his classes to participate in experiments, or he advertises for subjects in a college newspaper. Subjects may or may not be paid for participation in such experiments.

In relation to the norm of *generalizability* in science, it is clear that this tendency represents a potential defect in social scientific research. Most simply put, college undergraduates are not typical of the public at large. There is a danger, therefore, that we may become knowledgeable about the attitudes and actions of college undergraduates without learning very much about social attitudes and actions in general.

However, this potential defect is less significant in terms of explanatory research than it would be in the case of description. Having noted the level of antiblack prejudice that existed among a group of college undergraduates, we would have little confidence that the same level existed among the public at large. If a documentary film, on the other hand, were found to reduce prejudice among those undergraduates, we would have more confidence—without being certain—that it would have a similar effect in the community at large. Social processes and *patterns* of causal relationships simply appear to be more generalizable and more stable than *specific* characteristics.

Aside from the question of generalizability, the cardinal rule of subject selection and experimentation concerns the comparability of experimental and control groups. Ideally, the control group represents what the experimental group would have been like had it not been exposed to the experimental stimulus. It is essential, therefore, that experimental and control groups be as similar as possible. There are several ways of accomplishing this.

Probability Sampling

The earlier discussions of the logic and techniques of probability sampling offer one method of selecting two groups of people very similar to each other. Beginning with a sampling frame comprised of all the people in the population under study, the researcher might select two probability samples. If two probability samples each resemble the total population from which they are selected, they should also resemble each other.

Recall also, however, that the degree of resemblance (representativeness) achieved by probability sampling is largely a function of the sample size. As a rule of thumb, probability samples of less than 100 are not likely to be terribly representative, and social scientific experiments seldom involve that many subjects in either experimental or control groups. As a result, then, probability sampling is seldom used in the selection of subjects for experiments, except in the following way.

Randomization

Frequently, a somewhat special use of probability sampling is employed in experimentation. Having recruited, by whatever means, a total group of subjects, the experimenter may *randomly* assign those subjects to either the experimental or control group. This might be accomplished by numbering all of the subjects serially and selecting numbers by means of a random number table, or the experimenter might assign the odd-numbered subjects to the experimental group and the even-numbered subjects to the control group.

Let's return again to the basic concept of probability sampling. If the experimenter has recruited a group of forty subjects altogether, in response to a newspaper advertisement, for example, there is no reason to believe that the forty subjects are necessarily representative of the entire population from which they have been drawn. Nor can we assume that the twenty subjects randomly assigned to the experimental group represent that larger population. We may have greater confidence, however, that the twenty subjects randomly assigned to the experimental group will be reasonably similar to the twenty assigned to the control group.

All this notwithstanding, the *number* of subjects involved is important. In the extreme, if we recruited only two subjects and assigned, by the flip of a coin, one as the experimental subject and one as the control, there would be no reason to assume that the two subjects would be similar to each other. With larger numbers of subjects, however, randomization makes more sense.

Matching

The comparability of experimental and control groups may be achieved more directly through a **matching** process similar to the *quota sampling* methods discussed in Chapter 6.

If twelve of your subjects were young white men, you might assign six of those at random to the experimental group and the other six to the control group. If fourteen were middle-aged black women, you might assign seven to each of the groups. The overall matching process could be most

efficiently achieved through the creation of a *quota matrix* constructed of all
the most relevant characteristics. (Figure 10-2 provides a simplified illustration of this.) Ideally, the quota matrix would be so constructed as to result in
an even number of subjects in each cell of the matrix. Then, half the subjects
in each cell would go into the experimental group, and half into the control
group.

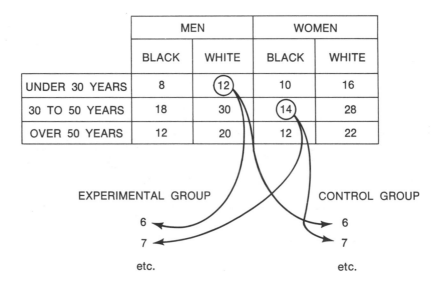

Figure 10-2. "Quota Matrix" Illustration

Alternatively, you might recruit more subjects than are required by
your experimental design. You might then examine many characteristics of
the large initial group of subjects. Whenever you discover a pair of very
similar subjects, you might assign one at random to the experimental group
and the other to the control group. Potential subjects who were unlike anyone
else in the initial group might be left out of the experiment altogether.

Whatever method is employed, the end result desired is the same.
The overall average description of the experimental group should be the
same as that of the control group. For example, they should have about the
same average age, the same sex composition, the same racial composition,
and so forth. (*Note:* This same test of comparability should be employed
whether the two groups are created through probability sampling or through
randomization.)

Thus far, I have referred to the "important" variables without saying
clearly what those variables are. I cannot, of course, give a definitive answer
to this question, any more than I could specify, earlier, which variables should
be used in stratified sampling. The answer, ultimately, depends on the nature

and purposes of the experiment. As a general rule, however, the two groups should be comparable in terms of those variables that are likely to be related to the dependent variable under study. In some cases, moreover, the experimenter may delay the assignment of subjects to experimental and control groups until he has initially measured the dependent variable. Thus, for example, he might administer a questionnaire measuring subjects' prejudice and then undertake a matching of experimental and control groups so as to assure himself, additionally, that the resulting two groups exhibited the same overall level of prejudice.

10.5
Modified Experimental Design

The preceding discussions have described the most fundamental experimental design. Subjects are recruited and assigned to either the experimental group or the control group. Each of the groups is observed and described in terms of the dependent variable under study. An experimental stimulus, representing an independent variable, is administered to the experimental group only. Finally, both groups are again observed and described in terms of the dependent variable; differences between the two groups are then attributed to the effect of the experimental stimulus. This experimental design is sometimes referred to as the "Before-and-after experiment with one control."

There are a number of possible modifications to this basic experimental design. Some of these are described below.

Increasing Variables and Groups

In the preceding discussions, I have spoken in terms of a single independent variable and a single dependent one. Experiments need not be limited in this fashion. For example, a single experiment might test the impact of one independent variable on several dependent variables. In the example of prejudice and the documentary film, we might wish to study the possible impact of the film—dealing with black history—on prejudice against a variety of minority groups. Thus, for example, we might study several dependent variables: antiblack prejudice, anti-Semitism, anti-Catholic prejudice, and so forth. Each of these dependent variables would be measured both before and after the showing of the film. We might then determine whether the film reduced prejudice in general, reduced only antiblack prejudice, or had no effect on prejudice whatever. Such a study could be conducted with a single experimental group and a single control group.

It would also be possible to study several independent variables: i.e., several experimental stimuli. In the prejudice research example, we might wish to study the impact of (1) a documentary film on black history, (2) a book on black history, and (3) a lecture on black history. An experiment examining each of these different experimental stimuli would require several experimental groups: at least one experimental group per experimental stimulus. Each of the experimental groups would be exposed to a different experimental stimulus. An even better experimental design in this case would include experimental groups exposed to different *combinations* of the stimuli. Thus, one experimental group might see the film and read the book, another would see the film and hear the lecture, another would read the book and hear the lecture, and still another would be exposed to all three. In addition, of course, a control group would be exposed to none of the stimuli. Figure 10-3 presents a diagram of such a study design.

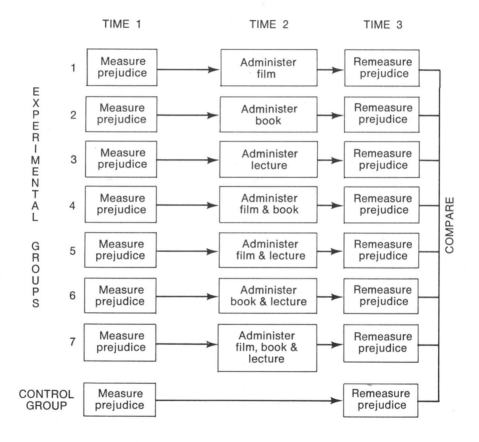

Figure 10-3. Illustration of Experimental Design with Three Experimental Stimuli

These latest examples should further clarify the basic principle of the experimental model. The effect of an independent variable is determined by comparing groups that are similar in all respects save that of the independent variable under examination. The more complicated experimental design just described would offer a number of comparisons in this respect. Suppose, for example, that the group viewing the film declined in prejudice while the control group did not. Suppose further that the group viewing the film and reading the book declined in prejudice more than the group that only read the book; and that the group viewing the film and hearing the lecture declined in prejudice more than the group only hearing the lecture; and, finally, that the group exposed to all three stimuli declined in prejudice more than the group exposed only to the book and the lecture. Each of these experimental results would provide independent evidence of the film's effectiveness in reducing prejudice.

Increasing Observations over Time

In describing the basic experimental model, I have indicated only two measurements of the dependent variable: before and after the administration of the experimental stimulus. Some research projects, however, would suggest the advisability of several measurements over time. Let's stick to our current example: we might suspect that repeated exposure to the black history film would have a cumulative effect on prejudice. Thus, for example, we might measure prejudice among our experimental and control groups, show the film to the experimental group, measure prejudice among the two groups again, wait a few weeks, show the film again to the experimental group, and remeasure prejudice in those groups.

Or from a different perspective, we might show the film only once and remeasure prejudice among both groups periodically over time. The purpose of this design would be to determine the long-range effect of the film. Does it have a long-lasting effect in reducing prejudice, or does it have merely a temporary effect?

Realize that a somewhat more complex design could treat the number of exposures to the film as an experimental variable, requiring more than one experimental group. One experimental group might be exposed to the film at the beginning of the experiment, and simply be remeasured in terms of prejudice at several points in time subsequent to the viewing of the film. Another experimental group might be reexposed to the film at each of those points in time and then measured again in terms of prejudice.

"After-Only" Experiment

In many cases, it does not make sense to measure the dependent variable—especially when it is a behavior—before the administration of the experimental stimulus. Let us consider, for a moment, the earlier example of small group interaction. Suppose we wish to discover the effect of different reward systems on cooperation and competition in small group problem-solving. We might imagine, for example, that telling subjects that the group member contributing most to the solution of the problem will receive an additional financial reward would lead to individual competition within the group, whereas telling them that all members would share equally in an additional reward for solving the problem would tend to stimulate cooperation.

It would probably not be appropriate in this situation to attempt to measure cooperation and competition prior to specifying the reward system. If a small group of subjects were initially assigned a problem to solve, they might develop patterns of interaction that would persist despite subsequent specifications of the reward system. Thus, we might initially specify a different reward system to each of the two groups and merely observe differences in their cooperation and competition.

Realize, of course, that the experimental design just described is open to the danger that the different groups might be—through the individual orientations of their members—differently inclined to cooperation and competition from the outset. Thus, differences in their observed behaviors might merely reflect those variations rather than the effect of the two reward systems. This danger, however, might be guarded against through random assignment of subjects to groups, and through *replication.* By repeating the experiment several times, using new groups of experimental subjects, the researcher might find that the democratic reward system consistently produced cooperation while the other produced competition. This would strengthen his confidence in the general research conclusion.

The "Double-Blind" Experiment

Mention was made earlier of the problem in medical experimentation that patients often improve when they *think* they are receiving a new drug; thus, it is often necessary to administer a placebo to a control group.

Sometimes, experimenters are subject to this same tendency to prejudge results. In medical research, the experimenters are sometimes more likely to "observe" improvement among patients receiving the experimental drug than among those receiving the placebo. (This would be most likely, perhaps, for the researcher who developed the drug.) The "double-blind" experiment is one in which neither the experimental subjects nor the experimenters know which is the experimental group and which the control. In the medical case, those researchers who are responsible for administering the drug and for noting improvements would not be told which subjects were receiving the drugs and which were receiving the placebo. Conversely, the researcher who knew which subjects were in which group would not be responsible for the administration of the experiment.

In social scientific experiments, as in medical experiments, the danger of experimenter bias is further reduced to the extent that the operational definitions of the dependent variables are clear and precise. Thus, the medical researcher would be less likely to unconsciously bias his reading of a patient's temperature than he would be to unconsciously bias his assessment of how lethargic the patient was. For the same reason, the small group researcher would be less likely to misperceive which subject spoke, or to whom he spoke, than whether the subject's comments were "in the spirit" of cooperation or competition.

As indicated several times already in this book, it is seldom possible to devise operational definitions and measurements that are wholly precise and unambiguous. It may be appropriate sometimes, therefore, to employ a double-blind design in social research experiments.

10.6
"Natural" Experiments and Evaluation Research

Although we tend to equate the terms "experiment" and "laboratory experiment," many important social scientific experiments occur outside of laboratories, often in the course of normal social events. Sometimes nature designs and executes experiments that we are able to observe and analyze; sometimes social and political decision-makers serve this "natural" function.

Let's imagine, for example, that a hurricane has struck a particular town. Some residents of the town suffer severe financial damages while others escape relatively lightly. What, we might ask, are the behavioral consequences of suffering a natural disaster? Are those who suffer most more likely to take precautions against future occurrences than are those who suffer less? To find the answers to these questions, we might interview residents of the town at some time subsequent to the hurricane. We might question them regarding their precautions prior to the hurricane and precautions that they are currently taking, comparing those who suffered greatly from the hurricane with those who suffered relatively little. In this fashion, we might take advantage of a "natural" experiment, whereas we could not have arranged it even if we were perversely willing to do so.

A similar example may be taken from the annals of social research surrounding World War II. Following the cessation of the war, social researchers undertook retrospective surveys of wartime morale among civilians in a number of German cities. One of the chief purposes of this research was to determine the effect of mass bombing on the morale of civilians, and the reports of wartime morale were compared for residents of heavily bombed cities and cities that received relatively little bombing. (*Note:* Bombing did not reduce morale.)

Increasingly, social researchers have become involved at the request of social planners in what is known as *evaluation research*. Whenever new social programs are put into effect, social researchers may be asked to evaluate the impact and success of those programs. Such situations are essentially large-scale experiments within natural social settings.

Let's suppose, for example, that a state decides to modify its welfare system in such a manner as to encourage welfare recipients to undergo job training and to become self-sufficient. Social researchers might be asked to evaluate the effectiveness of the new program.

The experiment and its evaluation might be undertaken in a number of ways. If the new welfare regulations were legislated for all recipients, the researcher would be primarily concerned with examining the employment patterns and self-sufficiency of recipients before and after the legislation. If the program were to provide for optional job training, he might also compare those recipients participating in the training with those who were not.

In some instances, the social researcher might work together with the social planners in designing and executing a more controlled experiment. Suppose that a state were considering the abolition of bail for certain classes of criminal offenses. A social researcher might cooperate with the courts in a pilot test of the program. Persons charged with the offenses in question during a certain period of time might be randomly assigned to experimental and control groups. The control group might be required to post the customary bail while the experimental group might all be released on their own recognizance. The researcher would then examine the extent to which members of the two groups reported for their court hearings or, alternatively, fled from the state.

In the design of evaluation research, it is essential that you begin with a fairly clear conceptualization and even operationalization of the criteria of success or failure in that which you are evaluating. This is essential more, perhaps, for practical reasons than for scientific ones, but then evaluation research is supposed to be practical. Perhaps an illustration will clarify this point.

Let's imagine that the Department of Political Science decides to revise its undergraduate curriculum in an attempt "to improve instructional quality." Since the faculty members are good social scientists, they decide to incorporate an evaluation research component in the program revision. It would be *absolutely essential* that they begin by specifying what is meant by "instructional quality," ultimately settling on empirical indicators of high and low quality. In all likelihood, they would fail initially in this task. In simple point of fact, many if not most of the things that are to be improved in experiments subject to evaluation are impossible to specify satisfactorily. One person's "quality" is another's irrelevance.

It would be more likely that the faculty in the political science department might agree on certain situational indicators that might be associated with "quality," whatever that is: small class sizes, active student-faculty interactions, or things of that sort. Very frequently, such elusive variables as "quality of instruction" are measured indirectly in terms of *outcomes* associated with them: the percentage of undergraduate majors who later attend graduate school, their average scores on Graduate Record exams, or their subsequent occupational success, for example. In many cases, of course, outcomes are the clear and direct criteria for success. The goal of prison reforms may be explicitly a reduction in the recidivism rate (percentage of released prisoners returning to prison for subsequent crimes). The goal of a traffic safety campaign in the mass media may be the reduction of traffic accidents.

Whatever the goal, it must be specified and agreed to in advance. Otherwise, the evaluation project may show, for example, that political science undergraduates are enjoying smaller classes *and* doing more poorly on Graduate Record exams. Such a finding is unlikely to produce consensus on the "success" or "failure" of the curriculum revision.

Once the goal of the experiment has been specified, it is usually appropriate to collect current baseline data. What is the current status of the criterion variable that will indicate success or failure later on? What is the average class size now in political science? What is the average score now being recorded on Graduate Record exams? Or, what is the current traffic accident rate, the current recidivism rate for the prison? Often, such data are routinely recorded and their formal retrieval and tabulation can be safely delayed. Many times, however, this is not the case. If the purpose of an experiment is to "improve morale" or to "increase interaction," it is unlikely that baseline data will be routinely available. Also be wary that those data that "everyone knows are available" are very likely not *in fact* available.

Having made sure that the relevant baseline data are currently available, the political science department may then proceed to institute the curriculum revisions, continue the collection of relevant data, and, finally, determine whether the agreed-upon criteria for success have been met.

One additional practical point should be raised in this context. Much evaluation research involves the collaboration of social science researchers and administrators. In the case of a prison reform project, it might involve the collaboration of, say, a criminologist and a prison warden. Without going into the matter in much detail, I should point out that these two people are likely to have very different basic concerns in relation to the experiment and its evaluation. Suppose, for example, that the prison reform experiment calls for prisoners to be permitted to visit their families, unsupervised, on Sunday afternoons. Three of the first five prisoners granted this privilege do not come back to prison. The evaluation researcher would duly note those data and wish to determine the frequency of the phenomenon over the course of, say, a few hundred visits. Do sixty percent of all prisoners skip town, or does the rate of three out of five merely represent the small sample size? The prison warden is unlikely to wait around to find out. More likely, either he will terminate the experiment or the governor will terminate *him*.

This dilemma has plagued clinical research in medicine for years. The medical researcher with a new cure for terminal acne may get the cooperation of a group of sufferers and their physicians. The group would be divided at random into two groups, with one group receiving the current cure and the other group receiving the new one. If those receiving the new "cure" begin expiring faster than those receiving the current cure, neither the patients nor their physicians are likely to stay with the experiment until its apparent bitter end.

There has been growing interest in recent years in what are referred to as "social indicators studies."[2] Social indicators correspond roughly to the economic indicators (like gross national product and unemployment rates) that have been used for decades. A society's social health, like its economic and medical health, can be measured, and those measurements compared over time. Crime rates comprise one set of social indicators. The incidence of race riots is another.

---

2. For an excellent annotated bibliography on social indicators, see Leslie D. Wilcox, Ralph M. Brooks, George M. Beal, and Gerald E. Klongan, *Social Indicators and Societal Monitoring* (New York: Elsevier, 1972).

Social indicators such as these not only may be employed as a passive barometer of a society's well-being; they may also be employed in active social experimentation. The social indicators can afford measurements of important dependent variables. Thus, we might imagine an experiment involving the legalization of marijuana coupled with the monitoring of such social indicators as the incidence of juvenile arrests, traffic accidents, school dropouts, teenage runaways, and so forth. The continual monitoring of such social indicators would aid in the discovery of the consequences, if any, of legalizing marijuana.

The role of evaluation research in connection with social change is not new. Industrial sociologists, for example, have worked within industry in studying such things as worker morale, productivity, and efficiency. Often they have worked in close cooperation with management and workers in developing new work situations and evaluating their consequences. In recent years, however, evaluation research has been gaining popularity in many other areas.

10.7

Strengths and Weaknesses of the Experimental Method

The chief advantage of a controlled experiment lies in the isolation of the experimental variable and its impact over time. This is seen most clearly in terms of the basic experimental model. A group of experimental subjects are found, at the outset of the experiment, to have a certain characteristic; following the administration of an experimental stimulus, they are found to have a different characteristic. To the extent that subjects have experienced no other stimuli, we may conclude that the change of characteristics is attributable to the experimental stimulus.

Another advantage is that, since individual experiments are often rather limited in scope, requiring relatively little time and money, it is often possible to replicate a given experiment several times, utilizing several different groups of subjects. (This is not always the case, of course, but it is usually easier to repeat experiments than, say, survey research.) As in all other forms of scientific research, replication of research findings strengthens our confidence in the validity and generalizability of those findings.

The greatest weakness of laboratory experiments lies in their artificiality. Social processes observed to occur within a laboratory setting might not necessarily occur within more natural social settings. If we may return to the example used frequently in this chapter, a black history film might genuinely reduce prejudice among a group of experimental subjects. That would not necessarily mean, however, that the same film shown in neighborhood movie theaters throughout the country would reduce prejudice among the general public. Artificiality is not as much a problem, of course, in the case of "natural" experiments as in the case of those conducted in the laboratory.

A second danger is one I have mentioned about research in general: the possible effect of an experiment upon that which is being examined. First, the people being studied may modify their behavior because of the fact that they are being studied. Second, the experimenters themselves are subject to selective perceptions based on their involvement in the experiment. These problems are inherent in most social research, but they are especially critical in connection with experimentation.

10.8
Summary

The experiment is a frequently used research method in the physical sciences, and it is an important one in social research as well. Experiments are especially appropriate to explanatory research purposes, particularly when the number of variables is rather limited.

We noted that the sampling considerations in experiments are somewhat different from those in surveys or content analysis. In part, this is because experiments seldom have a descriptive purpose. Hence, it is less important that the group of subjects studied in an experiment be representative of some real population.

The chief sampling concern in experiments is the presumed similarity of the experimental and control groups. Unless these groups are the same in terms of all variables save the experimental ones, the researcher cannot be sure that observed effects are attributable to the experimental stimuli. *Randomization* and *matching* are two common methods for insuring the similarity of control and experimental groups.

The "classical" experimental model is as follows. Subjects are divided into two groups: an experimental group and a control group. A pretest administered to both groups insures that both groups are the same in terms of some dependent variable. Then, an experimental stimulus is administered to the experimental group only. Subsequently, a posttest determines any differences between the experimental and control groups in terms of the dependent variable. Finally, any observed difference is then attributed to the effects of the experimental stimulus.

Having described the "classical" experimental model, Chapter 10 described some possible modifications of the model: increasing the number of variables under study, increasing the number of experimental and control groups, and increasing the number of observations over time. The "double-blind" experiment was discussed as a method of guarding against experimenter bias.

Although the term "experiment" is commonly associated with laboratories, we saw next that some experiments in social research are not conducted in laboratories. First, it is sometimes possible for social researchers to make "natural experiments," those experiments that involve studying the course of events in the real world. Also, we discussed the growing field of "evaluation research," which involves social scientists in the development, execution, and modification of social innovations.

The chapter concluded with a discussion of the special strengths and weaknesses of the use of experiments in social research. The rigorously controlled conditions under which experiments typically are conducted provide the chief advantage—isolating the effects of particular variables. The chief weaknesses involve the "artificiality" of such tightly controlled experimental conditions and the risk that the experimental situation will influence what is being studied.

10.9
Main Points

1. Experiments are an excellent vehicle for the controlled testing of causal processes.

2. The "classical" experiment tests the effect of an experimental stimulus on some dependent variable through the pretesting and posttesting of experimental and control groups.

3. It is generally less important that a group of experimental subjects be representative of some larger population than that experimental and control groups be similar to one another.

4. *Randomization* and *matching* are two common methods for insuring the similarity of the experimental and control groups.

5. "Natural experiments" often occur in the course of social life in the real world, and social researchers can study those in somewhat the way they would design and conduct laboratory experiments.

6. Evaluation research is an increasingly important form of social research, in which researchers cooperate with policy-makers and administrators in the design, execution, and modification of innovative social programs. The implementation of the innovative program may be organized like an experiment, thereby permitting the researcher to evaluate the effects of the program just as he would evaluate the effects of an experimental stimulus.

10.10
Annotated Bibliography

Anderson, Barry, *The Psychology Experiment* (Belmont, California: Brooks/Cole, 1971). An excellent overview of experimental methods. This readable little book begins with an examination of scientific inquiry in general and proceeds to describe the specific techniques available to the experimenter. Considerable attention is given to the analysis of experimental data.

Bales, Robert, *Interaction Process Analysis: A Method for the Study of Small Groups* (Reading, Mass.: Addison-Wesley, 1950). An old but classic overview of small group research. Bales discusses the theory and techniques appropriate to the examination of social interaction in small groups under controlled laboratory conditions.

Berleman, William, and Steinburn, Thomas, "The Execution and Evaluation of a Delinquency Prevention Program," *Social Problems*, 14:413–423 (Spring, 1967). An illustration of the use of experimental methods and evaluation research. The authors examine the success of a small settlement house program in Seattle in preventing juvenile delinquency. The report is also reprinted in Phillip Fellin, Tony Tripodi, and Henry Meyer (eds.), *Exemplars of Social Research* (Itasca, Ill.: F. E. Peacock Publishers, Inc., 1969), 19–31, which also contains other excellent illustrations of social research experiments.

Campbell, Donald, and Stanley, Julian, *Experimental and Quasi-Experimental Designs for Research* (Chicago: Rand McNally, 1963). An excellent analysis of the logic and methods of experimentation in social research. This book is especially useful in its application of the logic of experiments to other social research methods.

Deutsch, Morton, and Collins, Mary Evans, *Interracial Housing: A Psychological Evaluation of a Social Experiment* (Minneapolis: University of Minnesota Press, 1951). An old but classic illustration of experimental evaluation research in a natural setting. The authors examined the effects of segregated and integrated residential patterns on the attitudes of whites toward blacks in New York and New Jersey housing projects. An abridged version of their report is contained in William Petersen (ed.), *American Social Patterns* (Garden City, N.Y.: Doubleday Anchor Books, 1956), 7–61.

Moursund, Janet, *Evaluation: An Introduction to Research Design* (Monterey, California: Brooks/Cole, 1973). An excellent overview of evaluation research. This readable little book begins with a discussion of the place of evaluation research within the administration of social experiments and proceeds to describe and illustrate ways of collecting and analyzing evaluation data. This book manages to present the "big picture" while also providing a wealth of specific practical information.

11
Survey Research

11.1
Introduction

Chapter 11 discusses survey research, a mode of observation that has been anticipated in earlier chapters of this book. In a typical survey, the researcher selects a sample of respondents and administers a standardized questionnaire to them. Since sampling and questionnaire construction have already been discussed in a more general context, this chapter will mostly address two basic methods of administering questionnaires to a sample of respondents.

11.2
Topics Appropriate to Survey Research

Surveys may be used for descriptive, explanatory, and exploratory purposes. They are chiefly used in studies that have individual people as the units of analysis. Although this method can be used for other units of analysis, such as groups or interactions, it is necessary that some individual persons be used as respondents or informants. Thus, it would be possible to undertake a survey in which divorces were the units of analysis, but the survey questionnaire would need to be administered to the participants in the divorces (or to some other informants).

Survey research is probably the best method available to the social scientist interested in collecting original data for purposes of describing a population too large to observe directly. Careful probability sampling provides a group of respondents whose characteristics may be taken as representative of those of the larger population; and carefully constructed standardized questionnaires provide data in the same form from all respondents. Formal government censuses differ from surveys only in that all members of the larger population are studied rather than a sample.

Surveys are also excellent vehicles for the measurement of attitudes and orientations prevalent within a large population. Public opinion polls are a well-known example of this use. Probability sampling and standardized questionnaires provide the means of discovering the prevailing attitudes among a large population.

11.3
Self-Administered Questionnaires

There are two main methods of administering survey questionnaires to a sample of respondents. This section will deal with the method in which respondents are asked to complete the questionnaires themselves—*self-administered* questionnaires—and the following section will deal with surveys that are administered by staff interviewers.

Although the mail survey is the typical method used in self-administered studies, there are several additional methods commonly used. In some cases, it may be appropriate to administer the questionnaire to a group of respondents gathered at the same place at the same time. A survey of students taking Introductory Psychology might be conducted in this manner during class. High school students might be surveyed during homeroom period.

Some recent experimentation has been conducted with regard to the home delivery of questionnaires. A research worker delivers the questionnaire to the home of sample respondents and explains the study. Then, the questionnaire is left for the respondent to complete, and it is picked up subsequently by the researcher.

Home delivery and the mail can be used in combination as well. In many parts of the country, the 1970 United States Census was conducted in this fashion. Questionnaires were mailed to families, and then census enumerators visited homes to pick up the questionnaires and check them for completeness. In just the opposite method, questionnaires have been hand delivered by research workers with a request that the respondents mail the completed questionnaires to the research office.

On the whole, the appearance of a research worker, either delivering the questionnaire, picking it up, or both, seems to produce a higher completion rate than is normally true for straightforward mail surveys. Additional experimentation with this method is likely to point to additional techniques for improving completion while reducing costs.

Mail surveys are the typical form of self-administered survey, however, and the remainder of this chapter is devoted specifically to that type of study.

Mail Distribution and Return

The basic method for data collection through the mail has been the transmission of a questionnaire, accompanied by a letter of explanation and a return envelope. The respondent then completes the questionnaire and returns it to the research office through the mail, using the envelope provided for that purpose.

In some cases, it is possible to further facilitate this process through the use of a *self-mailing* questionnaire. The questionnaire is constructed in such a manner that the research office's return address and postage are printed on the questionnaire itself. Upon completion, then, it can be dropped in the mail without requiring an envelope.

The researcher should plan this method with caution, however, as the post office has special requirements regarding the form of materials that can be mailed. In particular, questionnaires must be sealed in some manner. This can be accomplished in a number of ways.

If the questionnaire is printed in the form of a booklet, it may be possible to obtain a three-panel rather than two-panel cover. In this form, the back cover has a fold-out panel with an adhesive strip on it. When questionnaires are mailed out, the fold-out panel is tucked inside the back of the questionnaire. Upon completion of the questionnaire, the respondent may unfold the extra panel, lick the adhesive, and fold the panel around the questionnaire booklet. If the research office return address and postage are already printed on the extra panel, the booklet can be placed directly in the mail for return.

This method simplifies the assembly of mailing pieces since it is unnecessary to include a return envelope. And the respondent cannot lose the return envelope without losing the questionnaire itself. Also, there is an added appeal to the respondent in this form of questionnaire. It has a certain "toy value." To some extent, the respondent may want to complete the questionnaire so that he can then play with the cover.

If it is not possible to produce a three-panel cover, the researcher may be able to have adhesive tabs affixed to the booklet. Rather than an entire panel that folds around the completed questionnaire, a smaller tab may be used to seal it.

Finally, the researcher may ask the respondent to close and seal the booklet himself—perhaps with a staple or scotch tape. This is a little risky, however, for several reasons. First, forcing the respondent to go to extra effort is likely to reduce the response rate. Perhaps he will not have anything readily available for sealing the booklet at the time of completion, put it off, and eventually forget to return the questionnaire. Second, the variety of sealing methods that respondents will devise will probably hinder the processing of returned questionnaires. (I have received questionnaires sealed with glue, trading stamps, paper clips, string, and so forth.) And besides, many respondents will neglect to seal the questionnaires at all, and the researcher may have difficulty getting them delivered by the post office.

Ultimately, self-mailing questionnaires have many advantages in terms of ease, economy, and response rate, but they should be planned and pretested with care. It is vital, moreover, for all experimental models to be cleared with the post office.

Postal Options and Relative Costs

In a mail survey, the researcher has a number of options available for the transmission of questionnaires—both outgoing and incoming. Postal rates change frequently; the researcher should, of course, check current postal rates in planning his study, and he should allow some extra funds for this purpose to prevent delay in getting the study into the field.

First class and bulk rate are the primary postal-class options available to the researcher. First class is more expensive, but it is also more flexible and better. Nevertheless, bulk-rate postage can often be used effectively.

In bulk-rate mailing, each mailing piece must be printed with a bulk-rate permit. This permit may be set in type for printing on the envelope, it may be mimeographed, or a rubber stamp may be created and used. The researcher must obtain a permit number from the post office, however. (*Note:* Universities or other agencies may already have a number, which the researcher could use.) This bulk-rate mailing permit on the envelope takes the place of a stamp.

To take advantage of bulk-rate mailing, the researcher must send a minimum of 250 pieces, and these must be arranged in bundles according to zip codes. (Check with the post office for specific details.) Thus the post office is able to transmit bundles of questionnaires to a given zip code area without separating and sorting them.

Both first-class and bulk-rate mail seem to move at the same speed through the mails, so time is not a consideration for bulk-rate mailing. Changes of addresses can present a problem, however. Technically, bulk-rate pieces will be forwarded only within a given city, but in practice there are variations in both directions. Some bulk-rate pieces are not forwarded even within a city, and others are forwarded between cities. First-class mail is clearly safer in this regard.

The primary advantage of bulk rate is cost, being only a fraction of first-class rates. When hundreds or thousands of pieces are involved, the savings are considerable.

Finally, bulk-rate mailing can be used only for outgoing question-naires. They must be returned by first class mail.

Two basic options are available with regard to return postage for questionnaires. The researcher may affix stamps to the envelopes or self-mailing questionnaires to cover postage, or he may have them imprinted with a business-reply mailing permit. Researchers differ in their assessments of the relative merits of these two methods.

The business-reply permit is similar to the bulk-rate permit in that it is printed on the mailing piece in place of postage stamps. (Check with the post office for additional format requirements.) Business-reply rates are those of first-class mail, however, plus a surcharge of around 5 cents per piece returned through the mail. As a result, the researcher pays postage only on those returned, but he pays more per questionnaire than if stamps were used. If stamps are affixed to the envelopes, however, the researcher is paying postage whether the questionnaires are returned or not.

As a general rule, then, the researcher will save money using stamps if he achieves a very high return rate, and he will save money with business-reply postage if the rate is low. Other factors are involved in the decision, however.

Business-reply postage is easier for the researcher in that permits can be printed quickly and inexpensively, and he avoids the time and cost of licking and sticking hundreds or thousands of stamps. On the other hand, some researchers feel that the presence of postage stamps on the envelopes will be regarded as a sign of sincerity, and respondents will be more likely to return the questionnaires. (Others fear that respondents will steam the stamps off for use on other mail.)

The methodological studies of this issue do not appear to have resolved the matter. My personal preference is to use business reply permits for reasons of ease and efficiency.

Monitoring Returns

The mailing of questionnaires sets up a new research question that may prove very valuable to the study. As questionnaires are returned to the researcher, he should not sit back idly, but should undertake a careful recording of the varying rates of return among respondents.

An invaluable tool in this activity will be a return rate graph. The day on which questionnaires were mailed should be labeled Day 1 on the graph; and, every day thereafter, the number of returned questionnaires should be logged on the graph. Since this is a rather minor activity, it is usually best to compile two graphs. One should show the number returned each day—rising, then dropping. Another should report the *cumulative* number or percentage. In part, this activity provides the researcher with gratification as he gets to draw a picture of his successful data collection. More important, however, it is his guide to how the data collection is going. If he plans follow-up mailings, the graph provides a clue as to when such mailings should be launched. (The dates of subsequent mailings should be noted on the graph.)

As completed questionnaires are returned, each should be opened, perused, and assigned an identification number. These numbers should be assigned serially as the questionnaires are returned—even if other identification (ID) numbers have already been assigned. This can have important advantages. Two examples should illustrate these.

Let's assume that the researcher is studying attitudes toward a political figure. In the middle of the data collection, let's further assume that the figure in question is discovered to be supporting a mistress. By knowing the date of that public disclosure and the dates when questionnaires have been received, the researcher is in a position to determine the effects of the disclosure.

In a less sensational way, serialized ID numbers can be valuable in estimating nonresponse biases in the survey. Barring more direct tests of bias, the researcher may wish to assume that those respondents who failed to answer the questionnaire will be more like those who delayed answering than like those who answered right away. An analysis of questionnaires received at different points in the data collection might then be used for estimates of sampling bias. For example, if grade-point averages (GPA) reported by students decrease steadily through the data collection, with those replying right away having higher GPAs and those replying later having lower GPAs, then the researcher might tentatively conclude that those who failed to answer at all have lower GPAs yet. Although it would not be advisable to make statistical estimates of bias in this fashion, the researcher could take advantage of approximate estimates.

If respondents have been identified for purposes of follow-up mailing, then preparations for those mailings should be made as the questionnaires are returned. The case study that follows in this chapter will discuss this in greater detail.

Follow-up Mailings

The methodological literature on follow-up mailings strongly suggests this is an effective method for increasing return rates in mail surveys. In general, the longer a potential respondent delays replying, the less likely he is to do so at all. Properly timed follow-up mailings, then, provide additional stimuli for responding.

The effects of follow-up mailings will be seen in the response rate curves recorded during data collection. The initial mailing will be followed by a rise and subsequent subsiding of returns; the follow-up mailing will spur a resurgence of returns; and more follow-ups will do the same. In practice, three mailings (an original and two follow-ups) seems the most efficient.

The timing of follow-up mailings is also important. Here the methodological literature offers less precise guides, but it has been my experience that two or three weeks is a reasonable space between mailings. (This period might be increased by a few days if the mailing time—out and in—is more than two or three days.)

When the researcher conducts several surveys over time to the same population, such experience should help him to develop more specific guidelines in this regard. The Survey Research Office at the University of Hawaii conducts frequent student surveys and has been able to refine the mailing and remailing procedure considerably. Indeed, a consistent pattern of returns has been found, which appears to transcend differences of survey content, quality of instrument, and so forth. Within two weeks after the first mailing, approximately 40 percent of the questionnaires are returned; within two weeks after the first follow-up, an additional 20 percent are received, and within two weeks after the final follow-up an additional 10 percent are received. There are no grounds for assuming that a similar pattern would appear in surveys of different populations, but this illustration should indicate the value of carefully tabulating return rates for every survey conducted.

Follow-up mailings may be administered in a number of ways. In the simplest, nonrespondents are simply sent a letter of additional encouragement to participate. A better method, however, is to send a new copy of the survey questionnaire with the follow-up letter. If potential respondents have not returned their questionnaires after two or three weeks, there is a good likelihood that the questionnaires will have been lost or misplaced. Receiving a follow-up letter might encourage them to look for the original questionnaire, but if it is not easily found, the letter may go for naught. (The response rates reported in the above paragraph all involved the sending of additional questionnaires.)

If the individuals in the survey sample are not identified on the questionnaires, it may not be possible to remail only to nonrespondents. In such a case, the researcher should send his follow-up mailing to all initial members of the sample, thanking those who may have already participated and encouraging those who have not to do so. (The case study reported in a later section of this chapter describes another method that may be used in an anonymous mail survey.)

Acceptable Response Rates

A question that new survey researchers frequently ask concerns the percentage return rate that should be achieved in a mail survey. It bears repeating here that the body of inferential statistics used in connection with survey analysis assumed that *all* members of the initial sample complete and return their questionnaires. Since this almost never happens, response bias becomes a concern, with the researcher testing (and hoping for) the possibility that the respondents are essentially a random sample of the initial sample, and thus a somewhat smaller random sample of the total population.[1]

Nevertheless, overall response rate is one guide to the representativeness of the sample respondents. If a high response rate is achieved, there is less chance of significant response bias than if a low rate is achieved. But what is a *high* response rate?

A quick review of the survey literature will uncover a wide range of response rates. Each of these may be accompanied by a statement something like "This is regarded as a relatively high response rate for a survey of this type." (A United States senator made this statement regarding a poll of constituents that achieved a 4 percent return rate.) Despite the great variety of actual return rates and reactions to those rates, there are some rules of thumb that might be followed.

I feel that a response rate of at least 50 percent is *adequate* for analysis and reporting. A response rate of at least 60 percent is *good.* And a response rate of 70 percent or more is *very good.* The reader should bear in mind, however, that these are only rough guides, they have no statistical basis, and a demonstrated lack of response bias is far more important than a high response rate.

In computing response rates, the accepted practice is to omit all those questionnaires that could not be delivered. In his methodological report, the researcher should indicate the initial sample size, then subtract the number that could not be delivered due to bad addresses, death, and the like. Then the number of completed questionnaires is divided by the *net* sample size to produce the response rate. As a result, the response rate is really a measure of the researcher's success in persuading sample members to participate, and he does not count against himself those whom he could not even contact.

---

1. For more detailed examinations of nonresponse biases, see Marjorie N. Donald, "Implications of Nonresponse for the Interpretation of Mail Questionnaire Data," *Public Opinion Quarterly*, vol. 24, no. 1 (1960), pp. 99–114, and K. A. Brownlee, "A Note on the Effects of Nonresponse on Surveys," *Journal of the American Statistical Association*, vol. 52, no. 277 (1957), pp. 29–32.

Although this is the accepted practice, the reader should be aware of the logical assumption upon which it is based: that nondeliverable questionnaires represent a random sample of the initial sample. Of course, this may not be the case at all. Persons whose questionnaires cannot be delivered are, at the very least, probably more mobile than others in the sample, and mobility may be related to a variety of other variables. Here again, tests for nonresponse bias are the best guide.

A Case Study

The steps involved in the administration of a mail survey are many and can best be appreciated in a walkthrough of an actual study. We shall conclude this section, then, with a detailed description of a survey conducted among University of Hawaii students in the spring of 1969. As the reader will note shortly, the study did not represent the theoretical ideal for such studies, but in that regard it serves present purposes all the better.

The sample design and selection for this study have been reported as a case study in Chapter 7. By way of general overview, it will be recalled that approximately 1,100 students were selected from the university registration tape through a stratified, systematic sampling procedure. For each student so selected, six self-adhesive mailing labels were printed by the computer.

By the time the research team was prepared to distribute the questionnaires, it became apparent that their research funds were inadequate to cover several mailings to the entire sample of 1,100 students. (Questionnaire printing costs were higher than anticipated.) As a result, a systematic two-thirds sample of the mailing labels was chosen, yielding a subsample of 770 students.

An earlier decision had been made to keep the survey anonymous in the hope of encouraging more candid responses to some sensitive questions. (Subsequent surveys of the same issues among the same population indicate this was unnecessary.) Thus, the questionnaires would carry no identification of students on them. At the same time, it was hoped that follow-up mailing costs could be reduced by remailing only to nonrespondents.

To achieve both of these aims, a special postcard method was devised. Each student was mailed a questionnaire that carried no identifying marks, plus a postcard addressed to the research office—with one of his mailing labels affixed to the reverse side of the card. The introductory letter asked him to complete and return the questionnaire—assuring him anonymity—and to return the postcard simultaneously. Receipt of the postcard would tell the researchers that he had returned his questionnaire—without indicating *which* questionnaire was his. This procedure would then facilitate follow-up mailings. (See below.)

The 32-page questionnaire was printed in the form of a booklet (photo-offset and saddle-stitched). A three-panel cover—described elsewhere in this chapter—permitted the questionnaire to be returned without an additional envelope.

A letter introducing the study and its purposes was printed on the front cover of the booklet. It explained why the study was being conducted (to learn how students feel about a variety of issues), how students had been selected for the study, the importance of each student's responding, and the mechanics of returning the questionnaire.

Students were assured that the study was anonymous, and the postcard method and rationale were explained. A statement followed about the auspices under which the study was being conducted, and a telephone number was provided for those who might want more information about the study. (About five students called for information.)

By printing the introductory letter on the questionnaire, we avoided the necessity of enclosing a separate letter in the outgoing envelope, thereby simplifying the task of assembling mailing pieces.

The assembly of materials for the initial mailing involved the following steps. (1) One mailing label for each student was stuck on a postcard. (2) Another label was stuck on an outgoing manila envelope. (3) One postcard and one questionnaire were placed in each envelope—with a glance to insure that the name on the postcard and on the envelope were the same in each case.

This was accomplished through an assembly-line procedure involving the several members of the research team. Although the procedure was somewhat organized in advance, it should be noted that a certain amount of actual practice was required before the best allocation of tasks and persons was discovered.

It is also worth noting that the entire process was delayed several days while the initial batch of manila envelopes were exchanged for larger ones. This delay could have been avoided if a walkthrough of the assembly process had been carried out in advance.

The distribution of the survey questionnaires had been set up for a bulk-rate mailing. Once the questionnaires had been stuffed into the envelopes, they were grouped by zip codes, tied in bundles, and delivered to the post office.

Shortly after the initial mailing, questionnaires and postcards began arriving at the research office. Questionnaires were opened, perused, and assigned identification numbers as described earlier in the chapter.

The processing of postcards, however, pointed to an oversight in sample design. Recall from the earlier discussion of the sample design (Chapter 7) that the final arrangement of students in the sampling frame had been by social security number, thereby providing a quasi-stratification by region of origin. As a result, the mailing labels were printed in that order (within class strata). Social security numbers had not been printed on the mailing labels, however, as they were not relevant to the study.

Given a postcard bearing a particular name and address, then, it was very difficult to locate the corresponding labels among those remaining in the several sheets of computer printout. Thus it was necessary to cut apart all the labels from the printout sheets and alphabetize them. Then it was possible to locate a given student's labels with a minumum of effort. (*Note:* The labels could have been printed in alphabetical order initially, if this problem had been anticipated.) For every postcard received, then, a search was made for that student's label, and they were destroyed.

After a period of two or three weeks, all the mailing labels remaining were used to organize a follow-up mailing. The assembly procedures described above were repeated with one exception. A special separate letter of appeal was prepared and included in the mailing piece. The new letter indicated that many students had returned their questionnaires already, but that it was very important for all others to do so as well. The letter also indicated that the research office records might be in error, and if the student had already returned his questionnaire, he should ignore the second appeal and accept our thanks for his assistance. If he had not already participated, he was encouraged to do so.

The follow-up mailing stimulated a resurgence of returns as expected, and the same logging procedures were continued. The returned postcards told us which additional mailing labels to destroy. Unfortunately, time and financial pressures made it impossible to undertake a third mailing as had been initially planned, but the two mailings resulted in an overall return rate of 62 percent.

11.4

Interview Surveys

This section essentially parallels the prior one; it describes an alternative method of data collection in connection with surveys. Rather than asking respondents to read questionnaires and enter their own answers, interviewers ask the questions orally and record respondents' answers. **Interviewing** is typically done in a face-to-face encounter, and this section will focus on such interviewing situations. However, telephone interviewing should follow most of the same guidelines. Also, most interview surveys require more than one interviewer, although you might undertake a small-scale interview survey yourself. Portions of this section will discuss methods for training and supervising a staff of interviewers assisting you on the survey.

The Role of the Interviewer

There are a number of advantages in having a questionnaire administered by an interviewer rather than by the respondent himself. To begin, interview surveys typically attain higher response rates than mail surveys. A properly designed and executed interview survey ought to achieve a completion rate of at least 80 to 85 percent. (Federally funded surveys often require this.) It would seem that respondents are more reluctant to turn down an interviewer standing on their doorstep than they are to throw away a mail questionnaire.

Within the context of the questionnaire, the presence of an interviewer generally decreases the number of "don't knows" and "no answers." If minimizing such responses is important to the study, the interviewer can be instructed to probe for answers. ("If you had to pick one of the answers, which do you think would come closest to your feelings?")

Interviewers can also provide a guard against confusing questionnaire items. If the respondent clearly misunderstands the intent of a question or indicates that he does not understand, the interviewer can clarify matters, thereby obtaining relevant responses. (Such clarifications must be strictly controlled, however, through formal *specifications*. See below.)

Finally, the interviewer can observe as well as ask questions. For example, the interviewer can note the respondent's race if this is considered too delicate a question to ask. Similar observations can be made regarding the quality of the dwelling, the presence of various possessions, the respondent's ability to speak English, the respondent's general reactions to the study and so forth. In one survey of students, respondents were given a short self-administered questionnaire to complete—concerning sexual attitudes and behavior—during the course of the interview. While a student completed the questionnaire, the interviewer made detailed notes regarding the dress and grooming of the respondent.

Neutral Role of Interviewer Survey research is of necessity based on an unrealistic *stimulus–response* theory of cognition and behavior. It must be assumed that a questionnaire item will mean exactly the same thing to every respondent, and every given response must mean the same when given by different respondents. Although this is an impossible goal, survey questions are drafted in such a way as to closely approximate the ideal.

The interviewer must also fit into this ideal situation. The interviewer's presence should not affect a respondent's perception of a question nor the answer given. The interviewer, then, should be a *neutral* medium through which questions and answers are transmitted.

If this goal is successfully accomplished, different interviewers would obtain exactly the same responses from a given respondent. This neutrality has a special importance in area samples. To save time and money, a given interviewer is typically assigned to complete all the interviews in a particular geographical area—a city block or group of nearby blocks. If the interviewer does anything to affect the responses obtained, then the bias thus interjected might be interpreted as a characteristic of the area under study.

Let's suppose that a survey is being done to determine attitudes toward low-cost housing, to help in the selection of a site for a new government-sponsored development. An interviewer assigned to a given neighborhood might—through word or gesture—communicate his own distaste for low-cost housing developments. His respondents might thereby tend to give responses generally in agreement with his own position. The results of the survey would indicate that the neighborhood in question would strongly resist construction of the development in their area.

General Rules for Interviewing

The manner in which interviews ought to be conducted will vary somewhat by survey population and will be affected somewhat by the nature of the survey content as well. Nevertheless, it is possible to provide some general guidelines that would apply to most if not all interviewing situations.

Appearance and Demeanor As a general rule, the interviewer should dress in a fashion fairly similar to that of the people he or she will be interviewing. A richly dressed interviewer will probably have difficulty getting good cooperation and responses from poorer respondents. And a poorly dressed interviewer will have similar difficulties with richer respondents.

To the extent that the interviewer's dress and grooming differ from those of her respondents, it should be in the direction of cleanliness and neatness in modest apparel. If cleanliness is not next to godliness, it appears to be next to neutrality. Although middle-class neatness and cleanliness may not be accepted by all sectors of American society, they remain the primary norm and are more likely to be acceptable to the largest number of respondents.

Dress and grooming are typically regarded as signals to a person's attitudes and orientations. At the time this is being written, a man wearing colorful clothes, beads, and sandals, and sporting long hair, sideburns, and a beard communicates—correctly or incorrectly—that he is politically on the left, sexually permissive, antiwar, favorable to drug use, and so forth. His appearance will communicate these orientations to a respondent as much as if he began the interview by saying "Hi there, I'm a hippie!"

In demeanor, the interviewer should be pleasant if nothing else. Since he will be prying into the respondent's personal life and attitudes, he must communicate a genuine interest in getting to know the respondent without appearing to be a spy. He must be relaxed and friendly without being too casual or clinging. One of the most important natural abilities that interviewers must have is the ability to determine very quickly the kind of person the respondent will feel most comfortable with; the kind of person the respondent would most enjoy talking to. There are two aspects of this. Clearly, the interview will be more successful if the interviewer can become the kind of person the respondent is comfortable with. Second, since the respondent is asked to volunteer a portion of his time and to divulge personal information about himself, he deserves the most enjoyable experience that the researcher and the interviewer can provide.

Familiarity with Questionnaire If the interviewer is unfamiliar with the questionnaire, the study suffers and an unfair burden is placed on the respondent. In the latter respect, the interview is likely to take more time than necessary and be generally unpleasant. Moreover, the interviewer cannot acquire familiarity by skimming through the questionnaire two or three times. It must be studied carefully, question by question, and the interviewer must practice reading it aloud. (See "coordination and control" later in this chapter.)

Ultimately, the interviewer must be able to read the questionnaire items to respondents without error, without stumbling over words and phrases. A good model for interviewers is the actor reading lines in a play or motion picture. The lines must be read as naturally as though they constituted a natural conversation, but that conversation must follow exactly the language set down in the questionnaire. Of course, the interviewer should not attempt to memorize the questionnaire.

By the same token, the interviewer must be familiar with the specifications (to be discussed shortly) prepared in conjunction with the questionnaire. Inevitably some questions will not exactly fit a given respondent's situation, and a question will arise as to how the question should be interpreted in that situation. The specifications provided to the interviewer should give adequate guidance in such cases, but the interviewer must know the organization and contents of the specifications sufficiently to permit efficient reference to them. It would be better for the interviewer to leave a given question unanswered than to spend five minutes searching through the specifications for clarification or trying to interpret the relevant instructions.

Follow Question Wording Exactly An earlier chapter discussing conceptualization and instrument construction pointed to the significance of question wording for the responses obtained. Thus, a slight change in the wording of a given question may lead a respondent to answer "yes" rather than "no."

Although the researcher will very carefully phrase his questionnaire items in such a way as to obtain the information he needs and to insure that respondents will interpret items in a manner appropriate to those needs, all this effort will be wasted if interviewers rephrase questions in their own words.

Record Responses Exactly Whenever the questionnaire contains open-ended questions, those soliciting the respondent's own answer, it is very important that the interviewer record that answer exactly as given. No attempt should be made to summarize, paraphrase, or correct bad grammar. The response should be written down exactly as given.

This is especially important since the interviewer will not know how the responses are to be coded prior to processing—indeed, the researcher may not know this until he has had an opportunity to read a hundred or so such responses. For example, the questionnaire might ask respondents how they feel about the traffic situation in their community. One respondent might answer that there were too many cars on the roads and that something should be done to limit their numbers. Another might say there was a need for more roads. If the interviewer recorded these two responses with the same summary—"congested traffic"—the researcher would not be able to take advantage of the important differences in the original responses.

Sometimes, the respondent may be so inarticulate that the verbal response is too ambiguous to permit interpretation. However, the interviewer may be able to understand the intent of the response through the respondent's gestures or tone. In such a situation, the exact verbal response should still be recorded, but the interviewer should add marginal comments giving his interpretation and his reasons for arriving at it.

More generally, it will be useful to the researcher to have any marginal comments explaining aspects of the response not conveyed in the verbal record, such as the respondent's apparent uncertainty in answering, anger, embarrassment, and so forth. In each case, however, the exact verbal response should also be recorded.

Probing for Responses   Sometimes respondents will respond to a question with an inappropriate answer. For example, the question may present an attitudinal statement and ask the respondent to "strongly agree, agree somewhat, disagree somewhat, or strongly disagree." The respondent, however, may reply: "I think that's true." The interviewer should follow this reply with: "Would you say you strongly agree or agree somewhat?" If necessary, the interviewer might explain that he must check one or the other of the categories provided. If the respondent adamantly refuses to choose, the interviewer should write in the exact response given by the respondent.

Probes are more frequently required in eliciting responses to open-ended questions. For example, in response to the previous question about traffic conditions, the respondent might simply reply, "Pretty bad." The interviewer could obtain an elaboration on this response through a variety of probes. Sometimes the best probe is silence; if the interviewer sits quietly with pencil poised, the respondent will probably fill the pause with additional comments. (This is a technique used effectively by newspaper reporters.) Appropriate verbal probes might be "How is that? In what ways?" Perhaps the most generally useful probe is "Anything else?"

It is frequently necessary to probe for answers that will be sufficiently informative for analytical purposes. In every case, however, it is imperative that such probes be completely *neutral.* The probe must not in any way affect the nature of the subsequent response. Whenever the researcher anticipates that a given question may require probing for appropriate responses, he should present one or more useful probes next to the question in the questionnaire. This practice has two important advantages. First, he will have more time to devise the best, most neutral probes. Second, all interviewers will use the same probes whenever they are needed. Thus, even if the probe is not perfectly neutral, all respondents will be presented with the same stimulus. This is the same logical guideline discussed for question wording. Although a question should not be loaded or biased, it is essential that every respondent be presented with the same question, even a biased one.

Coordination and Control

As indicated earlier in this section, most interview surveys require the assistance of several interviewers. In large-scale surveys, of course, such interviewers are hired and paid for their work. As a student researcher, you might find yourself recruiting friends to assist you in interviewing. Whenever more than one interviewer is involved in a survey, it is essential that their efforts be carefully controlled. There are two essential aspects to this: training interviewers, and supervising them after they begin work.

Interviewer training should be done in a group, rather than training each interviewer separately. The latter approach will inevitably result in more superficial training.

The interviewer training session should begin with a description of what the study is all about. Even though the interviewers may be involved only in the data collection phase of the project, it will be useful to them to understand what will be done with the interviews they conduct and what purpose will be served. Morale and motivation are usually low when interviewers do not know what is going on.

The training on how to interview should begin with a discussion of general guidelines and procedures, such as those discussed earlier in this chapter. Then, you should turn to the questionnaire itself. The whole group should go through the questionnaire together—question by question. Do not simply ask if anyone has any questions about the first page of the questionnaire. Read the first question aloud, explain the purpose of the question, and then entertain any questions or comments the interviewers may have. Once all their questions and comments have been handled, go on to the next question in the questionnaire.

It is always a good idea to prepare what are called *specifications* to accompany an interview questionnaire. This is a document made up of explanatory and clarifying comments about the handling of difficult or confusing situations that may occur with regard to specific questions in the questionnaire. When you are drafting the questionnaire, you should try to think of all the problem cases that might arise—the bizarre circumstances that might make a question difficult to answer. The survey specifications should provide detailed guidelines on how to handle such situations. As an example, such a simple matter as "age" might present problems. When asked how old he is, a respondent might report that he will be 25 next week. The interviewer might not be sure whether to take the respondent's current age or his nearest one. The specifications regarding that question in the questionnaire should explain what should be done. (Probably, you would specify that age as of last birthday should be recorded in all cases.)

If you have prepared a set of specifications, you should go over those with the interviewers at the same time that you go over the individual questions in the questionnaire. Make sure that your interviewers fully understand the specifications as well as the questions themselves.

This portion of the interviewer training is likely to generate a number of troublesome questions from your interviewers. They will ask: "What should I do if . . . ?" In such cases, you should never give a quick answer. If you have specifications, be sure to show how the solution to the problem could be determined from the specifications. If you do not have specifications prepared, show how the preferred handling of the situation fits within the general logic of the question and the purpose of the study. Giving offhand, unexplained answers to such questions will only confuse the interviewers, and they will probably not take their work very seriously. If you do not know the answer to such a question when it is asked, you would do well to admit that and ask for some time to decide on the best answer. Then think out the situation carefully and be sure to give all the interviewers your answer, explaining your reasons.

Once you have gone through the whole questionnaire as described above, you should conduct one or two demonstration interviews in front of everyone. Preferably, *you* should interview someone else. Realize that your interview will be a model for those you are training, and make it good. It would be best, moreover, if the demonstration interview were done as realistically as possible. Do not break up the course of the demonstration to point out how you have handled a complicated situation; handle it, and then explain later. It is irrelevant if the person you are "interviewing" gives real answers or takes on some hypothetical identity for the purpose, just so long as the answers are consistent.

After the demonstration interviews, you should pair off your interviewers and have them practice on each other. When they have completed the questionnaire, have them reverse roles and do it over again. Interviewing is the best training for interviewing. As your interviewers are practicing on each other, you should try to wander around, listening in on the practice so that you will know how well they are doing. Once the practice is completed, the whole group should discuss their experiences and ask any additional questions they may have.

The final stage of the training for interviewers should involve some "real" interviews. Have them conduct some interviews under the actual conditions that will pertain in the final survey. You may want to assign them people to interview, or perhaps they may be allowed to pick people themselves. Do not have them practice on people you have selected in your sample, however. After each interviewer has completed three to five interviews, have him check back with you. Look over the completed questionnaires to see if there is any evidence of misunderstanding. Again, answer any questions that individual interviewers may have. Once you are convinced that a given interviewer knows what is to be done, assign some real interviews— using the sample you have selected for the study.

It is essential that you continue supervising the work of interviewers over the course of the study. It is probably unwise to let them conduct more than twenty or thirty interviews without seeing you. You might assign twenty interviews, have the interviewer bring back those questionnaires when they are completed, look them over, and assign another twenty or so. Although this may seem overly cautious, you must continually protect yourself against misunderstandings that may not be evident early in the study.

If you are the only interviewer in your study, the preceding comments may not seem relevant to you. This is not wholly the case, however. You would be advised, for example, to prepare specifications for potentially troublesome questions in your questionnaire. Otherwise, you run the risk of making ad hoc decisions during the course of the study that you will later regret or forget. Also, the emphasis that has been placed on *practice* applies equally to the one-man project and to the complex funded survey with a large interviewing staff.

11.5

Comparison of Two Survey Methods

We have now examined two methods of data collection appropriate for survey research. Although I have touched on some of the relative advantages of each, it will be worth looking at this issue directly.

Self-administered questionnaires have the advantages of being generally cheaper and quicker than interview surveys. These are likely to be important considerations for an unfunded student wishing to undertake a survey in connection with a term paper or a thesis. Using the self-administered mail format, it costs no more to conduct a national survey than a local one, moreover; the cost difference between a local and a national interview survey would be enormous. Also, mail surveys typically require a small staff: one person can conduct a reasonably good mail survey alone, although you should not underestimate the work involved.

Finally, self-administered surveys are more appropriate in dealing with especially sensitive issues, when they offer complete anonymity. Respondents might be reluctant to report controversial or deviant attitudes or behavior in a face-to-face interview, but might do so more willingly in response to an anonymous self-administered questionnaire.

Interview surveys have many advantages, also. As touched on earlier, interview surveys generally produce fewer incomplete questionnaires. Although respondents may skip questions in a self-administered questionnaire, interviewers are trained not to do this. Interview surveys, moreover, typically achieve higher return rates than self-administered ones.

Although self-administered questionnaires may be more effective in dealing with sensitive issues, interview surveys are definitely more effective in dealing with complicated ones. The prime example of this would be the enumeration of household members and the determination as to whether a given household address contained more than one housing unit. Although the concept "housing unit" has been refined and standardized by the Bureau of the Census, and interviewers can be trained to deal with the concept in the field, it would be extremely difficult to devise a self-administered questionnaire dealing with this issue that could be understood by respondents. This advantage of interview surveys pertains more generally to all complicated contingency questions.

Using interviewers, it is possible to conduct a survey based on a sample of addresses. An interviewer can arrive at an assigned address, introduce the survey, and even—following instructions—choose the appropriate person at that address to respond to the survey. Self-administered mail questionnaires addressed to "occupant" receive a notoriously low response.

Finally, interviewers are able to make important observations aside from responses to questions asked in the interview. They may, in a household interview, note characteristics of the neighborhood, the dwelling unit, and so forth. They may note characteristics of the respondents or their interaction with the respondents, such as that a respondent had difficulty communicating or was hostile.

Ultimately, you must balance all these advantages and disadvantages of the two methods in relation to (a) your research needs and (b) your resources.

11.6
Strengths and Weaknesses of Survey Research

Like other modes of observation in social scientific research, surveys have special strengths and special weaknesses. It is important to know these in determining whether the survey format is appropriate to your research goals.

As noted earlier in this chapter, surveys are particularly useful in describing the characteristics of a large population. A carefully selected probability sample in combination with a standardized questionnaire offers the possibility of making refined descriptive assertions about a student body, a city, a nation, or other large population. Surveys determine unemployment rates, voting intentions, and the like with uncanny accuracy. Although the examination of official documents—such as marriage, birth, or death records—can provide such accuracy in regard to a few topics, no other method of observation can provide this general capability.

Surveys—especially self-administered ones—make very large samples feasible. Surveys of two thousand respondents are not unusual. A large number of cases is very important for both descriptive and explanatory analyses. Whenever several variables are to be analyzed simultaneously, it is essential to have a large number of cases.

In one sense, surveys are flexible. Many questions may be asked on a given topic, affording the researcher considerable flexibility in his analyses. Although experimental design may require the researcher to commit himself in advance to a particular operational definition of a concept, the survey analyst is able to develop operational definitions on the basis of actual observations.

Finally, standardized questionnaires have an important strength in regard to measurement generally. Earlier chapters have discussed the ambiguous nature of most concepts: they have no ultimately *real* meanings. One person's "religiosity" is quite different from another's. Although the researcher must be able to define concepts in ways most relevant to his research goals, he may not find it easy to apply the same definitions uniformly to all subjects. The survey researcher is bound to this requirement by having to ask exactly the same questions of all his subjects and having to impute the same intent to all respondents giving a particular response.

Survey research has a number of weaknesses. First, the requirement for standardization just mentioned often seems to result in the fitting of round pegs into square holes. Standardized questionnaire items often represent the "least common denominator" in assessing people's attitudes, orientations, circumstances, and experiences. By designing questions that will be at least minimally appropriate to all respondents, the researcher seldom taps what is most appropriate to many respondents. It is in this sense that surveys often appear superficial in their coverage of complex topics. Although this problem can be partly offset through sophisticated analyses, it is inherent in survey research.

Similarly, survey research can seldom deal with the *context* of social life. Although questionnaires can provide information in this area, the survey researcher can seldom develop the "feel" for the total life situation in which respondents are thinking and acting—in contrast, say, with the participant observer.

Although surveys are flexible in the sense mentioned earlier, they are inflexible in other ways. Studies involving direct observation can be modified as field conditions warrant, but surveys typically require that an initial study design remain unchanged throughout. As the field researcher, for example, becomes aware of an important new variable operating in the phenomenon he is studying, he may begin making careful observations of it. The survey researcher would likely be unaware of the new variable's importance, and could do nothing about it in any event.

Finally, surveys are subject to the "artificiality" mentioned earlier in connection with experiments. Few studies are aimed at the act of completing questionnaires or of being interviewed, and yet finding out that a person gives conservative answers to a questionnaire does not necessarily mean the person is conservative; finding out that a person gives prejudiced answers to a questionnaire does not necessarily mean that the person is prejudiced. This shortcoming is especially salient in the realm of action. Surveys cannot measure social action; they can only collect self-reports of recalled past action, or of prospective or hypothetical action. There are two aspects of this problem. First, the topic of study may not be amenable to measurement through questionnaires. Second, the act of studying that topic—an attitude, for example—may affect it. A survey respondent may have given no thought to whether the governor should be impeached until asked for his opinion by an interviewer. He may, at that point, form an opinion on the matter.

As with all methods of observation, a full awareness of the inherent or probable weaknesses of survey research can partially resolve them in some cases. Ultimately, the researcher is on the safest ground when he is able to employ a number of different research methods in studying a given topic.

11.7
Summary

Chapter 11 has discussed survey research, a mode of observation that has been very popular in the social sciences in recent years. The chapter began with an examination of the topics most appropriate to survey research. We saw that it is particularly valuable as a method for providing *descriptions* of large populations, and that survey data can be used for explanatory purposes as well. Surveys typically, though not necessarily, have people as their units of analysis.

Data are collected in surveys through the use of questionnaires (described in Chapter 5) and they typically involve the administration of those questionnaires to samples selected from larger populations (described in Chapters 6 and 7).

There are two basic methods for the administration of questionnaires to respondents. *Self-administered* questionnaires may be mailed or handed to respondents who then complete them on their own. The chapter discussed some of the considerations involved in this form of questionnaire administration, discussing such matters as various postal options, methods for monitoring the returned questionnaires, follow-up mailings, and response rates. A case study was provided to give a clearer picture of the several steps involved in the use of a self-administered questionnaire.

Sometimes, questionnaires are administered by *interviewers*—specially trained people who contact respondents, read the questionnaire items to them, and record respondents' answers. The chapter discussed the role of the interviewer in this research process and provided a set of general guidelines for interviewing. In addition, some suggestions were made for the coordination and control of interviewers, just in case you find yourself supervising a team of interviewers.

The relative advantages of these two methods of survey administration were then discussed, and, finally, the special strengths and weaknesses of survey research were presented. Against the advantages of economy and standardization, we noted that surveys can be somewhat artificial and superficial.

11.8
Main Points

1. Survey research, a popular social research method, is the administration of questionnaires to a sample of respondents selected from some population.

2. Survey research is especially appropriate for making *descriptive* studies of large populations; survey data may be used for *explanatory* purposes as well.

3. Questionnaires may be administered in two basically different ways: *self-administered* questionnaires may be completed by the respondents themselves; *interviewers* may administer questionnaires, reading the items to respondents and recording the answers.

4. It is generally advisable to plan *follow-up* mailings in the case of self-administered questionnaires: sending new questionnaires to those respondents who fail to respond to the initial appeal.

5. A proper monitoring of questionnaire returns will provide a good guide as to when a follow-up mailing is appropriate.

6. The essential characteristic of interviewers is that they be *neutral*; their presence in the data-collection process must not have any effect on the responses given to questionnaire items.

7. Interviewers must be carefully trained to be familiar with the questionnaire, to follow the question wording and question order exactly, and to record responses exactly as they are given.

8. A *probe* is a neutral, nondirective question designed to elicit an elaboration on an incomplete or ambiguous response, given in an interview in response to an open-ended question. Examples would include: "Anything else?" "How is that?" "In what ways?"

9. The advantages of a self-administered questionnaire over an interview survey are: economy, speed, lack of interviewer bias, and the possibility of anonymity and privacy to encourage more candid responses on sensitive issues.

10. The advantages of an interview survey over a self-administered questionnaire are: fewer incomplete questionnaires and fewer misunderstood questions, generally higher return rates, and greater flexibility in terms of sampling and special observations.

11. Survey research in general has advantages in terms of economy and the amount of data that can be collected. The standardization of the data collected represents another special strength of survey research.

12. Survey research has the weaknesses of being somewhat artificial and potentially superficial. It is difficult to gain a full sense of social processes in their natural settings through the use of surveys.

11.9
Annotated Bibliography

Babbie, Earl, *Survey Research Methods* (Belmont, California: Wadsworth, 1973). A comprehensive overview of survey methods. (You thought I'd say it was lousy?) This textbook, although overlapping somewhat with the present one, covers aspects of survey techniques that are omitted here.

Glock, Charles (ed.), *Survey Research in the Social Sciences* (New York: Russell Sage Foundation, 1967). An excellent collection of essays on the use of survey methods in the several social sciences. This book is especially useful in illustrating the somewhat different ways in which different disciplines regard and utilize a given research method. The several chapters also provide extensive bibliographies, citing examples of survey projects.

Hyman, Herbert, *Survey Design and Analysis* (New York: Free Press, 1955.) An old but classic and important overview of survey methods. Although incomplete or outdated in its treatment of survey techniques, it provides an excellent statement of the logic of survey in social research, illustrating that logic with several research examples. Paul Lazarsfeld's foreword is especially important.

Lazarsfeld, Paul, Berelson, Bernard, and Gaudet, Hazel, *The People's Choice* (New York: Columbia University Press, 1948). An old but classic survey. This panel survey, conducted in Erie County, Ohio, examined the ways in which voters reached their final presidential preference during the 1940 election campaign. Survey research is currently so popular in the social sciences that citing recent examples is at once very easy and very difficult. I have chosen, therefore, to cite this one for its historical value and because its methodological and substantive values remain current several decades later.

Stouffer, Samuel, *Communism, Conformity, and Civil Liberties* (New York: John Wiley, 1955). Another old but classic survey. This massive survey examined the impact of (Joe) McCarthyism on the attitudes of both the general public and community leaders, asking whether the repression of the early 1950s affected support for civil liberties. Like *The People's Choice* (see above), this maintains its methodological and substantive importance today.

12

Other Modes of Observation

12.1
Introduction

The preceding chapters in Part Three have been addressed to some of the more popular methods or modes of observation used by social scientists. The list these chapters provide, however, is far from complete. In the present chapter, I would like to describe, more briefly, some other research methods used by social scientists, though even these additions hardly exhaust the possibilities available to social scientists. We shall consider historical research, the use of existing records and statistics, unobtrusive measures, secondary analysis, and computer simulation modeling.

12.2
Historical Research

The academic discipline of history is one of those that lie on the borderline between two major academic divisions. Some regard history as a social science, while others regard it as a humanity. Its ultimate assignment is, of course, irrelevant to our purposes. What is important, however, is that historical research is often effectively used by social scientists.

You will recall from Chapter 1 of this book that scientists seek *generalized understanding*. Rather than seeking to understand a specific event fully, the scientist attempts to develop general principles or laws that permit the understanding of broad classes of events. The historian is somewhat different in this regard. His goal is to reconstruct prior events in all their relevant aspects. Although his efforts may not be limited solely to description, his attempts at explanation are typically limited to the specific event under study. What were the most important causes of the French Revolution? Why did the American revolutionaries establish a republican form of government rather than a monarchy?

Social scientists, when they engage in historical research, share the historian's concern for understanding a particular event fully, but they usually are motivated also to generate generalized understanding. The social scientist then may seek, within a particular event, clues to understanding more general processes operating in other events.

Max Weber's studies of Confucianism,[1] Hinduism,[2] Judaism,[3] and Protestantism[4] examined the historical development of particular religions within particular social contexts. At the same time, Weber sought to discover, from a full understanding of these specific religions, general principles regarding the role of religion in society. Among other things, he was interested in understanding the operation of religious authority, the interrelation between religion and economy, and, more generally, the role of ideas in determining social action and evolution.

Presumably the historical researcher merely assembles all the facts pertaining to a particular event. His sources of facts are many and varied. He will undoubtedly read the histories other people have written. He may examine official documents relevant to the occurrence. He may examine letters and diaries written at the time, perhaps by participants. If he is studying a recent event, he may be able to interview some of the people who took part. (This latter technique is sometimes called *oral history.*)

If you recall the discussions of Part Two of this book, you may have already suspected that assembling "facts" is not as simple and straightforward as it may appear. "Facts" about a particular event often seem to contradict one another. Contradictory or not, the historical researcher is likely to find himself deluged with facts. As Robert Bellah reports in his excellent research biography:

> The usual textbook notion of social research is that one forms a hypothesis and then proceeds to gather data to confirm or negate it. In many instances, this may be a tolerably accurate description; but, at least in the field of comparative and historical research, the researcher often finds himself with an abundance of data, and the problem is how to make sense of it.[5]

It bears repeating that *content analysis* sometimes offers one systematic method for organizing and summarizing such data.

Historical research is in many ways most like field research. Like all social science, it may be motivated by the desire to test a general theory or a more limited hypothesis, or by an unstructured interest in the particular event. The researcher compiles a mass of information with the intent of developing conclusions or hypotheses from his full and deep understanding of what has transpired. Historical research is, at the same time, subject to the same problems of validity and generalizability that characterize field research.

---

1. Max Weber, *The Religion of China*, Hans H. Gerth, Trans. (Glencoe, Ill.: Free Press, 1951).
2. ——————*The Religion of India* (Glencoe, Ill.: Free Press, 1958).
3. ——————*Ancient Judaism* (Glencoe, Ill.: Free Press, 1952).
4. ——————*The Protestant Ethic and Spirit of Capitalism* (New York: Charles Scribner's, 1958).
5. Robert Bellah, "Tokugawa Religion," in Phillip E. Hammond, Ed., *Sociologists at Work* (New York: Basic Books, 1964), p. 159.

12.3

Analyzing Existing Statistics

Frequently it is possible or necessary to undertake social scientific research through the use of official statistics. In any event, this possible source of data should never be overlooked, even when some other mode of observation is also being employed.

One of the foremost examples of this type of research may be found in Emile Durkheim's classic study, *Suicide*.[6] Basically, Durkheim was attempting to discover the causes of suicide. Quite clearly, this research interest did not lend itself to such research methods as participant observation, experimentation, or survey research. Aside from the obvious problems involved in using such methods to study suicide, Durkheim faced the additional problem that the topic of his research was relatively rare.

Durkheim discovered, however, that most European nations routinely compiled and reported summary statistics on suicides. Although these official data obviously said nothing about the motivations for suicide and said little about the characteristics of persons committing suicide, Durkheim was nonetheless able to undertake a rather ingenious analysis. He was able, for example, to examine the effects of living in the country or living in cities by comparing the suicide rates of towns and cities of different sizes. More importantly for his ultimate thesis, he was able to examine the possible effects of religion by comparing the suicide rates in Protestant countries and Catholic ones and by comparing suicide rates in predominantly Protestant and predominantly Catholic regions of a single country. Even though Durkheim was unable to examine directly the suicide rates of Protestants and Catholics, he was able to examine this indirectly.

Another excellent example may be found in the work of Samuel Stouffer. Stouffer and his colleagues, some years ago, were interested in learning about the effect of the Depression of the 1930s on the stability of marriages and families. Stouffer initially designed and proposed a sample survey for this purpose; lacking the money necessary to conduct this survey, however, Stouffer did not give up his research interest nor his intent to study the issue empirically. Rather, he reviewed the available official statistics regarding marriages and divorces. Having determined what data were readily available for analysis, Stouffer asked what sorts of trends should be expected to appear in those official statistics if the Depression had indeed made marriages and families more unstable.[7]

Among other things, Stouffer suggested that the Depression might have resulted in what he called "impulsive marriages." One indicator of such a marriage, he suggested, would be that it was performed outside the bride's and groom's state of residence. Stouffer's analysis of statistics indicated an increase of out-of-state marriages during and immediately following the Depression.

---

6. Emile Durkheim, *Suicide* (Glencoe, Ill.: Free Press, 1951).
7. Reprinted in Samuel A. Stouffer, *Social Research to Test Ideas* (New York: Basic Books, 1960).

Stouffer suggested another possible indicator that the Depression might have resulted in the breakdown of traditional marriage and family patterns; an increase in religiously mixed marriages. His analysis of the relevant official statistics indicated that this hypothesis also was correct.

The volume of official statistics relevant to social scientific analyses is simply enormous, and that volume increases each year. The United States Census Bureau may be the largest single contributor to this volume of statistics, but other governmental bureaus, agencies, and departments should not be overlooked. The United States Departments of Labor, Agriculture, Commerce, and Health, Education, and Welfare regularly report many statistical series, and the same is true at their state and local counterparts. Law enforcement agencies report crime statistics. The list could go on and on.

Government agencies are not the only source of such statistics, moreover. Corporations, for example, publish annual reports, and business-oriented magazines often summarize the reports of many corporations. Other kinds of nongovernmental organizations collect and publish data in a similar fashion.

On the whole, then, there is a rich abundance of statistical data appropriate and readily available for the analysis of a variety of social scientific topics. The researcher's first task is simply to locate and extract the data which he requires.

There are two major problems involved in the use of this type of data, and these problems correspond roughly to the concepts of *validity* and *reliability* discussed earlier in this book. First, in terms of validity, the variables that are represented by the data available for analysis may not correspond exactly to the variables that you wish to study. You must decide, then, whether the data that *are* available provide at least useful indicators of the variables and concepts which interest you. Thus, for example, Stouffer did not have data that directly represented "impulsive marriages"; he reasoned, however, that the available data on out-of-state marriages would provide an *approximate indicator* of his concept.

Second, the analysis of available statistics may raise problems of reliability and comparability. If, for example, you wish to analyze the corporate profits of several corporations, or the crime rates of several cities, you may find that the individual units of analysis define and measure the variables in question somewhat differently. This will be less of a problem, of course, if all the data have been collected and compiled by a single agency. As a rule, you may guard against this general problem through carefully checking the different definitions and measurement methods utilized.

One of the chief advantages of this mode of observation is low cost. Also, it is often quicker than other modes of observation. Realize, of course, that this does not mean that all research projects utilizing existing statistics will be cheap or fast on any absolute standard. Such projects would be typically less expensive and faster, however, than projects that required the collection of original data in order to address the same topic.

The analysis of available statistics may often be used to advantage in conjunction with other research methods.

12.4
Unobtrusive Measures

There is another advantage to the analysis of existing statistics that was not mentioned in the previous section. Such a mode of observation avoids one of the inherent problems of most social research methods: the effect of the study on that which is being studied. Clearly, analyzing suicide statistics has no influence whatever on the suicides themselves, whereas, by comparison, interviewing someone who was standing on the top of a tall building or sitting with his head in a gas oven might conceivably influence whether or not the suicide occurred.

In recent years, Eugene Webb and his colleagues[8] have drawn attention to a variety of *unobtrusive measures:* methods for observing and measuring social phenomena while having little or no impact on that which is being measured. These social scientists have shown that scientific ingenuity is almost limitless. We are reminded again that the scientist is very much like a detective.

How can we measure the relative popularity of different radio stations? The social scientist's first idea would probably be to conduct a survey, asking people what station they prefer or what station they are listening to at the time of the interview. This mode of observation, however, is likely to affect the variables being studied or, at least, to be unreliable in some indeterminate number of cases. We do not know how many respondents have turned down the volume on their favorite soap opera, answered the interviewer's telephone call, and reported that they were listening to *Meet the Press.* Webb and his colleagues suggest a radically different way of measuring radio listenership: we might simply arrange for some auto mechanics to check the dial settings on the radios of cars left at service stations and garages.

How would we determine the most popular exhibit at a museum? Again, many social scientists would immediately recommend a survey. Others might suggest participant observation, and still others might recommend an experiment in which subjects would be exposed to a variety of exhibits. Webb and his colleagues suggest that another method would be to examine the floor tiles immediately in front of several exhibits in the museum. Those exhibits with the most worn-down tile would be presumably more popular than those exhibits whose tiles are relatively unworn. Or, we might check the museum maintenance records to discover where floor tiles have been most frequently replaced. Similarly, those exhibits whose glass cases are the most smudged with mucus are likely to be the most popular with runny-nosed little kids.

Aside from the inherent advantage of being unobtrusive, this mode of observation is simply fun in that it requires a great deal of imagination and ingenuity on the part of the researcher. Like the police detective, the social scientist searches for clues. If a museum exhibit were popular, for example,

---

8. Eugene J. Webb, Donald T. Campbell, Richard D. Schwartz, and Lee Sechrest, *Unobtrusive Measures: Nonreactive Research in the Social Sciences* (Chicago: Rand McNally, 1966).

what traces of that popularity might have been left behind by the participants in its popularity?

There are inherent problems in this mode of observation as well. Like the analysis of existing statistics, the use of unobtrusive measures in general may face problems of validity. Do the indirect indicators of research concepts and variables adequately tap what is to be studied? There are problems of reliability: suppose museum officials installed a higher quality tile in front of those exhibits they considered would be popular.

These indirect, unobtrusive measures may also present difficulties, or at least uncertainties, with regard to *representativeness.* In the example of the museum floor tile, we run the risk of overrepresenting the preferences of heavy people, people who shuffle their feet when they walk, or people with abrasive soles on their shoes. Or, in the car radio example, we might overrepresent the listening habits of people who have a lot of trouble with their cars or people who are the most diligent in terms of preventive maintenance.

These latest remarks should not be taken as an invalidation of unobtrusive measures; rather, they are meant to suggest the full extent of ingenuity that must be exercised by the social scientist in using this, as in any other, method of research.

12.5
Secondary Analysis

With the growth in the use of computers for analyzing social scientific data has come an extremely valuable new source of data for social scientific research. As more and more social researchers have undertaken original data collection—through surveys, content analyses, or other means —and have prepared these data for computer analyses, it has become apparent that such data need not and should not be discarded once they have been analyzed by the original researcher. Indeed, international networks of *data archives* have been organized for the storage and sharing of such data.

Let's suppose, for example, that Researcher A has received a foundation grant of $200,000 to conduct a national survey on the topic of religiosity and prejudice. His survey questionnaire generates a variety of data relevant to these two concepts, but he also collects data relevant to other concepts and variables that he feels might shed some light on his primary research concern: political party affiliation and alienation, for example. Researcher A might then expend his $200,000 grant executing his national survey and analyzing the relationship between religiosity and prejudice.

Researcher B might have a special research interest in the relationship between alienation and political party affiliation. However, he might lack the $200,000 required to undertake a national survey to study that relationship. He might be able to obtain, at a cost of perhaps $40 or $50, a copy of the data cards or magnetic tapes containing the data collected in Researcher A's survey.

In addition to reanalyzing each other's data, academic researchers frequently utilize data files generated by commercial polling firms such as Gallup, Harris, and Roper. Also, the United States Census Bureau selects a *public use sample* from its decennial census for this purpose.

Realize that this form of secondary analysis differs importantly from the analysis of existing statistics. In secondary analysis, the researcher is not limited to the manipulation and interpretation of published statistics. Rather, he has added flexibility in his analyses because, by possessing a copy of the original data used in the publication of such official statistics, he can organize and analyze the data in new ways.

One example of this type of research method is the study of politics and prejudice by Seymour Martin Lipsett and Earl Raab.[9] These social scientists wished to study the relationship between extremist political movements and prejudice over the course of American history. In analyzing those political movements that occurred early in American history, they made use of published statistics. In connection with more recent political movements, they often were able to obtain copies of the original data collected in public opinion polls and other surveys. Regardless of the published reports produced by those several studies, Lipsett and Raab were in a position to reanalyze the data in ways more directly appropriate to their own interests.

Several networks of data archives have, in recent years, sprung up across the country and throughout the world. The chief ones are the Interuniversity Consortium for Political Research at the University of Michigan, the Roper Center at Williams College, and the International Data Library and Reference Service at the University of California, Berkeley. The National Opinion Research Center (NORC) at the University of Chicago, another data repository, has also begun conducting a General Social Survey for the express purpose of providing researchers with an omnibus data set for secondary analysis.

Each of these institutes has assumed the responsibility of collecting from original researchers the data obtained in major research projects. Such data are then maintained in a fashion similar to the maintenance of books in a conventional library. Researchers wishing to undertake secondary analyses may then obtain copies of the data files from these central repositories. In addition to use by professional researchers for secondary analyses, many individual universities obtain and maintain some such data sets as a resource for student instruction in research methods.

Secondary analyses have become increasingly popular in the social sciences in recent years, largely due to the time and money saved by this form of research. There are, at the same time, problems inherent in secondary analysis.

The chief problem facing a secondary analyst is that of *validity.* Very often an original researcher may not have collected data in precisely the form required by the secondary analyst. It may be necessary, then, to utilize indirect indicators of research concepts and variables. For example, the secondary analyst may be interested in studying the sources of political

9. Seymour Martin Lipset and Earl Raab. *The Politics of Unreason* (New York: Harper & Row, 1970).

involvement and activity. He goes to the data file, looks up several possible sources, and finds very little information regarding political involvement and activity: perhaps in one study respondents were asked only whether they had voted in the most recent election, for example. The prospective secondary analyst, then, must weigh the potential saving in time and money against the uncertain validity of the measures available in the original data sets available to him.

12.6
Computer Simulation Modeling

Chapter 12 concludes with a brief overview of a rather different mode of observation currently being explored by social scientists. Sometimes it is possible for scientists, on the basis of prior theoretical and empirical research, to construct a computerized model of a social process. Such a model may then be manipulated and observed as a *simulation* of the real thing.

Let's consider a hypothetical example in the field of demography. Demographers are chiefly concerned with the dynamic process of change in the size and characteristics of human populations. Chief among their tools in this effort is the *age-sex profile.*

An age-sex profile describes the numbers of men and women in different age categories within a population. This is especially important to demographers as a clue to future fertility and population growth. Most simply put, the more men and women there are in the child-bearing ages, the greater is population growth likely to be in subsequent years. By estimating future birth rates, demographers are then able to estimate the future age-sex profiles of that society.

It would be possible to construct a computerized model of a given society's age-sex profile and build a reproductive component into that model, thereby making a dynamic model. Working with such a computer simulation model, demographers would be able to determine the probable conse-quences of, say, a war which killed half the young men, a general trend towards smaller families, or similar events. The possible event simply would be programmed into the computer model, and the demographer would observe the subsequent changes in that model, just as though he were actually observing the changes in a real population.

The potential for computer simulation seems almost limitless. Dyadic (two-person) interactions such as a fist fight or a debate might be simulated, computer models might be constructed to simulate small group interaction, or, as indicated above, whole societies might be simulated.

Computer simulation would seem to be especially valuable in the area of social and environmental planning. To the extent that it is possible to construct computer models of social processes, prospective social changes might be tested out by computer prior to trying them out in real life. The importance of this has become particularly evident in recent years as we have discovered that well-intentioned social change often has unhappy inadvertent consequences. The introduction of modern public health methods into an underdeveloped country, for example, has often resulted in rapid population growth and consequent starvation. Or although DDT has indeed produced a greater abundance of farm crops, we are now discovering some of its very negative environmental consequences.

The utility and effectiveness of computer simulation in this respect depend on the comprehensiveness of the computer models and the extent to which they adequately reproduce the actual social processes under study. Computer simulation will be more effective, therefore, in the study of phenomena involving relatively few variables that have relatively clear and regular relationships.

12.7
Summary

In Chapter 12, the final chapter of Part Three, I have attempted to provide a brief overview of some additional research methods available to social researchers. This final list is intended as more suggestive than exhaustive, so realize that there are many more tricks in the social scientist's bag.

The chapter began with a brief description of historical research, very akin to what an historian does except that social researchers—as scientists—are interested in generalized understanding. Whereas the historian seeks to provide detailed descriptive accounts of past events, the social scientist engaging in historical research is more concerned with discovering general patterns and relationships. The work of historians may serve as the data that such a social researcher utilizes.

Next, we looked at the various uses of existing statistics in social research. The world around us is filled with collected and published data, in the form of governmental and nongovernmental reports. The social researcher can often obtain and analyze such data for the purpose of answering important research questions.

The term "unobtrusive measures" refers to a wide variety of research methods, including content analysis and some types of field research. The term refers to all those modes of observation that have no impact on what is being observed. Although surveys and experiments, for example, represent a clear intrusion into what is being studied, a little ingenuity can often suggest ways of getting relevant data without intruding.

Secondary analysis is an increasingly important research method in the social sciences. Most typically associated with survey research, it refers to the subsequent reanalysis of data collected originally by some other researcher. The purpose of the secondary analysis, moreover, may be quite different from the purpose of the original study. The greatest advantage of secondary analysis lies in its economy, and a network of *data libraries* has grown up in recent years to support this method.

Computer simulation modeling is very different from any of the research methods discussed earlier. Although there are many different forms of simulation, the term generally refers to the construction, in the form of computer programs, of models of real world processes. To the extent that the processes built into the computer models are an accurate reflection of the real world, experimentation with and observation of those models can shed considerable light on what happens in the real world. Computer simulation will no doubt grow increasingly important in connection with evaluation research in the future.

12.8
Main Points

1. There are a great many different research methods available to the social researcher.

2. Each of the available methods has special strengths and weaknesses.

3. The "best" research project would be one that brought to bear several different methods on the same research question. To the extent that several different methods yielded the same general conclusion, the researcher's confidence in that conclusion would be increased.

12.9
Annotated Bibliography

Historical Research

Bellah, Robert, *Tokugawa Religion: The Values of Pre-Industrial Japan* (Glencoe, Ill.: Free Press, 1957). An excellent illustration of historical research in the social sciences. Bellah examines the rise of capitalist economic values in pre-*Meiji* Japan in comparison with the rise of capitalism in the West (see Weber below). Bellah provides an excellent biography of the project, discussing the methods of historical research, in Phillip Hammond (ed.), *Sociologists at Work* (New York: Basic Books, 1964).

Weber, Max, *The Protestant Ethic and the Spirit of Capitalism*, Talcott Parsons (trans.) (New York: Charles Scribner's, 1958). One of the great classics in social research. Weber examines the effects of religious values—puritan asceticism—on the development of the capitalist model of reinvestment and economic growth. Among other things, Weber's analysis was offered as a counterbalance to the Marxian notion that economic factors shaped ideas rather than the other way around. This study and Weber's studies of the religions of India, China, and ancient Israel, together provide an unparalleled example of *comparative* historical research in social science.

Analyzing Existing Statistics

Durkheim, Emile, *Suicide*, John Spalding and George Simpson (trans.) (Glencoe, Ill.: Free Press, 1951). Another classic study. Durkheim set out to understand the reasons for suicide, analyzing the suicide rates for different types of areas. For example, Durkheim examined the effects of religion by analyzing the suicide rates of Catholic and Protestant countries and regions of countries.

Stouffer, Samuel, *Social Research to Test Ideas* (New York: Free Press of Glencoe, 1962), Chapter 6: "Effects of the Depression on the Family." A minor, little-known study by a master, that illustrates what can be done with existing statistics when specially collected data are not available. Wishing to learn whether the Depression of the 1930s had substantially altered traditional marriage and family patterns, Stouffer asks how such an alteration would show up in regularly compiled government statistics and then looks to see. Also instructive is Chapter 7, which examines the effects of radio on newspaper circulation.

Unobtrusive Measures

Webb, Eugene, Campbell, Donald, Schwartz, Richard, and Sechrest, Lee, *Unobtrusive Measures: Nonreactive Research in the Social Sciences* (Chicago: Rand McNally, 1966). A stimulating and delightful statement on unobtrusive measures. As noted in the present book, there are many unobtrusive ways of studying social phenomena, and many of those have been discussed separately: e.g., content analysis, participant observation, historical research, and the analysis of existing statistics may be regarded as unobtrusive. The book by Webb *et al.*, however, examines the general notion of unobtrusiveness, and the many ingenious illustrations provide a perfect portrayal of the social researcher as a detective.

Secondary Analysis

Hyman, Herbert, *Secondary Analysis of Sample Surveys: Principles, Procedures, and Potentialities* (New York: John Wiley, 1972). A comprehensive overview of secondary analysis. Hyman examines the role of this method within the broader context of social scientific inquiry, discusses methods of secondary analysis, and provides many illustrations.

Lipset, Seymour, and Raab, Earl, *The Politics of Unreason: Right-wing Extremism in America: 1790–1970* (New York: Harper & Row, 1970). An excellent illustration of the potential of secondary analysis. The authors undertake a historical examination of the relationship between right-wing political movements and prejudice in America. Much of the analysis of recent movements is based on the secondary analysis of Gallup Poll and other public opinion poll data.

Nasatir, David, "Social Science Data Libraries," *The American Sociologist*, 2:207–212 (November, 1967). An excellent overview of data libraries available for the support of secondary analysis. Nasatir discusses the potential for secondary analysis, citing examples, and provides a directory of data libraries. Although some of the organizational and institutional information is now outdated, this still remains a very useful reference.

Part Four:
Quantitative Data Analysis

In this final part of the book, we shall be discussing several aspects of what is the most exciting portion of the research process: the analysis of data and the development of generalized understanding about social phenomena. In the chapters comprising Part Four, we shall examine the steps that separate observation from the final reporting of findings.

Chapter 13 is addressed to the quantification of the data collected through the modes of observation discussed in Part Three. Today, much social science data is analyzed by machine: computers and other data-processing devices. Chapter 13 provides a brief overview of some of the equipment involved and describes the processes required to convert observations into forms suitable for machine processing.

The first of several discussions on the logic of data analysis is presented in Chapter 14. We shall begin with an examination of methods of analyzing and presenting the data related to a single variable. Then we will turn to the relationship between two variables and learn how to construct and read simple percentage tables. The chapter ends with a preview of multivariate analysis.

Chapter 15 is addressed to measurement, a matter that has been discussed several times earlier in the book. This chapter specifically examines techniques of constructing indexes and scales—composite measures of variables.

In their attempt to develop generalized understanding, scientists seek to discover patterns of interrelationships among variables. Very often, these interrelationships take a cause-and-effect form. Chapter 16 is addressed to the logic of causation as appropriate to social scientific research. This theoretical chapter lays the basis for the following ones on analytical techniques.

Chapter 17 describes the elaboration model of data analysis developed by Paul Lazarsfeld at Columbia University. The concluding theme in Chapter 14 will be picked up again and developed further. This chapter will present the logic of causal analysis through the use of percentage tables. The same logic will then be applied in the use of other statistical techniques in subsequent chapters.

Chapter 18 provides an introduction to some of the more commonly used statistical methods in social science research. Rather than merely showing how to compute statistics by these methods (computers can do that), I have attempted to place them in the context of the earlier theoretical and logical discussions. Thus, you should come away from this chapter knowing when to use various statistical measures as well as how to compute them.

The book ends with an overview of some of the more advanced methods of multivariate analysis. Again, the emphasis is on understanding the logic of their use rather than how to compute them.

13
Quantifying Data

13.1
Introduction

The chapters of Part Three have dealt with a variety of methods of collecting social science data through direct or indirect observation. Chapter 13 will deal with the steps involved in converting such data into a form appropriate to *quantitative* analyses. Realize that this is a different approach than the *qualitative* analyses discussed in Chapter 8 (field research).

Put somewhat differently, the purpose of this chapter is to describe methods of converting social science data into a *machine-readable* form—a form that can be read and manipulated by computers and similar machines used in data analysis. Although discussions in Chapters 4 and 9 have touched on this subject, we shall carry it through to its termination here. Once the steps described in this chapter have been completed in a real research project, the researcher will have converted his data into the form of data cards (sometimes known by the trade name, IBM cards), magnetic tape, or something similar.

To insure that you understand what machine-readable data look like, the first section of this chapter will present a brief overview of common data-processing and analysis hardware. Then we shall discuss coding and, finally, the several options available for keypunching.

13.2
A Quick Look at Hardware

People often object to social research for attempting to reduce living, breathing human beings to holes punched in cards. Part One of this book dealt with this as a philosophical issue; this section and the rest of this chapter will deal with the mechanics of accomplishing it.

An IBM card (Figure 13-1) is divided into 80 vertical columns which are usually numbered, running from left to right. All of the mechanized data-processing equipment is designed to locate (and read) any specified columns. Data are stored on cards by punching holes within the columns. Each vertical column is further divided into 12 spaces. Ten of those spaces are numbered: 0, 1, 2, 3, 4, 5, 6, 7, 8, 9, from top to bottom. Above the 0 space, two unnumbered spaces are provided: moving up from 0, they are designated minus (−) and plus (+) or sometimes called 11 and 12, or X and Y, respectively.

A keypunch machine punches holes in the spaces in columns of IBM cards. Using a keyboard similar to that of a typewriter, the keypunch operator can punch specified holes (0, 1, 2, . . .) into specified columns of a given card. Alphabetical letters and special characters may also be punched, in the form of multiple punches in a column; but for our purposes, we shall consider only single-punch, numerical data.

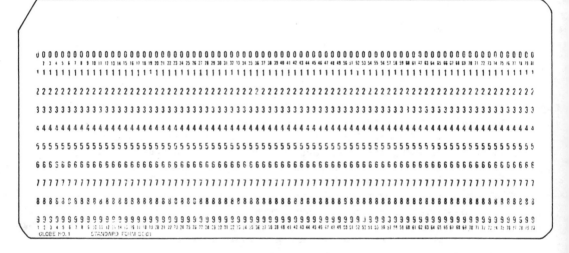

Figure 13-1

The keypunch machine also has the capacity to read the punches in a given column of one card and transfer those punches to the same column of the card following it in the deck (duplicate option). Finally, the keypunch machine may be programmed to carry out certain operations automatically; these will be mentioned in a later section of this chapter.

Data are put in machine-readable form by assigning one or more specific columns of a data card (a "field") to a variable, and assigning punches within that column to the various attributes comprising that variable. For example, an experimental subject's sex might be recorded in column 5 of the card. If the subject were a male, a 1 might be punched in that column; if a female, a 2. The subject's age might be assigned to columns 6 and 7 (a two-column code); if the subject were 35 years of age, 3 and 5, respectively, would be punched in those columns. Or ages could be recorded in categories and stored in a single column: for example, 1-punch for under 20, 2-punch for 20 to 29, and so forth.

A given card, then, represents the data provided by or about a given subject—the unit of analysis. If the units of analysis were newspaper editorials being examined in a content analysis, each data card would represent an editorial. The columns of each card would be assigned to specific variables describing that editorial. For example, two columns might be assigned to storing the last two digits of the year in which the editorial appeared.

In survey research, a data card may stand for a questionnaire, with columns assigned to the various items contained in the questionnaire. Column 34 might store answers to the question "Have you ever smoked marijuana?" A 1-punch could represent "yes," and a 2-punch represent "no." The key ideas for you to grasp are that each card represents a single research unit of analysis, and that each *field* of one or more card columns is used for storing the same variable on each card. For example, each survey respondent may have his answer to the marijuana question stored in column 34.

Several pieces of equipment are capable of reading data cards. The basic machine among these is the counter-sorter. This machine may be set to read a given column. Then when the cards are fed into it, they are sorted into pockets corresponding to the punches found in the column, and a counter indicates the number having each of the punches. If sex is recorded in column 5, the sorter would be set on that column, and men and women would be sorted into the 1 and 2 pockets, respectively.

The counter-sorter can be used for tabulating the distributions of responses given to questions in a survey simply by counting the punches to be found in the columns assigned to the questions. The counter-sorter can also be used to examine the relationships between variables.

Suppose the researcher wished to determine whether men or women attend church more often. Having separated the respondents by sex as described above, the counter-sorter should then be set to read the column containing responses to the question: "On the average, how often do you attend church services?" All the men would then be rerun through the counter-sorter to determine the frequency of church attendance as indicated by the punches contained in that column. The same procedure would be repeated for the women, and the distributions of responses would then be compared.

The counter-sorter has three basic limitations for the analysis of data. First, it is limited to counting and sorting cards. While the researcher may use these capabilities for extremely sophisticated analyses, the machine itself cannot perform sophisticated manipulations of data. Second, the counter-sorter is rather slow in comparison with other available machines. Third, it is limited to the examination of one card per unit of analysis in the analysis of relationships among variables. In effect, the researcher is thereby limited to 80 columns of data per unit of analysis. (*Note:* Other machines provide for the construction of "work-decks" containing all the data required for a particular phase of the analysis. Data contained on several different cards can be transferred to a single deck, thereby permitting the use of the counter-sorter.)

Most sophisticated analysis today is conducted by the use of computers. The computer—through manipulation programs—can solve all the limitations of the counter-sorter. First, it can go beyond simple counting and sorting to perform intricate computations and provide sophisticated presentations of the results. The computer can be programmed to examine several variables simultaneously and to compute a variety of statistics. Second, if the data are stored on magnetic tape or magnetic disc rather than on cards, those data can be passed through the machine much faster than is possible by the use of cards and the counter-sorter. Moreover, the capability for simultaneous extensive manipulations and computations further speeds the overall analysis. Finally, the computer can analyze data contained on several cards per unit of analysis.

This chapter will discuss the steps (and options) involved in converting data into forms amenable to the use of counter-sorters and computers. Following a brief presentation of selected data-processing terminology, we shall discuss the coding process and then turn to an enumeration of the several methods of keypunching the data.

13.3

Selected Data-Processing Terminology

The present section defines some of the terms commonly used in data processing. The later sections of this chapter will utilize those terms that are most likely to be familiar to inexperienced researchers. Nonetheless, you should become familiar with the other terms frequently used.

File

A file is the collection of data pertaining to a given case. Thus, all the information obtained from or about a survey respondent, for example, would constitute his data file. All the data describing the experiences and behavior of an experimental subject over the course of an experiment would constitute that subject's file.

Case

The term "case" refers to a concrete instance of the unit of analysis in a study. For example, in a survey, each respondent would be a case. In a content analysis of popular songs, each song would be a case. Each subject in an experiment would be a case. The *number of cases* (typically designated by the letter *n*) is the number of respondents in a survey, subjects in an experiment, and so forth.

Record

A file is comprised of one or more records. Typically, a record is a data card, and the data file for a particular subject might be recorded on one or more cards. When data are stored on magnetic tapes or discs, the term "card" becomes somewhat artificial, and records may have different configurations (see *record length* below). Even when tapes and discs are used, however, the card format is often maintained.

Whenever a file contains more than one record, a description of the location of a specific data item (for example, a questionnaire item) must include an indication of the appropriate record. Let's imagine a study in which each case is assigned three cards for the storage of its data file. These cards would be identified as card 1, card 2, and card 3. Each such card would contain a specified set of information. Thus, for example, the length of time required for an experimental subject to complete a given task on a particular trial might be stored in column 30 of card 2. This piece of information would be stored in column 30 of card 2 for each experimental subject. Column 30 of card 1 would contain some other piece of information.

Deck

A deck is the set of records containing the same items of information—for all subjects. *Deck 1*, then, would consist of all the card 1's punched for all subjects. In the coding and keypunching of data consisting of more than one record per case, a deck identification is required to distinguish the different records comprising each case's file. (This will be illustrated in the discussion of codebooks later in this chapter.)

Byte

"Byte" is a technical computer term that generally corresponds to the notion of a data card column in the present context. It specifies a location within a record. Whenver data are stored on magnetic tapes or discs, and the card form is abandoned, the term "column" becomes somewhat anachronistic, and "byte" is more appropriate.

Code

"Code" is also a technical term; it generally corresponds to the notion of "punch" in the language surrounding data cards. Since magnetic tapes and discs do not have holes punched in them, the term "punch" seems as inappropriate as "card" and "column." (*Note:* The coding process discussed in connection with content analysis and to be discussed again in this chapter refers to the assignment of numerical codes to represent the several attributes comprising variables.)

Record Length

Whenever the data record is a card, the record length is 80 columns or 80 bytes, regardless of whether all 80 are actually used. Using tapes and discs, however, the researcher need not be constrained by the conventional 80-column format. With his data initially punched on, say, three cards per case, the researcher might create, on tape or disc, files each comprised of one record, 240 bytes in length. It would be as though he had manufactured a long card with 240 columns. A given data item, then, might be located at byte 200 rather than at column 40 of card 3.

13.4
Coding

To permit quantitative analyses, data must be converted to the form of numerical codes representing attributes of variables which, in turn, are assigned for storage in specified locations in data files. The conversion of data into this form is called **coding**. This process has been discussed somewhat in two earlier sections of this book.

The discussion of questionnaire construction in Chapter 5 dealt with the precoding of questionnaires. Questionnaire items were assigned to specific cards and columns, and each closed-ended response category was assigned a numerical punch. For the most part, no special coding process is required for converting closed-ended questionnaire items into machine-readable format.

The discussion of content analysis in Chapter 9 dealt with the coding process in a manner much closer to our present concern. Recall that the content analyst must develop methods of assigning individual paragraphs, editorials, books, songs, and so forth with specific classifications or attributes. In content analysis, the coding process is inherent in data collection or observation.

When other research methods are employed, it is often necessary to engage in a coding process after the data have been collected. For example, open-ended questionnaire items result in nonnumerical responses, which must be coded prior to analysis. Or a field researcher might wish to undertake a quantitative analysis based on his qualitative field notes. He might wish, for example, to quantify the open-ended interviews he conducted with participants in some social event under study.

As with content analysis, the task here is one of reducing a wide variety of idiosyncratic items of information to a more limited set of attributes comprising a variable. Suppose, for example, that a survey researcher has asked respondents "What is your occupation?" The responses to such a question would vary considerably. While it would be possible to assign each separate occupation reported a separate numerical code, this procedure would not facilitate analysis, which typically depends on several subjects having the same attribute.

In the matter of occupation, there are a number of preestablished coding schemes (none of them very good, however). One such scheme would distinguish "professional and managerial occupations," "clerical occupations," "semiskilled occupations," and so forth. Another scheme distinguishes among different sectors of the economy: manufacturing, health, education, commerce, and so forth. Still others combine both.

The occupational coding scheme used should be appropriate to the analyses intended in the study. From one perspective, it might be sufficient to code all occupations as either "white-collar" or "blue-collar." From another perspective, "self-employed" and "not self-employed" might be sufficient. Or a peace researcher might wish to know only whether the occupation was dependent on the defense establishment or not.

While the coding scheme ought to be tailored to meet the particular requirements of the analysis, one general rule of thumb should be kept in mind. If the data are coded so as to maintain a great deal of detail, code categories can always be combined during an analysis that does not require such detail. If the data are coded into relatively few, gross categories, however, there is no way during analysis for recreating the original detail. Thus, the researcher would be well advised to code his data in somewhat more detail than he plans to use in the analysis.

There are two basic approaches to the coding process. First, you may begin with a relatively well-developed coding scheme, derived from your research purpose. Thus, as suggested above, the peace researcher might want to code occupations in terms of their relationship to the defense establishment. Or let's suppose, for example, that you have been engaging in participant observation of an emerging new religion. You have been keeping very careful notes of the reasons new members have given for joining. Perhaps you have developed the impression that new members seem increasingly to regard the religion as a substitute for a family. You might, then, wish to review your notes more carefully—coding each new member's comments in terms of whether this aspect of the religion was mentioned. You might also wish to code their comments in terms of their own family status: whether they have a family or not.

If you are fortunate enough to have assistance in the coding process, your task would be to refine your definitions of code categories and train your coders so that they will be able to assign given responses to the proper categories. You should explain the meaning of the code categories you have developed and give several examples of each. To insure that your coders fully understand what you have in mind, it would be useful for you to code several cases. Then your coders should be asked to code the same cases, without knowing how you coded them, and your coders' work should be compared with your own. Any discrepancies will indicate an imperfect communication of your coding scheme to your coders. Even if there is perfect agreement between you and your coders in this regard, you should still continue to *check-code* at least a portion of the cases throughout the coding process.

If you are not fortunate enough to have assistance in coding, it is still important to obtain some verification of your own reliability as a coder. Nobody is perfect, especially a researcher hot on the trail of a finding. In the case of the participant observer quantifying his notes regarding reasons for joining a new religion, let's suppose further that he has the impression that persons who do not have a regular family will be more likely to regard the new religion as a family substitute. There is a danger, then, that whenever he discovers a subject who reports no family, the researcher will unconsciously try to find some evidence in the subject's comments that the religion is a family-substitute. If at all possible, then, you should try to get someone else to code a portion of. your cases—explaining the meaning of your coding scheme—to see if someone else would make the same assignments that you have made. (Note how this relates to the characteristic of *intersubjectivity* in science.)

The second approach to coding is appropriate whenever you are not sure initially how your data should be coded—you do not know what variables they represent among your subjects of study. Suppose, for example, that you have asked, in a questionnaire, "What do you think about the John Birch Society?" Although you might anticipate coding responses as being positive, negative, or neutral, it is unlikely that you would be able to anticipate the full range of variation in responses. In such a situation, it would be useful to prepare a list of perhaps fifty or one hundred actual responses to this open-ended question. You could then review that list, noting the different dimensions that those responses reflect. Perhaps you would find that several of the positive responses contained references to the fight against domestic communism; perhaps a number of the negative responses referred to racial prejudice.

Once you have developed a coding scheme based on the list of fifty or one hundred responses, you should insure that each of the listed responses would fit into one of the code categories so developed. Then you would be ready to begin coding the remainder of the responses. If you have coding assistance, the previous comments regarding the training and checking of coders would apply here; if you do not, the comments on having your own work checked apply.

Like the set of attributes comprising a variable, and like the response categories in a closed-ended questionnaire item, code categories should be both exhaustive and mutually exclusive. Every piece of information being coded should fit into *one and only one* code category. Problems arise whenever a given response appears to fit equally into more than one code category, or when it fits into none.

Since code category assignments for individual cases will ultimately be converted into punches in specific columns of cards, it is essential that you understand that you should *never* punch more than one punch in a given column for a given case—that is, do not plan on *multiple punching.* Most computer programs that you might use simply do not accept multiple punches, and complications arise even in the use of those machines, such as the counter-sorter, that do read multiple punches. Assign a single code category to each observation being coded; punch a single punch in each column being punched.

This means that if a subject has two jobs—one within the defense establishment and one outside it—or if a questionnaire respondent checks both "strongly agree" and "agree," you cannot assign both codes to that case. There are a number of methods of resolving such situations. For example, you may be able to establish a logical order of priorities among code categories. In the example of defense-related occupations, you might wish to code a case as having a defense-related occupation even if there is also a nondefense-related occupation. In the example of Likert items, you might want to code multiple answers to the extremes, coding "strongly agree" in the above example.

Another solution to this problem is the assignment of a special code for multiple classifications. In the example of the defense-related occupation, you might want to assign a code of 1 for those with such an occupation *only*, a code of 2 for those without a defense-related occupation, and a code of 3 for those with both kinds.

Sometimes you may want to allow for more than one code category for each case. Let's suppose you are conducting a laboratory experiment in which subjects are given a difficult task to perform, and you wish to analyze their emotional responses to that difficulty. Perhaps you are interested in such reactions as anger, sorrow, humor, violence, resignation, diligence, and so forth. During the course of the experiment, you have noted that many subjects exhibit more than one of these reactions, and you have recorded all that appear. You should not attempt to punch several punches, representing different reactions, in a single column assigned to this variable. There are two ways in which you might handle this situation.

First, you might assign a single column to each of the possible reactions to the situation, and code each subject in terms of whether or not each reaction was exhibited. You might assign column 28 to anger, and use a code of 1 to indicate that the subject exhibited anger and a code of 2 to indicate that he did not. Column 29 might be assigned to sorrow, and so forth. This procedure will require the assignment of several columns to subjects' reactions to the experimental situation, but data card columns are about the cheapest resource in research.

As an alternative, you might assign only as many columns to this piece of information as there are different code categories applicable to a given case. Suppose that three reactions was the largest number exhibited by a single subject. Three columns might then be assigned to recording reactions. Each of the possible reactions would be assigned a numerical code: anger could be 1, sorrow could be 2, humor could be 3, and so forth. If a given subject exhibited anger and sorrow, a 1-punch could be put in the first column assigned, a 2-punch could be put in the second column, and the third column could be left blank. If a subject exhibited only humor, then a 3-punch should be put in the first of the columns and the other two should be left blank. This method for handling multiple classifications is most effective if you have access to a computer program that has the capacity to read several columns simultaneously—treating them as a multiple-punched, single column. If you do not have access to such a program, you would do better to use the first alternative described.

Finally, a comment on the use of "blanks" is in order. If you are planning to analyze your data using a counter-sorter, blanks in columns being analyzed present no immediate problem. If you plan to utilize computer programs, however, you should be warned against the use of blanks. Leaving a column blank (unless it is assigned as a blank column for all cases) is inadvisable for two reasons. First, this procedure creates a quality control problem in data processing. Discovering that a given case is blank in a particular column, you will not be sure whether the blank occurred intentionally or is the result of an error—that the keypuncher failed to punch the appropriate punch in that column. Even "no answer" should be assigned a numerical punch, then.

The second difficulty created by the use of blanks is more technical. Some computers or computer programs assign a special value to blanks as part of their internal operations. Depending on the type of analysis being conducted, a blank may confuse or abort the desired computations.

In the previous example relating to the solution of multiple classifications through the assignment of, say, three columns for coding emotional reactions to an experimental situation, it would be more appropriate to enter a standard punch such as 0 in each column in which no reaction is coded.

13.5
Codebook Construction

The end product of the coding process is the conversion of data items into numerical codes representing attributes comprising variables, which, in turn, are assigned card and column locations within a data file. A codebook is a document that describes the locations of variables and the code assignments to the attributes comprising those variables. A codebook serves two essential functions. First, it is the primary guide used in the coding process. Second, it is your guide for locating variables and interpreting punches in your data file during analysis. If you decide to correlate two variables as a part of your analysis of your data, the codebook tells you where to find the variables and what the punches represent.

Figure 13-2 illustrates portions of the codebook appropriate to the survey questionnaire illustrated in Chapter 5, a questionnaire requiring more than one card per case for data storage. (It would be useful for you to refer back to the questionnaire—paying special attention to the precoding notations.)

Note that columns 1 through 4 of *each deck* have been assigned to the respondent's identification number (case ID). Since there is more than one card per case, this number would be punched into each card so as to permit us to relate all the cards making up a single respondent's data file. Column 5 in the example has been assigned for recording the card or deck identification. Column 5 is used for this purpose in each card, but the number punched is different: appropriately, a 1 is punched in all the card 1's, a 2 in all the card 2's, and so forth.

Only portions of only three of the six decks have been illustrated here. The actual codebook was, of course, much longer.

If we wished to know how much involvement students reported in "social action or political groups," the codebook in Figure 13-2 would show us that this information is contained in column 8 of card 5, and that all respondents who have a 1-punch in that column reported "much" participa-

DECK 1 CODEBOOK

COLUMN   *DESCRIPTION*

1-4   Respondent identification number
5   Deck identification number: 1
6   A-1a. "It would be a good thing if the United Nations
                were someday converted into a world government."
                1. Strongly agree
                2. Agree
                3. Disagree
                4. Strongly disagree
                5. Don't know
                0. no answer
7   A-1b. "People who defile the American flag should be
                put in prison."
                1. Strongly agree
                2. Agree
                3. Disagree
                4. Strongly disagree
                5. Don't know
                0. no answer

. . . .

DECK 3 CODEBOOK

COLUMN   *DESCRIPTION*

1-4   Respondent identification number
5   Deck identification number: 3
6   B-9.   "How important is it to you to have the instruc-
                tor comment on your remarks in class?"
                1. Very important
                2. Fairly important
                3. Not very important
                4. Not at all important
                0. no answer
7   B-10. "In terms of your own personal satisfaction,
                how much importance do you attach to getting
                good grades?"
                1. A great deal of importance
                2. A fair amount of importance
                3. Only a little importance
                4. No importance at all
                0. no answer

. . . .

Figure 13-2

DECK 5 CODEBOOK

```
COLUMN       DESCRIPTION

  1-4        Respondent identification number
   5         Deck identification number: 5
             E-1.   "In general, how would you characterize your
                     participation in the following activities
                     during the time you have been in college?"
   6         E-la.  "Varsity athletics"
                     1.  Much
                     2.  Some
                     3.  Little
                     4.  None
                     0.  no answer
   7         E-lb.  "Intramural athletics"
                     1.  Much
                     2.  Some
                     3.  Little
                     4.  None
                     0.  no answer
   8         E-lc.  "Social action or political groups"
                     1.  Much
                     2.  Some
                     3.  Little
                     4.  None
                     0.  no answer
```

. . . .

Figure 13-2 (Continued)

tion, those with a 2-punch reported "some" participation, and so forth. Either a counter-sorter or a computer could be used to discover how many students were given each of the punches in question.

If we were interested in the possible relationship between participation in social action and political groups, on the one hand, and attitudes toward the importance of good grades, on the other, the codebook would tell us we must correlate the punches in column 8 of card 5 and column 7 of card 3. How to examine the relationship between two variables such as these will be discussed in Chapter 14.

13.6
Coding and Keypunching Options

There are a number of ways in which the coding process may be integrated with the keypunching process so as to provide the desired end product: a set of cards containing the numerically coded data. I shall discuss five different options in this section.

Transfer Sheets

The traditional method of data processing involves the coding of data and the transfer of code assignments to a "transfer sheet" or "code sheet." Such sheets are ruled off in 80 columns corresponding to the data card columns and in rows representing individual cards. Coders write numbers corresponding to the desired punches in the appropriate columns of the sheets.

The code sheets are then given to the keypunchers who punch cards corresponding to the sheets. Once they are punched, the cards are then *verified*. A *verifier* looks very much like a keypunch machine, but instead of punching holes in cards, it reads the punches that have already been punched. The verifier operator loads the deck of punched cards (instead of blank cards) and then simulates the repunching of the code sheets. Whenever the "punch" attempted for a given column by the verifier operator is the same as the punch already in that column of the card, the card advances to the next column. If the "punch" attempted by the verifier operator differs from that found in the column, a red light goes on and the machine stops. The verifier operator has two more chances to "punch" the correct number. If an incorrect punch was entered initially, the card is notched over the erroneous column for later correction. After verification and correction, the researcher is provided with a deck of cards that accurately represent the data contained in the questionnaires or other data source-documents. (Incidentally, this method works even when the researcher is the "coder," "keypuncher," and "verifier operator.")

Edge-Coding

Edge-coding is a data-processing method that does away with the need for code sheets. The outside margin of each page of a questionnaire or other data source-document is left blank or is marked with spaces corresponding to data card columns. Rather than transferring code assignments to a separate sheet, the codes are written in the appropriate spaces in the margins.

The edge-coded source-documents are then used for keypunching and verification instead of code sheets.

Punching Directly

Discussions of precoding earlier in this book were presented in anticipation of this method of data processing. It is especially useful with lengthy questionnaires which would present a formidable coding task. If the questionnaires have been adequately designed and precoded, keypunchers may *punch directly* from them without the need for separate code sheets or even edge-coding. The precoded questionnaire would contain indications of the columns and the punches to be assigned to questions and responses, and the keypunchers and verifier operators could directly transfer responses to data cards.

When a *punch-direct* method is to be used, it is essential that questionnaires be *edited* prior to punching. An editor should read through each questionnaire to insure that every question has been answered (enter a 0 or some other standard code when no answer is given), to insure there are no multiple answers (change to a single code according to a uniform procedure), and to clarify any unclear responses.

If most of the questionnaire is amenable to direct punching (that is, closed-ended questions presented in a clear format), it is also possible to code a few open-ended questions on the questionnaire and still punch directly. In such a situation, the editor should enter the code for a given question in a specified location near the question to ease the keypuncher's job.

The layout of the questionnaire is extremely important for effective direct punching. The several question and reponse categories must be arranged in a logical "flow." If most response categories are presented on the right-hand side of the page but one set is presented on the left-hand side, keypunchers frequently miss the deviant set. (*Note:* Many respondents will make the same mistake, so a questionnaire carefully designed for keypunching will be more effective for data collection as well.)

Direct punching can be made more effective by careful questionnaire design. Since the keypunch machine can be programmed to perform certain operations automatically, the keypuncher can speed up his work by using that feature. If a blank column is assigned to the bottom of each questionnaire page or at the end of a section of the questionnaire page, the keypunch machine can be programmed to skip those columns automatically. This practice reduces the need for the keypuncher to continually compare the card column being punched with the column that is supposed to be punched. The keypuncher simply punches a whole page (or designated section) without checking columns. If the keypunch machine automatically skips a column at the appropriate point in the questionnaire, the keypuncher knows he is on the right column.

To use this feature of the keypunch machine, it is necessary for multicard files to be punched one card at a time. If each respondent is to have two cards, for example, the keypuncher must punch card 1 for all respondents, since the location of blank columns will differ on the two cards, and then punch card 2 for all respondents. This in itself has an advantage, however. If the keypuncher is able to punch the same set of questions over and over on several questionnaires, his growing familiarity with the questionnaire format will speed up the punching and will increase accuracy.

Ideally, the questionnaire should be designed to permit its separation into "packets" corresponding to the different cards. (An identification number must be used to insure that the several portions of a given questionnaire can be related to one another later.) This facilitates the keypunching described above and also makes it possible for several keypunchers to be working on the questionnaire at the same time.

Once the cards are keypunched, the punched decks and questionnaires (or packets) are given to a verifier operator as discussed in the earlier sections.

In those situations such as content analysis in which coding takes place during data collection, it makes sense to record the data in a form amenable to direct punching. Perhaps a precoded form would be appropriate, or, in some cases, the data might be recorded directly on transfer sheets.

Coding to Optical Scan Sheets

Manual keypunching can be avoided through the use of an *optical scanner*. This machine reads black pencil marks on a special code sheet and punches cards to correspond with those marks. (These sheets are frequently called *mark-sense* sheets.)

It is possible for coders to transfer data to such special sheets in the form of black marks rather than in the form of numbers on a code sheet. The sheets are then fed into an optical scanner and data cards are automatically punched. In some instances, it may be necessary to "translate" the initial punches through the use of a special computer program. In any event, the researcher is ultimately provided with a deck of data cards without the necessity of manual punching. Moreover, it is unnecessary to verify the punching separately.

This use of the optical scanner provides greater accuracy and speed of keypunching. There are several disadvantages, however, which should be mentioned. Some coders find it very difficult to transfer data to the special sheets. Using a conventional code sheet, the coder simply writes the appropriate code number in the next blank space on the sheet. The configuration of op-sense sheets, however, hampers this. Often, it is more difficult to locate the appropriate column, and once the appropriate column is found, the coder must search for the appropriate space to blacken. (The severity of this problem can be appreciated only by attempting to code in both manners.) Past experience suggests that these difficulties result in a greater expenditure of time and greater inaccuracy, which offset the gains.

Second, the optical scanner has relatively rigid tolerances. Unless the black marks are sufficiently black, the scanner may fail to read and punch. (The researcher will have no way of knowing when this has happened until he begins his analysis.) Moreover, if the op-sense sheets are folded or multilated, the scanner may refuse to read them at all.

Direct Use of Optical Scan Sheets

In handling questionnaire data, it is sometimes possible to use optical scan sheets a little differently and possibly avoid the difficulties they may offer coders. Persons asked to complete questionnaires may be asked to record their responses directly on such sheets. Either standard sheets can be provided with instructions on their use, or special sheets can be prepared for the particular study. Questions can be presented with the several answer categories, and the respondents could be asked to black in the spaces provided beside the answers they choose. If such sheets are properly laid out, the optical scanner can then read and punch the answers directly.

This procedure avoids the necessities of both coding and keypunching (although the sheets should be edited). It can be rather effective when used with respondents who have had previous experience with such sheets (for example, students). There are limitations inherent in this method, however.

The researcher is limited to asking closed-ended questions. Only those that can be answered through the selection of a previously coded response can be handled. If the respondent is unwilling to select any of the answers provided, he is unable to communicate his answer to the researcher. Furthermore, the dangers of insufficiently blackened spaces and mutilated sheets are present here as in the previous example. (This would hamper the administration of mail surveys, although it might be possible with proper planning and testing.)

13.7
Data Cleaning

Whichever data processing method has been used, you will now have a set of cards that purport to represent the data collected in your study. The next important step is the "cleaning" of those data (eliminating errors).

No matter how, or how carefully, the data have been transferred to cards, some errors are inevitable. Depending on the data-processing method, these errors may result from incorrect coding, incorrect reading of written codes, incorrect sensing of blackened marks, and so forth. Even keypunch verification is not perfect.

Two types of cleaning should be done: *possible-punch* cleaning and *contingency* cleaning. First, for any given variable, there is a specified set of legitimate attributes, translated into a set of possible punches. In the variable "sex," there will be perhaps three possible punches: 1 for male, 2 for female, and 0 for no answer. If a case is found to contain, say, a 7-punch in the column assigned to sex, it is clear that an error has been made.

Possible-Punch Cleaning

Possible-punch cleaning can be accomplished in two different ways. First, the researcher may have access to computer programs designed for this purpose. He may be able to specify the possible punches associated with each card column, and the computer will then read all the data cards and indicate those cards that have one or more errors. Alternatively, the researcher can examine the distribution of punches in each column (using either the computer or the sorter) and determine whether there are any inappropriate punches. If the column assigned to sex has a 7-punch reported, the researcher might use the sorter to locate the card having this punch. Then he could locate the source-document corresponding to that card (using the ID number), determine what the punch should have been, and make the necessary correction.

Contigency Cleaning

Contingency cleaning is more complicated. The logical structure of the data may place special limits on the responses of certain respondents. For example, a questionnaire may ask for the military draft status of *male respondents only*. All male respondents, then, should have a response punched (or a special code for failure to answer), while no female respondent should have a punch (or should have a special punch indicating the question is inappropriate). If a given female respondent is punched as having a 1-A draft status, an error has been made and should be corrected.

Contingency cleaning may be accomplished through computer programs, if available, or through the use of the counter-sorter. In either event, however, the process is more complicated than is true of possible-punch cleaning. Computer programs will require a rather complicated set of "if-then" statements. Manual cleaning will require two or more passes through the counter-sorter to clean each set of items.

Although data cleaning is an essential step in data processing, it should be acknowledged that it may be safely avoided in certain cases. Perhaps the researcher will feel he can safely exclude the very few erroneous punches that appear in a given column—if the exclusion of those cases will not significantly affect his results. Or, some inappropriate contingency responses may be safely ignored. If some women respondents have been given a draft status, he can limit his analysis of this variable to male respondents. These comments notwithstanding, however, the researcher should not use them as rationalizations for sloppy research. "Dirty" data will almost always produce misleading research findings.

13.8
Summary

Chapter 13 has dealt with the quantification of data: what is often called data processing. The procedures described in this chapter might be applied to data collected in most of the different ways discussed in Part Three. Regardless of how observations initially have been made, the purpose of this phase of research is the same: to transform the records of those observations into standardized, numerical forms suitable for machine processing.

The chapter began with a brief overview of some of the mechanical equipment—hardware—involved in data processing and quantitative data analysis. We discussed keypunch machines, verifiers, sorters, and computers. In that connection, we looked at the manner in which numerical data are stored on data cards: essentially, variables are assigned locations in the form of card columns, and the attributes of those variables are represented by different numerical punches within the appropriate columns.

Following a brief data-processing glossary, the coding process was discussed. We noted that this process is essentially the same as the process of the same name in content analysis. Our discussion focused on the procedures involved in the coding of other types of data, such as experimental or survey data. In this connection, codebooks were discussed and illustrated.

Then, the chapter discussed and described the several different options available to the social researcher in data processing. Some of these options involve manual coding and keypunching, while other options are more mechanized. The relative advantages and disadvantages of each were discussed.

The chapter concluded with a discussion of data cleaning. The purpose of this final stage of data processing is to eliminate any errors that may have been made in coding or keypunching.

13.9
Main Points

1. The quantification of data is necessary in order to permit subsequent statistical manipulations and analyses.

2. The observations describing each unit of analysis must be transformed into standardized, numerical codes for retrieval and manipulation by machine.

3. A given variable is assigned a specific location in the data storage medium: in terms of IBM card columns, for example. That variable is assigned the same location in all the data files containing the data describing the different cases about which observations were made.

4. The attributes of a given variable are represented by different punches in the columns assigned to that variable. (If cards are not being used, other terms apply, but the general ideal is the same.)

5. A codebook is the document that describes the locations assigned to different variables and the punches assigned to represent different attributes.

6. A transfer sheet is a special coding sheet upon which numerical codes are recorded. Keypunchers use these transfer sheets to know how to punch the data cards.

7. Edge-coding is an alternative to the use of transfer sheets. The numerical coding is done in the margins of the original documents—such as questionnaires—instead of on transfer sheets.

8. "Precoding" refers to the assignment of variable locations and appropriate punches for attributes printed on a questionnaire or similar document. Keypunchers are able to punch directly from such original documents if they are properly precoded and edited.

9. Optical scan sheets or mark-sense sheets may be used in some research projects to save time and money in data processing. These are the familiar sheets used in examinations, on which answers are indicated by black marks in the appropriate spaces. Optical scanners are machines that read the black marks and transfer the same information to data cards by punching them.

10. "Possible-punch cleaning" refers to the process of checking punches to see that only those punches assigned to particular attributes— possible punches—appear in given card columns. This process guards against one class of data-processing error.

11. "Contingency cleaning" is the process of checking that only those cases that *should* have data on a particular variable do in fact have such data. This process guards against another class of data-processing error.

14
Elementary Analyses

14.1
Introduction

Most social science analysis falls within the general rubric of **multivariate analysis,** and the bulk of Part Four of this book is devoted to the varieties of multivariate analysis. The term simply refers to the examination of several variables simultaneously. The analysis of the simultaneous associations among age, education, and prejudice would be an example of multivariate analysis.

You should realize that multivariate analysis is not a specific form of analysis; specific techniques for conducting a multivariate analysis are factor analysis, smallest-space analysis, multiple correlation, multiple regression, and path analysis, among others. The basic logic of multivariate analysis can best be seen through the use of simple tables, called contingency tables or cross-tabulations. Thus the present chapter is devoted to the construction and understanding of such tables.

Furthermore, multivariate analysis cannot be fully understood without a firm understanding of even more fundamental analytic modes: univariate and bivariate analyses. The chapter, therefore, will begin with these.

14.2
Univariate Analysis

Univariate analysis is the examination of only one variable at a time. We shall begin with the logic and formats for the analysis of univariate data.

The most basic format for presenting univariate data would be the reporting of all individual cases: reporting the attributes describing each case under study in terms of the variable in question. Suppose in a study of corporate executives, you are interested in their ages. (Your data might have been taken from *Who's Who in America.*)

The most direct manner of reporting the ages of corporate executives would be to list them: 63, 57, 49, 62, 80, 72, 55, and so forth. Such a report would provide your reader with the fullest details of the data, but it would be too cumbersome for most purposes.

In the present example, you could report your data in a somewhat more manageable form without losing any of the detail by reporting that 5 executives were 38 years old, 7 were 39, 18 were 40, and so forth. Such a format would avoid duplicate entries, but it would permit the reader to reconstruct completely the original data on this variable.

For an even more manageable format—with a certain loss of detail—you could report executives' ages as a **frequency distribution** of *grouped data:* 256 executives under 45 years of age, 517 between 45 and 50 years of age, and so forth. In this case, your reader would have fewer data to examine and interpret, but he would not be able to reproduce fully the original ages of all the executives. Thus, for example, he would have no way of knowing how many executives were 41 years of age.

Frequency distributions are often referred to by the term "marginals," and this term will be used in the following discussions. The above examples have presented marginals in the form of raw numbers. An alternative form would be the use of *percentages.* Thus, for example, you could report that x percent of your corporate executives were under 45, y percent were between 45 and 50, and so forth.

In computing percentages, you frequently must make a decision regarding the *base* from which to compute: that number that represents 100 percent. In the most straightforward case, the base would be the total number of cases under study. A problem arises, however, whenever some cases have missing data. Let's assume, for example, that a researcher has conducted a survey in which respondents were asked to report their ages. If some of the respondents failed to give an answer to the question being reported, however, the researcher has two alternatives. First, he might still base his percentages on the total number of respondents, with those failing to give their ages being reported as a percentage of the total. Second, he could use the number of persons giving an answer as the base from which to compute the percentages. (He should still report the number who did not answer, but they would not figure in the percentages.)

The choice of a base depends wholly on the purposes of the analysis. If, for example, the researcher wishes to compare the age distribution of his survey sample with comparable data describing the population from which the sample was drawn, he will probably want to omit the "no answers" from the computation. His best estimate of the age distribution of all respondents is to be found in the distribution discovered among those answering the question. Since "no answer" is not a meaningful age category, its presence among the base categories would confuse the comparison of sample and population figures.

Moving beyond the reporting of marginals, you may choose to present your data in the form of summary averages. Your options in this regard include the **mode** (the most frequent attribute, either grouped or ungrouped), the arithmetic **mean,** or the **median** (the *middle* attribute in the ranked distribution of observed attributes). Thus, you might report that most of the corporate executives were between 50 and 55 years of age (mode), that the mean age was 53, or that the median age was 54. Averages have the special advantage to the reader of reducing the raw data to the most manageable form: a single number (or attribute) can represent all the detailed data collected in regard to the variable. This advantage comes at a cost, of course, since the reader cannot reconstruct the original data from an average.

This disadvantage of averages can be somewhat alleviated through the reporting of summaries of the **dispersion** of responses. The simplest measure of dispersion is the **range.** Thus, in addition to reporting a mean age of 35, you might also indicate that the ages reported ranged from 18 to 69. A somewhat more sophisticated measure of dispersion is the *standard deviation.* The standard deviation for a distribution of values is the range from the mean within which approximately 34 percent of the cases fall, provided the values are distributed in a *normal curve.* Other measures of dispersion would be interquartile range and similar statistics.

Throughout the above discussions, we have explored variations in the reporting of a continuous variable, age. If the data being analyzed generated a nominal or limited ordinal variable, then some of the techniques discussed above would not be applicable. If the variable in question were sex, for example, marginals in terms of either raw numbers or percentages would be appropriate and useful. The modal response would be legitimate, but it would convey little useful information to the reader. Reports of mean, median, or dispersion summaries would be inappropriate.

In presenting univariate—and other—data, you will be constrained by two often conflicting goals. On the one hand, you should attempt to provide the reader with the fullest degree of detail regarding those data. On the other hand, the data should be presented in a manageable form. As these two goals often go directly counter to each other, you will find yourself continually seeking the best compromise between the two goals. One useful solution, however, is to report a given set of data in more than one form. In the case of age, for example, you might report both the marginals on ungrouped ages plus the mean age and standard deviation.

This concludes the introductory discussion of univariate analysis. You should have concluded that this seemingly simple matter can be rather complex. The lessons of this section, in any event, will be important as we move now to a consideration of subgroup descriptions and bivariate analyses.

14.3
Subgroup Comparisons

Univariate analyses serve the purpose of *describing* the units of analysis of a study and, if they are a sample drawn from some larger population, for making descriptive inferences about the larger population. Bivariate and multivariate analyses are aimed primarily at *explanation.* Before turning to explanation, however, we should consider the intervening case of subgroup description.

Often you may wish to describe subsets of your subjects. In a straightforward univariate analysis, you might wish to present the distribution of the ages of corporate executives. In exploring this variable in more depth, however, you might want to compare the ages of executives leading "new" corporations (in terms of the date of incorporation) and "old" ones. In analyzing a survey of attitudes toward the Ku Klux Klan, you might want to describe the attitudes of whites and blacks separately. In analyzing attitudes toward equal rights for women and men, you might want to analyze the attitudes of men and women separately.

In computing and presenting stratified descriptions, you follow the same steps as outlined in the section on univariate analysis, but the steps are followed independently for each of the relevant subgroups. For example, all men in the sample would be treated as a total sample representing 100 percent, and the distributions of responses or summary averages would be computed for the men. The same would be done for women. Then, you could report that 75 percent of the women approved of sexual equality, and that 63 percent of the men approved. Each group would have been subjected to a simple, univariate analysis. Frequency distributions for subgroups are often referred to as *stratified* marginals.

In some situations, the researcher presents stratified marginals or other subgroup descriptions for purely descriptive purposes. The reporting of census data often has this purpose. The average value of dwelling units on different census blocks may be presented for descriptive purposes. The reader may then note the average house value for any given block.

More often, the purpose of subgroup descriptions is comparative. In the study of sexual equality, you would clearly be interested in determining whether women were *more likely* to approve of the proposition than were men. Moreover, this comparison is not motivated by idle curiosity in most cases. Typically, it is based on an expectation that the stratification variable will have some form of causal effect on the description variable. Whether a subject is a man or a woman should be expected to affect the attitude toward equality of the sexes. Similarly, whether a subject is black or white should be expected to affect his attitude toward the Ku Klux Klan. When the analysis is motivated by such expectations, we move into the realm of explanation rather than description. At this point, it is appropriate to turn to a discussion of bivariate analysis.

14.4
Bivariate Analysis

Explanatory, **bivariate analysis** is basically the same as subgroup descriptions with certain special constraints. In subgroup descriptions, you are completely free to pick whatever stratification variable you desire and to describe each subgroup in terms of any other variable. In the example of sexual equality, you may separately describe men and women in terms of the percentages approving or disapproving (see Table 14-1).

Or you might describe those approving and those disapproving in terms of the percentages of men and women (see Table 14-2).

Either of these tables would be a legitimate presentation of subgroup descriptions. The data presented in the two tables would be read differently,

Table 14-1. "Do you approve or disapprove of the
proposition that men and women should be treated
equally in all regards?" (Hypothetical Data)

	Men	Women
Approve	63%	75%
Disapprove	37	25
	100%	100%
	(400)*	(400)

* The figures shown in parentheses represent the *base* from which the
percentages were computed. In this instance, there are 400 men
altogether, 63 percent (252 of the men) of whom "approve." Thirty-
seven percent (148 of the men) "disapprove."

however. From Table 14-1, we would note that 63 percent of the men in the
sample approved of sexual equality, as compared with 75 percent of the
women. From Table 14-2, we would note that of those approving, 46 percent
are men whereas of those disapproving, 60 percent are men; or, respectively,
that 37 percent of the 400 men disapprove, compared with 25 percent of the
400 women (Table 14-1), and that of those approving, 54 percent are women,
whereas of those disapproving, 40 percent are women (Table 14-2).

Table 14-2

		Approve	Disapprove
Men		46%	60%
Women		54	40
		100%	100%
	100% =	(552)	(248)

In an explanatory, bivariate analysis, however, only Table 14-1 would
make sense. The reasoning behind this assertion may best be presented as a
series of propositions:

1. Women generally are accorded an inferior status in American
society; thus they should be more supportive of the proposed equality of the
sexes.

2. A respondent's sex should therefore affect (cause) his or her
response to the questionnaire item: women should be more likely to approve
than men.

3. If the male and female respondents in the survey are described
separately in terms of their responses, a higher percentage of the women
should approve than of the men.

Following this logic, then, Table 14-1 divides the sample into two groups—men and women—and then describes the attitudes of the two groups separately. The percentages approving in the two groups are then compared, and we see that women are indeed more likely to approve than are men.

If Table 14-2 were presented as an explanatory, bivariate analysis, the logic of that table would be as follows. Attitudes on sexual equality affect the sex of the person holding that attitude. Approving of sexual equality will tend to make the person a woman more than it will make the person a man. This reasoning is, of course, absurd. Respondents' sexes are predetermined long before attitudes regarding sexual equality. Different attitudes on sexual equality can have no effect on whether the person holding a given attitude will be a man or a woman.

Realize, however, that Table 14-2 would be legitimate from the standpoint of subgroup description and even for purposes of *prediction*. If for some reason we knew a given respondent's attitude on sexual equality and wanted to predict whether that person was a man or a woman, Table 14-2 would be the appropriate source for such a prediction. If we knew the respondent approved of sexual equality, we would predict that the respondent was a woman. (*Note:* If we made several independent predictions of this sort, we would be wrong 46 percent of the time.) If we knew the respondent disapproved of sexual equality, we would guess that respondent was a man (and be wrong 40 percent of the time in repeated tests).

For purposes of explanation, however, only Table 14-1 is legitimate. In explanation, the reader must understand the logic of *independent* and *dependent* variables. Basically, the researcher attempts to explain values of the dependent variable on the basis of values about the independent variable. In this sense, he reasons that the independent variable *causes* the dependent variable (typically, in a probabilistic sense). In the above example, attitudes toward sexual equality comprise the dependent variable, while respondents' sexes comprise the independent variable. Thus, sex causes attitudes toward sexual equality. (The logical aspect of causation is discussed in more detail in Chapter 16.)

One problem which often confuses inexperienced researchers should be commented on: Should a table be percentaged "down" or "across"? Should a *column* of percentages total 100 percent or should a *row* of percentages? The answer to these questions is altogether arbitrary. In this book, I have tended to standardize the procedure by percentaging down, so that columns of percentage figures equal 100 percent, but this is only a matter of personal taste and habit.

A very useful guideline follows from this general issue, however. If a table is percentaged down, it should be read across. If it is percentaged across, it should be read down. Taking Table 14-1 as an example, we find it has been percentaged down in the sense that the percentages in each column total 100 percent. This table is interpreted by reading across: 63 percent of the men approve as compared with 75 percent of the women.

Dogged adherence to this general rule for table construction and interpretation will avoid a common error. Many inexperienced researchers would read Table 14-2 as follows: "Sixty-three percent of the men approve of sexual equality as compared with 37 percent who disapprove. Therefore, men are more likely to approve." This interpretation is misleading. While it is true that men are more likely to approve of sexual equality *than to disapprove,* this has no significance outside of a simple description of men's attitudes. The more important observation is that men are less likely to approve *than are women.* Since the table is percentaged down, it should be read across.

Let's take another example. Suppose we are interested in learning something about newspaper editorial policies regarding the legalization of marijuana. Assume we undertake a content analysis of editorials on this subject, during a given year, that have appeared in a sample of daily newspapers across the nation. Each editorial has been classified as "favorable," "neutral," or "unfavorable" toward the legalization of marijuana. Perhaps we might wish to examine the relationship between editorial policies and the types of communities in which the newspapers are published, thinking that rural newspapers might be more conservative in this regard than urban ones. Thus, each newspaper (hence, each editorial) has been classified in terms of the population of the community in which it is published.

Table 14-3 presents some hypothetical data describing the editorial policies of rural and urban newspapers. Note that the unit of analysis in this example is the individual editorial. Table 14-3 tells us that there were 127 editorials regarding marijuana in our sample of newspapers published in communities with populations under 100,000. (*Note:* This "cutting point" is chosen for simplicity of illustration and does not mean that "rural" refers to a community of less than 100,000 in any absolute sense.) Of these, 11 percent (14 editorials) were favorable toward legalization of marijuana, 29 percent were neutral, and 60 percent were unfavorable. Of the 438 editorials that appeared in our sample of newspapers published in communities of more than 100,000 residents, 32 percent (140 editorials) were favorable toward legalizing marijuana, 40 percent were neutral, and 28 percent were unfavorable. (Remember, this is all hypothetical.)

Table 14-3. Hypothetical Data Regarding Newspaper Editorials on the Legalization of Marijuana

Editorial Policy toward Legalizing Marijuana		Community Size	
		Under 100,000	Over 100,000
Favorable		11%	32%
Neutral		29	40
Unfavorable		60	28
	100% =	(127)	(438)

When we compare the editorial policies of "rural" and "urban" newspapers in our imaginary study, we find—as expected—that rural newspapers are less favorable toward the legalization of marijuana than are urban ones. This is determined by noting that a larger percentage (32 percent) of the urban editorials were favorable than of the rural ones (11 percent). We might note, as well, that rural editorials were more unfavorable

(60 percent) than were the urban ones (28 percent). Note that this table shows percentages in such a manner as to assume that the size of a community might affect its newspapers' editorial policies on this issue, rather than that editorial policy might affect the size of communities.

Constructing and Reading Tables

Before turning to an introduction to multivariate analysis, it will be useful to review the steps involved in the construction of explanatory bivariate tables. They are as follows:

1. The cases are divided into groups according to their attributes of the independent variable.

2. Each of these subgroups is then described in terms of attributes of the dependent variable.

3. Finally, the table is read by comparing the independent variable subgroups with one another in terms of a given attribute of the dependent variable.

Let's repeat the analysis of sex and attitudes on sexual equality following these steps. For the reasons outlined above, sex is designated as the independent variable; attitudes toward sexual equality constitute the dependent variable. Thus, we proceed as follows:

1. The cases are divided into men and women.

2. Each sex subgrouping is described in terms of approval or disapproval of sexual equality.

3. Men and women are compared in terms of the percentages approving of sexual equality.

In the example of editorial policies regarding the legalization of marijuana, size of community would be the independent variable and a newspaper's editorial policy would be the dependent variable. The table would be constructed as follows:

1. Divide the editorials into subgroups according to the sizes of the communities in which the newspapers are published.

2. Describe each subgroup of editorials in terms of the percentages favorable, neutral, or unfavorable toward the legalization of marijuana.

3. Compare the two subgroups in terms of the percentages favorable toward the legalization of marijuana.

Bivariate analyses typically have an explanatory causal purpose. These two hypothetical examples have hinted at the nature of causation as it is used by social scientists. I hope the rather simplified approach to causation employed in these examples will have a common-sense acceptability for you at this point. This rather superficial, common-sense view of causation will assist you in understanding this chapter and the next. Chapter 16 will take a much closer look at causation. A fundamental understanding of the subjects covered in this chapter and the next one should assist you in understanding more fully the complex nature of causation.

Bivariate Table Formats

The format for presenting contingency table data has never been standardized, with the result that a variety of formats will be found in research literature. As long as a table is easily read and interpreted, there is probably no reason to strive for standardization. At the same time, however, there are a number of guidelines that should be followed in the presentation of most tabular data.

1. A table should have a heading or a title that succinctly describes what is contained in the table.

2. The original content of the variables should be clearly presented — in the table itself if at all possible—or in the text with a paraphrase in the table. This is especially critical when a variable is derived from responses to an attitudinal question, since the meaning of the responses will depend largely on the wording of the question.

3. The attributes of each variable should be clearly indicated. In the case of complex categories, these will have to be abbreviated, but the meaning should be clear in the table and, of course, the full description should be reported in the text.

4. When percentages are presented in the table, the base upon which they are computed should be indicated. Note that it is redundant to present all of the raw numbers for each category since these could be reconstructed from the percentages and the bases. Moreover, the presentation of both numbers and percentages often confuses a table and makes it more difficult to read.

5. If any cases are omitted from the table due to missing data ("no answer" for example), their numbers should be indicated in the table.

Table 14-4 is an example of a good table.

Table 14-4. "Do you approve or disapprove of the
general proposition that men and women should be
treated equally in all regards?"

	Men	Women
Approve	63%	75%
Disapprove	37	25
	100%	100%
	(400)	(400)
No answer =	(12)	(5)

14.5

Introduction to Multivariate Analysis

The logic of multivariate analysis is the topic of later chapters in this book—especially Chapter 17. At this point, however, it will be useful to discuss briefly the construction of multivariate tables: those constructed from several variables.

Multivariate tables may be constructed on the basis of a more complicated subgroup description—following essentially the same steps outlined above for bivariate tables. Instead of one independent variable and one dependent variable, however, we will have more than one independent variable. Instead of explaining the dependent variable on the basis of a single independent variable, we shall seek an explanation through the use of more than one independent variable.

Let's return to the example of attitudes toward sexual equality; suppose that the researcher believed that age would also affect such attitudes: that young people would approve of sexual equality more than would older people. As the first step in table construction, we would divide the total sample into subgroups based on the various attributes of both independent variables simultaneously: young men, old men, young women, and old women. Then the several subgroups would be described in terms of the dependent variable, and comparisons would be made. Table 14-5 is a hypothetical table that might result.

Table 14-5. "Do you approve or disapprove of the proposition that men and women should be treated equally in all regards?"

	Under 30		30 and Over	
	Women	Men	Women	Men
Approve	90%	78%	60%	48%
Disapprove	10	22	40	52
	100%	100%	100%	100%
	(200)	(200)	(200)	(200)
No answer =	(2)	(10)	(3)	(2)

Following the convention of this textbook, this table has also been percentaged down, and it should, therefore, be read across. The interpretation of this table warrants several conclusions:

1. Among both men and women, younger people are more supportive of sexual equality than are older people. Among women, 90 percent and 60 percent, respectively, approve.

2. Within each age group, women are more supportive than are men. Among those respondents under 30 years of age, 90 percent of the women approve, compared with 78 percent of the men. Among those 30 and over, 60 percent of the women and 48 percent of the men approve.

3. As measured in the table, age would appear to have a stronger effect on attitudes than sex. For both men and women, the effect of age may be summarized as a 30 percentage point difference. Within each age group, the percentage point difference between men and women is 12.

4. Both age and sex have independent effects on attitudes. Within a given attribute of one independent variable, different attributes of the second still affect attitudes.

5. Similarly, the two independent variables have a cumulative effect on attitudes. Young women are the most supportive, while older men are the least supportive.

Chapter 17 on the *elaboration model* will examine the logic of multivariate analysis in much greater detail. Before concluding this section, however, it will be useful to note an alternative format for presenting such data.

Several of the tables presented in this chapter are somewhat inefficient. When the dependent variable—attitude toward sexual equality—is dichotomous (two attributes), knowing one attribute permits the reader to easily reconstruct the other. Thus, if we know that 90 percent of the women under 30 years of age approve of sexual equality, then we know automatically that 10 percent disapprove. Reporting the percentages who disapprove, then, is unnecessary. On the basis of this recognition, Table 14-5 could be presented in the alternative format of Table 14-6.

In Table 14-6, the percentages approving of sexual equality are reported in the cells representing the intersections of the two independent variables. The numbers presented in parentheses below each percentage represent the number of cases upon which the percentages are based. Thus, for example, the reader knows that there are 200 women under 30 years of age in the sample, and 90 percent of those approved of sexual equality. This tells him, moreover, that 180 of those 200 women approved, and that the other 20 (or 10 percent) disapproved. This new table is easier to read than the former one, and it does not sacrifice any detail.

Table 14-6. "Do you approve or disapprove of the proposition that men and women should be treated equally in all regards?"

Percent Who "Approve"	Women	Men
Under 30	90 (200)	78 (200)
30 and over	60 (200)	48 (200)

14.6
Summary

Chapter 14 has introduced some of the more elementary methods of quantitative data manipulations. This introduction is based on the belief that you cannot appreciate and understand complex analytical methods unless you fully understand those that seem fairly simple.

The chapter began with univariate analysis: the analysis of a single variable. In short order, we discovered that the social researcher faces a very wide range of options in the analysis and presentation of even a single variable. We looked at different methods of data reduction: ways of summarizing a set of observations, all the while attempting to maintain the greatest amount of detail. We discussed frequency distributions, percentages, grouped data, averages, and measures of dispersion.

Next, the chapter turned to the concept of subgroup comparisons. In this case, we were concerned with univariate analyses of different subsets of the total population of observations. The univariate descriptions of those subsets were then compared.

Bivariate analysis, examined next, is nothing more than a slightly different interpretation of subgroup comparisons. That slightly different interpretation, however, involves the concepts of causation and explanation. Rather than simply comparing subgroups of a population, the purpose in bivariate analysis is to begin examining the relationships between variables.

Considerable attention was given to the construction and interpretation of bivariate percentage tables, since these are very common in social research, their seeming simplicity is deceptive, and they contain within them the basic logic of explanatory data analysis.

Finally, the chapter turned to an introduction to multivariate analysis. This critical topic will be pursued in considerably more detail in Chapter 17.

14.7
Main Points

1. Univariate analysis is the analysis of a single variable.

2. The full original data collected with regard to a single variable are, in that form, usually impossible to interpret. *Data reduction* is the process of summarizing the original data so as to make them more manageable, all the while maintaining as much of the original detail as possible.

3. A frequency distribution shows the number of cases having each of the attributes of a given variable.

4. Grouped data are created through the combination of attributes of a variable.

5. *Averages* (the mean, median, and mode) reduce data to an easily manageable form, but they do not convey the detail of the original data.

6. Measures of dispersion give a summary indication of the distribution of cases around an average value.

7. To undertake a subgroup comparison: (a) divide cases into the appropriate subgroups, (b) describe each subgroup in terms of a given variable, and (c) compare those descriptions across the subgroups.

8. Bivariate analysis is nothing more than a different interpretation of subgroup comparisons: (a) divide cases into subgroups in terms of their attributes on some *independent variable*, (b) describe each subgroup in terms of some *dependent variable*, (c) compare the *dependent variable* descriptions of the subgroups, and (d) interpret any observed differences as a statistical association between the independent and dependent variables.

9. As a rule of thumb in interpreting bivariate percentage tables: (a) "percentage down" and "read across" in making the subgroup comparisons *or* (b) "percentage across" and "read down" in making subgroup comparisons.

10. Multivariate analysis is a method of analyzing the simultaneous relationships among several variables, and may be used in more fully understanding the relationship between two variables.

14.8
Annotated Bibliography

Cole, Stephen, *The Sociological Method* (Chicago: Markham, 1972). A readable introduction to analysis. Cole begins with the general question of what social scientific inquiry is, and then illustrates with easily understood examples. He goes on to an introduction of the elaboration model, and it is useful in that regard also.

Davis, James, *Elementary Survey Analysis* (Englewood Cliffs, N.J.: Prentice-Hall, 1971). An extremely well-written and well-reasoned introduction to analysis. In addition to covering the materials of the present book's Chapter 14, Davis' book is well worth reading in terms of measurement, statistics, and the elaboration model.

Labovitz, Sanford, and Hagedorn, Robert, *Introduction to Social Research* (New York: McGraw-Hill, 1971). Another useful introduction to analysis. Against the background of more general concerns for social scientific inquiry, the authors provide a very readable and useful introduction to elementary analyses in their Chapter 6. Like Cole and Davis, they then go on to a consideration of multivariate analysis and the elaboration model.

Zeisel, Hans, *Say It With Figures* (New York: Harper & Row, 1957). An excellent discussion of table construction and other elementary analyses. Though several years old, this is still perhaps the best available presentation of this specific topic. It is eminently readable and understandable and has many concrete examples.

15

Index and Scale Construction

15.1
Introduction

Chapter 15, like Chapters 4 and 5, is addressed to the matter of measurement. It is a logical continuation of the earlier discussion of conceptualization and operationalization. The earlier discussions examined some of the ways in which measurement is dealt with in the design of a social research study; the present chapter describes the continuation of that concern during the analysis of data.

This chapter discusses the construction of indexes and scales as composite measures of variables. A short section at the end of the chapter considers typologies. These different types of composite or cumulative measures are very frequently used in social research. Each type involves the combination of several empirical indicators of a variable into a single measure.

There are several reasons for the frequent use of composite measures. First, despite the care taken in designing studies so as to provide valid and reliable measurements of variables, the researcher seldom is able to develop in advance single indicators of complex concepts. This is especially true with regard to attitudes and orientations. The survey researcher, for example, is seldom able to devise single questionnaire items that adequately tap respondents' degrees of prejudice, religiosity, political orientations, alienation, and the like. More likely, he will devise several items, each of which provides *some* indication of the variables. Each of these, however, is likely to prove invalid or unreliable for many respondents.

You should realize that *some* variables are rather easily measured through single indicators. We may determine a survey respondent's sex by asking: Sex: [ ] Male [ ] Female. We may determine a newspaper's circulation by merely looking at the figure the newspaper reports. The number of times an experimental stimulus is administered to an experimental group is clearly defined in the design of the experiment. Nonetheless, social scientists, using a variety of research methods, frequently wish to study variables that have no clear and unambiguous single indicators.

Second, the researcher may wish to employ a rather refined ordinal measure of his variable, arranging cases in several ordinal categories from—for example—very low to very high on a variable. A single data item might not have sufficient categories to provide this range of variations, but an index or scale formed from several items would.

Finally, indexes and scales are *efficient* devices for data analysis. If considering a single data item gives us only a rough indication of a given variable, considering several data items may give us a more comprehensive and more accurate indication. For example, a single newspaper editorial may give us some indication of the political orientations of that newspaper. Examining several editorials, on the other hand, would probably give us a better assessment, but the manipulation of several data items simultaneously could be very complicated. Indexes and scales (especially scales) are efficient *data-reduction devices:* Several indicators may be summarized in a single numerical score, while sometimes very nearly maintaining the specific details of all the individual indicators.

15.2
Indexes Versus Scales

The terms "index" and "scale" are typically used imprecisely and interchangeably in social research literature. Before considering the distinctions that this book will make between indexes and scales, let's first see what they have in common.

Both scales and indexes are typically *ordinal* measures of variables. Scales and indexes are constructed in such a way as to rank-order people (or other units of analysis) in terms of specific variables such as religiosity, alienation, socioeconomic status, prejudice, or intellectual sophistication. A person's score on a scale or index of religiosity, for example, gives an indication of his relative religiosity vis-a-vis other people.

As the terms will be used in this book, both scales and indexes are *composite measures of variables:* measurements based on more than one data item. Thus, a survey respondent's score on an index or scale of religiosity would be determined by the specific responses he gave to several questionnaire items, each of which would provide some indication of his religiosity. Similarly, a person's I.Q. score is based on his answers to a large number of test questions. The political orientation of a newspaper might be represented by an index or scale score reflecting the newspaper's editorial policy on a number of political issues.

For the purposes of this book, we shall distinguish indexes and scales through the manner in which scores are assigned. An **index** is constructed through the simple accumulation of scores assigned to *individual* attributes. A **scale** is constructed through the assignment of scores to *patterns* of attributes. A scale differs from an index by taking advantage of any *intensity structure* that may exist among those attributes. A simple example should clarify this distinction.

Suppose we wished to measure support of civil liberties for Communists. We might ask in a questionnaire whether a Communist should be allowed to pursue the following occupations: (1) lawyer, (2) doctor, (3) minister, (4) engineer, (5) newspaper reporter. Some people would be willing to allow a Communist to pursue all of the occupations listed; some would be unwilling to permit any. Many, however, would feel that some were permissible while others were not. Each person who gave a mixed set of responses presumably would be indicating that he felt some of the occupations to be more important than others. The relative priorities of the different occupations would vary from person to person, however; there is no absolute ranking inherent in the occupations themselves. Given the responses to such a questionnaire, the researcher might construct an index of respondents' relative commitments to civil liberties for Communists on the basis of the *number* of occupations they would hold open to Communists. The respondent who would permit a Communist to hold all the occupations clearly would support a greater degree of civil liberty than one who would close all occupations to a Communist. Moreover, the researcher would assume that the respondent who would permit a Communist to hold three of the occupations would be more supportive of a Communist's civil liberties than the respondent who would hold open only one or two of the occupations, regardless of which one, two, or three occupations are involved. Such an index might provide a useful and accurate ordinal measure of attitudes about civil liberties.

Suppose for a moment, however, that the occupations used in the above example had been: (1) ditch digger, (2) high school teacher, and (3) President of the United States. In this situation, there is every reason to believe that these three items have an *intensity structure*. The person who would permit a Communist to be President would surely permit him to be a high school teacher and a ditch digger. On the other hand if he would permit Communists to dig ditches, he might or might not permit them in the other two occupations. In all likelihood, in this study, knowing the *number* of occupations approved for Communists would tell the researcher *which* occupations were approved. In such a situation, a composite measure comprised of the three items would constitute a *scale* as I have used the term.

It should be apparent that scales are generally superior to indexes, if for no other reason than that scale scores convey more information than do index scores. Still the reader should be wary of the common misuse of the term "scale"; clearly, calling a given measure a scale rather than an index does not make it better. The reader should be cautioned against two other misconceptions about scaling. First, whether the combination of several data items results in a scale almost always depends on the particular sample of observations under study. Certain items may form a scale among one sample but not among another, and the reader should not assume that a given set of items *are* a scale because they have formed a scale among a given sample. Second, the use of certain *scaling techniques* to be discussed does not insure the creation of a scale any more than the use of items that have previously formed scales can offer such insurance.

An examination of the substantive literature based on social science data will show that indexes are used much more frequently than scales. Ironically, however, the methodological literature contains little if any discussion of index construction, while discussions of scale construction abound. There appear to be two reasons for this disparity. First, indexes are more frequently used because scales are often difficult or impossible to construct from the data at hand. Second, methods of index construction are not discussed because they seem obvious and straightforward.

Index construction is not a simple undertaking. Furthermore, I feel that the general failure to develop index-construction techniques has resulted in the creation of many bad indexes in social research. With this in mind, I have devoted most of this chapter to the methods of index construction. Once the logic of this activity is fully understood, the reader will be better equipped to attempt the construction of scales. Indeed, the carefully constructed index may turn out to be a scale anyway.

15.3
Index Construction

Item Selection

A composite index is created for the purpose of measuring some variable. The first criterion for selecting items to be included in the index is *face validity* (or logical validity). If the researcher wishes to measure political conservatism, for example, each of the items considered should appear on its face to indicate conservatism (or its opposite: liberalism). Political party affiliation would be one such item. If people were asked to approve or disapprove of the views of a well-known conservative public figure, their responses might, logically, provide another indication of their conservatism. A researcher interested in constructing an index of religiosity might consider church attendance, acceptance of certain religious beliefs, and frequency of prayer; each of these would appear to offer some indication of religiosity.

Typically, the methodological literature on conceptualization and measurement stresses the need for *unidimensionality* in scale and index construction: a composite measure should represent only one dimension. Thus, items reflecting religiosity should not be included in a measure of political conservatism, even though the two variables might be empirically related to one another. In this sense, an index or scale should be unidimensional.

At the same time, the researcher should be constantly aware of the subtle nuances that may exist within the general dimension he is attempting to measure. Thus in the example of religiosity, the indicators mentioned above represent different *types* of religiosity. If the researcher wished to measure ritual participation in religion, he should limit the items included in the measure to those specifically indicating this: church attendance, communion, confession, and the like. If, on the other hand, he wished to measure religiosity in a more general way, he would want to include a balanced set of items, representing each of the different types of religiosity. Ultimately, the nature of the items included will determine how specifically or generally the variable is measured.

In selecting items for inclusion in an index, the researcher must also be concerned with the amount of *variance* provided by those items. If an item provider an indication of political conservatism, for example, the researcher should note what proportion of respondents were identified as conservatives by the item. In the extremes, if a given item identified no one as a conservative or everyone as a conservative, the item would not be very useful in the creation of an index. If nobody indicated approval of a radical right political figure, an item about him would not be of much use in the construction of an index.

With regard to variance, the researcher has two options. First, he may select several items on which responses divide people about equally in terms of the variable. Thus he might select several items, each of which attains responses that are about half conservative and half liberal. Although none of these items would justify the characterization of a person as "very conservative," a person who appeared conservative on all of them might be so characterized.

The second option is the selection of items differing in variance. One item might identify about half the subjects as conservative, while another might identify few of the respondents as conservative. (*Note:* This latter option is necessary for scaling, but it is reasonable for the construction of an index as well.)

Bivariate Relationships among Items

The second step in index construction is the examination of the bivariate relationships among the items being considered for inclusion. If each of the items does indeed give an indication of the variable—as suggested on grounds of face validity—then the several items should be related to one another empirically. For example, if several items all reflect conservatism or liberalism, then those who appear conservative in terms of one item should appear conservative in terms of others. Recognize, however, that such items will seldom if ever be perfectly related to one another; persons who appear conservative on one item will appear liberal on another. (This disparity creates the need for constructing composite measures in the first place.) Nevertheless, persons who appear conservative on item A should be more likely to appear conservative on item B than do persons who appear liberal on item A.

The researcher should examine all the possible bivariate relationships among the several items being considered for inclusion in the index to determine the relative strengths of relationships among the several pairs of items. Either percentage tables or correlation coefficients, or both, may be used for this purpose. The primary criterion for evaluating these several relationships is the strength of the relationships. The use of this criterion, however, is rather subtle.

Clearly, the researcher should be wary of items that are not related to one another empirically. It is unlikely that they measure the same variable if they are unrelated. More to the point, perhaps, a given item that is unrelated to several of the other items probably should be dropped from consideration.

At the same time a *very* strong relationship between two items is another danger sign. At the extreme, if two items are perfectly related to one another, then only one is necessary for inclusion in the index, since it completely conveys the indications provided by the other. (This problem will become even clearer in the next section.)

To illustrate the steps in index construction, an example from the substantive literature of survey research may be useful.[1] A recent survey of medical school faculty members was concerned with the consequences of the "scientific perspective" on the quality of patient care provided by physicians. The primary intent was to determine whether more scientifically inclined doctors were more impersonal in their treatment of patients than were other doctors.

The survey questionnaire offered several possible indicators of respondents' scientific perspectives. Of those, three items appeared—in terms of face validity—to provide especially clear indications of whether or not the doctors were scientifically oriented. The three items were:

1. "As a medical school faculty member, in what capacity do you feel you can make your greatest *teaching* contribution: as a practicing physician or as a medical researcher?"

2. "As you continue to advance your own medical knowledge, would you say your ultimate medical interests lie primarily in the direction of total patient management or the understanding of basic mechanisms?"

3. "In the field of therapeutic research, are you generally more interested in articles reporting evaluations of the effectiveness of various treatments or articles exploring the basic rationale underlying the treatments?"

In each of the items above, the second answer would indicate a greater scientific orientation than the first answer. Taking the responses to a single item, we might conclude that those respondents who chose the second answer are more scientifically oriented than those who chose the first answer. This *comparative* conclusion is a reasonable one, but we should not be misled into thinking that respondents who chose the second answer to a given item are "scientists" in any absolute sense. They are simply *more scientific* than those who chose the first answer to the item. This important point will become clearer when we examine the distribution of responses produced by each of the items.

In terms of the first item—best teaching role—only about one-third of the respondents appear scientifically oriented. (Approximately one-third said they could make their greatest teaching contribution as medical researchers.) This does not mean that only one-third of the sample are "scientists," however, for the other two items would suggest quite different conclusions in this regard. In response to the second item—ultimate medical interests—ap-

---

1. The example, including tables presented, is taken from Earl R. Babbie, *Science and Morality in Medicine* (Berkeley: University of California Press, 1970).

proximately two-thirds chose the scientific answer, saying they were more interested in learning about basic mechanisms than learning about total patient management. In response to the third item—reading preferences—about eighty percent chose the scientific answer.

To repeat, these three questionnaire items cannot tell us how many "scientists" there are in the sample, for none of the items is related to a set of criteria for what constitutes being a scientist in any absolute sense. Using the items for this purpose would present us with the problem of three, quite different, estimates of how many scientists there were in the sample.

Rather, these three questionnaire items provide us with three independent indicators of respondents' relative inclinations toward science in medicine. Each item separates respondents into the *more* scientific and the *less* scientific. In view of the different distribution of responses produced by the three items, it is clear that each of the resulting groupings of more or less scientific respondents will have a somewhat different membership from the others. Respondents who seem scientific in terms of one item will not seem scientific in terms of another. Nevertheless, to the extent that each of the items measures the same general dimension, we should find some correspondence among the several groupings. Respondents who appear scientific in terms of one item should be more likely to appear scientific in their responses to another item than would those who appeared nonscientific in their responses to the first. We should find an association or correlation between the responses given to two items.

Table 15-1 shows the associations among the responses to the three items. Three bivariate (two-variable) tables are presented, showing the conjoint distribution of responses for each pair of items. Although each single item produces a different grouping of "scientific" and "nonscientific" respondents, we see in Table 15-1 that the responses given to each of the items correspond, to a degree, to the responses given to each of the other items.

An examination of the three bivariate relationships presented in Table 15-1 supports the belief that the three items all measure the same variable: scientific orientations. Let's begin by looking at the first bivariate relationship in the table. Faculty assessments of their best teaching roles and their expressions of their ultimate medical interests both give indications of scientific orientations. Those who answer "researcher" in the first instance would appear more scientifically inclined than those who answered "physician." Those who answered "basic mechanisms" would appear more scientifically inclined than those who answered "total patient management" in reply to the question concerning ultimate interests. If both these items do indeed measure the same thing, those appearing scientific on one ("researchers") should appear more scientific in answering the second ("basic mechanisms") than those who appeared nonscientific on the first ("physicians"). Looking at the data, we see that 87 percent of the "researchers" are scientific on the second item, as opposed to 51 percent of the "physicians." (*Note:* The fact that the "physicians" are about evenly split in their ultimate medical interests is irrelevant. It is only relevant that they are *less* scientific in their medical interests than are the "researchers.") The strength of this relationship may be summarized as a 36 percentage point difference.

Table 15-1. Bivariate Relationships of Scientific Orientation Items

		Best Teaching Role	
		Physician	Researcher
Ultimate Medical Interest	Total patient management	49%	13%
	Basic mechanisms	51	87
	100% =	(285)	(196)

		Reading Preferences	
		Effectiveness	Rationale
Ultimate Medical Interest	Total patient management	68%	30%
	Basic mechanisms	32	70
	100% =	(132)	(349)

		Reading Preferences	
		Effectiveness	Rationale
Best Teaching Role	Physician	85%	64%
	Researcher	15	36
	100% =	(132)	(349)

The same general conclusion is to be reached in regard to the other bivariate relationships. The strength of the relationship between reading preferences and ultimate medical interests may be summarized as a 38 percentage point difference; the strength of the relationship between reading preferences and the two teaching roles may be summarized as a 21 percentage point difference.

Initially the three items were selected on the basis of face validity—each appeared to give some indication of faculty members' orientations to science. By examining the bivariate relationship between the pairs of items, we have found support for the initial belief that they all measure basically the same thing.

Multivariate Relationships among Items

The discovery of the expected bivariate relationships between pairs of items further suggests their appropriateness for inclusion in a composite index. This is not a sufficient justification, however. The next step in index construction is the examination of the multivariate relationships among the items. The researcher must examine the simultaneous relationships among the several variables before combining them in a single index.

Recall that the primary purpose of index construction is the development of a method of classifying respondents in terms of some variable such as political conservatism, religiosity, scientific orientations, or whatever. An index of political conservatism should identify respondents who are very conservative, moderately conservative, not very conservative, and not at all conservative (or moderately liberal and very liberal, respectively, in place of the last two categories). The several gradations in terms of the variable are provided by the combination of responses given to the several items included in the index. Thus, the respondent who appeared conservative on all the items would be considered very conservative overall.

For an index to provide meaningful gradations in this sense, it is essential that each item add something to the evaluation of each respondent. Recall from the preceding section that it was suggested that two items perfectly related to one another would not be appropriate for inclusion in the same index. If one item were included, the other would add nothing to our evaluation of respondents. The examination of multivariate relationships among the items is another way of eliminating "deadwood." It also determines the overall power of the particular collection of items in measuring the variable under consideration.

The purposes of this multivariate examination will become clearer if we return to the earlier example of measuring scientific orientations among a sample of medical school faculty members. Table 15-2 presents the trivariate relationship among the three items.

Table 15-2. Trivariate Relationship Among Scientific Orientation Items

Percent Interested in Basic Mechanisms		Best Teaching Role	
		Physician	Researcher
Reading Preferences	Effectiveness	27% (66)	58% (12)
	Rationale	58% (219)	89% (130)

Table 15-2 has been presented somewhat differently from Table 15-1. In this instance, the sample respondents have been categorized in four groups according to: (1) their best teaching roles and (2) their reading preferences. The numbers in parentheses indicate the number of respondents in each group. (Thus 66 faculty members said they could best teach as physicians and also said they preferred articles dealing with the effectiveness of treatments.) For each of the four groups, the percentage saying they are ultimately more interested in basic mechanisms has been presented. (Of the 66 faculty mentioned above, 27 percent are primarily interested in basic mechanisms.)

The arrangement of the four groups is based on a previously drawn conclusion regarding scientific orientations. Those in the upper left corner of the table are presumably the least scientifically oriented of the four groups: in terms of their best teaching roles and their reading preferences. Those in the lower right corner of the table are presumably the most scientifically oriented in terms of those items.

Recall that expressing a primary interest in "basic mechanisms" was also taken as an indication of scientific orientations. As we should expect, then, those in the lower right corner are the most likely to give this response (89 percent) and those in the upper left corner are the least likely (27 percent). The respondents who gave mixed responses in terms of teaching roles and reading preferences have an intermediate rank in their concern for basic mechanisms (58 percent in both cases).

This table tells us many things. First, we may note that the original relationships between pairs of items are not significantly affected by the presence of a third item. Recall, for example, that the relationship between teaching role and ultimate medical interest was summarized as a 36 percentage point difference. Looking at Table 15-2, we see that among only those respondents who are most interested in articles dealing with the effectiveness of treatments, the relationship between teaching role and ultimate medical interest is 31 percentage points (58 percent minus 27 percent: first row), and the same is true among those most interested in articles dealing with the rationale for treatments (89 percent minus 58 percent: second row). The original relationship between teaching role and ultimate medical interest is essentially the same as in Table 15-1, even among those respondents judged as scientific or nonscientific in terms of reading preferences.

The same conclusion may be drawn as we examine the columns in Table 15-2. Recall that the original relationship between reading preferences and ultimate medical interests was summarized as a 38 percentage point difference. Looking only at the "physicians" in Table 15-2, we see the relationship between the other two items is now 31 percentage points. The same relationship is found among the "researchers" in the second column.

The importance of these observations becomes clearer when we consider what might have happened. Table 15-3 presents hypothetical data to illustrate this.

Table 15-3. Hypothetical Trivariate Relationship among Scientific Orientation Items

Percent Interested in Basic Mechanisms		Best Teaching Role	
		Physician	Researcher
Reading Preferences	Effectiveness	51%	87%
	Rationale	51%	87%

The hypothetical data in Table 15-3 tell a much different story than did the actual data reported in Table 15-2. In this instance, it is evident that the original relationship between teaching role and ultimate medical interest persists, even when reading preferences are introduced into the picture. In each row of the table the "researchers" are more likely to express an interest in basic mechanisms than are the "physicians." Looking down the columns, however, we note that there is no relationship between reading preferences and ultimate medical interests. If we know whether a respondent feels he can best teach as a physician or as a researcher, knowing his reading preference adds nothing to our evaluation of his scientific orientations. If something like Table 15-3 resulted from the actual data, we would conclude that reading preferences should not be included in the same index as teaching roles, since it will contribute nothing to the composite index.

In the present example, only three questionnaire items were involved. If more were being considered, then more complex multivariate tables would be in order. In this instance, we have limited our attention to the trivariate analysis of the three items. The purpose of this step in index construction, again, is to determine the simultaneous interaction of the items to determine whether they are all appropriate for inclusion in the same index.

Index Scoring

When the researcher has arrived at the best items for inclusion in the index, the next step is the assignment of scores for particular responses, thereby creating a single composite index out of the several items. There are two basic decisions to be made in this regard.

First, the researcher must decide the desirable range of the index scores. Certainly one of the primary advantages of an index over a single item is the range of gradations it offers in the measurement of a variable. As noted earlier, political conservatism might be measured from "very conservative" to "not at all conservative" (or "very liberal"). How far to the extremes, then, should the index extend?

In this decision, the question of variance enters once more. Almost always, as the possible extremes of an index are extended, fewer cases are to be found at each end. The researcher who wishes to measure political conservatism to its greatest extreme may find he has almost no one in that category.

The first decision, then, concerns the conflicting desires for (1) the range of measurement in the index and (2) the adequate number of cases at each point in the index. The researcher will be forced to reach some kind of compromise between these conflicting desires.

The second decision concerns the actual assignment of scores for each particular response. Basically the researcher must decide whether to give each item an equal weight in the index or to give them different weights. As we shall see later, scale construction is quite different in this regard, but this is an open issue in index construction. While there are no firm rules to be followed in this regard, I would suggest—and practice tends to confirm this—that items should be weighted equally unless there are compelling reasons for differential weighting. That is, the burden of proof should be on differential weighting; equal weighting should be the norm.

Of course, this decision must be related to the earlier issue regarding the balance of items chosen. If the index is to represent the composite of slightly different aspects of a given variable, then the researcher should give each of those aspects the same weight. In some instances, however, he may feel that, say, two items reflect essentially the same aspect, while the third reflects a different aspect. If he wished to have both aspects equally represented by the index, he might decide to give the different item a weight equal to the combination of the two similar ones. In such a situation, he might wish to assign a maximum score of 2 to the different item and maximum scores of 1 to each of the similar ones.

Although the rationale for scoring responses should take such concerns as these into account, the researcher typically will experiment with different scoring methods, examining the relative weights given to different aspects but at the same time worrying about the range and distribution of cases provided. Ultimately, the scoring method chosen will represent a compromise among these several demands. (*Note:* In this activity, as in most survey activities, the decision is open to revision on the basis of later examinations. Validation of the index, to be discussed shortly, may lead the researcher to recycle his efforts and to construct a completely different index.)

In the example taken from the medical school faculty survey, the decision was made to weight each of the items equally, since they had been chosen, in part, on the basis of their representing slightly different aspects of the overall variable—scientific orientations. On each of the items, the respondents were given a score of 1 for choosing the "scientific" response to the item and a score of 0 for choosing the "nonscientific" response. Each respondent, then, had a chance of receiving a score of 0, 1, 2, or 3, depending on the number of "scientific" responses he chose. This scoring method provided what was considered a useful range of variation—four index categories—and also provided sufficient cases in each category for analysis.

Handling Missing Data

Regardless of the data collection method used by a social researcher, he must frequently face the problem of missing data. In a content analysis of the political orientations of newspapers, for example, he may discover that a particular newspaper has never taken an editorial position on one of the issues being studied; e.g., it may never have taken a stand on the United Nations. In an experimental design involving several retests of subjects over time, some subjects may be unable to participate in some of the sessions. In virtually every survey, some respondents fail to answer some questions (or choose a "don't know" response). Although missing data presents a problem at all stages of analysis, it is especially troublesome in index construction. (Again, scaling is different in this regard.) There are, however, several methods of dealing with this problem.

First, if there are relatively few cases with missing data, the researcher may decide to exclude them from the construction of the index and the analysis. (In the medical school faculty example discussed above, this was the decision made regarding missing data.) The primary concerns in this instance are whether the numbers available for analysis will still be sufficient, and whether the exclusion will result in a biased sample whenever the index is used in the analysis. The latter possibility can be examined through a comparison—on other relevant variables—of those who would be included and those excluded from the index.

Second, the researcher may have grounds for treating missing data the same as if the respondent had given one of the available responses. For example, if a questionnaire has asked respondents to indicate their participation in a number of activities by checking "yes" or "no" for each, many respondents may have checked some of the activities "yes" and left the remainder blank. In such a case, the researcher might decide that a failure to answer meant "no," and score missing data in this case as though the respondents had checked the "no" space.

Third, a careful analysis of missing data may yield an interpretation of their meaning. In constructing a measure of political conservatism, for example, the researcher may discover that those respondents who failed to answer a given question were generally as conservative—in terms of other items—as those who gave the conservative answer. As another example, a recent survey measuring religious beliefs found that respondents who answered "don't know" about a given belief were almost identical to the "disbelievers" in their answers regarding other beliefs. (*Note:* You should not take these examples as empirical guides in your own studies, but only as suggestive of ways of analyzing your own data.) Whenever the analysis of missing data yields such interpretations, then, the researcher may decide to score such cases accordingly.

Fourth, the researcher may decide to assign an *intermediate* score for missing data. For example, in creating an index of the political orientations of newspapers, the researcher might assign a score of 0 to a conservative editorial on a given issue, a score of 2 to a liberal editorial, and a score of 1 in those instances in which a newspaper had taken no editorial position on the issue. (This is the same logic whereby the survey response "undecided" is often scored as lying between "agree" and "disagree.")

Fifth, the researcher may assign index scores *proportionately* on the basis of the data available. For example, let's assume that six items are being combined in an index, with scores of 0 or 1 being assigned for each item. The maximum score that might be assigned to a given case then is 6. If a given case has one missing data item, but receives a score of 5 on the five data items that are present, that case might be given a proportionate score of $5/5 \times 6 = 6$ on the index. The case receiving a score of 2 with only 4 data items available might be given a final score of $2/4 \times 6 = 3$. Where these computations result in fractional results, some method for rounding off should be employed to simplify the final index scores.

Finally, the researcher may be unwilling to utilize any of these methods for handling missing data, but he may require that all cases in the study be scored for purposes of later analysis. In such a situation, he may decide to assign scores for missing data on a random basis. For an item assigned the possible scores of 0, 1, and 2, the first case missing that item might receive a score of 1, the second a score of 0, the third a score of 2, and so forth. This method is the most conservative from a research analysis standpoint, as the researcher is "stacking the deck" against himself. If the resultant index proves a powerful tool in his analysis, he might conclude that it would have been even more powerful if all cases had complete data. (Of course, if his purpose is to show the index is *unrelated* to other variables, he has stacked the deck in his favor.)

The choice of a particular method to be used depends so much on the research situation as to preclude the suggestion of a single "best" method or a ranking of the several I have described. Excluding all cases with missing data can bias the representativeness of subsequent findings, while including such cases by assigning scores to missing data can influence the nature of the subsequent findings. The safest and most exemplary method would be to construct the index using alternative methods and see whether the same findings follow from each. Understanding one's data is the final goal of analysis anyway.

Index Validation

Up to this point, we have discussed all the steps involved in the selection and scoring of items that result in a composite index purporting to measure some variable. If each of the above discussed steps is carried out carefully, the likelihood of the index actually measuring the variable is enhanced. To prove success, however, there must be *validation* of the index. The basic logic of validation is the following. We assume that the composite index provides a measure of some variable; that is, the successive scores on the index arrange cases in a rank order in terms of that variable. An index of political conservatism rank-orders people in terms of their relative conservatism. If the index does this successfully, then persons scored as relatively conservative in terms of the index should appear relatively conservative in terms of all *other indications* of political orientations, such as questionnaire items. There are several methods for validating a composite index.

Item Analysis   The first step in index validation is an internal validation called *item analysis.* The researcher should examine the extent to which the composite index is related to (or predicts responses to) the items included in the index itself. If the index has been carefully constructed through the examination of bivariate and multivariate relationships among several items, this step should confirm the validity of that index. In a complex index containing many items, this step provides a more parsimonious test of the independent contribution of each item to the index. If a given item is found to be poorly related to the index, it may be assumed that other items in the index are washing out the contribution of that item. The item in question, then, contributes nothing to the index's power, and it should be excluded.

While item analysis is an important first test of the index's validity, it is scarcely a sufficient test. If the index adequately measures a given variable, it should successfully predict other indications of that variable. To test this, we must turn to items not included in the index.

External Validation Persons scored as politically conservative on an index should appear conservative in their responses to other items in the questionnaire. It must be realized, of course, that we are talking about *relative* conservatism, as we are unable to make a final absolute definition of what constitutes "conservatism" in any ultimate sense. However, those respondents scored as the most conservative in terms of the index should be the most conservative in answering other questions. Those scored as the least conservative on the index should be the least conservative on other items. Indeed, the ranking of groups of respondents on the index should predict the ranking of those groups in answering other questions dealing with political orientations.

In our example of the scientific orientation index, there were several questions in the questionnaire that offered the possibility of further validation. Table 15-4 presents some of those items.

Table 15-4. Validation of Scientific Orientations Index

	Index of Scientific Orientations			
	Low 0	1	2	High 3
Percent interested in attending scientific lectures at the medical school	34	42	46	65
Percent who say faculty members should have experience as medical researchers	43	60	65	89
Percent who would prefer faculty duties involving research activities only	0	8	32	66
Percent who engaged in research during preceding academic year	61	76	94	99

These items provide several lessons regarding index validation. First, we note that the index strongly predicts the responses to the validating items in the sense that the rank order of scientific responses among the four groups is the same as the rank order provided by the index itself. At the same time, each of the items gives a different *description* of scientific orientations overall. For example, the last validating item indicates that the great majority of *all* faculty were engaged in research during the preceding year. If this were the only indicator of scientific orientation, we would conclude that nearly all faculty were scientific. Nevertheless, those scored as more scientific in terms of the index are more likely to have engaged in research than those who were scored as relatively less scientific. The third validating item provides a different *descriptive* picture: Only a minority of the faculty overall say they would prefer duties limited exclusively to research. Nevertheless, the percentages giving this answer correspond to the scores assigned on the index.

Bad Index versus Bad Validators A dilemma that must be faced by nearly every index constructor is the apparent failure of external items to validate the index. If the internal item analysis shows inconsistent relationships between the items included in the index and the index itself, something is wrong with the index. But if the index fails to predict strongly the external validation items, the conclusion to be drawn is more ambiguous. The researcher must choose between two possibilities: (1) the index does not adequately measure the variable in question, or (2) the validation items do not adequately measure the variable and thereby do not provide a sufficient test of the index.

The researcher who has worked long and conscientiously on the construction of the index will find the second conclusion very compelling. Typically, he will feel he has included the best indicators of the variable in the index; the validating items are, therefore, second-rate indicators. Nevertheless, he should recognize that the index is purportedly a very powerful measure of the variable; thus, it should be somewhat related to any item that taps the variable even poorly.

When external validation fails, the researcher should reexamine the index before deciding that the validating items are insufficient. One method of doing this involves the examination of the relationships between the validating items and the individual items included in the index. If he discovers that some of the index items relate to the validators while others do not, this will improve his understanding of the index as it was initially constituted.

There is no cookbook solution to this dilemma; it is an agony the serious researcher must learn to survive. Ultimately, the wisdom of his decision regarding the index will be determined by its utility in his later analyses involving that index. Perhaps he will initially decide that the index is a good one and that the validators are defective, and later find that the variable in question (as measured by the index) is not related to other variables in the ways expected. At that point, he may return again to the composition of the index.

Likert Scaling

Earlier in this chapter, I defined a scale as a composite measure constructed on the basis of an *intensity structure* among items comprising the measure. In scale construction, response patterns across several items are scored, whereas in index construction, individual responses are scored and those independent scores are summed. By this definition, the measurement method developed by Rensis Likert, called Likert scaling, represents a more systematic and refined means for constructing indexes from questionnaire data. I shall discuss this method here, therefore, rather than in the sections on scaling to follow.

The term "Likert scale" is associated with a question format that is very frequently used in contemporary survey questionnaires. Basically, the respondent is presented with a *statement* in the questionnaire and is asked to indicate whether he "strongly agrees," "agrees," "disagrees," "strongly disagrees," or is "undecided." Modifications of the wording of the response categories (for example, "approve") may be used, of course.

The particular value of this format is the unambiguous *ordinality* of response categories. If respondents were permitted to volunteer or select such answers as "sort of agree," "pretty much agree," "really agree," and so forth, it would be impossible to judge the relative strength of agreement intended by the various respondents. The Likert format easily resolves this dilemma.

The Likert format also lends itself to a rather straightforward method of index construction. Whereas identical response categories will have been used for several items intended to measure a given variable, each such item might be scored in a uniform manner. With five response categories, scores of 0 to 4 or 1 to 5 might be assigned, taking the "direction" of the items into account (for example, assign a score of 5 to "strongly agree" for positive items and to "strongly disagree" for negative items). Each respondent would then be assigned an overall score representing the summation of the scores he received for his several responses to the individual items.

The Likert method is based on the assumption that the overall score based on responses to the many items seeming to reflect the variable under consideration provides a reasonably good measure of the variable. These overall scores are not the final product of index construction; rather, they are used for purposes of an *item analysis* resulting in the selection of the *best* items. Essentially, each of the individual items is correlated with the large, composite measure. Items that correlate highest with the composite measure are assumed to provide the best indicators of the variable, and only those items would be included in the index ultimately used for analyses of the variable.

It should be noted that the uniform scoring of Likert-item response categories assumes that each item has about the *same intensity* as the rest. This is the key respect in which the Likert method differs from scaling as the term is used in this book.

The reader should also realize that Likert-type items can be used in a variety of ways; the researcher is by no means bound to the method described above. Such items can be combined with other types of items in the construction of simple indexes; and, similarly, they can be used in the construction of scales. However, if all the items being considered for inclusion in a composite measure are in the Likert format, then the method described above should be considered.

Now we shall turn our attention from indexing methods to a selection of scaling techniques. While many methods are available to the survey researcher, we shall consider only Bogardus, Thurstone, and Guttman scales.

15.4
Scale Construction

Good indexes provide an ordinal ranking of cases on a given variable. All indexes are based on the assumption that this is true: a person with two indications of being scientifically inclined should be more scientific than the person with only one such indication. What an index may fail to take into account, however, is that not all indications of a variable are equally important. (Of course, the researcher may attempt to resolve this by weighting indicators differently.)

Scales offer more assurance of ordinality by tapping *structures* among the indicators. The several items going into a composite measure may have different *intensities* in terms of the variable. The three scaling procedures described below will illustrate the variety of techniques available.

Bogardus Social Distance Scale

A good example of a scale is the **Bogardus Social Distance Scale.** Let us suppose that the researcher is interested in the extent to which people are willing to associate with blacks. They might be asked the following questions:

1. Are you willing to permit blacks to live in your country?
2. Are you willing to permit blacks to live in your community?
3. Are you willing to permit blacks to live in your neighborhood?
4. Would you be willing to let a black live next door to you?
5. Would you let your child marry a black?

Note that the several questions increase in the closeness of contact which the respondent may or may not want with black Americans. Beginning with the original concern to measure willingness to associate with blacks, we have developed several questions indicating differing degrees of intensity on this variable.

The clear differences of intensity suggest a structure among the items. Presumably if a person is willing to accept a given kind of association, he would be willing to accept all those preceding it in the list—those with lesser intensities. For example, the person who is willing to permit blacks to live in his neighborhood will surely accept them in his community and his nation, but he may or may not be willing to accept them as his next-door neighbors or as relatives. This, then, is the logical structure of intensity inherent among the items.

Empirically, one would expect to find the largest number of people accepting co-citizenship and the fewest accepting intermarriage. In this sense, we speak of "easy items" (co-citizenship) and "hard items" (intermarriage). More people agree to the easy items than to the hard ones. With some inevitable exceptions, logic demands that once a person has refused a relationship presented in the scale, he will also refuse all those harder ones that follow it.

The Bogardus Social Distance Scale illustrates the important economy of scaling as a data-reduction device. By knowing *how many* relationships with blacks a given respondent will accept, we know *which* relationships were accepted. Thus, a single number can accurately summarize five or six data items without a loss of information.

Thurstone Scales

Often the inherent structure of the Bogardus Social Distance Scale is not appropriate to the variable being measured. Indeed, such a logical structure among several indicators is seldom apparent. **Thurstone scaling** is an attempt to develop a format for generating groups of indicators of a variable that have at least an *empirical* structure among them. One of the basic formats is that of "equal-appearing intervals."

A group of "judges" is given perhaps a hundred items felt to be indicators of a given variable. Each judge is then asked to estimate how strong an indicator of the variable each item is—by assigning scores of perhaps 1 to 13. If the variable were prejudice, for example, the judges would be asked to assign the score of 1 to the very weakest indicators of prejudice, the score of 13 to the strongest indicators, and intermediate scores to those felt to be somewhere in between.

Once the judges have all completed this task, the researcher examines the scores assigned to each item by all the judges to determine which items produced the greatest agreement among the judges. Those items on which the judges disagreed broadly would be rejected as ambiguous. Among those items producing general agreement in scoring, one or more would be selected to represent each scale score from 1 to 13.

The items selected in this manner might then be included in a survey questionnaire. Respondents who appeared prejudiced on those items representing a strength of 5 would then be expected to appear prejudiced on those having lesser strengths and, if some of those respondents did not appear prejudiced on the items with a strength of 6, it would be expected that they would also not appear prejudiced on those with greater strengths.

If the Thurstone Scale items were adequately developed and scored, the economy and effectiveness of data reduction inherent in the Bogardus Social Distance Scale would appear. A single score might be assigned to each respondent (the strength of the hardest item accepted), and that score would adequately represent the responses to several questionnaire items. And as is true of the Bogardus scale, a respondent scored 6 might be regarded as more prejudiced than one scored 5 or less.

Thurstone scaling is seldom if ever used in research today, primarily because of the tremendous expenditure of energies required for the "judging" of items. Several (perhaps 10 or 15) judges would have to spend a considerable amount of time for each of them to score the many initial items. Since the quality of their judgments would depend on their experience with and knowledge of the variable under consideration, the task might require professional researchers. Moreover, the meanings conveyed by the several items indicating a given variable tend to change over time. Thus an item having a given weight at one time might have quite a different weight later on.

For a Thurstone scale to be effective, it would have to be periodically updated.

Guttman Scaling

A very popular scaling technique used by researchers today is the one developed by Louis Guttman. Like both Bogardus and Thurstone scaling, **Guttman scaling** is based on the fact that some items under consideration may prove to be "harder" indicators of the variable than others. If such a structure appears in the data under examination, we may say that the items form a Guttman scale. One example should suffice to illustrate this.

In the earlier example of measuring scientific orientations among medical school faculty members, we recall that a simple index was constructed. As we shall see shortly, however, the three items included in the index essentially form a Guttman scale. This possibility first appears when we look for relatively "hard" and "easy" indicators of scientific orientations.

The item asking respondents whether they could best serve as practicing physicians or as medical researchers is the hardest of the three: only about one-third would be judged scientific if this were the single indicator of the variable. If the item concerning ultimate medical interests (total patient management versus basic mechanisms) were used as the only indicator, almost two-thirds would be judged scientific. Reading preferences (effectiveness of treatments versus the underlying rationales) is the easiest of the three items: about 80 percent of the respondents would be judged as scientific in terms of this item.

Table 15-5. Scaling Scientific Orientations

	Reading Preference	Ultimate Interests	Teaching Role	Number of Cases
	+	+	+	116
Scale Types:	+	+	−	127
Total = 383	+	−	−	92
	−	−	−	48
	−	+	−	18
Mixed Types:	+	−	+	14
Total = 44	−	−	+	5
	−	+	+	7

To determine whether a scale structure exists among the responses to all three items, we must examine the several possible response patterns given to all three items simultaneously. In Table 15-5, all the possible patterns have been presented in a schematic form. For each of the three items, pluses and minuses have been used to indicate the scientific and nonscientific responses, respectively. (A plus indicates a scientific response, while a minus indicates a nonscientific response.)

The first four response patterns in the table comprise what we would call the *scale types:* those patterns that form a scalar structure. Following those respondents who selected all three scientific responses (line 1), we see (line 2) that those with only two scientific responses have chosen the two easier ones; those with only one such response (line 3) chose the easiest of the three. And finally, there are those respondents who selected none of the scientific responses (line 4).

The second part of the table presents those response patterns that violate the scalar structure of the items. The most radical departures from the scalar structure are the last two response patterns: those who accepted only the hardest item, and those who rejected only the easiest one.

The final column in the table indicates the number of survey respondents who gave each of the response patterns. It is immediately apparent that the great majority (90 percent) of the respondents fit into one of the scale types. The presence of mixed types, however, indicates that the items do not form a perfect Guttman scale.

We should recall at this point that one of the chief functions of scaling is efficient data reduction. Scales provide a technique for presenting data in a summary form while maintaining as much of the original information as possible.

When the scientific orientation items were formed into an index in our earlier discussion, respondents were given one point on the index for each scientific response they gave. If these same three items were scored as a Guttman scale, some respondents would receive different scores than were received on the index. Respondents would be assigned those scale scores that would permit the most accurate reproduction of their original responses to all three items.

Respondents fitting into the scale types would receive the same scores as were assigned in the index construction. Persons selecting all three scientific responses would still be scored 3. Note that if we were told a given respondent in this group received a score of 3, we could predict accurately that he selected all three scientific responses. For persons in the second row of the table, the assignment of the scale score of 2 would lead us accurately to predict scientific responses to the two easier items and a nonscientific response to the hardest. In each of the four scale types we could predict accurately all the actual responses given by all the respondents.

The mixed types in the table present a problem, however. The first mixed type (− + −) was scored 1 on the index to indicate only one scientific response. If 1 were assigned as a scale score, however, we would predict that all respondents in this group had chosen only the easiest item (+ − −), thereby making two errors for each such respondent. Scale scores are assigned, therefore, with the aim of minimizing the errors that would be made in reconstructing the original responses given. Table 15-6 illustrates the index and scale scores that would be assigned to each of the response patterns in our example.

As mentioned above, the original index scoring for the four scale types would be maintained in the construction of a Guttman scale, and no errors would be made in reproducing the responses given to all three items. The mixed types would be scored differently, however, in an attempt to reduce errors. Note, however, that one error is made for each of the

Table 15-6. Index and Scale Scores

	Response Patterns			Number of Cards	Index Scores	Scale Scores*	Total Scale Errors
Scale Types:	+	+	+	116	3	3	0
	+	+	−	127	2	2	0
	+	−	−	92	1	1	0
	−	−	−	48	0	0	0
Mixed Types:	−	+	−	18	1	2	18
	+	−	+	14	2	3	14
	−	−	+	5	1	0	5
	−	+	+	7	2	3	7

* This table presents one common method for scoring "mixed types," but the reader should be advised that other methods are also used.

respondents in the mixed types. In the first mixed type we would predict erroneously a scientific response to the easiest item for each of the 18 respondents in this group, making a total of 18 errors.

The extent to which a set of empirical responses form a Guttman scale is determined in terms of the accuracy with which the original responses can be reconstructed from the scale scores. For each of the 427 respondents in this example, we will predict three questionnaire responses, for a total of 1,281 predictions. Table 15-6 indicates that we will make 44 errors using the scale scores assigned. The percentage of *correct* predictions is called the *coefficient of reproducibility:* the percentage of "reproducible" responses. In the present example, the coefficient of reproducibility is 1,237/1,281 or 96.6 percent.

Except for the case of perfect (100 percent) reproducibility, there is no way of saying that a set of items does or does not form a Guttman scale in any absolute sense. Virtually all sets of such items *approximate* a scale. As a rule of thumb, however, coefficients of 90 percent or 95 percent are the commonly used standards in this regard. If the observed reproducibility exceeds the level set by the researcher, he will probably decide to score and use the items as a scale.[2]

One concluding remark should be made with regard to Guttman scaling: it is based on the structure observed among the *actual data under examination.* This is an important point that is often misunderstood by researchers. It does not make sense to say that a set of questionnaire items (perhaps developed and used by a previous researcher) constitutes a Guttman scale. Rather, we can say only that they form a scale within a given body of data being analyzed. Scalability, then, is a sample-dependent,

---

2. The decision as to criteria in this regard is, of course, arbitrary. Moreover, a high degree of reproducibility does not insure that the scale constructed in fact measures the concept under consideration, although it increases confidence that all the component items measure the same thing. Finally, the reader should be advised that a high coefficient of reproducibility is more likely when few items are involved.

empirical question. While a set of items may form a Guttman scale among one sample of survey respondents, for example, there is no guarantee that they will form such a scale among another sample. In this sense, then, a set of questionnaire items in and of themselves never form a scale, but a set of empirical observations may.

15.5
Typologies

We shall conclude this chapter with a short discussion of typology construction and analysis. Recall that indexes and scales are constructed to provide ordinal measures of given variables. We attempt to assign index or scale scores to cases in such a way as to indicate a rising degree of prejudice, religiosity, conservatism, and so forth. In these regards, we are dealing with single dimensions.

Often, however, the researcher wishes to summarize the intersection of two or more dimensions. He may, for example, wish to examine political orientations separately in terms of domestic issues and foreign policy. The four-fold presentation in Table 15-7 describes such a typology.

Table 15-7. A Political Typology of Newspapers

Domestic Policy	Foreign Policy	
	Conservative	Liberal
Conservative	A	B
Liberal	C	D

Newspapers in cell A of the table are conservative on both foreign policy and domestic policy; those in cell D are liberal on both. Those in cells B and C are conservative on one and liberal on the other. (For purposes of analysis, each of the cell types might be represented by a data card punch (A = 1, B = 2, C = 3, D = 4) and could be easily manipulated in examining the typology's relationship to other variables.)

Frequently, the researcher arrives at a typology in the course of his attempt to construct an index or scale. The items that he felt represented a single variable appear to represent two. In the present example, the researcher may have been attempting to construct a single index of political orientations but discovered—empirically—that foreign and domestic politics had to be kept separate.

In any event, the researcher should be warned against a difficulty inherent in typological analysis. Whenever the typology is used as the *independent variable,* there will probably be no problem. In the example above, the researcher might compute and present the percentages of newspapers in each cell that normally endorse Democratic candidates; he could then easily examine the effects of both foreign and domestic policies on political endorsements.

It is extremely difficult, however, to analyze a typology as a *dependent variable*. If the researcher wants to discover why newspapers fall into the different cells of the typology, he is in trouble. This becomes apparent when we consider the ways in which he might construct and read his tables. Assume, for example, that he wants to examine the effects of community size on political policies. With a single dimension, he could easily determine the percentages of rural and urban newspapers that were scored conservative and liberal on his index or scale. With a typology, however, he would have to present the distribution of the urban newspapers in his sample among types A, B, C, and D. Then he would repeat the procedure for the rural ones in the sample and compare the two distributions. Let us suppose that 80 percent of the rural newspapers are scored as type A (conservative on both dimensions) as compared with 30 percent of the urban ones. Moreover, suppose that only 5 percent of the rural newspapers are scored as type B (conservative only on domestic issues) compared with 40 percent of the urban ones. It would be incorrect to conclude from an examination of type B that urban newspapers are more conservative on domestic issues than rural ones, since 85 percent of the rural newspapers, compared with 70 percent of the urban ones, have this characteristic. The relative sparsity of rural newspapers in type B is due to their concentration in type A. It should be apparent that an interpretation of such data would be very difficult in anything other than description.

In reality, the researcher would probably examine two such dimensions separately, especially if the dependent variable has more categories of responses than did the example given.

The reader should not think that typologies should always be avoided in social research; often they provide the most appropriate device for understanding the data. The reader should be warned, however, against the special difficulties involved in using typologies as dependent variables.

15.6
Summary

Chapter 15 returns to the issue of measurement, discussed earlier in Chapters 4 and 5. Although the pre-data-collection efforts to conceptualize and operationalize are aimed at effective measurement, we have seen that the researcher can refine his measurements during the analysis phase as well. This chapter has dealt with different types of composite measures: indexes, scales, and typologies.

The chapter began with an acknowledgment that most social science concepts cannot be satisfactorily measured on the basis of single observations. There is no single piece of information that can tell a person's socioeconomic status to the satisfaction of all social scientists. Any single indicator, such as income, would probably "misrepresent" the status of some people. Composite measures, then, are an answer to this problem. By measuring concepts on the basis of several different indicators, we gain confidence and consensus in the validity of our ultimate characterization of the people or other units of analysis we are studying.

Both indexes and scales are intended as ordinal measures. As we have seen, the manner in which scales are constructed provides us with a greater assurance of ordinality, since scales take advantage of logical or empirical structures that may exist among the individual indicators of a variable. Since relatively less has been written previously about the methods of index construction, however, the bulk of this chapter was addressed to that theme. Scale construction was given a somewhat briefer treatment.

Index construction begins with the initial selection of individual items or indicators that might be included in the index. This is accomplished on the basis of *face validity:* the extent to which the items *seem* to be valid indicators of the variable under consideration. Next, the bivariate relationships among the items selected are examined. If two items are, in fact, indicators of the same variable, then they should be related empirically to one another.

The examination of bivariate relationships among the items should provide a check on their validity as measures of the variable. Any item that appears unrelated to any of the others probably is not measuring the variable in question. On the other hand, if two items are *very* strongly related to each other, including both in the index would be redundant. The interpretation of bivariate relationships, then, should reduce the number of items considered for inclusion in the index.

The next step in index construction is the examination of multivariate relationships. The nature of this step will depend on the number of items still under consideration for inclusion in the index and the number desired ultimately. All the possible multivariate relationships should be examined. The goal of this step is the discovery of a group of items that demonstrate a cumulative set of interrelationships with one another: each of the items should contribute independently to the interrelationships.

Once the items have been selected, scores should be assigned to the different attributes of the selected items. The discussion of this step presented various scoring methods and several options for handling missing data.

The final step in index construction is *index validation*. If the index is a valid measure of the variable under consideration, it should predict other items in the data files. The discussion of this process illustrated assorted methods of index validation.

The discussion of scale construction began with a brief consideration of the *Bogardus Social Distance Scale,* an excellent illustration of the logical structure that may exist among indicators of a variable. We saw that it is sometimes possible to reduce the answers to several questions to a single number that would be sufficient for us to reproduce all the details of the original data. The Bogardus Social Distance Scale, then, is an efficient data-reduction device.

Next, the chapter considered the *Thurstone Scale*. We saw that this technique could yield excellent measures of variables, but a number of practical problems have limited its use in social research.

Guttman Scaling is probably the most popular scaling method used by social researchers today. It is based on the discovery of empirical structures among several indicators of a given variable. Some indicators reflect a greater "intensity" on the variable than others, and cases having the attributes that reflect a great intensity usually also have the attributes that reflect a lesser intensity. Thus, it is often possible to represent a set of attributes by a single scale score that would permit the researcher to reproduce most of the original attributes. The extent to which the original data can be reproduced from a knowledge of the scale scores may be computed as a *coefficient of reproducibility.*

The chapter closed with a brief discussion of typologies in social research. As we saw, typologies are typically a nominal rather than ordinal measure. Thus, they are especially troublesome when used as dependent variables, although they may be effectively used as independent variables.

15.7
Main Points

1. Single indicators of variables seldom have sufficiently clear validity to warrant their use.

2. Composite measures, such as scales and indexes, are a solution to this problem, by including several indicators of a variable in one summary measure.

3. Both scales and indexes are intended as ordinal measures of variables, though scales typically satisfy this goal better than indexes.

4. Indexes are based on the simple cumulation of indicators of a variable.

5. Scales take advantage of any logical or empirical intensity structures that exist among the different indicators of a variable.

6. Face validity is the first criterion for the selection of indicators to be included in a composite measure; the term means that an indicator seems, on face value, to provide some measure of the variable.

7. If different items are indeed indicators of the same variable, then they should be related empirically to one another. If, for example, frequency of church attendance and frequency of prayer are both indicators of religiosity, then those people who attend church frequently should be found to pray more than those who attend church less frequently.

8. Once an index or a scale has been constructed, it is essential that it be validated. "Internal validation" refers to the relationships between individual items included in the composite measure and the measure itself. "External validation" refers to the relationships between the composite measure and other indicators of the variable—indicators *not* included in the measure.

9. The *Bogardus Social Distance Scale* is a device for measuring the varying degrees to which a person would be willing to associate with a given class of people, such as an ethnic minority. Subjects are asked to

indicate whether or not they would be willing to accept different kinds of association. The several responses produced by these questions can be adequately summarized by a single score, representing the "closest" association that is acceptable, since those willing to accept a given association also would be willing to accept more distant ones.

10. *Thurstone Scaling* is a little-used technique for creating indicators of variables that have a clear intensity structure among them. Judges determine the intensities of different indicators.

11. *Likert Scaling* is a measurement technique based on the use of standardized response categories (e.g., strongly agree, agree, disagree, strongly disagree) for several questionnaire items. While Likert "scaling" is not often used in social research today, the Likert format for questionnaire items is very popular and extremely useful. Likert-format items may be used appropriately in the construction of either indexes or scales.

12. *Guttman Scaling* is probably the most popular scaling technique in social research today. It is a method of discovering and utilizing the empirical "intensity" structure among several indicators of a given variable.

13. A *coefficient of reproducibility* is a measure of the extent to which all the particular responses given to the individual items included in a scale can be reproduced from the scale score alone.

14. A *typology* is a nominal composite measure often used in social research. Typologies may be used effectively as independent variables, but interpretation is difficult when they are used as dependent variables.

15.8
Annotated Bibliography

Glock, Charles, Ringer, Benjamin, and Babbie, Earl, *To Comfort and to Challenge: A Dilemma of the Contemporary Church* (Berkeley: University of California Press, 1967). An empirical study illustrating composite measures. Since the construction of scales and indexes can be most fully grasped through concrete examples, this might be a useful study to examine. The authors utilize a variety of different composite measures, and they are relatively clear about the methods used in constructing them.

Lazarsfeld, Paul, and Rosenberg, Morris (eds.), *The Language of Social Research* (New York: Free Press, 1955), especially Section I. An excellent collection of conceptual discussions and concrete illustrations. The construction of composite measures is presented within the more general area of conceptualization and measurement.

Miller, Delbert, *Handbook of Research Design and Social Measurement* (New York: David McKay, 1970). An excellent compilation of frequently used and semi-standardized scales. The many illustrations reported in Part 4 of the Miller book may be directly adaptable to studies or at least suggestive of modified measures. Studying the several different illustrations, moreover, may also give a better understanding of the logic of composite measures in general.

Oppenheim, A. N., *Questionnaire Design and Attitude Measurement* (New York: Basic Books, 1966). An excellent presentation on composite measures, with special reference to questionnaires. Although Oppenheim says little about index construction, he gives an excellent presentation of the logic and the skills of scale construction—the kinds of scales discussed in Chapter 15 of the present book and many not discussed here.

16
The Logic of Causation

16.1
Introduction

Implicit in much of what has been said in prior chapters of this book are the notions of *cause* and *effect*. One of the chief goals of the scientist, social or other, is to explain things: to explain why things are the way they are. Typically, we do this by specifying the causes for the way things are: some things are caused by other things.

The general notion of *causation* is at once very simple and very complex. I imagine, on the one hand, that I could have ignored the issue altogether in this book—simply using the terms "cause" and "effect"—and most readers would have had little difficulty understanding the use of the terms. On the other hand, an adequate discourse on causation would require a whole book in its own right, or a series of books. However, let me attempt a middle-ground treatment of the subject, providing something more than a common-sense perspective on causation without attempting to be definitive.

Chapter 16 will begin with a review and an expansion of the previously mentioned subject of *determinism* in social science. Having done that, we shall return briefly to the topic of deductive and inductive logic. Next we shall consider some appropriate and inappropriate criteria for causality. The chapter will then conclude with a discussion of the links between measurement and association.

16.2
Determinism and Social Science

Chapters 1 and 2 of this book touched briefly on the deterministic perspective of science and of social science. Recall in particular that this perspective was juxtaposed to the *free-will* image of man and his behavior. The latter perspective suggests that each person is the master of his own destiny, the captain of his fate. Faced with alternative, possible actions, the free-will image of man suggests that a person makes an individual choice reflecting his own volition. The deterministic perspective, on the other hand, suggests that such choices are the result of factors over which the individual has no control.

Taken to its extreme, the deterministic perspective suggests there is no free choice whatever. Every action we might observe is totally determined by the whole collection of prior actions, events, and situations. Given that whole collection of prior actions, events, and situations, no action other than the observed one would be possible. We might illustrate this perspective through a dialogue such as the following.

A Dialogue on Voting

Let's consider the following hypothetical dialogue between a student who has said that he voted in the 1972 presidential election and a deterministic questioner.

Q: For whom did you vote in the 1972 presidential election?
A: I voted for George McGovern.
Q: Why did you vote for George McGovern?
A: I thought he was the best man for the job.
Q: Can you tell me more specifically why? Why did you think he was the best man for the job?
A: I was opposed to the war in Vietnam, and he seemed the most likely to end the war.
Q: Fine. What other reasons did you have?
A: I am concerned about social problems such as poverty and racial discrimination, and I thought he would do more to solve those problems.
Q: Fine. What other reasons did you have?
A: He seemed more concerned about environmental pollution and the depletion of natural resources, and these issues are important to me.
Q: Fine. What other reasons did you have for voting for George McGovern?
A: I'm a student, and he seemed more sensitive to the problems of students.
Q: I get that. Why else did you vote for McGovern?
A: Well, I consider myself generally to be a Democrat rather than a Republican, since I think Democrats have a better political philosophy on the whole.
Q: Fine. What other reasons did you have?
A: I consider myself a liberal, and McGovern was more liberal than Nixon.
Q: Fine. What other reasons did you have for voting for George McGovern?
A: Well, as a black American, I felt that McGovern would be more sensitive to the needs of my people.
Q: I can understand that. Why else did you vote for McGovern?
A: George is a personal friend of my father's from years back, and our family thinks highly of him as a human being.
Q: Fine. Why else did you vote for him?
A: I just didn't trust Nixon.

Q: Fine. Why else did you vote for McGovern?

A: I discussed the campaign with my friends and all of them agreed that McGovern was the best man.

Q: Fine. Why else did you vote for McGovern?

A: I can't think of any other reasons. What more do you want from me, anyway?

Q: I can understand why any black, liberal, Democratic student who believed McGovern to be more sensitive to the problems of blacks and of students, someone who was opposed to the Vietnam War and felt McGovern was more likely to end it, who was concerned about poverty and discrimination and believed McGovern the more capable of solving those problems, who was concerned about environmental pollution and the depletion of resources and believed McGovern more capable of handling those problems, someone who considered McGovern a personal friend and thought highly of him as a human being, who didn't trust Nixon, and whose friends were all voting for McGovern—*anyone* with all of those considerations and who felt, in general, that McGovern was the best man for the job would have voted for McGovern. Everyone exactly like that would have voted for McGovern. I want to know why *you* voted for McGovern.

I have called the preceding dialogue "hypothetical," because I doubt that anyone would stand still for that kind of cross-examination. If a real dialogue had lasted that long, however, what would be the answer to the final question? Why did the student being questioned—as an idiosyncratic person, leaving aside the considerations he shared with other people—vote for McGovern? As the questioner points out, *anyone* with exactly the same concerns, characteristics, and considerations as the student would have voted as the student did. Yet, sharing all of those things in common hardly makes all such people the same individual—they remain separate individuals who differ in other ways. But, can we say each of them made a personal, individual choice—separate from the considerations they shared in common —to vote for McGovern? The deterministic posture suggests that their decisions and their actions were based *precisely* on their common considerations rather than on whatever was left over when those considerations were taken out of the equation.

Imagine yourself under a cross-examination similar to the one illustrated above. Substitute the presidential candidate of your choice, of course, or examine any other action you have taken in the past. Ask yourself for all the characteristics and *considerations* that went into your decision to take the action in question. Once you have exhausted them all, ask yourself whether you can imagine anyone else with exactly those same characteristics and considerations would have made a different decision. Then ask yourself who *you* are except the sum of all those considerations. Isn't any action you take simply a result of such considerations?

Realize further that each of your considerations or characteristics— being liberal or being conservative—is simply a result of other, prior considerations. Seriously ask yourself to enumerate all the reasons why you are a liberal or a conservative—or why you consider yourself a middle-of-the-road moderate, for that matter. Eventually, it will appear that the *real you* is simply a collection of considerations that, in turn, are the products of prior considerations.

Despite the tone of the foregoing paragraphs, this chapter is not intended as an exercise in psychotherapy or in self-discovery. Nevertheless, a serious effort at understanding who you are in this fashion will help you get in touch with the deterministic perspective, which lies at the base of scientific explanation. The extreme deterministic perspective suggests that everything —*everything*—is the inevitable result of prior causes that, in turn, are the inevitable results of other prior causes.

I realize that personally experiencing this perspective may be rather unsettling if you have not seriously confronted it before. Let me hasten to add, therefore, that few if any among even the most deterministic scientists fully or consciously employ this perspective in their daily lives. All of us tend to act as though we possessed and exercised free will. Nevertheless, we shift gears somewhat when we engage in scientific—and sometimes in nonscientific— explanation. Let's examine two importantly different models used in that regard.

Idiographic and Nomothetic Models of Explanation

The preceding dialogue concerning the hypothetical student's decision to vote for McGovern might be regarded as an *idiographic model of explanation,* one that explains through the enumeration of the very many, seemingly idiosyncratic, considerations that lie behind a given action. Of course, we seldom go as far as the illustration did in the search for causes, and we surely never truly exhaust them in a given case. Nevertheless, it is important to realize that the idiographic model is employed frequently and in many different contexts.

Traditional historians, for example, tend to use the idiographic model, enumerating all the special causes of the French Revolution, or of the United States' decision to enter World War II. Clinical psychologists may tend to employ this model in seeking an explanation for the aberrant behavior of a patient. A criminal court, in response to a plea of extenuating circumstances, may seek to examine all the various considerations that have resulted in the crime in question. And most of us employ the idiographic model in attempting to understand the actions of others around us in everyday life.

Scientists, including social scientists, often employ a different model, which we will call the *nomothetic model of explanation.* This latter model does not involve an exhaustive enumeration of all the considerations that result in a *particular* action or event. Rather, it is a consciously parsimonious model that seeks to discover those considerations that are most important in explaining general classes of actions or events. To further distinguish these two models of explanation, let's return for a moment to the illustration of the student who voted for McGovern.

The idiographic model of explanation would involve—as in the illustration—an enumeration of the many considerations that, put together, provide a *complete* explanation of why the *particular* student voted the way he did. The nomothetic model of explanation, on the other hand, would involve the isolation of those *relatively few* considerations that would provide a *partial* explanation for the voting behavior of *many* people or of all people. For example, we might well imagine that political orientations—liberal or conservative—would be a consideration of great *general* importance in determining the voting behavior of the electorate as a whole. Most of those sharing the attribute "liberal" probably voted for McGovern, while most of those sharing the attribute "conservative" probably voted for Nixon. Realize that this single consideration would not provide a complete explanation for all voting behavior. Some liberals voted for Nixon; some conservatives voted for McGovern. The goal of the nomothetic model of explanation is to provide the greatest amount of explanation with the fewest number of causal variables: to uncover *general* patterns of cause and effect.

The nomothetic model of explanation is inevitably *probabilistic* in its approach to causation. The specification of a few considerations seldom if ever provides complete explanation. (We might discover, of course, that everyone who believed Nixon was the best man voted for him, but this would not be a very satisfying explanation.) In the best of all practical worlds, the nomothetic model indicates there is a very high (or very low) probability or likelihood that a given action will occur whenever a limited number of specified considerations are present. Adding more, specified considerations to the equation typically increases the degree of explanation, and the inherent parsimony of the model calls for a balancing of a high degree of explanation with a small number of considerations being specified.

The Problem of Dehumanization

As acknowledged earlier in this book, social scientists sometimes are criticized for *dehumanizing* the people they study. This charge is lodged specifically against the nomothetic model of explanation; the severity of the charge is increased when social scientists analyze matters of great human concern. Religious people, for example, are likely to feel robbed of their human individuality when a social scientist reports that their religiosity is largely a function of their sex, age, marital status, and social class. Any religious person will quickly report that there is much more than that to the strength of his convictions. And indeed there is, as the use of the idiographic model in the case of any individual person would reveal. Is the idiographic model any less *dehumanizing* than the nomothetic, however?

If everything—including being religious—is a product of prior considerations, is it any more dehumanizing to seek partial but general explanations utilizing only a few of those considerations than to seek total explanation utilizing them all? I suspect the true source of concern, underlying the charges of dehumanization, is based on the more direct confrontation with determinism that the nomothetic model represents. It is important to realize, however, that a careful listing of all the private individual reasons for being religious, or for voting for Candidate X, or any other action, involves the acknowledgment of a deterministic perspective: one that is logically no different from the deterministic perspective that permits us to specify four variables that are the most important in causing religiosity.

16.3
Criteria for Causality

None of the preceding provides much in the way of practical guidance in the discovery of causal relationships in scientific research. This section will discuss three specific criteria for causality as suggested by Paul Lazarsfeld. The actual use of these criteria in research practice will be illustrated in the following chapter on the *elaboration model*.

The first requirement in a causal relationship between two variables is that *the cause precede the effect in time*. It makes no sense, in science, to imagine something being caused by something else that happened later on. A bullet leaving the muzzle of a gun does not cause the gunpowder to explode; it works the other way around.

As simple and obvious as this criterion may seem, we will discover endless problems in this regard in the analysis of social science data. Often, the time order connecting two variables is simply unclear. Which comes first: authoritarianism or prejudice? Even when the time order seems essentially clear, exceptions can often be found. For example, we would normally assume that the educational level of parents would be a cause of the educational level of their children. Yet, some parents may return to school as a result of the advanced education of their own children.

The second requirement in a causal relationship is that the two variables be empirically correlated with one another. It would make no sense to say that exploding gunpowder causes bullets to leave the muzzles of guns if, in observed reality, the bullets did not come out after the gunpowder exploded.

Again, social science research experiences difficulties in regard to this seemingly obvious requirement. In the probabilistic world of nomothetic models of explanation at least, there are few perfect correlations. We are forced to ask, therefore, how great the empirical relationship must be for it to be considered causal.

The third requirement is that the observed empirical relationship cannot be "explained away" as being due to the influence of some third variable that causes both of them. For example, I may observe that my left knee generally aches just before it rains, but this does not mean that my joints affect the weather. A third variable, relative humidity, is the cause of both my aching knee and the rain. (This requirement for causality will be one of the main topics of discussion in Chapter 17. The terms "spuriousness" and "explanation" will be used in that context.)

From the perspective of this textbook, we shall consider two variables to be causally related—that is, one causes the other—if (a) the cause precedes the effect in time, (b) there is an empirical correlation between them, and (c) the relationship is not found to be the result of the effects of some third variable on each of the two initially observed. Any relationship satisfying all these criteria will be regarded as causal, and these are the only criteria.

To emphasize this last point more strongly, it will be useful to examine briefly some other criteria sometimes employed, especially by nonscientists, that will be regarded as inappropriate. In this discussion, I am indebted to Travis Hirschi and Hanan Selvin for an excellent article on this subject and its subsequent expansion in the context of their book on *Delinquency Research*.[1]

Necessary and Sufficient Causes

First, to review a point made earlier in the chapter, a *perfect* correlation between variables is *not* a criterion of causality in social science research (or in science generally for that matter). Put another way, exceptions, although they do not prove the rule, do not necessarily deny the rule either. In probabilistic models, there are almost always exceptions to the posited relationship. If a few liberals voted for Nixon and a few conservatives voted for McGovern, that would not deny the general causal relationship between political orientations and voting in the election.

Within this probabilistic model, it is useful to distinguish two types of causes: *necessary* and *sufficient* causes. A necessary cause represents a condition that must be present for the effect to follow. For example, it is necessary for a person to be a woman in order to become pregnant, even though not all women do become pregnant. A sufficient cause, on the other hand, represents a condition which, if it is present, inevitably results in the effect. Enlisting in the army is a sufficient cause for being given a uniform, even though there are other ways of acquiring uniforms.

The discovery of a *necessary and sufficient cause* is, of course, the most satisfying outcome in research. If cancer were the effect under examination, it would be nice to discover a single condition that (a) had to be present for cancer to develop and (b) always resulted in cancer. In such a case, you would surely feel that you knew precisely what caused cancer. Unfortunately, we seldom discover causes that are both necessary and sufficient, nor, in practice, are the causes perfectly necessary or perfectly sufficient. From the standpoint of this textbook, *either* necessary *or* sufficient causes—even imperfect ones—can be the basis for a causal relationship.

I suspect that many readers will have greater difficulty accepting the notion of a necessary cause than of a sufficient one. Even in the two examples given at the outset of this discussion, it is no doubt more comfortable to say that enlisting in the Army causes you to be given a uniform than to say that being a woman causes you to become pregnant. Everyone

---

1. Travis Hirschi and Hanan Selvin, *Delinquency Research: An Appraisal of Analytic Methods* (New York: Free Press, 1967). See especially pp. 114–136. The original article appeared in *Social Problems*, 13, 1966, pp. 254–268.

who enlists is given a uniform, but not every woman becomes pregnant. The difficulty in accepting necessary causes is usually even greater when a majority of those *caused* to do something do not do it. Let's postulate, for example, that being an anti-Semite is a necessary cause of murdering Jews in the streets. Non-anti-Semites don't do it. This causal relationship is not at all diminished by the fact that the vast majority of anti-Semites do not murder Jews in the streets.

16.4
Linking Measurement and Association

As we have seen in Section 16.3, one of the key elements in the determination of causation in science is an empirical association between the "cause" and the "effect." All too often, however, the process of *measuring* variables is seen as separate from that of determining the *associations* between variables. This view is, I think, incorrect, or at the very least, misleading.

This section addresses the intimate links between measurement and association within the context of causal inference. To do this, we shall review the traditional, deductive model of science, presenting it graphically. Then we shall examine some alternative, more appropriate, images of science in practice. In this latter regard, we shall consider the notions of "the interchangeability of indexes" and "fixed-point analysis."

The Traditional Deductive Model

The traditional perspective on the scientific method is based on a set of serial steps, which scientists are believed to follow in their work. These steps may be summarized as follows:

1. Theory construction
2. Derivation of theoretical hypotheses
3. Operationalization of concepts
4. Collection of empirical data
5. Empirical testing of hypotheses

Let's illustrate this view of the scientific research process with an example.

Theory Construction   Faced with an aspect of the natural or social world that interests him, the scientist is believed to create an abstract deductive theory to describe it. This is presumably a purely logical exercise. Let us assume for the moment that a social scientist is interested in deviant behavior. He presumably constructs—on the basis of existing sociological theory—a theory of deviant behavior. Among other things, this theory includes a variety of concepts relevant to the causes of deviant behavior.

Derivation of Theoretical Hypotheses On the basis of his total theory of deviant behavior, the scientist presumably derives hypotheses relating to the various concepts comprising his theory. This, too, is a purely logical procedure. Following the above example, let us suppose that the scientist logically derives the hypothesis that juvenile delinquency is a function of supervision: as supervision increases, juvenile delinquency decreases.

Operationalization of Concepts The next step in the traditional view of the scientific method is the specification of empirical indicators to represent the theoretical concepts. Although theoretical concepts must be somewhat abstract and perhaps vague, the empirical indicators must be precise and specific. Thus, in our example, the scientist might operationalize the concept "juvenile" as anyone under 18 years of age; "delinquency" might be operationalized as being arrested for a criminal act; and "supervision" might be operationalized as the presence of a nonworking adult in the home.

The effect of operationalization is to convert the theoretical hypothesis into an empirical one. In the present case, the empirical hypothesis would be: among persons under 18 years of age, those living in homes with a nonworking adult will be less likely to be arrested for a criminal act than will those without a nonworking adult in the home.

Collection of Empirical Data Based on the operationalization of theoretical concepts, the scientist then presumably collects data relating to the empirical indicators. In the present example, he might conduct a survey of persons under 18 years of age. Among other things, the survey questionnaire would ask of each whether the person lived in a home with a nonworking adult and whether the person had ever been arrested for a criminal act.

Empirical Testing of Hypotheses Once the data have been collected, the final step is the statistical testing of the hypothesis. The scientist determines, empirically, whether those juveniles with nonworking adults in the home are less likely to have been arrested for criminal acts than those lacking nonworking adults. The confirmation or disconfirmation of the empirical hypothesis is then used for purposes of accepting or rejecting the theoretical hypothesis.

Figure 16-1 depicts the traditional image of science in schematic form. We note that the scientist begins with a particular interest about the world, creates a general theory about it, and uses that deductive theory to generate a hypothesis regarding the association between two variables. This hypothesis is represented in the form: $Y = f(X)$. This expression would be read "Y is a function of X," meaning that values of Y are determined or caused by values of X. In our example, delinquency (Y) is a function of supervision (X).

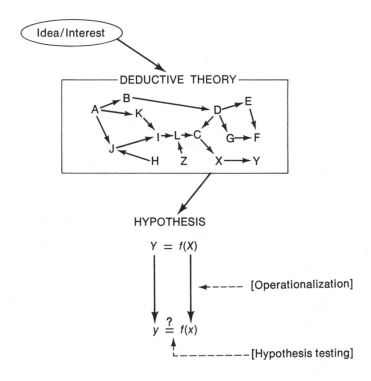

Figure 16-1. The Traditional Image of Science

    Next the scientist operationalizes the two variables by specifying empirical measurements to represent them in the real world. He collects data relevant to such measurements and, finally, tests the expected relationship empirically.

    The preceding description of the traditional deductive model of science tends to make scientific research seem a relatively routine activity. All the scientist must do is to move faithfully through steps 1 to 5 and he will have discovered truth.

    As pointed out elsewhere in this book, scientific research is not that neat. The empirical world that the scientist studies is not that neat. There are two basic problems that prevent the easy application of this deductive model in practice.

First, theoretical concepts seldom if ever permit unambiguous operationalization. Whereas concepts are abstract and general, every specification of empirical indicators must be an approximation. In the previous example, it is unlikely that the general concept of "supervision" is adequately represented by the presence of a nonworking adult in the home. The presence of such an adult does not assure supervision of the juvenile; in some homes lacking such an adult, other arrangements may be made for the juvenile's supervision.

Being arrested for a criminal act cannot be equated with the abstract concept "delinquency." Some juveniles may engage in delinquent behavior without being arrested. Others may be arrested falsely. Moreover, the specification of "juvenile" as a person under 18 years of age is an arbitrary one. Other specifications might have been made, and probably none would be unambiguously correct.

Furthermore, it is not sufficient to argue that the scientist should have specified "better" indicators of his concepts. The key point here is that there are almost never perfect indicators of theoretical concepts. Thus, every empirical indicator has some defects; all could be improved upon, and the search for better indicators is an endless one.

Second, the empirical associations between variables are almost never perfect. In the previous example, if all juveniles with nonworking adults in the home had never been arrested and all those without such adults had been arrested, we might conclude that the hypothesis had been confirmed. Or if both groups had exactly the same arrest records, we might conclude that the hypothesis had been rejected. Neither eventuality is likely in practice, however. Nearly all variables are related empirically to one another "to some extent." (Recall the earlier graphic illustrations of the deductive and inductive methods in Chapter 2.) Specifying the "extent" that represents acceptance of the hypothesis and the "extent" that represents rejection, however, is also an arbitrary act. (See Chapter 18 for a discussion of tests of statistical significance.)

Ultimately, then, the scientist uses approximate indicators of theoretical concepts to discover partial associations. And these problems conspire with one another against the researcher. Suppose that he specifies an extent of association that will constitute acceptance of the hypothesis, and the empirical analysis falls short. He will quite naturally ask himself whether different indicators of the concepts might have produced the specified extent of association.

The purpose of the preceding comments has been to demonstrate that the traditional view of the routine scientific method is inappropriate to research in practice. Research does not happen simply through the dogged traverse through steps 1 to 5. The realization of this should not be the source of dismay, however, but should serve as a challenge to the researcher. It should not be taken as a denial of the possibility of scientific research but it should lay the basis for enlightened, truly scientific, research.

Measurement and association are interrelated concepts. The scientist must handle both simultaneously and logically. Rather than moving through a fixed set of steps, the scientist moves back and forth through them endlessly. Often his theoretical constructions are built around the previously observed associations between empirical indicators. Partial theoretical constructions may suggest new empirical data to be examined, and so forth. It is hoped that, after each activity, the scientist understands his subject matter a little better. The "critical experiment" that ultimately determines the fate of an entire theory is a rare thing indeed.

Scientific research, then, is a never-ending enterprise aimed at the understanding of some phenomenon. To that end, the scientist continually measures and examines associations, and he must constantly be aware of their interrelations. The following sections should clarify the nature of the interrelations.

The Interchangeability of Indexes

Paul Lazarsfeld, in his discussions of the "interchangeability of indexes," has provided an important conceptual tool for our understanding of the relationship between measurement and association, and as a partial resolution of the two problems discussed in the previous section.[2] His comments grow out of the recognition that there are several possible indicators for any concept.

Let us return for the moment to the notion of a theoretical hypothesis: $Y = f(X)$. Lazarsfeld recognizes that there are several possible indicators of a concept like supervision; we might write these as x_1, x_2, x_3, and so forth. Although there may be reasons for believing that some of the possible indicators are better than others, they are essentially interchangeable. Thus, the scientist faces the dilemma of which to use in the testing of the hypothesis: $Y = f(X)$.

The solution to the dilemma lies in the use of *all* indicators. Thus, the scientist tests the following empirical hypotheses: $y = f(x_1)$, $y = f(x_2)$, $y = f(x_3)$, and so forth. Rather than having one test of the hypothesis, he has several, as indicated schematically in Figure 16-2.

You already may have anticipated a new dilemma. If the scientist following the traditional view of the scientific method faced the problem that the single empirical association might not be perfect, the present scientist will be faced with several empirical associations, none of which will be perfect and some of which may conflict with one another. Thus, even if he has specified a particular extent of association that will be sufficient to confirm the hypothesis, he may discover that the tests involving x_1, x_3, and x_5 meet that specified criterion, but the tests involving x_2 and x_4 do not. His dilemma is seemingly compounded. In fact, however, the situation really may be clarified.

In terms of the notion of "the interchangeability of indexes," the theoretical hypothesis is accepted as a *general* proposition if it is confirmed

---

2. Paul F. Lazarsfeld, "Problems in Methodology," in Robert K. Merton (ed.), *Sociology Today* (New York: Basic Books, 1959), pp. 39–78.

by all the specific empirical tests. If, for example, juvenile delinquency is a function of supervision in a broadly generalized sense, then juvenile delinquency should be empirically related to every empirical indicator of supervision.

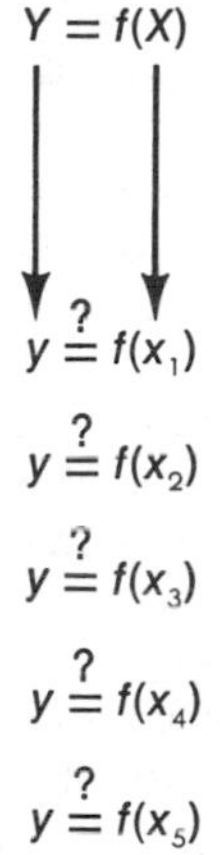

$$Y = f(X)$$

$$y \overset{?}{=} f(x_1)$$

$$y \overset{?}{=} f(x_2)$$

$$y \overset{?}{=} f(x_3)$$

$$y \overset{?}{=} f(x_4)$$

$$y \overset{?}{=} f(x_5)$$

Figure 16-2. The Interchangeability of Indexes

If, however, the scientist discovers that only certain indicators of supervision have this property, then he has specified the kinds of supervision for which the proposition holds. In practice, this may help him to reconceptualize "supervision" in more precise terms. Perhaps, for example, juvenile delinquency is a function of structural constraints, and some kinds of supervision are indicators of constraints, while others really are not.

It is very important to realize what the scientist will have accomplished through this process. Rather than routinely testing a fixed hypothesis relating to supervision and delinquency, he will have gained a more well-defined understanding of the nature of that association. This will make sense, however, only if we view the goal of science as understanding rather than simply as theory construction and hypothesis testing.

There is one additional step required, however, before our understanding of the scientific process is clear. That is to comprehend what I have called "fixed-point analysis." The notion of interchangeable indexes discussed above focused on the variability of *one* of the concepts, when in fact *all* concepts have this property. This will be the theme of the next section.

Fixed-Point Analysis

In the preceding section, we noted that given the theoretical hypothesis $Y = f(X)$, there are several possible indicators of X, written as x_1,

x_2, x_3 and so forth. It should also be evident that Y may be specified in several ways: y_1, y_2, y_3, and so forth. In short, no theoretical concepts have unambiguous empirical indicators. Thus, in a two-variable hypothesis, the number of possible tests is manifold. And the interpretation of so many tests—given many indicators—will be severely taxing.

The dilemma facing the scientist at this point may be represented in a paraphrase of William James as "a buzzing, whirling mess of variables" wherein no indicator can be accepted as a true measure of a given concept, illustrated schematically in Part I of Figure 16-3. There is no safe anchoring point from which the scientist can begin to build his analysis. Given such total uncertainty, the inexperienced researcher may give up in despair or retreat into the comfort of the traditional view of the scientific method as a serial set of routine steps.

The experienced scientist extricates himself from this morass through careful pragmatism and a healthy tolerance of ambiguity. One way he might deal with the situation is fixed-point analysis. The following discussion tells how he does this.

He begins by recognizing that he has, say, five possible indicators of delinquency and five indicators of supervision. Realizing that there is no natural fixed point from which to proceed, he arbitrarily fixes one. For example, he may specify, based on his best judgment, that y_1 will be fixed as the indicator of Y (arrest as an indicator of delinquency). He does this knowing full well that it may not be the best possible indicator.

Having fixed Y as y_1, he then permits himself to vary the possible measures of X, following the general procedure described in the section on the interchangeability of indexes. (See also Part II of Figure 16-3.) He does this as though there were no ambiguity as to the measurement of delinquency. The result of this activity is a better understanding of the nature of his possible indicators of X. As suggested above, he will discover that some indicators of X (supervision) are associated with y_1 (being arrested) while others are not. This discovery should lead to a reconceptualization of the types and nature of supervision. In the present illustration, let's assume he has decided the best measure of supervision is a combination of x_1, x_3, and x_4 (combined in a composite *index*, perhaps).

Once he has achieved a better understanding of X in this fashion, he then turns the process around: he "fixes" X and allows Y to vary (Part III of Figure 16-3). If $(x_1 x_3 x_4)$ now seems closest to his general concept of supervision—on the basis of the initial analyses—he uses that combination of measures as *the* measure of supervision. His subsequent analyses ask *which* indicators of Y (delinquency) are indeed functions of the newly fixed indicator of X (supervision). The result of these analyses will be a better understanding of the types and nature of his indicators of delinquency. Thus the fixed indicator of supervision may be associated importantly with whether or not a juvenile is arrested for a delinquent act, but not associated with whether or not he commits one. Thus the two indicators of delinquency are not interchangeable indexes of the same general concept in the context of the analysis.

Once the scientist has gained a better conceptualization of delinquency, he may then turn the process around again—using his new conceptualization to refine his understanding of the different indicators of supervision (Part IV of Figure 16-3). This procedure can, of course, go on endlessly (Part V). If you think about research as a line of scientific inquiry rather than a particular research project, you will see that the procedure does indeed go on endlessly.

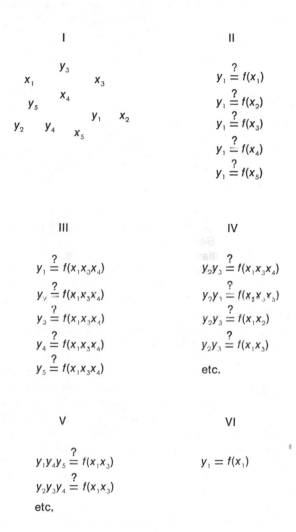

Figure 16-3. Fixed-Point Analysis

The ultimate result of this procedure should be carefully examined, as it is quite different from what is suggested by the traditional view of the scientific method. The scientist neither asks nor answers the question "*Is Y* a function of *X*?" Rather, he asks: "*How* is *Y* a function of *X*?" (Under what operationalizations is *Y* a function of *X*?) He does not address himself to the straightforward question of *whether* delinquency is decreased by increasing supervision. Rather, he asks: "What kinds of delinquency are affected by what kinds of supervision in what kinds of ways?" (The answer to this question is presented in Part VI of Figure 16-3 with the subscript *i* used to indicate the most useful indexes of *X* and *Y*.) In practice, of course, the researcher might arrive at several such answers. This latter line of inquiry is more appropriate than the former to the kinds of phenomena that scientists typically study, and the understanding generated by it will be more sophisticated and more useful as well.

The implication of the preceding comments is that measurement and association are importantly intertwined. The measurement of a variable makes little sense outside the empirical and theoretical contexts of the associations to be tested. Asked "How should I measure social class?" the experienced scientist will reply, "What is your purpose for measuring it?" The "proper" way of measuring a given variable depends very heavily on the variables to be associated with it. One further example should make this point clearer.

A controversy has raged recently in the sociology of religion concerning the relationship between religiosity and prejudice. A book by Charles Y. Glock and Rodney Stark entitled *Christian Beliefs and Anti-Semitism*[3] reported empirical data indicating that Christian church members holding orthodox beliefs were more likely to be anti-Semitic than were less orthodox members. The book's findings stirred considerable discussion within the churches, and it resulted in follow-up research on the same topic by other researchers.

One subsequent research project arrived at a conclusion directly opposite from that of Glock and Stark. The researchers reported that as orthodoxy increased, prejudice decreased. Upon closer examination, however, it was noted that the measures of orthodoxy in that study were based on acceptance of questionnaire statements of the traditional Christian doctrines of "All men are brothers" and "Love thy neighbor." Not surprisingly, survey respondents who accepted the statements based on these doctrines appeared less prejudiced than those who rejected them. Normally, these research findings would be (and were) challenged on the grounds of "contamination": the two variables being examined (religious orthodoxy and prejudice) actually measured the same or similar qualities. Calling one set of indicators "orthodoxy" and the other "prejudice" does not prove that prejudice decreases with increasing orthodoxy in a general sense. (Of course the measurement of orthodoxy in terms of brotherly love and equality might be extremely useful in some other context.)

The discussions of this chapter suggest a somewhat different reaction to the two kinds of research findings. Asking *how* orthodoxy and prejudice are associated with each other rather than asking *whether*, we would conclude that orthodoxy measured in terms of the Glock-Stark

---

3. (New York: Harper & Row, 1967).

indicators (belief in God, the divinity of Jesus, miracles, and the like) is positively associated with prejudice, while orthodoxy measured as commitment to the norms of brotherly love and equality is negatively associated with prejudice. Both conclusions are empirically correct; neither conclusion answers the more general question of *whether* religion and prejudice are related. The final remaining step, of course, is to evaluate the relative utility of the conclusions. The finding that orthodoxy and prejudice are negatively associated would probably be disregarded as either tautological or trivial.

16.5
Summary

Chapter 16 has dealt with the knotty subject of causation in social research. Although most people have some idea about what causation is, it is a far more complicated notion than it first appears. The purpose of this chapter has been to get you in touch with the complexities of causation without fully resolving the issue, since it cannot be fully resolved.

The chapter began with a discussion of determinism in relation to social research. We saw that there are two importantly different images of man's ultimate freedom. The *free-will* image suggests that each person is the ultimate master of his own destiny, personally choosing how he will behave in any given situation. The *deterministic* image, on the other hand, suggests that human behavior is a product of socioenvironmental factors—determinants—over which the actor has little or no control, that man is nothing more than a stimulus-response machine, albeit a complex one.

The logic of the deterministic image of man was illustrated, in part, through a hypothetical dialogue concerning the reasons for a particular voting "decision." The purpose of this extended treatment of determinism lies in the fact that explanatory, social research depends on a deterministic image of man, at least a partially deterministic image. It makes no sense at all to seek to explain why some people are more prejudiced than others unless we assume that prejudice is caused by factors other than personal, idiosyncratic decisions to be prejudiced or unprejudiced.

The general topic of causation was pursued through a discussion of two different explanatory models. The *idiographic* model aims at total explanation of a particular phenomenon through an exhaustive consideration of all relevant factors. This is the model typically employed by historians, for example. The *nomothetic* model of explanation, on the other hand, aims at partial, but generalized, understanding of a *class* of phenomena through the consideration of the relatively few, most relevant factors. This is the model typically employed by social scientists, and it is more parsimonious than the idiographic.

Since social scientific research, especially in regard to its deterministic image of man and its nomothetic model of explanation, is frequently charged with dehumanizing the people under study, this change was discussed in the chapter. I attempted to show that the seeming dehumanization is more a product of the scientist's explicitness than of his philosophical regard or disregard for people.

Having dealt with these general philosophical issues regarding the notion of causation, the chapter turned to more practical matters. Three basic criteria for causality were discussed: (1) empirical association, (2) time order, and (3) the lack of spuriousness. This discussion was followed by an examination of some common, though inappropriate, criteria for causality. In this latter connection, the notions of *necessary cause* and *sufficient cause* were introduced.

The chapter concluded with a discussion of the link between measurement and association. Having learned earlier in the book that there is no "true" measure for any variable, we discovered in this chapter that the "best" measure of a variable depends—in explanatory research—on the variables with which it is to be associated. Through the discussion of "the interchangeability of indexes" and "fixed-point analysis," the point was made that the question: "Is *X* related to *Y*?" is less meaningful than the question: "In what ways is *X* related to *Y*?"

16.6
Main Points

1. Explanatory scientific research depends implicitly on the notion of cause and effect.

2. Explanatory *social* scientific research depends implicitly on a *deterministic image of man*, at least in part.

3. The *idiographic* model of explanation aims at a complete understanding of a particular phenomenon, utilizing all relevant causal factors.

4. The *nomothetic* model of explanation aims at a general understanding—not necessarily complete—of a *class* of phenomena, utilizing the smallest number of most relevant causal factors. The nomothetic model is more parsimonious than the idiographic model, and it is the one most typically employed in social scientific research.

5. Although social scientists may seem to take a rather dehumanized view of the people they study, this merely reflects their parsimonious point of view. When a social scientist says that political party affiliation is the best predictor of voting behavior, this does not mean that he disregards or denies all other influences; he simply is interested in discovering the most important ones.

6. Most explanatory social research utilizes a *probabilistic* model of causation. *X* may be said to *cause Y* if it is seen to have *some* influence on *Y*.

7. There are two important types of causal factors: *necessary* causes and *sufficient* causes. *X* is a necessary cause of *Y* if *Y* cannot happen without *X* having happened. *X* is a sufficient cause of *Y* if *Y* always happens

when X happens. The scientifically most satisfying discovery is a necessary *and* sufficient cause.

8. There are three basic criteria for the determination of causation in scientific research: (1) The independent (cause) and dependent (effect) variables must be empirically related to one another; (2) the independent variable must occur earlier in time than the dependent variable; and (3) the observed relationship cannot be "explained away" as the artificial product of the effect of another, earlier variable. (This final criterion will be discussed more fully in Chapter 17.)

9. A perfect statistical relationship between two variables is *not* an appropriate criterion for causation in social research. We may say that a causal relationship exists between X and Y, then, even though X is not the *total* cause of Y.

10. The *interchangeability of indexes* suggests that if several specific, though imperfect, indicators of one variable are similarly related to another variable, then we may assume that the first variable—*in general*—is related to the second. Thus, we may conclude that X is related to Y, even though we cannot satisfactorily define X.

11. *Fixed-point analysis* is a logical model for varying the definitions of variables in such a way as to discover the *different* relationships that exist between variables according to the operational definitions employed. This model suggests that it is more fruitful to ask: "In what ways are X and Y related?" than it is to ask "Are X and Y related?"

12. *Contamination* of indicators means that the operational measure of one of two variables whose relationship is being examined may be construed as a measure of the other variable as well. For example, it would be an inappropriate test of the relationship between religiosity and prejudice if the measure of religiosity might be seen as a measure of prejudice as well.

16.7
Annotated Bibliography

Hirschi, Travis, and Selvin, Hanan, *Delinquency Research* (New York: Free Press, 1967), especially Part II. Excellent statements on causation within a practical framework. I can think of no better discussions of causation within the context of particular research findings than this. It is readable, stimulating, and generally just plain excellent.

Kaplan, Abraham, *The Conduct of Inquiry* (San Francisco: Chandler, 1964). A philosopher's perspective on social research. Especially in his discussions of explanation (Part 9), Kaplan lays the logical foundation for an understanding of the nature and analysis of causal relationships in social science.

Lazarsfeld, Paul, Foreword in Hyman, Herbert, *Survey Design and Analysis* (New York: Free Press, 1955). A classic and still valid statement of causation in social science. In the context of the elaboration model, Lazarsfeld provides a clear statement of the criteria for determining causation.

Rosenberg, Morris, *The Logic of Survey Analysis* (New York: Basic Books, 1968). A clear and practical statement of how the social researcher addresses causation. In his opening chapter, Rosenberg discusses the general meaning of causal relationships. In the concluding two chapters, he describes the process through which a researcher may arrive at causal conclusions.

17

The Elaboration Model

17.1
Introduction

Chapter 17 is devoted to a perspective on social scientific analysis that is referred to variously as "the elaboration model," "the interpretation method," "the Columbia school," or "the Lazarsfeld method." This varied nomenclature derives from the fact that the method we shall be discussing aims at the *elaboration* on an empirical relationship among variables in order to *interpret* that relationship in the manner developed by Paul *Lazarsfeld* while at *Columbia* University.

The elaboration model is used to understand the relationship between two variables through the simultaneous introduction of additional variables. It was developed primarily through the medium of contingency tables, but later chapters of this book will show how it may be used with other statistical techniques.

It is my firm belief that the elaboration model offers the researcher the clearest picture of the logic of analysis that is available. Especially through the use of contingency tables, this method portrays the logical processes of scientific analysis. Moreover, if the reader is able to comprehend fully the use of the elaboration model using contingency tables, he should be in a far better position to use and understand more sophisticated statistical techniques.

17.2
History of the Elaboration Model

The historical origins of the elaboration model are especially instructive for a realistic appreciation of scientific research in practice. During World War II, Samuel Stouffer organized and headed a special social research branch within the United States Army. Throughout the war, this group conducted a large number and variety of surveys among American servicemen. Although the objectives of these studies varied somewhat, they generally focused on the factors affecting soldiers' combat effectiveness.

Several of the studies examined the issue of morale in the military. Since morale was believed to affect combat effectiveness, the improvement of morale would increase the effectiveness of the war effort. Stouffer and his research staff, then, sought to uncover some of the variables that affected morale. In part, the group sought to confirm, empirically, some commonly accepted propositions. Among them were the following:

1. Promotions surely affected soldiers' morale, and it was expected that those soldiers serving in units with low promotion rates would have relatively low morale.

2. Given racial segregation and discrimination in the South, it was expected that Negro soldiers being trained in Northern training camps would have higher morale than those being trained in the South.

3. Those soldiers with more education would be more likely to resent being drafted into the army as enlisted men than would those soldiers with less education.

Each of these propositions made sense logically, and common wisdom held each to be empirically true. Stouffer decided to test each empirically. To his surprise, none of the propositions was confirmed.

First, soldiers serving in the Military Police—where promotions were the slowest in the army—had fewer complaints about the promotion system than did those serving in the Army Air Corps—where promotions were the fastest in the army. This finding was derived from responses to a question asking whether the soldier believed the promotion system to be generally fair.

Second, Negro soldiers serving in Northern training camps and those serving in Southern training camps seemed to differ little if at all in their general morale.

Third, the less educated soldiers were more likely to resent being drafted into the Army than were those with greater amounts of education.

Faced with data such as these, many researchers no doubt would have tried to hide the findings, as a poor reflection on their scientific abilities. Others would have run tests of statistical significance and then tried to publish the results. Stouffer, instead, asked *Why?*

Stouffer found the answer to this question within the concepts of "reference group" and "relative deprivation." In the simplest overview, Stouffer suggested that soldiers did not evaluate their positions in life in accord with absolute, objective standards, but on the basis of their relative position vis-à-vis others around them. The people they compared themselves with were their "reference group," and they felt "relative deprivation" if they did not compare favorably in that regard.

Within the concepts of "reference group" and "relative deprivation," Stouffer found an answer to each of the anomalies in his empirical data. Regarding promotion, he suggested that soldiers judged the fairness of the promotion system on the basis of their own experiences relative to others around them. In the Military Police, where promotions were few and slow, few soldiers knew of a less qualified buddy who had been promoted faster than they had. In the Army Air Corps, however, the rapid promotion rate meant that many soldiers knew of less qualified buddies who had been promoted faster than seemed appropriate. Thus, ironically, the MP's said the promotion system was generally fair while the Air Corpsmen said it was not.

A similar explanation seemed appropriate in the case of the Negro soldiers. Rather than simply comparing conditions in the North with those in the South, they compared their own status—as Negro soldiers—with the status of the Negro civilians around them. In the South, where discrimination was at its worst, they found being a soldier somewhat insulated them from adverse cultural norms in the surrounding community. Whereas Southern Negro civilians were grossly discriminated against and denied self-esteem, good jobs, and so forth, Negro soldiers had a slightly better status. In the North, however, many of the Negro civilians they encountered were holding down well-paying defense jobs. And with discrimination less severe, being a soldier did not help one's status in the community.

Finally, "reference group" and "relative deprivation" seemed to explain the anomaly of highly educated draftees accepting their induction more willingly than was true of those with less education. Stouffer reasoned as follows:[1]

1. A person's friends will, on the whole, have about the same educational status as the person himself.

2. People with less education will be more likely to engage in semiskilled production-line occupations and farming than will those with much education.

3. During wartime, many production-line industries and farming were declared vital to the national interest; production-line workers in those industries and farmers would be exempted from the draft.

4. A person with little education was more likely to have friends who were in draft-exempt occupations than the person with more education.

5. The draftee of little education would be more likely to feel discriminated against than would the draftee with more education, by virtue of each comparing himself with his friends.

These were the explanations that Stouffer suggested to unlock the mystery of the three anomalous findings. Because they were not part of a preplanned study design, he lacked empirical data for testing them, however. Nevertheless, Stouffer's logical exposition provided the basis for the later development of the elaboration model: understanding the relationship between two variables through the controlled introduction of other variables.

The formal development of the elaboration model was the work of Paul Lazarsfeld and his associates at Columbia University. In a methodological review of Stouffer's army studies, Lazarsfeld and Patricia Kendall

---

1. Samuel A. Stouffer *et al.*, *The American Soldier* (Princeton, N.J.: Princeton University Press, 1949), vol. I, pp. 122 ff., esp. p. 127.

Table 17-1. Summary of Stouffer's Data on
Education and Acceptance of Induction

	High Ed.	Low Ed.
Should *not* have been deferred	88%	70%
Should have been deferred	12	30
	100%	100%
	(1731)	(1876)

Tables 17-1, 17-2, 17-3, 17-4 are modified with permission of the Macmillan
Company from *Continuities in Social Research: Studies in the Scope and Method
of "The American Soldier"* by Robert K. Merton and Paul F. Lazarsfeld. Copyright
1950 by The Free Press, a Corporation.

presented hypothetical tables that would have proved Stouffer's contention
regarding education and acceptance of induction had the empirical data
been available.[2]

Kendall and Lazarsfeld began with Stouffer's data showing the
positive association between education and acceptance of induction (see
Table 17-1).

Following Stouffer's explanation, Kendall and Lazarsfeld created a
hypothetical table, compatible with the empirical data, to show that education
was related to whether one had friends who were deferred. In Table 17-2, we
note that 19 percent of those with high education reported having friends who
were deferred, as compared with 79 percent among those with less education.

Stouffer's explanation next assumed that soldiers with friends who
had been deferred would be more likely to resent their own induction than
would those who had no deferred friends. Table 17-3 presents the hypothetical data from Kendall and Lazarsfeld that would have supported that
assumption.

The hypothetical data presented in Tables 17-2 and 17-3 confirm the
linkages that Stouffer had specified in his explanation. First, soldiers with low

Table 17-2. Hypothetical Relationship between
Education and Deferment of Friends

		High Ed.	Low Ed.
	Yes	19%	79%
Friends deferred?			
	No	81	21
		100%	100%
		(1731)	(1876)

2. Patricia L. Kendall and Paul F. Lazarsfeld, "Problems of Survey Analysis," in Robert K. Merton
and Paul F. Lazarsfeld (eds.), *Continuities in Social Research: Studies in the Scope and Method of
"The American Soldier"* (New York: Free Press, 1950), pp. 133–196.

Table 17.3 Hypothetical Relationship between
Deferment of Friends and Acceptance of One's
Own Induction

	Friends Deferred?	
	Yes	No
Should not have been deferred	63%	94%
Should have been deferred	37	6
	100%	100%
	(1819)	(1818)

education were more likely to have friends who were deferred than those with more education. And, second, having friends who were deferred made a soldier more likely to think he should have been deferred. Stouffer had suggested that these two relationships would clarify the original relationship between education and acceptance of induction. Kendall and Lazarsfeld created the hypothetical table that would confirm that ultimate explanation (see Table 17-4).

Recall that the original finding was that draftees with high education were more likely to accept their induction into the Army as fair than those with less education. In Table 17-4, however, we note that level of education has no effect on the acceptance of induction among those who report having friends deferred: 63 percent among *both* educational groups say they should not have been deferred. Similarly, educational level has no significant effect on acceptance of induction among those who reported having no friends deferred: 94 and 95 percent say they should not have been deferred.

On the other hand, among those with high education the acceptance of induction is strongly related to whether or not one's friends were deferred: 63 percent versus 94 percent. And the same is true among those with less education. The hypothetical data in Table 17-4, then, support Stouffer's contention that education affected acceptance of induction only through the

Table 17-4. Hypothetical Data Relating Education to Acceptance of
Induction through the Factor of Having Friends Who Were Deferred

	Friends Deferred		No Friends Deferred	
	High Ed.	Low Ed.	High Ed.	Low Ed.
Should not have been deferred	63%	63%	94%	95%
Should have been deferred	37	37	6	5
	100%	100%	100%	100%
	(335)	(1484)	(1426)	(392)

medium of having friends deferred. Highly educated draftees were less likely to have friends deferred and, by virtue of that fact, were more likely to accept their own induction as fair. Those with less education were more likely to have friends deferred and, by virtue of that fact, were less likely to accept their own induction.

It is important to recognize that neither Stouffer's explanation nor the hypothetical data denied the reality of the original relationship. As educational level increased, acceptance of one's own induction also increased. The nature of this empirical relationship, however, was interpreted through the introduction of a third variable. The variable, deferment of friends, did not deny the original relationship; it merely clarified the mechanism through which the original relationship occurred. This, then, is the heart of the elaboration model and of multivariate analysis.

Having observed an empirical relationship between two variables, the researcher seeks to understand the nature of that relationship through the effects produced by introducing other variables. Mechanically, he accomplishes this by first dividing his sample into subsets on the basis of the *control* or *test* variable. For example, having friends deferred or not is the control variable in our present example, and the sample is divided into those who have deferred friends and those who do not. The relationship between the original two variables is then recomputed separately for each of the subsamples. The tables produced in this manner are called the *partial tables*, and the relationships found in the partial tables are called the *partial relationships*. The partial relationships are then compared with the initial relationship discovered in the total sample.

17.3
The Elaboration Paradigm

This section presents guidelines for the reader to follow in the understanding of an elaboration analysis. To begin, we must know whether the test variable is *antecedent* (prior in time) to the other two variables or

Figure 17-1

whether it is *intervening* between them, as these suggest different logical relationships in the multivariate model. If the test variable is intervening, as in the case of education, deferment of friends, and acceptance of induction, then the relationships of Figure 17-1 are posited.

The logic of this multivariate relationship is as follows: the Independent variable (educational level) affects the intervening test variable (having friends deferred or not), which in turn affects the dependent variable (accepting induction).

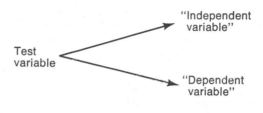

Figure 17-2

If the test variable is antecedent to both the independent and dependent variables, a very different multivariate relationship is posited (see Figure 17-2).

In this second situation, the test variable affects both the "independent" and "dependent" variables.[3] Because of their individual relationships to the test variable, the "independent" and "dependent" variables are empirically related to each other, but there is no causal link between them. Their empirical relationship is merely a product of their coincidental relationships to the test variable. (Subsequent examples will further clarify this.)

Table 17-5 is a guide to the understanding of an elaboration analysis. The two columns in the table indicate whether the test variable is antecedent or intervening in the sense described above. On the left side of the table is indicated the nature of the partial relationships as compared with the original relationship between the independent and dependent variables. In the body of the table are given the technical notations assigned to each case.

Table 17-5. The Elaboration Paradigm

Partial Relationships Compared with Original	Test Variable	
	Antecedent	Intervening
Same relationship	REPLICATION	
Less or none	EXPLANATION	INTERPRETATION
Split*	SPECIFICATION	

* One partial the same or greater, while the other is less or none.

3. Realize, of course, that the terms "independent variable" and "dependent variable" are, strictly speaking, used incorrectly in the diagram. In fact, we have one independent variable (the "test variable") and two dependent variables. The incorrect terminology has been used only to provide continuity with the preceding example.

Replication

Whenever the partial relationships are essentially the same as the original relationship, the term "replication" is assigned to the result, regardless of whether the test variable is antecedent or intervening. The meaning here is essentially the same as common sense would dictate. The original relationship has been replicated under test conditions. If, in our previous example, education still affected acceptance of induction both among those who had friends deferred and those who did not, then we would say the original relationship had been replicated. Note, however, that this finding would not confirm Stouffer's explanation of the original relationship. Having friends deferred or not would not be the mechanism through which education affected the acceptance of induction.

Researchers frequently use the elaboration model rather routinely in the hope of replicating their findings among subsets of the sample. The researcher who discovered a relationship between education and prejudice, for example, might introduce such test variables as age, region of the country, race, religion, and so forth, to test the stability of that original relationship. If the relationship were replicated among young and old, among persons from different parts of the country, and so forth, he might thereby conclude that the original relationship was a genuine and general one.

Explanation

Explanation is the term used to describe a *spurious relationship:* an original relationship that is "explained away" through the introduction of a test variable. Two conditions are required for this. The test variable must be antecedent to both the independent and dependent variables, and the partial relationships must be zero or significantly less than was found in the original. Three examples make this clear.

There is an empirical relationship between the number of storks in different areas and the birthrates for those areas. The more storks in an area, the higher the birthrate. This empirical relationship might thereby lead one to assume that the number of storks affects the birthrate. An antecedent test variable "explains away" this relationship, however. Rural areas have both more storks and higher birthrates than urban areas. Within rural areas, there is no relationship between the number of storks and the birthrate; nor is there a relationship within urban areas.

Second, there is a positive relationship between the number of fire trucks responding to a fire and the amount of damage done. If more trucks respond, more damage is done. One might assume from this, then, that the fire trucks themselves cause the damage. An antecedent test variable, however, explains away the original relationship: the size of the fire. Large fires do more damage than small ones, and more fire trucks respond to large fires than to small ones. Looking only at large fires, the original relationship would vanish (or perhaps reverse itself); and the same would be true looking only at small fires.

Finally, there is an empirical relationship between the region of the country in which a medical school faculty member attended medical school, and his attitude toward Medicare.[4] To simplify matters, only the East and the South will be examined. Of faculty members attending Eastern medical schools, 78 percent said they approved of Medicare, compared with 59 percent of those attending Southern medical schools. This finding makes sense in view of the fact that the South seems generally more resistant to such programs than the East, and medical school training should presumably affect a doctor's medical attitudes. This relationship is explained away through the introduction of an antecedent test variable: the region of the country in which the faculty member was raised.

Of faculty members raised in the East, 89 percent attended medical school in the East, and 11 percent in the South. Of those raised in the South, 53 percent attended medical school in the East and 47 percent in the South. Moreover, the area in which faculty members were raised is related to attitudes toward Medicare. Of those raised in the East, 84 percent approved of Medicare, as compared with 49 percent of those raised in the South.

Table 17-6 presents the three-variable relationship among region in which raised, region of medical school training, and attitudes toward Medicare.

Table 17-6. Region of Origin, Region of Schooling, and Attitudes toward Medicare

Percent Who Approve of Medicare		Region in which Raised	
		East	South
Region of Medical School Training	East	84	50
	South	80	47

Source: Babbie, 181.

Those faculty members raised in the East are quite likely to approve of Medicare, regardless of where they attended medical school. Those raised in the South are relatively less likely to approve of Medicare, but, again, the region of their medical school training has little or no effect. These data indicate, therefore, that the original relationship between region of medical training and attitudes toward Medicare was spurious; it was due only to the coincidental effect of region of origin on both region of medical training and on attitudes toward Medicare. When region of origin is *held constant* as we have done in Table 17-6, the original relationship disappears in the partials.

Interpretation

Interpretation is similar to explanation, except for the time placement of the test variable and the implications that follow from that difference. The

4. Earl R. Babbie, *Science and Morality in Medicine* (Berkeley: University of California Press, 1970), see esp. p. 181.

earlier example of education, friends deferred, and acceptance of induction is an excellent illustration of interpretation. In the terms of the elaboration model, the effect of education on acceptance of induction is not explained away; it is still a genuine relationship. In a real sense, educational differences *cause* differential acceptance of induction. The intervening variable, deferment of friends, merely helps to interpret the mechanism through which the relationship occurs.

Note an important point here. The researcher might have begun his analysis with the observation that having friends deferred made draftees less willing to accept their own induction as fair. In the attempt to better understand this original finding, he might have introduced education as an antecedent test variable. Had he done this, however, he would have found that the relationship between friends being deferred and acceptance of induction was *replicated* among the highly educated and among the lesser educated soldiers (see Table 17-4). He would have also noted that highly educated soldiers were less likely to have friends deferred, but the original relationship would not have been explained away.

As a final example of interpretation, it has been observed by researchers in the past that children from homes with working mothers are more likely to become delinquent than those whose mothers do not work. This relationship may be interpreted, however, through the introduction of "supervision" as a test variable. Among children who are supervised, delinquency rates are not affected by whether or not their mothers work. The same is true among those who are not supervised. It is the relationship between working mothers and lack of supervision that produced the original relationship.

Specification

Sometimes the elaboration model produces partial relationships that differ significantly from each other. For example, one partial relationship may look very much like the original two-variable relationship, while the second partial relationship is near zero. This situation is referred to as *specification* in the elaboration paradigm. The researcher has specified the conditions under which the original relationship occurs.

In a study of the sources of religious involvement, Glock and his associates discovered that among Episcopal church members, involvement decreased as social class increased.[5] This finding is reported in Table 17-7, which examines mean levels of church involvement among women parishioners at different levels of social class.

Glock interpreted this finding in the context of others in the analysis, and concluded that church involvement provides an alternative form of gratification for those people who are denied gratification in the secular society. This explained why women were more religious than men, why old

---

5. Charles Y. Glock, Benjamin B. Ringer, and Earl R. Babbie, *To Comfort and to Challenge* (Berkeley: University of California Press, 1967), p. 92.

Table 17-7. Social Class and Mean Church
Involvement among Episcopal Women

| | Social Class Levels | | | | |
	Low 0	1	2	3	High 4
Mean Involvement	.63	.58	.49	.48	.45

Source: Glock et al, 85. Note that mean scores rather than percentages have
been used here.

people were more religious than young people, and so forth. Glock reasoned
that people of lower social class (measured by income and education) had
fewer chances to gain self-esteem from the secular society than did people of
higher social class. To illustrate this, he noted that social class was strongly
related to the likelihood that a woman had ever held an office in a secular
organization (see Table 17-8).

Table 17-8. Social Class and the Holding of Office
in Secular Organizations

| | Social Class Levels | | | | |
	Low 0	1	2	3	High 4
Percent who have held office in a secular organization	46	47	54	60	83

Source: Glock et al, 92. Note that percentages are used in this table.

Glock then reasoned that if social class was related to church
involvement only by virtue of the fact that lower-class women would be denied
opportunities for gratification in the secular society, the original relationship
should not hold among women who were getting gratification. As a rough
indicator of the receipt of gratification from the secular society, he used as a
variable the holding of secular office. In terms of this test, then, social class
should be unrelated to church involvement among those who had held such
office (see Table 17-9).

Table 17-9 presents an example of a specification. Among women
who have held office in secular organizations, there is essentially no
relationship between social class and church involvement. In effect, the table
specifies the conditions under which the original relationship holds: among
those women lacking gratification in the secular society.

The term "specification" is used in the elaboration paradigm regardless of whether the test variable is antecedent or intervening. In either case,
the meaning is the same. The researcher has specified the particular
conditions under which the original relationship holds.

*Table 17-9. Church Involvement by Social Class and
Holding Secular Office*

	Social Class Levels				
	Low				High
Mean Church Involvement	0	1	2	3	4
Have held office	.46	.53	.46	.46	.46
Have not held office	.62	.55	.47	.46	.40

Source: Glock *et al*, 92.

Refinements to the Paradigm

The preceding sections have presented the primary logic of the elaboration model as developed by Lazarsfeld and his colleagues. Morris Rosenberg has offered an excellent presentation of the paradigm described above, and he goes beyond it to suggest additional variations.[6]

Rather than reviewing the comments made by Rosenberg, we might find it useful at this point to consider the logically possible variations. Some of these points may be found in Rosenberg's book; others were suggested by it.

First, the basic paradigm assumes an initial relationship between two variables. It might be useful, however, for a more comprehensive model to differentiate between positive and negative relationships. Moreover, Rosenberg suggests the application of the elaboration model to an original relationship of *zero*—with the possibility that relationships will appear in the partials.

Rosenberg cites as an example of this a study of union membership and attitudes toward having Jews on the union staff.[7] The initial analysis indicated that length of union membership did not relate to the attitude: those who had belonged to the union less than four years were as willing to accept Jews on the staff as were those who had belonged to the union for longer than four years. The *age* of union members, however, was found to *suppress* the relationship between length of union membership and attitudes toward Jews. Overall, younger members were more favorable to Jews than were older members. At the same time, of course, younger members were not likely to have been in the union as long as the old members. Within specific age groups, however, those in the union longest were the most supportive of having Jews on the staff. Age, in this case, was a *suppressor variable*, concealing the relationship between length of membership and attitudes toward Jews.

Second, the basic paradigm focuses on partials being the same or weaker than the original relationship, but does not provide guidelines for specifying what constitutes a significant difference between the original and the partials. Every researcher using the elaboration model will frequently find

---

6. Morris Rosenberg, *The Logic of Survey Analysis* (New York: Basic Books, 1968).
7. *Ibid.*, pp. 88–89.

himself making an arbitrary decision as to whether a given partial is significantly weaker than the original. This, then, suggests another dimension to the paradigm.

Third, the limitation of the basic paradigm to partials that are the same as or weaker than the original neglects two other possibilities. A partial relationship might be *stronger* than the original. Or, on the other hand, a partial relationship might be the reverse of the original—negative where the original was positive.

Rosenberg provides a hypothetical example of this by first suggesting that a researcher might find working-class respondents in his study more supportive of the civil-rights movement than middle-class respondents.[8] He further suggests that *race* might be a *distorter variable* in this instance, distorting the true relationship between class and attitudes. Presumably, black respondents would be more supportive of the movement than whites, but blacks would also be overrepresented among working class respondents and underrepresented among the middle class. Middle-class black respondents might be more supportive of the movement than working-class blacks, however; and the same relationship might be found among whites. *Holding race constant*, then, the researcher would conclude that support for the civil-rights movement was greater among the middle class than among the working class.

All these new dimensions further complicate the notion of specification. If one partial is the same as the original, while the other partial is even stronger, how should the researcher react to that situation? He has specified one condition under which the original relationship holds up, but he has also specified another condition under which it holds even more clearly.

Finally, the basic paradigm focuses primarily on dichotomous test variables. In fact, the elaboration model is not so limited—either in theory or in use—but the basic paradigm becomes more complicated when the test variable divides the sample into three or more subsamples. And the paradigm becomes more complicated yet when more than one test variable is used simultaneously.

These comments are not made with the intention of faulting the basic elaboration paradigm. To the contrary, my intention is to impress upon the reader that the elaboration model is not a simple algorithm—a set of procedures through which analysis is accomplished. The elaboration model is primarily a logical device for assisting the researcher in the understanding of his data. A firm understanding of the elaboration model will facilitate a sophisticated analysis. It does not suggest which variables should be introduced as controls, however, nor does it suggest definitive conclusions as to the nature of elaboration results. For all these things, the researcher must look to his own ingenuity. Such ingenuity, moreover, will come only through extensive experience. By pointing to the oversimplifications in the basic elaboration paradigm, I have sought to bring home the point that the model provides only a logical framework. Sophisticated analysis will be far more complicated than the examples used to illustrate the basic paradigm.

---

8. *Ibid.*, pp. 94–95.

At the same time, the elaboration paradigm is a very powerful logical framework. If the reader fully understands the basic model, he will be in a far better position for understanding other techniques such as correlations, regressions, factor analyses, and so forth. The next chapter will attempt to place such techniques as partial correlations and partial regressions in the context of the elaboration model.

17.4
A Computer Simulation of the Elaboration Model

Although the previous section indicated that the elaboration model is a logical framework rather than a set of specific statistical computations, it is possible that this situation may change somewhat in the near future. I have recently been engaged in an attempt to develop a *computer simulation* of the elaboration model; that is, I have attempted to teach a computer to undertake an elaboration analysis of social scientific data. While this model is still under development and not ready for distribution, the initial results are interesting and may provide a useful review of the logic of elaboration. It also provides another illustration of the potential of computer simulation in the social sciences. (Cf. Chapter 12.)

The simulation model utilizes a computer *time-sharing* system. Sitting at a remote terminal, which resembles a typewriter, the researcher simply types instructions to the computer on the typewriter and receives the computer response almost immediately, typed on the same typewriter. In the simulation of the elaboration model, the researcher enters the data to be analyzed, and once he has done this, the computer undertakes an analysis closely approximating what a trained elaboration analyst would conduct.

The illustration presented in Figure 17-3, which should be familiar, shows the initial round of interaction between the program and the user. The user begins by typing the name of the program: ELABORATION MODEL. The program responds with a brief description of its purpose and informs the user of what he will be required to do.

Having presented the introduction, the program then asks the user if he is prepared to continue. The user answers "Yes," and the program proceeds to solicit names for the three variables and the dichotomous code categories for each. The user enters each name as requested.

Once the names have been entered, the program proceeds to print a trivariate table, using the variable and code names assigned. The last statement from the program, at the bottom of the illustration, instructs the user to roll the terminal typewriter back to the top of the page and begin entering cell frequencies, one row at a time. The illustration has been terminated at this point, to give a picture of what the printout looks like before the data have been entered.

Figure 17-4 shows the table as it looks once the cell frequencies have been entered by the user.

```
ELABORATION MODEL

THIS PROGRAM UNDERTAKES AN ELABORATION ANALYSIS OF
THE SIMULTANEOUS RELATIONSHIPS AMONG ANY THREE
DICHOTOMOUS VARIABLES.  TO USE THE PROGRAM, YOU
MUST NAME THE THREE VARIABLES, INDICATING TIME
ORDER, NAME THE DICHOTOMOUS CODE CATEGORIES FOR
EACH, AND ENTER THE TRIVARIATE TABLE OF FREQUENCES.
ARE YOU READY TO TRY IT?  TYPE YES OR NO.
YES
TYPE THE NAME OF THE VARIABLE WHICH OCCURS FIRST
IN TIME.
EDUCATION
NAME THE FIRST CODE CATEGORY OF EDUCATION
HIGH
NAME THE SECOND CATEGORY OF EDUCATION
LOW
NAME THE VARIABLE WHICH OCCURS NEXT IN TIME.
WHETHER FRIENDS WERE DEFERRED
NAME THE FIRST CODE CATEGORY OF WHETHER FRIENDS WERE DEFERRED
YES
NAME THE SECOND CATEGORY OF WHETHER FRIENDS WERE DEFERRED
NO
OKAY, NAME THE LAST VARIABLE
WHETHER RESP. SHOULD HAVE BEEN DEFERRED
NOW NAME THE FIRST CODE CATEGORY OF WHETHER RESP. SHOULD HAVE BEEN DEFERRED
YES
NAME THE SECOND CATEGORY OF WHETHER RESP. SHOULD HAVE BEEN DEFERRED
NO


OKAY, SIT TIGHT FOR A MINUTE

EDUCATION:                                    HIGH

WHETHER FRIENDS WERE DEFERRED:                    YES       NO

WHETHER RESP. SHOULD HAVE BEEN DEFERRED:     YES

                                 NO



EDUCATION:                                    LOW

WHETHER FRIENDS WERE DEFERRED:                    YES       NO

WHETHER RESP. SHOULD HAVE BEEN DEFERRED:     YES

                                 NO

NOW ROLL YOUR TYPEWRITER BACK TO THE TOP
OF THE TABLE AND BEGIN ENTERING YOUR DATA
ONE ROW AT A TIME.
□:
```

Figure 17-3

As indicated by the final statement in Figure 17-4, nothing more is required of the user once the data have been entered. The illustrations presented in Figure 17-5 are all the work of the program. It begins by presenting and evaluating each of the bivariate tables. Then, it constructs a trivariate table and compares the effects under controlled conditions of education and whether friends were deferred with their original, uncontrolled effects. Finally, the program announces that the data represent an *interpretation* and explains what that means in the context of the present data.

Note that the program correctly identifies the data as representing an *interpretation*. Furthermore, it indicates that the "fit" is .94, and not perfect. "Fit" is a somewhat arbitrary statistic computed by the program to indicate

```
EDUCATION:                                        HIGH

WHETHER FRIENDS WERE DEFERRED:                              YES    NO

WHETHER RESP. SHOULD HAVE BEEN DEFERRED:    YES    124    86
                                     []:
                                            NO     211    1340


EDUCATION:                                        LOW

WHETHER FRIENDS WERE DEFERRED:                              YES    NO
                                     []:
WHETHER RESP. SHOULD HAVE BEEN DEFERRED:    YES    549    20
                                     []:
                                            NO     935    372

NOW ROLL YOUR TYPEWRITER BACK TO THE TOP
OF THE TABLE AND BEGIN ENTERING YOUR DATA
ONE ROW AT A TIME.
[]:

OKAY, YOU CAN SIT BACK AND RELAX WHILE I TRY TO
GET PAUL LAZARSFELD ON THE TELEPHONE.
```

Figure 17-4

how closely a set of data approximate the elaboration outcome identified. A perfect case would have a fit of 1.0. Recall that the zero-order relationship between education and attitudes toward induction was represented by an 18 percentage point difference. A perfect interpretation would require that this relationship be reduced to zero in both of the partial tables. This is the case for those respondents who had friends deferred from the army. Among those with no friends deferred, however, there is a 1 percentage point difference— which represents one-eighteenth or about six percent of the original relationship. Thus, the fit is .94.

The careful reader, however, will note that the data really are "better" than a perfect *interpretation,* since the remaining relationship is in the opposite direction from the original. The relationship is, in a sense, *less* than zero. The present version of the program fails to notice this fact, since it deals only with the absolute values of *epsilon* (percentage point differences). A revised version of the program will take account of such situations as well as the more extreme case of what Rosenberg has called *distorter variables.*.

The next illustration is taken from the study of medical school faculty members mentioned earlier. The initial analysis of attitudes toward Medicare pointed to the effects of geographical factors in two forms. Both region of origin and region in which medical training was received were found to relate to faculty members' attitudes toward Medicare. To simplify matters, only East and South are considered in the illustration.

Recall that it was found that faculty members raised in the East were more supportive of Medicare than those raised in the South. Similarly, those who received their M.D. degrees in the East were more supportive than those trained in the South. However, region of origin and region of medical training were related to each other, with faculty members showing some tendency to attend school in the same area where they were raised. The question, then, was: which of these regional factors *really* affected attitudes toward Medicare?

TABLE 1: DOES EDUCATION AFFECT WHETHER FRIENDS WERE DEFERRED?

EDUCATION:		HIGH	LOW
WHETHER FRIENDS WERE DEFERRED:	YES	19	79
	NO	81	21
		100	100
		(1761)	(1876)

THIS TABLE SUGGESTS THERE IS A VERY STRONG
RELATIONSHIP BETWEEN EDUCATION AND WHETHER FRIENDS WERE DEFERRED
REPRESENTING A 60 PERCENTAGE
POINT DIFFERENCE.

TABLE 2: DOES EDUCATION AFFECT WHETHER RESP. SHOULD HAVE BEEN DEFERRED?

EDUCATION:		HIGH	LOW
WHETHER RESP. SHOULD HAVE BEEN DEFERRED:	YES	12	30
	NO	88	70
		100	100
		(1761)	(1876)

THIS TABLE SUGGESTS THERE IS A MODERATE
RELATIONSHIP BETWEEN EDUCATION AND WHETHER RESP. SHOULD HAVE BEEN DEFERRED
REPRESENTING A 18 PERCENTAGE POINT DIFFERENCE.

TABLE 3: DOES WHETHER FRIENDS WERE DEFERRED AFFECT WHETHER RESP. SHOULD HAVE BEEN DEFERRED?

WHETHER FRIENDS WERE DEFERRED:		YES	NO
WHETHER RESP. SHOULD HAVE BEEN DEFERRED:	YES	37	6
	NO	63	94
		100	100
		(1819)	(1818)

THIS TABLE SUGGESTS THERE IS A STRONG
RELATIONSHIP BETWEEN WHETHER FRIENDS WERE DEFERRED AND WHETHER RESP. SHOULD HAVE BEEN DEFERRED
REPRESENTING A 31 PERCENTAGE POINT DIFFERENCE.

TABLE 4: TRIVARIATE RELATIONSHIP

PERCENT WHO ARE
YES ON WHETHER RESP. SHOULD HAVE BEEN DEFERRED

EDUCATION:		HIGH	LOW
WHETHER FRIENDS WERE DEFERRED:	YES	37	37
		(335)	(1484)
	NO	6	5
		(1426)	(392)

EVALUATION

1. RECALL THAT THE OVERALL RELATIONSHIP BETWEEN EDUCATION
    AND WHETHER RESP. SHOULD HAVE BEEN DEFERRED WAS REPRESENTED BY A 18
    PERCENTAGE POINT DIFFERENCE. WHEN WE CONTROL
    FOR WHETHER FRIENDS WERE DEFERRED IN TABLE 4, WE NOTE THAT AMONG
    RESPONDENTS WHO ARE YES ON WHETHER FRIENDS WERE DEFERRED,
    THE DIFFERENCE IS 0
    PERCENTAGE POINTS, AND AMONG THOSE WHO ARE NO,
    THE DIFFERENCE IS 1 PERCENTAGE POINTS.

2. RECALL THAT THE OVERALL RELATIONSHIP BETWEEN WHETHER FRIENDS WERE DEFERRED
    AND WHETHER RESP. SHOULD HAVE BEEN DEFERRED WAS REPRESENTED BY A 31
    PERCENTAGE POINT DIFFERENCE. WHEN WE CONTROL
    FOR EDUCATION IN TABLE 4, WE NOTE THAT AMONG
    RESPONDENTS WHO ARE HIGH ON EDUCATION,
    THE DIFFERENCE IS 31 PERCENTAGE POINTS,
    AND AMONG THOSE WHO ARE LOW,
    THE DIFFERENCE IS 32 PERCENTAGE POINTS.

WITH A 'FIT' OF 0.94 YOUR DATA
REPRESENT AN INTERPRETATION. THAT IS,
YOU HAVE INTERPRETTED THE RELATIONSHIP BETWEEN
EDUCATION AND WHETHER RESP. SHOULD HAVE BEEN DEFERRED. EDUCATION AFFECTS
WHETHER FRIENDS WERE DEFERRED WHICH, IN TURN,
AFFECTS WHETHER RESP. SHOULD HAVE BEEN DEFERRED, BUT EDUCATION HAS LITTLE DIRECT
EFFECT ON WHETHER RESP. SHOULD HAVE BEEN DEFERRED BY ITSELF. YOU HAVE INTERPRETTED
THE PROCESS THROUGH WHICH EDUCATION AFFECTS WHETHER RESP. SHOULD HAVE BEEN DEFERRED

Figure 17-5

```
        ELABORATION 134 16 25 4 19 16 19 18
ENTER NAME OF FIRST VARIABLE AND
NAMES OF THE CODES--ONE AT A TIME
REGION OF ORIGIN
EAST
SOUTH
REPEAT FOR SECOND VARIABLE
REGION OF MEDICAL TRAINING
EAST
SOUTH
REPEAT FOR THIRD VARIABLE
ATTITUDE TOWARD MEDICARE
APPROVE
DISAPPROVE


TABLE 1:  DOES REGION OF ORIGIN AFFECT REGION OF MEDICAL TRAINING?

REGION OF ORIGIN:                    EAST     SOUTH

REGION OF MEDICAL TRAINING:   EAST    89       53

                              SOUTH   11       47

                                      100      100
                                     (179)    (72)

THIS TABLE SUGGESTS THERE IS A STRONG
RELATIONSHIP BETWEEN REGION OF ORIGIN AND REGION OF MEDICAL TRAINING
REPRESENTING A 36 PERCENTAGE
POINT DIFFERENCE:


TABLE 2:  DOES REGION OF ORIGIN AFFECT ATTITUDE TOWARD MEDICARE?

REGION OF ORIGIN:                            EAST     SOUTH

ATTITUDE TOWARD MEDICARE:   APPROVE          84       49

                            DISAPPROVE       16       51

                                             100      100
                                            (179)    (72)

THIS TABLE SUGGESTS THERE IS A STRONG
RELATIONSHIP BETWEEN REGION OF ORIGIN AND ATTITUDE TOWARD MEDICARE
REPRESENTING A 35 PERCENTAGE POINT DIFFERENCE.
```

Figure 17-6

Figure 17-7 illustrates *specification* and is based on hypothetical data involving sex (male or female), intercourse, and pregnancy. The elaboration-minded reader will already anticipate the result: sex specifies the conditions under which intercourse is related to pregnancy. Such a reader will be surprised by the program's conclusion: a true and logical conclusion, which might be expected from a computer program, that is more logical than sexual.

It bears repeating that this computer simulation of the elaboration model is still under development. Even after it is fully developed, however, I anticipate that it will be most useful as a device for teaching the elaboration method rather than for doing the analyses.

The illustrations in Figure 17-6 answer the question. Another option of the program is also illustrated. Since the normal input procedures of the program are rather time-consuming and aggravating for the user experienced

TABLE 0. DOES REGION OF MEDICAL TRAINING AFFECT ATTITUDE TOWARD MEDICARE?

REGION OF MEDICAL TRAINING:		EAST	SOUTH
ATTITUDE TOWARD MEDICARE:	APPROVE	78	59
	DISAPPROVE	22	41
		100	100
		(197)	(54)

THIS TABLE SUGGESTS THERE IS A MODERATE
RELATIONSHIP BETWEEN REGION OF MEDICAL TRAINING AND ATTITUDE TOWARD MEDICARE
REPRESENTING A 19 PERCENTAGE POINT DIFFERENCE.

TABLE 4: TRIVARIATE RELATIONSHIP

PERCENT WHO ARE
APPROVE ON ATTITUDE TOWARD MEDICARE

REGION OF ORIGIN:		EAST	SOUTH
REGION OF MEDICAL TRAINING:	EAST	84	50
		(159)	(38)
	SOUTH	80	47
		(20)	(34)

EVALUATION

1. RECALL THAT THE OVERALL RELATIONSHIP BETWEEN REGION OF ORIGIN
   AND ATTITUDE TOWARD MEDICARE WAS REPRESENTED BY A 35
   PERCENTAGE POINT DIFFERENCE. WHEN WE CONTROL
   FOR REGION OF MEDICAL TRAINING IN TABLE 4, WE NOTE THAT AMONG
   RESPONDENTS WHO ARE EAST ON REGION OF MEDICAL TRAINING,
   THE DIFFERENCE IS 34
   PERCENTAGE POINTS. AND AMONG THOSE WHO ARE SOUTH,
   THE DIFFERENCE IS 33 PERCENTAGE POINTS.

2. RECALL THAT THE OVERALL RELATIONSHIP BETWEEN REGION OF MEDICAL TRAINING
   AND ATTITUDE TOWARD MEDICARE WAS REPRESENTED BY A 19
   PERCENTAGE POINT DIFFERENCE. WHEN WE CONTROL
   FOR REGION OF ORIGIN IN TABLE 4, WE NOTE THAT AMONG
   RESPONDENTS WHO ARE EAST ON REGION OF ORIGIN,
   THE DIFFERENCE IS 4 PERCENTAGE POINTS.
   AND AMONG THOSE WHO ARE SOUTH,
   THE DIFFERENCE IS 3 PERCENTAGE POINTS.

WITH A 'FIT' OF 0.78 YOUR DATA
REPRESENT AN EXPLANATION. THAT IS, THE
SEEMING RELATIONSHIP BETWEEN REGION OF MEDICAL TRAINING AND
ATTITUDE TOWARD MEDICARE IS MERELY A FUNCTION OF THE FACT THAT
REGION OF ORIGIN AFFECTS BOTH REGION OF MEDICAL TRAINING
AND ATTITUDE TOWARD MEDICARE.
THUS, THE SEEMING RELATIONSHIP BETWEEN REGION OF MEDICAL TRAINING
AND ATTITUDE TOWARD MEDICARE IS SPURIOUS.

Figure 17-6 (Continued)

with the program, a fast input option is provided.

Rather than typing the name ELABORATION MODEL to initiate the program, a user may merely type ELABORATION followed by the cell frequencies—in the order in which they would have otherwise been requested. If this is done, the program then asks for the variable and code names in a somewhat more abbreviated fashion and launches into the analysis as soon as the names have been entered.

```
        ELABORATION 0 0 100 100 80 0 20 100
ENTER NAME OF FIRST VARIABLE AND
NAMES OF THE CODES--ONE AT A TIME
RESPONDENT'S SEX
MALE
FEMALE
REPEAT FOR SECOND VARIABLE
HAVING INTERCOURSE
YES
NO
REPEAT FOR THIRD VARIABLE
GETTING PREGNANT
YES
NO
```

TABLE 1:   DOES RESPONDENT'S SEX AFFECT HAVING INTERCOURSE?

RESPONDENT'S SEX:		MALE	FEMALE
HAVING INTERCOURSE:	YES	50	50
	NO	50	50
		100	100
		(200)	(200)

THIS TABLE SUGGESTS THERE IS A ZERO
RELATIONSHIP BETWEEN RESPONDENT'S SEX AND HAVING INTERCOURSE
REPRESENTING A 0 PERCENTAGE
POINT DIFFERENCE.

TABLE 2:   DOES RESPONDENT'S SEX AFFECT GETTING PREGNANT?

RESPONDENT'S SEX:		MALE	FEMALE
GETTING PREGNANT:	YES	0	40
	NO	100	60
		100	100
		(200)	(200)

THIS TABLE SUGGESTS THERE IS A STRONG
RELATIONSHIP BETWEEN RESPONDENT'S SEX AND GETTING PREGNANT
REPRESENTING A 40 PERCENTAGE POINT DIFFERENCE.

TABLE 3:   DOES HAVING INTERCOURSE AFFECT GETTING PREGNANT?

HAVING INTERCOURSE:		YES	NO
GETTING PREGNANT:	YES	40	0
	NO	60	100
		100	100
		(200)	(200)

THIS TABLE SUGGESTS THERE IS A STRONG
RELATIONSHIP BETWEEN HAVING INTERCOURSE AND GETTING PREGNANT
REPRESENTING A 40 PERCENTAGE POINT DIFFERENCE.

TABLE 4:   TRIVARIATE RELATIONSHIP

PERCENT WHO ARE
YES ON GETTING PREGNANT

RESPONDENT'S SEX:		MALE	FEMALE
HAVING INTERCOURSE:	YES	0	80
		(100)	(100)
	NO	0	0
		(100)	(100)

Figure 17-7

```
EVALUATION

1.  RECALL THAT THE OVERALL RELATIONSHIP BETWEEN RESPONDENT'S SEX
    AND GETTING PREGNANT WAS REPRESENTED BY A 40
    PERCENTAGE POINT DIFFERENCE.  WHEN WE CONTROL
    FOR HAVING INTERCOURSE IN TABLE 4, WE NOTE THAT AMONG
    RESPONDENTS WHO ARE YES ON HAVING INTERCOURSE,
    THE DIFFERENCE IS 80
    PERCENTAGE POINTS, AND AMONG THOSE WHO ARE NO,
    THE DIFFERENCE IS 0 PERCENTAGE POINTS.

2.  RECALL THAT THE OVERALL RELATIONSHIP BETWEEN HAVING INTERCOURSE
    AND GETTING PREGNANT WAS REPRESENTED BY A 40
    PERCENTAGE POINT DIFFERENCE.  WHEN WE CONTROL
    FOR RESPONDENT'S SEX IN TABLE 4, WE NOTE THAT AMONG
    RESPONDENTS WHO ARE MALE ON RESPONDENT'S SEX,
    THE DIFFERENCE IS 0 PERCENTAGE POINTS,
    AND AMONG THOSE WHO ARE FEMALE,
    THE DIFFERENCE IS 80 PERCENTAGE POINTS.

WITH A 'FIT' OF 1, YOUR DATA
REPRESENT A SPECIFICATION.  THAT IS, YOU HAVE
SPECIFIED THE CONDITIONS UNDER WHICH RESPONDENT'S SEX
AFFECTS GETTING PREGNANT.  AS WE SEE IN TABLE 4, THE EFFECT
PRIMARILY OCCURS AMONG THOSE WHO ARE
YES ON HAVING INTERCOURSE.
```

Figure 17-7 (Continued)

17.5

Elaboration and Ex Post Facto Hypothesizing

Before we leave the discussion of the elaboration model, one further word is in order regarding its power in connection with an unfortunate sacred cow in the traditional norms of scientific research. The reader of methodological literature will find countless references to the fallacy of *"ex post facto hypothesizing."* The intentions of such injunctions are correct, but the inexperienced researcher is sometimes led astray.

When the researcher observes an empirical relationship between two variables and then simply suggests a reason for that relationship, this is sometimes called ex post facto hypothesizing. He has generated a hypothesis linking two variables after their relationship is already known. We will recall, from an early discussion in this book, that all hypotheses must be subject to disconfirmation. Unless the researcher (or theorist) can specify empirical findings that would disprove his hypothesis, it is essentially useless. It is reasoned, therefore, that once the researcher has *observed* a relationship between two variables, any hypothesis regarding that relationship cannot be disproved.

This is a fair assessment in those situations in which the researcher does nothing more than dress up his empirical observations with deceptive hypotheses after the fact. Having observed that women are more religious than men, he should not simply assert that women will be more religious than men because of some general dynamic of social behavior and then rest his case on the initial observation.

The unfortunate spin-off of this injunction against ex post facto hypothesizing is in its inhibition of good, honest hypothesizing after the fact. Inexperienced researchers are often led to believe that they must make all their hypotheses before examining their data—even if this means making a lot of poorly reasoned ones. Furthermore, they are led to ignore any empirically observed relationships that do not confirm some prior hypothesis.

Surely, few researchers would now wish that Sam Stouffer had hushed up his anomalous findings regarding morale among soldiers in the Army. Stouffer noted peculiar empirical observations and set about hypothesizing the reasons for those findings. And his reasoning has proved invaluable to subsequent researchers.

There is a further, more sophisticated, point to be made here, however. Whereas anyone can generate hypotheses to explain observed empirical relationships in a body of data, the elaboration model provides the logical tools for *testing* those hypotheses within the same body of data. A good example of this may be found in the earlier discussion of social class and church involvement. Glock explained the original relationship in terms of social deprivation theory. If he had stopped at that point, his comments would have been interesting but hardly persuasive. He went beyond that point, however. He noted that if the hypothesis were correct, then the relationship between social class and church involvement should disappear among those women who were receiving gratification from the secular society—those who had held office in a secular organization. This was then subjected to an empirical test. Had the new hypothesis not been confirmed by the data, he would have been forced to reconsider.

These additional comments should further illustrate the point that data analysis is a continuing process, demanding all the ingenuity and perseverance the researcher can muster. The image of a researcher carefully laying out hypotheses and then testing them in a ritualistic fashion results only in ritualistic research.

For the reader who is concerned that the strength of ex post facto proofs seems to be less than that of the traditional kinds, let me repeat the earlier assertion that "scientific proof" is a contradiction in terms. Nothing is ever proved *scientifically*. Hypotheses, explanations, theories, or hunches can all escape a stream of attempts at disproof, but none can be proved in any absolute sense. The acceptance of a hypothesis, then, is really a function of the extent to which it has been tested and not disconfirmed. No hypothesis, therefore, should be considered sound on the basis of one test—whether the hypothesis was generated before or after the observation of empirical data. With this in mind, the researcher should not deny himself some of the most fruitful avenues available to him in data analysis. He should always try to reach an honest understanding of his data, develop meaningful theories for more general understanding, and not worry about the manner of reaching that understanding.

17.6
Summary

Chapter 17 has discussed the *elaboration model* developed by Paul Lazarsfeld and his colleagues. It provides a logical model for the analysis and interpretation of the relationships among variables. As such, it provides a useful basis for a later understanding of other modes of analysis in social research.

The basic form of the elaboration model is as follows: (a) a relationship between two variables is observed; (b) a third variable—a *control* variable or *test* variable—is then used to subdivide the cases under study; (c) the original relationship between two variables is computed within each of the subgroups; and (d) the comparison of the original *zero-order* relationship with each of the *partial* relationships observed within the subgroups provides the basis for a better understanding of the original relationship itself.

The chapter began with a brief historical overview of the development of the elaboration model. We saw that it arose in connection with the research activities of Samuel Stouffer, working for the United States Army during World War II. Stouffer offered an interesting interpretation of certain anomalous findings, and Lazarsfeld went on to develop the empirical analyses that would have been necessary to confirm Stouffer's interpretation. This effort resulted in a much broader logical model.

Next, the chapter addressed the fundamental paradigm embodied within the elaboration model. We discovered that two important considerations are involved: (1) whether the *control* variable is *antecedent* or *intervening* and (2) the outcome of the comparison between the original relationship and the partial relationships. The possible results are that: (a) the partial relationships are the same as the original one, (b) the partial relationships all disappear, or (c) one partial relationship disappears while the other is the same as the original relationship. The various outcomes are given the names: *replication, interpretation, explanation,* and *specification,* and each outcome has a different implication for our understanding of the original relationship.

To further illustrate the logic of the elaboration model, a tentative computer simulation of elaboration was presented briefly. The chapter concluded with a discussion of the issue of *ex post facto hypothesizing* in connection with the use of the elaboration model in the analysis of social research data.

17.7
Main Points

1. The elaboration model is one method of multivariate analysis appropriate to social research.

2. It was developed by Paul Lazarsfeld in connection with research undertaken by Samuel Stouffer.

3. The elaboration model is primarily a logical model that can illustrate the basic logic of other multivariate methods.

4. The basic steps in elaboration are as follows: (a) a relationship is observed to exist between two variables; (b) a third variable is held constant in the sense that the cases under study are subdivided according to the attributes of that third variable; (c) the original two-variable relationship is recomputed within each of the subgroups; and (d) the comparison of the original relationship with the relationships found within each subgroup provides a fuller understanding of the original relationship itself.

5. An *intervening* control variable is one that occurs in time between the occurrence of the independent variable and the occurrence of the dependent variable.

6. An *antecedent* control variable is one that occurs earlier in time than either the independent or the dependent variables.

7. A *zero-order* relationship is the observed relationship between two variables *without* a third variable being held constant or controlled.

8. A *partial* relationship is the observed relationship between two variables—within a subgroup of cases based on some attribute of the control variable. Thus, the relationship between age and prejudice among men only (i.e., controlling for sex) would be a partial relationship.

9. If a set of partial relationships is essentially the same as the corresponding zero-order relationship, this outcome is called a *replication,* regardless of whether the control variable is intervening or antecedent. This means, simply, that the originally observed relationship has been replicated within smaller subgroups, and that the control variable has no influence on that original relationship.

10. If a set of partial relationships is reduced essentially to zero when an *antecedent* variable is held constant, this outcome is called an *explanation,* meaning that the originally observed "relationship" was a *spurious* or ungenuine one. This outcome suggests that the control variable has a causal effect on each of the variables examined in the zero-order relationship, thus

resulting in a statistical relationship between those two that does not represent a causal relationship in itself.

11. If a set of partial relationships is reduced essentially to zero when an *intervening* variable is held constant, this outcome is called an *interpretation,* meaning that we have interpreted the manner in which the independent variable has its influence on the dependent variable: the independent variable influences the intervening variable, which, in turn, influences the dependent variable. In this instance, we conclude that the original relationship was a genuine causal relationship; we have shed further light on how that causal process operates.

12. If one partial relationship is reduced essentially to zero while the other remains about the same as the original one, this outcome is called a *specification,* regardless of whether the control variable was intervening or antecedent. This means, simply, that we have specified the conditions under which the originally observed relationship occurs.

13. *Ex post facto hypothesizing* refers to the development of hypotheses "predicting" relationships that have already been observed. This is invalid in science since it is impossible to disconfirm such hypotheses. Of course, nothing prevents a scientist from suggesting reasons that observed relationships may be the way they are; he simply should not frame those reasons in the form of "hypotheses." More important, one observed relationship and possible reasons for it may suggest hypotheses about other relationships that have not been examined. The elaboration model is an excellent logical device for this kind of "unfolding" analysis of data.

17.8
Annotated Bibliography

Glock, Charles (ed.), *Survey Research in the Social Sciences* (New York: Russell Sage Foundation, 1967), Chapter 1. An excellent discussion of the logic of elaboration. Glock's own chapter in this book presents the elaboration model, providing concrete illustrations.

Hirschi, Travis, and Selvin, Hanan, *Delinquency Research: An Appraisal of Analytic Methods* (New York: Free Press, 1967). Excellent logical discussions and concrete examples. This book examines the empirical research in the field of delinquency from a rigorously logical perspective. Critiques of specific research examples often set the stage for important and insightful general discussions of elaboration and other aspects of the logic of scientific inquiry.

Hyman, Herbert, *Survey Design and Analysis* (New York: Free Press, 1955). A somewhat dated but milestone statement of the elaboration model. The fundamental paradigm is discussed and illustrated through a number of real surveys. Lazarsfeld's foreword is the most available "classic" statement of the logic of elaboration. This was and still is an important book. Later sections of the book illustrate the relationship between the logical model and the nitty-gritty details of analyzing data by counter-sorter, an excellent method of developing hand-brain coordination in social research.

Lazarsfeld, Paul, and Rosenberg, Morris (eds.), *The Language of Social Research* (New York: Free Press, 1955). An excellent and classic collection of conceptual discussions and empirical illustrations. Section II is especially relevant, though the logic of elaboration runs throughout most of the volume.

Rosenberg, Morris, *The Logic of Survey Analysis* (New York: Basic Books, 1968). The most comprehensive statement of elaboration available. Rosenberg presents the basic paradigm, and goes on to suggest logical extensions of it. It is difficult to decide what is most important, this aspect of the book, or the voluminous illustrations. Both are simply excellent, and this book serves an important instructional purpose.

18
Social Statistics

18.1
Introduction

Many people are intimidated by empirical research because they feel uncomfortable with mathematics and statistics. And indeed, many research reports are filled with a variety of semispecified computations. The role of statistics in social research is very important, but it is equally important that that role be seen in its proper perspective.

Empirical research is first and foremost a logical operation rather than a mathematical one. If a person is fully conversant with the logic of science, he will be able to understand and use the appropriate mathematics. Mathematics is merely a convenient and efficient language for accomplishing the logical operations inherent in good data analysis. Statistics is the applied branch of mathematics especially appropriate to a variety of research analyses.

This chapter will consider two types of statistics: *descriptive* and *inferential.* **Descriptive statistics** is a medium for describing data in manageable forms. **Inferential statistics,** on the other hand, assists the researcher to draw conclusions from a sample that apply to the population from which the sample has been drawn.

18.2
Descriptive Statistics

Data Reduction

It is useful to begin the discussion of descriptive statistics with a brief look at the raw-data matrix produced by a research project. Table 18-1 presents such a raw-data matrix.

For our purposes, we may think of the variables in Table 18-1 as punch-card columns. Each column represents a coded set of data. Column V_3, for example, might represent sex: 1 for male and 2 for female. The "cases" in the left column of Table 18-1 would represent the people for whom data were coded.

A raw-data matrix contains all the original coded information that a researcher collects about his cases. It is worth noting, moreover, that the

Table 18-1. Typical Raw-Data Matrix

					Variables						
	V_1	V_2	V_3	V_4	V_5	V_6	V_7	V_8	V_9	$\cdots$	V_n
Case 1	2	5	1	4	3	3	9	2	7	$\cdots$	6
Case 2	3	2	1	1	8	5	9	1	6	$\cdots$	1
Case 3	1	3	2	3	2	5	3	7	5	$\cdots$	2
Case 4	2	1	2	2	5	2	7	4	4	$\cdots$	3
Case n	1	3	1	2	4	4	6	7	1	$\cdots$	4

researcher often sees his data in just this form. If the data are coded on transfer sheets for keypunching, those sheets form a raw-data matrix like the one in Table 18-1. And after keypunching the data, the researcher often has the computer list his data file, and the result is a raw-data matrix.

Recalling the earlier discussion of univariate analysis in Chapter 14, we note that the raw-data matrix has the advantage of representing all the available information. If the reader of a research report were provided with the raw-data matrix, he would have all the information available to the researcher himself.

The prime difficulty of such a data matrix is that it is a very inefficient presentation of the data. Imagine for a moment a matrix containing perhaps 200 variables for each of 2,000 cases. Such a matrix would contain nearly half a million entries. Neither the researcher nor the reader would be able to sift through so many numbers to recognize meaningful patterns in them.

Descriptive statistics provides a method of reducing large data matrices to manageable summaries to permit easy understanding and interpretation. Single variables can be summarized by descriptive statistics, and so can the associations among variables.

Chapter 14 discussed the various methods of summarizing univariate data: frequency distributions in either raw numbers or percentages, either grouping the data into categories or leaving them ungrouped; averages such as the mean, median, or mode; and measures of dispersion such as the range, the standard deviation, and so forth. The reader should keep in mind the inherent trade-off between summarization and the maintenance of the original data. The prime goal of univariate descriptive statistics is efficiency: the maximum amount of information should be maintained in the simplest summary form. We shall turn now to an extension of those concerns in an examination of the descriptive statistics available for summarizing associations among variables.

Measures of Association

The association between any two variables also may be represented by a data matrix, this time produced by the joint frequency distributions of the two variables. Table 18-2 presents such a matrix.

Table 18-2. Association between Variables
as a Data Matrix

	Variable X					
	X_1	X_2	X_3	X_4	X_5	X_6
Y_1	35	27	26	12	15	7
Y_2	38	48	38	22	35	13
Y_3	32	41	75	64	46	22
Y_4	28	45	63	80	79	45
Y_5	20	35	53	90	103	87
Y_6	23	12	76	80	99	165
Y_7	5	8	43	60	73	189

The data matrix presented in Table 18-2 provides all the necessary information for determining the nature and extent of the relationship between variables X and Y. The column headings in the table represent the values of variable X, while the row headings represent the values of variable Y. The numbers in the body of the matrix represent the number of cases having a particular pattern of attributes. For example, 35 cases have the pattern X_1 Y_1; 43 cases are X_3 Y_7.

Like the raw-data matrix presented in Table 18-1, this one gives the reader more information than he can easily comprehend. The careful reader will note that as values of variable X increase from X_1 to X_7, there is a general tendency for values of Y to increase from Y_1 to Y_7, but no more than a general impression is possible. A variety of descriptive statistics permits the summarization of this data matrix, however. Selecting the appropriate measure depends initially on the nature of the two variables.

We shall turn now to some of the options available to the researcher for summarizing the association between two variables. This discussion and those to follow are taken largely from the excellent statistics textbook by Linton C. Freeman.[1]

Each of the measures of association to be discussed in the following sections is based on the same model—*proportionate reduction of error* (PRE). The logic of this model is as follows. First, let's assume that the researcher is asked to "guess" respondents' attributes on a given variable; for example, whether they answered "yes" or "no" to a given questionnaire item. To assist him, let's assume further that the researcher knows the overall distribution of responses in the total sample—say, 60 percent said "yes" and 40 percent said "no." The researcher would make the fewest errors in this process if he always guessed the *modal* (most frequent) response: "yes."

Second, let's assume that the researcher knows the empirical relationship between the first variable and some other variable: say, sex. Now, each time we ask the researcher to guess whether a respondent said "yes" or "no," we shall tell him whether the respondent is a man or a woman. If the two variables are related to each other, the researcher should make fewer errors the second time. It is possible, therefore, to compute the PRE by knowing the

1. Linton C. Freeman, *Elementary Applied Statistics* (New York: John Wiley, 1968).

relationship between the two variables: the greater the relationship, the greater the reduction of error.

This basic PRE model is modified slightly to take account of different levels of measurement—nominal, ordinal, or interval. The following sections will consider each level of measurement and present one measure of association appropriate to each. The reader should realize that the three measures discussed are only an arbitrary selection from among many appropriate measures.

Nominal Variables   If the two variables consist of nominal data (for example, sex, religious affiliation, race), lambda (λ) would be one appropriate measure. As discussed above, lambda is based on the researcher's ability to "guess" values on one of the variables: the PRE achieved through knowledge of values on the other variable. A simple hypothetical example will illustrate the logic and method of lambda.

Table 18-3. Hypothetical Data Relating Sex to Employment Status

	Men	Women	Total
Employed	900	200	1,100
Unemployed	100	800	900
Total	1,000	1,000	2,000

Table 18-3 presents hypothetical data relating sex to employment status. Overall, we note that 1,100 people are employed, while 900 are unemployed. If the researcher were to predict whether or not people were employed, knowing only the overall distribution on that variable, he would always predict "employed," since this would result in fewer errors than always predicting "unemployed." Nevertheless, this strategy would result in 900 errors out of 2,000 predictions.

Let's suppose that the researcher had access to the data shown in Table 18-3 and that he was told each person's sex prior to making his prediction of employment status. His strategy would change in that case. For every man, he would predict "employed," while for every woman, he would predict "unemployed." In this instance, he would make 300 errors—the 100 unemployed men and the 200 employed women—or 600 fewer errors than would have been made in ignorance of their sexes.

Lambda, then, represents the reduction in errors as a proportion of the errors that would have been made on the basis of the overall distribution. In this hypothetical example, lambda would equal .67: 600 fewer errors divided by 900 errors based on the total distribution of employment status alone. In this fashion, lambda provides a measure of the statistical association between sex and employment status.

If sex and employment status were statistically independent of one another, we would have found the same distribution of employment status for men and women. In this case, knowing sexes would not have affected the number of errors made in predicting employment status, and the resulting lambda would have been zero. If, on the other hand, all men were employed and all women were unemployed, the researcher would have made no errors in predicting employment status, knowing sex. He would have made 900 fewer errors (out of 900) and lambda would have been 1.0—representing a perfect statistical association.

Lambda is only one of several measures of association appropriate to the analysis of two nominal variables. The reader is referred to Freeman[2] for discussion of other appropriate measures.

Ordinal Variables If the variables being related were ordinal in nature (for example, social class, religiosity, alienation), gamma (γ) would be one appropriate measure of association. Like lambda, gamma is based on the researcher's ability to guess values on one variable by knowing values on another. Instead of guessing exact values, however, gamma is based on the ordinal arrangement of values. For any given *pair* of cases, the researcher guesses that their ordinal ranking on one variable will correspond (positively or negatively) to their ordinal ranking on the other. Gamma is the proportion of pairs that fit this pattern.

Table 18-4. Hypothetical Data Relating Social Class to Prejudice

Prejudice	Lower Class	Middle Class	Upper Class
Low	200	400	700
Medium	500	900	400
High	800	300	100

Table 18-4 presents hypothetical data relating social class to prejudice. An inspection of the table will indicate the general nature of the relationship between these two variables: as social class increases, prejudice decreases. There is a negative association between social class and prejudice.

Gamma is computed from two quantities: (1) the number of pairs having the same ranking on the two variables and (2) the number of pairs having the opposite ranking on the two variables. The pairs having the same ranking are computed as follows. The frequency of each cell in the table is multiplied by the sum of all cells appearing below and to the right of it—with all these products being summed. In the present example, the number of pairs with the same ranking would be 200(900 + 300 + 400 + 100) + 500(300 + 100) + 400(400 + 100) + 900(100) or 340,000 + 20,000 + 20,000 + 90,000 = 470,000.

---

2. *Op. cit.*

The pairs having the opposite ranking on the two variables are computed as follows: The frequency of each cell in the table is multiplied by the sum of all cells appearing below and to the left of it—with all these products being summed. In this example, the numbers of pairs with opposite rankings would be 700(500 + 800+ 900 + 300) + 400(800 + 300) + 400(500.+ 800) + 900(800) or 1,750,000 + 440,000 + 520,000 + 720,000 = 3,430,000.

Gamma is computed from the numbers of same-ranked pairs and opposite-ranked pairs as follows:

$$Gamma = (same - opposite) \div (same + opposite)$$

In the present example, gamma would equal: (470,000 − 3,430,000) divided by 470,000 + 3,430,000) or −.76. The negative sign in this answer indicates the negative association suggested by the initial inspection of the table. Social class and prejudice, in this hypothetical example, are negatively associated with one another. The numerical figure for gamma indicates that 76 percent more of the pairs examined had the opposite ranking than had the same ranking.

Note that while values of lambda vary from 0 to 1, values of gamma vary from −1 to +1, representing the *direction* as well as the magnitude of the association. Since nominal variables have no ordinal structure, it makes no sense to speak of the direction of the relationship. (A negative lambda would indicate that the researcher had made more errors in predicting values on one variable while knowing values on the second than he made in ignorance of the second.)

Gamma is only one of several measures of association appropriate to ordinal variables. Again, the reader is referred to Freeman[3] for a more comprehensive treatment of this subject.

Interval or Ratio Variables   If the variables being associated are interval or ratio in nature (for example, age, income, grade point average, and so forth), one appropriate measure of association would be Pearson's product-moment correlation (r). The derivation and computation of this measure of association is sufficiently complex to lie outside the scope of the present book, so only a few general comments will be made.

Like both gamma and lambda, r is based on guessing the value of one variable on the basis of knowing the other. For continuous interval or ratio variables, however, it is unlikely that the researcher would be able to predict the *precise* value of the variable. But on the other hand, predicting only the ordinal arrangement of values on the two variables would not take advantage of the greater amount of information conveyed by an interval or ratio variable. In a sense, r reflects *how closely* the researcher can guess the value of one variable through his knowledge of the value of the other.

---

3. *Op. cit.*

To understand the logic of r, it will be useful to consider the manner in which a researcher might hypothetically "guess" values that cases have on a given variable. With nominal variables, we have seen that the researcher might always "guess" the modal value. This is not an appropriate perspective for interval or ratio data, however. Instead, the researcher would minimize his errors by always guessing the mean value of the variable. Although this would produce few if any perfect guesses, the extent of his errors would be minimized.

In the computation of lambda, we noted the number of errors produced by always guessing the modal value. In the case of r, "errors" are measured in terms of the sum of the squared differences between the actual value and the mean. We shall refer to this later as the *total variance.*

To improve his "guessing," the researcher constructs a *regression line* (see Chapter 19), stated in the form of a regression equation that permits the estimation of values on one variable from values on the other. The general format for this equation is $Y' = a + b(X)$, where a and b are computed values, where X is a given value on one variable, and Y' is the estimated value on the other. The values of a and b are computed in such a way as to minimize the differences between actual values of Y and the corresponding estimates (Y') based on the known value of X. The sum of squared differences between actual and estimated values of Y is called the *unexplained variance,* in that it represents errors that still exist even when estimates are based on known values of X.

The *explained variance* is the difference between the total variance and the unexplained variance. Dividing the explained variance by the total variance produces a measure of the *proportionate reduction of error* corresponding to the similar quantity in the computation of lambda. In the present case, this quantity is the correlation *squared: r^2.* Thus, if $r = .7$, then $r^2 = .49$: meaning that about *half* the variance has been explained.

In practice, the researcher will compute r rather than r^2, since the product-moment correlation can take either a positive or negative sign, depending on the direction of the relationship between the two variables. (Computing r^2 and taking a square root would always produce a positive quantity.) The reader is referred to Freeman[4] or any other standard statistics textbook for the method of computing r, although it is anticipated that most readers using this measure will have access to computer programs designed for this function.[5]

Mixed Types of Variables Often, the researcher will find that his interest lies in the association between two variables that differ in type: one

4. *Op. cit.*
5. Although r is based on a regression model, r is a *symmetrical* measure. (Gamma is also symmetrical, but lambda is not.) We shall see in the next chapter that predicting values of Y from values of X produces a different equation than predicting values of X from values of Y. Thus, while the linear regression model is asymmetrical, the computation of r is such as to produce a symmetrical solution.

ordinal variable and one nominal variable. A variety of special statistics are appropriate to these different possibilities, and the reader is encouraged to examine Freeman[6] for the appropriate statistics for his particular situation.

This is an opportune point for a general comment regarding types of variables and the appropriateness of statistical measures. A quick review of social scientific research literature will yield countless examples of statistical measures applied to data that do not meet the logical requirements of the measures. The computation of Pearson's r for ordinal data is perhaps the most typical example. One's response to this practice seems largely a matter of personal taste. The person who argued against it would be correct on statistical grounds: correlation coefficients assume interval data, and ordinal data do not meet that criterion. On the other hand, it is my personal orientation to accept, and even to encourage, the use of whatever statistical techniques help the researcher (and the reader) to understand the body of data under analysis. If the computation of r from ordinal data serves this purpose, then it should be encouraged. However, I strongly object to (and discuss in the next section) the practice of making statistical inferences on the basis of such computations. The researcher is justified in bending the rules if it helps him understand his data, but he must be aware of the implications of bending those rules.

18.3
Inferential Statistics

Many, if not most, social scientific research projects involve the examination of data collected from a sample drawn from a larger population. A sample of people may be interviewed in a survey; a sample of divorce records may be coded and analyzed; a sample of newspapers may be examined through content analysis. Samples are seldom if ever studied for the sole purpose of describing the samples per se; in most instances, the ultimate purpose is to make assertions about the larger population from which the sample has been selected. Frequently, then, the researcher will wish to interpret his univariate and multivariate sample findings as the basis for *inferences* about some population.

This section will examine the statistical measures available to the researcher for making such inferences and the logical bases for them. We shall begin with univariate data and move to multivariate.

Univariate Inferences

The opening sections of Chapter 14 dealt with methods of presenting univariate data. Each summary measure was intended as a method of

---

6. *Op. cit.*

describing the sample studied. Now we have come to the point of using those measures to make broader assertions about the population. This section is addressed to two univariate measures: percentages and means.

If 50 percent of a sample of people say they have had colds during the past year, the researcher's best estimate of the similar proportion of the total population from which the sample has been drawn is 50 percent. (This assumes a simple random sample, of course.) It is rather unlikely, nonetheless, that *precisely* 50 percent of the population have had colds during the year, however. If a rigorous sampling design for random selection has been followed, however, the researcher will be able to estimate the expected range of error when the sample finding is applied to the population.

Chapter 6 on sampling theory covered the procedures for making such estimates, so they will be only reviewed here. In the case of a percentage, the quantity $\sqrt{pq/n}$, where p is a percentage and q equals $1 - p$, and where n is the sample size, is called the *standard error*. As noted in Chapter 6, this quantity is very important in the estimation of sampling error. The researcher may be 68 percent "confident" that the population figure falls within plus or minus one standard error of the sample figure, he may be 95 percent "confident" that it falls within plus or minus two standard errors, and 99.9 percent "confident" that it falls within plus or minus three standard errors.

Any statement of sampling error, then, must contain two essential components: the *confidence level* (for example, 95 percent) and the *confidence interval* (for example ± 2.5 porocnt). If 50 percent of a sample of 1,600 people say they have had colds during tho year, the researcher might say he is 95 percent confident that the population figure is between 47.5 percent and 52.5 percent.

Recognize in this example that he has moved beyond simply describing the sample into the realm of making estimates (inferences) about the larger population. In doing this, the researcher must be wary of several assumptions.

First, the sample must be drawn from the population about which inferences are being made. A sample taken from a telephone directory cannot legitimately be the basis for statistical inferences about the population of a city.

Second, the inferential statistics assume simple random sampling, which is virtually never the case in sample surveys. The statistics assume sampling with replacement, which is almost never done; but this is probably not a serious problem. Although systematic sampling is used more frequently than random sampling, this probably presents no serious problem if done correctly. Stratified sampling, since it improves representativeness, clearly presents no problem. Cluster sampling does present a problem, however, as the estimates of sampling error may be too small. Quite clearly, street-corner sampling does not warrant the use of inferential statistics. Also assumed is a 100 percent completion rate. This problem increases in seriousness as the completion rate decreases.

Third, the inferential statistics are addressed to sampling error only; they do not take account of *nonsampling* errors. Thus, it might be quite correct to state that between 47.5 percent and 52.5 percent of the population (95 percent confidence) would *say* that they had had colds during the previous year, but their reports might be essentially worthless. The researcher could confidently guess the proportion of the population who would *report* colds, but not the proportion who had had them. Whereas nonsampling errors are probably larger than sampling errors in a respectable sample design, the researcher should be especially cautious in generalizing from his sample findings to the population.

Tests of Statistical Significance

What constitutes a *significant* association between two variables? This question, like many, has no reasonable answer. Nevertheless, it is frequently answered in an unreasonable manner.

There is no scientific answer to the question of whether a given association between two variables is "significant," strong, important, interesting, or worth reporting. Perhaps the ultimate test of significance rests with the researcher's ability to persuade his audience (present and future) of the association's significance.

At the same time, there is a body of inferential statistics that may assist the researcher in this regard: the body of *parametric tests of significance.* As the name suggests, "parametric" statistics are those that make certain assumptions about the parameters describing the population from which the sample is selected.

Although tests of significance are widely reported in social scientific literature, the logic underlying them is rather subtle and is often misunderstood. Tests of significance are based on the same sampling logic that has been discussed elsewhere in this book. To understand the logic of these tests, let's return for a moment to the concept of sampling error in regard to univariate data.

Recall that a sample statistic normally provides the best single estimate of the corresponding population parameter, but that it is seldom the case that the statistic and the parameter precisely correspond. Thus, the researcher reports the probability that the parameter falls within a certain range (confidence interval). The degree of uncertainty within that range is due to normal sampling error. The corollary of such a statement is, of course, that it is *improbable* that the parameter would fall outside the specified range only as a result of sampling error. Thus, if the researcher estimates that a parameter (99.9 percent confidence) lies between 45 percent and 55 percent, he says by implication that it is *extremely improbable* that the parameter is actually, say, 90 percent if his only error of estimation is due to normal sampling. This is the basic logic behind tests of significance.

Given a specified degree of association between two variables, tests of significance represent the likelihood that such an association could be due only to normal sampling error in the case where there is *no association* between the variables in the population. In a sense, the researcher assumes no association in the population (called the **null hypothesis**) and then asks whether his measured association in the sample could be due only to sampling error. If the measured association could not reasonably be attributed to sampling error, he will then assume that an association exists between the variables in the population.

There is a corollary to confidence intervals in tests of significance: representing the probability of the measured association being due *only to sampling* error. This is called the **level of significance.** Like confidence intervals, levels of significance are derived from a logical model in which several samples are drawn from a given population. In the present case, we assume that there is no association between the variables in the population, and then ask what proportion of the samples drawn from that population would produce associations at least as great as those measured in the empirical data. Three levels of significance are frequently used in research reports: .05, .01, and .001. These mean, respectively, that the chances of obtaining the measured association as a result of sampling error are 5/100, 1/100, and 1/1,000.

Researchers who use tests of significance normally follow one of two patterns in this regard. Some prefer to specify in advance the level of significance that they will regard as sufficient. If any measured association is statistically significant at that level, they will regard it as representing a genuine association between the two variables. In other words, they are willing to discount the possibility of it resulting from sampling error only.

Other researchers prefer to report the specific level of significance for each association, disregarding the conventions of .05, .01, and .001. Rather than reporting that a given association was significant at the .05 level, they would indicate that it was significant at the .023 level, indicating the chances of it having resulted from sampling error as 23 out of 1,000.

Chi-square is a frequently used test of significance in social science. It is based on the *null hypothesis:* the assumption that there is no relationship between the two variables in the total population. Given the observed distribution of values on the two separate variables, the researcher computes the conjoint distribution that would be expected if there were no relationship between the two variables. The result of this operation is a set of *expected frequencies* for all the cells in the contingency table. The researcher then compares this expected distribution with the distribution of cases actually found in the sample data, and he determines the probability that the discovered discrepancy could have resulted from sampling error alone. An example will illustrate this procedure.

Let's assume that a researcher is interested in the possible relationship between church attendance and sex among the members of a particular church. To test this relationship, he has selected a sample of 100 church members at random. Assume further that he finds his sample is made up of 40 men and 60 women. And, finally, assume that 70 percent of his sample report having attended church during the preceding week, while the remaining 30 percent say they did not.

If there were no relationship between sex and church attendance, then we should expect 70 percent of the men in the sample to have attended church during the preceding week and should expect that 30 percent did not. Moreover, we should expect the same proportional results from women.

Table 18-5 (Section A) presents the expected frequencies based on this model. Thus, we should expect that 28 men and 42 women would have attended church, while 12 men and 18 women would not have attended church.

Table 18-5. A Hypothetical Illustration of Chi-Square

Section A. Expected cell frequencies

	Men	Women	Total
Attended church	28	42	70
Did not attend church	12	18	30
Total	40	60	100

Section B. Observed cell frequencies

	Men	Women	Total
Attended church	20	50	70
Did not attend church	20	10	30
Total	40	60	100

Section C. (Observed − expected)^2 / expected

	Men	Women
Attended church	2.29	1.52
Did not attend church	5.33	3.56

$\chi^2 = 12.70$, $p = .001$

Section B of Table 18-5 presents the hypothetically observed cell frequencies discovered among the sample of 100 church members. We note that 20 of the men report having attended church during the preceding week, while the remaining 20 say they did not. Among the women in the sample, 50 attended church and 10 did not. Comparing the expected and observed frequencies (Sections A and B), we note that somewhat fewer men attended church than expected, while somewhat more women than expected attended.

Chi-square is computed as follows. For each cell in the tables, the researcher (1) subtracts the expected frequency for that cell from the observed frequency, (2) squares this quantity, and (3) divides the squared difference by the expected frequency. This procedure is carried out for each cell in the tables, and the several results are added together. (Section C of Table 18-5 presents the cell-by-cell computations.) The final sum is the value of chi-square: 12.70 in the example.

The value that we have now computed is the overall discrepancy between the observed conjoint distribution in the sample and the distribution that we should have expected if the two variables were unrelated to one another. Of course, the mere discovery of a discrepancy does not prove that the two variables are related, since normal sampling error might produce discrepancies even when there was no relationship in the total population. The magnitude of the value of chi-square, however, permits us to estimate the probability of this having happened.

To determine the statistical significance of the observed relationship, we must utilize a standard table of chi-square values. This will require the computation of the *degrees of freedom*. In the case of chi-square, the degrees of freedom are computed as follows: the number of rows in the table, minus one, is multiplied by the number of columns, minus one. This may be written as $(r - 1)(c - 1)$. In the present example, we have two rows and two columns (discounting the *totals*), so there is 1 degree of freedom.

Turning to a table of chi-square values (see Appendix F), we find that for one degree of freedom and random sampling from a population in which there is no relationship between two variables, 10 percent of the time we should expect a chi-square of at least 2.7. Thus, if we selected 100 samples from such a population, we should expect about 10 of those samples to produce chi-squares equal to or greater than 2.7. Moreover, we should expect chi-squares of at least 6.6 in 1 percent of the samples. Chi-square values of 10.8 should be expected in only .1 percent of the samples. Thus, the lower the computed chi-square value, the more probable it is that the value could be attributed to sampling error alone. The higher the chi-square value, the less probable it is that it could be due to sampling error alone.

In the present, hypothetical, example, the computed value of chi-square is 12.70. If there were no relationship between sex and church attendance in the whole church member population, and a large number of samples had been selected and studied, then we would expect a chi-square of this magnitude in fewer than .1 percent of those samples. Thus, the probability of obtaining a chi-square of this magnitude is less than .001, if random sampling has been used and there is no relationship in the population. We report this finding by saying the relationship is statistically significant "at the .001 level." Since it is so improbable that the observed relationship could have resulted from sampling error alone, we are likely to reject the null hypothesis and assume that there is a relationship between the two variables in the total population of church members.

Most measures of association can be tested for statistical significance in a similar manner. Standard tables of values permit the researcher to determine whether a given association is statistically significant and at what level. Any standard statistics textbook provides instructions on the use of such tables, and we shall not pursue the matter further here.

Tests of significance have the advantage of providing an objective yardstick against which to estimate the significance of associations between variables. They assist the researcher in ruling out associations that may not represent genuine relationships in the population under study. The researcher who uses or reads reports of significance tests should remain wary of several dangers in their interpretation, however.

First, we have been discussing tests of *statistical* significance; there are no objective tests of *substantive* significance. Thus, the researcher may be legitimately convinced that a given association is not due to sampling error, but he may be in the position of asserting without fear of contradiction that two variables are only slightly related to one another. Recall that sampling error is an inverse function of sample size; the larger the sample, the smaller the expected error. Thus, a correlation of, say, .1 might very well be significant (at a given level) if discovered in a large sample, whereas the same correlation between the same two variables would not be significant if found in a smaller sample. Of course, this makes perfectly good sense if one understands the basic logic of tests of significance: in the larger sample, there is less chance that the correlation could be simply the product of sampling error. In both samples, however, it might represent a very weak and essentially zero correlation.

Second, tests of significance are based on the same sampling assumptions as were assumed in the computation of confidence intervals. To the extent that these assumptions are not met by the actual sampling design, the tests of significance are not strictly legitimate.

Third, the researcher should be wary of applying tests of significance to data that represent a total population rather than a sample. If, for example, he has studied *all* the newspapers in the country and discovered a correlation of .3 between two variables, he should not report that the association is significant at the .001 level. Since he has not sampled, there is *no* chance that the association could be due to sampling error. The association between the two variables as measured in the population is *precisely* a correlation of .3—whether that degree of association is a *substantively significant* one, whether it is important, cannot be answered through any objective test. Some researchers feel a test of significance in such a case indicates the probability that the relationship is a general one over time—that it describes newspapers over time and not just at the time of the study.

As is the case for most matter covered by this book, I have a personal prejudice. In this instance, it is against tests of significance. My objection is not to the statistical logic of those tests, since it is sound. Rather, I am concerned that such tests seem to mislead more than they enlighten. My principal reservations are the following:

1. Tests of significance make sampling assumptions that are virtually never satisfied by actual sampling designs.

2. They assume the absence of nonsampling errors, a questionable assumption in most actual empirical measurements.

3. In practice, they are too often applied to measures of association that have been computed in violation of the assumptions made by those measures (for example, product-moment correlations computed from ordinal data).

4. Statistical significance is too easily misinterpreted as "strength of association," or substantive significance.

At the same time, I feel that tests of significance can be a valuable asset to the researcher—useful tools for the understanding of data. My view in this regard is perhaps paradoxical. While the above comments suggest an extremely conservative approach to tests of significance—that you should use them only when all assumptions are met—my general perspective is just the reverse. I would encourage you to use any statistical technique—any measure of association or any test of significance—on any set of data if it will help you to understand your data. If the computation of product-moment correlations among nominal variables and the testing of statistical signifi-cance in the context of uncontrolled sampling will meet this criterion, then I would encourage such activities. I say this in the spirit of what Hanan Selvin has referred to as "data-dredging" techniques. Anything goes, it if leads ultimately to the understanding of data and of the social world under study.

The price that must be paid for this radical freedom, however, is the giving up of strict, statistical interpretations. You would not be able to demonstrate the ultimate importance of your finding solely on the basis of your correlation being significant at the .05 level. Whatever the avenue to discovery, empirical data must ultimately be presented in a legitimate manner, and their importance must be argued logically.

18.4
Summary

In Chapter 18, I have attempted to provide a brief overview of the different kinds of statistical measures that may be used in quantitative social research. I have made no attempt to be exhaustive in this regard, nor have I attempted to discuss any one statistical measure in full detail. Rather, I have tried to provide a general logical framework within which you might go on to learn statistics.

The chapter began with a discussion of descriptive statistics, those techniques that assist the researcher in summarizing the data being analyzed. In this regard, we returned to the notion of data-reduction, this time in terms of summarizing the relationships between variables. The statistical computations that summarize the relationships between variables are called *measures of association.*

Many measures of association are based on the model of the *proportionate reduction of error* (PRE). The logic of this model was discussed, and specific measures of association appropriate to different levels of measurement were described.

Next, the chapter turned to inferential statistics. We noted that few social research projects have the ultimate goal of determining the associations among variables within a particular set of observations. More typically, the researcher wishes to generalize his findings to larger, real populations. Inferential statistics, then, provide means whereby the generalizability of observed associations—among a survey sample, for example—to some larger population may be determined. This discussion began with a consideration of univariate inferences, involving a return to the earlier concepts of probability sampling: sampling distribution, standard error, confidence level, and confidence interval.

Next, we examined *tests of statistical significance.* These measures estimate the likelihood that an observed level of association—in a sample—could have been produced solely by sampling error, with there being no association between the variables in the larger population from which the sample was selected. *Chi-square* was discussed as an illustration of tests of significance. The chapter concluded with a discussion of the common misuses of tests of statistical significance.

18.5
Main Points

1. Descriptive statistics are used to summarize data under study. Some descriptive statistics summarize the distribution of attributes on a single variable; others summarize the associations between variables.

2. Inferential statistics are used to estimate the generalizability of findings arrived at in the analysis of a sample to the larger population from which the sample has been selected. Some inferential statistics estimate the single-variable characteristics of the population; others—tests of statistical significance—estimate the relationships between variables in the population.

3. Descriptive statistics summarizing the relationships between variables are called *measures of association.*

4. Many measures of association are based on a *proportionate reduction of error* (PRE) model. This model is based on a comparison of (a) the number of "errors" we would make in attempting to "guess" the attributes of a given variable for each of the cases under study—if we knew nothing but the distribution of attributes on that variable—and (b) the number of "errors" we would make if we knew the joint distribution overall and were told for each case the attribute of one variable each time we were asked to "guess" the attribute of the other.

5. *Lambda* (λ) is an appropriate measure of association to be used in the analysis of two *nominal* variables, and it also provides a clear illustration of the PRE model.

6. *Gamma* (γ) is an appropriate measure of association to be used in the analysis of two *ordinal* variables.

7. *Pearson's product-moment correlation* (r) is an appropriate measure of association to be used in the analysis of two *interval* or *ratio* variables.

8. Inferences about some characteristic of a population—such as the percentage of voters favoring Candidate A—must contain an indication of a *confidence interval* (the range within which the value is expected to be; e.g., between 45% and 55% favor Candidate A) and an indication of the *confidence level* (the likelihood that the value does fall within that range; e.g., 95% confidence). Computations of confidence levels and intervals are based on probability theory and assume that conventional probability sampling techniques have been employed in the study.

9. Inferences about the generalizability to a population of the associations discovered between variables in a sample involve *tests of statistical significance.* Most simply put, these tests estimate the likelihood that an association as large as the observed one could result from normal sampling error if no such association exists between the variables in the larger population. Tests of statistical significance, then, are also based on

probability theory and assume that conventional probability sampling techniques have been employed in the study.

10. Statistical significance must not be confused with *substantive* significance, the latter meaning that an observed association is strong, important, meaningful, or worth writing home to your mother about.

11. The *level of significance* of an observed association is reported in the form of the probability that that association could have been produced merely by sampling error. To say that an association is "significant at the .05 level" is to say that an association as large as the observed one could not be expected to result from sampling error more than 5 times out of a hundred.

12. Social researchers tend to utilize a particular set of levels of significance in connection with tests of statistical significance: .05, .01, and .001. This is merely a convention, however.

13. Tests of statistical significance, strictly speaking, make assumptions about data and methods that are almost never satisfied completely by real social research. Despite this, the tests can serve a very useful function in the analysis and interpretation of data. You should be wary of interpreting the "significance" of the test results too precisely, however.

18.6
Annotated Bibliography

Freeman, Linton, *Elementary Applied Statistics* (New York: John Wiley, 1968). An excellent introductory statistics textbook. Everyone has his favorite statistics text, and this is simply mine. It is clear, well-organized, and understandable. In addition to describing the most frequently used statistical methods in detail, Freeman provides briefer descriptions of many more that might be appropriate in special situations.

Kish, Leslie, *Survey Sampling* (New York: John Wiley, 1965). The definitive reference for sampling statistics. In addition to discussing the logic of statistical inference, Kish provides formulas to cover just about any aspect of sampling that is likely to be encountered.

Morrison, Denton and Henkel, Ramon (eds.), *The Significance Test Controversy: A Reader* (Chicago: Aldine-Atherton, 1970). A compilation of perspectives—pro and con—on tests of statistical significance. The question of the validity, utility, or "significance" of tests of statistical significance is one that reappears periodically in social science journals. Each reappearance is marked by an extended exchange between different points of view. This collection of such articles offers an excellent picture of the persistent debate.

19

Advanced Modes of Analysis

19.1
Introduction

For the most part, this book has focused on rather rudimentary forms of data manipulation in social scientific analysis. I have suggested that the logic of data analysis can be most clearly seen through the use of contingency tables and percentages. The elaboration model of analysis was presented in this form.

The preceding chapter has dealt with some other statistical techniques that may be applied to data—especially within the context of contingency tables. Now we shall move one step further and consider briefly a few more complex methods of data analysis and presentation. Each of the techniques examined in this chapter will be presented from the logical perspective of the elaboration model. Four methods of analysis will be discussed: regression analysis, path analysis, factor analysis, and smallest-space analysis. The reader should realize that these four techniques represent only an arbitrary selection from among the many that are available to the analyst.

19.2
Regression Analysis

At several points in this text, I have referred to the general formula for describing the association between two variables: $Y = f(X)$. Recall from Chapter 16 that this formula is read "Y is a function of X," meaning that values of Y can be explained in terms of variations in the values of X. Stated more strongly, we might say that X causes Y, so the value of X determines the value of Y. **Regression analysis** is a method of determining the specific function relating Y to X.

The regression model can be seen most clearly in the case of a perfect linear association between two variables. Figure 19–1 is a scattergram presenting in graphic form the conjoint values of X and Y as produced by a hypothetical study.

A quick perusal of Figure 19–1 indicates that for the four cases in our study, the values of X and Y are identical in each instance. The case with a value of 1 on *X* also has a value of 1 on *Y*, and so forth. The relationship between the two variables in this instance could be described by the equation *Y* = *X*; this would be the *regression equation.* Since all four points lie on a straight line, we could superimpose that line over the points; this would be the *regression line.*

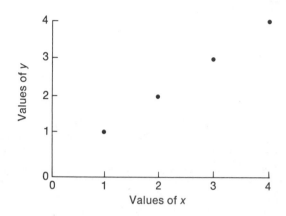

Figure 19-1. Simple Scattergram of Values of *X* and *Y*

The regression model has important descriptive uses. The regression line offers a graphic picture of the association between *X* and *Y.* And the regression equation is an efficient form for summarizing that association. The regression model has inferential value as well. To the extent that the regression equation correctly describes the *general* association between the two variables, it may be used to predict other sets of values. If, for example, we know that a new case has a value of 3.5 on *X,* we can predict the value of 3.5 on *Y* as well.

In practice, of course, studies are seldom limited to four cases, and the associations between variables are seldom as clear as the one presented in Figure 19-1. A somewhat more realistic example is presented in Figure 19-2.

Two observations may be made regarding Figure 19-2. As was the case in our previous example, we note that the values of *Y* generally correspond to those of *X;* and as values of *X* increase, so do values of *Y.* At the same time, however, the association is not nearly as clear as was the case in Figure 19-1.

While it is not possible on Figure 19-2 to superimpose a straight line that will pass through all the points in the scattergram, an approximate line could be constructed. This line would provide the best possible linear representation of the several points.

The statistical procedures for computing the regression line can be found in any standard statistics text, so we shall consider only the *logic* of that procedure here. Assume for the moment that we have drawn through the scattergram a line that seems to represent fairly closely the general pattern of the points. This line would permit us to predict roughly values of Y on the basis of values of X.

For a given value of X, we could locate that value on the approximate regression line and determine the value of Y at that point on the line. Since the several points clearly do not lie directly on the line, however, it is certain that we shall make errors in most predictions of Y on the basis of X. For all those cases with values of X equal to 10 in Figure 19-2, we note that the actual values of Y range between 5 and 15. Given our approximate regression line, then, it is possible to measure the errors in predicting each value of Y from each value of X; these errors can be represented as distances along the Y axis between the points and the line. Figure 19-3 illustrates this with fewer points.

The linear regression line is the straight line that has the property of minimizing the *squared distances* between points and the line—as measured along the Y axis. Thus, the regression line is referred to as the *least-squares line*. The line having this property, then, provides the best summary description of the association between X and Y. Moreover, any straight line can be expressed as an equation, as was the case in Figure 19-1.

The general form of the regression equation is $Y = a + bX$. In this equation, a indicates the value of Y when $X = 0$. (Note in the equation that for $X = 0$, $Y = a$.) This is referred to as the *Y-intercept*. In the equation, b represents the number of units changed in Y for every increase of *one* unit in the value of X. This is referred to as the *slope*. Note that in the simpler example in Figure 19-1, $a = 0$ and $b = 1$, which reduced the equation to $Y = X$.

Let's assume for the moment that the regression equation for the points in Figure 19-2 is $Y = 2 + 1.3X$. For every given value of X, then, we would be able to estimate the value of Y. If X equals 23, then we would estimate Y as $2 + 1.3(23) = 31.9$.

It is important to note that the regression line that best predicts values of Y on the basis of values of X is different from the regression line that best predicts values of X from values of Y. This will become clear when the reader experiments with scattergrams and approximate regression lines— comparing errors along the Y axis with errors along the X axis. The regression model, then, assumes a designation of independent and dependent variables.

Before moving to more complex methods of regression analysis, it will be useful to detour for a moment to consider the logic of scattergrams in normal research conditions. It is traditional to introduce the notion of regression through the use of a scattergram of points produced by two continuous variables. I have done this in Figure 19-2. In practice, however, social scientific research seldom involves the analysis of continuous variables: typically data is collected in—or reduced to—a limited set of categories. Let's illustrate this with a hypothetical example of an analysis of approval of Medicare on the basis of general political orientations.

Let's assume that the researcher believes that attitudes toward Medicare are based on general political orientations. His data on Medicare attitudes are in the form of the responses: Strongly Approve (SA), Approve

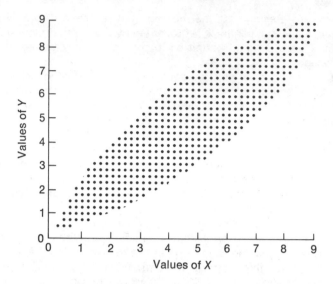

Figure 19-2. Complex Scattergram of Values of X and Y

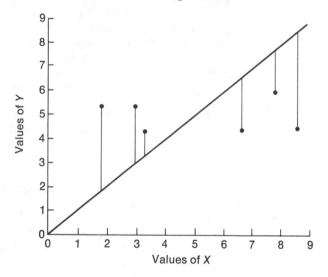

Figure 19-3. Measuring Distances Between Points and Regression Line

(A), Disapprove (D), and Strongly Disapprove (SD). His data on general political orientations are in the form of subjects' self-characterizations as Very Conservative (VC), Moderately Conservative (MC), Moderately Liberal (ML), and Very Liberal (VL). The scattergram of points produced by these variables is presented in Figure 19-4.

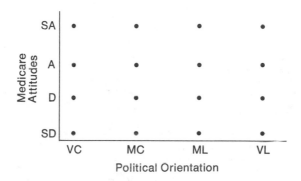

Figure 19-4. Scattergram for Grouped Data

Clearly, Figure 19-4 tells us nothing about the association between political orientations and attitudes toward Medicare, since the points are evenly distributed with no apparent pattern. This is due to the fact that each point represents more than one case; since the data are grouped, the individual points have been "piled up" on top of each other.

Figure 19-5 is more useful. The several points have been replaced by numbers representing the number of cases giving a particular response pattern. For example, we discover that 100 "very conservative" subjects said they "strongly disapproved" of Medicare; 50 "moderately conservative" subjects "approved" of Medicare.

Figure 19-5 conveys considerably more information than Figure 19-4. Another interesting observation is in order. Figure 19-5 is nothing more or less than a *contingency table*. A firm understanding of the logic of contingency tables, then, may offer a better base for understanding the logic of the regression model, especially when it is applied to grouped data.

Multiple Regression

Thus far, we have limited our discussion to the linear regression between two variables. The basic regression model, however, is more general than this implies. It is possible to extend the model to more than two variables, just as the elaboration model can be so extended.

From the discussion of the elaboration model, we recall that some dependent variables may be affected by more than one independent variable. By constructing more complex contingency tables, the researcher can determine the joint contribution of several independent variables to the prediction of values on the dependent variable.

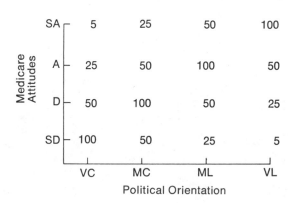

Figure 19-5. Scattergram of Grouped Data with Frequencies

If, for example, the researcher believes that both age and education affect prejudice, he could construct tables appropriate for testing this. Presumably, if his data confirm his belief, he would find that the oldest subjects having the least education would be the most prejudiced, while the youngest subjects having the most education would be the least prejudiced. This would show him the joint effects of age and education on prejudice.

Multiple regression is based on the same logic. Although it is difficult to present a regression line in more than two dimensions, the multiple regression equation can be presented: $P = a + bE + cA$, where P is prejudice, E is education, and A is age. If more independent variables were involved, the equation would simply be extended to take those into account.

Partial Regression

In the discussion of the elaboration model, special attention was paid to the relationship between two variables when a third, test, variable was held constant. Thus, we might have examined the effect of education on prejudice with age held constant, testing the independent effect of education. To do this, we would have computed the tabular relationship between education and prejudice separately for each age group.

Partial regressions are based on this same logical model. The equation summarizing the relationship between two variables is computed on the basis of the test variables remaining constant. As in the case of the elaboration model, the result may then be compared with the "uncontrolled" relationship between the two variables to clarify further the nature of the overall relationship.

Curvilinear Regression

Up to now, we have been discussing the association among variables as represented by a straight line—though in more than two dimensions. The regression model is even more general than this implies.

The reader with a knowledge of geometry will already know that curvilinear functions also can be represented by equations. For example, the equation $X^2 + Y^2 = 25$ describes a circle with a radius of 5. Raising variables to powers greater than 1 has the effect of producing curves rather than straight lines. And from the standpoint of empirical research, there is no reason to assume that the relationship among every set of variables will be linear. In some cases, then, curvilinear regression analysis can provide a better understanding of empirical relationships than can any linear model.

Although curvilinear functions are more difficult to identify and interpret in contingency tables, our previous discussion of scattergrams and tables suggests the possibility of a contingency table similar to the one presented in Figure 19-6.

	X_1	X_2	X_3	X_4	X_5	X_6	X_7
Y_4	0	25	50	100	50	25	0
Y_3	0	50	100	0	100	50	0
Y_2	0	100	25	0	25	100	0
Y_1	100	50	0	0	0	50	100

Figure 19-6. Curvilinear Relationship in a Contingency Table

The data presented in Figure 19-6 roughly describe a curvilinear relationship between X and Y. All cases having the value of X_1 also have the value of Y_4. As we move across the table to X_4, we note the tendency for increasing values of Y; then the values of Y decrease again as we move past X_4 until we discover that all cases with X_7 are also Y_4. Thus the relationship is a curvilinear one, not adequately represented by any straight line.

Curvilinear regression analysis would provide a neater summary of the relationship apparent in Figure 19-6. Moreover, the regression equation would permit one estimate of Y values from X values.

The potential of curvilinear regression analysis is very great, although this has scarcely been approached in practice. Most collections of points representing the coincidence of two variables could be perfectly represented by an equation. With normal social scientific data, however, such an equation would be complex indeed, involving variables raised to very high powers. Such a complex equation might have little practical value, and its theoretical value might be minimal as well.

Recall that a regression line serves two functions. It describes a set of empirical observations, and it provides a general model of the relationship between two variables in the general population that the observations represent. A very complex equation might result in a rather erratic line that would indeed pass through every individual point. In this sense, it would perfectly describe the empirical observations. There would be no guarantee, however, that such a line would adequately predict new observations, or that it in any meaningful way represented the relationship between the two variables in general. Thus, it would have little or no inferential value.

Earlier in this book, we discussed the need for balancing detail and utility in data reduction. The researcher attempts to provide the most faithful, yet also the simplest, representation of his data. This is essentially the same problem facing the researcher using regression analysis. He wishes to represent his data in the simplest fashion (thus, linear regressions are most frequently used), but in such a way as to best describe the actual data. Curvilinear regression analysis adds a new option to the researcher in this regard, but it does not solve his problems altogether. Nothing does that.

Cautions in Regression Analysis

The use of regression analysis for statistical inferences makes certain assumptions of which the researcher should be aware. These are the same ones assumed by correlational analysis, concerning simple random sampling, the absence of nonsampling errors, and continuous interval data. Since social scientific research seldom completely satisfies these assumptions, the reader should use caution in assigning ultimate meaning to the results of regression analyses.

As indicated earlier, however, I would encourage the use of these techniques—even though they may not be statistically justified—in any situation in which their use assists the researcher in understanding his data and, by extension, the world around him.

19.3
Path Analysis

Path analysis offers another graphic presentation of the interrelations among variables. It is based on regression analysis, but it can provide a more useful graphic picture of relationships among several variables than is possible through other means.

Path analysis is a *causal* model for understanding relationships between variables. It assumes that the values on one variable are caused by the values on another, so it is essential that independent and dependent variables be distinguished in path analysis.

By way of an introduction to path analysis, let's consider the simple case of two variables causally related. *X* is the independent variable and *Y* the dependent. We might describe this causal relationship by the graphic notation of Figure 19-7a. We may improve the communicative value of the diagram by adding to the arrow the standardized regression coefficient describing the strength of their empirical relationship, as shown in Figure 19-7b. This is called the *path coefficient* in path analysis.

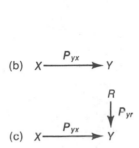

Figure 19-7. Causal Relationship Between Two Variables

In a sense, path analysis represents a closed system of analysis. Whereas the present example is based on the explanation of variance in variable *Y*, path analysis aims at explaining *all* of that variance. Clearly, however, *X* is probably not sufficient for that purpose. Since we know how much of the variance in *Y* is explained by *X*, however, it is possible to compute the *unexplained variance* as a residual. To close the analytical system, the path analyst posits a hypothetical variable that combines all the remaining explanatory variables. This variable (*R*) is added to the path diagram, as shown in Figure 19-7c.

Clearly, the path analysis describing the relationship between only two variables is little more than a different presentation of the standardized regression cofficient describing their relationship. As additional variables are added to the model, however, the special value of path analysis becomes clearer. Note the example (Figure 19-8) in which independent variables *X* and *Y* are seen as causes of the dependent variable *Z*.

This latest diagram differs from the earlier one in several fashions.

First, the notation P_{zx} represents the *partial* relationship between Z and X with Y held constant. The notation P_{zy} represents the partial relationship between Z and Y with X held constant. In other words, the arrow connecting X and Z represents the causal effect of X on Z *independent* of the effects of Y, and so forth.

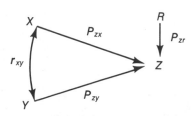

Figure 19-8. Path Diagram for Three Variables

Second, note that the relationship between the two independent variables has also been indicated in the diagram. This arrow has two heads, to indicate that there is no causal direction implied in the relationship. Finally, P_{zr} still represents the hypothetical relationship between Z and all the residual explanatory variables.

The power of path analysis becomes even clearer when we add a new variable—an intervening variable between the independent variables and the dependent variable. For this purpose, let's designate the independent variables as X and Y, the intervening variable as I, and the dependent variable as Z (see Figure 19-9).

This more complex example provides even more paths between variables. To begin, both X and Y are believed to causally affect I, and these are represented as paths with appropriate path coefficients. And I is believed to causally affect Z, with this being represented as well. At the same time, however, both X and Y can have independent effects on Z—independent of each other and independent of the role played by I.

The interpretation of this diagram is not possible without a knowledge of the actual path coefficients, so let's insert some hypothetical figures (see Figure 19-10).

In the latest diagram, it is clear that the strongest predictor of Z is the intervening variable, I. Looking further in the diagram, we note a strong partial relationship between Y and I, and, at the same time, a rather weak partial relationship between Y and Z. This suggests that Y primarily affects Z through the intervening variable. X, on the other hand, shows a rather strong direct relationship with Z, with a weaker relationship between X and I. Here we would conclude that X affects Z directly more than working that effect through the intervening variable.

Even this rather simple example should indicate the general complexity of path analysis. As additional variables are added to the diagram, its interpretation becomes more difficult. At the same time, the reader should

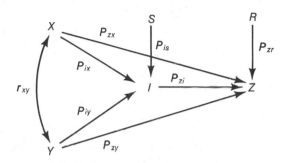

Figure 19-9. Path Diagram for Four Variables

have noted a striking similarity between the interpretation of a path diagram and the use of the multivariate elaboration model. In the latter case, the researcher compares partial tables to determine the effect of control variables

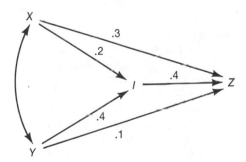

Figure 19-10. Hypothetical Path Diagram

on the initially observed association between two other variables. The path analyst does this through the use of standardized regression coefficients arranged in a logical schematic diagram. The basic logic is the same.

19.4
Factor Analysis

Factor Analysis is a different approach to multivariate analysis. Its statistical basis is sufficiently complex and sufficiently different from the foregoing discussions as to suggest a very general discussion here.

Factor analysis is used to discover patterns among the variations in values of several variables. This is done essentially through the generation of artificial dimensions (factors) that correlate highly with several of the real variables and that are independent of one another. A computer must be used to perform this complex operation.

Let's suppose for the moment that our data file contains several indicators of subjects' prejudice. Each of the items should provide some indication of prejudice, but none of them would give a perfect indication. All of these items, moreover, should be highly intercorrelated empirically. In a factor analysis of the data, it is likely that an artificial dimension would be created that would be highly correlated with each of the items measuring prejudice. Each subject would essentially receive a value on that artificial dimension, and the value assigned would provide a good predictor of the observed attributes on each item.

Suppose now that the same study provided several indicators of subjects' mathematical ability. It is likely that the factor analysis would also generate an artificial dimension highly correlated with each of those items.

The output of a factor analysis program consists of columns representing the several factors (artificial dimensions) generated from the observed relations among variables plus the correlations between each variable and each factor—called the *factor loadings*.

In the above example, it is likely that one factor would more or less represent "prejudice" while another would more or less represent "mathematical ability." Data items measuring prejudice would have high loadings on (correlations with) the prejudice factor and low loadings on the mathematical ability factor. Data items measuring mathematical ability would have just the opposite pattern.

In practice, however, factor analysis does not proceed in this fashion. Rather, the variables are input to the program, and a series of factors with appropriate factor loadings are the output. The researcher must then determine the meaning of a given factor on the basis of those variables that load highly on it. The generation of factors, however, has no reference to the meaning of variables, only to their empirical associations. Two criteria are taken into account: (1) a factor must explain a relatively large proportion of the variance found in the study variables; and (2) every factor must be more or less independent of every other factor.[1]

There are a number of advantages in factor analysis. First, it is an efficient method of discovering predominant patterns among a large number of variables. Instead of the researcher being forced to compare countless

---

1. This is not true of all factor analytical methods (for example, *oblique* solutions).

correlations—simple, partial, and multiple—to discover those patterns, factor analysis can be used for this task. Incidentally, here is a good example of a helpful use of computers.

Second, factor analysis presents data in a form that can be interpreted by the reader or researcher. For a given factor, the reader can easily discover the variables loading highly on it, thus noting clusters of variables. Or, he can easily discover which factors a given variable is or is not loaded highly on.

Factor analysis has disadvantages as well. First, as noted above, factors are generated without any regard to substantive meaning. Often the researcher will find factors producing very high loadings for a group of substantively disparate variables. He might find, for example, that prejudice and religiosity have high positive loadings on a given factor with education having an equally high negative loading. Surely the three variables are highly correlated, but what does the factor represent? All too often, inexperienced researchers will be led into naming such factors as "religio-prejudicial lack of education," or with a similarly nonsensical name.

Second, factor analysis is often criticized on basic philosophical grounds. Recall an earlier statement that to be legitimate, a hypothesis must be disconfirmable. If the researcher is unable to specify the conditions under which his hypothesis would be disproved, his hypothesis is in reality either a tautology or useless. In a sense, factor analysis suffers this defect. No matter what data are input, factor analysis produces a solution in the form of factors. Thus if the researcher were asking "Are there any patterns among these variables?" the answer always would be "yes." This fact must also be taken into account in evaluating the results of factor analysis. The generation of factors by no means insures meaning.

My personal view of factor analysis is the same as presented in regard to other complex modes of analysis. It can be an extremely useful tool for the social science researcher. Its use should be encouraged whenever such activity may assist the researcher in his understanding of a body of data. As in all cases, however, the researcher must maintain an awareness that such tools are only tools and never magical solutions.

19.5
Smallest-Space Analysis

Smallest-space analysis (SSA) is rather different from the previously discussed methods of multivariate analysis; and, although it is still relatively new, it appears to hold considerable potential for the understanding of data.

Smallest-space analysis is based on the correlations between variables. Any measure of association may be used for this purpose, although we shall use Pearson's r in the examples to follow. Let's begin with a simple correlation matrix describing the associations among variables: A, B, and C (Table 19-1).

Now let's plot these three variables as points on a plane, letting the distance between two points represent the *inverse* of the correlation between

Table 19-1

	A	B	C
A	x	.8	.2
B		x	.5
C			x

the two variables. That is, if two variables are highly correlated, they will be close together; if they are weakly correlated, they will be farther apart. The following diagram would satisfy this design.

$$A \qquad B \qquad C$$

Since A and B are the most highly correlated variables, they have been placed relatively close together. The next highest correlation is between B and C, and the distance between these two points is the next shortest. Finally, the correlation between A and C is the weakest of the three correlations, and the distance between A and C is the longest distance in the diagram.

Now let's enlarge our correlation matrix by adding variable D (Table 19-2).

Table 19-2

	A	B	C	D
A	x	.8	.2	.1
B		x	.5	.3
C			x	.9
D				x

It is still possible to plot these four points in such a fashion that the distance between two points corresponds to the inverse of the correlation between the two variables. It should be noted, however, that the distances do not *equal* the inverse of the correlations. The metric distances are irrelevant; thus SSA is referred to as a *nonmetric* technique. However, the *rank order* of distances between points should be the inverse of the rank order of correlations. The diagram in Figure 19-11 would satisfy the latest correlation matrix.

To clarify the new diagram, the points have been connected by lines, which in turn have been labeled with the correlations between the pairs of variables. An examination of the diagram will indicate that the longest distance (*AD*) corresponds to the weakest correlation. The shortest distance (*CD*) corresponds to the strongest correlation. The same is true for all other distances and correlations. (An understanding of plane geometry will help to explain how the diagram was constructed.)

Many readers will have already realized that there are some correlation matrices that could not be represented in accordance with the rules laid down. This is especially true as more and more variables are added. Given such a situation, SSA permits the researcher to move in two different directions.

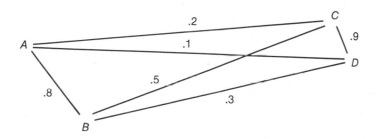

Figure 19-11. Smallest-Space Analysis: Four Variables

First, SSA is not limited to two dimensions (although this textbook essentially is). Like multiple regressions, SSA can employ an unlimited number of geometric dimensions. As a general guideline, n variables can be plotted perfectly in SSA format within $n-1$ dimensions. Thus, any two variables can be plotted on a line, any three can be plotted on a plane, any four can be plotted in three dimensions, and so forth. As we have seen in other contexts, however, such liberties can lead the researcher into uninterpretable situations.

The second solution to this problem lies in the familiar area of compromise. Perhaps the researcher cannot plot six variables perfectly within two dimensions (a graphic presentation that would be easily read), but he may be able to come close. Thus, it may be possible to plot the points in such a manner that they more or less satisfy the correspondence of rankings between correlations and distances.

At this point, and with the addition of many variables generally, hand tabulations and hand-drawn diagrams become too difficult. But this is the sort of task that the computer handles easily. Computer programs now exist to generate SSA diagrams from an input in the form of a correlation matrix. The researcher must specify the number of dimensions desired in his solution, and the computer works on that basis. In addition to the diagram, moreover, the computer provides a summary statistic called the **coefficient of alienation.** Although this statistic has no commonsensible interpretation, it represents the extent to which the SSA diagram violates the rules of correspondence between distances and correlations. The lower the coefficient, the better the fit of the diagram to the rules.

The computer output from an SSA program will look something like the configuration shown in Figure 19-12.

Since each of the letters in this diagram represents a study variable, the diagram would be interpreted in terms of the observed clustering of variables. For example, we note that variables *J, K, L,* and *M* are closely clustered, and *A-B-C-D* forms another cluster, with both of these clusters being rather distant from the cluster *N-O-P-Q.*

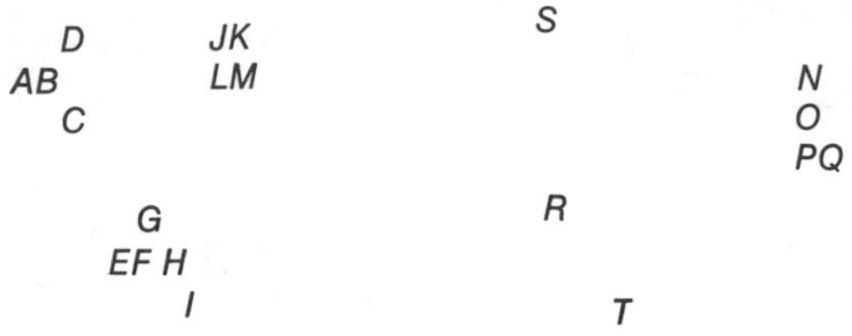

Figure 19-12. Sample Smallest-Space Analysis Results—Hypothetical

The reader will note from the previous section of this chapter that SSA is quite similar to factor analysis, and it is sometimes referred to as a "nonmetric factor analysis."

19.6
Summary

I suspect that my own bias in connection with data analysis has become pretty clear. In case it has not, let me clarify it here: I personally am most inclined toward the use of the elaboration model in the form of simple percentage tables. However, I would not want you to conclude that this is the only "really good" method of multivariate analysis or even that I hold that belief. In this concluding chapter, therefore, I have provided a series of brief descriptions of other more complex modes of analysis. In each instance, I have sought to indicate how the basic logic of a given mode is essentially the same as that inherent in the elaboration model. That should not be too surprising, of course, if we can assume that social research is scientific.

The chapter began with discussions of the different methods of *regression analysis*. We noted how regressions are related to the notion of product-moment correlations. The end product of a regression analysis is an equation that summarizes the relationship observed between variables. In the simplest case, a dependent variable is shown as equaling some constant value (*a*) plus another value (*b*) that is multiplied by the value of the independent variable. This is a simple *linear regression equation.* Later discussions touched on *multiple* regressions, *partial* regressions, and *curvilinear* regressions.

Next, we looked at *path analysis,* which affords a graphic presentation of the network of causal relationships observed among a large number of variables. Based on regression coefficients, this method provides an excellent vehicle for communicating the nature of extremely complex interrelationships.

Factor Analysis was discussed next, very briefly. This analytical technique—feasible by computer only—derives a set of artificial dimensions (*factors*) that appear to best represent the different dimensions reflected by the actual data under study. If the data being analyzed contain indicators of a number of variables representing different political orientations, factor analysis might discover the existence of a general dimension of, say, liberalism-conservatism. None of the actual indicators would provide a perfect measure of this general dimension, but several indicators would be strongly associated with it.

The chapter concluded with a description of *smallest-space analysis* (*SSA*), which is sometimes called a *nonmetric* factor analysis. Like path analysis, SSA is presented in a graphic form. Variables are represented in SSA as points, and the associations between variables are represented as the distances between points: the greater the distance between two points, the weaker the association; the shorter the distance, the greater the association. SSA is nonmetric in the sense that the final plotting of points aims at maintaining the inverse correspondence of the rank-order of distances and the rank-order of associations. The actual metric distances do not correspond to the actual metric measures of association. The output of SSA, then, is the plotting of many points, each of which represents a variable. Those points clustered together represent variables that are relatively highly associated with one another. *Clusters* that are far apart from one another represent *clusters* of variables that are very weakly (or negatively) associated with each other.

At the close of Part Three, it was suggested that the "best" research effort would be one that combined different modes of observation; that if different observational methods produced essentially the same conclusions, the researcher might have a greater confidence in those conclusions. A similar point should be made here. The "best" data analysis would be one that examined a given set of data through many different analytical techniques. If each of those analyses pointed to the same conclusions, the researcher might place a greater confidence in them.

19.7
Main Points

1. Regression analysis represents the relationships between variables in the form of equations, which can be used to predict the values of a dependent variable on the basis of values of one or more independent variables.

2. The basic regression equation—for a simple linear regression—is of the form: $Y = a + bX$. Y in this case is the value (estimated) of the dependent variable; a is some constant value; b is another numerical value, which is multiplied by X, the value of the independent variable.

3. Regression equations are computed on the basis of a *regression line:* that geometric line that represents, with the least amount of discrepancy, the actual location of points in a scattergram.

4. A *multiple* regression analysis results in a regression equation, which estimates the values of a dependent variable from the values of several independent variables.

5. A *partial* regression analysis examines the effects of several independent variables, but with each independent variable's effect expressed separately while the effects of all others are held constant.

6. A *curvilinear* regression analysis permits the "best-fitting" regression line to be something other than a straight line. The curvature of the regression line is achieved by permitting the values of the independent variables to be raised to powers greater than 1; e.g., squared, cubed, and so forth.

7. *Path analysis* is a method of presenting graphically the networks of causal relationships among several variables. It illustrates graphically the primary "paths" of variables through which independent variables cause dependent ones.

8. *Path coefficients* are standardized regression coefficients, representing the partial relationships between variables.

9. *Factor analysis,* feasible only by computer, is an analytical method of discovering the general dimensions represented by a collection of actual variables. These general dimensions, or *factors,* are calculated hypothetical dimensions that are not perfectly represented by any of the empirical variables under study, but that are highly associated with groups of the empirical variables.

10. A *factor loading* indicates the degree of association between a given empirical variable and a given factor.

11. *Smallest-space analysis* (SSA) is a nonmetric method of graphically displaying the associations between a large number of variables.

12. Variables in SSA are represented by points, and the associations between variables are represented by the distances between points, with short distances representing high associations and long distances representing low associations.

13. The primary rule in SSA is that the rank-order of the distances between points should be the inverse of the rank-order of the associations between the variables those points represent.

14. The *coefficient of alienation* is a measure of the extent to which an actual SSA display fails to follow the rank-order rule exactly.

15. The "best" analysis of data would be one that employed several different analytical modes and resulted in the same set of conclusions from each mode.

19.8
Annotated Bibliography

Regression Analysis

Ezekiel, Mordecai and Fox, Karl, *Methods of Correlation and Regression Analysis: Linear and Curvilinear* (New York: John Wiley, 1959). A rather comprehensive presentation of correlation and regression methods. This book begins with a very simple introduction to the subject and then moves progressively to more complex aspects. In addition to describing a wide variety of statistical computations, the authors are sensitive to the practical considerations that apply to the use of correlation and regression in social research.

Path Analysis

Borgatta, Edgar (ed.), *Sociological Methodology, 1969* (San Francisco: Jossey-Bass, 1969), especially Chapters 1 and 2. Good discussions of the logic and techniques of path analysis. The chapters by Kenneth Land and David Heise examine a variety of aspects of path analysis and its potential contribution to social research, especially in regard to the discovery of causal relationships. These are both more advanced than would be desired in an introductory presentation, but good introductions to path analysis are hard to find.

Stark, Rodney, Foster, Bruce, Glock, Charles, and Quinley, Harold, *Wayward Shepherds: Prejudice and the Protestant Clergy* (New York: Harper & Row, 1971), pp. 80-84. An easily understood illustration of the use of path analysis. Having conducted an elaboration analysis of their data, using percentage tables, the authors present a path analysis of their major conclusions. This dual analysis should further clarify the interpretation of path analyses for readers more comfortable with percentage tables.

Factor Analysis

Harmon, Harry, *Modern Factor Analysis* (Chicago: University of Chicago Press, 1967). A rather comprehensive presentation of factor analytic methods. Harmon discusses both the logic and the specific computational techniques associated with this method of social scientific analysis.

Smallest-Space Analysis

Bloombaum, Milton, "Tribes and Traits," *American Anthropologist*, 70:328–330 (April, 1968). A simple illustration of the use of SSA. This reanalysis of anthropological data describing different societies gives a clear example of SSA results and their meaning.

Katz, Elihu, Gurevitch, Michael, and Haas, Hadassah, "On the Use of the Mass Media for Important Things," *American Sociological Review*, 38:164–181 (April, 1973). A more complex illustration of SSA. In addition to evaluating the relative roles played by the different mass media in Israel, the authors present their data in several analytical formats, further clarifying the interpretation of the SSA.

Appendix A   The Research Report

This book has considered the variety of activities that comprise the *doing* of social research. In this appendix, we shall turn to an often neglected subject: reporting the research to others. Unless the research is properly communicated, all the efforts devoted to previously discussed procedures will go for naught.

Before proceeding further on this topic, I should suggest one absolutely basic guideline. Good social scientific reporting requires good English (unless you are writing in a foreign language). Whenever we ask the "figures to speak for themselves," they tend to remain mute. Whenever we use unduly complex terminology or construction, communication is reduced. Every researcher should read and reread (at approximately three-month intervals) an excellent small book by William Strunk, Jr., and E. B. White, *The Elements of Style*.[1] If he does this faithfully, and if even 10 percent of the contents rub off, he stands a rather good chance of making himself understood and his findings perhaps appreciated.

Scientific reporting has several functions, and it is a good idea to keep these in mind. First, the report communicates to an audience a body of specific data and ideas. The report should provide those specifics clearly and with sufficient detail to permit an informed evaluation. Second, the scientific report should be viewed as a contribution to the general body of scientific knowledge. While remaining appropriately humble, the social scientist should always regard his research report as an addition to what we know about social behavior. Finally, the report should serve the function of stimulating and directing further inquiry.

Some Basic Considerations

Despite these general guidelines, different reports serve different purposes. A report appropriate for one purpose might be wholly inappropriate

---

1. (New York: Macmillan, 1959). The following are other useful references on writing:

H. W. Fowler, *A Dictionary of Modern English Usage* (New York: Oxford University Press, 1965).

Billy J. Franklin, and Harold W. Osborne (eds.), *Research Methods: Issues and Insights* (Belmont, Calif.: Wadsworth, 1971), part 8.

for another. This section of the appendix deals with some of the basic considerations in this regard.

Audience

Before drafting his report, the researcher must ask himself who he hopes will read it. Normally, he should make a distinction between fellow scientists and laymen. If written for the former, he may make certain assumptions as to their existing knowledge and may perhaps summarize certain points rather than explaining them in detail. Similarly, he may appropriately use more technical language than would be appropriate for an audience of laymen.

At the same time, the researcher should remain always aware that any science is composed of factions or cults. Terms and assumptions acceptable to his immediate colleagues may only confuse other scientists. This applies with regard to substance as well as techniques. The sociologist of religion writing for a general sociology audience, for example, should explain previous findings in more detail than would be necessary if he were addressing an audience of other sociologists of religion.

Form and Length of Report

I should begin this subsection by saying that my comments apply both to written and oral reports. These two forms, however, will affect the nature of the report.

It is useful to think about the variety of reports that might result from a research project. To begin, the researcher may wish to prepare a short *research note* for publication in an academic or technical journal. Such reports should be approximately one to five pages in length (double-spaced, typed) and should be concise and direct. In a short amount of space, the researcher will not be able to present the state of the field in any detail, and his methodological notes must be somewhat abbreviated as well. Basically, he should tell the reader why he feels a brief note is justified by his findings, and then tell what those findings are.

Often, researchers must prepare reports for the sponsors of their research. These may vary greatly in length, of course. In preparing such a report, however, the researcher should bear in mind the audience for the report—scientific or lay—and their reasons for sponsoring the project in the first place. It is both bad politics and bad manners to bore the sponsor with research findings that have no interest or value to him. At the same time, it may be useful to summarize the ways in which the research has advanced basic scientific knowledge (if it has).

Working papers or monographs are another form of research reporting. Especially in a large and complex project, it will be useful for the researcher to obtain comments on his analysis and the interpretation of his data. A working paper constitutes a tentative presentation with an implicit request for comments. Working papers can also vary in length, and they may present all of the research findings of the project or only a portion of them. Since the researcher's professional reputation is not at stake in a working paper, he should feel free to present tentative interpretations that he cannot altogether justify—identifying them as such and asking for evaluations.

Many research projects result in papers delivered at professional meetings. Often, these serve the same purpose as working papers. The researcher is able to present findings and ideas of possible interest to his colleagues and ask for their comments. Although the length of professional papers may vary depending on the organization of the meetings, the reader is strongly encouraged to say too little rather than too much. Whereas a working paper may ramble somewhat through a variety of tentative conclusions, conference participants should not be forced to sit through an oral unveiling of the same. Interested listeners can always ask for more details later, and uninterested ones can gracefully escape.

Probably the most popular research report is the article published in an academic journal. Again, lengths vary and the researcher should examine the lengths of articles previously published by the journal in question. As a rough guide, however, 25 typed pages is as good as any. A subsequent section on the organization of the report is primarily based on the structure of a journal article, so I shall say no more at this point, except to indicate that student term papers should be written on this model. As a general rule, a term paper that would make a good journal article would also make a good term paper.

A book, of course, represents the most prestigious form of research report. It has all the advantages of the working paper—length, detail—but it should be a more polished document. Since the publication of research findings as a book gives those findings an appearance of greater substance and worth, the researcher has a special obligation to his audience. Although he will still hope to receive comments from his colleagues, possibly leading him to revise his ideas, he must realize that other readers may be led to accept his findings uncritically.

Aim of the Report

Earlier in this book, we considered the different *purposes* of social research projects. In preparing his report, the researcher should keep these same differences in mind.

Some reports may focus primarily on the *exploration* of a topic of interest. Inherent in this aim is the tentativeness and incompleteness of the conclusions. The researcher should clearly indicate to his audience the exploratory aim of the study and point to the shortcomings of the particular project. An important aspect of an exploratory report is to point the way to more refined research on the topic.

Most studies have a *descriptive* purpose, and the research reports from such studies will have a descriptive element. The researcher should carefully distinguish for the reader those descriptions that apply only to the sample and those that are inferred to the population. Whenever inferential descriptions are to be made, the researcher should give his audience some indication of the probable range of error in those descriptions.

Many reports have an *explanatory* aim; the researcher wishes to point to causal relationships among variables. Depending on the probable audience for his report, the researcher should carefully delineate the rules of explanation that lie behind his computations and conclusions; and, as in the case of description, he must give his readers some guide to the relative certainty of his conclusions.

Finally, some research reports may have the aim of *proposing action*. For example, the researcher of prejudice may wish to suggest ways in which prejudice may be reduced, on the basis of his research findings. This aim often presents knotty problems for the researcher, as his own values and orientations may interfere with his proposals. While it is perfectly legitimate for his proposals to be motivated by personal values, he must insure that the specific actions he proposes are warranted by his data. Thus, he should be especially careful to spell out the logic by which he moves from empirical data to proposed action.

Organization of the Report

Although the organization of reports differs somewhat on the basis of form and purpose, it is possible to suggest a general format for presenting research data. The following comments apply most directly to a journal article, but with some modification they apply to most forms of research reports.

Purpose and Overview

It is always helpful to the reader if the researcher begins with a brief statement of the purpose of the study and the main findings of the analysis. In a journal article, this may sometimes be accomplished in the form of an *abstract* or *synopsis.*

Some researchers find this difficult to do. For the researcher, his analysis may have involved considerable detective work, with important findings revealing themselves only as a result of imaginative deduction and data manipulation. He may wish, therefore, to lead the reader through the same exciting process, chronicling the discovery process with a degree of suspense and surprise. To the extent that this form of reporting gives an accurate picture of the research process, I feel it has considerable instructional value. Nevertheless, many readers may not be interested in following the entire research account, and not knowing the purpose and general conclusions in advance may make it difficult for them to understand the significance of the study.

An old forensic dictum says: "Tell them what you're going to tell them; tell them; and tell them what you told them." Researchers would do well to follow this dictum in the preparation of research reports.

Review of the Literature

Since every research report should be placed in the context of the general body of scientific knowledge, it is important for the researcher to indicate where his report fits in that picture. Having presented the general purpose of his study, he should then proceed to bring the reader up to date on the previous research in the area, pointing to general agreements and disagreements among the previous researchers.

In some cases, the researcher may wish to challenge previously accepted ideas. He should carefully review the studies that have led to the acceptance of those ideas, and then indicate the factors that have not been previously considered or the logical fallacies present in the previous research.

When the researcher is concerned with resolving a disagreement among previous researchers, he should organize his review of the literature around the opposing points of view. He should summarize the research supporting one view, then summarize the research supporting the other, and finally suggest the reasons for the disagreement.

To an extent, the researcher's review of the literature serves a bibliographic function for readers, indexing the previous research on a given topic. This can be overdone, however, and the researcher should avoid an opening paragraph that runs three pages, mentioning every previous study in the field. The comprehensive bibliographic function can best be served by a bibliography at the end of the report, and the review of the literature should focus only on those studies that have direct relevance to the present study.

Study Design and Execution

A research report containing interesting findings and conclusions can be very frustrating when the reader is unable to determine the methodological design and execution of the study. The worth of all scientific findings depends heavily on the manner in which the data were collected and analyzed.

In reporting the design and execution of a survey, for example, the researcher should always include the following: the population, the sampling frame, the sampling method, the sample size, the data collection method, the completion rate, and the method of data processing and analysis. Comparable details should be given if other methods are used. The experienced researcher is able to report these details in a rather short space, without omitting anything required for his reader's evaluation of the study.

Analysis and Interpretation

Having set the study in the perspective of previous research and having described the design and execution of it, the researcher should then proceed to present his data. The following major section will provide further guidelines in this regard. For now, a few general comments are in order.

The presentation of data, the manipulations of those data, and the researcher's interpretations should be integrated into a logical whole. It is frustrating to the reader to discover a collection of seemingly unrelated analyses and findings with a promise that all the loose ends will be tied together later on in the report. Every step in the analysis should make sense—at the time it is taken. The researcher should present his rationale for a particular analysis, present the data relevant to it, interpret the results, and then indicate where that result leads next.

Summary and Conclusions

Following the forensic dictum mentioned earlier, I believe it is essential to summarize the research report. The researcher should avoid reviewing every specific finding, but he should review all of the significant ones, pointing once more to their general significance.

The report should conclude with a statement of what the researcher has discovered about his subject matter and where future research might be directed. A quick review of recent journal articles will probably indicate a very high frequency of the concluding statement: "It is clear that much more research is needed." This is probably always a true conclusion, but it is of little value unless the researcher can offer pertinent suggestions as to the nature of that future research. He should review the particular shortcomings of his own study and suggest ways in which those shortcomings might be avoided by future researchers.

Guidelines for Reporting Analyses

The presentation of data analyses should be such as to provide a maximum of detail without being cluttered. The researcher can accomplish this best by continually examining his report to see whether it achieves the following aims.

Quantitative data should be presented in such a way as to permit recomputations by the reader. In the case of percentage tables, for example, the reader should be able to collapse categories and recompute the percentages. He should be given sufficient information as to permit him to compute percentages in the table in the opposite direction from the researcher's presentation.

All aspects of the analysis should be described in sufficient detail to permit a secondary analyst to replicate the analysis from the same body of data. This means that he should be able to create the same indexes and scales, produce the same tables, arrive at the same regression equations, obtain the same factors and factor loadings, and so forth. This will seldom be done, of course, but if the report is presented in such a manner as to make it possible, the reader will be far better equipped to evaluate the report.

A final guide to the reporting of methodological details is that the reader should be in a position to completely replicate the entire study independently. It should be recalled from an earlier discussion that replicability is an essential norm of science generally. A single study does not prove a point; only a series of studies can begin to do this. Unless studies can be replicated, there can be no meaningful series of studies.

I have previously mentioned the importance of integrating data, analysis, and interpretations in the report. A more specific guideline can be offered in this regard. Tables, charts, and figures, if any, should be integrated into the text of the report—appearing near that portion of the text discussing them. Sometimes students describe their analyses in the body of the report, and place all the tables in an appendix at the end. This procedure greatly impedes the reader. As a general rule, it is best to (1) describe the purpose for presenting the table, (2) present it, and (3) review and interpret it.

Be explicit in drawing conclusions. Although research is typically conducted for the purpose of drawing general conclusions, the researcher should carefully note the specific basis for such conclusions. Otherwise he may lead his reader into accepting unwarranted conclusions.

Point to any qualifications or conditions warranted in the evaluation of conclusions. Typically, the researcher himself is in the best position to know the shortcomings and tentativeness of his conclusions, and he should give the reader the advantage of that knowledge. Failure to do this can misdirect future research and result in the waste of research funds.

I will conclude with a point made at the outset of this appendix, as it is extremely important. Research reports should be written in the best possible literary style. Writing clearly is easier for some people than for others, and it is always harder than writing poorly. The reader is again referred to the Strunk and White volume. Every researcher would do well to follow this procedure: Write. Read Strunk and White. Revise. Reread Strunk and White. Revise again. This will be a difficult and time-consuming endeavor, but so is science.

A perfectly designed, carefully executed, and brilliantly analyzed study will be altogether worthless unless the researcher is able to communicate his findings to others. This appendix has attempted to provide some general and specific guidelines toward that end. The best guides are logic, clarity, and honesty. Ultimately, there is probably no substitute for practice.

Appendix B   Research Ethics

A theoretically oriented textbook on social research methods would provide the student with only an ideal image of how research should be conducted. In the previous portions of this book, I have sought to impress upon the reader that a variety of administrative and practical concerns impinge upon the research process, so that it is not always possible to live up to the ideal model. The enlightened researcher should be aware of those additional constraints and be able to balance administrative and scientific factors so as to arrive at the best possible compromise.

This appendix is addressed to another nonscientific constraint—the ethics of research. These ethical concerns are not a part of the scientific method. Nevertheless, they comprise a set of norms that scientists in most disciplines are obliged to follow. In many instances, these ethical norms directly conflict with scientific procedures, just as administrative concerns do. The researcher should, therefore, be aware of the possible conflicts so as ultimately to conduct the most scientific, ethical research.

Science in and of itself is *amoral*. The law of gravity and the correlation between education and prejudice are neither moral nor immoral. Scientists, however, are not amoral, and neither are those who may use the results of scientific inquiry. Thus, scientific research may be conducted and used for either moral or immoral purposes. And, of course, one man's morality is another man's immorality. These are lessons that the nuclear physicists learned decades ago—lessons that social scientists are still learning today.

There is no way of insuring that all scientists will always be motivated by ethical concerns when they engage in scientific research. Nor is there any way to insure that scientific findings will be used only for ethical purposes. It is possible, however, to point to a set of more or less agreed-upon ethical norms relating to the execution of research.[1] This appendix will present some of the more common ethical problems that appear in social research and will suggest ethical solutions to them that do not seriously endanger the "scientific" quality of the research itself.

---

1. Some commonly agreed-upon ethical norms are discussed in the following:

American Association for Public Opinion Research, "Code of Professional Ethics and Practices," printed in *Public Opinion Quarterly* (Fall 1960).

Gideon Sjoberg, *Ethics, Politics, and Social Research* (Cambridge, Mass.: Schenkman, 1967).

Voluntary Participation

Social research often, though not always, represents an intrusion into the lives of people. The interviewer's knock on the door or the arrival of a questionnaire in the mail signals the beginning of an activity that the "respondent" has not requested and one that may require a significant portion of his time and energy. Participation in a social experiment represents a disruption in the subject's regular activities. The arrival of the participant observer can and often does interfere with the social process under study.

Social research, moreover, often requires that people reveal personal information about themselves—personal things that may be unknown to their friends and associates. And social research often requires that such information be revealed to strangers.

Other professionals, such as physicians and lawyers, also require such information. Their requests may be justified, however, on the grounds that the information is required for them to serve the personal interests of the respondent. The social researcher can seldom make this claim. Like the medical scientist, he can only argue that the research effort may ultimately help all mankind.

A major tenet of medical research ethics is that experimental participation must be *voluntary*. (Interestingly, the indictment of Nazi medical experimentation was based not so much on the cruelty of the experiments—such research is often unavoidably cruel—but on the fact that prisoners were forced to participate.) The same norm applies to social research. No one should be forced to participate. This norm is far easier to accept in theory than to apply in practice, however.

Again, medical research provides a useful parallel. Many experimental drugs are tested on prisoners. In the most rigorously ethical cases, the prisoners are told the nature—and the possible dangers—of the experiment; they are told that participation is completely voluntary; and they are further instructed that they can expect no special rewards—such as early parole—for participation. Even under these conditions, it is often clear that volunteers are motivated by the belief that they will personally benefit from their cooperation.

When the instructor in an introductory sociology class asks his students to fill out a questionnaire that he hopes to analyze and publish, he should always impress upon them that their participation in the survey is completely voluntary. Even so, it should be clear that most students will fear that nonparticipation will somehow affect the grades they receive in the course. In such a case, the instructor should be especially sensitive to the implied sanctions, and make special provisions to obviate them. Perhaps he might leave the room while the questionnaires are completed and dropped in a box. Or, he might ask students to return the questionnaires by mail, or put them at a box near the door upon arriving at the next meeting of the course.

Often, a faculty member may require subjects for social experiments, and students in his classes are a convenient resource. If he asks them to participate as experimental subjects, however, he must make it clear that they will in no way be penalized for nonparticipation.

You should be clear that this norm of voluntary participation goes directly against a number of scientific concerns. In the most general terms, the scientific goal of *generalizability* is threatened if experimental subjects or survey respondents are all the kinds of people who willingly participate in such things. This orientation probably reflects more general personality traits; possibly, then, the results of the research will not be generalizable to all kinds of people. Most clearly, in the case of a descriptive survey, a researcher cannot generalize his sample survey findings to an entire population unless a substantial majority of his scientifically selected sample actually participate—the willing respondents and the somewhat unwilling.

As discussed in Chapter 8, field research has its own ethical dilemmas in this regard. Very often, the researcher cannot even reveal that a study is being done, for fear that that revelation might significantly affect the social processes being studied. Clearly, the subjects of study in such cases are not even given the opportunity to volunteer or refuse to participate.

You should realize that the norm of voluntary participation is an important one, and you should also know that it is often impossible to follow it. In those cases where you feel ultimately justified in violating it, it is all the more important that you observe the other ethical norms of scientific research, such as bringing no harm to the people under study.

No Harm to the People Being Studied

Social research should never injure the people being studied, regardless of whether they volunteer for the study. Perhaps the clearest instance of this norm in practice concerns the revealing of information that would embarrass them or endanger their home life, friendships, jobs, and so forth. This norm is discussed more fully in the next section.

It is possible for subjects of study to be harmed psychologically in the course of a study, however, and the researcher must be aware of the often subtle dangers and guard against them. Very often, research subjects are asked to reveal deviant behavior, attitudes they feel are unpopular, or demeaning personal characteristics such as low income, the receipt of welfare payments, and the like. Revealing such information is very likely to make them feel at least uncomfortable.

Often, social research projects force participants to face aspects of themselves that they do not normally consider. This can happen even when the information is not revealed directly to the researcher. In retrospect, a certain past behavior may appear unjust or immoral. The project, then, can be the source of a continuing, personal agony for the subject. Perhaps he will begin questioning whether he is as religious or as ethical as he feels he ought to be, and this will continue to bother him long after the research project is over.

By now, you should have realized that just about any research you might conduct runs the risk of injuring other people in some of these regards. My purpose in this is not to paralyze you, to prevent you from ever doing research. I would just like you to be sensitive to these issues and be aware constantly that you are intruding in the lives of other human beings—usually uninvited.

There is no way for the researcher—whose study design involves the collection of information from and about people directly—to insure against all these possible injuries. Yet, some study designs make such injuries more likely than others. If a particular research procedure seems likely to produce unpleasant effects for subjects—asking survey respondents to report deviant behavior, for example—the researcher should have the firmest of scientific grounds for doing it. Unless it is vital to his research aims, he should not do it. If it is essential and also likely to be unpleasant for subjects, he will find himself in an ethical nether world and may find himself forced to do some personal agonizing. Although agonizing has little value in itself, it may be a healthy sign that he has become sensitive to the problem.

Although the fact often goes unrecognized, subjects can be harmed by the analysis and reporting of data. Every now and then, research subjects read the books published about the studies they participated in. A reasonably sophisticated subject will be able to locate himself in the various indexes and tables. Having done this, he may find himself characterized—though not identified by name—as bigoted, unpatriotic, irreligious, and so forth. At the very least, this is likely to trouble him and threaten his self-image. Yet the whole purpose of the research project may be to explain why some people are prejudiced while others are not.

I conducted a survey some years back of churchwomen. Ministers in a sample of churches were asked to distribute questionnaires to a specified sample of members, collect them, and return them to the research office. One of these ministers read through the questionnaires from his sample before returning them, and then proceeded to deliver a hell-fire and brimstone sermon to his congregation, saying that many of them were atheists and going to hell. Even though he could not know or identify the respondents who gave particular responses, it seems certain that many respondents were personally harmed by the action.

Like voluntary participation, not harming people is an easy norm to accept in theory, but it is often difficult to insure in practice. Sensitivity to the issue and experience with its applications, however, should improve the researcher's tact in delicate areas of research.

Anonymity and Confidentiality

The clearest concern in the protection of the subject's interests and well-being is the protection of his identity, especially in survey research. If revealing his survey responses would injure him in any way, adherence to this norm becomes all the more important. Two techniques—*anonymity* and *confidentiality*—assist the researcher in this regard, although the two are often confused.

Anonymity

A respondent may be considered *anonymous* when the researcher himself cannot identify a given response with a given respondent. This means that an interview survey respondent can never be considered anonymous, since an interviewer collects the information from an identifiable respondent. (This assumes that standard sampling methods are followed.) An example of anonymity would be the mail survey in which no identification numbers are put on the questionnaires prior to their return to the research office.

Of course, anonymity complicates any follow-up plans for increasing response rates. If the researcher does not know who among his sample have failed to reply, he cannot contact only them. As an alternative, however, he could mail again to all members of the original sample, asking those who had already replied to ignore the second appeal; or he could employ the postcard technique discussed in Chapter 11.

Despite the difficulties attendant upon insuring anonymity, there are some situations in which the researcher may be advised to pay the necessary price. In a recent study of drug use among university students, the researchers decided that they specifically did not want to know the identity of respondents. There were two reasons for this. First, they felt that honestly assuring anonymity would increase the likelihood and accuracy of responses. Second, they did not want to be in the position of being asked by authorities for the names of drug offenders. In the few instances in which respondents volunteered their names, such information was immediately obliterated on the questionnaires.

Confidentiality

In a *confidential* survey, the researcher is able to identify a given person's responses but essentially promises that he will not do so publicly. In an interview survey, for example, the researcher would be in a position to make public the income reported by a given respondent, but the respondent is assured that this will not be done.

There are a number of techniques whereby the researcher can better insure his performance on this guarantee. To begin, interviewers and others with access to respondent identifications should be trained in their ethical responsibilities. As soon as possible, all names and addresses should be removed from questionnaires and replaced by identification numbers. A master identification file should be created linking numbers to names—to permit the later correction of missing or contradictory information—but this file should not be available except for legitimate purposes.

Whenever a survey is confidential rather than anonymous, it is the responsibility of the researcher to make that fact clear to the respondent. The use of the term "anonymous" to mean "confidential" should never be tolerated.

Inferred Identity

Even in a truly anonymous survey, it is sometimes possible to identify a given respondent. This is particularly true with open-ended questions. If the respondent lists his occupation (or his father's occupation) as "President of ABC Company," the cat is out of the bag. Sometimes the multivariate analysis of closed-ended questions will permit the identification of a given respondent.

Since this is always a possibility in any survey, anonymous or not, the researcher cannot rule it out altogether. He should never attempt to make such identifications, however, and should insure that his research workers do not make such attempts. And, moreover, he should never report aggregated data in such a way that will permit readers to make such identifications. It is for this reason that the United States Census Bureau will not report aggregated data containing fewer than 15 cases per cell in a table.

Hidden Identification

Occasionally some researchers conduct surveys in which respondents are insured anonymity when in fact they are identifiable. Sometimes the return address of the research office contains a "box number" with that number being different for each respondent. On occasions, researchers have entered identification numbers under the stamps placed on return envelopes. Probably some have written numbers with lemon juice.

I suspect that in virtually all such cases—and they are probably few—the researchers have attempted to maintain the confidentiality of the data and have made no attempt to harm respondents. (It is my impression that those researchers most convinced of their personal morality are the most willing to engage in this devious practice.)

Whatever the motivations or scientific value, I am personally repelled by such practices and feel they should not be tolerated. If a survey is confidential rather than anonymous, the respondent should be so informed. Finally, *all surveys should be at least confidential.*

Concealing Identities

Recall that field researchers often do not even reveal their own identities to their subjects of study; much less are they invited to conduct their research. They have a special obligation, then, with regard to the protection of subjects' identities. As a result, field researchers often employ fictitious names in their research reports. Often the group under study—if there is one—is given a fictitious name, and all the individual participants *must* be protected in this fashion.

Analysis and Reporting

Just as the researcher has ethical obligations to respondents, so he has ethical obligations to his readers in the scientific community. As these latter norms are not often considered in the ethical realm, a few comments are in order.

In any rigorous study, the researcher should be more familiar with the technical shortcomings of the study than anyone else, and he should make these shortcomings known to his readers.

Negative findings should be reported if they are at all related to the analysis being reported. There is an unfortunate myth in scientific reporting that only positive discoveries are worth reporting (and journal editors are sometimes guilty of believing this as well). From the standpoint of the scientific community, however, it is often as important to know that two variables are not related to each other as to know that they are. Sometimes—as in *The American Soldier*[2]—the lack of expected correlations can be even more useful. Researchers must learn that there is no embarrassment inherent in nonrelationships.

Similarly, researchers should not fall victim to the temptation to "save face" by describing empirical findings as the products of preplanned analytical strategy when this is not the case. It is simply a fact of life that many findings arrive unexpectedly—even though they seem patently obvious in retrospect. Embroidering such events with descriptions of fictitious hypotheses is both dishonest and tends to mislead inexperienced researchers into thinking that all scientific inquiry is preplanned.

If an unexpected association between variables appears, it should be presented as unexpected. If the entire analytical strategy was radically restructured during the course of the study, the reader should be let in on the secret. This is especially beneficial since other researchers should be aware of the fact that another—seemingly functional—strategy is not appropriate to the subject matter. Science generally progresses through honesty and is retarded by ego-based deception.

Ethics—Relevant Illustrations

The ethics of social research—or of any scientific research—are not clear-cut. In this appendix, I have pointed to relatively few firm guidelines, and most of those are subject to debate, since they represent my own personal orientations.

My primary concern has been to make you more *sensitive* to ethical issues in social research. It will be far more important if you are able to recognize ethical considerations in real research situations than if you simply

2. Samuel A. Stouffer *et al.* (Princeton, N.J.: Princeton University Press, 1949). The study is discussed in Chapter 17.

memorize a set of ethical norms. With this in mind, the appendix concludes with the description of several research situations—most of them real, some hypothetical—that I believe have no clear-cut solutions, but I hope that the reader will be able to recognize the ethical issues in them.

1. An instructor in introductory sociology asks his students to complete questionnaires that he will then use for the analysis of a research problem of interest to him.

2. In a proposed study of attitudes among new law school gradu- ates, an agreement is made with the state bar association to include a questionnaire in the bar exam materials. Completion of the questionnaire will be a requirement for licensing.

3. The university contracts to conduct a study for the local city government. Since the city government is in general disfavor with the public, research workers are instructed to say only that they are doing the study for a group of university researchers.

4. The researcher's analysis of his data has produced so many surprises that his initial hypotheses have been wholly displaced by the findings that have appeared in his hectic and often confused analysis. The final conclusions are such that he is ashamed for not having begun with hypotheses appropriate to them. To save face, he writes his report as though he had.

5. After a field study of deviant behavior during a riot, law enforce- ment officials demand that the investigator identify for them those people observed to be looting during the recent riot. Rather than be an accomplice after the fact, the investigator complies.

6. At the completion of his analysis, the researcher discovers that 25 of the 2,000 survey interviews were falsified by the interviewers. He chooses to ignore the fact in his report.

7. A person who was not selected in the sample for a survey contacts the researcher and insists on being interviewed. The interview is conducted, and the questionnaire is then discarded.

8. Researchers obtain a list of right-wing radicals they wish to study. The researchers then contact this group with the explanation that they have been "selected at random."

9. Race matching is considered essential for a survey of racial prejudice. This means, however, that in the large city being studied, black interviewers will be working under generally poorer conditions than white interviewers.

10. A college instructor administers an hour exam to both sections of his course. The overall performance of the two sections is essentially the same. The grades of one section are artificially lowered, however, and the

instructor berates them for performing so poorly. The purpose of this experiment is to test the effect of such berating. He then administers the same final exam to both sections, and he discovers that the unfairly berated section performs more poorly. His hypothesis is confirmed.

11. A researcher in higher education wishes to examine the effect of various background factors on academic achievement. To measure achievement, he obtains students' grade point averages from the university administration.

12. Respondents are assured that a questionnaire they are asked to complete is anonymous. In fact, a serial number has been placed inconspicuously on the questionnaire to permit the analysis of other information collected about the respondents from other sources.

13. In a study of sexual behavior, the investigator wants to overcome subjects' reluctance to report what they will consider deviant behavior. Thus, he uses the following item: "Everyone masturbates now and then; about how often do you masturbate?"

14. Respondents are told that a survey is being conducted simply to determine how people feel about a series of public issues. In fact, the researcher is interested in determining sources of opposition to a particular issue.

15. A researcher discovers that 85 percent of the university student body smoke marijuana regularly. Publication of this finding will probably create a furor in the community. Since he is not planning to analyze drug use in depth, he decides to ignore the finding.

16. A researcher is contracted to conduct a study and prepare a report for the sponsor regarding a particular topic. He finds the data provide an opportunity to examine a related issue, although one that the sponsor is not concerned with. He uses project funds to cover the costs of analysis and typing for a paper, which he then delivers to a professional association meeting.

17. To test the extent to which people may try to save face by expressing attitudes on matters they are wholly uninformed about, the researcher asks for their attitudes regarding a fictitious issue.

18. A research questionnaire is circulated among students as part of their university registration packet. Although students are not told they must complete the questionnaire, the hope is that they will believe they must, thus insuring a higher completion rate.

19. A participant observer pretends to join a radical, political group in order to study it. He eventually becomes a member of the inner planning group. What should he do if the group plans:
(a) a peaceful, though illegal, demonstration?
(b) the bombing of a public building during a time it is sure to be unoccupied?
(c) the assassination of a public official?

20. An experimenter wishes to study the effects of emotional feelings among members of a group on their task performance. He asks each member of the group to report, confidentially, his feelings about the other members of the group. Regardless of what is reported, he tells each member of the experimental group that the other members don't like him very much.

The Importance of Ethical Concerns

The basic requirements of *scientific* research sorely tax the researcher's imagination and ingenuity. Practical, administrative constraints further complicate matters by often ruling out the ideal research procedures. Ethical concerns are likely to place an additional burden on the researcher. Having discovered that he has neither the time nor the money to execute the best possible study, the researcher may arrive at a brilliant compromise that is both administratively feasible and scientifically sound only to discover that it violates ethical concerns.

As repeated throughout this book, good scientific research is often difficult; ethical, scientific research may be harder yet, but the researcher cannot afford to give up on any of these concerns. He must conduct research that is scientifically sound, administratively feasible, and ethically defensible. He must not hurt people in the attempt to help them.

Appendix C   Random Numbers

10480	15011	01536	02011	81647	91646	69179	14194	62590	36207	20969	99570	91291	90700
22368	46573	25595	85393	30995	89198	27982	53402	93965	34095	52666	19174	39615	99505
24130	48360	22527	97265	76393	64809	15179	24830	49340	32081	30680	19655	63348	58629
42167	93093	06243	61680	07856	16376	39440	53537	71341	57004	00849	74917	97758	16379
37570	39975	81837	16656	06121	91782	60468	81305	49684	60672	14110	06927	01263	54613
77921	06907	11008	42751	27756	53498	18602	70659	90655	15053	21916	81825	44394	42880
99562	72905	56420	69994	98872	31016	71194	18738	44013	48840	63213	21069	10634	12952
96301	91977	05463	07972	18876	20922	94595	56869	69014	60045	18425	84903	42508	32307
89579	14342	63661	10281	17453	18103	57740	84378	25331	12566	58678	44947	05585	56941
85475	36857	53342	53988	53060	59533	38867	62300	08158	17983	16439	11458	18593	64952
28918	69578	88231	33276	70997	79936	56865	05859	90106	31595	01547	85590	91610	78188
63553	40961	48235	03427	49626	69445	18663	72695	52180	20847	12234	90511	33703	90322
09429	93969	52636	92737	88974	33488	36320	17617	30015	08272	84115	27156	30613	74952
10365	61129	87529	85689	48237	52267	67689	93394	01511	26358	85104	20285	29975	89868
07119	97336	71048	08178	77233	13916	47564	81056	97735	85977	29372	74461	28551	90707
51085	12765	51821	51259	77452	16308	60756	92144	49442	53900	70960	63990	75601	40719
02368	21382	52404	60268	89368	19885	55322	44819	01188	65255	64835	44919	05944	55157
01011	54092	33362	94904	31273	04146	18594	29852	71585	85030	51132	01915	92747	64951
52162	53916	46369	58586	23216	14513	83149	98736	23495	64350	94738	17752	35156	35749
07056	97628	33787	09998	42698	06691	76988	13602	51851	46104	88916	19509	25625	58104

Abridged from *Handbook of Tables for Probability and Statistics*, Second Edition, edited by William H. Beyer (Cleveland: The Chemical Rubber Company, 1968.) Reproduced by permission of the publishers, The Chemical Rubber Company.

48663	91245	85828	14346	09172	30168	90229	04734	59193	22178	30421	61666	99904	32812
54164	58492	22421	74103	47070	25306	76458	26384	58151	06646	21524	15227	96909	44592
32639	32363	05597	24200	13363	38005	94342	28728	35806	06912	17012	64161	18296	22851
29334	27001	87637	87308	58731	00256	45834	15398	46557	41135	10367	07684	36188	18510
02488	33062	28834	07351	19731	92420	60952	61280	50001	67658	32586	86679	50720	94953
81525	72295	04839	96423	24878	82651	66566	14778	76797	14780	13300	87074	79666	95725
29676	20591	68086	26432	46901	20849	89768	81536	86645	12659	92259	57102	80428	25280
00742	57392	39064	66432	84673	40027	32832	61362	98947	96067	64760	64584	96096	98253
05366	04213	25669	26422	44407	44048	37937	63904	45766	66134	75470	66520	34693	90449
91921	26418	64117	94305	26766	25940	39972	22209	71500	64568	91402	42416	07844	69618
00582	04711	87917	77341	42206	35126	74087	99547	81817	42607	43808	76655	62028	76630
00725	69884	62797	56170	86324	88072	76222	36086	84637	93161	76038	65855	77919	88006
69011	65795	95876	55293	18988	27354	26575	08625	40801	59920	29841	80150	12777	48501
25976	57948	29888	88604	67917	48708	18912	82271	65424	69774	33611	54262	85963	03547
09763	83473	73577	12908	30883	18317	28250	35797	05998	41688	34952	37888	38917	88050
91567	42595	27958	30134	04024	86385	29880	99730	55536	84855	29080	09250	79656	73211
17955	56349	90999	49127	20044	59931	06115	20542	18059	02008	73708	83517	36103	42791
46503	18584	18845	49618	02304	51038	20655	58727	28168	15475	56942	53389	20562	87333
92157	89634	94824	78171	84610	82834	09922	25417	44137	48413	25555	21246	35509	20463
14577	62765	35605	81263	39667	47358	56873	56307	61607	49518	89656	20103	77490	18062
98427	07523	33362	64270	01638	92477	66969	98420	04880	45585	46565	04102	46880	45709
34914	63976	88720	82765	34476	17032	87589	40836	32427	70002	70663	88863	77775	69348
70060	28277	39475	46473	23219	53416	94970	25832	69975	94884	19661	72828	00102	66794
53976	54914	06990	67245	68350	82948	11398	42878	80287	88267	47363	46634	06541	97809
76072	29515	40980	07391	58745	25774	22987	80059	39911	96189	41151	14222	60697	59583
90725	52210	83974	29992	65831	38857	50490	83765	55657	14361	31720	57375	56228	41546
64364	67412	33339	31926	14883	24413	59744	92351	97473	89286	35931	04110	23726	51900
08962	00358	31662	25388	61642	34072	81243	35648	56891	69352	48373	45578	78547	81788
95012	68379	93526	70565	10592	04542	76463	54328	02349	17247	28865	14777	62730	92277
15664	10493	20492	38391	91132	21999	59515	81652	27195	48223	46751	22923	32261	85653

16408	81899	04153	53381	79401	21438	83035	92350	36693	31238	59649	91754	72772	02338
18629	81953	05520	91962	04739	13092	97662	24822	94730	06496	35090	04822	86774	98289
73115	35101	47498	87637	99016	71060	88824	71013	18735	20286	23153	72924	35165	43040
57491	16703	23167	49323	45021	33132	12544	41035	80780	45393	44812	12515	98931	91202
30405	83946	23792	14422	15059	45799	22716	19792	09983	74353	68668	30429	70735	25499
16631	35006	85900	98275	32388	52390	16815	69298	82732	38480	73817	32523	41961	44437
96773	20206	42559	78985	05300	22164	24369	54224	35083	19687	11052	91491	60383	19746
38935	64202	14349	82674	66523	44133	00697	35552	35970	19124	63318	29686	03387	59846
31624	76384	17403	53363	44167	64486	64758	75366	76554	31601	12614	33072	60332	92325
78919	19474	23632	27889	47914	02584	37680	20801	72152	39339	34806	08930	85001	87820
03931	33309	57047	74211	63445	17361	62825	39908	05607	91284	68833	25570	38818	46920
74426	33278	43972	10119	89917	15665	52872	73823	73144	88662	88970	74492	51805	99378
09066	00903	20795	95452	92648	45454	09552	88815	16553	51125	79375	97596	16296	66092
42238	12426	87025	14267	20979	04508	64535	31355	86064	29472	47689	05974	52468	16834
16153	08002	26504	41744	81959	65642	74240	56302	00033	67107	77510	70625	28725	34191
21457	40742	29820	96783	29400	21840	15035	34537	33310	06116	95240	15957	16572	06004
21581	57802	02050	89728	17937	37621	47075	42080	97403	48626	68995	43805	33386	21597
55612	78095	83197	33732	05810	24813	86902	60397	16489	03264	88525	42786	05269	92532
44657	66999	99324	51281	84463	60563	79312	93454	68876	25471	93911	25650	12682	73572
91340	84979	46949	81973	37949	61023	43997	15263	80644	43942	89203	71795	99533	50501
91227	21199	31935	27022	84067	05462	35216	14486	29891	68607	41867	14951	91696	85065
50001	38140	66321	19924	72163	09538	12151	06878	91903	18749	34405	56087	82790	70925
65390	05224	72958	28609	81406	39147	25549	48542	42627	45233	57202	94617	23772	07896
27504	96131	83944	41575	10573	08619	64482	73923	36152	05184	94142	25299	84387	34925
37169	94851	39117	89632	00959	16487	65536	49071	39782	17095	02330	74301	00275	48280
11508	70225	51111	38351	19444	66499	71945	05422	13442	78675	84081	66938	93654	59894
37449	30362	06694	54690	04052	53115	62757	95348	78662	11163	81651	50245	34971	52924
46515	70331	85922	38329	57015	15765	97161	17869	45349	61796	66345	81073	49106	79860
30986	81223	42416	58353	21532	30502	32305	86482	05174	07901	54339	58861	74818	46942
63798	64995	46583	09785	44160	78128	83991	42865	92520	83531	80377	35909	81250	54238

```
82486  84846  99254  67632  43218  50076  21361  64816  51202  88124  41870  52689  51275  83556
21885  32906  92431  09060  64297  51674  64126  62570  26123  05155  59194  52799  28225  85752
60336  98782  07408  53458  13564  59089  26445  29789  85205  41001  12535  12133  14645  23541
43937  46891  24010  25560  86355  33941  25786  54990  71899  15475  95434  98227  21824  19535
97656  63175  89303  16275  07100  92063  21942  18611  47348  20203  18534  03862  78095  50136

03299  01221  05413  38982  55758  92237  26759  86367  21216  98442  08303  56613  91511  75928
79626  06486  03574  17663  07785  76020  79924  25651  83325  88428  85076  72811  22717  50585
85636  68335  47539  03129  65651  11977  02510  26113  99447  68645  34327  15152  55230  93448
18039  14367  61337  06177  12143  46609  32989  74014  64708  00533  35398  58408  13261  47908
08362  15656  60627  36478  65648  16764  53412  09013  07832  41574  17639  82163  60859  75567

79556  29068  04142  16268  15387  12856  66227  38358  22478  73373  88732  09443  82558  05250
92608  82674  27072  32534  17075  27698  98204  63863  11951  34648  88022  56148  34925  57031
23982  25835  40055  67006  12293  02753  14827  23235  35071  99704  37543  11601  35503  85171
09915  96306  05908  97901  28395  14186  00821  80703  70426  75647  76310  88717  37890  40129
59037  33300  26695  62247  69927  76123  50842  43834  86654  70959  79725  93872  28117  19253

42488  78077  69882  61657  34136  79180  97526  43092  04098  73571  80799  76536  71255  64239
46764  86273  63003  93017  31204  36692  40202  35275  57306  55543  53203  18098  47625  88684
03237  45430  55417  63282  90816  17349  88298  90183  36600  78406  06216  95787  42579  90730
86591  81482  52667  61582  14972  90053  89534  76036  49199  43716  97548  04379  46370  28672
38534  01715  94964  87288  55680  43772  39560  12918  86537  62738  19636  51132  25739  56947
```

Appendix D   Normal Curve Areas

z	.00	.01	.02	.03	.04	.05	.06	.07	.08	.09
0.0	.0000	.0040	.0080	.0120	.0160	.0199	.0239	.0279	.0319	.0359
0.1	.0398	.0438	.0478	.0517	.0557	.0596	.0636	.0675	.0714	.0753
0.2	.0793	.0832	.0871	.0910	.0948	.0987	.1026	.1064	.1103	.1141
0.3	.1179	.1217	.1255	.1293	.1331	.1368	.1406	.1443	.1480	.1517
0.4	.1554	.1591	.1628	.1664	.1700	.1736	.1772	.1808	.1844	.1879
0.5	.1915	.1950	.1985	.2019	.2054	.2088	.2123	.2157	.2190	.2224
0.6	.2257	.2291	.2324	.2357	.2389	.2422	.2454	.2486	.2517	.2549
0.7	.2580	.2611	.2642	.2673	.2704	.2734	.2764	.2794	.2823	.2852
0.8	.2881	.2910	.2939	.2967	.2995	.3023	.3051	.3078	.3106	.3133
0.9	.3159	.3186	.3212	.3238	.3264	.3289	.3315	.3340	.3365	.3389
1.0	.3413	.3438	.3461	.3485	.3508	.3531	.3554	.3577	.3599	.3621
1.1	.3643	.3665	.3686	.3708	.3729	.3749	.3770	.3790	.3810	.3830
1.2	.3849	.3869	.3888	.3907	.3925	.3944	.3962	.3980	.3997	.4015
1.3	.4032	.4049	.4066	.4082	.4099	.4115	.4131	.4147	.4162	.4177
1.4	.4192	.4207	.4222	.4236	.4251	.4265	.4279	.4292	.4306	.4319
1.5	.4332	.4345	.4357	.4370	.4382	.4394	.4406	.4418	.4429	.4441
1.6	.4452	.4463	.4474	.4484	.4495	.4505	.4515	.4525	.4535	.4545
1.7	.4554	.4564	.4573	.4582	.4591	.4599	.4608	.4616	.4625	.4633
1.8	.4641	.4649	.4656	.4664	.4671	.4678	.4686	.4693	.4699	.4706
1.9	.4713	.4719	.4726	.4732	.4738	.4744	.4750	.4756	.4761	.4767
2.0	.4772	.4778	.4783	.4788	.4793	.4798	.4803	.4808	.4812	.4817
2.1	.4821	.4826	.4830	.4834	.4838	.4842	.4846	.4850	.4854	.4857
2.2	.4861	.4864	.4868	.4871	.4875	.4878	.4881	.4884	.4887	.4890
2.3	.4893	.4896	.4898	.4901	.4904	.4906	.4909	.4911	.4913	.4916
2.4	.4918	.4920	.4922	.4925	.4927	.4929	.4931	.4932	.4934	.4936
2.5	.4938	.4940	.4941	.4943	.4945	.4946	.4948	.4949	.4951	.4952
2.6	.4953	.4955	.4956	.4957	.4959	.4960	.4961	.4962	.4963	.4964
2.7	.4965	.4966	.4967	.4968	.4969	.4970	.4971	.4972	.4973	.4974
2.8	.4974	.4975	.4976	.4977	.4977	.4978	.4979	.4979	.4980	.4981
2.9	.4981	.4982	.4982	.4983	.4984	.4984	.4985	.4985	.4986	.4986
3.0	.4987	.4987	.4987	.4988	.4988	.4989	.4989	.4989	.4990	.4990

This table is abridged from Table I of *Statistical Tables and Formulas*, by A. Hald (New York: John Wiley & Sons, Inc., 1952). Reproduced by permission of A. Hald and the publishers, John Wiley & Sons, Inc.

Appendix E   Critical Values of Chi-Square

d.f.	$\chi^2 0.995$	$\chi^2 0.990$	$\chi^2 0.975$	$\chi^2 0.950$	$\chi^2 0.900$
1	0.0000393	0.0001571	0.0009821	0.0039321	0.0157908
2	0.0100251	0.0201007	0.0506356	0.102587	0.210720
3	0.0717212	0.114832	0.215795	0.351846	0.584375
4	0.206990	0.297110	0.484419	0.710721	1.063623
5	0.411740	0.554300	0.831211	1.145476	1.61031
6	0.675727	0.872085	1.237347	1.63539	2.20413
7	0.989265	1.239043	1.68987	2.16735	2.83311
8	1.344419	1.646482	2.17973	2.73264	3.48954
9	1.734926	2.087912	2.70039	3.32511	4.16816
10	2.15585	2.55821	3.24697	3.94030	4.86518
11	2.60321	3.05347	3.81575	4.57481	5.57779
12	3.07382	3.57056	4.40379	5.22603	6.30380
13	3.56503	4.10691	5.00874	5.89186	7.04150
14	4.07468	4.66043	5.62872	6.57063	7.78953
15	4.60094	5.22935	6.26214	7.26094	8.54675
16	5.14224	5.81221	6.90766	7.96164	9.31223
17	5.69724	6.40776	7.56418	8.67176	10.0852
18	6.26481	7.01491	8.23075	9.39046	10.8649
19	6.84398	7.63273	8.90655	10.1170	11.6509
20	7.43386	8.26040	9.59083	10.8508	12.4426
21	8.03366	8.89720	10.28293	11.5913	13.2396
22	8.64272	9.54249	10.9823	12.3380	14.0415
23	9.26042	10.19567	11.6885	13.0905	14.8479
24	9.88623	10.8564	12.4011	13.8484	15.6587
25	10.5197	11.5240	13.1197	14.6114	16.4734
26	11.1603	12.1981	13.8439	15.3791	17.2919
27	11.8076	12.8786	14.5733	16.1513	18.1138
28	12.4613	13.5648	15.3079	16.9279	18.9392
29	13.1211	14.2565	16.0471	17.7083	19.7677
30	13.7867	14.9535	16.7908	18.4926	20.5992
40	20.7065	22.1643	24.4331	26.5093	29.0505
50	27.9907	29.7067	32.3574	34.7642	37.6886
60	35.5346	37.4848	40.4817	43.1879	46.4589
70	43.2752	45.4418	48.7576	51.7393	55.3290
80	51.1720	53.5400	57.1532	60.3915	64.2778
90	59.1963	61.7541	65.6466	69.1260	73.2912
100	67.3276	70.0648	74.2219	77.9295	82.3581

From "Tables of the Percentage Points of the χ^2-Distribution." *Biometrika,* Vol. 32 (1941), pp. 188–189, by Catherine M. Thompson. Reproduced by permission of Professor E. S. Pearson.

$\chi^2 0.100$	$\chi^2 0.050$	$\chi^2 0.025$	$\chi^2 0.010$	$\chi^2 0.005$	d.f.
2.70554	3.84146	5.02389	6.63490	7.87944	1
4.60517	5.99147	7.37776	9.21034	10.5966	2
6.25139	7.81473	9.34840	11.3449	12.8381	3
7.77944	9.48773	11.1433	13.2767	14.8602	4
9.23635	11.0705	12.8325	15.0863	16.7496	5
10.6446	12.5916	14.4494	16.8119	18.5476	6
12.0170	14.0671	16.0128	18.4753	20.2777	7
13.3616	15.5073	17.5346	20.0902	21.9550	8
14.6837	16.9190	19.0228	21.6660	23.5893	9
15.9871	18.3070	20.4831	23.2093	25.1882	10
17.2750	19.6751	21.9200	24.7250	26.7569	11
18.5494	21.0261	23.3367	26.2170	28.2995	12
19.8119	22.3621	24.7356	27.6883	29.8194	13
21.0642	23.6848	26.1190	29.1413	31.3193	14
22.3072	24.9958	27.4884	30.5779	32.8013	15
23.5418	26.2962	28.8454	31.9999	34.2672	16
24.7690	27.5871	30.1910	33.4087	35.7185	17
25.9894	28.8693	31.5264	34.8053	37.1564	18
27.2036	30.1435	32.8523	36.1908	38.5822	19
28.4120	31.4104	34.1696	37.5662	39.9968	20
29.6151	32.6705	35.4789	38.9321	41.4010	21
30.8133	33.9244	36.7807	40.2894	42.7956	22
32.0069	35.1725	38.0757	41.6384	44.1813	23
33.1963	36.4151	39.3641	42.9798	45.5685	24
34.3816	37.6525	40.6465	44.3141	46.9278	25
35.5631	38.8852	41.9232	45.6417	48.2899	26
36.7412	40.1133	43.1944	46.9630	49.6449	27
37.9159	41.3372	44.4607	48.2782	50.9933	28
39.0875	42.5569	45.7222	49.5879	52.3356	29
40.2560	43.7729	46.9792	50.8922	53.6720	30
51.8050	55.7585	59.3417	63.6907	66.7659	40
63.1671	67.5048	71.4202	76.1539	79.4900	50
74.3970	79.0819	83.2976	88.3794	91.9517	60
85.5271	90.5312	95.0231	100.425	104.215	70
96.5782	101.879	106.629	112.329	116.321	80
107.565	113.145	118.136	124.116	128.299	90
118.498	124.342	129.561	135.807	140.169	100

Appendix F Estimated Sampling Error
for a Binomial
(95% Confidence Level)

How to use this table: Find the intersection between the sample size and the approximate percentage distribution of the binomial in the sample. The number appearing at this intersection represents the estimated sampling error, at the 95% confidence level, expressed in percentage points (plus or minus).

Example: In a sample of 400 respondents, 60% answer "Yes" and 40% answer "No." The sampling error is estimated at plus or minus 4.9 percentage points. The confidence interval, then, is between 55.1% and 64.9%. We would estimate (95% confidence) that the proportion of the total population who would say "Yes" is somewhere within that interval.

Sample size	Binomial Percentage Distribution				
	50/50	60/40	70/30	80/20	90/10
100	10	9.8	9.2	8	6
200	7.1	6.9	6.5	5.7	4.2
300	5.8	5.7	5.3	4.6	3.5
400	5	4.9	4.6	4	3
500	4.5	4.4	4.1	3.6	2.7
600	4.1	4	3.7	3.3	2.4
700	3.8	3.7	3.5	3	2.3
800	3.5	3.5	3.2	2.8	2.1
900	3.3	3.3	3.1	2.7	2
1000	3.2	3.1	2.9	2.5	1.9
1100	3	3	2.8	2.4	1.8
1200	2.9	2.8	2.6	2.3	1.7
1300	2.8	2.7	2.5	2.2	1.7
1400	2.7	2.6	2.4	2.1	1.6
1500	2.6	2.5	2.4	2.1	1.5
1600	2.5	2.4	2.3	2	1.5
1700	2.4	2.4	2.2	1.9	1.5
1800	2.4	2.3	2.2	1.9	1.4
1900	2.3	2.2	2.1	1.8	1.4
2000	2.2	2.2	2	1.8	1.3

Appendix G   Square Roots

Number	Square root	Square	Number	Square root	Square
1	1	1	51	7.1414	2601
2	1.4142	4	52	7.2111	2704
3	1.7321	9	53	7.2801	2809
4	2	16	54	7.3485	2916
5	2.2361	25	55	7.4162	3025
6	2.4495	36	56	7.4833	3136
7	2.6458	49	57	7.5498	3249
8	2.8284	64	58	7.6158	3364
9	3	81	59	7.6811	3481
10	3.1623	100	60	7.746	3600
11	3.3166	121	61	7.8102	3721
12	3.4641	144	62	7.874	3844
13	3.6056	169	63	7.9373	3969
14	3.7417	196	64	8	4096
15	3.873	225	65	8.0623	4225
16	4	256	66	8.124	4356
17	4.1231	289	67	8.1854	4489
18	4.2426	324	68	8.2462	4624
19	4.3589	361	69	8.3066	4761
20	4.4721	400	70	8.3666	4900
21	4.5826	441	71	8.4261	5041
22	4.6904	484	72	8.4853	5184
23	4.7958	529	73	8.544	5329
24	4.899	576	74	8.6023	5476
25	5	625	75	8.6603	5625
26	5.099	676	76	8.7178	5776
27	5.1962	729	77	8.775	5929
28	5.2915	784	78	8.8318	6084
29	5.3852	841	79	8.8882	6241
30	5.4772	900	80	8.9443	6400
31	5.5678	961	81	9	6561
32	5.6569	1024	82	9.0554	6724
33	5.7446	1089	83	9.1104	6889
34	5.831	1156	84	9.1652	7056
35	5.9161	1225	85	9.2195	7225
36	6	1296	86	9.2736	7396
37	6.0828	1369	87	9.3274	7569
38	6.1644	1444	88	9.3808	7744
39	6.245	1521	89	9.434	7921
40	6.3246	1600	90	9.4868	8100
41	6.4031	1681	91	9.5394	8281
42	6.4807	1764	92	9.5917	8464
43	6.5574	1849	93	9.6437	8649
44	6.6332	1936	94	9.6954	8836
45	6.7082	2025	95	9.7468	9025
46	6.7823	2116	96	9.798	9216
47	6.8557	2209	97	9.8489	9409
48	6.9282	2304	98	9.8995	9604
49	7	2401	99	9.9499	9801
50	7.0711	2500	100	10	10000

Number	Square root	Square	Number	Square root	Square
101	10.0499	10201	151	12.2882	22801
102	10.0995	10404	152	12.3288	23104
103	10.1489	10609	153	12.3693	23409
104	10.198	10816	154	12.4097	23716
105	10.247	11025	155	12.4499	24025
106	10.2956	11236	156	12.49	24336
107	10.3441	11449	157	12.53	24649
108	10.3923	11664	158	12.5698	24964
109	10.4403	11881	159	12.6095	25281
110	10.4881	12100	160	12.6491	25600
111	10.5357	12321	161	12.6886	25921
112	10.583	12544	162	12.7279	26244
113	10.6301	12769	163	12.7671	26569
114	10.6771	12996	164	12.8062	26896
115	10.7238	13225	165	12.8452	27225
116	10.7703	13456	166	12.8841	27556
117	10.8167	13689	167	12.9228	27889
118	10.8628	13924	168	12.9615	28224
119	10.9087	14161	169	13	28561
120	10.9545	14400	170	13.0384	28900
121	11	14641	171	13.0767	29241
122	11.0454	14884	172	13.1149	29584
123	11.0905	15129	173	13.1529	29929
124	11.1355	15376	174	13.1909	30276
125	11.1803	15625	175	13.2288	30625
126	11.225	15876	176	13.2665	30976
127	11.2694	16129	177	13.3041	31329
128	11.3137	16384	178	13.3417	31684
129	11.3578	16641	179	13.3791	32041
130	11.4018	16900	180	13.4164	32400
131	11.4455	17161	181	13.4536	32761
132	11.4891	17424	182	13.4907	33124
133	11.5326	17689	183	13.5277	33489
134	11.5758	17956	184	13.5647	33856
135	11.619	18225	185	13.6015	34225
136	11.6619	18496	186	13.6382	34596
137	11.7047	18769	187	13.6748	34969
138	11.7473	19044	188	13.7113	35344
139	11.7898	19321	189	13.7477	35721
140	11.8322	19600	190	13.784	36100
141	11.8743	19881	191	13.8203	36481
142	11.9164	20164	192	13.8564	36864
143	11.9583	20449	193	13.8924	37249
144	12	20736	194	13.9284	37636
145	12.0416	21025	195	13.9642	38025
146	12.083	21316	196	14	38416
147	12.1244	21609	197	14.0357	38809
148	12.1655	21904	198	14.0712	39204
149	12.2066	22201	199	14.1067	39601
150	12.2474	22500	200	14.1421	40000

Number	Square root	Square	Number	Square root	Square
201	14.1774	40401	251	15.843	63001
202	14.2127	40804	252	15.8745	63504
203	14.2478	41209	253	15.906	64009
204	14.2829	41616	254	15.9374	64516
205	14.3178	42025	255	15.9687	65025
206	14.3527	42436	256	16	65536
207	14.3875	42849	257	16.0312	66049
208	14.4222	43264	258	16.0624	66564
209	14.4568	43681	259	16.0935	67081
210	14.4914	44100	260	16.1245	67600
211	14.5258	44521	261	16.1555	68121
212	14.5602	44944	262	16.1864	68644
213	14.5945	45369	263	16.2173	69169
214	14.6287	45796	264	16.2481	69696
215	14.6629	46225	265	16.2788	70225
216	14.6969	46656	266	16.3095	70756
217	14.7309	47089	267	16.3401	71289
218	14.7648	47524	268	16.3707	71824
219	14.7986	47961	269	16.4012	72361
220	14.8324	48400	270	16.4317	72900
221	14.8661	48841	271	16.4621	73441
222	14.8997	49284	272	16.4924	73984
223	14.9332	49729	273	16.5227	74529
224	14.9666	50176	274	16.5529	75076
225	15	50625	275	16.5831	75625
226	15.0333	51076	276	16.6132	76176
227	15.0665	51529	277	16.6433	76729
228	15.0997	51984	278	16.6733	77284
229	15.1327	52441	279	16.7033	77841
230	15.1658	52900	280	16.7332	78400
231	15.1987	53361	281	16.7631	78961
232	15.2315	53824	282	16.7929	79524
233	15.2643	54289	283	16.8226	80089
234	15.2971	54756	284	16.8523	80656
235	15.3297	55225	285	16.8819	81225
236	15.3623	55696	286	16.9115	81796
237	15.3948	56169	287	16.9411	82369
238	15.4272	56644	288	16.9706	82944
239	15.4596	57121	289	17	83521
240	15.4919	57600	290	17.0294	84100
241	15.5242	58081	291	17.0587	84681
242	15.5563	58564	292	17.088	85264
243	15.5885	59049	293	17.1172	85849
244	15.6205	59536	294	17.1464	86436
245	15.6525	60025	295	17.1756	87025
246	15.6844	60516	296	17.2047	87616
247	15.7162	61009	297	17.2337	88209
248	15.748	61504	298	17.2627	88804
249	15.7797	62001	299	17.2916	89401
250	15.8114	62500	300	17.3205	90000

Number	Square root	Square	Number	Square root	Square
301	17.3494	90601	351	18.735	123201
302	17.3781	91204	352	18.7617	123904
303	17.4069	91809	353	18.7883	124609
304	17.4356	92416	354	18.8149	125316
305	17.4642	93025	355	18.8414	126025
306	17.4929	93636	356	18.868	126736
307	17.5214	94249	357	18.8944	127449
308	17.5499	94864	358	18.9209	128164
309	17.5784	95481	359	18.9473	128881
310	17.6068	96100	360	18.9737	129600
311	17.6352	96721	361	19	130321
312	17.6635	97344	362	19.0263	131044
313	17.6918	97969	363	19.0526	131769
314	17.72	98596	364	19.0788	132496
315	17.7482	99225	365	19.105	133225
316	17.7764	99856	366	19.1311	133956
317	17.8045	100489	367	19.1572	134689
318	17.8326	101124	368	19.1833	135424
319	17.8606	101761	369	19.2094	136161
320	17.8885	102400	370	19.2354	136900
321	17.9165	103041	371	19.2614	137641
322	17.9444	103684	372	19.2873	138384
323	17.9722	104329	373	19.3132	139129
324	18	104976	374	19.3391	139876
325	18.0278	105625	375	19.3649	140625
326	18.0555	106276	376	19.3907	141376
327	18.0831	106929	377	19.4165	142129
328	18.1108	107584	378	19.4422	142884
329	18.1384	108241	379	19.4679	143641
330	18.1659	108900	380	19.4936	144400
331	18.1934	109561	381	19.5192	145161
332	18.2209	110224	382	19.5448	145924
333	18.2483	110889	383	19.5704	146689
334	18.2757	111556	384	19.5959	147456
335	18.303	112225	385	19.6214	148225
336	18.3303	112896	386	19.6469	148996
337	18.3576	113569	387	19.6723	149769
338	18.3848	114244	388	19.6977	150544
339	18.412	114921	389	19.7231	151321
340	18.4391	115600	390	19.7484	152100
341	18.4662	116281	391	19.7737	152881
342	18.4932	116964	392	19.799	153664
343	18.5203	117649	393	19.8242	154449
344	18.5472	118336	394	19.8494	155236
345	18.5742	119025	395	19.8746	156025
346	18.6011	119716	396	19.8997	156816
347	18.6279	120409	397	19.9249	157609
348	18.6548	121104	398	19.9499	158404
349	18.6815	121801	399	19.975	159201
350	18.7083	122500	400	20	160000

Number	Square root	Square	Number	Square root	Square
401	20.025	160801	451	21.2368	203401
402	20.0499	161604	452	21.2603	204304
403	20.0749	162409	453	21.2838	205209
404	20.0998	163216	454	21.3073	206116
405	20.1246	164025	455	21.3307	207025
406	20.1494	164836	456	21.3542	207936
407	20.1742	165649	457	21.3776	208849
408	20.199	166464	458	21.4009	209764
409	20.2237	167281	459	21.4243	210681
410	20.2485	168100	460	21.4476	211600
411	20.2731	168921	461	21.4709	212521
412	20.2978	169744	462	21.4942	213444
413	20.3224	170569	463	21.5174	214369
414	20.347	171396	464	21.5407	215296
415	20.3715	172225	465	21.5639	216225
416	20.3961	173056	466	21.587	217156
417	20.4206	173889	467	21.6102	218089
418	20.445	174724	468	21.6333	219024
419	20.4695	175561	469	21.6564	219961
420	20.4939	176400	470	21.6795	220900
421	20.5183	177241	471	21.7025	221841
422	20.5426	178084	472	21.7256	222784
423	20.567	178929	473	21.7486	223729
424	20.5913	179776	474	21.7715	224676
425	20.6155	180625	475	21.7945	225625
426	20.6398	181476	476	21.8174	226576
427	20.664	182329	477	21.8403	227529
428	20.6882	183184	478	21.8632	228484
429	20.7123	184041	479	21.8861	229441
430	20.7364	184900	480	21.9089	230400
431	20.7605	185761	481	21.9317	231361
432	20.7846	186624	482	21.9545	232324
433	20.8087	187489	483	21.9773	233289
434	20.8327	188356	484	22	234256
435	20.8567	189225	485	22.0227	235225
436	20.8806	190096	486	22.0454	236196
437	20.9045	190969	487	22.0681	237169
438	20.9284	191844	488	22.0907	238144
439	20.9523	192721	489	22.1133	239121
440	20.9762	193600	490	22.1359	240100
441	21	194481	491	22.1585	241081
442	21.0238	195364	492	22.1811	242064
443	21.0476	196249	493	22.2036	243049
444	21.0713	197136	494	22.2261	244036
445	21.095	198025	495	22.2486	245025
446	21.1187	198916	496	22.2711	246016
447	21.1424	199809	497	22.2935	247009
448	21.166	200704	498	22.3159	248004
449	21.1896	201601	499	22.3383	249001
450	21.2132	202500	500	22.3607	250000

Number	Square root	Square	Number	Square root	Square
501	22.383	251001	551	23.4734	303601
502	22.4054	252004	552	23.4947	304704
503	22.4277	253009	553	23.516	305809
504	22.4499	254016	554	23.5372	306916
505	22.4722	255025	555	23.5584	308025
506	22.4944	256036	556	23.5797	309136
507	22.5167	257049	557	23.6008	310249
508	22.5389	258064	558	23.622	311364
509	22.561	259081	559	23.6432	312481
510	22.5832	260100	560	23.6643	313600
511	22.6053	261121	561	23.6854	314721
512	22.6274	262144	562	23.7065	315844
513	22.6495	263169	563	23.7276	316969
514	22.6716	264196	564	23.7487	318096
515	22.6936	265225	565	23.7697	319225
516	22.7156	266256	566	23.7908	320356
517	22.7376	267289	567	23.8118	321489
518	22.7596	268324	568	23.8328	322624
519	22.7816	269361	569	23.8537	323761
520	22.8035	270400	570	23.8747	324900
521	22.8254	271441	571	23.8956	326041
522	22.8473	272484	572	23.9165	327184
523	22.8692	273529	573	23.9374	328329
524	22.891	274576	574	23.9583	329476
525	22.9129	275625	575	23.9792	330625
526	22.9347	276676	576	24	331776
527	22.9565	277729	577	24.0208	332929
528	22.9783	278784	578	24.0416	334084
529	23	279841	579	24.0624	335241
530	23.0217	280900	580	24.0832	336400
531	23.0434	281961	581	24.1039	337561
532	23.0651	283024	582	24.1247	338724
533	23.0868	284089	583	24.1454	339889
534	23.1084	285156	584	24.1661	341056
535	23.1301	286225	585	24.1868	342225
536	23.1517	287296	586	24.2074	343396
537	23.1733	288369	587	24.2281	344569
538	23.1948	289444	588	24.2487	345744
539	23.2164	290521	589	24.2693	346921
540	23.2379	291600	590	24.2899	348100
541	23.2594	292681	591	24.3105	349281
542	23.2809	293764	592	24.3311	350464
543	23.3024	294849	593	24.3516	351649
544	23.3238	295936	594	24.3721	352836
545	23.3452	297025	595	24.3926	354025
546	23.3666	298116	596	24.4131	355216
547	23.388	299209	597	24.4336	356409
548	23.4094	300304	598	24.454	357604
549	23.4307	301401	599	24.4745	358801
550	23.4521	302500	600	24.4949	360000

Number	Square root	Square	Number	Square root	Square
601	24.5153	361201	651	25.5147	423801
602	24.5357	362404	652	25.5343	425104
603	24.5561	363609	653	25.5539	426409
604	24.5764	364816	654	25.5734	427716
605	24.5967	366025	655	25.593	429025
606	24.6171	367236	656	25.6125	430336
607	24.6374	368449	657	25.632	431649
608	24.6577	369664	658	25.6515	432964
609	24.6779	370881	659	25.671	434281
610	24.6982	372100	660	25.6905	435600
611	24.7184	373321	661	25.7099	436921
612	24.7386	374544	662	25.7294	438244
613	24.7588	375769	663	25.7488	439569
614	24.779	376996	664	25.7682	440896
615	24.7992	378225	665	25.7876	442225
616	24.8193	379456	666	25.807	443556
617	24.8395	380689	667	25.8263	444889
618	24.8596	381924	668	25.8457	446224
619	24.8797	383161	669	25.865	447561
620	24.8998	384400	670	25.8844	448900
621	24.9199	385641	671	25.9037	450241
622	24.9399	386884	672	25.923	451584
623	24.96	388129	673	25.9422	452929
624	24.98	389376	674	25.9615	454276
625	25	390625	675	25.9808	455625
626	25.02	391876	676	26	456976
627	25.04	393129	677	26.0192	458329
628	25.0599	394384	678	26.0384	459684
629	25.0799	395641	679	26.0576	461041
630	25.0998	396900	680	26.0768	462400
631	25.1197	398161	681	26.096	463761
632	25.1396	399424	682	26.1151	465124
633	25.1595	400689	683	26.1343	466489
634	25.1794	401956	684	26.1534	467856
635	25.1992	403225	685	26.1725	469225
636	25.219	404496	686	26.1916	470596
637	25.2389	405769	687	26.2107	471969
638	25.2587	407044	688	26.2298	473344
639	25.2784	408321	689	26.2488	474721
640	25.2982	409600	690	26.2679	476100
641	25.318	410881	691	26.2869	477481
642	25.3377	412164	692	26.3059	478864
643	25.3574	413449	693	26.3249	480249
644	25.3772	414736	694	26.3439	481636
645	25.3969	416025	695	26.3629	483025
646	25.4165	417316	696	26.3818	484416
647	25.4362	418609	697	26.4008	485809
648	25.4558	419904	698	26.4197	487204
649	25.4755	421201	699	26.4386	488601
650	25.4951	422500	700	26.4575	490000

Number	Square root	Square	Number	Square root	Square
701	26.4764	491401	751	27.4044	564001
702	26.4953	492804	752	27.4226	565504
703	26.5141	494209	753	27.4408	567009
704	26.533	495616	754	27.4591	568516
705	26.5518	497025	755	27.4773	570025
706	26.5707	498436	756	27.4955	571536
707	26.5895	499849	757	27.5136	573049
708	26.6083	501264	758	27.5318	574564
709	26.6271	502681	759	27.55	576081
710	26.6458	504100	760	27.5681	577600
711	26.6646	505521	761	27.5862	579121
712	26.6833	506944	762	27.6043	580644
713	26.7021	508369	763	27.6225	582169
714	26.7208	509796	764	27.6405	583696
715	26.7395	511225	765	27.6586	585225
716	26.7582	512656	766	27.6767	586756
717	26.7769	514089	767	27.6948	588289
718	26.7955	515524	768	27.7128	589824
719	26.8142	516961	769	27.7308	591361
720	26.8328	518400	770	27.7489	592900
721	26.8514	519841	771	27.7669	594441
722	26.8701	521284	772	27.7849	595984
723	26.8887	522729	773	27.8029	597529
724	26.9072	524176	774	27.8209	599076
725	26.9258	525625	775	27.8388	600625
726	26.9444	527076	776	27.8568	602176
727	26.9629	528529	777	27.8747	603729
728	26.9815	529984	778	27.8927	605284
729	27	531441	779	27.9106	606841
730	27.0185	532900	780	27.9285	608400
731	27.037	534361	781	27.9464	609961
732	27.0555	535824	782	27.9643	611524
733	27.074	537289	783	27.9821	613089
734	27.0924	538756	784	28	614656
735	27.1109	540225	785	28.0179	616225
736	27.1293	541696	786	28.0357	617796
737	27.1477	543169	787	28.0535	619369
738	27.1662	544644	788	28.0713	620944
739	27.1846	546121	789	28.0891	622521
740	27.2029	547600	790	28.1069	624100
741	27.2213	549081	791	28.1247	625681
742	27.2397	550564	792	28.1425	627264
743	27.258	552049	793	28.1603	628849
744	27.2764	553536	794	28.178	630436
745	27.2947	555025	795	28.1957	632025
746	27.313	556516	796	28.2135	633616
747	27.3313	558009	797	28.2312	635209
748	27.3496	559504	798	28.2489	636804
749	27.3679	561001	799	28.2666	638401
750	27.3861	562500	800	28.2843	640000

Number	Square root	Square	Number	Square root	Square
801	28.3019	641601	851	29.1719	724201
802	28.3196	643204	852	29.189	725904
803	28.3373	644809	853	29.2062	727609
804	28.3549	646416	854	29.2233	729316
805	28.3725	648025	855	29.2404	731025
806	28.3901	649636	856	29.2575	732736
807	28.4077	651249	857	29.2746	734449
808	28.4253	652864	858	29.2916	736164
809	28.4429	654481	859	29.3087	737881
810	28.4605	656100	860	29.3258	739600
811	28.4781	657721	861	29.3428	741321
812	28.4956	659344	862	29.3598	743044
813	28.5132	660969	863	29.3769	744769
814	28.5307	662596	864	29.3939	746496
815	28.5482	664225	865	29.4109	748225
816	28.5657	665856	866	29.4279	749956
817	28.5832	667489	867	29.4449	751689
818	28.6007	669124	868	29.4618	753424
819	28.6182	670761	869	29.4788	755161
820	28.6356	672400	870	29.4958	756900
821	28.6531	674041	871	29.5127	758641
822	28.6705	675684	872	29.5296	760384
823	28.688	677329	873	29.5466	762129
824	28.7054	678976	874	29.5635	763876
825	28.7228	680625	875	29.5804	765625
826	28.7402	682276	876	29.5973	767376
827	28.7576	683929	877	29.6142	769129
828	28.775	685584	878	29.6311	770884
829	28.7924	687241	879	29.6479	772641
830	28.8097	688900	880	29.6648	774400
831	28.8271	690561	881	29.6816	776161
832	28.8444	692224	882	29.6985	777924
833	28.8617	693889	883	29.7153	779689
834	28.8791	695556	884	29.7321	781456
835	28.8964	697225	885	29.7489	783225
836	28.9137	698896	886	29.7658	784996
837	28.931	700569	887	29.7825	786769
838	28.9482	702244	888	29.7993	788544
839	28.9655	703921	889	29.8161	790321
840	28.9828	705600	890	29.8329	792100
841	29	707281	891	29.8496	793881
842	29.0172	708964	892	29.8664	795664
843	29.0345	710649	893	29.8831	797449
844	29.0517	712336	894	29.8998	799236
845	29.0689	714025	895	29.9166	801025
846	29.0861	715716	896	29.9333	802816
847	29.1033	717409	897	29.95	804609
848	29.1204	719104	898	29.9666	806404
849	29.1376	720801	899	29.9833	808201
850	29.1548	722500	900	30	810000

Appendix G Square Roots

Number	Square root	Square	Number	Square root	Square
901	30.0167	811801	951	30.8383	904401
902	30.0333	813604	952	30.8545	906304
903	30.05	815409	953	30.8707	908209
904	30.0666	817216	954	30.8869	910116
905	30.0832	819025	955	30.9031	912025
906	30.0998	820836	956	30.9192	913936
907	30.1164	822649	957	30.9354	915849
908	30.133	824464	958	30.9516	917764
909	30.1496	826281	959	30.9677	919681
910	30.1662	828100	960	30.9839	921600
911	30.1828	829921	961	31	923521
912	30.1993	831744	962	31.0161	925444
913	30.2159	833569	963	31.0322	927369
914	30.2324	835396	964	31.0483	929296
915	30.249	837225	965	31.0644	931225
916	30.2655	839056	966	31.0805	933156
917	30.282	840889	967	31.0966	935089
918	30.2985	842724	968	31.1127	937024
919	30.315	844561	969	31.1288	938961
920	30.3315	846400	970	31.1448	940900
921	30.348	848241	971	31.1609	942841
922	30.3645	850084	972	31.1769	944784
923	30.3809	851929	973	31.1929	946729
924	30.3974	853776	974	31.209	948676
925	30.4138	855625	975	31.225	950625
926	30.4302	857476	976	31.241	952576
927	30.4467	859329	977	31.257	954529
928	30.4631	861184	978	31.273	956484
929	30.4795	863041	979	31.289	958441
930	30.4959	864900	980	31.305	960400
931	30.5123	866761	981	31.3209	962361
932	30.5287	868624	982	31.3369	964324
933	30.545	870489	983	31.3528	966289
934	30.5614	872356	984	31.3688	968256
935	30.5778	874225	985	31.3847	970225
936	30.5941	876096	986	31.4006	972196
937	30.6105	877969	987	31.4166	974169
938	30.6268	879844	988	31.4325	976144
939	30.6431	881721	989	31.4484	978121
940	30.6594	883600	990	31.4643	980100
941	30.6757	885481	991	31.4802	982081
942	30.692	887364	992	31.496	984064
943	30.7083	889249	993	31.5119	986049
944	30.7246	891136	994	31.5278	988036
945	30.7409	893025	995	31.5436	990025
946	30.7571	894916	996	31.5595	992016
947	30.7734	896809	997	31.5753	994009
948	30.7896	898704	998	31.5911	996004
949	30.8058	900601	999	31.607	998001
950	30.8221	902500	1000	31.6228	1000000

Glossary

Area Probability Sample   A form of multistage CLUSTER SAMPLE in which geographical areas such as census blocks or tracts serve as the first-stage sampling unit. Units selected in the first stage of sampling are then "listed"—all the households on each selected block would be written down after a trip to the block—and such lists would be subsampled. See discussions in Chapter 6 and the description of the Oakland sample in Chapter 7.

Attributes   Characteristics of persons or things. See VARIABLES and Chapter 4.

Average   An ambiguous term generally suggesting "typical" or "normal." The MEAN, MEDIAN, and MODE are specific examples of mathematical *averages*.

Bias   (1) That quality of a measurement device which tends to result in a misrepresentation of what is being measured in a particular direction. For example, the questionnaire item "Don't you agree that the President is doing a good job?" would be *biased* in that it would generally encourage more favorable responses. See Chapter 5 for more on this. (2) The thing inside you that makes other people or groups seem consistently better or worse than they really are. (3) What a nail looks like after you hit it crooked. (If you drink, don't drive.)

Binomial   (1) A variable which has only two attributes is binomial. "Sex" would be an example, having the attributes "male" and "female." (2) The advertising slogan used by the Nomial Widget Co.

Bivariate Analysis   The analysis of two variables simultaneously, for the purpose of determining the empirical relationship between them. The construction of a simple percentage table or the computation of a simple correlation coefficient would be examples of *bivariate analyses*. See Chapter 14 for more on this.

Bogardus Social Distance Scale   A measurement technique for determining the willingness of people to participate in social relations—of varying degrees of closeness—with other kinds of people. It is an especially efficient technique in that several discrete answers may be summarized without losing any of the original details of the data. This technique is described in Chapter 15.

Census An enumeration of the characteristics of some population. A *census* is often similar to a survey, with the difference that the *census* collects data from *all* members of the population while the survey is limited to a sample.

Cluster Sample (1) A multistage sample in which natural groups (*clusters*) are sampled initially, with the members of each selected group being subsampled afterward. For example, you might select a sample of United States colleges and universities from a directory, get lists of the students at all the selected schools, and then draw samples of students from each. This procedure is discussed in Chapter 6, and Chapter 7 illustrates different *cluster sample* designs. See also AREA PROBABILITY SAMPLE. (2) Pawing around in a box of macadamia-nut-clusters to take all the big ones for yourself.

Codebook (1) The document used in data processing and analysis that tells the location of different data items in a data file. Typically, the codebook identifies the card and column locations of data items and the meaning of the punches used to represent different attributes of variables. See Chapter 13 for more discussion and illustrations. (2) The document that cost you thirty-eight boxtops just to learn that Captain Marvelous wanted you to brush your teeth and always tell the truth. (3) The document that allows CIA agents to learn that Captain Marvelous wants them to brush their teeth.

Coding The process whereby raw data are transformed into standardized form suitable for machine processing and analysis. See Chapters 9 and 13.

Coefficient of Alienation (1) A measure of the extent to which a SMALLEST-SPACE ANALYSIS (SSA) solution satisfies the rule that the rank-order of distances between points must be the inverse of the rank-order of the correlations between the variables that the points represent. More accurately, the *coefficient of alienation* is a measure of the extent to which the solution *fails* to satisfy the rule: the smaller, the better. See Chapter 19. (2) The number of times you don't get invited to parties your friends get invited to.

Coefficient of Reproducibility (1) A measure of the extent to which a SCALE score allows the researcher to reconstruct accurately the specific data that went into the construction of the scale. See Chapter 15 for a fuller description and an illustration. (2) Fecundity.

Cohort Study A study in which some specific group is studied over time although data may be collected from different members in each set of observations. A study of the occupational history of the class of 1970, in which questionnaires were sent every five years, for example, would be a cohort study. See Chapter 3 for more on this (if you want more).

Conceptualization The mental process whereby fuzzy and imprecise notions (*concepts*) are made more specific and precise. So you want to study "prejudice." What do you *mean* by "prejudice"? Are there different kinds of prejudice? What are they? See Chapter 4, which is all about *conceptualization* and its pal, OPERATIONALIZATION.

Confidence Interval (1) The range of values within which a population parameter is estimated to lie. A survey, for example, may show 40 percent of a sample favoring Candidate A (poor devil). While the best estimate of the support existing among all voters would also be 40 percent, we would not expect it to be exactly that. We might, therefore, compute a *confidence interval* (e.g., from 35 percent to 45 percent) within which the actual percentage of the population "probably" lies. Note that it is necessary to specify a CONFIDENCE LEVEL in connection with every *confidence interval*. See Chapters 6 and 18. (2) How close you dare to get to an alligator.

Confidence Level The estimated probability that a population parameter lies within a given CONFIDENCE INTERVAL. Thus, we might be 95 percent *confident* that between 35 and 45 percent of all voters favor Candidate A. See Chapters 6 and 18.

Contingency Question A survey question that is to be asked only of *some* respondents, determined by their responses to some other question. For example, all respondents might be asked whether they belong to the Symbionese Liberation Army, and only those who said "yes" would be asked how often they go to SLA meetings and picnics. The latter would be a *contingency question*. See Chapter 5 for illustrations of this.

Contingency Table (1) A format for presenting the relationships among variables—in the form of percentage distributions. See Chapter 14 for several illustrations of this and for guides to doing it. (2) The card table you keep around in case your guests bring their seven kids with them to dinner.

Control Group In experimentation, a group of subjects to whom *no* experimental stimulus is administered and who should resemble the experimental group in all other respects. The comparison of the *control group* and the experimental group at the end of the experiment points to the effect of the experimental stimulus. See Chapter 10.

Control Variable A variable that is "held constant" in an attempt to further clarify the relationship between two other variables. Having discovered a relationship between education and prejudice, for example, we might "hold sex constant" by examining the relationship between education and prejudice among men only and then among women only. In this example, sex would be the *control variable*. See Chapter 17 to find out how important the proper use of control variables is in analysis.

Cross-Sectional Study A study that is based on observations representing a single point in time. Contrasted with a LONGITUDINAL STUDY.

Deduction (1) The logical model in which specific expectations or HYPOTHESES are developed on the basis of general principles. Starting from the general principle that all deans are meanies, you might anticipate that *this* one won't let you change courses. That anticipation would be the result of *deduction*. See also INDUCTION and Chapters 2 and 16. (2) What the Internal

Revenue Service said your good-for-nothing moocher of a brother-in-law technically isn't.

Dependent Variable   That variable that is assumed to *depend* on or be caused by another (called the INDEPENDENT VARIABLE). If you find that income is partly a function of amount of formal education, income is being treated as a *dependent variable*.

Descriptive Statistics   (1) Statistical computations describing either the characteristics of a sample *or* the relationships among variables in a sample. *Descriptive statistics* merely summarize a set of sample observations, whereas INFERENTIAL STATISTICS move beyond the description of specific observations to make inferences about the larger population from which the sample observations were drawn. (2) 36-24-36 (A male-chauvinist-pig-of-a-devil made me say that).

Dichotomy   A classification having only two categories. Chapter 10 discusses dichotomous variables. See also BINOMIAL.

Dispersion   The distribution of values around some central value, such as an AVERAGE. The RANGE is a simple example of a measure of *dispersion*. Thus, we may report that the MEAN age of a group is 37.9, and the range is from 12 to 89.

E.P.S.E.M.   *Equal probability of selection method.* A sample design in which each member of a population has the same chance of being selected into the sample. See Chapter 6.

External Validation   The process of testing the *validity* of a measure, such as an INDEX or SCALE, by examining its relationship to other, presumed indicators of the same variable. If the index really measures "prejudice," for example, it should correlate with other indicators of prejudice. See Chapter 15 for a fuller discussion of this and for illustrations.

Face Validity   (1) That quality of an indicator that makes it seem a reasonable measure of some variable. That the frequency of church attendance is some indication of a person's religiosity seems to make sense without a lot of explanation. It has *face validity*. (2) Putting the right face on your head when you get up in the morning.

Factor Analysis   A complex algebraic method for determining the general dimensions or *factors* that exist within a set of concrete observations. See Chapter 19 for more details on this.

Frequency Distribution   A description of the number of times the various attributes of a variable are observed in a sample. The report that 53 percent of a sample were men and 47 percent were women would be a simple example of a *frequency distribution*. Another example would be the report that 15 of the cities studied had populations under 10,000; 23 had populations between 10,000 and 25,000; and so forth.

Generalizability   (1) That quality of a research finding that justifies the inference that it represents something more than the specific observations upon which it was based. Sometimes this involves the *generalization* of findings from a sample to a population. Other times, it is a matter of concepts: if you are able to discover why people commit burglaries, can you *generalize* that discovery to other crimes as well? (2) The likelihood that you will ever be a general.

Guttman Scale A type of composite measure used to summarize several discrete observations and to represent some more general variable. See Chapter 15.

Hypothesis (1) An expectation about the nature of things derived from a theory. It is a statement of something that ought to be observed in the real world if the theory is correct. See DEDUCTION and also Chapters 2 and 3. (2) A graduate student paper explaining why hypopotamuses are the way they are.

Hypothesis-Testing (1) The determination of whether the expectations that a hypothesis represents are, indeed, found to exist in the real world. See Chapters 2 and 3. (2) An oral examination centering around a graduate student paper explaining why hypopotamuses are the way they are.

Independent Variable A variable whose values are *not* problematical in an analysis but are taken as simply given. An *independent variable* is presumed to cause or determine a DEPENDENT VARIABLE. If we discover that religiosity is partly a function of sex—women are more religious than men—"sex" is the *independent variable* and "religiosity" is the dependent variable. Note that any given variable might be treated as *independent* in one part of an analysis and dependent in another part of the analysis. "Religiosity" might become an *independent variable* in the explanation of crime.

Index A type of composite measure that summarizes several specific observations and represents some more general dimension. Contrasted with SCALE. See Chapter 15.

Induction (1) The logical model in which general principles are developed from specific observations. Having noted that Jews and Catholics are more likely to vote Democratic than Protestants are, you might conclude that religious minorities in the United States are more affiliated with the Democratic Party and explain why. This would be an example of *induction*. See also DEDUCTION and Chapters 2 and 16. (2) What you went to college to avoid.

Inferential Statistics The body of statistical computations relevant to making inferences from findings based on sample observations to some larger population. See also DESCRIPTIVE STATISTICS and Chapter 18. Not to be confused with "infernal statistics," which have something to do with the population of Hell.

Informant Someone well-versed in the social phenomenon that a researcher wishes to study and who is willing to tell the researcher what he knows. If you were planning participant observation among the members of a religious sect, you would do well to make friends with someone who already knew about them—possibly a member of the sect—who could give you some background information about them. Not to be confused with a RESPONDENT.

Interchangeability of Indexes   A term coined by Paul Lazarsfeld referring to the logical proposition that if some general variable is related to another variable, then all indicators of the variable should have that relationship. See Chapter 16 for a fuller description of this and a graphic illustration.

Internal Validation   The process whereby the individual items comprising a composite measure are correlated with the measure itself. This provides one test of the wisdom of including all the items in the composite measure. See also EXTERNAL VALIDATION and Chapter 15.

Interpretation   A technical term used in connection with the elaboration model. It represents the research outcome in which a CONTROL VARIABLE is discovered to be the mediating factor through which an INDEPENDENT VARIABLE has its effect on a DEPENDENT VARIABLE. See Chapter 17.

Intersubjectivity   That quality of science (and other inquiries) whereby two different researchers, studying the same problem, arrive at the same conclusion. Ultimately, this is the practical criterion for what is called OBJECTIVITY. We agree that something is "objectively true" if independent observers with different subjective orientations conclude that it is "true." See Chapter 2.

Interval Measure   A level of measurement describing a variable whose attributes are rank-ordered and have equal distances between adjacent attributes. The Fahrenheit temperature scale is an example of this, since the "distance" between 17° and 18° is the same as that between 89° and 90°. See Chapter 4 and also NOMINAL MEASURE, ORDINAL MEASURE, and RATIO MEASURE.

Interview   A data-collection encounter in which one person (an interviewer) asks questions of another (a RESPONDENT). *Interviews* may be conducted face-to-face or by telephone. See Chapter 11 for more information on interviewing as a method of survey research.

Judgmental Sample   A type of NONPROBABILITY SAMPLE in which the researcher selects the units to be observed on the basis of his own *judgment* about which ones will be the most useful or representative. Another name for this is PURPOSIVE SAMPLE. See Chapter 6 for more details.

Latent Content   As used in connection with content analysis, the underlying "meaning" of communications as distinguished from their MANIFEST CONTENT. See Chapter 9.

Level of Significance   In the context of TESTS OF STATISTICAL SIGNIFICANCE, the degree of likelihood that an observed, empirical relationship could be attributable to sampling error. A relationship is *significant* at the .05 *level* if the likelihood of its being only a function of sampling error is no greater than 5 out of 100. See Chapters 6 and 18.

Likert Scale   (1) A type of composite measure developed by Rensis *Likert* in an attempt to improve the levels of measurement in social research through the use of standardized response categories in survey QUESTIONNAIRES. "*Likert*-items" are those utilizing such response categories as "strongly agree," "agree," "disagree," and "strongly disagree." Such items may be used in the construction of true *Likert scales* and may also be used in the construction of other types of composite measures. See Chapter 15. (2) The device that tells how much Ren and Jane Likert weigh.

Longitudinal Study A study design involving the collection of data at different points in time, as contrasted with a CROSS-SECTIONAL STUDY. See also Chapter 4 and TREND STUDY, COHORT STUDY, and PANEL STUDY.

Manifest Content In connection with content analysis, the concrete terms contained in a communication, as distinguished from LATENT CONTENT. See Chapter 9.

Matching In connection with experiments, the procedure whereby pairs of subjects are *matched* on the basis of their similarities on one or more variables, and one member of the pair is assigned to the experimental group and the other to the CONTROL GROUP. See Chapter 10.

Mean (1) An AVERAGE, computed by summing the values of several observations and dividing by the number of observations. If you now have a grade-point-average of 4.0 based on 10 courses, and you get an F in this course, your new grade-point-(mean)-average will be 3.6. (2) The quality of the thoughts you might have if your instructor did that to you.

Median (1) Another AVERAGE, representing the value of the "middle" case in a rank-ordered set of observations. If the ages of five men are 16, 17, 20, 54, and 88, the *median* would be 20. (The MEAN would be 39.) (2) The dividing line between safe driving and exciting driving.

Mode (1) Still another AVERAGE, representing the most frequently observed value or attribute. If a sample contains 1000 Protestants, 275 Catholics, and 33 Jews, "Protestant" is the *modal* category. See Chapter 14 for more thrilling disclosures about averages. (2) Better than apple pie à la median.

Multivariate Analysis The analysis of the simultaneous relationships among several variables. Examining simultaneously the effects of age, sex, and social class on religiosity would be an example of *multivariate analysis*. See Chapters 14, 17, and 19.

Nominal Measure A level of measurement describing a variable whose different attributes are *only* different, as distinguished from ORDINAL, INTERVAL, or RATIO MEASURES. Sex would be an example of a nominal measure. See Chapter 4.

Nonprobability Sample A sample selected in some fashion other than those suggested by probability theory. Examples include JUDGMENTAL (PURPOS-IVE), QUOTA, and SNOWBALL SAMPLES. See Chapter 6.

Nonsampling Error (1) Those imperfections of data quality that are a result of factors other than sampling error. Examples include misunderstandings of questions by respondents, erroneous recordings by interviewers and coders, keypunch errors, and so forth. (2) The mistake you made in deciding to interview everyone rather than selecting a sample.

Null Hypothesis   In connection with HYPOTHESIS TESTING and TESTS OF STATISTICAL SIGNIFICANCE, that *hypothesis* that suggests there is *no* relationship between the variables under study. The researcher may conclude that two variables *are* related after having statistically rejected the *null hypothesis.*

Objectivity   See INTERSUBJECTIVITY.

Operationalization   One step beyond CONCEPTUALIZATION. *Operationalization* is the process of developing OPERATIONAL DEFINITIONS. Also, see Chapter 4.

Operational Definitions   The concrete and specific *definition* of something in terms of the *operations* by which observations are to be categorized. The *operational definition* of "earning an A in this course" might be: "correctly answering at least 90 percent of the final exam questions." See Chapter 4.

Ordinal Measure   A level of measurement describing a variable whose attributes may be *rank-ordered* along some dimension. An example would be "socioeconomic status" as comprised of the attributes "high, medium, low." See Chapter 4 and also NOMINAL MEASURE, INTERVAL MEASURE, and RATIO MEASURE.

P.P.S.   *Probability proportionate to size.* (This refers to a type of multistage CLUSTER SAMPLE in which clusters are selected, not with equal probabilities (see E.P.S.E.M.) but with *probabilities proportionate* to their *sizes*—as measured by the number of units to be subsampled. See Chapter 6 and the Episcopal Churchwomen and Oakland illustrations in Chapter 7.

Panel Study   A type of LONGITUDINAL STUDY, in which data are collected from the same sample (the *panel*) at several points in time. See Chapter 3.

Path Analysis   A form of MULTIVARIATE ANALYSIS in which the causal relationships among variables are presented in graphic format. See Chapter 19.

Probability Sample   The general term for a sample selected in accord with *probability* theory, typically involving some random-selection mechanism. Specific types of *probability samples* include AREA PROBABILITY SAMPLE, E.P.S.E.M., P.P.S., SIMPLE RANDOM SAMPLE, and SYSTEMATIC SAMPLE. See Chapters 6 and 7.

Probe   A technique employed in interviewing to solicit a more complete answer to a question. It is a nondirective phrase or question used to encourage a respondent to elaborate on an answer. Examples include "Anything more?" and "How is that?" See Chapter 11 for a discussion of interviewing.

Purposive Sample   See JUDGMENTAL SAMPLE and Chapter 6.

Qualitative Analysis   The nonnumerical examination and interpretation of observations, for the purpose of discovering underlying meanings and patterns of relationships. This is most typical of field research and historical research. See Chapter 8.

Quantitative Analysis The numerical representation and manipulation of observations for the purpose of describing and explaining the phenomena that those observations reflect. See Chapter 13 especially, and also the remainder of Part Four.

Questionnaire A document containing *questions* and other types of items designed to solicit information appropriate to analysis. *Questionnaires* are used primarily in survey research and also in experiments, field research, and other modes of observation. See Chapters 5 and 11.

Quota Sample A type of NONPROBABILITY SAMPLE in which units are selected into the sample on the basis of prespecified characteristics, so that the total sample will have the same distribution of characteristics as are assumed to exist in the population being studied. See Chapter 6.

Randomization A technique for assigning experimental subjects to experimental and CONTROL GROUPS: *randomly*. See Chapter 10.

Range A measure of DISPERSION, comprised of the highest and lowest values of a variable in some set of observations. In your class, for example, the *range* of ages might be from 17 to 37.

Ratio Measure A level of measurement describing a variable whose attributes have all the qualities of NOMINAL, ORDINAL, and INTERVAL MEASURES and in addition are based on a "true zero" point. "Age" would be an example of a *ratio measure*. See also Chapter 4.

Reductionism A fault of some researchers: a strict limitation (reduction) of the kinds of concepts to be considered relevant to the phenomenon under study. See Chapter 3.

Regression (1) A method of data analysis in which the relationships among variables are represented in the form of an equation, called a *regression* equation. See Chapter 19 for a discussion of the different forms of *regression* analysis. (2) What seems to happen to your knowledge of social research methods just prior to an examination.

Reliability That quality of a measurement method that suggests that the same data would have been collected each time in repeated observations of the same phenomenon. In the context of a survey, we would expect that the question "Did you attend church last week?" would have higher reliability than the question "About how many times have you attended church in your life?" This is not to be confused with VALIDITY. See also Chapter 4.

Replication Generally, the duplication of an experiment to expose or reduce error. It is also a technical term used in connection with the elaboration model, referring to the elaboration outcome in which the initially observed relationship between two variables persists when a CONTROL VARIABLE is held constant. See Chapter 17. See Chapter 2 and INTERSUBJECTIVITY.

Representativeness (1) That quality of a sample of having the same distribution of characteristics as the population from which it was selected. By implication, descriptions and explanations derived from an analysis of the sample may be assumed to *represent* similar ones in the population. *Representativeness* is enhanced by PROBABILITY SAMPLING and provides for GENERALIZABILITY and the use of INFERENTIAL STATISTICS. See Chapter 6. (2) A noticeable quality in the presentation-of-self of some U.S. Congressmen.

Respondent   A person who provides data for analysis by *responding* to a survey QUESTIONNAIRE.

Response Rate   The number of persons participating in a survey divided by the number selected in the sample, in the form of a percentage. This is also called the "completion rate" or, in self-administered surveys, the "return rate": the percentage of QUESTIONNAIRES sent out that are returned. See Chapter 11.

Sampling Frame   That list or quasi-list of units comprising a population, from which a sample is selected. If the sample is to be REPRESENTATIVE of the population, it is essential that the *sampling frame* include all (or nearly all) members of the population. See Chapters 6 and 7.

Sampling Interval   The standard distance between elements selected from a population for a sample. See Chapter 6.

Sampling Ratio   The proportion of elements in the population that are selected to be in a sample. See Chapter 6.

Scale   (1) A type of composite measure comprised of several items that have a logical or empirical structure among them. Examples of *scales* include BOGARDUS SOCIAL DISTANCE, GUTTMAN, LIKERT, and THURSTONE SCALES. Contrasted with INDEX. See also Chapter 15. (2) One of the less appetizing parts of a fish. (3) An early sign of the heartbreak of psoriasis. (4) Except for fish.

Secondary Analysis   (1) A form of research in which the data collected and processed by one researcher are reanalyzed—often for a different purpose—by another. This is especially appropriate in the case of survey data. Data archives are repositories or libraries for the storage and distribution of data for *secondary analysis.* (2) Estimating the weight and speed of an opposing team's linebackers.

Simple Random Sample   (1) A type of PROBABILITY SAMPLE in which the units comprising a population are assigned numbers, a set of *random* numbers is then generated, and the units having those numbers are included in the sample. Although probability theory and the calculations it provides assume this basic sampling method, it is seldom used for practical reasons. An equivalent alternative is the SYSTEMATIC SAMPLE (with a random start). See Chapter 6. (2) A random sample with a low I.Q.

Smallest-Space Analysis   A method of MULTIVARIATE ANALYSIS in which the correlations among variables are represented graphically in the form of distances separating points. See Chapter 19.

Snowball Sample   (1) A NONPROBABILITY SAMPLING method often employed in field research. Each person interviewed may be asked to suggest additional people for interviewing. See Chapter 8. (2) Picking the icy ones to throw at your methods instructor.

Specification Generally, the process through which concepts are made more specific. It is also a technical term used in connection with the elaboration model, representing the elaboration outcome in which an initially observed relationship between two variables is replicated among some subgroups created by the CONTROL VARIABLE and not among others. In such a situation, you will have *specified* the conditions under which the original relationship exists: e.g., among men but not among women. See Chapter 17.

Statistical Significance (1) A general term referring to the *un*likeliness that relationships observed in a sample could be attributed to sampling error alone. See TESTS OF STATISTICAL SIGNIFICANCE and Chapter 18. (2) How important it would really be if you flunked your statistics exam. I mean, you could always be a poet.

Stratification The grouping of the units comprising a population into homogeneous groups (or *strata*) prior to sampling. This procedure, which may be used in conjunction with SIMPLE RANDOM, SYSTEMATIC, or CLUSTER SAMPLING, improves the REPRESENTATIVENESS of a sample, at least in terms of the *stratification* variables. See Chapters 6 and 7.

Systematic Sample (1) A type of PROBABILITY SAMPLE in which every *k*th unit in a list is selected for inclusion in the sample: e.g., every 25th student in the college directory of students. *k* is computed by dividing the size of the population by the desired sample size, and is called the sampling interval. Within certain constraints, *systematic sampling* is a functional equivalent of SIMPLE RANDOM SAMPLING and usually easier to do. Typically, the first unit is selected at random. See Chapter 6. (2) Picking every third one whether it's icy or not. See SNOWBALL SAMPLE (2).

Test of Statistical Significance (1) A class of statistical computations that indicate the likelihood that the relationship observed between variables in a sample can be attributable to sampling error only. See INFERENTIAL STATISTICS and Chapter 18. (2) A determination of how important statistics have been in improving Man's lot in life. (3) An examination that can radically affect your grade in this course and your grade-point-average as well.

Thurstone Scale A type of composite measure, constructed in accord with the weights assigned by "judges" to various indicators of some variable. This technique is seldom used today, due to the time and effort it requires. See Chapter 15.

Trend Study A type of LONGITUDINAL STUDY in which a given characteristic of some population is monitored over time. An example would be the series of Gallup Polls showing the political-candidate preferences of the electorate over the course of a campaign, even though different samples were interviewed at each point in time. See Chapter 3.

Typology The classification (typically nominal) of observations in terms of their attributes on two or more variables. The classification of newspapers as "liberal-urban, liberal-rural, conservative-urban, conservative-rural" would be an example. See Chapter 15.

Units of Analysis The *what* or *whom* being studied. In social science research, the most typical units of analysis are individual people. See Chapter 3.

Univariate Analysis The analysis of a single variable, for purposes of description. FREQUENCY DISTRIBUTIONS, AVERAGES, and measures of DISPERSION would be examples of *univariate analysis*, as distinguished from BIVARIATE and MULTIVARIATE ANALYSIS. See Chapter 14.

Validity A descriptive term used of a measure that accurately reflects the concept that it is intended to measure. For example, your I.Q. would seem a more *valid* measure of your intelligence than would the number of hours you spend in the library. It is important to realize that the ultimate *validity* of a measure can never be "proven." Yet, we may agree to its relative *validity* on the basis of FACE VALIDITY, INTERNAL VALIDATION, and EXTERNAL VALIDATION. This must not be confused with RELIABILITY. See also Chapter 4.

Variables Logical grouping of ATTRIBUTES. The variable "sex" is made up of the attributes "male" and "female." See Chapter 4.

Weighting (1) A procedure employed in connection with sampling whereby units selected with unequal probabilities are assigned weights in such a manner as to make the sample REPRESENTATIVE of the population from which it was selected. See Chapters 6 and 7. (2) Olde English for hanging around for somebody who never gets there on time.

Index